Women and the American Civil War

D0872939

Women and the American Civil War

North-South Counterpoints

EDITED BY JUDITH GIESBERG

AND RANDALL M. MILLER

The Kent State University Press

KENT, OHIO

© 2018 by The Kent State University Press, Kent, Ohio 44242

ALL RIGHTS RESERVED

ISBN 978-1-60635-340-0

Manufactured in the United States of America

Cataloging information for this title is available at the Library of Congress.

22 21 20 19 18   5 4 3 2 1

To our students at Villanova University and Saint
Joseph's University, for all they teach us by asking and
exploring new questions about the Civil War era

Judy and Randall

February 2018

Contents

Preface and Acknowledgments

This book grew out of discussions among historians at conferences about the need to bring the Civil War into women's history and women's history into the Civil War. The historians recognized that the intersections of those histories were already underway, and with much profit, but they continued to ask for systematic comparative studies that looked at women across regional boundaries, rather than simply within them, and that extended the compass of inquiry across the Civil War era. From such discussions, we suggested that we all might gain new perspectives and understandings about women, and men, during the Civil War era by pairing essays on key issues affecting and reflecting women's interests, identities, and involvement in such subjects as politics, family, wartime mobilization, relief, religion, emancipation, Reconstruction, and memory. As in all such conversations, someone challenged any among us to try this approach. We took up that challenge. This book is the result.

In bringing together the various authors and agreeing on the subjects, we sought scholars whose work spoke to the issues. In order to cut across the sectional divide in scholarship that tended to focus on one section rather than engage in an ongoing investigation of people across regional lines, we paired essays on the North and South for each subject and encouraged the authors to share their work so that they would "speak" to one another throughout the book. Simply put, the purpose and the plan was to encourage comparisons and counterpoints. By pairing essays by subject, we wanted readers to see the people and the period as dynamic and even dialectic, rather than fixed by circumstance and geography.

We see our book as exploratory more than "definitive," and do not pretend to comprehensiveness in subject or range. The book is, rather, a series of investigations that we hope readers will take as invitations to continue the inquiry into discovering how gender and place—and race—especially informed what the Civil War era meant to its contemporaries and might mean to students of that time thereafter. Doing so will move us all closer to realizing what Walt Whitman famously said nobody would ever do—namely, get the "real war" into the books.

This book is the work of many hands. First, we thank all those historians wanting us to try such a project—and we toast you all for your confidence. We thank the authors for taking on the project with enthusiasm and intellectual rigor. We also benefited from the assistance of staff at various libraries, including most directly the Falvey Library at Villanova University, the Drexel Library at Saint Joseph's University, the Van Pelt Library at the University of Pennsylvania, the Magill Library at Haverford

College, the Historical Society of Pennsylvania, and the Library Company of Philadelphia. We also raise our glass to the bartenders and wait staff at Brick & Brew in Havertown, Pa., "the office," for letting us stake out window tables to work on this book while sampling various brews or wines to insure words would flow. We thank the readers at Kent State University Press for their instructive and useful comments, which did much to improve the book. And we very much thank the staff at Kent State University Press, especially Joyce Harrison and Will Underwood, for believing in this book from the beginning, providing most helpful advice on direction and scope all along the way, and guiding the book through the review and publication process. We also thank the DBD Fund for providing a grant to support this work. And throughout the gestation period of this project, we thank the patience and support of our spouses, Edward Fierros and Linda Patterson Miller, who knew we would get the work done and still be home for dinner.

Judith Giesberg, Havertown, Pa., and Randall M. Miller, Glen Mills, Pa.

Introduction

In 2002, surveying the literature on women and the Civil War, historian Thavolia Glymph concluded that "the period of the Civil War and Reconstruction remains the most racially gendered and regionally segregated historiographical space in U.S. history."[1] At the time, the scholarship was still relatively young, having only begun to mature in the previous decade. Since then, those, like Glymph, who teach and write on the subject have inspired and trained others, and as a result scholarship on women in the Civil War is far less elite and white than it once was. Much has been accomplished to uncover the lives of Southern slave and freedwomen and poor white women, for instance, and studies of the urban and rural communities in the North have moved beyond an exclusive focus on middle-class women's voluntary work. New work is underway on the great variety of wartime and postwar experiences of women in the West, including Native American, Chinese, and Mexican women. But yet much of it—except for perhaps this latter—remains "regionally segregated." Historians writing about Southern women rarely comment on or interact with those working on the North, and vice versa; questions and research methods employed in one place do not inform and are not replicated in the other. This leaves us asking: Are there two distinct models for studying women's Civil War? We think not, but the essays in this collection will allow us to consider that question carefully.

This volume brings historians together in a series of paired essays on critical issues relating to women and the American Civil War. Each pair assays a particular subject from the Southern and the Northern experience, thereby establishing a running comparative dynamic throughout the book. This organization will allow readers to see where the work overlaps, when questions posed of one group of women might rightfully be posed of another, and how sources discovered and methods employed in one case might, and even ought, to be used in the other.

While readers, we hope, will find the arrangement of these essays instructive, they will also be struck by how deep and richly textured is our understanding of women's Civil War. As the field has matured, historians have reconsidered what we thought we knew about the period's usual suspects—plantation mistresses, slave women, middle-class reformers, nurses, for instance—and added a panoply of new ones—female spies, smugglers, resisters, refugees, veterans, to name a few. This maturing is reflected in the essays that follow, which revisit with fresh eyes old favorites such as the politically savvy Jessie Frémont, contraband teacher and activist Harriet Jacobs, and Confederate nurse Kate Cumming. The essays continue the recovery work of women's history, giving us new names to consider, women like (in Chandra Manning's essay) Mrs. Maria Renfro, who organized a female-led church in Cairo, Illinois, that became the basis for the town's first African Methodist Episcopal Church, and (in Wendy Venet's essay) former slave and veteran's wife Julia Layton, who, at the 1897 national meeting of the Woman's Relief Corps, successfully stopped a measure that would have segregated the corps by calling instead for union. "Until we have union," Layton insisted, "this organization will not progress." Indeed, the same could be said about the postwar suffrage campaign that fractured and hopelessly floundered over the relationship between black civil rights and women's rights.

There are no angels here, though, and by this we mean that none of the scholars revisit the postwar urge to naturalize women's wartime contributions by saddling women with terms such as "angels" and "martyrs." But there are also *no angels* because the essays that follow—while they uncover women's self-emancipation, healing, and commemorative work—also make room for women whose wartime actions are less commendable: self-serving, perhaps; violent; and criminal, even. Readers will find the essays make spare reference to "agency," for instance, which no one here presumes to "give" to these women. They will find, though, Aggie Crawford (in Lisa Frank's essay) stealing newspapers during the war so her enslaved community could stay on top of war news and escaped slave Lydia Penney (in Libra Hilde's essay) enlisting as a regimental nurse with her husband's regiment, the 5th U.S. Colored Troops. Readers will also find (in Rebecca Capobianco's essay) slaveowning women demanding orders of protection to keep slaves from running away and white freedmen's teacher Mary Ames (in Chandra Manning's essay) unwittingly sending a young pupil to his death in a river rather than allow him into her school dirty.

Other essays attest to the work that still needs to be done examining postwar legal records to find freedwomen seeking—and getting (in Elizabeth Smith's essay)—equal justice in the courts and exploring women's spiritual lives and their religious expressions. "That day a-coming! There's a day a-coming . . . I hear the rumbling of the chariots . . . white folks blood is a running on the ground like a river . . . Oh Lord, hasten the day!" an enslaved Virginia woman named Aggy declared (in W. Scott Poole's essay), praying that "God allow her to live to see the day when 'I shall see white folks' die like wolves shot 'when they come hungry out the woods.'" Aggy's prayer is evidence that the scholarship on women in the Civil War has matured, making it possible to treat women not as heroes, angels, or martyrs but as complicated and fully human.

POLITICS

The Civil War resulted from the failure of political compromise. We start, then, with politics. In paired essays on women's politics, Stacey Robertson and Elizabeth Varon show that women's politics did not begin with the war or end there. Both authors argue that women's political interests and actions were varied, often contentious, and hardly marginal, and as such they did much to define political categories and shape men's political priorities and obligations. In Robertson's essay, female antislavery activists evidence women's growing political consciousness, and as the second party system collapsed, they proved essential in animating and informing mass politics through such practices as running petition campaigns and mass rallies. By broadening our understanding of "the political," Robertson invites readers to consider a number of ways the personal became political and shaped American politics during and through the Civil War era.

Elizabeth Varon's essay shares with Robertson's this expansive definition of politics, including white women's private expressions of support for slavery and the conservative social order that sustained it, as in proslavery novels and essays, and black women's harrowing accounts of experiencing and escaping slavery. Like Northern reformers, female slaveholders drew on their charge to uphold the honor of the family, in their case by arguing against the agitations and disruptions of Northern women. So, too, did enslaved women claim protection of family for their decision to go public with their stories of survival and escape. Varon also points to the ways that Southern women of color built on a long history of community politics, sharpening, in the lead up to the war, their tools of dissent and resistance in ways that brought the sectional political crisis to a head when they ran away and helped others to do so.

FAMILY

Whereas women, South and North, usually explained their forays into politics as a defense of family, when the war came it radically reordered many families, sometimes permanently so. In the next pair of essays, Jacqueline Campbell and Nicole Etcheson consider the war as a family crisis, not in the tired sense of it being a "brothers' war," but instead that it was endured/waged by sisters, mothers, wives, and daughters. Focusing on the wartime demands on families, Campbell's essay reveals that slaveholding white women's efforts to defend their families often put them in direct conflict with enslaved women's vigorous efforts to transform theirs by disrupting slavery, running away to Union lines, and supporting men who enlisted. This fundamental divide kept white and black women at war with one another long after Appomattox. For the Northern side, Nicole Etcheson tracks women's experience of war as something also determined by the "life course"—that is, that it mattered if women, black and white, were young, middle-aged, or old and if they were unmarried, married, or widowed. Each life stage came with cultural norms that shaped their experience of the war, and the ideology of separate spheres was as much about age as it was gender, race, class, religion, and region. Etcheson's approach offers historians new opportunities to do comparative work, say, on how the middle age of women like Northerner Mary Livermore framed her approach to war work and how youth informed Southerner Ada Bacot's—or perhaps it was her widowhood or the assistance of her enslaved cook, Savary (in Libra Hilde's essay). Conflicts between women about women's proper roles in wartime mobilization also broke along generational lines. Dorothea Dix, for example, had strong opinions about how nursing was inappropriate for young unmarried women, but young unmarried women nursed and did so well.

RELIEF

Libra Hilde and Jeanie Attie contribute essays on relief work, describing how very unprepared both governments were at the beginning of the war and how critical women's voluntary labor—nursing, for instance—was to successful mobilization. Southern and Northern white women raised supplies and provided medical care as the two war-making machines slowly came to life. Reading these essays alongside each other highlights the unique features of Confederate women's relief work, for there are no Northern counterparts (about which we are aware) to the South's ladies' gunboat societies or to examples of women surrendering their jewelry to outfit an ironclad or pooling their resources to buy a cannon. Regressive economic policies—Union taxes and Confederate impressment—depressed the reform urge and left working-class, yeoman, and poor women deeply suspicious of the federal government. In the South relief turned inward, Hilde shows, as suspicions and resentment mounted. Nothing in the North matched Southern women's bread riots, perhaps, but, as Attie notes, institutions such as the United States Sanitary Commission suffered as women withdrew their support from an institution associated with corruption and a federal government with a seemingly inexhaustible demand for men and matériel.

Of the long-term effects of women's successful mobilization, Attie says that "something ruptured during the war and the gendered crises that the war provoked reverberated in the postwar decades." Hilde's essay concludes the same about Southern women, except that the rupture she describes in Confederate hospitals fell sharply along lines of race, as enslaved women refused to countenance the abuse of their mistresses-turned-nurses and "deserted" to Union hospitals. When the war was over, Southern women relief workers, black and white, both claimed prerogatives as veterans—but of two separate wars.

Because we have filed these essays under the category of "relief" and the next two are marked "mobilization," a word about definition is in order. The distinction between "relief" and "mobilization" seems a rather fine one, for much of women's relief work was harnessed to state-sponsored mobilization. Women's wartime mobilization, like men's, was highly local. They conceived of their loyalty often to a locale and the men serving from home, rather than, or perhaps more than, to the state. Even so, as Attie explains in her essay on Northern women's relief, at times they "made public a reasoned loyalty to the federal government, defense of the Constitution, and opposition to the Southern threat." So might the same be said of the Southern women described by Hilde—well, surely white women. Women's work recruiting volunteers and outfitting them was critical to mobilization. Women serving as teachers, freedmen's aid workers, and some nurses—whom we might think of as engaged in the business of relief—explained their motivations in terms strongly connected to "the Cause." Of course, nurses often traveled with local regiments, motivated by the desire to support the men in uniform, and in that sense their work supported mobilization.

The distinction becomes even finer once women were doing the work. Readers will find in several essays that follow women who increasingly came to see the value of their work and committed or withheld it as they saw fit. Indeed, although Jessica Ziparo insists that through mobilization the state required women to "be complicit in their subordination," she concedes that women made "hundreds of thousands of negotiations and transactions" with the local and state officials for whom they worked, laying important foundations for labor and women's rights battles that would be waged later. And of course, whether we consider their work as mobilization or relief, women, black and white, remained skeptical of and critical of "the administration"—whether that meant the Davis or Lincoln administration, or that of North Carolina governor Zebulon Vance or Pennsylvania governor Andrew Curtin—for, as the war dragged on, women made few distinctions about the mounting demands made on them. Whether it was a new state-sponsored tax or an appeal for donations from a relief organization, it was often seen as an unwelcome and unfair demand. Surely this turn to definition has not made completely clear a distinction between what might be called mobilization and relief, but we hope it gives readers a sense of some of what the essays have taught us.

Mobilization

Jessica Ziparo points to the wartime problem of finding an "acceptable equilibrium" among the Union government's need for women's "labor and sacrifice, Northern women's ambition, and Victorian norms of appropriate female behavior." In following Northern women's movement into aid work as nurses and paid work as clerks, seamstresses, and arsenal employees, Ziparo finds that women's wartime work did not translate into new respect or rights for them as citizens. Rather, women were at times "complicit in their own subordination" when they accepted low wages, poor working conditions, and male authority as the condition for work. Women widowed by the war further became supplicants of the state by seeking pensions. Viewed from that perspective, Ziparo cautions against claiming too much progress for women's rights as a result of the rupture in gender relations.

As in the North, Southern mobilization included women feeding and supplying the armies, working as nurses and seamstresses and in other kinds of "women's work," and leaving the home places for jobs in factories, arsenals, and government offices. And for Southern women as for Northern women, as Lisa Frank shows, such work was underpaid and underappreciated. This work forced slaveholding women into new, and uncomfortable, responsibilities and pitted them against the interests of poorer women and enslaved women. At the same time, women of color—free and enslaved—took stock of their chances, measuring the weakness of the Confederacy and seizing the moments of Southern defeat and Union invasion to desert. The failure of Confederate mobilization was thus due in part to divisions among Southern women and women's priorities of serving their family interests over any loyalty to the state.

RELIGION

In paired essays on religion, Timothy Wesley and W. Scott Poole emphasize that millennialism defined Northern and Southern evangelical Protestants' understanding of God's design and humans' role and responsibilities in it. By Wesley's reckoning, the dominance and pervasiveness of millennialist thought among evangelical Protestants pushed Northern Christian women into social reform and politics and established Northern, or at least Republican, political priorities in millennialist terms. Using religious language and logic, evangelical Protestant women pressed Republicans to move directly against slavery, lobbied governments to support abolition, and kept the issue alive in political discourse. To them, abolition and Union victory seemed to fulfill the millennialist promise for America. In turn, W. Scott Poole argues that white and black Southern women also viewed the war and emancipation "in an eschatological fashion," but, for them, the war "reshaped their theology of apocalypse." Poole stresses how race and class significantly colored the religious meanings Southern women, and men, derived from the experience of war. For white women, religion was more than a comfort and strength during hard times; it also drove political engagement and demands for the maintenance of a hierarchical order based on slavery. Southern defeat raised questions about God's favor that white women struggled to understand after the war. Black women, Poole shows, drew on their own cultural and spiritual resources to resist attempts by white women to control their religious and social lives and in doing so realized their own theology of apocalyptic liberation. As such, Poole concludes that historians need be wary of insisting that religion, like gender, necessarily bound all women together.

EMANCIPATION

The benefits of having these scholars talk to each other are obvious in the section on emancipation. In their paired essays, Chandra Manning and Rebecca Capobianco examine how emancipation policies were negotiated on the ground, where Northern women volunteered at contraband camps and at freedmen's schools and where enslaved women and slaveholding Southern women administered a de facto emancipation in their homes and communities. Manning's essay shows how some women relief workers opened themselves up to learning from slaves, rather than instructing them, and in so doing discovered and acted in solidarity with them. The slaveholding women in Capobianco's essay, on the other hand, learned that they had to watch and now negotiate with enslaved women, those who ran away and the many, many more who stayed but sought a new relationship on their own terms. Capobianco's essay reminds us that, as we come to terms with how best to rewrite the history of emancipation, we should stay alert to how many times the paths enslaved women took to freedom led them back to where they started.

RECONSTRUCTION

Elizabeth Parish Smith's essay on Reconstruction shows how black and white Southern women sought to reunite family and reorganize labor around their families. They shared a new supposed equality in the law, and the experience of violence. Exploring court records, Smith reveals how women of color at times received justice in court when they sought to protect themselves against white employers. Her study suggests that we should not too readily dismiss the possibilities that opened up during Reconstruction for reordering relations of race—if not necessarily gender. Where Smith looks at court records to recover the gendered and racialized experiences of Reconstruction, Faye Dudden argues that newspapers fed Northern white suffragists' fears about Reconstruction and their racism. Women of color drew news about black enfranchisement from a wide community of teachers, activists, and black newspapers, shaping their unique activist vision that was at once feminist and antiracist. Both of these essays remind us that there is still much good work to be done excavating and assaying the rights—beyond suffrage—that women sought, gained, and exercised in the postwar period.

MEMORY

Wendy Venet traces efforts by Northern women to commemorate their wartime work, the volumes they produced in the process, and how their wartime commemorative efforts at times intersected with or informed their suffrage activism. Very few statues were constructed in commemoration of women's war work; Venet describes a couple of them in her essay. Female war veterans, Venet shows, fought for the memory of the war, too, against those who sought to erase from it the history of slavery. Micki McElya's work begins with a statue, the Contrabands and Freedmen's Cemetery Memorial in Alexandria, and uses it to explore the gendered and racialized "Civil War memorial cultures" that emerged after the war. The commemorative landscape that developed after the war was stubbornly resistant to including women and, as McElya shows, struggled with how to incorporate the story of the freedwomen who cooked, cared, washed, and spied for Union troops during the war.

CONCLUSION

In the years since Glymph diagnosed a problem in the emerging literature on women and the Civil War, scholars have borrowed questions, methods, and approaches from each other and have sought to draw parallels where they exist while keeping their eyes trained on the experiences unique to region. Nothing has been more destructive of regional segregation than the good work done on the experiences of women of color, working-class women, and others who had received scant attention before the 1990s. As historians continue to discover and delineate the stories of women beyond the planter elite and the Northern white middle class, without discounting or dismissing the place of such women in understanding the dynamics and directions of women's lives, historians are giving us a richer and more nuanced history of the U.S. Civil War. Or to put it another way, as the history has become less "racially gendered" it has also become less "regionally segregated." The essays in this collection point us toward that progress and the work that remains to be done.

NOTE

1. Thavolia Glymph, "The Civil War Era," in *A Companion to American Women's History,* ed. Nancy Hewitt (Oxford: Blackwell, 2002), 171.

PART

Politics

Southern Women and Politics in the Civil War Era

Elizabeth R. Varon

"Fiddle-dee-dee! War, war, war; this war talk is spoiling all the fun at every party this spring. I get so bored I could scream," proclaims the iconic Southern belle, Scarlett O'Hara, in the opening scenes of the 1939 movie *Gone with the Wind*. This image of Southern women's disdain for politics held sway in the public mind for much of the twentieth century. But the advent of women's history as a serious scholarly discipline has brought to light a far more compelling and complex set of images. Scholarship of the past fifty years has established that Southern women were integral to nineteenth-century politics. They played a limited, largely symbolic role in the formal realm of "high" electoral politics, as ardent supporters of political parties; they participated in moral reform societies on behalf of causes such as temperance and in memorialization societies such as the Mount Vernon Ladies Association; they were prominent in print culture, contributing polemics to the slavery debates; and they played a robust role in the broader realm of "infrapolitics," or the daily resistance of subordinate groups to the prevailing power structure.[1] Women's actions—the flight of female slaves from plantations, for example, or the efforts by white female writers to defend slavery against abolitionist critiques—deepened the alienation of the North from the South.

When war broke out, white women contributed to the Confederate cause in a wide range of ways, most visibly as hospital workers. But the scope and duration of the war tested women's patriotism, and thus a lively debate has taken shape among modern scholars over whether home front demoralization—white women's waning commitment to Southern nationalism—was a major factor in spelling the doom of the Confederacy. Recent scholarship has also challenged us to break the habit of equating the South with the Confederacy, and to take into consideration female Unionists in the Civil War South, black and white, and also those women who resided in the war-torn slaveholding border states. Understanding the scope and variety of Southern women's political activism is vital for understanding the war's causes, course, and consequences.

Recent scholarship has elaborated interlocking story lines that "gender" the familiar narrative of sectional alienation. One line traces the divergence of gender conventions in the North and South, as economic modernization gave rise to new understandings of masculinity and femininity in the North even as the white South defended traditional patriarchy. Another traces the politicization of women in the antebellum era, as they were drawn into the slavery debates—implicated both in resistance to and defense of the peculiar institution. A third story line concerns how the first two developments were perceived: how the *perception* that the Northern and the Southern social orders had grown incompatible fed the *conviction* that the two sections were politically irreconcilable.[2]

These storylines offer us new perspectives on some familiar characters and events on the road to Civil War. For example, we all know about Harriet Beecher Stowe's contribution, with her best-selling 1852 novel *Uncle Tom's Cabin,* to the antislavery cause. Stowe represented the centrality of Northern women to the abolitionist movement and the use of sentimental fiction for political purposes. Stowe's novel not only inflamed the proslavery press in the South, it also prompted a concerted response from white Southern female writers like Mary Eastman and Louisa Mc-Cord, who countered Stowe with rose-colored fantasies about the purported gentility and harmony of plantation life. Works like Eastman's *Aunt Phillis's Cabin; or, Southern Life As It Is,* published the same year as Stowe's book, were widely hailed in the proslavery press. Eastman offered readers a panoply of "contented" slaves and large doses of editorializing on slavery, in which she maintained that both the Bible and the Revolutionary forefathers had vouched for the institution. Such "anti-Tom" novels were the literary antecedents to that most enduring volley in the ongoing literary war over slavery, Margaret Mitchell's 1936 revival of the plantation-fiction genre, *Gone with the Wind.*[3]

Eastman and McCord represent the paradox of conservative women's political activism. They sought to defend the principle of social hierarchy: the doctrines of white supremacy and of "separate spheres" for men and women. According to the prevailing gender conventions of the era, the public sphere of politics, characterized by controversy, competition, and corruption, was the realm of men, while women were assigned to the safe and sedate private sphere of home and family. Women could exert influence, understood as gentle and noncoercive, as they did in a variety of charitable societies and church groups dedicated to aiding the unfortunate and spreading the gospel. But women should not exert power and court controversy. Southern critics of Harriet Beecher Stowe accused her of encroaching on the male terrain of politics and of representing the radical doctrine of women's rights; but, paradoxically, women like McCord and Eastman themselves entered the public fray in order to level such accusations at Stowe.[4]

In defending slavery as a positive good, Eastman and McCord also represent the eclipse of a tenuous tradition of "gradualism" in the South. Some reform-minded women in the Upper South, such as Mary Blackford of Fredericksburg, Virginia, had supported the American Colonization Society (ACS)—which encouraged the

Elizabeth R. Varon

manumission of slaves and their deportation to the African colony of Liberia—as a vehicle to promote the gradual, voluntary dismantling of slavery. Blackford, a staunch Episcopalian, trumpeted the religious benevolence of the cause, on the grounds that migrants to Africa would bring Christianity there and that she and her fellow ACS reformers were simply using familiar vehicles for benevolence, such as fundraising fairs and the distribution of tracts, to exhort their neighbors to good deeds. But these claims to benevolence did not insulate the ACS from criticism, as it came under withering attacks from abolitionists, who saw it as a front for proslavery interests, and slavery defenders, who saw it as a front for abolitionism. In the 1850s, as white Southerners closed ranks against the abolitionist threat, gradualism became politically suspect, and women like Blackford became marginalized.[5]

We all know the name of Harriet Tubman and recognize her role in leading the Underground Railroad in the 1850s. She was a remarkable, heroic individual.[6] But she was not alone. Recent scholarship has recovered the names and stories of scores of female fugitives from slavery and of female Underground Railroad operatives, white and black, Northern and Southern, who fought their own campaign along the border of the free and slave states. Their stories may be forgotten today, but they were national news back then.[7] When the slave Jane Johnson was rescued from her master (a prominent Southern politician) by the Underground Railroad in Philadelphia in 1855, her case became a national cause célèbre. Johnson risked recapture by testifying in public on behalf of her abolitionist allies and proclaiming the slave's natural yearning for freedom; to the antislavery press, she represented the courage and dignity of enslaved women. To the proslavery press, however, she represented the faithlessness of Northerners, who, in defiance of the 1850 Fugitive Slave Law, refused to act as slave catchers. The hundreds of enslaved women who risked life and limb to seek freedom thus directly impacted the course of the sectional crisis: among the principal grievances of secessionists was their complaint that the border between North and South was too porous, and the Upper South too vulnerable to slave flight.[8]

Women who fled slavery and found refuge in the North entered the literary war over slavery by publishing narratives of their experiences. The most influential of these was Harriet Jacobs's *Incidents in the Life of a Slave Girl,* published in 1861 under the penname Linda Brent. *Incidents* offered a searing indictment of the sexual predations of slaveholding men and the callous cruelty of plantation mistresses. "No pen can give an adequate description of the all-pervading corruption produced by slavery. The slave girl is reared in an atmosphere of licentiousness and fear," Jacobs explained. Jacobs points out that on the eve of the Civil War abolitionists were still fighting the problem of disbelief: the propensity of white Northerners to accept uncritically proslavery accounts of Southern life. "Reader, I draw no imaginary pictures of southern homes," Jacobs declared. "I am telling you the plain truth. Yet when victims make their escape from this wild beast of Slavery, northerners consent to act the part of bloodhounds, and hunt the poor fugitive back into his den, 'full of dead men's bones, and all uncleanness.'"[9]

Slave narratives, together with WPA interviews (conducted during the New Deal by the Works Progress Administration, to chronicle the prewar experiences of former slaves) and other firsthand accounts, have made it possible for historians to recover the wide spectrum of slave resistance, including the daily acts of resistance on the part of slave women, such as feigning illness, work slowdowns, tool-breaking, and truancy (short-term flight). As the scholar Stephanie Camp has demonstrated, seemingly "small" or even covert gestures of defiance by the enslaved—the holding of illegal parties, away from the master's gaze, or the display in the slave quarters of abolitionist images—created "rival geographies" on the plantation landscape, carving out zones of physical and psychological autonomy for slaves. Such acts must be regarded, Camp has persuasively argued, as "political," for they sustained a culture of opposition to white domination that stoked the anxieties of slaveholders and served as a foundation for more overt forms of black politics during and after the Civil War.[10]

Moreover, it was not just Southern women's actions but also *gender aspersions* that worked to escalate the sectional conflict. Attacks on the manhood and womanhood of one's political opponents—the charge that they were not "true" men and women—were a staple of antebellum politics. Lashing out against the gender egalitarianism of radical antislavery societies, which featured women, including South Carolina's anomalous Grimké sisters (elite slaveholders who repudiated slavery and the South), as orators and managers, antiabolitionists linked women's rights to the specter of disunion. When thousands of Northern women signed petitions to Congress demanding an end to slavery and rejected the annexation of Texas, Southern politicians offered them jarring chastisements. Rep. Jesse A. Bynum of North Carolina, for example, declared in 1837 that it was an "awful omen, when women were stepping into the political sphere, calling on men to act." Women's agitation would result in a "civil war . . . that would drench the fairest fields of this great republic with brothers' blood."[11]

Such attacks, which became more pointed in the 1850s, greatly eroded the trust between the North and South. Indeed, by the eve of war, many Northerners and Southerners had come to believe that the gender conventions of the two regions were antagonistic and incompatible. Defenders of slavery and "Southern rights" charged that Northern society, with its bent for social reform and its nascent women's rights movement, was fundamentally hostile to the patriarchal social order of the slave South. As the proslavery *Richmond Enquirer* put it in 1856, in a typical accusation, antislavery Northerners who supported the new Republican Party threatened all of the pillars of traditional society: they were "at war with religion, female virtue, private property, and distinctions of race."[12]

Gender politics continued to roil Congress as well. In 1856 Preston Brooks, a representative from South Carolina, savagely beat Sen. Charles Sumner on the floor of the Senate with a cane after Sumner insulted the "honor" of the South with a speech on slavery in Kansas. On its face, this seems the perfect illustration of the maxim that politics was a man's world. But when put in its context, the incident illustrates how gender aspersions were central to the slavery debates. Sumner's speech had indicted the forceful incursions by Southern settlers in the West, and their bid

Elizabeth R. Varon

to establish a proslavery regime in Kansas, as the "rape of a virgin territory." Such sexualized imagery fueled the abolitionist critique of Southern men as rapacious and uncivilized, and of Southern society as saturated by violence against women. Proslavery forces who rallied around Brooks, by contrast, claimed that Sumner's defenseless capitulation to Brooks's blows proved that Northern men were weak and submissive, slavelike in their subservience. This fueled the proslavery critique of the North as a world turned upside down, in which "strong-minded" abolitionist women and radical free blacks had raised the specter of social equality and effected the erosion of male authority.[13]

Even as they imputed gender transgressions to their opponents, antebellum politicians routinely called on women to join the ranks of political parties and movements. Of course, women could not yet vote, and there was a very strong social taboo in place against female public speaking; nonetheless, elite and middle-class women—to whom Victorian culture ascribed a penchant for piety and virtue—had a distinct role to play in electoral politics, both in influencing and mobilizing male voters and in lending an aura of moral sanctity to political causes. In the 1840s the Whig Party was more enthusiastic about female partisanship than the rival Democratic Party; the Whigs' agenda was one of economic modernization and moral reform, and women, especially in Northern cities and towns, had demonstrated that they could be effective agents of reform movements such as the temperance (anti-liquor) cause. Such activism could be and was justified as an extension of women's maternal, domestic duty to promote piety and virtue—and women's support for the Whigs could be seen, in turn, as an extension of their benevolent work. Whig women in Richmond, Virginia, for example, used their social connections and fundraising skills to erect a statue in that city to Whig idol Henry Clay; Clay was a symbol, in their eyes, of political moderation and compromise. The Democrats by contrast, committed to defending slavery, agrarianism, and traditional values, were at first ambivalent about women's partisanship. They singled out for condemnation the Republicans' celebration of Jessie Frémont in the presidential election campaign of 1856; for example, a September 1856 editorial in the *Richmond Daily Dispatch* associated Jessie with the dread Northern doctrine of women's rights and referred to her supporters disparagingly as the "old Amazonian phalanx, of which [feminist/ abolitionist] Abby Kelly is Generalissimo." But by the late antebellum period, such opposition to women's overt partisanship faded somewhat, as Democrats came to realize the utility of claiming that pious women favored them over the Whigs and then the Republicans. The Southern nationalist wing of the Democratic party appealed to white Southern women to embrace the cause of Southern independence.[14]

Women's partisanship coexisted uneasily with the notion that they should, as an extension of their moral purity, be sectional mediators. This view was articulated forcefully in the rhetoric of a national organization led by elite southern women: the Mount Vernon Ladies' Association (MVLA), dedicated to restoring and preserving George Washington's mansion and estate and gravesite, which had fallen into dilapidation. Originally the brainchild of Ann Pamela Cunningham of South

Carolina, the MVLA had its organizational base in Virginia. The association, which eventually succeeded in restoring Mount Vernon, generated a wealth of discourse on women's civic duty. Publicized in newspapers such as the *Richmond Enquirer* and journals such as the *Southern Literary Messenger,* the MVLA was perhaps the most celebrated of all antebellum women's associations. Those who spoke on behalf of the organization advanced the idea that women's patriotism was different in kind from men's—it was purer, more self-sacrificing, more enduring. No cause was better suited to women, Beverly Wellford Jr., a prominent Virginia lawyer and orator, proclaimed in a July 4, 1855, speech on behalf of the MVLA, than "the cause of extinguishing in our country, sectional feeling and sectional asperities"; by preserving the "Mecca of Republicanism," women could "silence the ravings of a besotted fanaticism." Despite their efforts to serve as representatives of disinterested patriotism, the women of the MVLA became enmeshed in partisan and sectional controversies, first in a feud with the Southern nationalist wing of Virginia's Democratic Party, and then with the alienation of the MVLA's Southern wing from its Northern wing on the eve of secession. In the wake of the MVLA's purchase of Mount Vernon in 1858, the public discourse on Southern women's civic duty would undergo a marked change. The notion that women were more patriotic than men would prove to be enduring; the notion that they should serve as sectional mediators would be eclipsed.[15]

Abolitionist John Brown's failed raid on Harpers Ferry in 1859 accelerated a political reorientation among white Southern women, as their antipathy toward abolitionists gave way to more widespread hostility to the Northern people in general. Amanda Virginia Edmonds of Fauquier County, Virginia, spoke for many enraged Southerners when she wrote of the Brown conspirators, "I would see the fire kindled and those who did it singed and burnt until the last drop of blood was dried within them and every bone smouldered to ashes." Brown's raid, by revealing, so secessionists claimed, the secret will of the North, primed the pump for secession. But the tradition of proslavery Unionism, which cast the Union as the best bulwark against abolition and slave flight and insurrection, remained strong among segments of the white South, particularly in Upper and border South states. By the time of the secession crisis, champions of Union and of Southern nationalism alike claimed the "ladies" were on their side. During the election campaign of 1860 and the subsequent secession convention debates in the South, women attended speeches, rallies, and processions; contributed their own polemics to the partisan press; and, fortunately for historians, left a treasure trove of firsthand accounts of the deepening crisis. These accounts—letters, diaries, memoirs, poems, and stories—furnish moving and astute analyses of the advent of secession. Such sources are the most powerful argument for recognizing the centrality of women to the story of the war's causes. "Every woman was to some extent a politician," Sallie A. (Brock) Putnam of Richmond wrote in her memoirs in 1867, looking back on Virginia's secession convention of 1861. According to Putnam, an ardent secessionist who went on to serve as a Confederate nurse, there was no doubt where Virginia women's loyalty lay during the secession crisis: "The fact was, that long before the ordinance of secession was passed by the

Elizabeth R. Varon

Convention, almost every women in Richmond had in her possession a Confederate flag—ready, at any moment, to run it out her window."[16]

Recent scholarship on masculinity has disclosed that there was a generational gap among white Southern men on the issue of secession, with young men, eager to achieve wealth and authority, enthusiastically embracing the Confederacy as a vehicle for their own ambitions while many older men, already established and invested in the status quo, were wary of abandoning the Union. A parallel dynamic seems to have existed among women. Mary Blackford, the Fredericksburg colonizationist, was a reluctant secessionist, as she felt her sons' enthusiasm for disunion marked her own failure to properly instruct them in the "sentiments of patriotism." Younger women, by contrast, less steeped in the image of women as sectional mediators who should curb men's passions, were more easily swept away in the excitement of secession. Virginia teenager Mary Hill of Rappahannock County lamented in January of 1861 that her native state was dragging its feet about secession and wished that Virginia "had a little more South Carolinian fire," while Elizabeth Randolph Preston Allan observed that young people in her hometown of Lexington were wearing the "blue cockade, the Confederate badge," while "older people . . . hoped to preserve the Union."[17]

The Southern public press urged women to shake off any ambivalence about secession and to "repress certain womanly feelings and expectations for the good of the Cause," the historian Drew Faust has noted. Women assumed a prominent role in the rituals of troop departures, presenting young volunteers with uniforms and flags, and affirming women's belief that defense of the homeland was, as North Carolinian Catherine Edmondston put it, "the highest exercise of men's highest & holiest duty!" Regret gave way to resolve. "An indescribable sadness weighs down my soul as I think of our once glorious but now dissolving Union," Mary Jones of Georgia wrote her son Charles in the winter of 1861. "We have no alternative," she added. "Necessity demands that we now protect ourselves from entire destruction at the hands of those who have rent and torn and obliterated every national bond of union, of confidence and affection. When your brother and yourself were very little fellows, we took you into old Independence Hall; and at the foot of Washington's statue I pledged you both to support and defend the Union. *That Union* has passed away, and you are free from your mother's vow."[18]

Even as the Confederacy mobilized white women, a beleaguered minority of whites held out against secession. In the eyes of white Southern Unionists, the nascent Confederacy was coercive in nature. There is no more chilling account of how it felt to be a Unionist in the midst of secession fever than that of Elizabeth Van Lew of Richmond, Virginia. Van Lew was a native-born white Southerner, but one who harbored a loathing for slavery and a belief that her state, as the mother of the Union, should represent moderation and compromise. As she watched a secessionist procession snake through the streets of Richmond in the wake of Virginia's vote to join the Confederacy, she knew the time for compromise had passed. "Such a sight!" Van Lew wrote. "The multitude, the mob, the whooping, the tin-pan music, and the fierceness of a surging, swelling revolution. This I witnessed. I thought of France and as the procession passed, I fell upon my knees under the angry heavens, clasped my hands and prayed, 'Father forgive them, for they know not what they do.'" For Van Lew, secession was a kind of collective madness that had descended on the South. Although she could have easily sought refuge in the North, she chose to stay in Richmond during the war so that she could put her political principles on the line as the leading Union spy in the Confederacy. Her Richmond home was the nerve center of an elaborate interracial espionage ring that funneled critical information to Grant's army.[19]

Van Lew was remarkable—but not anomalous. When the war started, countless Southern white women transgressed the prevailing definitions of female patriotism to serve their chosen cause.

If Scarlett O'Hara represents Southern women's purported disdain for politics, the character of Melanie Wilkes from *Gone with the Wind* has represented their heroic mobilization for war. For a long time, the standard narrative of Southern women and the Civil War, inscribed in scholarship and popular culture, was the story of their unflagging devotion to "the Cause." While male civic duty in wartime was synonymous with the exercise of courage on the battlefield, women's duty was synonymous with sacrifice and benevolence—the willingness to send their men off to war and to channel their domestic skills into helping the troops. This patriotic division of labor reflected the idea that women's proper place was in the domestic sphere of home and family. The vast majority of writing on women and the war, through the 1960s, told us how women fulfilled those duties—and suggested that the Confederacy was populated by just so many Melanie Wilkeses, willing and eager to sacrifice their menfolk on the altar of the Confederacy.[20]

Since the advent of women's history as a field in the 1970s, a more fascinating story has come to light—we now see the Civil War as a conflict over gender roles and relations, in which women contested their political subordination to men. Scholars have found provocative examples of women who felt the prevailing ideal of sacrifice and benevolence asked too much of them—women who resisted the demands of patriotism, in countless letters begging their men to desert the army or asking the government to exempt them from the draft, and, more dramatically, in bread riots against Confederate authorities. The most famous of these, the Richmond Bread Riot of April 1863, pitted working-class women against a government that failed to uphold the basic contract at the heart of the South's paternalistic social order: that in return for their subordination, women would be protected by men. Feeling exploited by Confederate policies such as conscription, taxation, and impressment (government seizure of civilian goods), the women raised the hue and cry of a "rich man's war but a poor man's fight"—the charge that common people had been made to bear the brunt of the sacrifice. The Confederate government responded with the threat of force and punishment, dispersing the rioters and trying the ring-leaders, and elite commentators on the riot showed little sympathy or solidarity, deriding the female protesters as unpatriotic and unworthy of sympathy. Expressions of disillusionment and dissent, including protestations of war weariness by elite women in their private letters and diaries, have led some scholars to conclude that the Confederate nation failed ultimately to command the loyalty of its women; high rates of desertion in the war's last year, as women implored their men to come home, seem to offer empirical proof. The very fact that women, across the social spectrum, saw fit to reach out to Confederate authorities with their requests, complaints, commentary, and protests, is itself significant: women crafted a new political identity as "soldiers' wives," and they demanded a hearing.[21]

And yet other scholars have seen the glass as half full, emphasizing the resilience of Confederate patriotism, and noting that expressions of war weariness should not be conflated with a withdrawal of support for the Confederacy. Indeed, scholars have found countless provocative examples of Southern women who felt that the prevailing ideal of female sacrifice asked *too little* of them, and who sought to do more for the Cause. A common lament in Southern women's wartime letters and diaries was "I wish I was a man"; in a society that valorized male courage as the highest virtue, these women wanted to give the last full measure of devotion. In that spirit, countless women transgressed the boundary of women's sphere and of home front and battlefront. Women filled the void left by men by taking on new responsibilities, as plantation managers and farmhands, teachers, clerks, and factory workers. Scores of women worked as spies and scouts for the Confederacy. Even more surprising is historians' discovery and documentation of 250 cases of women who disguised themselves as men and fought as soldiers in the Union and Confederate ranks.[22]

Women also achieved a new level of visibility and public influence in the literary realm, stoking the public's will to make the necessary sacrifices. Women such as the novelist Augusta Jane Evans and poet Margaret Junkin Preston produced heralded works of Confederate propaganda. Evans's bestselling 1864 novel *Macaria; or Altars of Sacrifice* featured heroines who found fulfillment through service to the Confederacy. Although she had written newspaper articles as well as fiction on behalf of the Confederacy, and shared her political opinions with Confederate leaders, Evans after the war—embodying the same paradox as Eastman and McCord—spoke out against women's political participation and women's suffrage. The prolific and ambitious Margaret Junkin Preston, sister-in-law to Confederate hero Stonewall Jackson, was a Northern transplant to the South who became ever more ardent in her Confederate loyalty as she witnessed the tragedies of war. While privately lamenting those tragedies in her private writings, she churned out verses proclaiming the righteousness of the Confederate cause and lauding the strength and fortitude of Southern women; her long narrative poem *Beechenbrook: A Rhyme of War,* published in 1865, helped to articulate themes that would become central to the "Lost Cause" mythologizing of the martyred Confederacy as morally pure. She reveled in the notion that women could serve the Cause with their pens as men did with their swords.[23]

Our best window into how gender roles were challenged and contested during the war is in the field of medicine. Thousands of female hospital workers, whose ranks were made up of orderlies, nurses, hospital managers, and even a few female physicians, surged forward to assist the wounded. Kate Cumming of Mobile, Alabama, was one of the many Confederate women who heeded the call to serve. Over her family's objections, she volunteered to work in the hospital division of the Army of Tennessee, and on the second day of the Battle of Shiloh (April 1862) she set out along with some forty other women from Mobile to Corinth, the Confederate base to which the wounded were being evacuated. Cumming's remarkable wartime diary provides a window into how she acclimated to her new duties. On April 11 she wrote, "My heart beat with expectation as we neared Corinth. As I had never been where there was a large army, and had never seen a wounded man, except in the cars, as they passed, I could not help feeling a little nervous at the prospect of now seeing both. . . . Mrs. Ogden tried to prepare me for the scenes which I should witness upon entering the wards. But alas! Nothing that I had ever heard or read had given me the faintest idea of the horrors witnessed here." Cumming quickly steeled herself, noting in the next day's journal entry that "the foul air from this mass of human beings at first made me giddy and sick, but I soon got over it. We have to walk, and when we give the man any thing kneel, in blood and water; but we think nothing of it at all." Cumming also gave voice to her distress over the "confusion and want of order" that characterized the wards; "the amount of good done is not near what it might be, if things were better managed," she lamented, adding "I trust that in a little time things will be better."[24]

As they took on greater responsibilities, Confederate women who filled the ranks of hospital workers pressed for recognition of their expertise, hard work, and patriotic sacrifices. But such recognition proved elusive, as male authorities remained ambivalent about the prospect of female authority. In Richmond, for example, women were pushed out of the business of managing their own private hospitals. In the first year of the war, sixteen female-run hospitals operated in the Confederate capital. But in the fall of 1862 the Confederate Medical Department, seeking more centralized control, fiscal efficiency, and military discipline in medical care, ordered the private hospitals closed. They were to be supplanted by state-run, male-run general hospitals. Only one hospital manager, Sally Tompkins, a well-connected member of Richmond's social elite, was permitted to keep her own hospital open, and she was required to adhere to regulations enforced by male inspectors.[25]

The move to close private hospitals did not deter female volunteers; indeed, the success of the private hospitals ensured that women would be called upon to contribute to the general hospitals, not only as nurses but as "matrons," namely superintendents of the kitchens, laundries, and wards. Chief matrons had considerable authority, supervising workforces consisting of poor white women, convalescing soldiers, free blacks, and slaves and acting as confidantes and advocates for the patients (helping them, for example, obtain furloughs). But such authority was always circumscribed by the supervision of male surgeons and military officers, who typically were high-handed or openly hostile to the women. For example, Phoebe Yates Pember, a matron, at Chimborazo Military Hospital in Richmond, drew the wrath of her male superiors when she "made a concerted effort to protect the hospital's liquor supply, which was rationed daily to the patients, from the predations of the surgeons and other male hospital staff." Contests over female authority would mul-

Elizabeth R. Varon

tiply as the war ground on. And yet women in the end made a decisive difference. Scholars have established that Confederate hospitals managed by matrons boasted lower mortality rates than hospitals run by male surgeons, without matrons; the women's attention to hygiene, nutrition, and soldier morale contributed materially to their patients' recovery rates.[26]

Between the poles of female dissent and patriotic devotion ran a current of ambivalence: some women gave themselves over to the Cause but not wholeheartedly. The preeminent symbol of such ambivalence is none other than the Confederate first lady, Varina Davis. A sophisticated thinker who chafed under the prevailing assumptions of women's inferiority and dependence, Davis never fully accepted the central tenets of the Confederate faith: that secession was necessary and justified; that the war was winnable; and that Northerners were irredeemable demons. During the war, she maintained secret ties with Northern friends and even nursed Union prisoners of war. She frequently came under fire from the Confederate public, both for rumors of her undue influence over her husband in matters of patronage and for her general pessimism about the Confederate cause. These doubts about Varina Davis's loyalty seemed to be borne out when, in the late nineteenth century, she befriended the widow of Ulysses S. Grant and publicly opined that it had been God's will that the North defeat the South.[27] Varina Davis's case alerts us to the perils of trying to generalize about the degree of white women's fealty to the Confederacy.

At issue in controversies over women's war work and patriotism was the question of female accountability: were women to be classed as "innocents" in wartime, or as political actors?[28] Punishments as well as rewards were at stake. The "Woman Order" is a case in point. On May 15, 1862, Union general Benjamin F. Butler, heading up the army of occupation in New Orleans, promulgated his notorious General Order No. 28. Butler was disgusted by the insolent and abusive behavior of the Confederate women of New Orleans toward the Union soldiers there: women turned up their noses at soldiers, spat upon them, hurled insults, threw decayed food, and even emptied chamber pots from their windows onto Union men in the streets below. And so he decreed that any woman who showed such contempt for federal soldiers would "be treated as a woman of the town, plying her avocation"—namely, she would be liable for arrest as a prostitute. The "Woman Order" courted controversy. Confederates interpreted it as a grant of license to Union soldiers to sexually assault Southern ladies. Innocent women, the *Richmond Dispatch* fumed, were to be made victims of Yankee soldiers' "brutal passions." Northerners were divided. Some felt Butler's order was unchivalrous and an embarrassment; others argued that women, through their public acts of defiance, had forfeited the protections of chivalry and must be punished. Butler noted in his defense that he did not actually follow through by arresting anyone—and that his rhetorical threat had worked to pacify the female population. But the damage had been done. Butler would be known to Confederates hereafter as "the Beast."[29]

Confederate women would retain their reputation among Northerners as zealous partisans, and the need to break their spirit would help to motivate the turn to "hard war" policies, targeting civilian morale, by Union generals such as William

Tecumseh Sherman. The brutal guerrilla warfare that churned up border regions, particularly in Missouri, often witnessed the complete breakdown of distinctions between home front and battlefront, and combatant and noncombatant, as guerrilla bands on both sides targeted civilians with random acts of terror, and as military authorities tried to hold civilians accountable for guerrilla actions. For example, in August 1863 Union general Thomas Ewing Jr. issued General Order No. 11, requiring Southern sympathizers in four rural counties in western Missouri to leave their homes and be exiled to the Confederacy, as a punishment for their complicity in supporting the brutal rebel guerrilla William Quantrill.[30]

Over the course of Sherman's March to the Sea and the Carolinas campaign, military and economic resources were the Federals' principal targets—industrial and military property, foodstuffs, cotton and other crops, mills, and railroad tracks and depots, for example—but private property and domestic spaces were targeted too. Sherman instructed his soldiers that as they meted out destruction, they should "discriminate between the rich, who are usually hostile, and the poor and industrious, usually neutral or friendly." Technically, only authorized details of foragers were supposed to seize resources for the army's use from civilians. These rules were observed in the breach, with bands of so-called Bummers wreaking havoc on Southern households, carrying away not only provisions to supply the army but valuables and souvenirs for their own use. The historian Lisa Tendrich Frank has shown that such tactics were a premeditated form of gendered psychological warfare on Sherman's part, intended to "break the will of elite female Confederates" by invading their private domestic spaces—parlors, kitchens, bedrooms—and laying hands on articles such as clothes, quilts, and jewelry in symbolic acts of violation. Elite women openly defied the Yankee invaders in verbal and sometimes even physical altercations, knowing full well that such recalcitrance would likely ratchet up the Yankees' desire for vengeance. Sherman's tactics, Frank concludes, had the effect of reinvigorating elite women's Confederate patriotism. In Camden, South Carolina, for example, Emma Holmes confronted two of Sherman's men with her "bottled wrath" and a warning that "we would never be subdued, for if every man, woman & child were murdered, our blood would rise up and drive them away." "I taunted them with warring on women & children," Holmes wrote her in diary, and "laughed at their pretence of 'fighting for the old flag.'"[31]

The issue of accountability loomed especially large for Southern women who risked all for the cause of Union. Long before emancipation became a Union war aim, blacks pushed the agenda of freedom, by fleeing farms and plantations and seeking refuge with the Union army. This flight—a mass exodus of roughly half a million people—destabilized slavery, gave the lie to proslavery claims of a supposedly contented slave population, and bolstered the Union war effort, as former slaves worked in a wide range of capacities for the Federal army—as scouts, spies, skilled and unskilled laborers, and eventually as soldiers. In other words, the kind of resistance to slavery that had so often been covert before the war now became overt.

Women such as Susie King Taylor, a Georgia slave who fled to Union lines, exemplify this kind of patriotic service; Taylor worked as a nurse and teacher for a black

Elizabeth R. Varon

regiment during the war and published a stirring postwar memoir of her experiences as a "camp follower." African American women played leadership roles in providing assistance to the fugitive slaves who converged in places like Alexandria, Virginia, and Washington, D.C., along the border. Both Elizabeth Keckley, a celebrated seamstress who worked for Mary Todd Lincoln, and writer/reformer Harriet Jacobs were active in "contraband relief" societies, supporting black refugees from the South and trying to cope with the massive humanitarian crisis that wartime refugeeing had brought on.[32]

The Union officials and rank-and-file soldiers who administered "contraband camps" were often ambivalent or hostile toward black refugees. Many were unsure of their obligations; in the military culture of the era, soldiers were not accustomed to regarding the care of refugees as their responsibility.[33] As three officers at Helena, Arkansas, the site of several refugee camps, complained, "The contrabands are left entirely to the mercy and rapacity of the unprincipled part of our army." Black laborers were routinely exploited—not paid at all, or paid in counterfeit money, or robbed, if they had been paid in real money, by Union soldiers. Black men had little protection for their families: "the wives of some have been molested by soldiers to gratify their licentious lust, and their husbands murdered in endeavoring to defend them," the Helena officers noted with horror. The lack of shelter, clothing, food and sanitation bred diseases such as typhoid fever, measles, small pox, pneumonia and dysentery, and medical care was woefully inadequate; the "negro hospital" at Helena was "notorious for filth, neglect, mortality & brutal whipping." The Helena officers asked plaintively, "For the sake of humanity, for the sake of Christianity, for the good name of our army . . . cannot something be done to prevent this oppression"?[34]

This push and pull between whites who were hostile to emancipation and blacks who were determined to shape it made camps at once places of "despair and death," the historian Thavolia Glymph has written, and sites "of refuge and hope and the making of freedom." Harriet Jacobs attested to this paradox. She did relief work among refugees in Alexandria, Virginia, and bore witness to their suffering, sending reports of the dire conditions there to the Northern press, to inspire the benevolent to step forward with aid. She described men, women, and children languishing in destitution—but still displaying faith in the Union, and clinging to those moments in which the promise of freedom seemed to materialize. "Amidst all this sadness, we would sometimes hear a shout of joy," she wrote. "Some mother had come in, and found her long-lost child; some husband his wife. Brothers and sisters meet."[35]

For Jacobs, the human dramas that unfolded in the camps were a powerful indictment of slavery itself. What but the love of freedom, she asked, could compel fugitive slaves to seek refuge in such flawed sanctuaries? To well-minded whites who had an interest in assisting the freed people, Jacobs preached empathy: "Trust them." In letters she sent north after the Emancipation Proclamation had been issued, Jacobs compiled evidence of progress in the camps—of weddings, night classes, sewing circles, and other manifestations of the so-called contrabands' fitness for full citizenship. "Many have found employment, and are supporting themselves and their families," Jacobs wrote to abolitionist Lydia Maria Child in March 1863. "They are quick, intelligent and full of the spirit of freedom." Small victories sustained her: "I can but feel with my heart the last chain is to be broken, the accursed blot wiped out."[36]

Black Southern Unionists, together with white ones, represent a tradition of indigenous Southern dissent. It is commonplace to equate the Confederacy and the South—to say the South lost the Civil War. But as a number of recent studies demonstrate, that shorthand glosses over crucial divisions within the South. The South was divided by a number of regional fault lines, most notably the line dividing the mountainous upcountry "white belts" from low-country "black belts," where plantation slavery predominated, and the line dividing what we might call the border South or Upper South—states like Virginia—from the Deep South. Upper South states had close cultural and economic ties to the North and stronger cohorts of Unionists than Deep South states did. There were, in a sense, many Souths.

We can translate these divisions into striking numbers, thanks to the work of William Freehling, the author of *The South v. The South*. He shows that some 450,000 men from slave states fought in the Union blue: 150,000 of these were African Americans; 200,000 were whites in the four slave states (Missouri, Kentucky, Delaware, and Maryland) that did not secede; and 100,000 were whites from Confederate states like Virginia. These statistics give us a new perspective on an old debate: did the Confederacy lose because of the overwhelming numbers and resources of the North, or did the Confederacy die of internal causes, because of its own failure of will? If we confront the presence of Unionists in the South, we can fuse these two explanations and see that internal divisions in the South contributed to the North's manpower advantage. The Confederacy could not and did not command the loyalty of the entire South.[37]

And yet if we survey elite white Southern women's accounts of Confederate defeat from the spring of 1865, what is most striking is the red thread of defiance that runs through many of them: elite women were loath, at the bitter end, to acknowledge the flaws or divisions in their society and pessimistic about the prospect of reconciliation with the hated Yankees. Many regarded the conciliatory surrender terms that U. S. Grant offered Robert E. Lee at Appomattox as a transparent bid to lure Southerners into accepting renewed subjugation. Emma LeConte of Columbia, South Carolina, a fervent Confederate with a keen intellect and acid pen, wrote in her diary in late April, "I used to dream about peace, to pray for it, but this is worse than war. What is such peace to us? . . . It is too horrible. What I most fear is a conciliatory policy from the North, that they will offer to let us come back as before. Oh no, no! . . . Let them oppress and tyrannize, but let us take no favors of them." Sarah Fowler Morgan Dawson, who produced a massive diary of life in wartime Baton Rouge and New Orleans, was equally unrepentant. She learned of Lee's surrender on April 13. To those around her who seemed to welcome the return of "blessed Peace," she had this to say: "Never! Let a great earthquake swallow us up first! Let us leave our land and emigrate to any desert spot of the earth, rather than return to the Union, even as it Was!"[38] Such protestations bespoke these women's deep investment in the Confederate cause and their profound bitterness at the loss of slavery and the world it had once made.

Elizabeth R. Varon

Historians of Southern women have long debated an irresistible question: what was the impact of war-time behavioral changes on postwar norms? Was the Civil War, as pioneering historian Anne Firor Scott proposed in 1970, a "watershed" for Southern women? Certainly we can find evidence that by the late nineteenth century, white Southern women had more public authority and opportunities, as reformers, suffragists, and wage earners, than they had before the war; Scott hypothesized that the war had weakened the foundations of patriarchy. Other scholars, such as Drew Faust and George Rable, have countered that there was no clear cause-and-effect relationship between the war and these changes, and they have brought to light abundant evidence that some Southern women emerged from war fiercely nostalgic for the past and eager to return to prewar norms. Recent scholarship has sought greater precision in our questions and case studies. Work on women's Confederate memorial societies such as the United Daughters of the Confederacy has shown that they were vehicles through which women could seek simultaneously to uphold traditional values by romanticizing the Lost Cause and to wield new public authority as keepers of the Confederate flame. The historian Jane Turner Censer's generational approach to the question of the war's impact on women's political status has shown that older women, who had come of age early in the antebellum era, were more resistant to postwar change than younger ones, who did seek a new sort of self-reliance and independence of thought and action after the war, in their reform work, wage work, and literary output.[39]

The historian Thavolia Glymph has questioned the "war as watershed" thesis from another angle, disputing the notion that white women gained new authority over the plantation regime while men were away at war. Glymph shows that plantation mistresses had been architects and enforcers of the slave system all along: they wielded violence—systematic, not episodic—against slave women, in a volatile environment characterized by "warring intimacy." In sources such as the Works Progress Administration interviews conducted in the 1930s, women who had been household slaves testify that they regarded mistresses as more cruel and brutal even than masters. Black women saw white women as the face of slaveholder authority, and when the war began, enslaved women sought to destabilize that authority through heightened acts of resistance. After the war, freedwomen resisted white women's efforts to salvage the prewar order and turn them into all-purpose servants; black women organized to claim control over labor conditions (by negotiating wage rates for certain tasks), to mobilize voters on behalf of the Republican Party, and to establish independent households, free of the pall of white surveillance and demands. As the freed people's civil rights protections eroded with the demise of Reconstruction, so too did the negotiating power of former household slaves.[40]

Freedwomen's resistance reverberated directly in the halls of power, as they bore witness to the resurgence of power by ex-Confederates following Lincoln's assassination and Andrew Johnson's accession to the presidency; emboldened by Johnson's extreme lenience and his own commitment to white supremacy, former rebels used punitive laws and vigilante violence to enforce black subordination. Tragic events in Memphis, Tennessee, dramatized the scope and toll of that violence. On May 1,

1866, a white mob, led by city policemen, began a wave of attacks against African Americans in South Memphis. The violence stretched out over three terror-filled days. The precipitating incident was a clash between recently discharged black Union soldiers and white policemen at a festive gathering of African Americans on South Street when the police tried to suppress the blacks' celebration of emancipation and Union. In the midst of false rumors that the black troops were staging an "uprising," white civilians poured into South Memphis, setting fire to shanties, schools, and churches, pillaging stores and residences, sexually assaulting black women, and murdering at least forty-six freed people. As historian Hannah Rosen explains, the context for the mob violence was white fear and resentment at the prospect of "social equality" between the races. Memphis whites justified the riot by representing black troops as lawless and domineering and black women as lewd and disorderly. What was needed, these whites insisted, was "a restoration of the old order of things."[41]

Gen. George Stoneman, the Union commander in Memphis, ordered the rioters to stand down and then charged a military commission to gather testimony from black witnesses to the tragedy. A congressional committee conducted its own investigation, interviewing some sixty-six freed people. In the end, "no rioters were arrested or charged with any crimes," but, Rosen notes, the African American witnesses, particularly women who had had the courage to speak out about the sexual assaults they had suffered, nonetheless shaped the public debate on Reconstruction. The congressional committee's final report, widely distributed across the North, condemned the "licentious brutality" of the mob and described black women as respectable and blameless victims of "fiends in human shape."[42]

A small minority of white female Unionists publicly protested the resurgence of Confederate power under Johnson and then championed the program of Congressional Reconstruction, the foundation of which was black male suffrage. Elizabeth Van Lew, the former Union spy, was in their vanguard. When U. S. Grant became president, he rewarded her for her wartime service to the Union by appointing her postmaster of Richmond, Virginia—a high-paying, plum patronage job. She used her postmastership as a bully pulpit, appointing women and African Americans to work, for the first time, in the Richmond post office; publicizing and decrying anti-black proscription and violence; and advocating women's suffrage. Ex-Confederates, although they had been blind to Van Lew's political agency during the war (thanks to her success at keeping her espionage work secret), held her accountable afterward for her wartime sins—they accused her of being mentally unstable and cast her as traitor, whose punishment for her disloyalty should be a lifetime of derision and ostracism. Van Lew was driven out of office in 1877 and lived out the remainder of her years in Richmond isolated and in fear for her life.

In 1906, just six years after Van Lew's death, John Goode, who had been a delegate to Virginia's secession convention in 1861, wrote this in his memoirs: "Throughout the war, from its commencement to its close, the women of the Confederacy, although its greatest sufferers, were the truest of the true. In all the trials and vicissitudes of the war, it was their unfailing constancy that nerved the arms and strengthened the hearts

Elizabeth R. Varon

of their fathers, husbands, sons, and brothers. . . . It is due to the truth of history to say that the women of the Confederacy made the men of the Confederacy what they were."[43] Goode was thus sweeping under the rug not only Van Lew's story but also that of Susie King Taylor, Varina Davis, and a host of other women who contravened the myth of Southern solidarity. His words remind us of the high stakes involved in how we as historians define politics: if we define politics broadly, to include not only electoral contests but a variety of battles for social authority, we bring into focus not only the stunning range of women's public activism, but also their private agonies and triumphs.

NOTES

1. On "infrapolitics," see James C. Scott, *Domination and the Arts of Resistance: Hidden Transcripts* (New Haven, Conn.: Yale Univ. Press, 1992); and Stephanie M. H. Camp, *Closer to Freedom: Enslaved Women and Everyday Resistance in the Plantation South* (Chapel Hill: Univ. of North Carolina Press, 2004).

2. For some noteworthy works of the last decade, see Stephen W. Berry, *All That Makes a Man: Love and Ambition in the Civil War South* (New York: Oxford Univ. Press, 2003); Camp, *Closer to Freedom;* Amy Greenberg, *Manifest Manhood and the Antebellum American Empire* (New York: Cambridge Univ. Press, 2005); Michael D. Pierson, *Free Hearts and Homes: Gender and American Antislavery Politics* (Chapel Hill: Univ. of North Carolina Press, 2007); and Kristen Tegtmeier Oertel, *Bleeding Borders: Race, Gender and Violence in Pre-Civil War Kansas* (Baton Rouge: Louisiana State Univ. Press, 2009). For a concise interpretive synthesis, see Nina Silber, *Gender and the Sectional Conflict* (Chapel Hill: Univ. of North Carolina Press, 2009).

3. Elizabeth R. Varon, *We Mean to Be Counted: White Women and Politics in Antebellum Virginia* (Chapel Hill: Univ. of North Carolina Press, 1998), 154; Elizabeth R. Varon, *Disunion! The Coming of the American Civil War, 1789–1859* (Chapel Hill: Univ. of North Carolina Press, 2008), 246; Elizabeth Moss, *Domestic Novelists in the Old South: Defenders of Southern Culture* (Baton Rouge: Louisiana State Univ. Press, 2002).

4. Varon, *We Mean to Be Counted.*

5. Ibid., 46–47.

6. See, for example, Catherin Clinton, *Harriet Tubman: The Road to Freedom* (New York: Little, Brown, 2004).

7. Eric Foner, *Gateway to Freedom: The Hidden History of the Underground Railroad* (New York: W. W. Norton, 2015); Manisha Sinha, *The Slave's Cause: A History of Abolition* (New Haven, Conn.: Yale Univ. Press, 2016).

8. Nat Brandt and Yanna Brandt, *In the Shadow of the Civil War: Passmore Williamson and the Rescue of Jane Johnson* (Columbia: Univ. of South Carolina Press, 2007).

9. Harriet Jacobs [Linda Brent], *Incidents in the Life of a Slave Girl* (Boston: For the Author, 1861), 56, 79.

10. Camp, *Closer to Freedom.*

11. Varon, *Disunion!,* 130.

12. Ibid., 268–70.

13. Ibid.

14. Varon, *We Mean to Be Counted,* 13; Christopher J. Olsen, *Political Culture and Secession in Mississippi: Masculinity, Honor, and the Antiparty Tradition, 1830–1860* (New York: Oxford Univ. Press, 2000).

15. Varon, *We Mean to Be Counted,* 124–36; http://www.mountvernon.org/digital-encyclo-pedia/article/ann-pamela-cunningham; Mount Vernon Ladies' Association, *Historical Sketch of Ann Pamela Cunningham* (New York: Marion Press, 1911).

16. Edmonds and Putnam, as qtd. in Varon, *We Mean to Be Counted,* 140, 154.

17. Berry, *All That Makes a Man;* Peter S. Carmichael, *The Last Generation: Young Virginians in Peace, War, and Reunion* (Chapel Hill: Univ. of North Carolina Press, 2005); Varon, *We Mean to Be Counted,* 152–53.

18. Drew Gilpin Faust, *Mothers of Invention: Women of the Slaveholding South in the American Civil War* (Chapel Hill: Univ. of North Carolina Press, 2003), 15–16; Mary Jones to Charles C. Jones Jr., Jan. 3, 1861, in Brooks D. Simpson, Stephen W. Sears, and Aaron Sheehan-Dean, eds., *The Civil War: The First Year Told by Those Who Lived It* (New York: Library of America, 2011), 178.

19. Elizabeth R. Varon, *Southern Lady, Yankee Spy: The True Story of Elizabeth Van Lew, a Union Agent in the Heart of the Confederacy* (New York: Oxford Univ. Press, 2003), 51.

20. See, e.g., Mary Elizabeth Massey, *Bonnet Brigades: American Women and the Civil War* (New York: Alfred A. Knopf, 1966).

21. Stephanie McCurry, *Confederate Reckoning: Power and Politics in the Civil War South* (Cambridge, Mass.: Harvard Univ. Press, 2010); Faust, *Mothers of Invention.*

22. George Rable, *Civil Wars: Women and the Crisis of Southern Nationalism* (Champaign-Urbana: Univ. of Illinois Press, 1989); Elizabeth Leonard, *All the Daring of a Soldier: Women of the Civil War Armies* (New York: W. W. Norton, 1999); DeAnne Blanton and Lauren M. Cook, *They Fought Like Demons: Women Soldiers in the Civil War* (Baton Rouge: Louisiana State Univ. Press, 2002).

23. http://www.georgiaencyclopedia.org/articles/arts-culture/macaria; http://www.en-cyclopediaofalabama.org/article/h-1072; Stacy Jean Klein, *Margaret Junkin Preston, Poet of the Confederacy: A Literary Life* (Columbia: Univ. of South Carolina Press, 2007); Jonathan Daniel Wells, *Women Writers and Journalists in the Nineteenth-Century South* (Cambridge: Cambridge Univ. Press, 2011), 153–59.

24. Kate Cumming, *Kate: The Journal of a Confederate Nurse,* ed. Richard Barksdale Harwell (Baton Rouge: Louisiana State Univ. Press, 1998), 14–19.

25. Libra R. Hilde, *Worth a Dozen Men: Women and Nursing in the Civil War South* (Charlottesville: Univ. of Virginia Press, 2012).

26. E. Susan Barber, "Sally Louisa Tompkins, Confederate Healer," in Cynthia A. Kierner and Sandra Gioia Treadway, eds., *Virginia Women: Their Lives and Times* (Athens: Univ. of Georgia Press, 2015), 1:352–54.

27. Joan E. Cashin, *First Lady of the Confederacy: Varina Davis's Civil War* (Cambridge, Mass.: Harvard Univ. Press, 2006).

28. On accountability as a theme, see Silber, *Gender and the Sectional Conflict.*

29. Earl J. Hess, *The Civil War in the West: Victory and Defeat from the Appalachians to the Mississippi* (Chapel Hill: Univ. of North Carolina Press, 2012), 84–91; Andrew S. Coopersmith, *Fighting Words: An Illustrated History of Newspaper Accounts of the Civil War* (New York: New Press, 2004), 97–101.

30. Hess, *Civil War in the West,* 84–91; Coopersmith, *Fighting Words,* 97–101; Michael Fellman, *Inside War: The Guerrilla Conflict in Missouri During the American Civil War* (New York: Oxford Univ. Press, 1990).

31. Lisa Tendrich Frank, *The Civilian War: Confederate Women and Union Soldiers during Sherman's March* (Baton Rouge: Louisiana State Univ. Press, 2015), 6–8, 60–62, 105–6; John F. Marszalek, ed., *Diary of Miss Emma Holmes, 1861–1866* (Baton Rouge: Louisiana State Univ. Press, 1979), 402.

32. Camp, *Closer to Freedom*; Susie King Taylor, *Reminiscences of My Life in Camp: An African American Woman's Civil War Memoir* (Athens: Univ. of Georgia Press, 2006); Jean Fagan Yellin, *Harriet Jacobs: A Life* (New York: Basic Books, 2005); Jennifer Fleischner, *Mrs. Lincoln and Mrs. Keckley: The Remarkable Story of the Friendship Between a First Lady and a Former Slave* (New York: Broadway Books, 2003).

33. Jim Downs, *Sick from Freedom: African-American Illness during the Civil War and Reconstruction* (New York: Oxford Univ. Press, 2012, 50–51, 55–56).

34. Halleck to Grant, Mar. 31, 1863; Officers' Report, Helena, Ark., Dec. 29, 1862; Eaton Questionnaire, Apr. 29, 1863, in Ira Berlin et al., eds., *Free at Last: A Documentary History of Slavery, Freedom, and the Civil War* (New York: New Press, 1992), 101–2, 180–81, 190–93.

35. Eaton Questionnaire, Apr. 29, 1863, in Berlin et al., *Free at Last,* 105; Thavolia Glymph, "Refugee Camp at Helena, Arkansas, 1863," in J. Matthew Gallman and Gary Gallagher, eds., *Lens of War: Exploring Iconic Photographs of the Civil War* (Athens: Univ. of Georgia Press, 2015), 139; "Harriet Jacobs to William Lloyd Garrison," in Stephen W. Sears, ed., *The Civil War: The Second Year* (New York: Library of America, 2012), 385–89; "Harriet Jacobs to Lydia Maria Child," Mar. 18, 1863, in Brooks D. Simpson, ed., *The Civil War: The Third Year Told by Those Who Lived It* (New York: Library of America, 2013), 99.

36. Jacobs to Child, Mar. 18, 1863, in Simpson, ed., *Civil War,* 99; Yellin, *Harriet Jacobs,* 167.

37. William Freehling, *The South vs. The South: How Anti-Confederate Southerners Shaped the Course of the Civil War* (New York: Oxford Univ. Press, 2001).

38. Emma LeConte, *When the World Ended: The Diary of Emma LeConte,* ed. Earl Schenck Miers (Lincoln: Univ. of Nebraska Press, 1987), 90–91; Sarah Morgan, *The Civil War Diary of a Southern Woman,* ed. Charles East (New York: Touchstone, 1992), 606.

39. On this debate, see Anne Firor Scott, *The Southern Lady: From Pedestal to Politics, 1830–1930* (Chicago: Univ. of Chicago Press, 1970); Faust, *Mothers of Invention;* Rable, *Civil Wars;* and Jane Turner Censer, *The Reconstruction of White Southern Womanhood, 1865–1895* (Baton Rouge: Louisiana State Univ. Press, 2003).

40. Thavolia Glymph, *Out of the House of Bondage: The Transformation of the Plantation Household* (Cambridge: Cambridge Univ. Press, 2008).

41. Hannah Rosen, *Terror in the Heart of Freedom: Citizenship, Sexual Violence, and the Meaning of Race in the Postemancipation South* (Chapel Hill: Univ. of North Carolina Press, 2009), 61–69.

42. Ibid., 81–82.

43. John Goode, *Recollections of a Lifetime* (Richmond: Neale, 1906), 53.

"All Ladies Have Politics"

Women, Morality, and Politics in the North

S t a c e y   M .   R o b e r t s o n

In the summer of 1856, amid a lively and contentious presidential campaign that pitted Democrat James Buchanan against two candidates from new parties, Millard Fillmore for the Know-Nothings and famed explorer John C. Frémont for the Republicans, a group of abolitionists met in Abington, Massachusetts, to celebrate the anniversary of the West Indian emancipation. Predictably, participants engaged in a heated discussion about the campaign. Wendell Phillips, the blue-blooded radical whose eloquence dazzled even his opponents, declared to the large audience, "I value politics, not for the men it elects, but for the discussion it permits. The canvass is worth a hundred fold more than the election." This particular canvass allowed for a serious national conversation about slavery and, indirectly, women and politics. While many Americans considered the Republican Party nominee to be the abolitionist candidate, Phillips questioned John Frémont's antislavery credentials and proclaimed that the *real* abolitionist—and the superior politician—in the Frémont family was John's wife Jessie: "*If Jessie is an Abolitionist, put her up for President (cheers); but do not put her husband up.*"[1]

As Phillips's proclamation suggests, Jessie Frémont was a central figure in the 1856 election, and her prominence highlights the extent to which women had already entered the political fray, primarily though not entirely through the Northern abolitionist movement. During the relentless partisan discussions and mass political meetings that occurred throughout the summer and into the fall of 1856, slavery was a dominant theme. Indeed, slavery had disturbed and rankled American politics for decades—and women had long since entered and perturbed, even disrupted, this contentious space. Beginning even before William Lloyd Garrison founded his abolitionist newspaper the *Liberator* in 1831, Northern women had forged a place for themselves in the national debate over slavery.[2] Who better, after all, to highlight the immorality and inhumanity of slavery than women? Who better to protect the sacred role of motherhood, which was so threatened by slavery, than women? Who better to defend enslaved women's virtue than women? Such questions informed and animated women's increasing involvement in antislavery and social reform politics. Thus, it should have been no surprise that women in the North participated in the 1856 presidential campaign in large numbers, larger indeed than ever before in a presidential election.[3] Jessie Frémont became a symbol of Northern women's partisanship and especially their moral opposition to slavery. As Phillips's comment suggests, Jessie's abolitionist credentials outshone her husband's and offered hope and inspiration to Northern opponents of slavery, men and women alike.

Northern women's partisanship began in earnest with the Whig Party in 1840, but the ground had been laid by abolitionist and reform women who carefully negotiated a space for themselves in the political arena, though not so much as partisan players than as guardians of virtue in the nation. This moral caretaker role would slowly expand, reaching directly into partisanship by the Civil War. The expansion was multilayered and complicated: abolitionist political parties invited women to the table in the 1840s and 1850s, while at the same time women novelists, journalists, and orators began writing and speaking about politics through a variety of venues. Southern women, as well, occasionally found ripe conditions to justify strategic partisan interventions. While antislavery sentiment was often the impetus for political engagement, women had become increasingly knowledgeable about and concerned with partisan developments in their communities and states, regardless of their position on slavery. As Ronald and Mary Zboray have shown in their examination of thousands of Northern women's diaries, more than 40 percent referred to reading political newspapers; discussing politics with friends, family, and neighbors; or participating in some type of political event. Amid this increasing politicization of Northern women, however, abolitionist women led the way in direct partisan engagement. For these women, a common theme emerged in their political efforts: the immorality of slavery trumped man's law. This Higher Law emphasis allowed women a rationale for intruding into a traditionally male space even as they began to "feminize" this space with discussions of morality and virtue. During and after the Civil War, women continued to insist that their voices be heard in the halls of legislatures across the North.

By the mid 1850s, when the Republican Party offered its first presidential candidate, the Northern public had come to expect at least a circumscribed place for women in campaigns, political discussions, and the larger cultural engagement with partisanship. To be sure, the acceptance of women's place in politics varied across party and region, but the persistence and consistency of women's voices in partisan discussions could not be denied. As one Ohio abolitionist wrote to a friend, "All Ladies *have politics* now."[4]

Women's partisan activism experienced a false start as early as the Revolution, when New Jersey lawmakers gave *any inhabitant* "worth fifty pounds" the right to vote. Although married women could not hold property, about one hundred single and widowed women joined New Jersey men in voting each year. This brief window of political opportunity closed in 1807, when New Jersey legislators rescinded the right to vote for all women and African American men.[5] Even without the vote, however, women slowly wedged back open the political window over the next three decades, relying on new assumptions about women's generous and virtuous nature. This process began with women's increased access to education; continued with their participation in collective women's organizations such as charitable and benevolent groups; and expanded further with their opportunity for paid employment and their involvement in abolition and women's rights. All of these activities and experiences broadened women's understanding of their civic identity and their place in "public," broadly defined to include everything from courthouses to schoolhouses to statehouses to the world of ideas. This potholed process took place over several decades, eventually leading to women's increased opportunity for partisan activity.[6] Not everyone took advantage of the opportunity, however. This was neither a linear nor an inevitable process. The complex rhythm of women's life cycles meant that involvement in political moments, such as listening to one's parents discuss a political issue or attending a partisan family barbecue, likely changed with marriage, childbirth, or employment. While this essay engages with the indirect and inconsistent involvement of Northern women in political moments, it is more interested in how this involvement led to and allowed for women's direct engagement with partisanship.

One of the most important developments for women's political engagement was the antislavery petition campaign of the 1830s. Starting in Ohio, women abolitionists developed a polite but insistent petition to Congress requesting the elimination of slavery in the District of Columbia. Known as the "Fathers and Rulers" petition, it offered a "humble memorial" that appealed to both Christianity and virtue in support of freedom for enslaved men and women in the nation's capital. While the petition's language was tame and its message supplicating, the process of gathering signatures on an antislavery petition required women to become politically knowledgeable and articulate as they discussed and debated slavery with friends, neighbors, and even strangers. This experience was a political awakening for many women. As one male abolitionist leader wrote to a colleague about women's antislavery petitioning, it is "worse than useless to advise females to take an active part in any public movement unless they feel within them a *self sustaining power, a confidence,* that no obstacle can weaken, no opposition subdue."[7] The Fathers and Rulers petition spread with a surprising ferocity and helped lead in 1837 to the "Gag Rule" in the U.S. House of Representatives that automatically tabled all antislavery petitions. Furious at the silencing of their political voices, abolitionists reacted by redoubling their petitioning efforts.[8]

By the 1840 presidential election, Whig partisan organizers recognized the political opportunity that women's support offered, and they engaged in a targeted and shrewd "mass mobilization" of women in support of their candidate, Henry Clay.[9] Whig leaders understood that it was helpful to highlight women's support for Clay in order to secure the moral upper hand in the election. As the nation's purported conscience, women's presence at Whig rallies meant that Clay could claim the mantle of virtue. Whig women responded with enthusiasm. They brought their children to Whig picnics, thus linking family to the party. Partisan events became opportunities for courtship, as newly politicized women expressed preference for Whig men. A scattering of Southern women even joined the excitement, including some single

Stacey M. Robertson

Tennessee women who fainted during Clay's speeches.[10] These Whig ladies were joined by thousands of women reformers and abolitionists, who had learned during the previous decade the potential of partisan engagement, particularly through their petitioning efforts.[11] Although these Northern women utilized their moral authority in order to claim a political voice, it is important to note that by the 1840s women's partisanship was not exclusively limited to moral issues. Like their fathers, husbands, sons, and brothers, women also favored a particular party because it best represented their economic, racial, and regional interests. These female partisans were motivated by "a blend of kin and neighborhood affiliation, party loyalty, and rational judgment of current economic and political issues."[12]

While the Whigs helped pave the road toward increased partisanship among women, it was abolitionist third parties that created the greatest opportunity for politically minded women. Interestingly, until recently historians argued that women abolitionists tended to side with William Lloyd Garrison, who opposed the creation of an abolitionist third party and would eventually discourage voting entirely due to the proslavery nature of the Constitution. Garrisonians worried that partisan politics would dilute abolitionism and lead to unnecessary and debilitating political compromises. They believed that the desire to win office would eventually outweigh all moral concerns. Scholars have suggested that women abolitionists generally favored this position because they were more concerned with the morality of slavery and they were excluded from partisan politics. But recent studies have shown that many women abolitionists became passionate supporters of antislavery politics. As Melanie Gustafson writes, "Third parties were broad entities that fused the civic world of benevolent and reform organizations with the electoral world of voting and legislating. As such, they provided women with a new path into partisan politics, as antislavery activism moved from moral suasion to practical politics."[13]

Many antislavery women were primed for partisanship. First, as abolitionists they understood that ending slavery was as much a political issue as a moral issue. They were familiar with political debates over slavery in the territories and in the District of Columbia through their petitioning work. They also knew that racial equality was subject to political will, and they sought to repeal racist laws and practices by working through state legislatures. Women abolitionists became familiar with political systems, partisan dynamics, and the importance of engaging with party leaders, politicians, and electoral processes. Moreover, like their male counterparts, they had become frustrated with the failures of moral suasion as a method to convince slaveholders to voluntarily end slavery. Although still committed to supporting abolition as a moral problem, they sought a more pragmatic method for ending slavery. Many were exhilarated, therefore, when the Liberty Party emerged in 1840 as a third party devoted to rolling back slavery and challenging legalized racial inequality.[14]

The Liberty Party of the 1840s boasted that it was an "anti-party" political party. This provided women with a perfect opportunity to engage in politics without seeming to be political.[15] Focused primarily on forcing the two major parties—the Whigs and the Democrats—into a national discussion about slavery, the Liberty Party emphasized the sinfulness of slavery and the wrong of racial discrimination. Women abolitionists had forged a leadership role in both of these areas throughout their involvement in the movement. Pointing to the sexual degradation of enslaved women and the tragic breakup of enslaved families, the immorality of slavery was a constant theme for female antislavery societies across the North. Women abolitionists also created schools for free blacks in the North and tried to repeal the infamous Black Laws that prevented free blacks from voting, serving on juries, and, in some cases, even residing in the jurisdiction.[16]

After honing their political skills in the Liberty Party, many women continued their partisanship with the new abolitionist Free Soil Party that emerged as a successor to the Liberty Party, which had fallen into disarray by the late 1840s. While the new party took a more conservative approach to abolition than the Liberty Party—focusing on the exclusion of slavery from the western territories as a benefit to the "free labor" of white men—it nonetheless attracted leftover Liberty Party supporters as well as antislavery-leaning Democrats and Whigs who had become disillusioned with their parties.

Many women abolitionists supported the Free Soil Party, hoping it might have more success than the Liberty Party. They entered the new decade determined to participate in national policy developments, but they were quickly disappointed. The passage of the Compromise of 1850—which ended a multiyear debate regarding the new territories acquired during the Mexican-American War—disgusted women Free Soilers, who felt betrayed by their politicians. While the Compromise admitted California as a free state, it allowed the residents in the Utah and New Mexico territories to decide the future of slavery in those locations and, most distressing, it created a more stringent Fugitive Slave Law, which forced Northerners to participate in returning freedom seekers to their purported owners. These political developments increased support for the Higher Law position among women abolitionists in particular. Recognizing the power of legislative rule and concerned that good men would support the Fugitive Slave Law because it was the law of the land, women sought to provide virtuous Northern voters with an alternative approach. God's law, they argued, trumped the immoral laws created by man. Women hoped to convince Free Soil Party leaders to adopt this "moral discourse" of the Higher Law. "Free Soil men greeted the women's efforts warmly," according to Michael Pierson, "knowing that women's moral attacks recruited new members and helped maintain the loyalty of party radicals."[17] Women Free Soilers were, in fact, among the most articulate, persuasive, and influential advocates of the Higher Law position.

Jane Swisshelm and Clarina Nichols edited Free Soil newspapers during the 1850s. Both women developed a following among abolitionists, and they wielded power within the party.[18] Frederick Douglass argued that "women are beginning to have much influence in politics. There are few papers exerting greater influence than the *Saturday Visiter*, edited by Mrs. Swisshelm, and the *Brattleboro Democrat*, edited by Mrs. Nichols."[19] Clarina Nichols, who founded the Vermont paper, used the pages of the *Brattleboro Democrat* to remind readers of the immorality of slavery. She

Stacey M. Robertson

reasoned that God's laws favored freedom over slavery and that to disobey God was to invite punishment. Swisshelm lived in Pennsylvania, and she had a long history of political antislavery activism. She began her newspaper in 1847 as a voice of the Liberty Party, eventually transferring her loyalty to the Free Soil Party. She relentlessly underscored the human element in slavery, focusing particularly on women and children. Constitutional compromises, she proclaimed, were simply excuses to provide Southern slaveholders with the right to "horsewhip a woman and sell her baby." Challenging politicians and voters who claimed that they were forced to defend slavery and the Fugitive Slave Law out of deference to the law of the land and the Constitution, Swisshelm scoffed: "Why is the voice of Nature and of God suppressed within us?"[20]

While Swisshelm and Nichols pushed to include the Higher Law position in the Free Soil platform, another influential author emerged and applied even more pressure on party leaders. One of the most successful writers in American history, Harriet Beecher Stowe also advocated for God's law above man's law in her astonishingly popular *Uncle Tom's Cabin*. This novel, which introduces readers to slavery through the experience of the enslaved, quickly captured a worldwide audience. It sold 10,000 copies in the United States during its first week, and over 1.5 million in Great Britain during its first year. Northerners in particular were drawn to Stowe's depiction of the inhumanity of slavery. One of the most compelling scenes in the novel occurs when a runaway slave mother and her son appear at the door of an Ohio state senator. Although the senator had recently rejected his wife's request to vote against the Ohio Fugitive Slave Law due to the immorality of capturing and returning slaves to bondage, his heart is moved when he confronts the human reality of slavery in the form of the desperate people at his door, and he is converted to the Higher Law position. This politician comes to question the man-made law he misguidedly helped pass and follows his Christian impulse to aid escaping slaves.[21]

It is important to note that *Uncle Tom's Cabin* was first published as a series of stories in the *National Era,* a Washington, D.C.–based Free Soil newspaper. Though historians have generally ignored this fact, it underscores the political impact of the book. Gamaliel Bailey, the editor of the *National Era,* admitted that *Uncle Tom's Cabin* forced him to publish more stories addressing the morality of slavery in his newspaper.[22] Bailey understood that Stowe's emphasis on the primacy of God's law contradicted the general consensus among Free Soilers that the Constitution was the highest law in the land. As Michael Pierson shows, Bailey linked the Higher Law position to women like Stowe, Swisshelm, and Nichols and thus gendered it "feminine" and moral. Men could continue to support the primacy of the Constitution even while sympathizing with morally driven women without threatening their political legitimacy. And women benefited from this gendered divide because it allowed them to jump into the political arena as the voice of virtue.

By the early 1850s, when *Uncle Tom's Cabin* became an international best seller, the nation was increasingly aroused over slavery. As abolitionists predicted, the 1850 Fugitive Slave Law led to an increase in the number of blacks kidnapped by slave-catchers and, in response, thousands of African Americans emigrated north to Canada. When Congress passed the Kansas-Nebraska Act in 1854, many outspoken Northerners became convinced that the Southern "Slave Power" would stop at nothing to force the entire nation into accepting slavery. Because the act eliminated the 36° 30' line above which slavery had been forbidden for thirty years, it seemed to antislavery-leaning Northerners that Southerners had betrayed the formerly sacred Missouri Compromise and made it impossible to trust their word on matters of slavery. Kansas-Nebraska helped initiate a dramatic shift in the political landscape. As historian Richard B. Sewell writes, "Before the [Kansas-Nebraska] tempest subsided it had splintered the Democratic Party, smashed the last remnants of organized Whiggery, and crystallized antislavery elements from all parties into a formidable new political coalition."[23] This new coalition became the Republican Party, and it attracted antislavery women from across the North. Like their Liberty and Free Soil Party predecessors, women emphasized the moral impetus of their partisan activism. And as the nation confronted more regional hostility and violence, Republican women's emphasis on the immorality of slavery became increasingly persuasive.

In their first presidential campaign, Republican women participated in what appeared to be greater numbers than ever before, due in part to the candidate's wife, Jessie Frémont.[24] Described as "beautiful, highly educated, accomplished," by abolitionist Gerrit Smith, Jessie worked closely with party organizers in the campaign for her husband.[25] The daughter of influential Southern Democrat and Missouri senator Thomas Hart Benton, Jessie defied her father to elope with Frémont. Benton opposed the marriage because he considered Frémont lacking in talent and ambition. Very close to his brilliant daughter, Benton had hoped for a more impressive match for Jessie. The elopement became a political tool for Republican Party strategists, who created a caricature of Benton as a wealthy arrogant Democrat. They depicted John and Jessie, on the other hand, as republican egalitarians dedicated to the free labor system. In this narrative, Jessie fell in love with John despite her father's objections because he was independent and hardworking. He had risen to success using only his own talents and perseverance, relying on the opportunities afforded by the free North. Jessie faithfully supported her spouse, occasionally using her wit and loyalty to aid him.[26] This romantic story fascinated Northerners who were desperate for virtuous and honest political leadership, as would be further evidenced by the popularity of the rail-splitting Abraham Lincoln image that would become so pervasive a few years later.

Jessie Frémont enthralled women. She emerged at a time when many Northerners felt increasingly anxious over heightened Southern aggressiveness. When South Carolina congressman Preston Brooks ruthlessly beat Massachusetts senator Charles Sumner with a cane in the hallowed halls of the U.S. Senate, Republicans reacted with shock and anger. The brutality of this attack sent a chill down the collective spine of Northern women. A defenseless Sumner sat pinned under his writing table while Brooks beat him repeatedly, continuing even after his cane broke. As Southern editorialists defended Brooks and hundreds of supporters sent him new canes,

Stacey M. Robertson

Northern women felt hopeless and helpless. The emergence of Jessie Frémont provided Republican Party women with renewed hope that feminine morality might influence the White House. They dove into the election with an unheralded exuberance.[27]

Jessie inspired thousands of women to become active in partisan meetings, parades, picnics, and dinners. Newspaper editors wrote stories about the Republican candidate that featured her: "Fremont and 'His Jessie,'" "Give 'Em Jessie," "No Bachelor for Jessie," "Our Jessie," and "Mrs. Fremont and Her Husband."[28] Republican women's groups sprang up across the North. There were the "Sisters of Jessie" in Massachusetts, "Jessie Clubs" in the mining towns of California, the "Tribe of Jessie" in Ohio and New York, and the "Ladies' Jessie Club" in Pennsylvania.[29] Republican organizers even set aside space to accommodate women at partisan gatherings. "During the Presidential campaign, every where the Republicans had said that there would be seats reserved for ladies at their meetings," explained women's rights and antislavery advocate Lucy Stone, "as when Mr. Fremont was to be seen in New York, there was no peace among the people until Jessie came out too. They all recognized woman's right to have something at least to do with politics."[30] At a large Frémont gathering in Buffalo, women's presence was expected: "A new feature in political gatherings was witnessed last evening in the presence of some 400 ladies' seats having been reserved. The ladies here 'go in' for Fremont and 'our JESSIE.'"[31]

Jessie's appeal was rooted in her willingness to stand up to the South combined with her moral opposition to slavery. Her defiance in marrying John Frémont against the will of her Southern Democratic father became a symbol of her strength, virtue, and bravery to resist the entire South. Moreover, her well-known opposition to slavery became a major theme in the campaign. "Mrs. Fremont told me," explained Gerritt Smith, "that her mother taught her to hate Slavery, and she did hate it. She said she would never own a slave, nor permit one to do her work. She did her own work, rather."[32] Slavery, in addition to being an abhorrent and inhumane institution, weakened and demoralized white slaveowners because they became dependent on the labor of others, growing lazy and soft. In opposition, Jessie was independent and determined. "Jessie has long been among our people a synonym for character and for force," asserted one editor. "In times of heated political excitement, when a word of unusual meaning may be caught up and adopted by the nation, it is no wonder that 'Jessie,' already expressive of the idea of power, should . . become a household word through the land. . . . [Should she reach the White House] we may look for a new era of glory, at least so far as her administration is concerned."[33] In a popular story about Jessie, retold again and again by Republican strategists, she was said to have helped keep California free by debating Southern women who wanted to see slavery admitted to the state. When these women wondered who would take care of their cooking and cleaning, Jessie replied that she would rather do her own cooking than accept slavery, thus shaming the Southern women by pointing to their failed femininity.[34]

Jessie also became a symbol of domesticity and virtue. Republicans contrasted the loving home of the Frémonts to the unmarried Democratic opponent James Buchanan. "There is a great hurrahing over J[essie] at this moment," asserted one writer to the *Liberator.* "The Democrats have no feminine element in their two-legged, walking platform; no Jessie to hurrah for; no Jessie to vitalize their manhood and kindle their enthusiasm! Theirs is a *bachelor* party, and it will be a *bachelor* Administration if they get it. No wife, no child, no home, to humanize and save them."[35] At a Republican rally in Michigan women hoisted a flag that pronounced on one side "'Is Liberty a crime?' and on the other 'Fremont men, or no husbands.'"[36] Only Frémont men would boast the character to attract Republican women. At another Republican meeting, a wagon full of ladies was adorned with a banner that read: "We are the tribe of Jess, for equal Rights and Free Discussion." A second wagon carried the banner: "No Bachelor for JESSIE: Free Hearts and Free Homes."[37] Jessie and John Frémont would save the United States from the wretched institution of slavery and return the nation to freedom and domesticity.

By the time of the 1856 presidential campaign, the debate about slavery's place in the nation was focused in and around the territory of Kansas. The Kansas-Nebraska Act, in addition to eliminating the Northern border of slavery, had also legislated that popular sovereignty would settle the future of slavery in Kansas. This meant that the residents of the territory would determine whether slavery or freedom would be the law of the land. As a result, hundreds of determined pro- and antislavery men and women relocated to the territory in order to affect the outcome of the vote. The predictable result of this stream of passionate new residents was conflict and violence. Missouri "ruffians," as the abolitionists called them, crossed into Kansas and bullied antislavery citizens. In response, New England abolitionist minister Henry Ward Beecher encouraged Northerners to send rifles to beleaguered antislavery residents of Kansas. Known as "Beecher's Bibles," these arms were purchased by Kansas Emigrant Aid Societies across the North and shipped to the territory. It should be no surprise, therefore, that Kansas became an important symbol for Republicans during the campaign. Women embraced the theatrical opportunity of Kansas during countless mass Republican rallies across the North in the form of a "float" that featured thirty-two (because Kansas would become the thirty-second state) attractive young single women. All of them wore white save one, who wore black and represented Kansas. This message was a creative critique of Southern violence and slavery in the territory. At another rally in Pennsylvania the procession of thirty-two "young ladies . . . made its appearance" directly following a speech about the history of slavery and the need to challenge its "ascendancy." The platform was then cleared to allow the young women a prominent place in the gathering.[38] Republican women at a mass rally in Beloit, Wisconsin, featured the same float, and it also raised funds for antislavery Kansas settlers by selling dinner to attendees. They eschewed political endorsements at their table in order to appear nonpartisan. Despite their wary negotiation of gender expectations, these Republican women worked closely with party organizers and engaged in self-conscious partisanship. Dozens of communities followed suit, hoisting young women onto floats and raising money to defend freedom in Kansas.[39]

The territorial violence in Kansas gave Republican women an opportunity to contrast the virtue of John and Jessie Frémont with the unbridled lawlessness represented by their opponents. These abolitionist women created Kansas Aid groups designed to help "'feed and clothe the destitute in Kansas—especially widows and orphans,'" thus creating a "feminine" rationale for activism. But these groups were also clearly designed to promote Republican electoral success. Carefully and quietly collaborating with Republican officials and politicians, women ensured that the aid groups developed goals in concert with political aims. The leadership of the Women's Kansas Aid Association in Jefferson, Ohio, for example, included the wives of leading Republican state politicians.[40] Spousal conversations about Kansas might lead to creative opportunities for the Kansas Aid association to help market the Republican Party. It also meant that support for widows and orphans might also include Beecher's Bibles or other types of arms designed to provide a different type of aid.

Republican women could not entirely avoid the wide-ranging violence that cut across Kansas. Sometimes, in fact, they highlighted tales of abolitionist women's bravery in the face of physical threats and aggression in Kansas. Under the headline "The Ladies of Lawrence," the *Anti-Slavery Bugle* reprinted an article about the critical role played by "Free State ladies" in the defense of Lawrence against antiabolitionist "invaders." Unlike the timid proslavery women who were whisked out of town during the violence, abolitionist women refused to leave and give up the right, and duty, to fight. "*Forty ladies of Lawrence enrolled their names secretly, with the determination of fighting by the sides of their husbands and sons as soon as the fighting commenced!*"[41] Many of the women practiced shooting with pistols, and one "young girl (a beauty of nineteen years)," even reported that she "dreamt last night of shooting three invaders." The courage, strength, and determination exhibited by this young female abolitionist reflected the popular image of Jessie Frémont. The article concluded with the story of two valiant women who risked their lives to sneak ammunition into Lawrence. When an enemy scout stopped their wagon, he "saw only a work-basket, which had purposely been filled with sewing materials." He casually dismissed the fluffy pillows—filled with gun powder—beneath their skirts, and allowed them to pass through to the town.

Though Jessie Frémont was a popular symbol for women amid the Kansas crisis and during the 1856 election, she was also a brilliant political strategist and organizer. She served on the exclusive committee that had the difficult job of preventing her husband from making political blunders by carefully limiting his public access. John Frémont was an outdoorsmen with little political experience or aptitude. He spent his time preceding the election "fencing, riding, and exercising," while Jessie and other close advisers managed the day-to-day campaign. According to one biographer, "Every morning she brought fruit and coffee into the dining room to meet with her 'private committee,' carrying a market basket brimming with letters. . . . For the first time in American history, the wife of a presidential candidate took an active role in a national campaign."[42] Jessie's calm demeanor and her political acumen convinced several party insiders that she was a better presidential prospect than her husband.[43]

Jessie's intelligence and effectiveness influenced both white and black women. While subject to a wide range of cruel and debilitating racial restrictions, black women nonetheless managed to participate in partisan activism throughout the 1850s. From

Kansas Aid groups to local elections, from lecturing to petitioning, African American women engaged in the political system in support of abolition and racial equality. Like their white counterparts, black women usually supported Republican Party policies but did not formally associate with the party. By promoting Kansas, or critiquing the Fugitive Slave Law, abolitionist speakers inevitably advanced the party. But in the violent environment of the Kansas period, African American women also risked bodily harm when they publicly advocated for these issues. When Frances Ellen Watkins canvassed Ohio during the late 1850s, she occasionally encountered mob opposition. During a lecture in Fairfield, Ohio, a group of rabble-rousers surrounded the lecture hall as Watkins spoke, yelling obscenities and breaking windows. Appalled by this criminal behavior, local citizens made sure that the "ruffians" were brought to justice. During the leader's trial, he referred to abolitionists as "maggoty-brained friends of the slave," and he was rewarded with a conviction of disturbing the peace.[44] Despite such occasional interventions, Watkins's Republican lectures in Ohio were persuasive and successful. As Salem resident Daniel Hise declared in his diary after hearing Watkins, "*Miss Watkins,* a colored lady made as good a speech as I ever listened to."[45]

A few years later another black women abolitionist lectured in the Midwest, and she experienced a more violent response from local racists. Sojourner Truth spoke at a courthouse in Angola, Indiana, in 1861.[46] Two months following Fort Sumter, but before the First Battle of Bull Run, the nation was tense. Truth expressed the desire to fight with the brave troops on the battlefield. "At this moment," according to local abolitionist Josephine Griffing, a mob "rushed up the stairs, and like a pack of hounds, with ears well rubbed, set upon this patriotic, noble woman, and with insolent threats and yells choked her down."[47] Unsatisfied with this assault, the next day the mob surrounded the home of Truth's host, "one of the oldest and wealthiest men in the county," and only failed to carry through on their "hellish plan" of violence because "they were soon too drunk for a riot." Still determined to expel Truth, the leaders of the mob prosecuted her for violation of the Black Laws.[48] After four different trials, Truth triumphed. Women's presence in the courtroom, according to Griffing, "produced a marked impression" and helped lead to a positive result. Even though Griffing herself had encountered innumerable violent opponents during her years as a radical antislavery lecturer, she concluded, "In my experience with mobs, I have never seen such determination. No dog ever hung to a bone as have these hungry hounds to Sojourner."[49]

The violent response to both Truth and Watkins is evidence of racism in the North, but also ambivalence about women's intrusions into civic spaces. This indecision continued during the national response to the 1859 raid on Harpers Ferry by abolitionist John Brown. The aftermath of Harpers Ferry—in which John Brown constructed himself as God's martyr for the sin of slavery—offered Republican women a chance to dive further into politics under the guise of religion. When a Cleveland newspaper accused Ohio resident Amanda Sturtevant of helping John Brown prior to the raid, she responded by boasting that she "invited and cordially welcomed" Brown to her home, and was "glad [to have] entertained so worthy a man." She freely confessed that she had known about his previous violent activities in Kansas and Missouri when she asked him into her home, concluding, "I am free to say that I approve it."[50] Sturtevant claimed that she had not known about Brown's Harpers Ferry plans, but she cheekily praised his "efforts to liberate the slaves" and said finally, "Any law, enactment, or custom which forbids me to aid suffering humanity wherever found, I utterly reject and despise." She then dared her enemies "to find a grand jury . . . who will indict me."[51]

Other women used the Higher Law position to defend Brown. "How in the name of common sense do Christians propose to do away with this enormous sin if not with John Brown's method?" one woman asked. "You know very well and every body knows that Southern slaveholders will not allow any kind of Christian teaching in all their borders only the christianity of devils and how is the great southern heart to be reached but by God's ministers of vengeance."[52] Josephine Griffing proclaimed Harpers Ferry "a necessary and lawful penalty for violated rights." Although, she concluded, "the attack was less beautiful than the sunshine, the rain, and the dew, of moral influence, it had nevertheless a place in the counsels of Heaven, as well as the whirlwind, the Earthquake and the Fire, in the physical economy of nature."[53] Another abolitionist woman proclaimed, "I do not approve of the Harper's Ferry tragedy because it was one of blood, and contrary to the peaceable kingdom. . . . But Slavery tramples all the precepts of Jesus under its feet."[54] Westerner Celestial Colby wrote: "The great heart of the North beats in sympathy with *the motive* that prompted to the deed."[55] Another Ohio woman explained that Brown was "following only the instincts of right, and the teachings of the golden rule."[56]

Women abolitionists understood Harpers Ferry as a prelude to further conflict, and they warned of the political implications of the raid. "A terrible baptism in blood" would occur if the nation did not heed the violence in Kansas and Harpers Ferry as a warning to abandon its "national sin"—slavery—and elect the Republicans. Often this discussion of the nation's future was couched in religious terms, with references to the "divine justice" which would be meted out to a nation that failed to reach its God-given potential for establishing a "heaven on earth." Many women abolitionists, influenced by the memories of Kansas and fugitive slave rescues, seemed more willing to consider seriously the possibility of disunion—and the creation of a new nation where freedom could flourish.

Many of the extant letters from women to John Brown as he lingered in prison, awaiting his execution, linked politics and religion. Harpers Ferry became an opportunity for a second Revolution, led by Republicans. "God writes national judgments upon national sins," opined Republican lecturer and poet Frances Ellen Watkins. "And what may be slumbering in the storehouse of divine justice we do not know."[57] "Your conviction was divinely inspired," declared Josephine Griffing, "and your adherence to it, the grandest service that God and Humanity could demand."[58] Harpers Ferry might result in national redemption if Americans embraced antislavery politics." Who shall say that in the Infinite Future, the same halo of glory shall not rest upon the hills of Harper's Ferry, that it shall not be remembered by coming generations as the Lexington, the Concord, the Bunker Hill of a *holier revolution,* than that for which our fathers fought," wondered Celestia Colby.[59] Another woman, who lived in the Old Northwest, marveled, "Treason is it, to help a Brother or a Sister, to life, liberty and the pursuit of happiness! What did you call it when you lifted the murderous hand against our mother, because of a few taxes?"[60] Many women agreed with C. B. Campbell's contention that Harpers Ferry must lead to "either the elimination of slavery or the dissolution of the Union."[61] One woman declared, "Union lovers, to save the union . . . have ignobly surrendered the great right of free speech, and are gulping down the poisonous anodynes of union-slavery."[62] She also linked the North's commitment to the Union as a sign of its sacrifice of "honor and manhood."

In the wake of Harpers Ferry, Republican women continued their active and vocal partisanship. During the 1860 presidential campaign, women supported the "Wide Awake" groups that emerged across the North. Determined to "awaken" the nation to the Republican Party candidate Abraham Lincoln, Wide Awakes held picnics, marches, meetings, and celebrations. Women initiated, organized, and supported such activities. Elizabeth Cady Stanton and other Seneca Falls, New York, abolitionist women presented their local Wide Awake group with an honorific banner. In response, the eager young Wide Awakes honored Stanton, Susan B. Anthony, and other guests at the Stanton household with martial music followed by dancing and celebrating. It was a memorable event that illuminated the increasing partisanship of women in the new party. Side by side, arm in arm, young men and women challenged the status quo and helped to bring victory to the Republicans.[63]

The nation was thus ready for young Anna Dickinson, a brilliant Republican Party lecturer, who emerged as one of the most persuasive, successful, and talented partisan orators in the nation during the Civil War. A Philadelphia native, Dickinson grew up in the Quaker faith, where preaching and public witnessing were open to women. She learned of women's oratorical skills from the many female speakers she heard in her own church. Mentored by the eloquent and wise Quaker abolitionist Lucretia Mott, Dickinson developed her own lecturing style very early in her life. She always supported both emancipation and racial equality, but she also managed to appeal to various constituencies and worked very closely with Republican Party strategists. Early in Dickinson's career, the New Hampshire Republican Party employed her as a full-time lecturer during a key election. The twenty-year-old electrified audiences, and some political strategists credited her with influencing the Republican victory.[64] So popular and persuasive was Dickinson, a contingent of U.S. congressmen requested that she speak in the House Chamber in 1864, and she received a standing ovation for her powerful oratory.[65] Known as the American Joan of Arc, Dickinson represented a new generation of young women who came of age in the 1850s amid a highly partisan decade when politics infiltrated many aspects of life.

As Dickinson captivated large audiences with her eloquence, Northern women continued their political activism through the Women's Loyal National League. Founded in 1863 by Elizabeth Cady Stanton and Susan B. Anthony, the league advocated emancipation as a political imperative of the Civil War. In an effort to convince Congress that a majority of Americans desired immediate abolition, it collected petitions demanding full emancipation for all slaves. As women took to the streets and collected thousands of signatures, they became increasingly politicized. Continuing to rely on the idea that women should act as stewards of morality in politics, Stanton and Anthony emphasized patriotic duty as a rationale for women's increasing intrusion into political spaces. The Women's Loyal National League attracted a younger leadership full of exuberance and confidence. They managed to gain 100,000 signatures within a year, inviting a new generation of women to join in shaping and directing the push for emancipation and in translating the end of slavery into a larger meaning for liberty.[66]

In conclusion, politically aware and active Northern women forged a meaningful and productive avenue into partisan politics through antislavery third parties. Some joined Liberty picnics, serving pies to attendees and listening closely to political speeches. Others edited Free Soil newspapers, reminding party leaders that antislavery was an inherently moral movement. Still others stood before crowds and added their voices to the growing antislavery chorus across the North. As the conflict over slavery intensified in the 1850s, women's voices became increasingly powerful and potent in political discussions and electoral campaigns. Harriet Beecher Stowe, Jane Swisshelm, and Jessie Frémont were leaders in this chorus—and their refrain was consistent and loud—namely, that the demands of the Higher Law superseded politics and man-made law and required virtuous men and women to courageously battle slavery in all its forms.

Such political activism must not be underestimated. Harriet Beecher Stowe's *Uncle Tom's Cabin* contributed to a large-scale shift in the political terrain of the 1850s. The immorality of the Slave Power made tangible through the writings of women like Stowe revealed the high stakes of every election in relation to the very meaning of American democracy. Jessie Frémont inspired Northern women to reenvision themselves—to make room for a political self that was intertwined with all other aspects of their identity. She smoothed the path for other women who would find political engagement both natural and desirable. Anna Dickinson's soaring popularity on platforms across the North is evidence of a new respect for women's partisanship, though this would be challenged and repeatedly negotiated for decades to come.

This essay suggests the importance of continuing to explore the range of women's participation in politics throughout U.S. history. While I focus on partisan politics and abolitionists, women interacted and engaged with political issues in countless ways. As the Zborays' research has shown, nearly half of New England women in the decade preceding the Civil War were reading and talking about politics on a regular basis. In order to include women's voices in our historical interpretations of politics we need to continue to broaden our understanding of the "political" to include activities and communications beyond traditional partisan boundaries. And following the lead of the Zborays, we need large-scale analyses of diaries and letters; microhistories of contentious moments; biographies of politically active women; and metahistories postulating about how women's political interventions have changed over time.

Such scholarship will also provide needed historical context for understanding women's political engagement after the Civil War and even today. Tracking the long history of women's multifaceted political participation also makes visible what has been invisible and thus makes possible refracting the experience of antebellum, wartime, and postwar politics through microscopic and panoramic lenses that reveal the full range of political actors and the complexity of political interests and identities. Observing and analyzing that experience also serves to legitimize, empower, and demand gender equity as essential to democracy.

Notes

1. "Speech of Wendell Phillips," *Liberator*, Aug. 8, 1856.

2. An excellent and thorough history of American women abolitionists is Julie Jeffrey, *The Great Silent Army of Abolitionism: Ordinary Women in the Antislavery Movement* (Chapel Hill: Univ. of North Carolina Press, 1999).

3. Michael D. Pierson, *Free Hearts and Free Homes: Gender and American Antislavery Politics* (Chapel Hill: Univ. of North Carolina Press, 2003), 140.

4. A. D. Hawley to Betsey Mix Cowles, July 6, 1840, Betsy Mix Cowles Papers, box 1, folder 9, Department of Special Collections and Archives, Kent State Univ. Library, Kent, Ohio (hereafter cited as BMC Papers, Kent).

5. Judith Apter Kinghoffer and Lois Elkis, "'The Petticoat Electors': Women's Suffrage in New Jersey, 1776–1807," *Journal of the Early Republic* 12 (Summer 1992): 159–93; Rosemarie Zagarri, *Revolutionary Backlash: Women and Politics in the Early American Republic* (Philadelphia: Univ. of Pennsylvania Press, 2007), 46–81. See also Catherine Allgor, *Partisan Politics: In Which the Ladies of Washington Help Build a City and a Government* (Charlottesville: Univ. of Virginia Press, 2002).

6. For more on women's increasing political presence in the antebellum period, see Anne Boylan, *The Origins of Women's Activism: New York and Boston, 1797–1840* (Chapel Hill: Univ. of North Carolina Press, 2002); Carol Lasser and Stacey M. Robertson, *Antebellum Women: Private, Public, Partisan* (New York: Rowman & Littlefield, 2010); and Ronald J. and Mary Saracino Zboray, *Voices without Votes: Women and Politics in Antebellum New England* (Durham: Univ. of New Hampshire Press, 2010).

7. Letter from Augustus Wattles to Betsey Mix Cowles, Apr. 9, 1836, BMC Papers, Kent, box 1, folder 3.

8. On the Fathers and Rulers petition, see Stacey M. Robertson, *Hearts Beating for Liberty: Women Abolitionists in the Old Northwest* (Chapel Hill: Univ. of North Carolina Press, 2010), chap. 1. On women's antislavery petitioning, see Susan Zaeske, *Signatures of Citizenship: Petitioning, Antislavery, and Women's Political Identity* (Chapel Hill: Univ. of North Carolina Press, 2003).

9. Boylan, *Origins of Women's Activism*, 137.

10. Jayne Crumpler DeFiore, "COME, and Bring the Ladies: Tennessee Women and the Politics of Opportunity during the Presidential Campaigns of 1840 and 1844," *Tennessee Historical Quarterly* 51 (1992): 204.

11. Boylan, *Origins of Women's Activism*, 137, 158.

12. Ronald J. Zboray and Mary Saracino Zboray, "Whig Women, Politics, and Culture in the Campaign of 1840: Three Perspectives from Massachusetts," *Journal of the Early Republic* 17 (Summer 1997), 281.

13. Melanie Susan Gustafson, *Women and the Republican Party, 1854–1924* (Urbana: Univ. of Illinois Press, 2001), 7.

14. See Robertson, *Hearts Beating,* chap. 2.

15. Ibid.

16. Ibid., chap. 1; Jeffrey, *Great Silent Army.*

17. Pierson, *Free Hearts,* 57.

18. Ibid.

19. Ibid.

20. Jane Swisshelm, "Letters of Mrs. Swisshelm—No. 2," *Farmer's Cabinet,* May 9, 1850.

21. Pierson, *Free Hearts,* 62–63.

22. Ibid., 64.

23. Richard H. Sewell, *Ballots for Freedom: Antislavery Politics in the United States, 1837–1860* (1976; repr., New York: Norton, 1980), 254.

24. Because women did not vote, it is difficult to determine the extent of their political involvement. This estimation is based on a review of newspaper references to women's participation in Republican Party activities. According to Michael Pierson, "It was, in fact, the largest outpouring of ordinary women's electoral participation since 1840, when the Whig Party had enlisted women's visible support for William Henry Harrison. In 1856, however, women engaged in a broader range of activities than Whig women had in 1840." Pierson, *Free Hearts,* 140.

25. "Gerritt Smith and Fremont," *National Era* (Washington, D.C.), Aug. 21, 1856.

26. Pierson, *Free Hearts,* 125.

27. For more on the Sumner assault, see David Donald's still-classic *Charles Sumner and the Coming of the Civil War* (New York: Alfred A. Knopf, 1960); Williamjames Hull Hoffer, *The Caning of Charles Sumner: Honor, Idealism, and the Origins of the Civil War* (Baltimore: Johns Hopkins Univ. Press, 2010); and Michael D. Pierson, "'All Southern Society Is Assailed by the Foulest Charges': Charles Sumner's 'The Crime against Kansas' and the Escalation of Republican Anti-slavery Rhetoric," *New England Quarterly* 68 (Dec. 1995): 831–57.

28. "Fremont and 'His Jessie,'" *Daily Citizen and News* (Lowell, Mass.), June 27, 1856; "Give 'Em Jessie," *Frederick Douglass's Paper,* Jan. 18, 1856; "The Rally of the River Counties," *New York Daily Tribune,* Oct. 17, 1856; "Political News," *Saturday Evening Post,* July 5, 1856; "The Night Before the Election," *Flag of our Union,* Dec. 20, 1856.

29. "The Fremont Barbeque: A Monster Meeting of the Republicans," *Liberator,* Aug. 29, 1856; "From California," *National Era,* Aug. 26, 1856; "Synopsis of News," *Frank Leslie's Weekly,* Oct. 25, 1856; "Political Items," *New York Daily Tribune,* Oct. 16, 1856; "Pennsylvania: The Canvass," *New York Daily Tribune,* Oct. 8, 1856.

30. "Woman's Rights Convention in New York," *Liberator,* Dec. 5, 1856.

31. "Fremont and Freedom in Buffalo," *New York Daily Tribune,* July 11, 1856.

32. "Gerritt Smith and Fremont," *National Era,* Aug. 21, 1856.

33. "Mrs. Jessie Fremont," *Frank Leslie's Weekly,* Oct. 25, 1856.

34. Pierson, *Free Hearts,* 130.

35. "A Northern Republic," *Liberator,* Oct. 3, 1856.

36. Ibid.

37. "The Rally of the River Counties," *New York Daily Tribune,* Oct. 17, 1856.

38. "Pennsylvania: The Canvass," *New York Daily Tribune,* Oct. 8, 1856.

39. Pierson, *Free Hearts,* 148.

40. Ibid.

41. "The Ladies of Lawrence," *Anti-Slavery Bugle* (Salem, Ohio), Jan. 12, 1856.

42. Sally Denton, *Passion and Principle: John and Jessie Frémont, the Couple whose Power, Politics, and Love Shaped Nineteenth-Century America* (New York: Bloomsbury, 2007).

43. William E. Gienapp, *The Origins of the Republican Party, 1852–1856* (New York: Oxford Univ. Press, 1987), 376–77.

44. "Border Ruffianism in Fairfield Township," *Anti-Slavery Bugle*, Nov. 27, 1858. See also "Letter from Frances E. Watkins," *Anti-Slavery Bugle*, Nov. 13, 1858.

45. Oct. 17, 1858, Daniel Hise Diary, Ohio History Center (formerly the Ohio Historical Society), Columbus, Ohio.

46. For more on Truth's lecturing experiences, see Victoria Ortiz, *Sojourner Truth: A Self-Made Woman* (Philadelphia: J. B. Lippincott, 1974), 68–73. See also Carleton Mabee, *Sojourner Truth: Slave, Prophet, Legend* (New York: New York Univ. Press, 1993); and Nell Irvin Painter, *Sojourner Truth: A Life, A Symbol* (New York: W. W. Norton, 1996). For references to Truth's early lectures in the Old Northwest, see *New Lisbon* (Ohio) *Aurora*, Aug. 27, 1851, and Mar. 3, 1852.

47. "Treason in Disguise," *Liberator*, June 21, 1861.

48. "Shameful Persecution," *Liberator*, June 28, 1861.

49. Ibid.

50. On the Missouri rescue, see Stephen Oates, *To Purge This Land With Blood: A Biography of John Brown* (New York: Harper & Row, 1970), 260–64.

51. "Mrs. Sturtevant," *Anti-Slavery Bugle*, Nov. 19, 1859.

52. Sarah Everett to "Jennie," Dec. 31, 1859, John Brown Papers, Kansas State Historical Society, qtd. in Oates, *To Purge This Land With Blood*, 317.

53. "The Salem Quarterly Meeting of Human Progress," *Anti-Slavery Bugle*, May 26, 1860.

54. "Remarks by a Woman," *Anti-Slavery Bugle*, Jan. 7, 1860.

55. Letter from Celestia R. Colby, "A Morning in December, Or a Leaf From My Journal," *Anti-Slavery Bugle*, Jan. 7, 1860.

56. "MN," to John Brown, Nov. 16, 1859, qtd. in James Redpath, ed., *Echoes of Harper's Ferry* (1860; repr., New York: Arno Press, 1969), 415–16.

57. FEW [Frances Ellen Watkins] to John Brown, in ibid., 418–19.

58. "Letter to Aaron D. Stevens," *Anti-Slavery Bugle*, Mar. 24, 1860.

59. Colby, "A Morning in December."

60. "Remarks by a Woman," *Anti-Slavery Bugle*, Jan. 7, 1860.

61. "John Brown Meeting in Iowa," *Liberator*, Jan. 6, 1860.

62. "The Union," *Anti-Slavery Bugle*, Apr. 21, 1860.

63. Ann D. Gordon, ed., *The Selected Papers of Elizabeth Cady Stanton and Susan B. Anthony, In the School of Anti-Slavery, 1840–1866* (New Brunswick, N.J.: Rutgers Univ. Press, 1997), 1:441–44.

64. On Dickinson, see J. Matthew Gallman, *America's Joan of Arc: The Life of Anna Elizabeth Dickinson* (New York: Oxford Univ. Press, 2008); Gustafson, *Women and the Republican Party*; James McPherson, *The Struggle for Equality: Abolitionists and the Negro in the Civil War and Reconstruction* (Princeton, N.J.: Princeton Univ. Press, 1967), 128–31; and Wendy Hamand Venet, *Neither Ballots nor Bullets: Women Abolitionists and the Civil War* (Charlottesville: Univ. Press of Virginia, 1991), 35–59.

65. McPherson, *Struggle for Equality*, 131.

66. Venet, *Neither Ballots nor Bullets*.

Stacey M. Robertson

PART

2

Wartime Mobilization

"With Hearts Nerved by the Necessity for Prompt Action"

Southern Women, Mobilization, and the Wartime State

LISA TENDRICH FRANK

The Union and Confederate governments understood that the Civil War had to be won on the home front as well as on the battlefield. Doing so required the enlistment and mobilization of households—the bedrock of representative democracy as well as of the nation's and region's economy—and waging the war required that the wartime state control and influence these households. With the majority of free men of military age deployed in the military at some point over the course of the war, white women became the heads of many Southern households. As a result, the Confederate government, like its Union counterpart, attempted to control the labor and behavior of these women. Sometimes women willingly mobilized themselves, in opposition to and in support of the Confederacy and with or without the state's aid or coordination. In other instances, the state coerced women into the war effort. The responses varied across households and across time. Some Southern women offered their labor while others refused or withdrew it; some encouraged while others resisted the enlistment of their men and the impressment of their household supplies.

The military strategies and policies of the Union and Confederate armies also shaped the lives of Southern women. Women felt the impact of the wartime state when armies occupied or evacuated towns, invaded home fronts, fought guerrillas, and otherwise waged war. At the same time, as the war brought hardships to their communities, Southern white women looked to the wartime state for its resources and sometimes for guidance. When the needs of their families conflicted with the needs of their nation, many Confederate women resisted or withdrew their support for the war. Some white women who remained steadfast in their support for their enlisted kin and neighbors became disappointed in what they deemed an ineffective Confederate government. Despite the diversity of experiences in the Confederacy, the wartime state imposed new pressures and obligations on female-led households that shaped the choices and experiences of all Southern women.

In the years immediately preceding the war, Southern women debated the ramifications of Republican Party victories in presidential and congressional elections. In their discussions of slavery, federalism, and state's rights, Southern white women's opinions ran the gamut from a desire to preserve the United States or to secede and create a new nation. When secession came, many Southern white women mobilized themselves to create and sustain a sense of Confederate nationalism as well as the resulting wartime state.[1] Women were excluded from voting or officially participating in secession conventions, but many white women found informal, yet often public, ways to support or refute the ideas being discussed by their representatives. Their close attention to politics—something that began long before 1860—allowed them to express educated opinions on secession, war, and the proper relationship between individuals and their government. The discussions consumed all of society, leading one slaveholder to note that "the election excitement runs so high, men, women, even children, take part."[2]

Only men could formally decide whether to create a Confederate state, but many women insisted that their voices be heard. In many instances, white women published their positions in local newspapers. For example, a group of "plain country women" in Florida took pains to explain how they had become informed citizens. In an 1860 letter to the editors of the *Jacksonville Standard*, "the ladies of . . . Broward's Neck" refuted the idea that women did not understand politics: "If any person is desirous to know how we come by the information to which we allude, we tell them in advance, by reading the newspapers and public journals for the ten years past and when we read we do so with inquiring minds peculiar to our sex." As a result, these secessionist women offered their "humble opinion that the single issue is now presented to the Southern people, will they submit to all the degradation threatened by the North toward our slave property."[3] Other white women found more informal means of expressing their political loyalties. They wore ribbons and jewelry that showed their support of their side of the secession debate, and they shaped the public discourse by encouraging neighbors and loved ones to do the same.

Discussions of secession split Southern white women into competing camps, as personal and national impulses pushed them in different directions. Some women actively supported their state's decision to leave the Union and became Southern nationalists, while others took flight and headed northward, showing their disagreement with their countrymen and their willingness to oppose the creation of an independent Southern state. As they voiced and acted upon their opinions, many of them struggled with their community's and their own sense that they were treading on new public terrain. Many Unionist women refrained from expressing their political opinions in public, especially when the enthusiasm for secession made their state's withdrawal from the Union unavoidable.[4] Secessionist women were typically more vocal than their Unionist counterparts. Ada Bacot, for example, declared that "I wonder sometimes if people think it strange I should be so warm a secessionist, but why should they, has not every woman a right to express her opinions upon such subjects, in private if not in public?"[5]

Once the secession conventions began, many Southern white women participated in the debates from the balconies of state houses. The galleries filled with female onlookers who excitedly listened to the debates and cheered on their advocates. In

Lisa Tendrich Frank

Richmond, so many women "spend so much time in the Senate that many of the ladies take their sewing or crocheting."[6] At Arkansas's secession convention, "every nook and corner [in the statehouse] was full . . . the galleries crowded—men jostled ladies, and ladies each other."[7] Denied access to the podium, women found other ways to express their politics. When a speaker declared his intended vote, raucous women in the galleries erupted with cheers or with threats and hisses. One Arkansas widow threw a bouquet at a representative's feet to show her support for opposing secession.[8] In 1860 a group of Florida women shamed legislators into voting for secession. To the "agitated matrons . . . throughout the South," these ladies "recommend to reserve their crinolines to present to our Southern Politicians who have compromised away the rights of the South."[9]

Although the galleries were primarily reserved for "ladies," and other women of wealth and stature, less affluent women also discussed secession and war. Some may have preferred to opt out of the debates, but the privileges of whiteness initially led many to support the Confederacy. Nonslaveholding women often hoped that independence would allow them to continue to benefit from enslaved labor and African Americans' lower position in society.[10] Southern whites of all statures understood the approaching war as a contest over "whether we should live as slaves or freemen."[11] However, in some areas, especially those not touched by slavery, many poor women opposed secession and war, criticizing it as a rich man's war and a poor man's fight. A letter to Georgia governor Joseph Brown expressed outrage that a poor elderly man had five sons in the Confederate army while the wealthy did not: "They want other people [to] do all the fighting and let them ly at home."[12]

The 1860 election and subsequent secession debates also shaped the lives of enslaved African American women. Although excluded from the public discussions of political events, many enslaved people listened carefully as white men and women discussed the sectional debate. They then discussed the issues among themselves and acted accordingly. The news of secession sometimes led to the escape of enslaved people who saw it as a chance to gain freedom. In South Carolina the Manigault family recognized the information being shared among their enslaved people and worried about its consequences. Several bondspeople ran away after overhearing discussions of secession, and they then evaded capture because slaves who remained on the plantation listened to conversations about attempts to capture the runaways. As a result, the Manigaults cautioned each other to watch their tongues. "No overseer or Planters should speak on such subjects before a small house boy or girl" because the information revealed on any topic made its way to those that should not have the information.[13] Talking about Lincoln's election, his presumed radical agenda, and the prospects for secession all aroused passionate opinions, and domestics worked in earshot of the heated discussions. With white Southerners declaring that the Confederacy was essential to protecting the institution of slavery, African Americans learned through the slave "grapevine" that among Northerners at least the political and social acceptance of slavery was eroding. They discussed the events among themselves, debated what would follow, and planned for the future.[14]

As the Confederate and state governments worked to mobilize troops, white women balanced the needs of the wartime state and their households. Before the fighting began, many women eagerly volunteered to become unofficial enlistment agents for the Confederacy, but women's participation became essential after Jefferson Davis authorized 100,000 volunteers to fight for the Confederacy on March 6, 1861, and then asked for an additional enlistment of 400,000 more men in May. This need for recruits continued throughout the war, and it brought increased struggles for families. Many white women struggled with the choices they faced, especially as the war grew longer and casualties mounted. Despite battlefield dangers, many Southern white women urged the men of their families to enlist in the Confederate army. They convinced, cajoled, and used whatever tools they had to raise an army. Union spy Emma Edmonds noted that Confederate women were "the best recruiting officers" because they refused "to tolerate, or admit to their society any young man who refuses to enlist."[15] Drawing on Southern ideals of honor and masculinity, some women shamed hesitant men into the military. In Arkansas women convinced Henry Morton Stanley to enlist by sending him "a chemise and petticoat, such as a negro lady's maid might wear." The women's message was clear: men who did not fight for their nation were not men.[16] Similar "gifts" were delivered to unenlisted men around the Confederacy. In Selma, Alabama, a woman reportedly sent her fiancé a petticoat and skirt, accompanied by a note that warned him to "wear these, or volunteer."[17]

Wartime demands proved to be too much for other Southern white women. Some considered the expected wartime sacrifices to be too great; others saw the Union as too precious. Like their "secesh" counterparts, these women mobilized themselves in opposition to the war. They encouraged men to hide from recruitment officers, pleaded for them to purchase substitutes, or encouraged their men to look for exemptions. In some areas women supported and hid men who deserted from the Confederate army. The aid that women provided deserters led to widespread condemnation in parts of the South. As one Confederate woman explained, "What can we expect but desertion from the army," considering the support deserters receive from disloyal "mothers, wives, and sisters?"[18] Other women stuck in Union-controlled areas supported men who had joined pro-Confederate guerrilla units.[19] At the same time, some white women in Confederate territory were staunch, but secret, Unionists. A significant "Union Circle" existed in Atlanta, Georgia, as did one in Richmond, Virginia. In both instances, local women regularly gave supplies to and fed imprisoned Union soldiers under the guise of humanitarianism.[20]

The mobilization of the Confederate South and widespread enlistment of men created new opportunities for enslaved women. As overseers and other white men left their homes to fulfill their military obligations to the state, many slaves feigned loyalty to their masters while simultaneously pursuing their self-interests. This deceit led one slaveholder to decry that "as to the idea of a *faithful servant, it is all a fiction.* I have seen the favourite & most petted negroes the first to leave in every instance."[21] Thousands of enslaved African American women escaped from bondage during the war. According to some accounts, enslaved women made up as many as 40 percent of wartime

Lisa Tendrich Frank

runaways.[22] The newspapers filled with runaway ads, and slaveholders struggled to figure out what to do. Virginian George Talbot, for example, offered a $2,000 reward for the return of "Nancy Ashby, a mulatto girl, fine looking" and "Sarah Gaskins, brown skin, fine looking."[23] Some escaped African American women, like Susie Baker King, made it to safety and volunteered to aid the Union war effort. In 1862 King had fled to Union lines in Savannah. After taking her freedom, she became a laundress, teacher, and nurse for the Union army, continuing to oppose the Confederate state by fighting against it.[24] Other enslaved women encouraged enslaved men to join the Union army, especially later in the war when invading troops were nearby and federal policy allowed for African American enlistment. In doing so, enslaved women also pursued their longstanding ambitions of freedom and used skills honed over generations to defy their enslavers and weaken the Confederacy in any way they could.

Even without leaving the plantation, enslaved women undermined their white masters and mistresses by slowing down work or refusing to work altogether. Enslaved women on one Alabama plantation, according to their mistress, refused to "do their duty."[25] The work habits of these and other enslaved women across the Confederacy did not go unnoticed. From North Carolina in 1863 Catherine Edmondston complained that "negro property is worse than useless for they do no work unless they choose."[26] Many owners tried to whip their slaves back into submission; some looked to sell them or hire them out.

Other enslaved women tried to cripple the Confederacy by pushing the United States more firmly against slavery. Formerly enslaved women like Sojourner Truth and Harriet Jacobs offered firsthand accounts of their lives in bondage to make the case for abolition. After escaping from slavery, Truth narrated her story to a friend, published it, and then traveled the North giving lectures on the horrors of slavery. Jacobs, too, detailed the horrors of slavery in her book in the hopes that it would help destroy the South's oppressive labor system.[27] Their efforts, combined with those of other formerly enslaved people and abolitionists, helped move the Union toward emancipation, which consequently dealt a hard blow to the Confederacy.

The Confederate government, lacking the resources and infrastructure to do so itself, relied on its citizens to supply the armies. When shortages occurred, many white women extended the obligations of the household to include the needs of their deployed loved ones and neighbors. Throughout the South, white women mobilized themselves into sewing and aid societies, all designed to outfit the soldiers that the government could not.[28] Those who could do so donated their labor and supplies, but many did not have extra resources. Some aid societies expected Confederate officials to help offset their material costs and asked the state to pay for the supplies they provided. In November 1861 the Augusta (Georgia) Ladies' Aid Society asked the captains of each company to help pay the costs of the supplies women needed to sew uniforms.[29] Often forcefully enlisting the help of enslaved women, these white women's activities drew upon a long history of sewing circles and other domestic work. Their antebellum experience knitting, spinning, dressmaking, and even doing decorative embroidery work gave them the skills to make uniforms and other supplies for the soldiers.

In many instances, women mobilized as a community to outfit locally raised units with adequate clothing and flags. Virginian Judith McGuire recorded that "our parlor was the rendezvous for our neighborhood, and our sewing-machine was in requisition for weeks." Together the women "were busily employed sewing for our soldiers. Shirts, pants, jackets, and beds, of the heaviest material, have been made by the most delicate fingers."[30] Through these actions, Confederate women showed their enthusiasm and support for the war, both at its outset and as it continued.[31] Soon after secession, for example, Little Rock's women met in Theatre Hall, where daily they made seventy-five pairs of pants and two hundred jackets for Confederate soldiers. A few weeks later they had produced "nearly or quite three thousand military suits, upwards of fifteen hundred haversacks, and probably five thousand shirts, and have also covered over twelve hundred canteens."[32] Confederate soldiers often appealed directly to their loved ones when they discovered the limited supplies of their quartermasters. Ellen House's sister, like countless others, received a request "to cut out a couple of shirts for two . . . who were going off tomorrow and needed them. Of course she did it."[33]

In addition to demands for uniforms, the Confederate government expected that women help feed the armies. Many elite women, especially early in the war when supplies and patriotic sentiments were at their greatest, gave more than requested, and in some instances, the largesse continued throughout the war. For example, North Carolinian Catherine Edmondston described the governor's request that they "collect voluntary subscriptions of meat, meal, & flour for the army. These supplies are to be over and above every man's *surplus* that the Government already has. It must be from his own stock of provisions, *what he denies himself for the sake of the army.*" As a result of her family's privileged position, even during wartime, she was able to "give 500 lbs of meat which we had intended for our own table. . . . Mr E gave 500 lbs of Meat & 1500 lbs of meal."[34] Few Southerners had the resources to give so much excess food at any point in the war, and as a result the Confederate government created a tax-in-kind program in April 1863. Under this controversial policy, the state impressed 10 percent of each household's agricultural output in order to feed the army and ease the suffering elsewhere in the Confederacy. This policy may have helped soldiers, but it also ensured that the state "was inside every household."[35] It also turned the patriotic provisioning of soldiers into a state-mandated act.

As late as 1865, many Confederate women actively worked to sustain the Confederate state. Fundraising efforts, instead of being crushed by the lengthy war, remained steady. In South Carolina a group of Columbia women that included Mary Amarinthia Snowden and other elite women sponsored and ran a fundraiser bazaar in the State House. Held in January 1865 as William Tecumseh Sherman's Union troops approached the city, the Columbia bazaar was deemed "a complete success."[36] It was not merely a local affair but instead also garnered support and contributions from around the South and overseas. Before it was forced to close early in the face of the arrival of Union troops, the Columbia bazaar raised several thousand dollars; the approaching end to the Confederate state did not end women's support of the bazaar or the Confederacy.[37]

Lisa Tendrich Frank

The wartime state required that cotton and other agricultural production continue in spite of a shortage of manpower. As a result, the Confederate government depended on women's successful renegotiation of a home front that had fewer men. Part of that readjustment required women to labor in positions that were previously held by white men or enslaved African Americans. For their part, plantation mistresses had to take control of the management of enslaved labor, a job that had usually been done by their husbands, sons, fathers, or brothers. The loss of overseers and other white male labor to the battlefield left white women with a more difficult situation at home. Mrs. C. C. Clay, in Alabama, struggled to get her slaves to work. When nothing seemed to help, she admitted that she "begged" her way to doing "what little is done."[38] North Carolinian Mag Bingham similarly struggled with her new responsibilities. She highlighted the problems she had managing the enslaved people, especially the women who were "insolent."[39] Less affluent white women had to take over the management of family farms—herding cattle, tending to chickens, engaging with local merchants, and tending to crops. Some women had to run shops and small businesses on their own.

These tasks were often taxing, especially when added to women's regular duties. Although some scholars have shown that women's work during the Civil War was an impetus for the women's rights movement—much more so in the North than the South—others have highlighted the difficult and frustrating nature of such work for women and their resulting desire to return to antebellum gender roles. Both experiences coexisted. White women may have been willing to construct new outhouses, manage the enslaved people, and till the land, but they did not necessarily feel liberated by the tasks.[40] While some women found the freedom of independent life to be empowering and satisfying, others resented the sudden requirement to assume "male" tasks, and while some women appreciated the "large experience which will be at all times useful," others complained of the drudgery of wartime life.[41] Lucy Buck of Virginia detailed her long day of chores. "Ma had made the fires and we commenced milking. . . . Finished ironing, got dinner and did some cleaning up." Her morning was busy, but she did not have time to rest. "In the afternoon there were pies to make for tomorrow, salt rising to bake, and supper to get besides milking, and washing the children. Oh such a weary time we had of it"—especially because nothing went easily. "The children were sleepy and fretful, the stove *wouldn't* get hot, the bread would not bake and the cows *would* run." After the children were in bed, Buck continued her labors. She had to bring in wood and water and clean up the kitchen.[42] Like Buck, other Southern white women felt overwhelmed and discouraged by their wartime lives and grew "so sick and tired of it."[43] Regardless of their attitudes toward wartime work, however, women who took on these roles provided the Confederate nation with much-needed labor and supplies. They produced clothing and food for soldiers, and freed Southern men from domestic responsibilities so they could serve their nation on the battlefield.

By fulfilling the needs of the wartime state, women brought to the forefront many of the skilled tasks that they had been doing in private for generations. The war, for example, created a new need for medical professionals. With over 400,000 sick and wounded Confederate soldiers and much of the fighting occurring in and near many Southern communities, the demand for medical assistance skyrocketed during the war. Prior to the war, women had been excluded from the profession on account of propriety; medicine was not seen as ladylike. Wartime demands for medical assistance allowed women to care for the sick and wounded, just as before the war they had tended to ailing loved ones at home. Women also provided hospitals and wounded soldiers with vital food and supplies. Although the Confederacy had no official counterpart to the Union's United States Sanitary Commission, Southern women drew upon their healing and nurturing responsibilities within the household to become effective nurses during the war. Some enslaved African American women were hired at hospitals as well, but matrons placed them in primarily menial positions.[44]

In September 1862 the Confederate government authorized positions for women in military hospitals and hired some women as nurses and hospital matrons. These paid positions were usually in large hospitals near urban areas. Women hired to be chief, assistant, or ward matrons received meager monthly salaries of $40, $35, or $30 that rarely covered the women's expenses. The official duties of Richmond's Chimborazo Military Hospital matron Phoebe Pember included keeping the hospital clean, preparing food, and distributing medications, but she also washed wounds and helped surgeons during amputations.[45] Other women opened private hospitals when the demand overwhelmed the available public resources. In Richmond, Virginia, for example, volunteer Sally Tompkins founded a hospital that was later commissioned as an official Confederate hospital. Recognizing her vital work, President Jefferson Davis made Tompkins an honorary captain in the Confederate army so that she could get paid and could continue to operate the hospital. Over the course of the Civil War Tompkins and her staff cared for more than thirteen hundred Confederate soldiers, most of whom survived their treatment.[46]

The presence of battles in one's neighborhood served as the gateway to nursing for many women in the South. After initially collecting supplies for wounded Confederate soldiers in her home of Mobile, Alabama, in April 1862 Kate Cumming headed to the Battle of Shiloh, in Mississippi, to volunteer as a nurse with the Army of Tennessee. After September 1862, when the Confederate government allowed hospitals to pay their female nurses, she became officially enlisted in the Confederate medical department. At the hospitals, she rolled bandages, supervised the work of soldiers and slaves as they dressed wounds, distributed food and drink to the wounded, and, as the war lengthened, tended to wounds. Cumming served in hospitals in Mississippi, Tennessee, and Georgia, often taking on the responsibility in close proximity to the battlefield. As a result, while at Gilmer Hospital in Chattanooga she noted that "it is impossible to feel that any thing connected with our army is permanent. The whole place is surrounded with breastworks, some of which are within a stone's throw of the hospital."[47]

The Confederacy had the resources to pay only a few nurses, so most women simply volunteered to care for the large numbers of casualties caused by the war.[48] Although the ability and desire to support the state eventually waned in parts of the

Confederacy, the women at Wayside Hospital in Columbia, South Carolina, provided a steady workforce. Founded by the wife of a local doctor, the hospital owed its existence to women and relied on the voluntary assistance of white women from throughout the community. Mary Boykin Chesnut explained that the women at the Columbia hospital were indispensible: they fed the soldiers, helped dress their wounds, and did "not for any cause [miss] one day's attendance."[49] Women around the Confederacy "went to the hospital as usual" each day to do their part for their nation.[50]

Other white women alleviated the state's responsibility for their men by opening up their homes and nursing wounded and sick soldiers. With hospitals either too far away or overwhelmed by demand, homes-turned-hospitals allowed many soldiers to receive medical care near the battlefields and their units. It also meant that private homes served remarkably public functions. For example, Judith McGuire noted that even though there were hospitals in Winchester, Virginia, "those who are very sick are taken to the private houses, and the best chambers in town are occupied by them."[51] In 1865, in North Carolina, Mrs. John Smith's house-turned-hospital was "full of wounded Confederate soldiers. . . . lying on the bare floor."[52] In these and other instances, female-centered households fulfilled a central obligation of the wartime state.

In addition to nursing, white women aided the war effort by taking on government jobs that men vacated when they left for the battlefield. Women were hired in clerical positions in the Treasury Department, Quartermaster Department, War Department, Commissary General, and Post Office Department. These government jobs were coveted because they paid decent salaries and offered women an option to support themselves. Although thousands applied for these jobs, they were primarily given to educated elite women who had connections to those in government. In particular, hundreds of white women worked for the Confederate Treasury, signing notes. The job was highly competitive; for each open position the Treasury Department received about 100 applications. In their applications women stressed their need for a position as well as the government's obligation to give them one in exchange for their support for and sacrifices on behalf of the Confederacy. "Treasury girls" earned $65 a month to work six hours a day for five days a week signing Confederate notes. Their job required extremely neat handwriting and careful attention to detail. In addition, over one hundred women secured posts in the Confederate War Department, earning $125 each month for their jobs as clerks. Government jobs, however, did not always pay well. Copyists in the War Department earned only twenty cents for each hundred words copied, and cleaning women only made $6 each month.[53]

Although munitions and textile factories employed women prior to the war, the increased needs of the wartime state made their integration into the workforce necessary. Poorer Southern white women frequently took the factory jobs, sometimes to help their nation, but more often to earn enough money to support themselves and their families. Some women helped manufacture war matériel at Confederate arsenals and ordnance factories, where they generally received lower wages than their male counterparts. Factory work was dangerous, especially when it involved the manufacture of ammunition. In March 1863 an explosion at an ordnance factory near Richmond, Virginia, killed thirty-four of its five hundred female workers and injured dozens more. Accidents at other ordnance factories, including an explosion in Jackson, Mississippi, killed female employees at an alarming rate.[54]

Other women found paid work sewing uniforms or producing the materials to make uniforms for Confederate soldiers. The Quartermaster Department paid some women by the piece: thirty cents per shirt and a quarter for underwear. Women who worked at the Georgia Soldiers Clothing Bureau were paid between $24 and $48 each month. Women who worked at the cotton and woolen mills in Roswell, Georgia, helped to produce uniforms, rope, blankets, tent cloth, and other supplies for Confederate soldiers. When Sherman's men arrived in Roswell, they recognized women's role in aiding the Confederate war effort and treated the women as enemies. Soldiers destroyed the mills and, by Sherman's order, expelled the women as traitors.

The labor of enslaved African American women also aided the war effort, though by compulsion rather than free will. With the loss of men and increased demands for local production, enslaved women faced larger workloads during the war. Their domestic tasks grew as blockades stopped the import of cloth and finished goods. As a result, enslaved women had to spin more cotton than usual to make homespun material. They also had to make more clothing so that they could outfit themselves as well as their white mistresses and Confederate soldiers. In addition, because the Confederate state had impressed so many African American men to serve as laborers in the Confederate army, enslaved women had to take on additional responsibilities in the fields. Nicey Kinney recalled that her elderly master "sho seed dat us done our wuk." During the war, the former Georgia housemaid had to "plant all our cleared g[r]ound, and sho has done some hard wuk down in dem ol bottom lands, plowin', hoein', pullin' codn and fodder, and Ise even cut cordwood and split rails. Dem was hard times."[55] The wartime needs of the Confederate household—many of which suffered from the impressment of private property—transformed enslaved life. Some African American women, especially in urban areas, hired themselves out for small wages, which could be used to weaken the Confederacy. For example, one enslaved woman used the money she earned washing Confederate soldiers' clothes to make bread for Union prisoners of war. "She got in to the prisoners through a hole under the jail-yard fence; knowing all the while she'd be shot if caught at it."[56] Many enslaved women discovered that their wartime circumstances allowed them to oppose their mistresses. During the war, Aggie Crawford stole newspapers so she and the rest of her enslaved community could keep up to date on current events.[57] Black women regularly ignored orders and slowed down their work pace.[58]

Both Confederate and Union military policies also resulted in wartime displacement.[59] The Confederate government did not necessarily intend for it to happen, but its military frequently abandoned individual families as a matter of military expediency. Elite women often blamed the failures of the wartime state when they moved their families to join those of other female family members or friends as a precaution or as enemy troops neared. Reports abound of combined households filled with extended family or close friends. From her home in Paris, Virginia, Amanda Edmonds

Lisa Tendrich Frank

visited "some Alexandria refugees, who are making their home in the country (Miss Parrott's)." They were not people she had known before the war, but "we were invited to spend the evening with them and a very pleasant one we spent—thirteen ladies and not a single gentleman."[60] Some women had to leave their homes after Union troops arrived, further delegitimizing the authority of the Confederate state. Late in the war, Ellen House recorded her forced migration from a Union-occupied area: "It is almost nine months since I was ordered to leave Knoxville by Gen Carter. . . . We spent three months in Abingdon Va. . . . and received kindness from Tenn refugees there that I will never forget."[61]

The wartime state (Union and Confederate) also created military policies that impacted the lives of white and black women across the South. These effects were especially felt in the bombardment and sieges of towns, like Vicksburg, and the forced evacuation of others, like Atlanta. Occupying Union forces also changed women's relationship with their government and those around them. Indeed, the citizens of many Southern towns and cities suffered when Union soldiers cut off their supply lines. When invading Union troops occupied Confederate towns, many women took to the road to look for safety. In August 1862 Sarah Morgan's family fled Baton Rouge in such a hurry that "one single dress did my running bag contain."[62] When they arrived a safe distance from the shelling, the house was "already crowded to overflowing" with "three families from Baton Rouge. . . . There was so many of us, that there was not room on the balcony to turn."[63]

Other white women moved to urban areas to find work so they could support their families. As a result, urban populations swelled during the Civil War. Richmond's population, which began the war at 38,000 grew to between 130,000 and 150,000 by the end of the war. Atlanta, the fourth largest Southern urban area in 1860 with a population of 9,554, housed 22,000 people by 1864. This population explosion led many civilians to complain that they were being overrun. One resident of Richmond complained that the town was "unnaturally swollen." Another described it as "crowded as Broadway, New York; it is said that every border-house is full."[64] The explosion of urban populations created new demands on the state and Confederate governments, especially as food shortages became rampant. Southern governments—whether national or local—lacked the resources to resolve the issue, and in most instances families were left to fend for themselves.

Enslaved African American women exploited the disruptions caused by the war to work against the Confederate state. They visited relatives and friends on other plantations, where they exchanged information that frequently weakened the Confederate war effort. The informal slave grapevine—which helped slaves pass personal and political communication between communities prior to the war—became a powerful tool of resistance during the war. Enslaved women used the information they learned to run to Union lines or help others reach them. Still others used the gathered and shared information to hurt the Confederate military; they passed relevant military information to Union officials, who used it to defeat Confederate forces. Union military policies similarly encouraged the mobility of African Americans. The close proximity of Union forces encouraged the escape of enslaved African Americans, who claimed their freedom and sometimes aided the Union army.[65]

Women's constant motion on the home front necessarily changed the structure of the Southern household, as well as women's relationship to their government. Instead of relying solely on community members, Southern women increasingly felt justified in bringing their requests to the national government. For example, North Carolinian Louise Medway, who represented "a number of Ladies here [who] have established a Soldiers's Aid Society for the purpose of ministering to the wants of the sick & wounded *en route,*" appealed to President Jefferson Davis for assistance. She justified her request by explaining that the aid society had "been very successful & have fed & sometimes partially clothed from 6 to 8,000 per month besides having wounds dressed &c." The problem was that the Custom House would not release donations to her because of her sex and lack of official appointment. Medway requested from the president "a permit for all articles coming to me for use of our Soldiers." This permit, she hoped, would allow those abroad with more means and opportunities to help the Confederacy, whose "means are so small & the wants of our soldiers so many."[66] Recognizing the importance of her work to the Confederacy and its soldiers, Davis approved Medway's request.

Other women appealed to the president and wartime state for protection from invading soldiers. From South Carolina in December 1864, one woman told Davis she was "very anxious respecting Sherman's advance," because she was confident that "should he get into S[outh] Carolina our fate will be most deplorable." Despite her fears, she confirmed her loyalty to the Confederate state. She assured the president that she could "bear up under it all could we only have a hope that Sherman will be stopped in his wicked course." She made one last plea to Davis on behalf of her dedication to the state: "I therefore hope you will do for us what you can in this sad dilemma and stop the advance of our vile enemy. [I]n behalf of my native State I entreat you to think of us."[67] Confederate women's loyalty, she asserted, should assure them protection by their government. As a result, some women in the path of Sherman's invading troops lost confidence in the Confederate government and its ability to wage a successful war, even as these women retained their secessionist desires and hatred for the Union.[68]

Notions of reciprocity encouraged women to claim the right of protection from their local, state, and national government. If women were willing to give up their men to the battlefield and their supplies to the soldiers, they assumed that in return they would be able to support their families on the home front. When the state did not provide the services to which these women felt entitled, women took to the pen and to the streets to protest. They wrote countless letters to local officials and to Davis, appealing for help and listing the sacrifices that warranted such assistance. They also sent letters to wartime governors and legislators requesting aid to feed and clothe themselves and their children. One North Carolina woman beseeched the governor to help her get "a few bunches of cotton yarn to clothe myself and little children."[69]

Lisa Tendrich Frank

Others published their complaints in newspapers, highlighting the hardships they faced and the aid they felt they deserved.

As conditions worsened and officials ignored their pleas for help, Southern white women took to the streets to make their displeasure known and to get results. Bread riots in urban areas were the most visible manifestation of Southern women's belief that the government owed them something for their wartime work and sacrifices. In extreme cases, women staged public demonstrations against inflation and shortages. Desperate women banded together to protest the state's neglect of their basic needs. In Salisbury, North Carolina, Confederate soldiers' wives and mothers took to the streets in March 1863 to protest the price of food and other necessities. The women demanded fair prices—namely, the military rate for flour, molasses, salt, and other basic provisions. When their requests were ignored and denied, they broke into local stores and seized the items they needed.[70] Women protested in other North Carolina towns, including in Jonesville, where "a band of *women,* armed with axes . . . came down on the place, to press the tithe corn &c. brought wagons along to carry it off." There was "a similar attack . . . on Hamptonville a few days ago. . . . with more success."[71] Similar food riots occurred in Georgia, Alabama, and urban areas in other Confederate states. The largest bread riot occurred in Richmond, Virginia, in April 1863. Upset by out-of-control inflation that made it impossible to afford food and supplies, approximately one thousand hungry women marched together to the capitol, demanding a meeting with Confederate president Jefferson Davis. When they were turned away, they broke into local shops to take bread and other supplies to feed their families. Instead of recognizing the desperate straits faced by these Confederates and the unfulfilled expectations of the wartime state, many newspapers branded the protesters as prostitutes and "very wicked and ignorant women."[72] Politicians publicly followed suit, but often acknowledged that local governments had failed their constituencies. Seemingly missing the point of the food riots, Gov. Zebulon Vance of North Carolina urged the women to let the state deal with it: "When forcible seizures have to be made to avert starvation, let it be done by your county or state agents."[73]

Poor women, especially those whose husbands were away fighting, participated in bread riots and lobbied the government to meet their needs.[74] As a result, the Confederate government and some individual states made accommodations for suffering civilians. Public welfare, rare on the local and national level in earlier years, became common in almost all Confederate states by 1863. For example, in February 1863 the North Carolina General Assembly allotted $1 million to be used to help the "wives and families of indigent soldiers."[75] It did not match the need.[76] Virginia enacted similar measures in 1864, allotting $1 million to help families of soldiers in occupied areas and suspending state taxes. Encouraged by state governments, local aid societies run by wealthier white women in the community also played a large part in disbursing funds and supplies to soldiers' families in need on the Confederate home front.[77] In 1864 the Confederate government, responding to the protests of soldiers' wives and other women who were suffering from shortages, taxes, and impressment, exempted them from the Confederacy's tax-in-kind policy, despite its detriment to the state's wartime objectives.

Even if he did not always allocate the resources to help alleviate the shortages faced by Confederate civilians, President Jefferson Davis confirmed the valuable service that Confederate women had given to their nation. He acknowledged that a "peculiar claim of gratitude is due to the fair country-wom[e]n" who "have gone to the hospital to watch by the side of the sick." Using the gender conventions of the time, he praised the women "who have nursed as if nursing was a profession—who have used their needle with the industry of sewing-women." In addition, he commended the women because they "have born[e] privation without a murmur, and . . . have given up fathers, sons, and husbands with more than Spartan virtue."[78]

The Confederacy depended on the labor of civilian women throughout the Civil War. Often the government requested women's efforts through official channels. Calls for women to aid Confederate soldiers both on and off the battlefield were a common refrain in newspapers, and praise for women who did so was publicly offered by politicians from all levels of government. At a meeting of the Ladies Clothing Association in Charleston, South Carolina, Rev. R. W. Barnwell asked for fifteen volunteers who would go to Virginia for approximately one month, to relieve the Virginia women who had been working tirelessly at the hospitals. He called upon the women of South Carolina to help because, "WITHOUT YOU, THIS WAR COULD NOT HAVE BEEN CARRIED ON, FOR THE GOVERNMENT WAS NOT PREPARED TO MEET ALL THAT WAS THROWN UPON IT."[79] Officials and other Confederate supporters similarly warned communities of the dangers of women who did not support the war effort. In 1863 President Davis urged women to keep men from deserting their posts. "I conjure . . . the wives, mothers, sisters, and daughters of the Confederacy—to use their all powerful influence in aid of this call . . . to take care that none who owe service in the field should be sheltered at home from the disgrace of having deserted their duty to their families, to their country and to their God."[80]

A number of white women also supported the Confederacy through espionage activities, some state-supported and some not. Female spies used their femininity to disguise their actions and intentions. Playing upon nineteenth-century assumptions that women understood little about politics and military matters, they eavesdropped on Union officeholders and soldiers. In some cases they even asked direct questions about Union military plans, hiding behind the facade of feminine ignorance and the social convention of making pleasant conversation. Some female spies pretended to be romantically interested in the Union soldiers stationed in their towns. They engaged the men in conversation and passed along the information they obtained to Confederate authorities. They hid messages under their large skirts, in their shoes, sewn into their jackets, and in their hair. Those who were caught were arrested and imprisoned. However, many saw the risk as a worthy one, because the information proved invaluable for the commanders who received it and it aided the Confederacy. In March 1862 Catherine Baxley described the group of women held with her at

Lisa Tendrich Frank

the Old Capitol Prison. "Mrs. Rose Greenhow and myself were the first female[s] brought to this old Union rat trap, but our number is gradually increasing." At the time of her writing it included "Mrs. Morris, still with us; the next a Mrs. J. Parton, alias Mrs. McCarter; . . . Then a party were brought here who were released in two or three days. Then Mrs. Morris of Baltimore . . . then two young ladies captured at Dranesville or thereabout."[81]

Some Southern women took advantage of the privileges of their race and class to aid or subvert the Confederate cause. One of the best-known female spies, Rose O'Neal Greenhow, played a large part in a Confederate spy ring in Washington, D.C. Greenhow, a Washington socialite, was able to obtain information from members of the United States Congress and the cabinet whom she entertained. Through encoded messages, she then shared the military information with her contacts in the Confederate government. Information provided by Greenhow helped P. G. T. Beauregard secure victory at the First Battle at Bull Run. After discovering her covert actions, Union Secret Service arrested Greenhow in August 1861. They initially placed her and her young daughter under house arrest, but in January 1862 they transferred her to the Old Capitol Prison.[82] Although some women's espionage work was done without official sanction and remains hidden, Greenhow's participation in the spy ring did not go unnoticed. Jefferson Davis recognized the vital nature of Greenhow's work. After her release from prison in June 1862, the Confederate president met with her in Richmond and acknowledged her contributions to the nation's victory at Bull Run. Thomas "Stonewall" Jackson similarly recognized the work of another female spy, Belle Boyd, when he awarded her an honorary commission as a captain and aide-de-camp for her efforts in Virginia.[83]

Other Southern white women provided intelligence for the Union. Elizabeth Van Lew, for example, ran a spy ring in Richmond, Virginia, that successfully passed information to Union officials and aided in the escape of Union prisoners of war.[84] Most notably, escaped slave Harriet Tubman undermined the Confederate state not only by her role in helping other enslaved people escape but also by providing valuable information about Confederate forces in South Carolina to Union officials. Throughout the war she served as a scout and a spy for the Union army. Her knowledge of the area and her ability to get information from enslaved people made her invaluable. In June 1863 Tubman led a successful raid up the Combahee River that resulted in the burning of several plantations; the confiscation of thousands of dollars of rice, corn, and cotton; and the freeing of more than 750 enslaved African Americans.[85]

Other women disguised themselves as men and enlisted in the military to fight for the Confederacy.[86] Although not sanctioned by the Confederate government or military, women's military service provided much needed support for the Southern nation. Once they passed the cursory initial exam for army service and joined a regiment, they fought alongside men and were rarely revealed to be women. Most female combatants were discovered only if they got sick, wounded, or pregnant. Some who were discharged after their discovery as women later reenlisted in other regiments. Southern women's varied reasons for enlistment included not only a commitment to the Confederate war effort but also the desire to remain with a male loved one, need for money, or hope for adventure. Once in the military, women served as did all soldiers: they performed picket duty, participated in daily drills, became scouts, fought on the front lines, and sometimes had hospital duty. Some rose through the ranks, with nobody the wiser as to their sex. Female combatants performed honorably for their nation. Two female Southern soldiers died of their wounds at Gettysburg, and a third's leg was amputated after the battle.[87]

In conclusion, the formation of the Confederacy and the declaration of war created a series of pressures and opportunities that shaped the lives of enslaved and free women across the South. In this context, white and black women pursued personal, communal, and national ambitions that both supported and conflicted with one another. At first the needs of the state and the desires of white women often reinforced one another. Although there were notable exceptions, white women initially volunteered to help mobilize their communities. They helped enlist soldiers, sew uniforms, and take on work in factories and hospitals that was once largely men's domain. They participated in public discussions of politics, and some even dressed as men in order to serve in the army. They also directed the labor of enslaved African Americans, who had little choice but to aid their mistresses as they worked to outfit and feed the Confederate army. As the war progressed, the relationship between women and the state changed. Many white women continued to offer their voluntary assistance to the Confederacy, but as the war lengthened, the government also made formal and often intrusive demands on its female citizens. The state's taxation and impressment of goods created frustrations among many, as did the growing requirements of war, including mounting casualties and the evictions of citizens from their homes and towns. Some white women resented the state for these increasingly difficult realities, and in their protests these women often chose to meet the immediate needs of their families over those of the state. They rioted in the streets for bread and hid deserting soldiers who sought refuge. As the Confederate state struggled to control its territory, enslaved African Americans found greater opportunities to subvert the government and slavery and otherwise obtain freedom. They refused to work for their owners, fled to Union lines, and used a loose network of communication, the so-called grapevine, to obtain and pass intelligence to invading soldiers. Despite these challenges, some Southern white women remained dedicated to the Confederate state and its goals. Southern women contributed much to the mobilization of the Confederacy's resources and the supply of the army, but by the time the military surrendered in 1865, the actions and frustrations of Southern women revealed a Confederate government that could not fulfill its responsibilities to them. Despite the failings of their government, however, few white women gave up on the idea of Southern independence. Although their support for the Confederate government was always conditional, their belief in the rightness of the Confederate cause and all it represented proved more durable.

　　　　　　　　　　　　Lisa Tendrich Frank

1. On the creation of a Confederate identity, see, e.g., Drew Gilpin Faust, *The Creation of Confederate Nationalism: Ideology and Identity in the Civil War South* (Baton Rouge: Louisiana State Univ. Press, 1988); Paul Quigley, *Shifting Grounds: Nationalism and the American South, 1848–1865* (New York: Oxford Univ. Press, 2012); Gary W. Gallagher, *Becoming Confederates: Paths to a New National Loyalty* (Athens: Univ. of Georgia Press, 2013). For selected works on women and gender during the Civil War, see, e.g., LeeAnn Whites, *The Civil War as a Crisis in Gender: Augusta Georgia, 1860–1890* (Athens: Univ. of Georgia Press, 1995); Lisa Tendrich Frank, *The Civilian War: Confederate Women and Union Soldiers during Sherman's March* (Baton Rouge: Louisiana State Univ. Press, 2015); LeeAnn Whites and Alecia P. Long, eds., *Occupied Women: Gender, Military Occupation, and the American Civil War* (Baton Rouge: Louisiana State Univ. Press, 2009).

2. Grace Brown Elmore, Oct. 18, 1860, Diary and Reminiscence [typescript], South Caroliniana Library, Univ. of South Carolina, Columbia. On the use of women as symbols for the Confederate state and the use of gendered language during secession conventions, see Stephanie McCurry, *Confederate Reckoning: Power and Politics in the Civil War South* (Cambridge, Mass.: Harvard Univ. Press, 2010), 25–30.

3. The Ladies of Broward's Neck, Nov. 6, 1860, in Samuel Proctor, ed., "The Call to Arms: Secession from a Feminine Point of View," *Florida Historical Quarterly* 35 (Jan. 1957): 267, 269.

4. Thomas G. Dyer, *Secret Yankees: The Union Circle in Confederate Atlanta* (Baltimore: Johns Hopkins Univ. Press, 1999), 26–52.

5. Ada Bacot, Jan. 19, 1861, as qtd. in Drew Gilpin Faust, *Mothers of Invention: Women of the Slaveholding South in the American Civil War* (Chapel Hill: Univ. of North Carolina Press, 1996), 11.

6. Margaret Sumner McLean, Jan. 9, 1861, in Katherine M. Jones, *Ladies of Richmond, Confederate Capital* (Indianapolis: Bobbs-Merrill, 1962), 34–35.

7. Qtd. in Michael B. Dougan, *Confederate Arkansas: The People and Politics of a Frontier State in Wartime* (Tuscaloosa: Univ. of Alabama Press, 1976), 62.

8. Lisa Tendrich Frank, "Domesticity Goes Public: Southern Women and the Secession Crisis," in Mark K. Christ, ed., *"The Die is Cast": Arkansas Goes to War, 1861* (Little Rock: Butler Center Books, 2010), 31–51.

9. The Ladies of Broward's Neck, "The Call to Arms," 270. On women and Southern honor, see Bertram Wyatt-Brown, *Southern Honor: Ethics and Behavior in the Old South* (New York: Oxford Univ. Press, 1982), esp. 226–53.

10. Stephanie McCurry, *Masters of Small Worlds: Yeoman Households, Gender Relations, and the Political Culture of the Antebellum South Carolina Low Country* (New York: Oxford Univ. Press, 1995); Nancy D. Bercaw, *Gendered Freedoms: Race, Rights, and the Politics of Household in the Delta, 1861–1875* (Gainesville: Univ. Press of Florida, 2003).

11. *Charleston Mercury*, Oct. 31, 1860.

12. Qtd. in Laura F. Edwards, *Scarlett Doesn't Live Here Anymore: Southern Women in the Civil War Era* (Urbana: Univ. of Illinois Press, 2000), 90.

13. G. E. Manigault to My Dear Brother [Louis], Jan. 21, 1861, and Charles Manigault to My Cher Louis, Jan. 19, 1861, as qtd. in McCurry, *Confederate Reckoning*, 234.

14. Steven Hahn, *A Nation under our Feet: Black Political Struggles in the Rural South from Slavery to the Great Migration* (Cambridge, Mass.: Harvard Univ. Press, 2003), 13–14, 65–68; Tera W. Hunter, *To 'Joy My Freedom: Southern Black Women's Lives and Labors after the Civil War* (Cambridge, Mass.: Harvard Univ. Press, 1997), esp. 4–20; Leslie A. Schwalm, "Between

Slavery and Freedom: African American Women and Occupation in the Slave South," in Whites and Long, *Occupied Women*, 137–54; Leslie A. Schwalm, *A Hard Fight for We: Women's Transition from Slavery to Freedom in South Carolina* (Urbana: Univ. of Illinois Press, 1997).

15. S. Emma E. Edmonds, *Nurse and Spy in the Union Army; Comprising the Adventures ad Experiences of a Woman in Hospitals, Camps and Battle-fields* (Hartford, Conn.: W. S. Williams, 1865), 332.

16. Henry Morton Stanley, *Sir Henry Morton Stanley: Confederate,* ed. Nathaniel Cheairs Huges Jr. (Baton Rouge: Louisiana State Univ. Press, 2000), 104; Wyatt-Brown, *Southern Honor.*

17. See William G. Stevenson, *Thirteen Months in the Rebel Army: Being a Narrative of Personal Adventures in the Infantry, Ordnance, Cavalry, Courier, and Hospital Services; With an Exhibition of the Power, Purposes, Earnestness, Military Despotism, and Demoralization of the South* (New York: A. S. Barnes & Burr, 1862), 195.

18. McCurry, *Confederate Reckoning,* 126.

19. On women's role in guerrilla warfare, see LeeAnn Whites, "Forty Shirts and a Wagon-load of White: Women, the Domestic Supply Line, and the Civil War on the Western Border," *Journal of the Civil War Era* 1 (Mar. 2011): 56–78.

20. See Dyer, *Secret Yankees.* On the Unionist network in Richmond, Virginia, see Elizabeth Varon, *Southern Lady, Yankee Spy: The True Story of Elizabeth Van Lew, A Union Agent in the Heart of the Confederacy* (New York: Oxford Univ. Press, 2003), esp. 85–86.

21. Catherine Edmondston, Sept. 9, 1863, *"Journal of a Secesh Lady": The Diary of Catherine Ann Devereux Edmondston, 1860–1866,* ed. Beth Gilbert Crabtree and James W. Patton (Raleigh, N.C.: Division of Archives and History, Department of Cultural Resources, 1979), 463.

22. McCurry, *Confederate Reckoning,* 250.

23. As qtd. in Edward L. Ayers, *In the Presence of Mine Enemies: War in the Heart of America, 1859–1863* (New York: W. W. Norton, 2003), 374.

24. See Susie King Taylor, *A Black Woman's Civil War Memoirs,* ed. Patricia W. Romero and Willie Lee Rose (Princeton, N.J.: Markus Weiner, 1988); Jane E. Schultz, *Women at the Front: Hospital Workers in Civil War America* (Chapel Hill: Univ. of North Carolina Press, 2004).

25. Mrs. C. C. Clay Sr., as qtd. in James L. Roark, *Masters Without Slaves: Southern Planters in the Civil War and Reconstruction* (New York: W. W. Norton, 1977), 82–83.

26. Edmondston, Sept. 9, 1863, *"Journal of a Secesh Lady,"* 463.

27. See Sojourner Truth, *The Narrative of Sojourner Truth, A Northern Slave,* ed. Olive Gilbert (Boston: Published for the Author, 1850); Harriet A. Jacobs, *Incidents in the Life of a Slave Girl. Written by Herself* (Boston: Published for the Author, 1861).

28. On Southern women's creation of and participation in aid societies, see Frank, *Civilian War,* 78–79, 183 n11; Faust, *Mothers of Invention,* 24–29. On Civil War fundraising fairs, see Beverly Gordon, *Bazaars and Fair Ladies: The History of the American Fundraising Fair* (Knoxville: Univ. of Tennessee Press, 1998), 59–60, 96–99.

29. Whites, *Civil War as a Crisis in Gender,* 85.

30. Judith W. McGuire, May 10, 1861, *Diary of a Southern Refugee during the War, by a Lady of Virginia* (Lincoln: Univ. of Nebraska Press, 1995), 12.

31. On wealthy Southern white women's continued enthusiasm for the war, see Frank, *Civilian War.*

32. *Weekly Arkansas Gazette* (Little Rock), June 15, 1861.

33. Ellen Renshaw House, Dec. 10, 1863, in *A Very Violent Rebel: The Civil War Diary of Ellen Renshaw House,* ed. Daniel E. Sutherland (Knoxville: Univ. of Tennessee Press, 1996), 64.

34. Edmondston, Mar. 15, 1865, *"Journal of a Secesh Lady,"* 678–79.

35. See McCurry, *Confederate Reckoning,* 154–56, quotation on p. 156.

36. S. C. Goodwyn to Husband, Jan. 22, 1865, Artemus Darby Goodwyn Papers, South Caroliniana Library, Univ. of South Carolina, Columbia.

37. See Frank, *Civilian War*, 76–77, 92–95; Gordon, *Bazaars and Fair Ladies*; John Hammond Moore, *Columbia and Richland County: A South Carolina Community, 1740–1990* (Columbia: Univ. of South Carolina Press, 1993).

38. Qtd. in Roark, *Masters Without Slaves*, 82–83.

39. Mag Bingham to Brother, Oct. 30, 1862, as qtd. in Victoria E. Bynum, *Unruly Women: The Politics of Social and Sexual Control in the Old South* (Chapel Hill: Univ. of North Carolina Press, 1992). On the relationships between plantation women and enslaved African American women, see, e.g., Thavolia Glymph, *Out of the House of Bondage: The Transformation of the Plantation Household* (New York: Cambridge Univ. Press, 2008).

40. For discussions of women's wartime work and their attitudes toward it, see Faust, *Mothers of Invention*; George C. Rable, *Civil Wars: Women and the Crisis of Southern Nationalism* (Urbana: Univ. of Illinois Press, 1991); Bynum, *Unruly Women*; Anya Jabour, *Scarlett's Sisters: Young Women in the Old South* (Chapel Hill: Univ. of North Carolina Press, 2007), 239–80.

41. Kate Corbin to Sally Munford, Nov. 19, 1862, as qtd. in Jabour, *Scarlett's Sisters*, 267.

42. Lucy Buck, June 13, 1863, *Shadows on My Heart: The Civil War Diary of Lucy Rebecca Buck of Virginia*, ed. Elizabeth R. Baer (Athens: Univ. of Georgia Press, 1997), 214.

43. Qtd. in Faust, *Mothers of Invention*, 38.

44. On enslaved African Americans' work in Confederate hospitals, see Libra R. Hilde, *Worth a Dozen Man: Women and Nursing in the Civil War South* (Charlottesville: Univ. of Virginia Press, 2012), 138–49; Jane Schultz, *Women at the Front: Hospital Workers in Civil War America* (Chapel Hill: Univ. of North Carolina Press, 2004), 21.

45. Carol C. Green, *Chimborazo: The Confederacy's Largest Hospital* (Knoxville: Univ. of Tennessee Press, 2004); Phoebe Yates Levy Pember, *A Southern Woman's Story* (Columbia: Univ. of South Carolina Press, 2002); Schultz, *Women at the Front*.

46. On the Hospital Act, see Faust, *Mothers of Invention*, 97–98. Robert S. Holtzman, "Sally Tompkins, Captain, Confederate Army," *American Mercury* 88 (1959): 127–30; Mary Elizabeth Massey, *Women in the Civil War* (Lincoln: Univ. of Nebraska Press, 1994), 47–48, 52.

47. Kate Cumming, Aug., 8, 1863, *Kate: The Journal of a Confederate Nurse*, ed. Richard Barksdale Harwell (Baton Rouge: Louisiana State Univ. Press, 1959), 124.

48. According to J. David Hacker, casualties in the Civil War numbered between 752,000 and 851,000. See J. David Hacker, "A Census-Based Count of the Civil War Dead," *Civil War History* 57 (Dec. 2011): 306–47.

49. Mary Boykin Chesnut, Aug. 19 and Oct. 28, 1864, *Mary Chesnut's Civil War*, ed. C. Vann Woodward (New Haven, Conn.: Yale Univ. Press, 1981), 637, 656. See also ibid., Aug. 29, Sept. 21, Nov. 6, Nov. 25, 1864, Jan. 7, 1865, 641, 644, 667–68, 677, 700. On Confederate women's continued patriotism late in the war, see Frank, *Civilian War*, esp. 124–47.

50. Frances Thomas Howard, Dec. 25, 1864, *In and Out of the Lines: An Accurate Account of the Incidents during the Occupation of Georgia by Federal Troops in 1864–65* (New York: Neale, 1905), 185.

51. McGuire, June 12, 1861, *Diary of a Southern Refugee*, 29.

52. Ellen Devereux Hinsdale to Child, Mar. 23, 1865, Hinsdale Family Papers, Duke Univ., Durham, N.C.

53. See Faust, *Mothers of Invention*, 88–91; Janet E. Kaufman, "Working Women of the South: 'Treasury Girls,'" *Civil War Times Illustrated* 25 (1986): 32–38; Rable, *Civil Wars*, 131–35.

54. Faust, *Mothers of Invention*, 90; Drew Gilpin Faust, *This Republic of Suffering: Death and the American Civil War* (New York: Vintage Books, 2008), 138; Rable, *Civil Wars*, 134–35;

Michael B. Chesson, "Harlots or Heroines?: A New Look at the Richmond Bread Riot," *Virginia Magazine of History and Biography* 92 (April 1984): 134–35.

55. Qtd. in Clarence L. Mohr, *On the Threshold of Freedom: Masters and Slaves in Civil War Georgia* (Athens: Univ. of Georgia Press, 1986), 212.

56. Qtd. in Hunter, *To 'Joy My Freedom,* 16.

57. Ibid., 16.

58. Ibid., 4–20.

59. See Yael A. Sternhell, *Routes of War: The World of Movement in the Confederate South* (Cambridge, Mass.: Harvard Univ. Press, 2012).

60. Amanda Virginia Edmonds, Sept. 19, 1861, *Journals of Amanda Virginia Edmonds,* 58.

61. Ellen Renshaw House, Jan. 1, 1865, in *A Very Violent Rebel,* 138–39.

62. Sarah Morgan, Aug. 10, 1862, in *Sarah Morgan: The Civil War Diary of a Southern Woman,* ed. Charles East (New York: Touchstone, 1992), 202–5.

63. Sarah Morgan, Aug. 11, 1862, in ibid., 206.

64. Mary Elizabeth Massey, *Refugee Life in the Confederacy* (Baton Rouge: Louisiana State Univ. Press, 1964), 75; McGuire, Feb. 5, 1862, *Diary of a Southern Refugee,* 88.

65. Steven Hahn, "'Extravagant Expectations' of Freedom: Rumour, Political Struggle, and the Christmas Insurrection Scare of 1865 in the American South," *Past and Present* 157 (Nov. 1997): 122–58.

66. Louise Medway to Jefferson Davis, Sept. 13, 1864, Jefferson Davis Papers, Duke Univ., Durham, N.C.

67. "A South Carolinian" to Jefferson Davis, Dec. 22, 1864, Davis Papers. See also Dunbar Rowland, ed., *Jefferson Davis, Constitutionalist: His Letters, Papers, and Speeches,* 10 vols. (Jackson: Mississippi Department of Archives and History, 1923), 7:4; Murrell, "'Of Necessity and Public Benefit,'" 77–100.

68. Frank, *Civilian War,* 124–47.

69. Lucinda Glenn to Governor [Zebulon] Vance, Oct. 29, 1863, Governors' Papers, Zebulon Vance, North Carolina Department of Archives and History, Raleigh.

70. *Carolina Watchman* 2 (Mar. 23, 1863): 2–3.

71. [?] to Sarah "Sade" Jones Lenoir, Jan. 22, 1865, Lenoir Family Papers, Southern Historical Collection, Univ. of North Carolina, Chapel Hill. For other descriptions of food riots, see "Agnes" to Mrs. Pryor, April 4, 1863, in Jones, ed., *Ladies of Richmond,* 155; Mary Waring, April 12, 1865, *Miss Waring's Journal: 1863–1865, Being the Diary of Miss Mary Waring of Mobile, During the Final Days of the War Between the States* (Chicago: Wyvern Press of S.F.E, 1964), 15.

72. As qtd. in Hunter, *To 'Joy My Freedom,* 8.

73. Zebulon Vance, *Greensborough* (N.C.) *Patriot.* April 9, 1863.

74. On "soldiers' wives" as a political force, see McCurry, *Confederate Reckoning.*

75. North Carolina General Assembly, "An Act for the Relief of the Wives and Families of Soldiers in the Army," in *Public Laws of the State of North Carolina Passed by the General Assembly at its Session of 1862-'63: Together with the Comptroller's Statement of Public Revenue and Expenditure* (Raleigh: W. W. Holden, Printer to the State, 1863), 63–64.

76. See Paul D. Escott, *Many Excellent People: Power and Privilege in North Carolina, 1850–1900* (Chapel Hill: Univ. of North Carolina Press, 1985), 32–58.

77. See Rable, *Civil Wars,* esp. 102–6.

78. Speech of President Davis in Columbia, Oct. 4, 1864, in Rowland, ed., *Jefferson Davis, Constitutionalist,* 6:354. See also Speech of President Davis at Macon, Georgia, Sept. 28, 1864, in ibid., 6:341–43; Speech of President Davis at Augusta, Oct. 5, 1864, in ibid., 6:359–60.

79. Emma Holmes, Dec. 2, 1861, in John M. Marszalek, ed., *The Diary of Miss Emma Holmes, 1861–1866,* ed. John M. Marszalek (Baton Rouge: Louisiana State Univ. Press, 1979), 101–2.

80. Jefferson Davis, Aug. 18, 1863, *Augusta Chronicle and Sentinel,* as qtd. in Whites, *Civil War as a Crisis in Gender,* 88–89.

81. C[atherine] V. B[axley] to Doctor, Mar. 14, 1862, *The War of the Rebellion: A Compilation of the Official Records of the Union and Confederate Armies,* ser. 2, vol. 2 (Washington, DC: Government Printing Office, 1897), 1319–20.

82. Rose O'Neal Greenhow, *My Imprisonment and the First Year of Abolition Rule in Washington* (London: Richard Bentley, 1863); Ishbel Ross, *Rebel Rose: Life of Rose O'Neal Greenhow, Confederate Spy* (New York: Harper & Row, 1954); William A. Tidwell with James O. Hall and David Winfred Gaddy, *Come Retribution: The Confederate Secret Service and the Assassination of Lincoln* (Jackson: Univ. Press of Mississippi, 1988).

83. Belle Boyd, *Belle Boyd in Camp and Prison* [1865], with Foreword by Drew Gilpin Faust and Introduction by Sharon Kennedy-Nolle (Baton Rouge: Louisiana State Univ. Press, 1998); Ruth Scarborough, *Belle Boyd: Siren of the South* (Macon, Ga.: Mercer Univ. Press, 1983).

84. See Varon, *Southern Lady, Yankee Spy.*

85. Catherine Clinton, *Harriet Tubman: The Road to Freedom* (New York: Little, Brown, 2004).

86. Although it is impossible to know the exact number of women who fought during the Civil War, scholars estimate that hundreds of women disguised as men fought for the Confederacy and Union. See DeAnne Blanton and Lauren M. Cook, *They Fought Like Demons: Women Soldiers in the Civil War* (Baton Rouge: Louisiana State Univ. Press, 2002); Elizabeth Leonard, *All the Daring of the Soldier: Women of the Civil War Armies* (New York: W. W. Norton, 1999); Richard Hall, *Patriots in Disguise: Women Warriors of the Civil War* (New York: Paragon House, 1993); C. Kay Larson, "Bonnie Yank and Ginny Reb," *Minerva Quarterly Report on Women and the Military* 8 (1990): 33–48; C. Kay Larson, "Bonnie Yank and Ginny Reb Revisited," *Minerva Quarterly Report on Women and the Military* 10 (1992): 35–61.

87. Blanton and Cook, *They Fought Like Demons,* 95–96.

Northern Women, the State, and Wartime Mobilization

JESSICA ZIPARO

A thorough and comprehensive examination of all women in the North during the Civil War era is beyond the bounds of any one essay. Just as it would be impossible to generalize how men in the North experienced and were changed by the Civil War and Reconstruction, women's wartime lives and how the war and its aftermath affected them varied depending on their class, race, age, ethnicity, religion, family composition, and where they lived, among myriad other factors. Women of the North did not all emerge from the Civil War having been changed in the same ways. Still, an overview of how some women responded to the challenges and opportunities posed by the national conflict, and how Northern society responded to those women, can be instructive, especially as regards to what did *not* happen: though women demonstrated that they could be valuable citizens to the wartime state, they were repeatedly undervalued and underappreciated and did not achieve significant advances in social or legal rights as a result of their vital contributions.[1]

The focus of this chapter is the wartime mobilization of Northern women, broadly defined as their actions preparing Northern soldiers to fight in, and the Union government to prosecute, the Civil War as well as their actions needed to maintain their homes and families and to help those affected by the conflict. As the wartime state mobilized female labor and formed new relationships with its female citizens, and as women mobilized themselves to assist in or simply survive the North's war effort, Northerners struggled to find an acceptable equilibrium among the Union's need for female labor and sacrifice, Northern women's ambition, and Victorian norms of appropriate female behavior. The federal government and businesses hired women but favored those who acknowledged their dependency and subordination. Women worked, out of choice and necessity, but they were paid less, if at all, and had to submit to male direction. Middle-class white women began to work in mixed-sex workplaces, but doing so cast serious doubts upon their morality and respectability. The government paid pensions to the widows of soldiers, but the women's private lives became closely monitored.

Writing in the 1880s, suffragists Elizabeth Cady Stanton and Susan B. Anthony declared that "the social and political condition of women was largely changed" by the Civil War and that the conflict "created a revolution in woman herself, as important in its results as the changed condition of the former slaves."[2] This, however, was not the case. Historian Nina Silber found that the war neither liberated women nor aggravated their oppression but rather did a bit of both. Silber notes that while women became more civically involved and politically savvy and enjoyed greater economic opportunities, "the Civil War imparted new lessons about submissiveness and subordination, making women more clearly aware of their second-class status outside the domestic realm."[3] We might take Silber's observation one step further, if we consider that during the war, through hundreds of thousands of negotiations and transactions, the state required that women who wanted to participate in the war effort or receive government work or assistance to be complicit in their own subordination.

Although American women's social and political conditions could—and arguably should—have been drastically altered by the events of the 1860s, in fact the end of the war resulted in the general reaffirmation of Northern women's subordination to the men in their homes, communities, and governments. While there was a subtle shift in gender relations as a result of women's wartime work, at least among the white middle class, with advances and augmented opportunities for women outside the home came greater scrutiny and supervision of them. There were important exceptions to this wartime and postbellum reinforcement of women's dependency, however, and although the Civil War may not have radically realigned the rights and roles of women in Northern society, it was a significant early marker on what was to be a long, and in some respects still unfinished, journey toward female equality in American society and government.[4]

In the Report of the Secretary of the Treasury on the State of the Finances, for the year 1864, Treasurer F. E. Spinner informed Congress that "but for the employment of females whose compensation is low, and in most cases too low, it would have been impossible to have carried on the business of the office."[5] The spirit of Spinner's observation could be applied more broadly. But for the contributions of women, whose efforts were often underappreciated and undercompensated by the governments and people of the North, it would have been impossible for the Union to have carried on the business of war. Women demonstrated their capabilities and developed political skills and confidence in a number of fields, including soldiers' aid, nursing, military supply manufacture, and clerical work. At home women did far more than keep the fires burning—caring for the farms and businesses men left in their charge. Despite these contributions, laws limiting the rights of women remained in place, and women's independence was seen as a wartime aberration to be righted with the cessation of the conflict.

When Confederates fired on Fort Sumter in April 1861, the immediate, most obvious and socially acceptable manner for women to participate in the conflict was to support in spirit and body the men who went to suppress the rebellion. The most common way women participated in the Union war effort remained the initial one:

providing supplies. Across the North, women young and old, poor and middle-class and wealthy, white and African American, worked in their own homes or those of friends, utilizing their domestic skills to produce food, clothing, bedding, and bandages for Union soldiers and organizing fundraising events. To do this work, the majority of women never had to leave their own communities, converting their familiar church groups and sewing circles into "soldiers' aid societies" or "ladies' aid societies," which coordinated efforts with other groups to distribute the materials produced and the funds raised.[6] Women who cared to were happy to have a way to support their loved ones and their nation.[7] Repurposing their efforts to soldier relief felt like a natural and appropriate transformation, and many women believed themselves to be well suited to the task of soldiers' aid, having already been engaged in benevolence and, to a lesser extent, antislavery work for years.[8]

Most soldier-relief efforts were comprised of white middle- to upper-class women who had the time and financial security to participate, but African American women also engaged in generating, collecting, and distributing assistance during the war.[9] Like white women, African American women's aid effort was not an entirely new undertaking: African American women had long performed benevolence work through their churches.[10]

For all women, the benevolence work required by the Civil War far surpassed anything they had done before in scope and scale. As the weeks became months and months became years, women engaged in relief efforts acquired new skills and moved into more complex commercial activities. Silber notes, for example, that the women of Melrose, Wisconsin, obtained nearby wheat donations and sold them to a market eighteen miles away, using the profits to buy materials for soldiers.[11] At the same time, male organizers sought to remove much of their autonomy and control the fruits of their labor. Federal and state governments, and organizations like the United States Sanitary Commission and the United States Christian Commission that sprang up to take advantage of women's critically needed aid work, coordinated their labor under male authority and pressured them to alter their methods and practices in ways women did not always agree with.[12] These entities also did not compensate the vast majority of women. Although a small number of mostly white middle- and upper-class women in positions of responsibility felt empowered and politically savvy after the war, most women, historian Jeanie Attie contends, did not benefit in those ways from the experience; instead they learned "that their unpaid household labor was too readily devalued, at best utilitarian and at worst instinctual."[13]

Nina Silber found that women's involvement in aid work heralded a new relationship between the federal government and its female citizens, one that taught women to be obedient to national governmental authority.[14] Silber writes that Northern women "learned to place a premium on obeying those men who, whether in positions of government or military authority, embodied the Union cause" in order to serve the soldiers.[15] In addition, women learned the value of expressing subordination to men in power, even when such sentiment was feigned, to achieve their goals. To cite one example, historian Elizabeth Leonard found that Annie Wittenmyer, who worked

Jessica Ziparo

for soldier's aid in the Midwest, eventually learned that women had to give "at least the impression of deference to ostensibly more official, typically male, institutions and styles, in order to avoid as much friction as possible and to allow the work to continue."[16] With few exceptions, for women to be successful and effective in the public they had to appear deferential to men, and to couch their contributions in the language and style of women's traditional work in the home. Whether or not this deference was genuine, these small concessions cumulatively reinforced for the public and the male power structure the conviction that women accepted and agreed with their subservient place in organizations and agencies, and as historian Judith Giesberg notes, they hid the contributions of necessarily modest women behind the egos of men in power.[17]

The rush of women seeking to contribute to the war effort by creating and collecting supplies was echoed in women seeking opportunities to serve as nurses in the conflict, even though that profession was not well defined in the 1860s.[18] Also, like benevolence work, nursing the sick and wounded seemed a natural extension of the caretaking women already performed in the home.[19] Historian Jane E. Schultz believes that estimates of the number of Union nurses serving during the war, including one estimate of over 21,000 women, have been too low. Schultz also found that "female hospital workers were as diverse as the population of the United States in 1860" in terms of race, class, age, and religion.[20] Whatever their exact number and composition, the nurses who served in the Civil War did so in hospitals, in makeshift triage units, on the battlefield, and on hospital ships. From the outset of the war the military leadership and military surgeons distrusted and sought to keep women from serving as nurses, and the public questioned such women's motives, morals, and respectability.[21] But wartime necessity and women's persistence kept women at work as nurses.

While women were eager to serve as nurses early in the war, it was far easier to determine how to send supplies to the front than it was to get oneself into a military hospital.[22] Resourceful women around the North began sending inquiries to the two most famous women in American medicine—Dr. Elizabeth Blackwell and Dorothea Dix—asking how they might volunteer.[23] Blackwell and Dix had very different ideas about what the female corps of nurses should look like. Blackwell, a practicing physician, sought to establish a trained, paid body of nurses who might continue to work after the war and was not concerned with the age or class of the women applying.[24] Dix, a reformer famous for her work improving the conditions of the incarcerated and mentally ill, was less concerned with training nurses but very much cared about the age and class of the women applying. She exclusively sought women who did not require to be paid for their work, were between thirty and forty-five years old, would submit to male authority, and who could present evidence of good moral character.[25] Despite their different visions, the two women worked together during the early crisis of the war, dispatching nurses to Washington.[26] After obtaining official War Department approval, however, Dix nudged Blackwell out of power and influence, and she became the channel through which many white middle-class women became nurses.

The result was the early preference for Dix's vision of an older, unpaid, morally policed, deferential, and white female nursing force.[27]

Going through Dix was not the only way women could become nurses. Some women attached themselves to regiments, typically one including a male relative, as they departed, signing on as nurses, laundresses, or cooks. Even if a woman left with the regiment as a laundress or cook, she was also likely to engage in nursing.[28] For African American women and poor women, enlisting in—or for newly freed slaves, being impressed into—regiments to serve as laundresses or cooks was the most likely way they could come to assist sick and injured soldiers and a means by which they could financially survive the war. Becoming involved in nursing through this channel had disadvantages besides inaccurate titles on payrolls: the designation of "laundress" or "cook" could also bring allegations of being a "camp follower," a label that implied prostitute.[29]

No matter the path Northern women took to become nurses during the Civil War—and evidence indicates that more women were willing to serve as nurses than the Union Army and benevolence agencies could or would effectively place—they faced some degree of public disapproval.[30] Victorian American ideas about what was proper for middle-class womanhood were contradictory when it came to female nurses. On the one hand, society believed that women were natural caretakers and lauded their careful, maternal ministrations of the sick and wounded when they occurred in the home.[31] Society also believed that middle-class white women had no place in the dangerous, dirty, decidedly masculine arena of war. Such women's senses, it was believed, were too delicate for the gruesome sights and smells of war and their constitutions too frail for camp tents and mess halls. Popular opinion held that it was especially inappropriate for young, unmarried white middle-class women to act as nurses, touching and healing the bodies of strange men and so far removed from parental and community oversight.[32] The stink of impropriety did not ever fully abate, and all women working as nurses had to vigilantly guard their reputations.[33] The more than twenty-one thousand women who went to war as nurses, therefore, had to face not only the emotional and physical hardships and dangers of their service, but also, especially at the beginning of the war, judgment and opprobrium of the communities they left behind.[34]

To dampen the public outcry, many nurses did their utmost to project themselves as respectable, morally upright, and deferential to doctors.[35] Some women also used the language of the home to describe their actions in the wards. The strange men whose bodies they comforted or healed were recognized as the brothers, sons, and husbands of other women, and nurses thought of themselves as proxy sisters and mothers.[36] Through these methods, female nurses and their supporters allayed societal fears and allowed women to continue to do the work but also diminished women's contributions as merely an extension of innately female nurturing instinct. The effect was to undercut women's efforts to command respect from doctors and society and to assert independence in caring for patients.[37]

Some white middle-class nurses managed to leverage their role as "mother" and "lady" to effect change in the way patients were treated in hospitals. Hannah Ropes, for one, requested an investigation into the treatment of patients at the Union Hotel Hospital, in Georgetown, writing that causing an inquiry to be launched would be "the best possible good a motherly woman could do."[38] Just as there were limits on the power of "mothers" and "ladies" in the home, there were limits on that purported authority in the wards. Moreover, African American nurses and working-class women had a more difficult time calling upon these lofty ideals in the face of male authority than did middle-class white women.[39] Female nurses served at the permission of the military generally, and specifically at the discretion of the surgeons and other male supervisors. Either could be revoked at any time. Women quickly learned the need to be obedient and subservient to men in authority if they wanted to stay in the wards.[40]

The federal government paid soldiers to fight, and their loyalty and reputation were never called into question because they received wages. The situation was not the same for nurses. Although eventually many nurses were compensated for their services, well-earned payment carried with it judgment, for respectable, white, middle-class women were not supposed to earn money for their services but rather to volunteer them in sacrifice to the nation. This may have been possible for upper- and some middle-class women, but poor women had little choice but to accept the public judgment over poverty. Women accepting pay were careful to stress that their primary motivation for nursing was patriotism, not money, in an effort to dampen the negative reaction against them. "To think that I, poor *Amy Bradley,* would come out here to work for *money* and that, the paltry sum of twelve dollars per month and Rations! . . . Thank God I had a higher motive than a high living & big salary," wrote Bradley, indignant at a surgeon's question about her pay.[41] Women's patriotism was genuine. The compensation white women received for nursing was quite small, and the pay African American women received even smaller, in relation to the gruesome, dangerous, heart- and back-breaking work of a Civil War nurse.[42] By downplaying the importance and inadequacies of the salaries women received, women undervalued their own work, but if they wanted to remain nurses and temper negative public reaction, they had little choice but to do so.

Unlike nurses and benevolence workers, women who sewed in factories, packed cartridges in arsenals, and clerked in government offices were not primarily mobilized to join the war effort by patriotism.[43] Women had been working outside the home long before the Civil War. The war, however, intensified demands on the government and left many women, including those with families to support, in need of work that paid. Historians cite contemporary estimates that indicate 300,000 women entered the labor market during the Civil War, many of them sewing garments to fill government contracts.[44] The new relationship between the federal government, businesses, and female employees began symbiotically—women needed work, and the government needed cheap goods and labor.

Female laborers played an important role in outfitting the Union Army. In his examination of the Union's military supply system, Mark Wilson found that "seamstresses comprised the largest group of military-industrial workers in the North."[45] Early in the war, state-run ordnance and garment-making operations from Pennsylvania to Wisconsin employed women to make military supplies because it was cheaper to hire women than it was to hire men.[46] As the war continued, the federal government took over the responsibility of outfitting soldiers. The federal government also employed women to produce ammunition, food, and medicines for the Union Army in locations throughout the Union.[47] While the military hired thousands of seamstresses to produce garments, women hired by private businesses contracting with the federal government stitched the bulk of the North's uniforms and tents.[48]

In addition to cost savings, army supply officers tried to maintain systems of public manufacture of goods, partially because of the women they employed. Such officers, and some congressmen, paternalistically believed that in directly hiring seamstresses the government provided important and deserved social welfare to needy women in precarious financial situations caused by the war.[49] Supervisors in arsenals around the North hired women early in the war because they could pay them significantly less than male employees and because arsenal supervisors made the gendered assumption that women would be more careful and obedient than were boys and men. Lt. Col. George D. Ramsay, commander of the Washington Arsenal, informed Congress in 1862 that he had dismissed two hundred "boys" in favor of "women" who were "more reliable in the laboratory."[50]

The federal government did not employ many women prior to the Civil War.[51] In 1859 there were eighteen women listed in biennial *Register of All Officers and Agents, Civil, Military, and Naval, in the Service of the United States*.[52] By 1871 that publication included the names of over nine hundred women in seven different departments. The *Register* tended to underreport women, however, and the federal government likely employed several thousands of women during the 1860s. In the women who pressed supervisors for employment through stories of helplessness and appealing to their benevolence, men discovered capable employees happy to work for half (or less) of the pay that male applicants found too low. The government never had to solicit women for employment; women were desperate for the jobs.[53] As word spread that Washington was hiring women, applications overwhelmed offices.[54]

Women performed a wide variety of jobs for the federal government in Washington in the 1860s, from copying to cartridge packing, printing to postal investigation, sewing to sweeping, and taxidermy to translation.[55] While most of the women employed by the government, especially in clerical positions, were white, African American women's names also appeared on federal payrolls in the 1860s. Although their race was not always noted in the records, making it difficult to find and quantify the number of female African American employees, a thorough cross-checking of payrolls and petitions with census records reveals that some black women did get federal work.[56] During the Civil War era, government employment became, and for decades would remain, an important means of social mobility for many African American men and women.[57]

An examination of women's applications to clerical positions in the Treasury and War Departments in the 1860s shows that women who had powerful men to advocate on their behalf and who wrote pathos-inducing letters were most successful. Although federal employment was an important opportunity for women, how women were able to obtain these limited positions reinforced paternalistic gender relations, rather than overturn them. Those who based their applications on their skills, experience, or political work alone did not typically meet with success. Women learned this lesson, and they tailored their applications accordingly, making the focus of their applications their desperate need and helplessness, and begging supervisors to rescue them from financial distress.[58] In January 1863, for example, Margaret C. Peters and Elizabeth Garretson penned a joint application to Secretary of the Treasury Salmon Chase from their hometown of Shreave in Wayne County, Ohio, to ask for jobs. The women wrote: "The war is now desolating our country has taken from us our husbands, one of whom (H. F. Peters) is now in a hospital in the enemy country–the other (John Garretson) for aught we know, may occupy a soldier's grave. The call of our country in taking our husbands, has taken our support, and want stares us and our children in the face. Now shall [we] leave things be? Can you—nay *will* you help us?"[59] Such appeals were common during the war.

The smaller salaries that women were willing to accept further reinforced, on a national stage, notions that the work of women was not and should not be valued equally with the work of men. The first federal department supervisors to hire women did so without official congressional approval. Congress officially approved the practice of supervisors in the March 1864 Deficiency Act, which explicitly authorized the employment of women. The act also formalized supervisors' practice of paying women half of what the lowest paid salaried men earned.[60]

Along with the paternalistic motivations for their hire and their smaller salaries, women working for the federal government, especially in mixed-sex work spaces such as the Treasury Department, faced much public attention. Rumors of sexual impropriety and immorality of female federal employees appeared frequently in the press. From arsenals to the Treasury Department, female federal employees were alleged to have obtained and retained their positions because they provided or dangled the hope of sexual favors to supervisors.[61] This negative attention threatened women's jobs, newspapers around the country issuing calls to abolish the practice of female federal employment during the Civil War era because of concerns about women's exploited or exploitative sexuality, causing women employed by the government to fall under intense public and state scrutiny.[62]

As female clerks, seamstresses, and arsenal employees became comfortable in their jobs and cognizant of their worth, they began to fight for greater pay and recognition of their labor, but their gains were limited. For example, the federal government subcontracted a significant amount of work to private employers, who paid seamstresses poorly during the Civil War.[63] Women fought the contracting-out system, seeking labor directly from the federal government, which paid higher wages than did contractors. Their argument was simple: why should private contractors earn profits at the expense of soldiers' widows and orphans (which many of them were, or claimed to be)?[64] In 1863, as the North suffered from the pinch of inflation, hundreds of working women met in New York to publicize their low wages and egregious working conditions.[65] Armed with a petition signed "Twenty Thousand Working Women of Philadelphia," seamstresses from Philadelphia traveled to Washington in 1864 to ask the War Department to modify the government contracting system they found exploitative and to raise their wages.[66] The seamstresses presented themselves "as American matrons and daughters, asking an equitable price for their labor."[67] Women clearly understood that their labor had value and that their wages should reflect that value. Secretary of War Edwin Stanton partially agreed to the seamstresses' requests, raising their wages by 20 percent and agreeing to hire more women directly. He did not, however, abolish private contracting or impose a minimum wage on the private sector, as the women had been requesting. Seamstresses from cities across the Union continued to push both Stanton and President Abraham Lincoln on these issues for the remainder of the war but were unsuccessful. Officials in the government did not want to relinquish the cost savings of private contracting (which were achieved by grossly underpaying female employees) and sought to shore up private industry as being in the best long-term interests of the nation.[68]

Female federal clerical workers and laborers in Washington also agitated for higher pay.[69] The efforts of these women to obtain greater and equal pay, including petitioning and politicking, forced Congress to debate the justice of unequal pay for women in three discussions in the Senate and one in the House of Representatives between 1867 and 1870. Although it came surprisingly close to succeeding, the movement ultimately failed, defeated by the economy of paying women reduced salaries and justified by the same paternalistic narratives of dependence and helplessness the government elicited from women seeking federal employment.[70]

Not all women underwent a dramatic shift during the Civil War in the type of work they performed. Historians estimate that approximately one-half of Northern soldiers were farmers or worked on farms. When these rural men left the corn and wheat fields for the battlefield, the wives, mothers, sisters, and daughters they left behind had to continue to care for family and perform the farm labor they had been doing prior to the war, as well as assume or replace the manual and managerial labor that had been done by now absent men. This work often had to be done in the face of acute financial stress, as pay from soldier husbands made it back to the farms irregularly and sometimes not at all.[71]

In her study of rural women in New York's rural Nanticoke Valley, an area west of Binghamton, Nancy Grey Osterud found that women survived the absence of men through mutual family aid and sharing residences and household responsibilities with kin. Judith Giesberg's examination of the Civil War experiences of rural Pennsylvania women found similar strategies employed there. Likewise, Ginette Aley found that rural midwestern women adjusted to wartime circumstances by assuming new responsibilities, when able, and enlisting support from kin networks. Many women had to learn not only how to manage the family's finances but what those finances were in the first place, something that they had not previously been privy to. Although historians have found that nineteenth-century rural women may have had more egalitarian marriages than did their urban and middle-class counterparts, due to the shared nature of farm work, husbands were not always forthcoming with such information, preferring to entrust the care of the family's finances to male relatives or other proxies.[72]

Even when husbands entrusted major financial transactions, including mortgage and debt management, to their wives, women, who had previously been excluded from such matters, were at a disadvantage in executing those transactions. Lack of experience, as well as ignorance of many details of transactions, hamstrung efforts. Moreover, the law often worked against them. Giesberg found that Pennsylvania property law was structured in a way that kept women dependent on men and limited women's freedom to contract.[73]

A dearth of postwar records makes it difficult for historians to draw conclusions as to how gender relations resettled in farms across the North when men returned from war. Two things are clear, however. One is that farm women's contributions during the war were often overlooked by the federal government. For instance, both Commissioner of Agriculture Isaac Newton and Secretary of War Stanton attributed the Union's impressive farm output during the war years to machinery and young men—not women.[74] Second, despite women's proven abilities during the war to manage property and finances, Giesberg found that after the war, "state laws worked powerfully to reinscribe their dependence," and that women returned to an "overall postwar climate that sought to limit women's property rights."[75]

In light of legal obstacles faced, the social stigma attached to middle-class women who worked outside the home, the lack of jobs open to women, and the paltry remuneration the majority of such jobs paid, Civil War widows' best, and many thought most appropriate, option for surviving the war in the absence of male support was social welfare.[76] There was precedent for women seeking assistance from the government after the loss of a male breadwinner in military service stretching back to the colonial era.[77] This, too, came with a price tag of dependence and supervision. Early in the conflict, when North and South both believed the war would be a brief one, state and local governments and charities cared for the families of soldiers. The federal government also provided for widows and orphans, but the system was inconsistent and inadequate. In the summer of 1862, after massive losses at the Battle of Shiloh and in Virginia, the number of men enlisting could not meet the Union's need for soldiers. According to historian Megan J. McClintock, the lack of manpower was in part due to men becoming increasingly concerned about the welfare of the families they would have to leave behind if they joined the army.[78]

The War Department modified its payment procedures to meet men's concerns, providing pay advances and paying a percentage of a man's enlistment bounty up front so that he could give it to his family upon his departure. But such measures were not enough. In an effort to induce men to enlist, Congress expanded federal pension benefits for the families of soldiers in July 1862, increasing pension rates and including mothers and sisters of soldiers in the pension program.[79] As McClintock outlines, however, for widows this government assistance came with a price—increased federal investigation of and supervision over women's private lives. The Northern public was concerned about corruption in the expanding federal government, and about the moral and social decline of society.[80] The Bureau of Pensions could not afford to be perceived as giving public funds to lying, sexually immoral women. First, the federal government scrutinized the marriages of women applying for pensions to determine their legitimacy. Determining whether or not a marriage was "legitimate," however, was difficult in the nineteenth century, when the procedures and recordkeeping of marriages were not strict. The federal government found it especially difficult to determine the validity of the marriages of formerly enslaved people, who because of their enslavement were deprived of the records and rituals white society deemed as legitimating marriage.[81]

In order to remain eligible for a widow's pension, a woman could not remarry, and on this second issue the government was better able to investigate women's private affairs. During the Civil War era and in the years that followed, the federal government monitored women's private lives to ensure that they had not remarried or were not cohabiting or engaging in sexual relations with men to skirt the remarriage disqualification. The commissioner of pensions believed women's defrauding of the government was a crisis, telling Congress in 1868 that widows were flagrantly cohabitating and also claiming that some purported war widows were prostitutes. The government helped to deflect public criticism by assuring the public it was being selective and morally upright in granting pensions only to respectable, worthy women.[82] If a woman wanted to secure her federal pension, she had to submit to government inquiries into her private life. Women could not avoid public intrusion into their private affairs by seeking state or local support either, as those entities also imposed standards of respectability and monitored the behavior of women seeking and receiving assistance to ensure those standards were met. Thus, Civil War widows' pensions reaffirmed and reinforced women's dependency on men and the government's paternalism over its female citizens.[83]

Women mobilized for war in ways that generated conflicting feelings in Victorian America, but society started to adjust, however reluctantly, to the idea of female benevolent workers, nurses, clerks, and farm laborers. Other occupations proved harder to accommodate into that Victorian ideal. Women who worked as soldiers or political activists during the Civil War resisted laboring under the restrictions society and the government imposed upon them as women. Women wanting to be soldiers abandoned their female identity, at least temporarily, and political activists endured censure for their transgressive actions until public opinion shifted.

Hundreds of women dressed as men and served as soldiers for both the Union and the Confederacy in the Civil War.[84] Women served in the military secretly, but it wasn't a secret during the Civil War that women were serving. Letters home and newspaper articles informed the public that not all of the Union army's soldiers were men.[85] Some on the home front were romanced by the derring-do—which in actuality was serious soldiering—of female soldiers who claimed they had enlisted as men because of a selfless love of country and a husband, father, or brother. While clearly breaking cultural norms by dressing as men and engaging in combat, women going to war because of ardent patriotism, or to be with and care for male relatives, generated some ambivalence in the public. The public treated far less favorably women who were motivated to go to war because they sought adventure or for a soldier's pay.[86] The U.S. Army exemplified American ambivalence over female service in the Civil War; the army denied that women ever fought in the Civil War into the twentieth century, despite the fact that Congress granted veteran Franklin Thompson (Sarah Edmonds) a pension for her service in 1886, after the secretary of war did not object to the "female soldier."[87]

Women also performed important political and intellectual labor during the Civil War era. Through fiery speeches, emotive poetry, reasoned prose, and laborious petitioning, female abolitionists helped to move the North from tolerating slavery during the antebellum period and early years of the war to ratifying a constitutional amendment granting African American men the right to vote in 1870.[88] Some of this work, such as writing poetry, was framed as consistent with women's proper place. Other aspects of the work represented a sharp departure from prevailing social norms. For instance, in the early twentieth century Ida Tarbell claimed that Anna Dickinson's lecturing on behalf of the Republicans during the Civil War "effectually ended popular opposition in the North to woman lecturers. The people began to feel that if a woman could render a patriotic service of this kind, the day had passed when there should be objection to her doing it."[89] While Tarbell's assessment was optimistic, a handful of mainly white middle- and upper-class women, by refusing to abandon the lecture circuit even in the face of public disapproval, expanded women's roles in the public square.

When the Civil War broke out, the women of the female suffrage movement agreed to place their fight aside and devote their time to helping the Union.[90] When the Union's war ended, Elizabeth Cady Stanton, Susan B. Anthony, Lucretia Mott, and other suffragists restarted theirs, believing that the contributions of Northern women who mobilized and labored during the conflict would be recognized and rewarded by federal and state governments. They were wrong. Much about women's legal status remained the same. In 1871 women in most states lacked the right to sign contracts, sue or be sued, or write wills without a husband's approval.[91] In fact, despite the inroads women made during the Civil War, the campaign for women's equal political status was in some ways made more difficult by the changes wrought by the conflict and its aftermath. Newly freed African American women found their masters' legal authority over them replaced, in large part, by their husbands'.[92] The word "male" for the first time appeared in the Constitution, and longtime allies in the fight for freedom, including Elizabeth Cady Stanton and Frederick Douglass, parted ways over how to proceed in the changed political landscape, causing a rift in the women's rights movement.[93] Women participated in the national conflict in critical ways, but invariably under paternalistic terms. Because of this, the Union and Northern society forced women to reify the idea that while women and their labor had value, neither they nor their contributions were as valuable as were men and male labor. This implicit and explicit denigration of women and their labor may, in part, explain why women failed to achieve greater rights in the postwar period.

NOTES

1. Portions of this chapter are adapted from *This Grand Experiment: When Women Entered the Federal Workforce in Civil War–Era Washington, D.C.* by Jessica Ziparo. Copyright © 2017, The University of North Carolina Press. Used with permission of the publisher.

2. Elizabeth Cady Stanton, Susan B. Anthony, and Matilda Joslyn Gage, eds., *History of Woman Suffrage.* 3 vols. (Rochester, N.Y.: Susan B. Anthony, 1881), 2:23.

3. Nina Silber, *Daughters of the Union: Northern Women Fight the Civil War* (Cambridge, Mass.: Harvard Univ. Press, 2005), 11–12; Jeanie Attie, *Patriotic Toil: Northern Women and the American Civil War* (Ithaca, N.Y.: Cornell Univ. Press, 1998), 5.

4. I am, of course, not the first to make the argument that the Civil War was not a watershed in women's rights. See Lyde Cullen Sizer, *The Political Work of Northern Women Writers and the Civil War, 1850–1872* (Chapel Hill: Univ. of North Carolina Press, 2000), xvii, 11; Silber, *Daughters of the Union,* 11–12; Attie, *Patriotic Toil,* 5. For more on women's political work during the Civil War era, see, e.g., Faye E. Dudden, *Fighting Chance: The Struggle Over Woman Suffrage and Black Suffrage in Reconstruction America* (New York: Oxford Univ. Press, 2011); Ellen Carol DuBois, *Feminism and Suffrage: The Emergence of an Independent Women's Movement in America, 1848–1869* (Ithaca, N.Y.: Cornell Univ. Press, 1978); Allison L. Sneider, *Suffragists in an Imperial Age: U.S. Expansion and the Woman Question, 1870–1929* (New York: Oxford Univ. Press, 2008); Melanie Susan Gustafson, *Women and the Republican Party, 1854–1924* (Chicago: Univ. of Illinois Press, 2001); and Rebecca Edwards, *Angels in the Machinery: Gender in American Party Politics from the Civil War to the Progressive Era* (New York: Oxford Univ. Press, 1997).

5. U.S. Treasury Department, Report of the Secretary of the Treasury on the State of the Finances, for the Year 1864, 1222 House Executive Document 3, Dec. 6, 1864, 76.

6. Judith Ann Giesberg, *Civil War Sisterhood: The U.S. Sanitary Commission and Women's Politics in Transition* (Boston: Northeastern Univ. Press, 2000), 14–16; Silber, *Daughters of the Union* 164–66.

7. Silber, *Daughters of the Union,* 163.

8. Giesberg, *Civil War Sisterhood,* 15; Lori Ginzberg, *Women and the Work of Benevolence: Morality, Politics, and Class in Nineteenth-Century United States* (New Haven, Conn.: Yale Univ. Press, 1990), 135–36; Susan Zaeske, *Signatures of Citizenship: Petitioning, Antislavery & Women's Political Identity* (Chapel Hill: Univ. of North Carolina Press, 2003), 21–22.

9. Silber, *Daughters of the Union,* 165–67; Ella Forbes, *African American Women during the Civil War* (New York: Garland, 1998), chap. 5; Jennifer Fleischner, *Mrs. Lincoln and Mrs. Keckley* (New York: Broadway Books, 2003), 248, 264.

10. Forbes, *African American Women during the Civil War,* 66.

11. Silber, *Daughters of the Union,* 170–72; Giesberg, *Civil War Sisterhood,* 99–101; Attie, *Patriotic Toil,* 83, 272.

12. Giesberg, *Civil War Sisterhood,* 99–101; Attie, *Patriotic Toil,* 83, 272.

13. Attie, *Patriotic Toil,* 272.

14. Silber, *Daughters of the Union,* 192.

15. Ibid., 192–93.

16. Elizabeth D. Leonard, *Yankee Women: Gender Battles in the Civil War* (New York: W. W. Norton, 1994), 85.

17. Giesberg, *Civil War Sisterhood,* 6.

18. Ibid., 15, 22; Silber, *Daughters of the Union,* 196–97.

19. Giesberg, *Civil War Sisterhood,* 24; Jane E. Schultz, *Women at the Front: Hospital Workers in Civil War America* (Chapel Hill: Univ. of North Carolina Press, 2004), 3.

Jessica Ziparo

20. Schultz, *Women at the Front,* 12, 20.

21. Ibid., 18.

22. Leonard, *Yankee Women,* 6, 12–14.

23. Giesberg, *Civil War Sisterhood,* 30, 35.

24. Ibid., 33–34, 41; Leonard, *Yankee Women,* 10; Silber, *Daughters of the Union,* 198.

25. Giesberg, *Civil War Sisterhood,* 18–19, 41; Leonard, *Yankee Women,* 16–17; Silber, *Daughters of the Union,* 198.

26. Giesberg, *Civil War Sisterhood,* 41–42.

27. Attie, *Patriotic Toil,* 43; Leonard, *Yankee Women,* 11.

28. Leonard, *Yankee Women,* 8–9; Silber, *Daughters of the Union,* 199; Schultz, *Women at the Front,* 20, 33.

29. Silber, *Daughters of the Union,* 197, 214–16; Jane E. Schultz, "Race, Gender, and Bureaucracy: Civil War Army Nurses and the Pension Bureau," *Journal of Women's History* 6 (Summer 1994): 47–48; Schultz, *Women at the Front,* 21, 56–57.

30. Schultz, *Women at the Front,* 63.

31. Giesberg, *Civil War Sisterhood,* 117.

32. Leonard, *Yankee Women,* 12–14; Silber, *Daughters of the Union,* 196; Schultz, *Women at the Front,* 49, 53–54.

33. Schultz, *Women at the Front,* 90.

34. Schultz, "Race, Gender, and Bureaucracy," 45; Schultz, *Women at the Front,* 20.

35. Silber, *Daughters of the Union,* 195–97.

36. Ibid., 202–3.

37. Schultz, *Women at the Front,* 3, 55.

38. Silber, *Daughters of the Union,* 203–6.

39. Schultz, "Race, Gender, and Bureaucracy," 45–46.

40. Schultz, *Women at the Front,* 4, 125; Silber, *Daughters of the Union,* 206–8. As Nina Silber notes, some women were comfortable with the superiority of men. Silber, *Daughters of the Union,* 208–12.

41. Schultz, *Women at the Front,* 43.

42. Silber, *Daughters of the Union,* 199–200; Leonard, *Yankee Women,* 23–30; Schultz, *Women at the Front,* 39, 42, 47–49. Not all women were satisfied with nurses' pay. Around the North, small numbers of women came together to protest the inadequacy of their wages. Some women pointed to the injustice of paying underqualified men more than qualified women earned. Schultz, *Women at the Front,* 40.

43. The arguments and ideas in this section about female government workers in Washington, D.C., are further developed in my *This Grand Experiment.* For more on women working in munitions factories during the Civil War, see Giesberg, *Civil War Sisterhood,* chap. 3.

44. Alice Kessler-Harris, *Out to Work: A History of Wage-Earning Women in the United States* (New York: Oxford Univ. Press, 1982), 76–77; Sizer, *Political Work of Northern Women Writers,* 115; and Judith Giesberg, *Army at Home: Women and the Civil War on the Northern Home Front* (Chapel Hill: Univ. of North Carolina Press, 2009), 120.

45. Mark R. Wilson, *The Business of Civil War: Military Mobilization and the State, 1861–1865* (Baltimore: Johns Hopkins Univ. Press, 2006), 73.

46. Ibid., 12–14.

47. Ibid., 74–75.

48. Ibid., 14–23, 73, and esp. chap. 3 for more on the public-private debate in the North during the Civil War. On women and work for federal contractors and in federal facilities, see also Phillip S. Paludan, *"A People's Contest": The Union and Civil War 1861–1865* (New York: Harper & Row, 1988), 182–83, 185–86; and Giesberg, *Army at Home,* 136–42.

49. Wilson, *Business of Civil War,* 87–88.

50. U.S. Congress, House of Representatives, *Loyalty of Clerks and Other Persons Employed By Government,* House Report No. 16, 37th Cong., 2d sess, 1862, 8; Giesberg, *Army At Home,* 76–78.

51. There were exceptions. During the antebellum period, women worked at the Government Hospital for the Insane, the Government Printing Office, and the Patent Office. Women were also sometimes employed as postmasters across the United States and as contract laborers in various cities .

52. The *United States, Register of All Officers and Agents, Civil, Military, and Naval, in the Service of the United States* (hereafter cited as *Federal Register*). The *Federal Register* was published every other year on odd years. Note that this publication underreported employees of both sexes, but as it is a consistent measure of female employment over the time period covered in this chapter, it functions as a gauge. For the underreporting issue, see Cindy S. Aron, "'To Barter Their Souls for Gold': Female Clerks in Federal Government Offices, 1862–1890," *Journal of American History* 67 (Mar. 1981): 835–53. Most notably for present purposes, the publication does not include statistics on the men and women employed in the Government Printing Office or most of the men and women employed in the Treasury Department's Bureau of Engraving and Printing. Ziparo, *This Grand Experiment,* 15.

53. Ziparo, *This Grand Experiment,* 39–66. None of the departments placed want ads or announcements with the exception of the Government Hospital for the Insane, which did occasionally run help wanted ads in local papers. See, e.g., "[want ad]," *Daily National Intelligencer* (Washington, D.C.), Oct. 1, 1862, 3. Ziparo, *This Grand Experiment,* 233n46.

54. Ziparo, *This Grand Experiment,* 25. See also Edward Winslow Martin, *Behind the Scenes in Washington* (New York: Continental Publishing Company, 1873), 466; "From Washington," *Public Ledger* (Philadelphia), Nov. 16, 1865, p. 1.

55. Ziparo, *This Grand Experiment.*

56. Ibid., 31. For example, the *Federal Register* for the Treasury Department provides no indication that 1860s messengers and laborers Sophia Holmes (*Federal Register* 1863, 1865, 1867; Census 1860, 1870, Washington, D.C.), Susan Bruce (*Federal Register* 1863, 1865, 1867; Census 1860, Washington, D.C.), Ruth Biggs (*Federal Register* 1867; Census 1870, Washington, D.C.), or Caroline Davis (*Federal Register* 1865, 1867; Census 1870, Washington, D.C.) were African Americans.

57. Kate Masur, "Patronage and Protest in Kate Brown's Washington," *Journal of American History* 99 (Mar. 2013): 1047–71. For the African American experience in the civil service in the early twentieth century, see Eric Yellin, *Racism in the Nation's Service: Government Workers and the Color Line in Woodrow Wilson's America* (Chapel Hill: Univ. of North Carolina Press, 2013).

58. Ziparo, *This Grand Experiment,* 39–66; Mary Clemmer Ames, *Ten Years in Washington: Life and Scenes in the National Capital, as a Woman Sees Them* (Hartford, Conn.: A. D. Worthington, 1873), 374.

59. File of Margaret C. Peters, Applications and Recommendations for Positions in the Washington, D.C., Offices of the Treasury Department, 1830–1910, entry 201, Records of the Division of Appointments, General Records of the Department of the Treasury, RG 56 (National Archives in College Park, Maryland), box 455 (Per to Pet); Ziparo, *This Grand Experiment,* 48.

60. Ziparo, *This Grand Experiment,* 22–23; An Act to Supply Deficiencies in the Appropriations for Service of Fiscal Year Ending June 30, 1864, and for Other Purposes, 38th Congress, ch. 30, 13 stat. 22, Mar. 14, 1864. See also Silber, *Daughters of the Union,* 78; U.S. Civil Service Commission, "Women in the Federal Service," Washington, D.C.: Government Printing Office, 1938, p. 4.

61. See, e.g., "The City," *The Critic* (Washington, D.C.), Nov. 30, 1869, 3. For the sexualizing of women in arsenals, see Giesberg, *Army at Home,* 84–87.

62. Ziparo, *This Grand Experiment,* 138–169. See, e.g., "The Investigation Into the Treasury Department and Washington—the Female Clerk System," *Daily Age* (Philadelphia), May 21, 1864, p. 1; "The Removal of Female Clerks from the Departments at Washington," *Evening Bulletin* (San Francisco), Dec. 19, 1866.

63. Sizer, *Political Work of Northern Women Writers,* 118.

64. Wilson, *Business of Civil War,* 92–96.

65. Kessler-Harris, *Out to Work,* 79; Wilson, *Business of Civil War,* 95–96.

66. Giesberg, *Army at Home,* 119–123; Wilson, *Business of Civil War,* 97–98.

67. "Twenty-Thousand Working Women," to Brigadier General Meigs, June 6, 1864, Old Military Records, National Archives and Records Administration, box 439, NM 81, e. 225, qtd. in Giesberg, *Army at Home,* 122.

68. Mark Wilson also argues that the government suffered from cash flow issues that made it easier to award large contracts to private businesses that would accept certificates than to pay thousands of workers cash on a monthly or weekly basis. Wilson, *Business of Civil War,* 98–103.

69. "Petition of Female Employees in the Treasury Department Praying an Increase of Salary," Jan. 30, 1865, Records of the U.S. Senate, RG 46, 38th Cong., 2nd sess., box No. 81, folder SEN 38H5–Jan. 27–Feb. 3 1865 (National Archives, Washington, D.C.). Female laborers also requested higher pay. For example, early in 1863 female press feeders at the Government Printing Office in Washington successfully struck for higher wages. "Strike of the Female Press Feeders at the Government Printing Office," *Daily Morning Chronicle,* Feb. 19, 1863, p. 3.

70. Ziparo, *This Grand Experiment,* 193–220; *Congressional Globe* (1869), 1774; Senate Discussion on H.R. no. 974, *Congressional Globe,* 41st Cong., 2nd sess., May 13, 1870, 3449–52, 3451–52.

71. Judith Ann Giesberg, "From Harvest Field to Battlefield: Rural Pennsylvania Women and the U.S. Civil War," *Pennsylvania History* 72 (Apr. 2005): 160–64.

72. Nancy Grey Osterud, "Rural Women during the Civil War: New York's Nanticoke Valley, 1861–1865," *New York History* 7 (Oct. 1990): 357–85; Giesberg, "From Harvest Field to Battlefield," 167–70; Ginette Aley, "Inescapable Realities: Rural Midwestern Women and Families During the Civil War," in Ginette Aley and J. L. Anderson, eds., *Union Heartland: The Midwestern Home Front During the Civil War* (Carbondale: Southern Illinois Univ. Press, 2013), 125–47.

73. Giesberg, "From Harvest Field to Battlefield," 172, 181; Giesberg, *Army at Home,* 38.

74. Giesberg, "From Harvest Field to Battlefield," 178–79, 183–84.

75. Ibid., 182.

76. Michael Thomas Smith, *The Enemy Within: Fears of Corruption in the Civil War North* (Charlottesville: Univ. of Virginia Press, 2011), 109. As Judith Giesberg has noted, working-class families understood and accepted the need for wives and daughters to earn supplemental income for the family. Giesberg, *Army at Home,* 73. For more on how the pension system functioned during and after the Civil War and how it affected later social welfare policies, see Theda Skocpol, *Protecting Soldiers and Mothers: The Political Origins of Social Policy in the United States* (Cambridge, Mass.: Belknap Press of Harvard Univ. Press, 1992).

77. Megan J. McClintock, "Civil War Pensions and the Reconstruction of Union Families," *Journal of American History* 83 (Sept. 1996): 456–80.

78. Ibid., 460–62.

79. Rebecca Edwards, *Angels in the Machinery: Gender in American Party Politics from the Civil War to the Progressive Era* (New York: Oxford Univ. Press, 1997), 29. The act raised the monthly pension paid to widows and orphans from $4 to $8. McClintock, "Civil War Pensions," 461–63, 479n15.

80. Smith, *Enemy Within*, 2–3.

81. McClintock, "Civil War Pensions," 466, 471–74. In recognition of this difficulty, Congress loosened evidentiary requirements in 1864 after the Fort Pillow Massacre.

82. In the late 1860s Congress refused to grant the commissioner the supervisory powers he sought. In 1882 Congress passed legislation terminating widow's benefits to women found to be cohabitating. McClintock, "Civil War Pensions," 471, 474, 476–77, 479–80.

83. LeeAnn Whites and Alecia P. Long, eds., *Occupied Women: Gender, Military Occupation, and the American Civil War* (Baton Rouge: Louisiana State Univ. Press, 2009), 192–93; Giesberg, "From Harvest Field to Battlefield," 174.

84. A commonly cited number is four hundred, but recent scholarship has suggested the number might be as high as one thousand. Elizabeth D. Leonard, "Introduction," in Sarah Emma Edmonds, *Memoirs of a Soldier, Nurse and Spy: A Woman's Adventures in the Union Army* (DeKalb: Northern Illinois Univ. Press, 1999), xiv. DeAnne Blanton and Lauren Cook found evidence of 250; see DeAnne Blanton and Lauren M. Cook, *They Fought Like Demons: Women Soldiers in the Civil War* (New York: Vintage Books, 2003), 7. For more on female soldiers in the Civil War, see Elizabeth D. Leonard, *All the Daring of the Soldier: Women of the Civil War Armies* (New York: W. W. Norton, 1999); Lauren Cook Burgess, ed., *An Uncommon Soldier: The Civil War Letters of Sarah Rosetta Wakeman, Alias Pvt. Lyons Wakeman, 153rd Regiment, New York State Volunteers, 1862–1864* (Pasadena, Md.: MINERVA Center, 1994); DeAnne Blanton, "Women Soldiers of the Civil War," *Prologue* 25 (Spring 1993): 27. Women also worked as spies during the Civil War. See, e.g., Elizabeth R. Varon, *Southern Lady, Yankee Spy: The True Story of Elizabeth Van Lew, A Union Agent in the Heart of the Confederacy* (New York: Oxford Univ. Press, 2003).

85. Blanton and Cook, *They Fought Like Demons*, 145–46; Blanton, "Women Soldiers of the Civil War," 27.

86. Blanton and Cook, *They Fought Like Demons*, 148–53, 162; Leonard, "Introduction" to *Memoirs of a Soldier*, xx–xxi.

87. Blanton and Cook, *They Fought Like Demons*, 167–68.

88. Wendy Hamand Venet, *Neither Ballots Nor Bullets: Women Abolitionists and the Civil War* (Charlottesville: Univ. Press of Virginia, 1991), x.

89. Ida Tarbell, "The American Woman," *American Magazine* 69 (1909–1910): 809; Venet, *Neither Ballots Nor Bullets*, 159; Silber, *Daughters of the Union*, 279–80.

90. DuBois, *Feminism and Suffrage*, 52.

91. Allison L. Sneider, *Suffragists in an Imperial Age: U.S. Expansion and the Woman Question, 1870–1929* (New York: Oxford Univ. Press, 2008), 45.

92. Amy Dru Stanley, "Instead of Waiting for the Thirteenth Amendment: The War Power, Slave Marriage, and Inviolate Human Rights," *American Historical Review* 115 (2010): 732–65.

93. Attie, *Patriotic Toil*, 268–269; Lisa Tetrault, *The Myth of Seneca Falls: Memory and the Women's Suffrage Movement, 1848–1898* (Chapel Hill: Univ. of North Carolina Press 2014), vol. 1, 19–23.

Emancipation

Southern Women and Emancipation during the Civil War

R E B E C C A   C A P O B I A N C O

In August of 1861 Betty Maury, an elite white woman living in Fredericksburg, Virginia, recorded a puzzling event in her diary. Maury reflected, "A black woman came here a few days ago to apply for the place of cook and gave her name as Henrietta Furgerson. The same woman who ran away . . . in New York when [Nanny] was a baby."[1] This moment is both intriguing and perplexing in its illustration of the complexities of freedom during the Civil War. Presumably something or somebody, likely a family member or child, brought Furgerson back to Fredericksburg after years of apparent freedom in the North. In August of 1861, just months into the Civil War, Furgerson's freedom was by no means protected or guaranteed in Virginia. Yet return she did. Social relations—like those between a mistress and an enslaved woman—were dramatically renegotiated during the war, leaving slaveholding women disoriented and puzzling over events such as this. Maury noted this curiosity in passing, but in the days and weeks ahead she found herself distracted by additional perceived improprieties perpetrated by her slaves.

There is no way to know what brought Henrietta Furgerson back to the doorstep of her former mistress, but the moment speaks to the peculiarities of freedom and the various ways in which women negotiated new spaces created by armed conflict. Furgerson's arrival appears personal, spurred not by a declaration of emancipation by Union forces but by an individual decision to act within her immediate context. Moreover, this incident demonstrates the difficulty in capturing the experience of Southern women and emancipation. Telling the story of Northern women and emancipation, historians often focus on the actions of women both black and white who worked to advance the cause of freedom. Among Southern women, though, it is necessary to speak of women working both for and against black freedom. Just as black women like Furgerson attempted to achieve freedom, white women like Maury sought to impede this process. Southern women often contended directly against one another, while simultaneously reckoning with life turned upside down by war. As women negotiated the realities of armed conflict, they found new and useful avenues for action while grappling with the deprivations produced by war. Despite their struggle with these limitations, women shaped the contours of emancipation as it evolved on the ground and in so doing influenced emancipation policy.

Historians have charted the development of emancipation policies and how the Union war effort determined where and when formal emancipation occurred. They have argued at length about whether or not emancipation came at the hands of liberating soldiers or the slaves themselves. Additionally, historians have highlighted the ways in which the burdens of maintaining slavery and the status quo during a time of chaos undermined white women's support for the Confederate war effort.[2] When these various narratives are brought into conversation with one another, it becomes clear that emancipation was layered and evolved in fits and spurts at the national and local level; as such, it is nearly impossible to define in a single, straightforward timeline. Southern women found themselves face to face at moments such as this, where emancipation was very much defined by local context rather than national policy.

Rebellion by the Southern states opened the way for rebellion by the slaves. Historians have charted the diverse paths to freedom African Americans took during the war—from finding refuge in the ranks of the Union army to escaping across contested boundaries. For women the war of emancipation, waged on the ground, in their homes and streets, differed from the familiar national narrative. In the absence of so many white men, the boundaries of slavery and the forces that held it in place underwent drastic change. The interests of slaveholders and the interests of slaves collided in this vacuum. As the Confederacy slowly deteriorated over four years of war, so too did the power whites had wielded over their peculiar world. On the home front, these changes manifested themselves in tangible ways as slaves contended with their white masters, left the plantation, or demanded wages.

Although Southern women confronted unique material constraints during the war, the ideological expectations of women's spheres of action remained the same for them as for Northern women. Women were defined as in need of protection from the wartime state, and as such they were supposed to steer clear of certain kinds of war work. As Chandra Manning shows in her essay in this collection, Northern women—particularly white women—who ventured into the South during the war found it difficult to find work, except perhaps as teachers or nurses, because of the strongly gendered notions of work that held sway in both North and South. This assumption extended to Southern white women as well, at times limiting their opportunities to labor for the Cause. In spite of these constraints, women's wartime efforts to protect their families and to manage emancipation on the ground remind us that the gendered ideals broke down under the strain of war and that women acted in ways that were politically and racially consequential—sometimes self-consciously so.

Historians have begun to synthesize studies of the small rebellions that occurred within the larger rebellion and to focus on the ways in which the path to emancipation took distinctly different routes for women than for men.[3] Women struggled for and against freedom on a local level and were most likely to negotiate emancipation at home. In the words and accounts of women themselves, the dimensions of this

Rebecca Capobianco

struggle are revealed. Women's stories move the process of emancipation along a different timeline than that of official policy and demonstrate that the personal decisions of individual people determined when and how emancipation occurred, and what it meant.

Almost immediately from the opening of hostilities, Union officials had to consider the state of fugitive slaves. By the end of July 1861, an estimated nine hundred slaves had come into Union lines in Hampton, Virginia.[4] Received by Gen. Benjamin F. Butler, who labeled them "contraband of war," such slaves were in an uncertain position, protected in practice by the Union army but without legal standing as "free" in any way.[5] In early August the United States Congress passed the first Confiscation Act, which declared the right of the Union army to "confiscate property" used in the Confederate war effort, including slaves.[6] James Oakes notes that the Union rout at the First Battle of Bull Run in July of 1861, just a month before Henrietta Furgerson appeared on Betty Maury's doorstep, began to push Congress to see that depriving the Confederate army of slaves would weaken its military power.[7] This idea informed nearly every federal move taken toward emancipation during the war, yet it was based on the assumption that slaves were male. By omission, federal emancipation policy left the fate of the women and children who had fled to Union lines undetermined, and it left enslaved women to navigate an uncharted and undefined path to freedom.

As Leslie Schwalm notes, Union policy toward confiscation in the early years of the war was marked by gendered notions of war as a masculine endeavor. Policy makers on both sides understood that only men could labor for war.[8] Left theoretically outside of the realm of war, and seemingly incapable of providing material assistance to the Confederate war effort, enslaved women were not protected by the first Confiscation Act. Yet men, women, and children sought refuge behind Union lines. In the first summer of the war, Butler wrote Washington asking for instruction, noting the ambiguity of U.S. confiscation policy and wondering what he should do with the women and children who still flocked to his lines.[9] Addressing Secretary of War Simon Cameron directly, Butler wondered of the more than nine hundred African Americans in his lines, "Are these men, women, and children, slaves? Are they free? Is their condition that of men, women, and children, or that of property, or is it a mixed relation?" To bring home the point, Butler added, "What their status was under the Constitution and laws, we all know. What has been the effect of rebellion and a state of war upon that status?"[10] The appearance of people who stood outside accepted notions of war moved Butler to press Washington for concrete answers to who fell under the category "contraband of war."

In an attempt to resolve this problem, Congress passed the Second Confiscation Act in July of 1862, expanding the terms of the first and allowing Union soldiers to confiscate slaves of any disloyal owner.[11] By targeting slaves belonging to disloyal owners rather than slaves engaged in production of the Confederate war effort, the Second Confiscation Act appeared to remove gender as a disqualifying factor for Union confiscation. However, as Eric Foner points out, the Lincoln administration left this second act "virtually unenforced," for fear of antagonizing loyal slaveowners and the Northern public.[12] Gen. Ulysses S. Grant captured the essence of Union policy in the early years of war, when in 1862, in reference to the fugitive slaves who had sought protection within his lines, he remarked, "I don't know what is to become of these poor people in the end, but it weakens the enemy to take them from them."[13] Still unsure of the ultimate fate of slavery, Union officials recognized that whatever the personal consequences of confiscation, it deprived the Confederacy of much-needed human labor.

On January 1, 1863, President Lincoln clarified this ambiguity by issuing the Emancipation Proclamation, freeing slaves in any area of the South still in rebellion on that date and inviting African American men to enlist in the Union army.[14] The Proclamation was a fundamental turning point in the war effort itself, transforming a war for restoration into a war for freedom.[15] Still, the problem of gender remained. While black men had the occasion to join the army's ranks, women did not, and the role they could play within Union lines remained unclear. Indeed, with each progressive move, U.S. authorities seemed unprepared to handle the questions raised by enslaved women and children who made their way to Union lines. Thavolia Glymph notes that the Preliminary Emancipation Proclamation and Emancipation Proclamation were "belated recognitions of the slaves' understanding that the war must result in their liberation."[16] As Benjamin Butler's complaints in 1861 made clear, Lincoln, Congress, and the U.S. Army were attempting to determine what to do with people who were already in their midst. Edward Ayers and Scott Nesbitt perhaps put it best in stating, "Emancipation was a deeply patterned, deeply contingent affair that depended on the interaction of processes occurring at multiple scales."[17]

A look at the situation in Fredericksburg, Virginia, provides a case study of that layered and contingent pattern of emancipation playing out. From Fredericksburg we can see not only the ambiguity of the timeline of emancipation, divorced from federal policy, but also the specific ways women encountered emancipation in the South. At Fredericksburg, as elsewhere, slaves began to move as soon as war broke out, taking advantage of the instability the war generated and in the case of Virginia the presence of the Union army.[18] Four major battles occurred in and around Fredericksburg, and the city changed hands multiple times over the course of the war. Fredericksburg became a gathering point for fugitive slaves who arrived from throughout Virginia to begin their flight to undefined freedom.

Betty Maury, daughter of naval commander Matthew Fontaine Maury, relocated to Fredericksburg, Virginia, from Washington, D.C., with her husband and young daughter, at the outset of the war, to "be with [the] people on the right side."[19] Written in the early years of the war, Maury's diary demonstrates that emancipation began unfolding well before it became federal policy and that it moved at a pace unconstrained by Union confiscation policy. Instead, emancipation depended on the individual choices of slaves and slaveholders.[20] In their diaries, slaveholding women, like Maury, registered their indignation at their slaves' behavior and their frustrations in attempting to control slaves' behavior through force or manipulation. Taken together, the many and constant small-scale conflicts between enslaved women and their mistresses—like those that Maury recorded—reveal a massive undercurrent of resistance that weakened both slavery and the Confederacy. At times Maury's complaints about the lack of help appear mundane, even grating, but they speak volumes about the steady scraping away of slaveholders' control and the unpredictable nature of a war that seemed to disrupt lives everywhere, from battlefield to home.[21]

In the absence of men, decisions about the protection of families and property in cities under siege fell to white women—including maintaining control over their slaves. Fanny Bernard Goolrick, a Fredericksburg resident, described an experience she shared not only with her neighbors but also with countless other Southerners throughout the Confederacy caught in the middle of armed conflict. She remembered taking refuge in the basement when a bombardment began, recalling how "the work of destruction began, and for long hours the only sound that greeted our ears were the whizzing and moaning of shells and the crash of falling bricks and timber."[22] The Goolricks shared their basement sanctuary with the family's slaves. Goolrick recalled how her "mother and we three children were seated on a low bed with Ca'line, a very small darkey, huddled as close to us children as she could get, trying to keep warm."[23] Yet Goolrick's aunt could not entirely forget propriety, and in the midst of the bombardment, she ordered one of her slaves to the kitchen to make food and coffee for the basement refugees. Despite the order, the enslaved woman—"Aunt B"—refused, carving out her own measure of freedom in this small moment.[24] Even as war stripped away the privileges of race and class, slaveholding white women sought to bind them up.[25]

As Union policy moved to endorse, however tentatively, the actions of runaway slaves, Southern white women did what they could to prevent their slaves from taking advantage of new opportunities. Maury reported on the effects of the Second Confiscation Act in July of 1862, remarking that the "Yankees have also passed a new confiscation bill seizing the property of all who refuse to take the oath. Uncle Jourdan was prepared to run this morning with the larger portion of his negroes."[26] Revealing her role in Uncle Jourdan's plan, Maury noted, "We have to be very cautious and careful in speaking of these things, for if the negroes had any suspicion that they were to be carried away they would run off."[27] The comment reveals, too, that Maury knew not to take the cooperation or loyalty of the family's slaves for granted. White women not only helped to deceive enslaved people, at times they also moved and ordered their slaves away on their own. Kate Stone recorded how her mother, overseeing a Louisiana plantation in the absence of white men, sent their family's slaves to Texas to keep them away from the Union army.[28] At other times, Stone's mother directed slaves to hide from Union soldiers.[29] Celina Roman wrote fearfully to her son from her Louisiana plantation, begging him to lock up their slaves "every night and Sunday and make them see that they are not free."[30] Though she remained on the plantation, Roman depended on her son to direct the control of the family's slaves from a distance and ensure her personal safety. Like Maury, Roman knew better than to take the loyalties of her family slaves for granted.

Despite their efforts, white women found themselves overseeing—and recording— the slow but steady disintegration of slavery. In June 1861 Betty Maury lamented that her slaves were already beginning to run off. She chronicled the drama of Fanny, the family's cook, who chose to leave "with all her possessions" rather than be relocated to a property outside the city.[31] Maury sent a constable to find her, but days later she had heard "no tidings of Fanny. I think she is too smart to be caught."[32] Fanny's departure was the first in a series of escapes that Maury recorded in her diary.[33] A few months later Maury noted that "seventeen of Mr. Mason's servants have run off. They stole all of cousin Nanny's dresses but three, and took both cloak and shawl. One party of them sent off in a wagon and carried their feather beds."[34] As the scale of escapes Maury recorded increased, so too did the liberties slaves felt comfortable taking when they left. In spite of the slow evolution of Union-sponsored emancipation and white women's attempts to keep them in bondage, slaves planned and executed individual and collective escapes. In the case of these runaways, the presence of the Union army was enough to prompt them to take leave of their masters.[35] Although male slaves were most likely to run away in the antebellum period alone, armed conflict altered both the opportunity for and the necessity for the escape of slave women.[36] During the war, enslaved women were just as likely as men to run away, with the exception of women with small children too young to survive the hazardous journey.[37]

Fanny's escape further illustrates the contingency of freedom. Three months after her successful departure, Fanny reappeared, "on her own accord." According to Maury, Fanny informed her master that she wanted "to be sold or hired out."[38] Thus, though she had come back, Fanny was determined that her return would be on her own terms. This pattern of flight followed by reappearance was not uncommon. John William determined to leave Fredericksburg with twenty-five of his slaves, but his slaves had other plans. On August 2, 1862, while the William family was at breakfast, "every one ran off." William sent another one of his slaves to find the fugitives and negotiate with them, offering them William's word that he would not send them away, but he was ultimately unsuccessful. While the group included mothers and their children, some of the mothers had no choice but to leave their children behind. By nightfall, two of the twenty-five runaways had returned—both of them mothers who came back for their children.[39] Kate Stone reported a similar episode in Louisiana in June of 1861, noting, "Aunt Lucy, the head of them all, ran away this morning, but was back by dinner . . . all of [the slaves] are demoralized."[40] Self-emancipation was fraught, dangerous, and often unsuccessful, particularly for women with children. Rather than leave permanently, enslaved women might run away as a temporary solution to a particular problem, joining a local group of fugitives who "marooned," or camped, nearby to keep an eye on family members and eventually return to work.

As Stephanie Camp has demonstrated, strategies of marooning and escape had a long history in slave communities. Enslaved women more regularly opted for truancy, a temporary departure for the span of a few days or weeks, as a means to gain personal space before resuming their work on the plantation.[41] Harriet Jacobs's seven-year confinement in her grandmother's attic crawl space allowed her to escape her vindictive master even as she kept an eye on her children.[42] Though strategies such as marooning

Rebecca Capobianco

were not new, in the chaos of war these tactics gained new salience, particularly in the absence of male overseers who normally regulated slave behavior and searched for runaways.[43] Enslaved women who remained on the plantation provided critical support, such as food, for maroon colonies.[44]

Close to the shifting lines of battle, Fredericksburg became a gathering point for escaped slaves in Virginia. Maury observed in June of 1862 that "runaway negroes from the country and around continue to come in every day. It is a curious and pitiful sight to see the foot sore and wearing [weary?] looking corn field hands with their packs on their backs and handkerchiefs tied over their heads—men, women, little children and babies coming in gangs of ten and twenty at a time."[45] Henrietta Furgerson's return had been the first indication, in Maury's world, that the war had created new opportunities for claiming freedom. This phenomenon had grown, however, and Maury watched daily as slaves from throughout the country followed this precarious path to freedom. Of these new arrivals, Maury opined, "They all look anxious and unhappy. Many of them are sent to the north. We hear that there is great want and suffering among those in Washington."[46] Though Maury could not know what these refugees felt upon arriving in Fredericksburg, her reflections on the "great want and suffering" in Washington were likely true. Realities for fugitive slaves who ended up in refugee camps in Washington and elsewhere were difficult—and in the case of black women, they were exceptionally challenging.

Left outside Union policy, black women faced violence and neglect at the hands of those mandated to protect them. As refugees from slavery, black women had to fend for themselves among soldiers who were unprepared for and often hostile to their presence.[47] In this vulnerable position, women suffered rape and violence in and around the refugee camps.[48] Women provided for themselves in camps, where there were few paid avenues for work. Laura Edwards points out that beyond field work, Union officials could only imagine black women "as cooks, laundresses, and prostitutes—although prostitution was officially discouraged."[49] The women pieced together resources, growing their own food or selling baked goods.[50] As more fugitives arrived in the camps, the problem of unemployment intensified. A Union soldier in the Mississippi Valley complained that after the Second Confiscation Act in 1862, he was "constantly besieged" by runaway slaves; he found their presence a nuisance.[51]

Former slaves also attested to the difficulties and dangers outside of Union refugee camps. Matilda Hatchett recalled traveling from her home in Sevier County, Arkansas, in a group of women and children finding their way to freedom in a makeshift camp. "We was freed and went to a place that was full of people," Hatchett recalled. "We had to stay in a church with about twenty other people and two of the babies died there on account of the exposure. Two of my aunts died, too, on account of exposure."[52] John Hawkins, a former slave who resided in Monroe County, Mississippi, also experienced emancipation's cruel ironies. Like Hatchett, he recalled how "the War brought freedom and starvation both to the slaves. I heard old people say they died in piles from exposure and hunger."[53] Outside Union camps, black women and men might protect themselves from violence, but even freedom on their own terms could be perilous.[54]

In areas where territory changed hands rapidly, like Fredericksburg and the Shenandoah Valley of Virginia, freedom gained could also be readily lost, ensuring that the experience of freedom was always contingent upon the ever fluctuating lines of battle.[55] For women and children, it was especially precarious. As Stephanie McCurry explains, refugee slaves' "presence in the rear of moving columns of troops or in ramshackle camps around the outskirts of encamped armies was entirely unwanted."[56] It is no small wonder then that reports of enslaved women's departures were often followed by news of their return.

Historians have focused on these stories of the slaves who left—fleeing into Union lines, enlisting in the U.S. Army, or marooning nearby—but the vast majority of slaves stayed put during the four years of Civil War. Whereas an estimated 500,000 slaves found refuge behind Union lines, roughly 3.5 million slaves remained in bondage until war's end.[57] We have as yet not fully considered how enslaved women and men who remained may have achieved some degree of autonomy, using their newfound leverage, as Fanny did, to negotiate the terms of their labor. The history of emancipation is exceptionally localized—slaves negotiated with "masters" to carve out measures of freedom within the context of an extremely unstable and unpredictable world. Even when slaves employed resistance tactics they had long utilized in the antebellum period, McCurry notes, "something fundamental" had changed.[58] As in the case of marooning, the absence of white males to exert power over slaves and punish their actions created space for old tactics to gain new ground.

Slaveholding women filled letters to their husbands, diary entries, and petitions to government officials with complaints of slaves becoming increasingly less productive or more vocal in their rejection of their mistresses' commands. Shortly after Maury's confrontation with Furgerson, in August of 1861, she found herself again challenged by new dynamics within her household, remarking on the departure of the family cook, Rebecca, and the behavior of her replacement, Robert. "There is talk of breaking up here and going to cousin Frank's in Albemarle," Maury reported after Rebecca's departure, for "we cannot get a cook and Robert behaves so badly we can't stand him much longer."[59] The departure of these enslaved women left the family weighing the possibility of relocating further into Confederate lines in hopes of preventing further disruption to their household.

Easy to overlook as minor grievances, these complaints evidence a massive case of slave resistance, spread widely over the landscape of the South. By simply refusing to work as they had before, slaves reduced the support their labor could lend to maintaining the Confederate war effort. Just as the Confederate soldier who took up arms and the white women who forged gunboats and wove tent cloth fought for the preservation of slavery, the slaves across the South who refused to pick up their plows, refused to cook for their families while under siege, or demanded wages for their work fought against it. Perhaps even more to the point, the sheer magnitude of slaves' rebellion and its subsequent impact on white women did much to undermine support for slavery itself over the course of the war.[60]

Rebecca Capobianco

For slaveholders, the situation only increased in frustration as the reach of the war expanded and the pace of emancipation accelerated. Again leveraging the presence of the Union army and the threat of flight, groups of slaves demanded wages in return for their labor. On May 16, 1862, Maury recorded, "Matters are getting worse and worse here every day with regard to the negroes. They are leaving their owners by the hundred and demanding wages. The citizens have refused to hire their own or other peoples slaves, so that there are a number of unemployed negroes in town."[61] Should a white resident break with this agreement, their peers were quick to correct them. Maury recounted such an instance, explaining, "Old Dr. Hall agreed to hire his servants but the gentlemen of the town held a meeting and wrote him a letter of remonstrance telling him that he was establishing a most dangerous precedent, that he was breaking the laws of Virginia and was a traitor to his state. So the old man refused to hire them and they all left him."[62] Evidently surrendering one's slaves was preferable to recognizing their ownership of their labor and suffering the ire of the white community in the process.

In her observations, Maury struggled to process slaves' efforts to utilize the opportunities of the moment to push for their own interests. In continuing to refer to people who had clearly loosed themselves of their bonds as "slaves," she denied their right to determine their own employment. Yet in subsequently documenting the presence of "a number of unemployed negroes," she recognized their ability to determine who would or would not benefit from their labor. Though still living behind Southern lines in the very presence of their former owners and not legally free, these "unemployed negroes" had claimed an autonomy for themselves that could not be ignored. In most cases, Southern women negotiated freedom in this contradictory space.

In some cases, even Union commanders found it impossible to conceptualize black freedom within the South's fluctuating boundaries, especially as the war progressed, black men enlisted, and remaining slave populations became disproportionately female. As in Fredericksburg, slaves in the Yazoo-Mississippi Delta emancipated themselves in advance of Union policy inviting them to do so. Unlike Fredericksburg, slaves in the Delta had the opportunity to take possession of the land they had worked as a result of absentee ownership that characterized plantation life in the harsh natural environment.[63] Beginning in 1862, freed people continued working the land but claimed ownership of their produce and entered into the cotton market independently. For nearly a year, until the Union army arrived, black men and women in the Delta operated their own system of freedom.[64] Unable or unwilling to tolerate the idea of former slaves retaining crops harvested from land they did not legally own, Union officials offered the land to white investors and forced black men and women who chose to stay to enter into a new system of dependency. In the case of the Delta, 69 percent of those remaining on the plantations under Union occupation were women.[65]

The drama of the local politics of resistance and freedom primarily transpired between white women left to oversee slave populations and black women, especially in areas where plantation slavery was the rule and white populations were small. Episodes like those Maury recorded occurred throughout the slave South over the course of the war.[66] As McCurry notes, slaves waged personal wars against their owners; in the context of war this often meant these wars were women against women.[67] From the outset, slave mothers taught their children they should be free, nourishing a politics of resistance that would feed slave resistance throughout the war.[68] Local resident and former slave Samuel Spottfort Clement remembered hearing the final sounds of battle at Appomattox Court House, Virginia, in April of 1865. As "the old field hands" listened to the gunfire, Clement recalled, they "prayed in concert that the Yankees might win the fight."[69] In Clement's estimation, "God heard their prayers that they had prayed, not only then but the prayers had been sent up three hundred years by the negro suffering slaves."[70] Though impossible to measure, enslaved mothers' work fostering an anticipation of freedom is evidenced by episodes like the one Clement observed and measures taken by slaves throughout the wartime South who acted like freedom was their birthright. Women stood at the center of slaves' political networks; enslaved women's position in or access to the household at times made them privy to privileged information that could be used to plan an escape or to time a planned resistance.[71]

In March 1863 Kate Stone reported from Louisiana similar confrontations with slaves who had stayed put but rejected their mistresses' attempts to control them. Stone observed, "Mr. Valentine came over last evening in very low spirits indeed. He says his Negroes will not even pretend to work and are very impudent . . . the Negro women marched off in their mistresses' dresses."[72] Elsewhere in the South, S. R. Hawley complained of comparable circumstances, writing in September of 1864 that slaves were "absenting themselves from the employment of their owners and some of them is going about in open daytime entering houses it matters not whether the familys are at Home or not and taking off just whatever they choose."[73] This pattern of staying put and yet emancipating themselves occurred throughout the South, in some cases by enslaved women who went to war with their mistresses.

Former slave Minerva Davis remembered stories her parents had told her of the dimensions of freedom in Tennessee. Though some slaves, like Davis's parents, had heard of their freedom, they chose not to act on that information immediately. However, when the opportunity presented itself, Davis's mother asserted her freedom within the context of a disagreement with her mistress. Davis remembered, "Mama was working for Miss Sallie Ann and done something wrong. Miss Sallie Ann says, 'I'm a good mind to whoop you . . . ' Mama says, 'Miss Sallie Ann, we is free; you ain't never got no right to whoop me no more care what I do.'" When Davis's mother's master returned home and questioned her, she did not back down. The disagreement over the state of her freedom led both to travel to the courthouse to settle the matter, and, predictably, the magistrate could not provide more clarity. Despite the apparent confusion, Davis stated, "Then papa took mama on Johnny Williams' place."[74] In moving to another plantation, Davis's mother remained enmeshed in slavery. Yet in her decision to move out she exercised a new level of autonomy and defined her freedom in terms that she determined for her family's welfare.

Rebecca Capobianco

Fear became a powerful tool female slaves used to their advantage in a world absent of white men. Kate Stone recorded a violent episode between two slaves, Jane and Aunt Lucy, on her family's Louisiana plantation, in which Jane "cut a great gash in Lucy's face." Though Jane did not attack any of the white members of the household and her anger seems to have been the result of a personal matter, the Stones feared her all the same. Kate remembered that her mother attempted to reprimand Jane, but the woman "showed a very surly, aggressive temper while Mamma was talking to her, and so Mama did not say much."[75] Eventually Jane took advantage of the white women's fears and "took her two children, a girl and boy about half-grown . . . [and] started for the [federal] camp at DeSoto." Relieved, Stone concluded, "I think we are all glad she has gone. We felt her a constant menace."[76] Stone's recollection suggests that Jane was never really a physical threat to these white women. Yet Jane took advantage of their fear as long as she stayed with the family and further when she chose to leave and take her children with her.

Laura Edwards has demonstrated that while violence did occur, slave women also made use of unique forms of resistance that were not necessarily physically threatening. Slave women misinterpreted instructions, broke tools, succumbed to sudden illnesses, stole supplies, or left for short periods of time to avoid punishment or to protest demands placed on them.[77] Though these tactics were not new, Emma Mordecai of Richmond identified how they differed from similar behaviors in the antebellum period. Mordecai lamented that "no one [is] asserting any authority over [the slaves]."[78] These efforts gained a new salience during the war as female slaves assumed more responsibilities because men were "conscripted" into use by the Confederate military. The fear and disorder caused by enslaved women's resistance prompted white women to complain to their soldier husbands and to entreat politicians to consider their plight.

In some cases, black women's resistance did take violent forms. Enslaved women's access to their master's homes gave them particular knowledge with which to wage local wars and the opportunity to take advantage of fears expressed by women like Kate Stone.[79] Irene Coates, a native of Georgia, was six years old when she gained her freedom. In an interview with the Federal Writers' Project, Coates recalled two incidents that "caused respect for the slaves by their masters and finally the Emancipation by Abraham Lincoln."[80] In one of these stories, Coates detailed an incident in which a female slave attacked an overseer, killing him and his horse. According to Coates, the slave in question "then calmly went to tell the master of the murder."[81] The master granted her a home on his plantation and her freedom on the spot.[82] While parts of her account seem highly unlikely, Coates recalled a story that had been handed down to her about slave women and the power of resistance. In retelling it, Coates invoked its power to "cause respect for the slaves."[83]

In March 1865, in Pineville, South Carolina, slave women led a violent uprising. Unrest between slaves and the remaining white population had been brewing for weeks, culminating on March 26 in an armed conflict between slaves and Confederate scouts. Susan Jervey, a local white resident, noted in February how she awoke in the middle of the night with her "head being full of Negroes and Yankees." Jervey explained, "What I most fear is not the Yankees, but the negroes, cut off from all help from across the river, and at their mercy, what will become of us?"[84] Isolated from their neighbors, a primarily female white population feared for their lives as their former slaves organized against them. Elizabeth Palmer Porcher was also afraid, stating that she had watched a group of slave rebels marching past who "intended to return . . . and play the mischief with us and give us no quarter."[85] Elsewhere in the South, white women wrote at length about a world turned upside down in which slaves were at war on a local scale with their would-be owners. Kate Stone reported from Louisiana in 1863 that "Negroes from all the inhabited places around commenced flocking to Mr. Hardison's, and they completely sacked the place in broad daylight, passing our gate loaded down with plunder until twelve at night." Before they began destroying property, the slaves had terrorized the white population, driving Stone and others to distraction. Stone and her family eventually fled.[86]

Tensions in Pineville culminated in an armed conflict between slaves and Confederate scouts. Reports spread that up to twenty-two slaves had been killed in the fight on March 26, and white residents immediately set about trying to find those who had escaped the hands of Confederate soldiers. At the center of this manhunt was a slave named Rose, who white residents were sure had been the ringleader of the rebellion. Thavolia Glymph notes the matter-of-fact way with which white women remarked on Rose's leadership and the lack of concern with which they recorded the slave rebels' brutal punishment. Having slave women involved in and leading an armed rebellion did not surprise slaveholders in the least. According to Alice Palmer, another white resident, townspeople left Rose's body "unburied on the field where she had been tied & dragged, & killed."[87] Two other slave women who were wounded in the fight were subsequently punished by being refused medical care.[88] Ultimately, white women's fears of being shown "no quarter" were misplaced, as it was in fact the female militants who were punished without remorse.

Though the violence at Pineville was unusual, it represents a culmination of forces at work throughout the duration of the war. As slaves chose to navigate the war on their own terms, demanding wages, speaking up against their mistresses, or taking up arms, they chipped away at white women's endurance, wearing them down and driving away their support for the Confederate cause.[89] Slaveholding women found themselves left to manage slavery as the institution crumbled from within and without.

Matters worsened as the war continued, the Confederacy's hope of success dwindled, and white women wrote to state officials, begging for their men to be sent home.[90] These pleas challenged the idea that women were wholeheartedly in support of the Cause, and some began to resent the institution of slavery that they had been left to defend alone. In the midst of trouble with her own slaves in February 1862, Maury admitted, "I cannot help being unpatriotic enough to feel a little selfish sometime and regret our peace and comfort in the old union."[91] Though slaveholding women's concerns were personal, many became increasingly political, and in so doing they undermined the possibility of Confederate success.

Rebecca Capobianco

As the war dragged on and slaves took liberties at home, women's "unpatriotic" feelings became more pronounced. Sarah Kenney of Tennessee asserted that she "would rather do all the work than be worried with a house full of servants that do what, how and when they please . . . if we could be compensated for their value [we] are better off without them."[92] An unidentified white woman wrote to North Carolina governor Zebulon Vance that she "believe[d] slavery is doomed to die out . . . God is agoing to liberate neggars, and fighting any longer is fighting against God."[93] Writing prophetically, W. W. Boyce asserted to her husband, a South Carolina congressman, "I tell you all this attention to farming is uphill work with me. I can give orders first-rate, but when I am not obeyed, I can't keep my temper. . . . I am ever ready to give you a helping hand, but I must say I am heartily tired of trying to manage free negroes."[94] Kate Foster, of Mississippi, extended her observations to the fugitives "flocking to the enemy in town," and complained, "we are all tired of them."[95] Slaveholding women's growing disillusionment with slavery manifested itself notably in declining support for the Confederate war effort.[96] In urging their husbands to desert, or declining to yield another loved one to the war effort, white women refused to continue to support the Cause, or at least the Confederacy, which was tantamount to a tacit resignation to Union victory and the end to slavery. Gertrude Thomas demonstrated this change in attitude, writing in 1864 in reference to slaves, "I am by no means so sure that we would not gain by having his freedom given him."[97] This was not abolitionism for abolition's sake, but rather a desire to free Southern whites of the burdens of slavery and the deprivations of war. Glymph has rightly suggested that "the home front story may turn out to have played a far larger and more significant role in 'the greatest slave rebellion in modern history' than scholars have credited."[98] Provided an opportunity to amplify their efforts during the war, slaves engaged in a war that furthered their own ends as well as that of the Union army by tearing at the cords that held the Confederacy together.

Former slaves remembered how their newfound freedom wreaked havoc on the white population of the South. Mary Bell, whose brother died while serving in the United States Colored Troops, remembered that her father's owner's son had taught him to read. This greatly irritated his owner, because Bell's father used that skill to read the "emancipation for freedom" to other slaves. Bell recalled that the slaves were "so happy, they could not work well, and they got so no one could manage them, when they found out they were to be freed in such a short time."[99] Bell's father turned his literacy and his leadership into leverage when his former master tried to convince him to stay on the Missouri plantation after freedom was declared, with the promise that "he would give him a nice house and lot for his family."[100] The respect did not run both ways. Bell's father remained for only six months and then took "eleven of the best slaves on the plantation" and traveled to Kansas City to enlist in the U.S. Army. When the men's owners attempted to reclaim them, according to Bell, "the officers said they were now enlisted U.S. Soldiers and could not be touched."[101] Bell's story illustrates how slaves mitigated their circumstances within slavery, bided their time, and periodically renegotiated the terms of their forbearance. Bell's father did not claim freedom as soon as he became aware of it but leveraged concessions from his master until such time as he was ready to move on.

Even where emancipation spread early in the war, its distribution was uneven at best and incomplete by war's end.[102] Louisa Everett and her husband, Sam, lived in relative isolation near Norfolk, Virginia, on a plantation with more than a hundred other slaves. Everett recalled that she and the other slaves did not learn of freedom until the fall of 1865. So successful was their master at insulating his slaves that "they had heard whisperings of the War but did not understand the meaning of it all."[103] The Everetts' testimony is particularly startling, given their relative proximity to Benjamin Butler's forces at Fort Monroe in Hampton, Virginia. Unlike the hundreds of slaves that marched into Union lines less than thirty miles from them, the Everetts did not know freedom could be so close at hand.

As news of Confederate defeat settled in Fredericksburg, Virginia, in April of 1865, Mary Caldwell groaned, "Noble old Virginia . . . She is to be trampled upon by those who have destroyed. Her slaves are, in all probability, to become her masters, for it is said the Yankees intend giving the negroes a vote. A negro to have a vote for our rulers. If that is to be so, as I told Mag, I feel as if I want to commit suicide and kill everyone else. A negro to rule over me. I think the women had better rise and take the rule, as men are found unfit to govern."[104] Caldwell continued to resist federal rule and confronted Union occupiers over the legality of secession. In May 1865 she recorded that "I have entered into several disputes with that gentleman on the slavery question, and, if sanity does not desert me, I think I have proven my point each time. He told me that he intends to bring up a little abolitionist chaplain to talk with me on the subject. I did not feel at all honored by the thought of an argument with an abolitionist."[105] Though Caldwell had limited success slowing the pace of emancipation, she was not discouraged; neither were those white women who sought to recreate some of the relationships of slavery that the war had swept away.

Caldwell remarked off-handedly, "Mag says women are the only free people in the South, for they [do] what they please while the men dare not."[106] By the end of the Civil War, nearly 30 percent of the adult male white population of the South was dead.[107] Of those who remained, many were wounded, and all suffered the stigma of defeat. Many remained disfranchised for some time and kept their politics to themselves. In the meantime, white women, as Mag observed, found opportunities to speak out under the protection of their womanhood. Mary Greenhow Lee perhaps put it most bluntly when she stated, "Political reconstruction might be unavoidable now, but social reconstruction we hold in our hands & might prevent."[108] White women utilized their positions not only to counter black freedom and equality but to reestablish control over black labor and, in the process, reclaim their own social position.[109]

Freedwomen, conversely, had their own ideas and sought to make their own decisions about whom they would work for and how to spend their leisure time.[110] Former slave Annie Burton remembered how, after emancipation, she chafed under the control of "Miss Mary," her employer. Unwilling to give up the role she played as a mistress before the war, Miss Mary attempted to control Burton's private life,

Rebecca Capobianco

including her intimate relationships. Burton rejected Mary's pretensions, pursuing a romance with a man her employer did not approve of and eventually marrying him. In retaliation for Burton's "ungratefulness," Mary refused Burton's request for a raise. Fed up, Annie left Miss Mary and sought new opportunities elsewhere.[111] Though many African American women worked as domestic workers in the decades after the Civil War, some, like Burton, were unwilling to do so on the uneven terms demanded by employers like Mary.[112] Standing on the ground they had gained during the war, freedwomen resisted their former mistresses' attempts to take it back.[113]

Southern women both black and white found a variety of ways to control the disorienting changes wrought by the war and pursued actions that were tangible, intentional, and significant. Sometimes these actions were subtle and have evaded our notice, like the myriad ways in which black women sought to establish some measure of "freedom" even as they remained enslaved. Yet the impact of their choices reverberated across the Southern landscape in ways no less significant for their variability and invisibility. To begin to fully understand the role Southern women played in the process of emancipation, historians must look beyond high politics to see how individuals pushed ahead of and against federal policies, carving out an emancipation that was meaningful to them even though we have only been able to detect it because of the strong reaction—in the letters, diaries, and memoirs described above—it elicited.

Notes

1. Betty Herndon Maury Diary, transcr. and annot. by Carolyn Carpenter, in *Fredericksburg History and Biography* 10 (2011): 32.

2. For particular examples, see Drew Gilpin Faust, *Mothers of Invention: Women of the Slaveholding South in the Civil War* (Chapel Hill: Univ. of North Carolina Press, 1996), who argues that the burdens of slavery weakened white women's support for the Confederate cause; Stephanie McCurry, *Confederate Reckoning: Power and Politics in the Civil War South* (Cambridge, Mass.: Harvard Univ. Press, 2010), who illuminates the ways in which poor white women and slaves undermined the Confederate nation; Steven Hahn, *A Nation under Our Feet: Black Political Struggles in the Rural South from Slavery to the Great Migration* (Cambridge, Mass.: Harvard Univ. Press, 2003), who powerfully reframes the definition of politics to identify the tangible ways slaves influenced the course of the war; and Glenn David Brasher, *The Peninsula Campaign and the Necessity of Emancipation: African Americans and the Fight for Freedom* (Chapel Hill: Univ. of North Carolina Press, 2012), who plots a new timeline for emancipation that begins with the movement of slaves into Union lines that forced Congress to address the question of "contraband" and evolved into military emancipation. Also significant is Amy Dru Stanley, "Instead of Waiting for the Thirteenth Amendment: The War Power, Slave Marriage, and Inviolate Human Rights," *American Historical Review* 115 (June 2010): 735. Stanley's point that Union policy failed to take black women into consideration when drafting wartime policy is a painful reminder of the gendered and unequal contours of freedom.

3. Caroline Janney has argued that white women's work during the war became expressly political and laid the foundation for further political resistance during Reconstruction. Caroline E. Janney, *Burying the Dead but Not the Past: Ladies' Memorial Associations and the Lost Cause.* (Chapel Hill: Univ. of North Carolina Press, 2008). Thavolia Glymph has illuminated

a particularly poignant episode of violent resistance orchestrated and led by slave women; see Thavolia Glymph, "Rose's War and the Gendered Politics of a Slave Insurgency in the Civil War," *Journal of the Civil War Era* 3 (2013): 501–32. Leslie Schwalm has examined how black women experienced life in Union refugee camps. Black women remained outside of Union policy, and as a result of their gender they were excluded from participating in war labor, limiting their options for providing for themselves and their families. Leslie Schwalm, "Between Slavery and Freedom: African American Women and Occupation in the Slave South," in LeeAnn Whites and Alecia P. Long, eds., *Occupied Women: Gender, Military Occupation, and the American Civil War* (Baton Rouge: Louisiana State Univ. Press, 2009), 137–53.

4. James Oakes, *Freedom National: The Destruction of Slavery in the United States, 1861–1865* (New York: W. W. Norton, 2014), 106.

5. Eric Foner, *A Short History of Reconstruction, 1863–1877* (New York: Harper & Row, 1990), 3.

6. James McPherson, *Battle Cry of Freedom: The Civil War Era* (New York: Oxford Univ. Press, 1988), 353.

7. Oakes, *Freedom National,* 127–28.

8. Schwalm, "Between Slavery and Freedom," 138. Drew Gilpin Faust examines how white women's labor forced Confederate officials to recognize that they could in fact provide valuable support even in the form of manufacturing such weapons of war as gunboats. For further discussion, see Faust, *Mothers of Invention.*

9. Oakes, *Freedom National,* 107.

10. Benjamin F. Butler to Secretary of War Simon Cameron, July 30, 1861, http://www.nytimes.com/1861/08/06/news/slave-question-letter-major-gen-butler-treatment-fugitive-slaves.html?pagewanted=all. Cameron responded in a letter dated August 8, 1861, reiterating the terms of the August 6 order and stating that "if persons held to service shall be employed in hostility to the United States the right to their services shall be forfeited and such persons shall be discharged there from." Simon Cameron to Maj. Gen. Benjamin F. Butler, Aug. 8, 1861, http://housedivided.dickinson.edu/sites/emancipation/files/2012/07/1861–08–08-Simon-Cameron-to-Benjamin-Butler.pdf.

11. Schwalm, "Between Slavery and Freedom," 144.

12. Foner, *A Short History of Reconstruction,* 71. Still unsure what to do with slave women who did make it into their lines, and viewing them as undesirable burdens who could not provide valuable work, the Union army attempted large-scale relocation of women out of army camps. Schwalm, "Between Slavery and Freedom," 146.

13. McPherson, *Battle Cry of Freedom,* 502.

14. Oakes, *Freedom National,* 340. James Oakes notes that in the days and weeks prior to issuing his official proclamation, Lincoln questioned whether or not a proclamation of its sort could have any significant effect on the ground.

15. Foner, *A Short History of Reconstruction,* 3.

16. Glymph, "Rose's War," 516–17.

17. Edward Ayers and Scott Nesbitt, "Seeing Emancipation: Scale and Freedom in the American South," *Journal of the Civil War Era* 1 (2011): 18.

18. For a close study of slave movements on the Virginia Peninsula, see Brasher, *Peninsula Campaign.*

19. Betty Herndon Maury Diary, 10.

20. While historians such as Edward Ayers have demonstrated that slaves often ran away when the Union army was close by, it is important to distinguish between proximity and policy. Particularly in the early years of war, as Glenn David Brasher has shown, slaves made the decision to seek refuge in Union lines before federal policy had invited or accepted them.

For useful maps of the relationship between the Union army's presence and slave escapes, see Ayers and Nesbitt, "Seeing Emancipation."

21. Maury's observations are all drawn from her diary.

22. Fanny Bernard Goolrick, "The Shelling of Fredericksburg: Recollections of One Who Was a Little Girl at That Time," *Fredericksburg* (Va.) *Daily Star,* Dec. 6, 1909, Records of Fredericksburg and Spotsylvania National Military Park. Celine Fremaux, a resident of Jackson, Louisiana, described an almost identical scene in August 1864. As she recalled, "It was then deep dusk [as an attack began] and even as he spoke [the boy who brought the news] we heard the Pop Pop of musketry, toward the college. Leon darted off before Ma thought of stopping him and we began to pray downstairs in the hall. Then we stepped out on the side walk. The booming of cannon mixed with the lighter shot and a sort of roar like many voices and trampling of feet and hoofs. The fighting came nearer and nearer." Celine Fremaux, qtd. in Walter Sullivan, *The War Women Lived: Female Voices from the Confederate South* (Nashville: J. S. Sanders, 1995), 209. The parallels between these two women's accounts illustrate that though Fredericksburg was in some ways unique, the experience of civilians on the ground was shared by countless others, particularly women, throughout the South.

23. Goolrick, "Shelling of Fredericksburg."

24. Ibid.

25. Even as the war accelerated toward emancipation, white women attempted to utilize the Union army's presence to enforce slavery's social and racial boundaries. In April 1863 Union soldier Henry Wood wrote to a commanding officer, "Complaints keep coming from the plantations around saying that their negroes refuse to work." Evidently white women had found a sympathetic ear, as Wood continued, "When practicable I sent some one to see them and instruct them to work." Henry Wood, qtd. in Stephanie Camp, *Closer to Freedom: Enslaved Women and Everyday Resistance in the Plantation South* (Chapel Hill: Univ. of North Carolina Press, 2004), 131.

26. Maury referred to the Second Confiscation Act, passed in July 1862, which expanded Union policy to officially free slaves who fled into Union lines. However, as Brasher astutely points out, this act was meant to solve a problem that already existed and answer the question of what to do with slaves who had fled into Union lines by the thousands without an assurance of freedom. The *North American and United States Gazette* reported that "between fifteen or twenty thousand combatants [slaves] against us on the Peninsula [of Virginia] have already been drawn from the slave population of eastern Virginia," indicating the extent to which slaves had chosen to leave in advance of policy protecting their flight. Brasher, *Peninsula Campaign,* 118.

27. Betty Herndon Maury Diary, 85.

28. Laura Edwards, *Scarlett Doesn't Live Here Anymore: Southern Women in the Civil War Era* (Champaign: Univ. of Illinois Press, 2000), 77.

29. Ibid., 78.

30. Celina Roman, qtd. in Camp, *Closer to Freedom,* 129. At times in their desperation, Southern white women even appealed to the U.S. military for "protection" from their slaves. McCurry, *Confederate Reckoning,* 254. In 1865 in South Carolina, six families begged the Federal Military Command to protect them from their former slaves, claiming the freedmen were "in the most disorderly & lawless condition, if not savage and barbarous." Petition to the Federal Military Command, Georgetown District, Mar. 6, 1865, qtd. in James L. Roark, *Masters Without Slaves: Southern Planters in the Civil War and Reconstruction* (New York: W. W. Norton, 1977), 84.

31. Betty Herndon Maury Diary, 12–13.

32. Ibid., 17.

33. Glenn David Brasher has pointed out that the election of Abraham Lincoln, and the subsequent secession by the Southern states, caused slaves to begin meeting and organizing to discuss what these national events meant for their future. Edmund Ruffin reported, "The negroes have received very general . . . impressions that the Northerners were operating for Negro emancipation." However, Brasher notes, these "impressions" were not a result of Union policy. As Lincoln made clear on his April 15, 1861, call for troops, he felt bound to protect the rights of Southern slaveholders under the restraints of the Constitution. Brasher, *Peninsula Campaign*, 30.

34. Betty Herndon Maury Diary, 63. Lizzie Alsop, another Fredericksburg resident, recorded a series of complaints echoing Maury's. In May 1862 she wrote, "Nine servants have gone from Sunny Side and as Mr. Weeden went home last Monday, there is no male upon the place except John (belonging to Mr. Samuel, who very kindly permits him to stay there)." Journal of Lizzie Maxwell Alsop, Wynne Family Papers, Virginia Historical Society, Richmond.

35. Episodes such as that described by Maury were not particular to the Fredericksburg area. Her words describing the departure of her slaves echoed across the South in the diaries and letters of white women. However, this exodus seems to have begun much earlier in Fredericksburg as a result of its proximity to battle lines and Union territory. In July 1863, Kate D. Foster, a resident of Mississippi, observed that two of her neighbors' household slaves had run off. Foster opined that had the slaves any pity, they would have stayed so that "Mrs D" would not be left to do all the housework. Kate D. Foster, qtd. in Camp, *Closer to Freedom*, 134. Writing in April 1863, Kate Stone of Louisiana similarly observed, "Negro women marched off in their mistress' dresses." Kate Stone, qtd. in ibid., 121.

36. Edwards, *Scarlett Doesn't Live Here Anymore*, 104.

37. McCurry, *Confederate Reckoning*, 246; Edwards, *Scarlett Doesn't Live Here Anymore*, 104.

38. Betty Herndon Maury Diary, 40.

39. Ibid., 85.

40. Edwards, *Scarlett Doesn't Live Here Anymore*, 104.

41. Camp, *Closer to Freedom*, 36.

42. Harriet Jacobs, *Incidents in the Life of a Slave Girl*, http://www.docsouth.unc.edu/fpn/jacobs/jacobs.html.

43. McCurry, *Confederate Reckoning*, 327. Slaves' narratives of their lives further support this point. During an interview with the Federal Writers' Project, F. H. Brown explained that his parents belonged to a Mrs. Rankins. Rankins's slaves, when threatened with punishment, would "run away sometimes and stay in the woods . . . but she would send for them to come on back and they wouldn't be whipped." F. H. Brown interview, *Born in Slavery: Slave Narratives from the Federal Writers' Project, 1936–1938*, Library of Congress, Washington, D.C., http://memory.loc.gov/cgi-bin/ampage?collId=mesn&fileName=021/mesn021.db&recNum=279&tempFile=./temp/~ammem_W9ci&filecode=mesn&next_filecode=mesn&prev_filecode=mesn&itemnum=39&ndocs=44. (276). Running away, particularly in the context of war, could be a means to an immediate end that did not necessarily result in permanent freedom but did gain slaves some level of power within their own particular contexts.

44. Camp, *Closer to Freedom*, 39.

45. Betty Herndon Maury Diary, 80.

46. Ibid. It is worth noting that while Maury's observations were not necessarily untrue, they demonstrate her own desire to cling both to slavery and to the paternalistic beliefs that anchored it in place. By insisting the runaway slaves were "unhappy," Maury assured herself that slaves were subsequently better off remaining in bondage.

47. McCurry, *Confederate Reckoning*, 9. Chandra Manning has also recently released an exceptional study of life in refugee camps entitled *Troubled Refuge: Struggling for Freedom in the*

Civil War (New York: Alfred A. Knopf, 2016). Manning notes that while particular circumstances of refugee camps differed throughout the South—for instance, they were less permanent in places where territory changed hands between the Union and Confederate armies—as the title suggests, one element remained constant: they were at best troubled refuges.

48. Edwards, *Scarlett Doesn't Live Here Anymore*, 109. The proliferation of violence against black women came in some part as a result of their problematic position of no longer belonging to white men as slaves and seemingly not belonging to black men as wives. Without the protection of legal ownership, their bodies were all the more unprotected. Abuses were so horrific that a group of Union chaplains operating in Helena, Arkansas, wrote their commanding general pleading for relief:

> The wives of some have been molested by soldiers to gratify thier licentious lust, and thier husbands murdered in endeavering to defend them, and yet the guilty parties, though known, were not arrested. . . . These grievances reported to us by persons in whom we have confidence, & some of which we know to be true, are but a few of the many wrongs of which they complain—For the sake of humanity, for the sake of christianity, for the good name of our army, for the honor of our country, cannot something be done to prevent this oppression.

Nancy Bercaw, *Gendered Freedoms: Race, Rights, and the Politics of the Household in the Delta, 1861–1875* (Gainesville: Univ. Press of Florida, 2003), 44. Samuel P. Sawyer, Pearl P. Ingall, and J. G. Forman to Maj. Gen. Samuel Curtis, Dec. 29, 1862, *Freedmen and Southern Society Project*. Univ. of Maryland, College Park, http://www.freedmen.umd.edu/Sawyer.html.

49. Edwards, *Scarlett Doesn't Live Here Anymore*, 111.

50. Ibid., 112. At Fort Monroe, the focus of emancipation and refugee policy in the early years of the war, in Virginia, Union officials recorded nine hundred female slaves, "earning substantially their own subsistence." Given traditionally female roles by the Union army, women were expected to care for themselves and essentially earn their keep. Schwalm, "Between Slavery and Freedom," 143.

51. Schwalm, "Between Slavery and Freedom, 144.

52. Matilda Hatchett interview, *Born in Slavery*, http://memory.loc.gov/cgi-bin/query/P?mesn:11:./temp/~ammem_W9ci:: (199).

53. John G. Hawkins, ibid., http://memory.loc.gov/cgi-bin/ampage?collId=mesn&fileName=023/mesn023.db&recNum=202&tempFile=./temp/~ammem_W9ci&filecode=mesn&next_filecode=mesn&prev_f (204).

54. In an effort to ease the growing tension between soldiers and refugee slaves, particularly women, the Union army implemented a plan of large-scale relocation to places like Cairo, Illinois. For those who made their way to privately run camps like that in Cairo, the situation could be much better. The Contraband Relief Society, a group of private citizens, helped prepare freed slaves for life in St. Louis, Missouri. However, racism and opposition to labor competition in the North forced another policy shift in 1863, and the army resorted to relocation to abandoned plantations instead. Schwalm, "Closer to Freedom," 146–49.

55. McCurry, *Confederate Reckoning*, 251.

56. Ibid.

57. Ibid., 8.

58. Ibid., 234. Stephanie McCurry further notes that slave owners, policymakers, and local officials observed and reported unprecedented levels of slave activity after the war broke out. For an excellent close-in study of the changing dynamics and directions of master-slave relationships during and because of the war, see Clarence L. Mohr, *On the Threshold of Freedom: Masters and Slaves in Civil War Georgia* (Athens: Univ. of Georgia Press, 1986).

59. Betty Herndon Maury Diary. 34.

60. Stephanie Camp notes that as the war dragged on, Confederates became increasingly concerned with the practical survival of the slave system for the purposes of providing basic necessities, going so far as to assert that the "question of food [was] today the most important question before us." Camp, *Closer to Freedom*, 131.

61. Betty Herndon Maury Diary, 74–75.

62. Ibid.

63. Bercaw, *Gendered Freedoms*, 29.

64. Ibid., 13.

65. Ibid., 34.

66. McCurry, *Confederate Reckoning*, 238.

67. Ibid., 232.

68. Ibid., 230.

69. Samuel Spottford Clement, "Memoir," *Documenting the American South Database*, Univ. of North Carolina, Chapel Hill.

70. Ibid. .

71. McCurry, *Confederate Reckoning*, 246.

72. Kate Stone, qtd. in Sullivan, *War Women Lived*, 90.

73. S. R. Hawley, qtd. in Edwards, *Scarlett Doesn't Live Here Anymore*, 114.

74. Minerva Davis interview, *Born in Slavery*, http://memory.loc.gov/cgi-bin/query/ P?mesn:14:./temp/~ammem_W9ci:: (128). Davis's account does not specify where in Tennessee her father resided.

75. Kate Stone, qtd. in Sullivan, *War Women Lived*, 89.

76. Ibid.

77. Edwards, *Scarlett Doesn't Live Here Anymore*, 59.

78. Emma Mordecai, qtd. in Camp, *Closer to Freedom*, 132.

79. Glymph, "Rose's War," 501–2.

80. Irene Coates interview, *Born in Slavery*, Dec. 16, 1936, http://memory.loc.gov/cgi-bin/ query/P?mesn:34:./temp/~ammem_W9ci:: (75).

81. Ibid., 76.

82. Ibid.

83. Ibid., 75.

84. Glymph, "Rose's War," 505–6.

85. Ibid., 503.

86. Sullivan, *War the Women Lived*, 90–93. This is a particular example described by Stone, but her account, much like those from Pineville, describes a white female population living in prolonged terror as a result of an empowered slave population going to war with their masters, invading and destroying homes without notice.

87. Glymph, "Rose's War," 511.

88. Ibid., 510.

89. Faust, *Mothers of Invention*, 56.

90. Ibid., 58.

91. Betty Herndon Maury Diary, 61.

92. Faust, *Mothers of Invention*, 73.

93. Edwards, *Scarlett Doesn't Live Here Anymore*, 85.

94. Faust, *Mothers of Invention*, 73.

95. Kate Foster, qtd. in Camp, *Closer to Freedom*, 134.

96. Faust, *Mothers of Invention*, 242.

97. Gertrude Thomas, qtd. in ibid., 74.

98. Glymph, "Rose's War," 522.

99. Mary A. Bell interview, *Born in Slavery,* Aug. 19, 1937, http://memory.loc.gov/cgi-bin /query/P?mesn:22:./temp/~ammem_W9ci:: (28).

100. Ibid., 29.

101. Ibid., 30.

102. Glenn David Brasher has skillfully argued that the actions of slaves in the Tidewater region of Virginia early in the war did much to move Union policy toward a more expansive emancipation. Slaves who chose to simply show up at places like Fort Monroe in Hampton, Virginia, forced Union soldiers to make a decision to welcome them or turn them away. In the case of the Tidewater area, Union policymakers welcomed escaped slaves and thereby spread emancipation before it was the rule of the day. Brasher, *Peninsula Campaign* .

103. Sam Everett and Louisa Everett interviews, *Born in Slavery,* Oct. 8, 1936, http://memory. loc.gov/cgi-bin/query/P?mesn:33:./temp/~ammem_W9ci:: (130).

104. Mary Caldwell Diary, Apr. 27, 1865, ed. Russel P. Smith, Collections of Fredericksburg and Spotsylvania National Military Park, National Park Service, U.S. Dept. of the Interior, Fredericksburg, Va.

105. Ibid., May 14, 1865.

106. Ibid., June 26, 1865.

107. Edwards, *Scarlett Doesn't Live Here Anymore,* 80.

108. Faust, *Mothers of Invention,* 248.

109. Ibid., 254. For a specific discussion of the evolution of the Southern household during and after the war, see Bercaw, *Gendered Freedoms.*

110. Yolanda Nicole Pierce, "Her Refusal to be Recast(e): Annie Burton's Narrative of Resistance," *Southern Literary Journal* 36 (2004): 8.

111. Ibid., 7.

112. Ibid., 12.

113. For further reading on the conflicts over memory and emancipation in the wake of the Civil War, see Caroline E. Janney, *Remembering the Civil War: Reunion and the Limits of Reconciliation* (Chapel Hill: Univ. of North Carolina Press, 2013); and David Blight, *Race and Reunion: The Civil War in American Memory* (Cambridge, Mass.: Harvard Univ. Press, 2001). Janney in particular notes that Southern women often took the lead arguing for memorialization and the silencing of emancipationist memory because that way they could safely voice their opinions in political spaces without fear of punishment.

Northern Women and Emancipation

Chandra Manning

"I WANT something to do." So begins *Hospital Sketches,* Louisa May Alcott's account of her experiences as an army nurse in the Civil War.[1] The capital letters in the first two words signal more than nineteenth-century type-setting convention. They expressed a longing that Alcott shared with many other Northern women who had been active in antislavery circles before the war. As soon as war broke out, women as well as men recognized it as the biggest public event likely to occur in their lifetimes, with towering stakes and enormous consequences. "They clamored for practical work, something for their hands to do," as one history written shortly after the war recalled.[2] Finding a way to be useful was less straightforward for women than for the men who rushed to Army recruiting offices, but many women managed to do so, and no understanding of slavery's destruction in the United States is complete without taking them into account.

Yet analysis of Northern women and emancipation matters for more than just making sure that all parties are represented in abolition's group portrait. The experiences of Northern antislavery women who went south differed from those of Northern women who remained at home, and from those of Northern antislavery men. The differences reveal something crucial about wartime emancipation that is otherwise easy to miss. Women who witnessed firsthand the humanitarian crises of slavery and its destruction saw how stark, vast, overwhelming material need could defeat the best of intentions and the most energetic of spirits. They, no less than the Southern women whose experiences of emancipation Rebecca Capobianco chronicles in this collection, had no choice but to realize that crushing material need could blunt the force of individual will. Likewise, Northern women grew up amid gender conventions that placed more limits on their actions and expectations than white men faced. Also like the Southern women described by Capobianco, they were more sensitized than most men to the constraints that *ideological* forces could place on individual agency.

Acutely aware that outside forces—material and ideological—could erect barriers in individuals' paths, Northern women who went south were uniquely attuned to how individual intent could be limited or stymied by tensions and forces that operated on large, national scales, even as their individual actions took place in the local context of the everyday. The Civil War was full of just such tensions and forces. Three that rested at the heart of wartime emancipation included the tensions between chaos and order, dependence and independence, and unyielding limits and resourcefulness. Some women were undone by those clashes, sapped of their energy and as depleted in their idealism as a tired nation would be in later decades when federal willingness to uphold freed people's rights waned. Others learned how to confront their own limitations and accept the inadequacy of their own efforts in the face of forces beyond their control, as well as their own shortcomings. When they accepted that they could not always control circumstances, and that they did not always know best, they loosed themselves from the need to be saviors or to transform freed people into mirror images of themselves. In exchange, they opened themselves up to learning from, not merely instructing, former slaves. Few Northern women were capable of sustaining that essentially humble viewpoint at all times (and some could not achieve it at all, any more than many of us can nowadays), but the ones who did discovered a solidarity that offers critical insight into both the achievements and limitations of wartime emancipation.

The story of Northern women who found opportunities to participate in wartime emancipation has often been told in one of three ways, each of which reveals something important, and each of which has been told often enough that it needs only brief mention, not full explication, here. The first is as a tale of opportunities opened by war, and then foreclosed after the crisis passed and a return to traditional gender roles ensued. A second approach, often adopted to safeguard against a triumphal tone, is to focus on the majority of Northern women who did not concern themselves with—or even actively opposed—emancipation. A third way is to acknowledge that abolitionist women counted for only a minority of the Northern female population, but aided the downfall of slavery despite their numbers, thereby making it necessary for any account of slavery's destruction to include their contributions.[3]

Louisa May Alcott and others like her would recognize partial truth in each of those standard narratives, but they would also notice that none of them made room for all that the war taught. Many antislavery advocates assumed, much as the leadership of the Republican Party did, that slavery was an outdated, localized institution that would crumble quickly and easily under the weight of its own inefficiency and moral rot, just as soon as the federal government stopped prolonging slavery's detestable life with artificial supports like the Fugitive Slave Act.[4] Yet Alcott and other Northern women who battled slavery soon discovered that slavery was embedded much more deeply into the central spine and nervous system of the nation than they had realized, incapable of removal without massive trauma. Alcott crashed up against immovable forces—in her case, typhoid fever and mercury poisoning—that no amount of determination or good will could budge. Those forces broke her and sent her home, work unfinished, but they also transformed her. The clash between her idealistic expectations and war's anguished reality moved Alcott off both pedestal and sidelines and into direct solidarity with people she once thought she was sent to help. She concluded *Hospital Sketches* by recognizing her and the nation's "large . . . debt" to black slaves-turned-soldiers, and by casting herself not as deliverer, healer, or ministering angel but as one of the "white relations" of African Americans, joined with rather than superior to the formerly enslaved.[5]

It took war and failure for Alcott to attain that level of discernment, but her experiences before the war helped prime her for it. She grew up in a Northern antislavery atmosphere in which abolitionist women found and exercised ways of opposing slavery, even as they sometimes railed against the barriers that nineteenth-century "true womanhood" gender conventions placed on their actions and instruments of protest.[6] Alcott's own literary career had not yet taken flight when war began, but numerous other women had taken up pens against slavery. Harriet Beecher Stowe's *Uncle Tom's Cabin* was an unrivaled publishing phenomenon when it came out as a novel, and it continued to reel in audiences as a play throughout the 1850s.[7] Decades earlier, Lydia Maria Child had published antislavery stories for children, as well as politically advanced (if awkwardly titled) analyses such as *An Appeal in Favor of that Class of Americans Called Africans, Authentic Anecdotes of American Slavery,* and the *Anti-Slavery Catechism.*[8] The South Carolina–born sisters Sarah and Angelina Grimké moved north, became Quakers, and wrote extensively against what they grew to perceive as the sin of slavery. Both contributed to the influential *American Slavery As It Is: Testimony of a Thousand Witnesses* compiled by Angelina's husband, Theodore Dwight Weld.[9] Women writers kept at their antislavery tasks right up through the outbreak of war: Harriet Jacobs, who escaped from bondage in North Carolina and resettled in Boston, published *Incidents in the Life of a Slave Girl,* a remarkably forthright account of the sexual predation she endured as a slave, in 1861.[10]

Other Northern women defied convention to speak out against slavery in public. The Grimké sisters became agents for the American Anti-Slavery Society, lecturing throughout New England about the evils inflicted on slaves. In 1838 Angelina even addressed the Massachusetts state legislature. Earlier that decade, African American orator Maria W. Miller Stewart held a Boston audience spellbound with an 1832 abolitionist testimony. Josephine Griffing spoke to gatherings of the Western Antislavery Society throughout Ohio, Indiana, and Michigan. Several firm advocates of women's rights, such as Lucretia Mott, also addressed public audiences on antislavery themes. The presidential election of 1860 launched the decades-long public speaking career of Anna Dickinson, a Philadelphia Quaker then still in her teens, who would blaze a fiery path through Northern public lecture circuits throughout the Civil War with radical denunciations of slavery and inequality.[11]

Many more women lodged their protests against slavery in ways that cultivated political consciousness without transgressing gender roles as dramatically as speaking in public did. They organized antislavery fairs to sell handicrafts and donated the proceeds to antislavery causes. They mounted boycotts of slave-grown products. So many joined women's antislavery organizations that by 1837 Massachusetts alone was home to forty-seven female antislavery societies. Northern women also flooded Congress and their state legislatures with petitions protesting slavery and other manifestations of racism.[12] Lydia Chase and her daughters, Lucy and Sarah, led numerous petition campaigns, such as an 1842 protest against a state law barring interracial marriage, this last on the grounds that such a law was "at variance with the Constitution of the State, since it denies that 'all men are born equal'" and was also "opposed to the spirit of free institutions, which know no difference among men, before the laws, except that of character and conduct."[13] When the Fugitive Slave Act passed in 1850, women launched a torrent of petitions, which did not let up for most of the decade. Sarah Chase signed one in 1855 asking for the removal of Judge of Probate Edward Greeley Loring because he enforced the odious law, as did Lydia Maria Child, while Louisa May Alcott signed one beseeching the legislature to remove any state official who complied with the hated federal statute.[14]

When war broke out in 1861, petitioning dipped, but women quickly redirected their efforts and energy. One week after U.S. forces evacuated Fort Sumter, Wisconsin governor Alexander Randall issued an appeal "To the Patriotic Women of Wisconsin," expressing his confidence that they would "contribute [their] aid in the present crisis" with as much "strength and courage and warm sympathies" as soldiers who "go bravely forward for God and Liberty."[15] Lucinda Park, the mother of "ten children all strong Republicans who are ready and willing to do all within their power," responded directly to Randall with the offer to "gladly aid in making garments" for anyone "going to fight for their country's freedom."[16] Because war aid was inseparable from emancipation effort to antislavery women, many gathered under hastily assembled umbrella organizations dedicated simultaneously to war aid and freed people's relief. One of the earliest was the Woman's National Loyal League, which Josephine Griffing immediately joined in 1861. Under its auspices, she continued to deliver lectures throughout the midwestern states. She used her platform to solicit donations of clothing and supplies for soldiers and for the enslaved men, women, and children who began running to Union army lines as soon as war erupted.[17] Griffing went on to work as an agent for the National Freedmen's Relief Association of Washington, pushing hard for both direct government relief and women's involvement in work with freed people.[18]

As the war progressed, slaves throughout the occupied South identified the Union army as a means of countering the power that masters held over them, and they acted on their longing for freedom by running to the army. Before war's end, nearly half a million would take refuge with the military, many gathering in what developed into giant, ad hoc refugee camps known as contraband camps, which were administered, overseen, and provisioned by the Union army.[19] Camps appeared wherever the army was, with the smallest sheltering hundreds of former slaves and the largest straining to absorb more than ten thousand. Women and children almost always outnumbered men, often by giant proportions, especially once black recruitment into the Union army began. Contraband camps rapidly developed crowding, shortages, disease, vulnerability to violence, and other features that characterize refugee camps the world over.[20] Armies exist to fight wars, not function as philanthropic relief organizations, and the Union army was no more equipped to minister to the needs of the sick, starving, destitute refugees from slavery than any other military force in human history has been capable of caring for the physical and mental needs of desperate refugees fleeing brutal regimes. Almost immediately, the Union army had a humanitarian crisis on its hands.

Refugees from slavery needed basic material necessities like food and clothing, which Northern relief, church, and freedmen's aid organizations, often spearheaded by women members, began to collect and ship south. In Cleveland, free African Americans collected bedding, warm clothing, shoes, and other supplies, and they delegated community members to carry the articles wherever they were needed.[21] Quakers from numerous Northern states sent blankets, books, and other provisions.[22] Antislavery societies quickly transformed into freedmen's aid societies dedicated to collecting and shipping relief supplies, such as the "22 quilts, 40 pillows & 17 tin cups" sent by the Freedmen's Association of New York in one shipment (of many) to Alexandria, Virginia.[23] The Northwestern Freedmen's Aid Commission marshalled the energies of societies throughout many western states and funneled a torrent of necessities through Chicago and down the western rivers for distribution to men, women, and children who had fled slavery. In 1864 alone the commission collected and disbursed $20,745.98 worth of relief, much of it in food, bolts of cloth, shoes, blankets, and farming implements, and some of it in the travel expenses of agents who transported the supplies south.[24] All relief societies drew on the efforts of women, and some were led by them. The St. Louis Ladies Contraband Relief Society, for example, set up shop in the Missouri Hotel on the corner of Main and Morgan Streets when a large group of former slaves sailed into the city from Helena, Arkansas. From those quarters, society members provisioned newcomers, responded to requests for supplies elsewhere in the city, swiftly assembled an employment clearinghouse service, and launched a hunt for suitable space to establish schools for freed people.[25]

Desperately needed as material assistance was, some of former slaves' needs required human presence, not just the contents of crates. Thousands of Northern women offered theirs, often viewing gender less as an obstacle than as a credential. Northern women's work among freed people in the South generally combined material relief with teaching; in fact, neither Northern women nor freed slaves perceived a clear separation between those two pursuits but rather regarded them as interconnected strands in the work of emancipation. "We need female teachers," Harriet Jacobs pleaded in the spring of 1863 as she surveyed "little ones" left to their own devices in Alexandria, Virginia, while their mothers desperately sought any work they could find to support their children.[26]

By that time, a student named Joanna Moore had already left her studies at Rockford Female Seminary in Illinois and headed down the Mississippi River, unsure of exactly how she would aid refugees from slavery, but certain that "Woman's hand and heart must supply their needs."[27] Born in Pennsylvania, Joanna Moore had been so determined to obtain an education that she knocked on the door of every house for miles around the Rockford Female Seminary in search of one that

Chandra Manning

would allow her to work for room and board, so that she could enroll at the young women's school. Her education was not cheaply bought: every day she did farm chores, kept house, cared for three difficult children, and covered six miles on foot to attend classes. Yet she walked away from the seminary with barely a glance once she was convinced of her call to serve the emancipated.[28] At a lecture she listened to a Baptist minister recently returned from a contraband camp paint a "panorama" of desperate and destitute women and children "stretching out empty hands." When the minister entreated, "What can a man do to help such a suffering mass of humanity? Nothing. A woman is needed, nothing else will do," Moore, in direct defiance of her mother's unrelenting criticism, sailed south.[29] Nothing about Joanna Moore's way was smooth, and in some ways being a woman made things harder. A Wisconsin school administrator traveling on the same boat as Moore dismissed her as frivolous and "gushing." When she first arrived at Island Number 10, a Union army officer laughed her off, and so did the first two freedwomen that she tried to help. On her first night, she said, she "cried myself to sleep."[30]

Like Joanna Moore, Charlotte Forten was unmarried and idealistic when war erupted, and she hesitated even less than Moore did to head south, but her eagerness did not inoculate her against frustration and disappointment. As a member of a prominent African American abolitionist family from Philadelphia, Forten was well educated and dedicated to the ideal of extending the benefits of education to black Americans. She was also extravagantly fond of New England, especially Salem, Massachusetts, where she first attended, and then taught, school. From Salem, Forten tried in 1862 to procure a commission to go to South Carolina as a teacher under the auspices of the New England Freedmen's Aid Commission, only to learn that the New England commission was not sending women at that time. Reluctantly, she returned to Philadelphia, obtained her commission in that city, and set sail for Port Royal, South Carolina, in the company of "an old Quaker gentleman [who] is going there to keep store, accompanied by his daughter."[31]

As Forten's and Moore's experiences indicated, being a woman in the mid-nineteenth-century United States made it challenging to be taken seriously, but in some ways the expectations and experiences of middle-class Northern women also uniquely positioned them to meet wartime emancipation's difficulties. By its very nature, war creates disorder. On the one hand, that very disorder was what made liberation possible, because it created opportunities for enslaved men, women, and children to run to freedom, and because it weakened the powerfully entrenched institution of slavery. But chaos also killed. As in all armed conflicts, wartime disorder in the Civil War South overthrew longstanding social structures, displaced large numbers of people, generated scarcities, disrupted resource distribution patterns, and created conditions perfect for the spread of disease. Meanwhile, the existence of war subordinated every other goal, including mitigating disruption, to the overarching one of fighting and winning a military conflict. From the Sea Islands to the Mississippi Valley, and from Louisiana's Gulf Coast to Virginia, former slaves often set off on desperate journeys, taking great risk but little else with them in their determination to escape bondage.

By the time they arrived at Union lines, they were generally weakened, exhausted, and malnourished. Their defenses against the new disease environment created by soldiers and thousands of vulnerable refugees—all subsisting in close proximity to each other in conditions of shortage—were compromised. Sanitation deteriorated, illness ran rampant, and former slaves suffered devastating hardship under conditions that militated against systematic relief. The farmers, shopkeepers, and laborers who made up the Union army concentrated on defeating the Confederacy more than they did on administering aid. Disorder, in short, sowed suffering even as it enabled emancipation.

Northern women could answer the tension between order and disorder more directly because they were not responsible for fighting and winning a military conflict and were therefore not pulled by cross purposes in the same way that Northern men were. As Union forces began bombarding Charleston in April 1863, Clara Barton stepped off a boat and onto ground reverberating from the force of nearby blasts.[32] Barton went to nurse sick soldiers, not to conduct a military campaign, so she was free to concentrate her efforts on relieving distress. While in South Carolina, Barton befriended Frances Gage, an Ohio woman serving as superintendent of contrabands on nearby Parris Island. When smallpox struck freed people throughout the Sea Islands, Army quarantine regulations prevented Barton from leaving her nursing post, but she did not let regulations stop her from trying to alleviate suffering. She boxed up "tons of comforts such as I thought them most in need of" and stashed them in the bottom of "little boats." She set the unmanned vessels to sail up "the mouths of creeks" to a former slave named Columbus Simonds, who became her partner, separated by distance and quarantine rules but connected by small boats, little waterways, and crates of needed supplies.[33] From South Carolina, Barton traveled to Virginia where she once again found herself among "a large number of colored people, mostly women & children," who had withstood the tromping back and forth of both Union and Confederate troops in territory that changed hands multiple times over the war. "In all cases they are destitute, having stood the sack of two opposing armies," Barton reflected. "What one army left them the other has taken," and in her view only system and order could combat the resulting misery. She turned her considerable energies to organizing food and lining up paid employment for mothers desperate to support their children.[34]

Massachusetts grandmother Abigail Dutton also took her formidable aptitude for systemization with her when she traveled to Nashville, Tennessee, to minister first to Union soldiers and then to freed people. Work was certainly not lacking in that railroad town, but adequate nutrition often was, and Dutton astutely observed that nobody (including former slaves) who was sick and malnourished was in much of a position to earn an adequate living no matter how prevalent jobs were, even if wages were promptly paid, which in Nashville they were not. Nor were the weakened likely to gain strength on a diet consisting of army-issued hardtack and bacon. In 1864 Dutton invented and established the "Special Diet Kitchen," where she prepared broths and ginger tea for the acutely ill and then worked convalescents up to fresh vegetables as they began to grow stronger. She also kept data on results, and she took that data to the superintendent of contrabands for Nashville to show him that "mortality . . . decreased ever so many per cent" as a result of her "S.D.K." Convinced by Dutton's evidence, Barnard, the superintendant, authorized the continuation of the Special Diet Kitchen in Nashville. Dutton trained other workers to follow her dietary guidelines so that the S.D.K. could persist in its work even after she herself was reassigned to an orphan's home in Nashville. Meanwhile, Superintendent Barnard traveled to other camps in Tennessee and Alabama to encourage the adoption of similar systems elsewhere.[35]

Antislavery Northern women familiar with the constraints that gender conventions placed on individual agency knew that banding together often offered the most promising solution to transcending crabbed and narrow limits, and many sought to foster associationism among African American women in the South for precisely that reason. The Northwest Freedmen's Aid Commission worked "to establish a seminary at New Orleans" for "colored girls" modeled "somewhat after the order of Mt. Holyoke."[36] By that time African American women in Cairo, Illinois, had already begun organizing themselves. Mrs. Maria Renfro opened her home on 15th Street to begin a new, female-led church congregation that offered refugees from slavery pouring into Cairo both material and spiritual sustenance. Renfro's congregation soon outgrew her house, becoming the nucleus for the African Methodist Episcopal Church in Cairo, which relocated to the corner of 16th Street and Washington Avenue and anchored the African American community in Cairo both during and after the war.[37]

Northern women's manner of confronting war's dislocations sometimes brought its own tragic consequences. Good order could help alleviate suffering, but overzealous dedication to standardization sometimes did its own damage. Mary Ames was fervently devoted to improving the lives of freed people on Edisto Island, South Carolina, and she had very definite ideas about how to go about doing so. Firm in her conviction that a solid education consisted of unyielding training in personal hygiene every bit as much as letters and numbers, she unwittingly sent a young boy to his death. A fourteen-year-old named John and his sister Eliza walked five miles to attend Ames's school. By the time they arrived, John was so covered in dirt that Ames felt duty bound to send him "into the creek to bathe" before permitting him to take his seat on the school bench. The trouble was that the creek was tidal and John could not swim. He drowned in the turning tide.[38] His tragedy serves as a reminder that Northern women's passion for organization amidst disorder often saved lives, but it also sometimes cost them, especially when good intentions blinded women to their own fallibility.

Limitations that Northern white middle-class women faced in their ability to act on their own independent will also sensitized them to a second tension at the heart of wartime emancipation: the tension between dependence and independence. Abolitionist women were products of a culture that pegged both moral gloss and fitness for political rights on self-reliance. As historians Nancy Fraser and Linda Gordon explain in their intellectual history of the American affinity for the concept of independence, "dependency was deemed antithetical to citizenship" by antebellum white Americans.[39] Well-meaning aid workers, therefore, faced a real dilemma when they found themselves among starving, freezing, and shelterless refugees from slavery, who so obviously needed immediate material assistance but who, in receiving it, would reinforce bigoted notions about black indolence and ineligibility for rights. How could Northern women respond to freed people's immediate need for life's necessities while also laying groundwork for long-term gains, a foundation best laid, in the words of missionaries among freed people in Arkansas, by demonstrating that "the people here are helping themselves"?[40]

Under ideal circumstances, many Northern women preferred to square that circle by helping to make it possible for former slaves to make or earn the money for the things they needed. Lucy and Sarah Chase and the freedwomen they befriended in eastern Virginia proved especially ingenious (and indefatigable) in this regard. Faced with shortages of bedding and clothing on Craney Island, Virginia, the Chase sisters and freedwomen gathered up corn husks and "a quantity of sacking," crafted sewing boxes from salvaged planks of the *Merrimack* (which had sunk nearby), and got to work stitching new beds and sturdy garments.[41] Josephine Griffing oversaw an employment bureau for freedwomen in Washington, D.C., just as the women of the Ladies Contraband Relief Society did in St. Louis, and other women made similar efforts elsewhere.[42] Harriet Tubman, already famous before the war for the daring slave escapes she had led after her own flight from bondage on Maryland's Eastern Shore, sailed to South Carolina in 1862. In Beaufort she built a washhouse and helped freedwomen set up a laundry business in it.[43] When everything went just right, efforts like those of the Chase sisters, Griffing, and Tubman could meet need and undercut notions about African American dependence at the same time.

Yet appealing as the prospect of helping freed people help themselves might seem, many Northern antislavery women who went south began to recognize exactly how naive and misplaced such a bromide could be amid the overwhelming hardship created by slavery and exacerbated by war; that realization set them apart from their counterparts who remained at home. Both the humanitarian crisis and the liberation of emancipation were inescapable to someone like Joanna Moore, who knew that neither the triumphal nor the tragic aspects of emancipation could be separated from each other. On Island Number 10 in the middle of the Mississippi River, Moore often found "children on the wharf with nothing on them but a part of a soldier's old coat." The island was fast stripped of its trees, and on most days, rooms "had no fire." Cheery notions of self-sufficiency had little place under such desperate circumstances and were also, as Moore glimpsed, tinged with hubristic overconfidence in human beings' ability to overpower their surroundings.[44] Self-sufficiency could prove very fleeting when buffeted by war's winds. The Beaufort women with the laundry enterprise met its bitter fickleness when the Union army commandeered their washhouse for soldiers' quarters, in effect wiping out the business.[45] Better, as women like Moore and Tubman knew, to recognize that the scale of need—unimaginable to the white middle-class reformers who comprised most of the ranks of Northern antislavery women who spent the war in the North—could quite simply overpower even the most determined and well-intentioned human efforts.

Chandra Manning

At the same time, antislavery women who worked among freed people were generally quicker than men to recognize that ideological forces could also sometimes prevail over individual will or effort. Horace James and Holland Streeter, administrators of contraband camps in eastern North Carolina, oversaw a colony established on Roanoke Island, North Carolina, as an experimental community designed specifically to demonstrate freed people's "personal responsibility for their own support." James was confident that a settlement of former slaves could become "self-supporting and independent, like free communities at the North," and thus vanquish white Northern skepticism about black Americans' readiness for freedom. The key, as he saw it, was to ensure that all necessities were purchased by rather than given to former slaves, who would use wages they earned working for the Union army. James worked hard to keep prices low and the reports flowing to Northern newspapers positive.[46] Trouble came when wages were held up for months on end, a problem that James tried vigorously to redress with the army paymaster but that he did not allow to dislodge his commitment to requiring freed people to purchase their necessities.[47] In the spring of 1865, aiming to demonstrate black capacity for independence to a doubting Northern electorate, James and Streeter cut off rations to freed people, including children, arguing that "*they have had too much* given them."[48] Women teachers on Roanoke could see immediately the damage that overzealous commitment to the goal of demonstrating freed people's self-sufficiency was about to do. "The sweeping reduction of the rations brings hundreds suddenly face to face with starvation," they exclaimed.[49]

Embedded within the tensions between chaos and order and dependence and independence was a third tension: the clash between human will and resourcefulness on one hand and the unyielding limits posed by harsh circumstances and structural forces on the other. As Christmas approached on Roanoke Island in 1863, new families of freed people arrived each day, and Elizabeth James was beside herself over "*where* to shelter them . . . in a camp where every nook and cranny is already crowded to excess." In one stoveless room James found twenty-eight "souls for whom Christ died," including several sick children, two of whom died within the week. "Should not the government provide, at least temporary shelter, for the crowds which come?" she implored, even as she recognized that no amount of human effort, even from the government, could magically devise enough room or the lumber to meet the need for sufficient housing on Roanoke Island. Where her cousin Horace saw weakness of will, Elizabeth saw the stark reality of a scale of need that was just plain larger than human capacity to meet it.[50]

In fact, all Northern women who went south to work for emancipation came face to face with failure, because no matter how much energy they exerted or resourcefulness they demonstrated, forces larger than individual human will simply did not yield. No matter who or where she was, if a Northern woman went south to teach or provide relief to refugees from slavery, some of the freed people she sought to help died, and often a great many of them did. Harriet Jacobs and Julia Wilbur, a white woman from upstate New York who worked in partnership with Jacobs, were tireless in their labors among suffering women and children in Alexandria, Virginia. They were also fearless in their battles with any Union authorities (like Superintendent of Contrabands Albert Gladwin) whom they believed to be heartless and inept in the administration of the occupied city. Jacobs and Wilbur succeeded in helping some women to find work, many children to stay alive, and scores of formerly enslaved people to claw their way out of bondage. Yet they still looked on helplessly as hundreds of former slaves succumbed to measles, diphtheria, scarlet fever, typhoid fever, smallpox, and sometimes to just plain exhaustion.[51]

Laura Haviland, a Michigan woman who taught and ministered to freed people in Cairo, Illinois, and in camps on islands in the Mississippi River, repeatedly encountered a collision between human resourcefulness and stubbornly unyielding limits. She steamed into ports along the river ready to distribute barrels of warm blankets, crisp cotton shirts, new socks and suits, and piles of little girls' dresses, each with a pocket containing a lovingly sewn two-inch rag doll.[52] But sometimes what she encountered was despair. On one day, Haviland could do nothing more than sit with a woman whose last remaining child, an eight-year-old boy, died in a shabby sick bed and then promise to get a coffin made so that the child's body would not be chewed by wharf rats as his mother made her lonely way to a new contraband camp, one not yet quite as crowded as the one where her son died.[53]

Not even the undauntable Chase sisters could always prevail. For months they tacked alphabet cards up on the walls so freedwomen could learn to read as they sewed. Sarah Chase even climbed to the top of abandoned houses to tear off roof slates for use in teaching writing. Yet neither the sisters' determination nor the freedwomen's formidable resilience could expand the limited carrying capacity of Craney Island or, for that matter, deflect the constant Confederate threats against it. Eventually, all but about three hundred former slaves had to be evacuated from Craney Island, to start all over again in camps in nearby Suffolk or Portsmouth.[54]

Women like the Chase sisters, Charlotte Forten, Laura Haviland, Harriet Tubman, Harriet Jacobs, and the thousands who went south to help make emancipation real came, sooner or later, to the realization that they could give every last ounce of energy they had and it would still not be enough to triumph over germs, warfare, poverty, prejudice, limited capacity, and other structural forces militating against real freedom. They had little choice but to concede that freed people's need was greater than women's power to meet it, and that the evil of slavery was bigger than any group of women's good intentions. To confront those truths changed the women who were forced to face them and set them apart from their sisters who stayed home for the duration of the war. In some cases, those truths broke women and sent them home as poisoned by bitterness, resentment, and resignation, as Louisa May Alcott had been by mercury. But other women managed to come face to face with those truths and keep going anyway, and those were the ones who made the most difference.

Northern women who accepted the limits to their own power were not saints, and they had their failings, but the ones who kept trudging as far as they could anyway generally did so because in recognizing their own weaknesses and limitations, they made themselves receptive to learning from the enslaved. Elizabeth Botume sailed

Chandra Manning

from Boston to Beaufort in the fall of 1864, and at first she was so sure that she brought all necessary knowledge with her that she missed the subtle cues and unspoken rules she would need to learn in order to work effectively with her students. She did not at first realize that Friday was washday, and nobody was going to come to school without undertaking that chore first. She did not understand local naming traditions, which made for difficulty in keeping track of who was who. She was caught unaware by the mutual suspicion between children born in Beaufort and those who had come from plantations further inland. All these oversights led her to make many early missteps, but once she set aside her certainties and began by respecting the "individuality and personal dignity" of each pupil, she and the children she taught began to make real progress together.[55] After Mary Ames's rigid certainties led to the teenage John's death by drowning, she grew more attentive to her inherent prejudices and preconceived notions. She could not always rise above them, but she tried to call herself on them, and sometimes she succeeded. She befriended a formerly enslaved couple named Jim and Sarah and their children, including their little boy, Ben. When Ben asked her one day if the reason she had never given him a kiss was because of his black skin, she stopped what she was doing, gathered him onto her lap, and held him in a genuine embrace until he fell asleep. So completely did Mary Ames learn to open herself up to solidarity with the family that when Sarah had a new baby soon thereafter, she and Jim named their daughter "Mary" in recognition of the woman who had become, not savior or leader, but *family* to them.[56]

When Northern women acknowledged their own limitations, they were more likely to see differences between freed people and themselves as sensible adaptations to learn from rather than defects to be suppressed. Planting and harvesting cotton on St. Helena in the South Carolina Sea Islands looked different from what Harriet Ware's New England sensibilities told her farming should look like, but she eventually realized that the "strong and graceful" women who organized their own work in the fields were the real experts, not her.[57] She also acknowledged that she needed the leadership of those women to make any headway in the work of education. Upon noticing that "Old Peggy" decided who "came into the Church" and who did not, Ware asked Peggy if she would make a special visit to school. Peggy did, and her approval lent Ware the credibility she needed.[58] Charlotte Forten arrived already armed with the determination to teach freed children "about the noble Touissant L'Ouverture" because she believed that knowing "what one of their own color c'ld do for his race" would "inspire them with courage and ambition (of a noble sort,) and high purpose." Still, she found that she did best when she paused in instructing long enough to be "quite *lifted out* of myself" by the children's own methods of praying and singing.[59]

Such an authentically humble stance was and is a rare thing among humans, and even women who could attain it sometimes often failed to sustain it at all times. Laura Towne came from Philadelphia to teach former slaves at Port Royal, South Carolina, and there was no question about her dedication: she remained there for the rest of her life. She was an utterly uncompromising abolitionist, tolerant of nothing less than root-and-branch absolutism among her fellow missionaries. Yet she did learn, sometimes, to subordinate her own firm ideas to the wisdom of former slaves. When she discovered that freedwomen had their own very definite sense of style, which looked nothing like the plain and somber dresses sent by well-meaning New England aid societies, she wrote to ask for cloth, needles, and thread rather than ready-made clothing because local women "prefer to make their own clothes and all know how to sew."[60] Yet at other times Towne retained her blind spots. She was especially intolerant of what she viewed as lapses in former slaves' morality and lamented, "I do not think they could work out their own civilization unless led up by white people."[61]

Women who could consistently embrace difference as a school from which to learn rather than a defect to stamp out were more exception than rule, but they were the most effective midwives attending the birth of freedom. Harriet Tubman did recognize and respect the initial hostility between Beaufort, South Carolina, freed people and the hundreds of inland South Carolinians she led out of bondage as part of the raids she conducted for the Union army, but she did not let it stop her from nursing, spying, raiding, or liberating.[62] Self-aware enough to realize her early efforts did "but little good" because at first she "only pitied those women," Joanna Moore stayed in the midst of, not to the side of or above, the formerly enslaved women and children that she initially expected to help. In Arkansas Moore sought out distant and remote places where no other teacher would go, and she ignored ridicule to do her work exactly there. She persuaded a soldier to build her an arbor on a desolate plantation, where she nailed a blackboard to a tree and joined forces with a black minister to teach and attend to the material and spiritual needs of the people she grew to "love as Jesus loved." She was hungry, dirty, exhausted, and often heartbroken by the number of children who had lost parents and by the lengths so many mothers had to go just to stay alive. But she also genuinely knew that she had a lot to learn from those mothers. Moore had grown up in a family with one blind sister and a large number of younger siblings, whose care fell to Joanna's responsibility. Early on, she learned that Rebecca, the blind sister, "was a great blessing to the whole household," in very practical, not sentimental, ways. Whereas at first Joanna's mother "was so sorry for [Rebecca's] blindness," that she was reluctant to ask anything of her, Joanna recognized her own need for precisely the gifts her sister had to offer. Rebecca "could shell the peas, grind the coffee, gather currants" and knit better than anyone else in the family. From Rebecca, Joanna learned to identify herself as recipient and beneficiary more than benefactor in her dealings with people who might at first glance seem to be in need of her, and she brought her aptitude for humility and solidarity into her work with former slaves. Every night she listened to her students and their families sing. She knew that their songs were not her familiar hymns but rather were freed people's own melodies, with a power large enough to embrace them all. For the rest of her life, Joanna Moore lived among African Americans and dedicated herself to working alongside formerly enslaved women and their daughters. She remained a staunch advocate for justice for freed people in an era when such a stance was not just unpopular but downright dangerous.[63]

Chandra Manning

Moore was exceptionally dedicated, but she was not the only Northern woman who stayed in the South to help make freedom real long after Confederate surrender ended formal hostilities in 1865. In fact, even though the total number of Southern-born (black and white combined) teachers outnumbered Northern ones 6,589 to 5,191 by the end of Reconstruction, the number of Northern women teaching freed people in the South rose every year from 1,405 in 1865 to 3,633 in 1870, and Northern women who went South to teach typically stuck to the task longer than Southern whites did (though not longer than typical African American teachers).[64] Individuals like Josephine Griffing remained at her work long after the war. Laura Towne continued to teach Sea Island children for the rest of her life.[65]

Women like Moore and Towne stayed in the South, but in later years the memory of women both black and white began to fade from familiar narratives of wartime and slavery's end. When the Fourteenth Amendment validated African American citizenship without ensuring black suffrage, male-led organizations like the National Equal Rights League and its state chapters focused their strategies on highlighting the particular worthiness of black men at the expense of women. Whereas women and men attended the annual convention of the Pennsylvania State Equal Rights Association in 1865 and passed resolutions that referred to "the people of this State, without distinction of sex or color," by the end of the decade, the association exclusively emphasized the rights that black soldiers had earned for black men.[66] Meanwhile, longstanding women's rights advocates who had once also championed abolition—women like Susan B. Anthony and Elizabeth Cady Stanton—began to resort to racist rhetoric that posited respectable white women's suitability for the ballot in preference to African American men's qualifications.[67] Such arguments were a far cry from Angelina Grimké's contention at an 1863 national convention of the women's rights movement—which Stanton and Anthony attended and endorsed—that "there can never be a true peace in this Republic until the civil and political rights of all citizens of African descent and all women are practically established."[68]

The ideal to which Grimké looked so hopefully in 1863, and to which women like Harriet Tubman, Joanna Moore, Laura Towne, Charlotte Forten, and others dedicated years of their lives, remained unrealized in the decades following the Civil War. To this day, their work remains unfinished and ongoing. The experiences and examples of Northern women who worked to make emancipation real still have the power to transform the goal they sought from unattainable pipe dream to work in progress, but only if there is room for failure as well as success in how we tell their stories.

NOTES

1. Louisa May Alcott, *Hospital Sketches* (1863; repr., Mineola, N.Y.: Dover, 2006), 1.

2. Elizabeth Cady Stanton, Susan B. Anthony, and Matilda Joslyn Gage, eds., *History of Woman Suffrage,* 3 vols. (Rochester, N.Y.: Charles Mann, 1887), 2:3.

3. Analyses of Northern women's involvement in wartime relief work among freed people include Ronald E. Butchart, *Northern Schools, Southern Blacks, and Reconstruction: Freedmen's*

Education, 1862–1875 (Westport, Conn.: Greenwood Press, 1980); Carol Faulkner, *Women's Radical Reconstruction: The Freedmen's Aid Movement* (Philadelphia: Univ. of Pennsylvania Press, 2004); Julie Roy Jeffrey, *The Great Silent Army of Abolitionism: Ordinary Women in the Antislavery Movement* (Chapel Hill: Univ. of North Carolina Press, 1998), chap. 6; Jacqueline Jones, *Soldiers of Light and Love: Northern Teachers and Georgia Blacks, 1865–1873* (Athens: Univ. of Georgia Press, 1992); Leslie Schwalm, *Emancipation's Diaspora: Race and Reconstruction in the Upper Midwest* (Chapel Hill: Univ. of North Carolina Press, 2009); Henry Lee Swint, *The Northern Teacher in the South, 1862–1870* (New York: Octagon Books, 1967).

4. For a concise treatment of Republican expectations for the end of slavery, see James Oakes, *The Scorpion's Sting: Antislavery and the Coming of the Civil War* (New York: W. W. Norton, 2014).

5. Alcott, *Hospital Sketches*, 73.

6. The classic account of antebellum, white, middle-class gender conventions is Barbara Welter, "The Cult of True Womanhood: 1820–1860," *American Quarterly* 18 (pt. 1, Summer 1966): 151–74.

7. Published in 1852, *Uncle Tom's Cabin* sold 300,000 copies in the U.S. as fast as printers could make new copies, and nearly 1million copies internationally. For a recent assessment of Stowe as an antislavery writer, see David S. Reynolds, *Mightier Than the Sword: Uncle Tom's Cabin and the Battle for America* (New York: W. W. Norton, 2011).

8. Lydia Maria Child, *An Appeal in Favor of that Class of Americans Called Africans, Authentic Anecdotes of American Slavery* (1838; repr., Newburyport, Mass: Charles Whipple, 1833); *From Slavery to Freedom: The African American Pamphlet Collection,* Library of Congress, Washington, D.C., memory.loc.gov); Lydia Maria Child, *Anti-Slavery Catechism* (Newburyport, Mass: Charles Whipple, 1839).

9. See, e.g., Sara Moore Grimké, *An Epistle to the Clergy of the Southern States* (Boston: n.p., 1836); Angelina Grimké, *An Appeal to the Women of the Nominally Free States* (Boston: n.p., 1837); and Theodore Dwight Weld, ed., *American Slavery As It Is: Testimony of a Thousand Witnesses* (New York: American Anti-Slavery Society, 1839).

10. Harriet Jacobs, *Incidents in the Life of a Slave Girl. Written by Herself* (Boston: Published for the Author, 1861). http://docsouth.unc.edu/fpn/jacobs/title.html.

11. On the Grimké sisters, see Gerda Lerner, *The Grimké Sisters from South Carolina: Pioneers for Women's Rights and Abolition* (New York: Oxford Univ. Press, 1998). On Stewart and Mott, see Karlyn Kohrn Campbell, ed., *Women Public Speakers in the United States, 1800–1925: A Biocritical Sourcebook* (Westport, Conn.: Greenwood Press, 1993); on Griffing, see Keith E. Melder, "Angel of Mercy in Washington: Josephine Griffing and the Freedmen, 1864–1872," *Records of the Columbia Historical Society,* 63–65 (1963–1965): 243–72; on Dickinson, see J. Matthew Gallman, *America's Joan of Arc: The Life of Anna Elizabeth Dickinson* (New York: Oxford Univ. Press, 2006).

12. Of all the signatures on antislavery petitions that reached Congress from the state of Massachusetts in 1837–1838, fully 80 percent belonged to women. See Lerner, *Grimké Sisters From South Carolina;* and Pat Harrison, "The Indomitable Grimké Sisters," *Schlesinger Library News* (Spring 2015): 10.

13. Petition of Lydia Earle Chase and others, 1842, Massachusetts Anti-Slavery and Anti-Segregation Petitions, House Unpassed Legislation 1842, Docket 1153, SC1/series 230, Massachusetts Archives, Boston, Mass., http://nrs.harvard.edu/urn-3:FHCL:10956456 and http://nrs.harvard.edu/urn-3:FHCL:11858131.

14. Petition of Lydia E. Capron and Others, Boston, 1855, Massachusetts Anti-Slavery and Anti-Segregation Petitions, House Unpassed Legislation 1855, Docket 18373, SC1/series 231, Massachusetts Archives, http://nrs.harvard.edu/urn-3:FHCL:11666564; Petition of Lydia Maria

Child and Others, Wayland, 1855, Massachusetts Anti-Slavery and Anti-Segregation Petitions, House Unpassed Legislation 1855, Docket 18373, SCI/series 231, http://nrs.harvard.edu/urn -3:FHCL:11666564?n=417; Petition of Samuel May and others, Boston, Feb. 2, 1855, Massachusetts Anti-Slavery and Anti-Segregation Petitions, Passed Acts; St. 1855, c. 489, SC1/series 229, Massachusetts Archives, http://nrs.harvard.edu/urn-3:FHCL:10520838?n=234. For more on the Fugitive Slave Act and aftermath, see Steven Lubet, *Fugitive Justice: Runaways, Rescuers, and Slavery on Trial* (Cambridge, Mass.: Harvard Univ. Press, 2010). Chapter 11 specifically discusses Judge Loring.

15. Alexander Randall, Apr. 22, 1861, Madison, Wis., in Reuben Gold Thwaites, ed. *Civil War Messages and Proclamations of Wisconsin War Governors* (Madison: Wisconsin History Commission, 1912), n51.

16. Lucinda Park to Gov. Alexander Randall, May 14, 1861, Black Earth, Dane County, Wis., in Wisconsin Governor Military Correspondence, ser. 49, box 42, State Historical Society of Wisconsin, Madison.

17. Stanton, Anthony, and Gage, *History of Woman Suffrage*, 2:28–29. Another organization, the Woman's National Loyal League, organized by Susan B. Anthony and Elizabeth Cady Stanton in 1863, mounted an energetic campaign in support of a constitutional amendment abolishing slavery. A February 1864 petition to Charles Sumner signed by 100,000 women boasted the signatures of 200,000 women by May 1864. See Stanton, Anthony, and Gage, *History of Woman Suffrage*, vol. 2; and Lerner, *Grimké Sisters from South Carolina*, 265.

18. Faulkner, *Women's Radical Reconstruction*, 1–2.

19. Ira Berlin et al., eds., *Freedom: A Documentary History of Emancipation, 1861–1867*, ser. 1, vol. 3 (New York: Cambridge Univ. Press, 1991), 77–80, counts at least 475,000 former slaves in direct contact with the Union army in contraband camps, working for the army, or serving as black soldiers (most of whom first went to contraband camps and enlisted from there) in the spring of 1865. That number does not count the thousands who had been in contraband camps at some earlier time and left or died, the addition of which would bring the total very close to 500,000. To place that number in perspective, it accounts for between 12 and 15 percent of the U.S. slave population, according to the 1860 census, and substantially exceeds the number of free African Americans living in the Northern states, according to that same census, which was approximately 221,702. See Inter-university Consortium for Political and Social Research, "Historical, Demographic, Economic, and Social Data: The United States, 1790–1970" [computer file] (Ann Arbor, Mich.: Inter-university Consortium for Political and Social Research, 1997).

20. For fuller discussions of contraband camps and more extensive bibliographical references, see Chandra Manning, "Working for Citizenship in Civil War Contraband Camps," *Journal of the Civil War Era* 4 (June 2014): 172–204; and Chandra Manning, *Troubled Refuge: Struggling for Freedom in the Civil War* (New York: Alfred A. Knopf, 2016). Several books and articles treat single or individual camps, e.g. Patricia Click, *Time Full of Trial: The Roanoke Island Freedmen's Colony, 1862–1867* (Chapel Hill: Univ. of North Carolina Press, 2001); and Cam Walker, "Corinth: The Story of a Contraband Camp," *Civil War History* 20 (Mar. 1975): 5–22.

21. John Eaton to H. B. Spellman, Oct. 2, 1863, Department of Tennessee, Record Group 105 (Records of the Bureau of Refugees, Freedmen, and Abandoned Lands), Microfilm 1914 (Pre-Bureau Records), reel 1, frame 40, National Archives and Records Administration, Washington, D.C. (hereafter cited as NARA).

22. See, e.g., Linda B. Selleck, *Gentle Invaders: Quaker Women Educators and Racial Issues During the Civil War and Reconstruction* (Richmond, Ind: Friends United Press, 1995), esp. chap. 3. Many individual women Quakers traveled to contraband camps as relief workers; several of them appear below.

23. Julia Wilbur to Sarah Wistar Cope, Feb. 7, 1863, Alexandria, Va., in Jean Fagin Yellin, ed., *The Harriet Jacobs Family Papers* (Chapel Hill: Univ. of North Carolina Press, 2008), 2:445. To cite just two other examples of similar societies, see the Records of the Freedmen's Aid Commission, Boston, Ms. N-101, Massachusetts Historical Society, Boston; and John Eaton to Martin Camp and the Contraband Committee of Summit County, Ohio, Nov. 2, 1863, Vicksburg, MS, Department of Tennessee, Record Group 105 (Records of the Bureau of Refugees, Freedmen, and Abandoned Lands), Microfilm 1914 (Pre-Bureau Records), reel 1, frame 45–46, NARA, Washington, D.C.

24. Northwestern Freedmen's Aid Commission, *Minutes of the First Annual Meeting . . . Held in the Second Presbyterian Church in Chicago, on Thursday Evening, April 14th, and on Friday Morning, April 15th, 1864*. With an appendix, containing a list of annual and life electors, and other data (Chicago: James Barnet, 1864), Newberry Library, Chicago.

25. Ladies Contraband Relief Society Testimony to the American Freedmen's Inquiry Commission (AFIC), Dec. 1863, Record Group 94, Microfilm 619, Records of the American Freedmen's Inquiry Commission (hereafter cited as AFIC Records), reel 201, frames 161–83, NARA; Major Lucien Eaton to Major General John Schofield, May 30, 1863, St. Louis, Mo., Department of Missouri, box 9, record group 393, Records of United States Army Continental Commands, 1821–1920 (cited as RG 393), pt. I, entry 2593, NARA; Contraband Relief Society Circular Letter, Feb. 1863, Civil War Collection folder B132, Missouri Historical Society, St. Louis.

26. Harriet Jacobs to Sella Martin, Apr. 13, 1863, Alexandria, Va., in Yellin, ed., *Harriet Jacobs Family Papers*, 2:478.

27. Joanna P. Moore, "Reminiscences," *Baptist Home Mission Monthly* 10 (1888): 291.

28. Joanna Moore, *In Christ's Stead: Autobiographical Sketches* (Chicago: Women's Baptist Home Mission Society, 1902), chap. 4.

29. Moore, *In Christ's Stead*, 22–24.

30. Moore, "Reminiscences," 291.

31. Charlotte Forten, *The Journal of Charlotte L. Forten* (New York: Dryden Press, 1953) 122, 123–28, 133, http://babel.hathitrust.org/cgi/pt?id=uc1.$b92760;view=1up;seq=8.

32. Clara Barton Diary, Apr. 7, 1863, Clara Barton Papers, reel 1, Library of Congress.

33. Clara Barton Diary, May 23, 1863, ibid.; Clara Barton to Brown and Duer, Editors of the *American Baptist*, Mar. 13, 1864, Washington, D.C. (but writing about Hilton Head), Clara Barton Papers, reel 63, Library of Congress, Washington, D.C.; David H. Burton, *Clara Barton: In the Service of Humanity* (Westport, Conn.: Greenwood Press, 1995), chap. 5; Ishbel Ross, *Angel of the Battlefield: The Life of Clara Barton* (New York: Harper & Row, 1956), chap. 5. On Barton and Gage, see Stephen B. Oates, *A Woman of Valor: Clara Barton and the Civil War* (New York: Free Press, 1994), pt. 3.

34. Barton to "My most esteemd & dear friend," July 5, 1864, Point of Rocks, Va., Clara Barton Papers, reel 63, Library of Congress, Washington, D.C.

35. For implementation of the Special Diet Kitchen, see Abigail Dutton to Dear Ones at Home, Nov. 4, 1864, and Nov. 7, 1864, Abigail Dutton Papers, Tennessee State Library and Archives, Nashville, Tenn. In February 1865 Dutton stayed with Superintendent Barnard's young children so that he and his wife could travel to Chattanooga, Huntsville, and Decatur to encourage the adoption of Special Diet Kitchens there. See Dutton to Father, Feb. 21, 1865, in ibid. By that time Dutton herself was reassigned to oversee the Orphan's Home at Nashville, run by the Freedmen's Aid Society (see letter of Feb. 5, 1865, in ibid.).

36. Northwestern Freedmen's Aid Commission, *Second Annual Report* (Chicago, 1865), 14, Newberry Library, Chicago.

37. "The African Methodist Episcopal Church of Cairo," Illinois Writers Project "Negro in Illinois" Collection, box 17, folder 3, Vivian G. Harsh Research Collection, Chicago Public Library, Chicago.

38. Mary Ames, *A New England Woman's Diary in Dixie* (Springfield, Mass., 1906), 25–26, http://docsouth.unc.edu/church/ames/menu.html.

39. Nancy Fraser and Linda Gordon, "A Genealogy of Dependency: Tracing a Keyword of the U.S. Welfare State," *Signs* 19 (Winter 1994): 309–36, esp. 312–15.

40. Observations of a group of five missionaries, including two women (Mrs. Eliza Austin and Mrs. F. M. Thomas) relayed in David Todd letter to brother, John, Apr. 16, 1864, Pine Bluff, Ark., David Todd and Charlotte Farnsworth Letters, Illinois History and Lincoln Collection, Univ. of Illinois. In her *Freedwomen and the Freedmen's Bureau: Race, Gender, and Public Policy in the Age of Emancipation* (New York: Fordham Univ. Press, 2010), Mary Farmer-Kaiser argues that after the war, agents of the Freedmen's Bureau, conditioned by nineteenth-century gender norms, expected a degree of dependency among freedwomen, and therefore freedwomen had recourse to more services in some respects than men did. While such a dynamic may well have held true after the war, during the war itself such gendered tolerance for dependency was suspended, as an "all hands on deck" attitude toward winning the war trumped –if temporarily—insistence on female dependency among white and black alike. It was not that gender did not matter in the war (it did), but rather that the same forces that made it possible for white women to take on roles during the war that ordinarily were off limits to them, precisely because of the demands of war, also made an unaffordable luxury of tolerance for dependence where African American women were concerned. In sum, there was a war to fight, and in zones of active conflict, women as well as men contributed to that war in ways that yielded both benefits and drawbacks. For more on this theme, see Manning, "Working for Citizenship."

41. Palmer Litts to S. S. Jocelyn, Dec. 1, 1862, Craney Island, Va., American Missionary Association Archives H1–4606, Amistad Research Center at Tulane Univ., accessed via Slavery and Anti-Slavery: A Transnational Archive, Gale-cengage; Lucy Chase Testimony, AFIC file 2, RG 94 M619, reel 200, frame 156, NARA; Lucy Chase to home folks, Jan. 26, 1863, entry in letter begun Jan. 20, 1863, in Henry L. Swint, ed., *Dear Ones at Home: Letters from Contraband Camps* (Nashville: Vanderbilt Univ. Press, 1966), 29. Freedwomen also made clothing from bolts of cloth donated by Northern aid societies.

42. For notice of Griffing's establishment of the Freedmen's Intelligence and Employment Agency, see *Freedmen's Record*, May 1865, 80; Ladies Contraband Relief Society Testimony to the AFIC, Dec. 1863, Record Group 94 Microfilm 619, AFIC Records, reel 201, frames 161–83, NARA.

43. Manuscript History concerning the Pension claim of Harriet Tubman, written by Charles Wood, Records of the House of Representatives, 1789–2011, Accompanying Papers of the 55th Congress, RG 233, NARA. See also Kate Clifford Larson, *Bound for the Promised Land: Harriet Tubman, Portrait of an American Hero* (New York: Ballantine Books, 2004), chap. 10.

44. Moore, *In Christ's Stead*, 26–28.

45. Manuscript History concerning the Pension claim of Harriet Tubman, written by Charles Wood, Records of the House of Representatives, 1789–2011, Accompanying Papers of the 55th Congress, RG 233, NARA.

46. Horace James Report to AFIC, Nov. 13, 1863, New Bern, N.C, AFIC Records, box 3, folder 55, p. 11, Houghton Library, Harvard Univ., Cambridge, Mass.; Horace James, *Annual Report of the Superintendent of Negro Affairs in North Carolina, 1864, With An Appendix Containing the History and Management of the Freedmen in this Department to June 1st, 1865* (Boston: W. F. Brown, 1865), 16, 18, 22.

47. Horace James Report to AFIC, Nov. 13, 1863.

48. Captain Horace James, Freedmen's Bureau Superintendent, to Col. J. S. Fullerton, July 10, 1865, New Berne, N.C., Letters Received, ser. 15, Washington Headquarters, RG 105, NARA.

49. Northern schoolteachers report, quoted with James's report in Ira Berlin et al., eds., *Freedom: A Documentary History of Emancipation, 1861–1867,* ser. 1, vol. 2 (New York: Cambridge

Univ. Press, 1993), 235. Among female teachers on Roanoke was Horace James's own cousin, Elizabeth James. See Elizabeth James's account of her time on Roanoke in her letters to George Whipple of the American Missionary Association in American Missionary Association Archives (note 50 below).

50. Elizabeth James to George Whipple, Dec. 19, 1863, Roanoke Island, N.C., American Missionary Association Archives, 1839–1882, 99726, Amistad Research Center at Tulane Univ., accessed via Slavery and Anti-Slavery: A Transnational Archive, Gale-cengage.

51. See Yellin, ed., *Harriet Jacobs Family Papers,* vol. 2, pts. 7 and 8; and the Julia Wilbur letters in the Rochester Ladies' Anti-Slavery Society Papers, 1851–1868, William L. Clements Library, Univ. of Michigan, Ann Arbor, transcr. by Alexandria Archaeology Association.

52. Laura Haviland, *A Woman's Life Work: Labors and Experiences* (Cincinnati: Walden & Stowe, 1882), 252–55.

53. Haviland, *A Woman's Life Work,* 246–47.

54. Lucy Chase to Home Folks, Jan. 26, 1863, entry in letter begun Jan. 20, 1863, in Swint, ed., *Dear Ones at Home,* 29; Lucy Chase Testimony, AFIC, File RG 94 M619, reel 200, frames 152, 158–59, NARA.

55. Elizabeth Hyde Botume, *First Days Amongst the Contrabands* (Boston: Lee and Shepard, 1893), 41–49, 62, 66. Freedpeople referred to refugees who came to Beaufort either singly or as a result of Union raids as "Combees"; see, e.g., ibid., 93.

56. Ames, *New England Woman's Diary in Dixie,* 88–90.

57. Harriet Ware, May 22, 1862, St. Helena, S.C., in Elizabeth Ware Pearson, ed., *Letters from Port Royal: Written at the Time of the Civil War* (Boston: W. B. Clarke, 1906), 52.

58. Harriet Ware, May 13, 1862, St. Helena, S.C., in Pearson, ed., *Letters from Port Royal,* 43.

59. Forten, *Journal,* 133, 146.

60. Laura Towne, Apr. 27, 1862, St. Helena, S.C., in *Letters and Diary of Laura M. Towne: Written from the Sea Islands of South Carolina, 1862–1884,* ed. Rupert Sargent Holland (Cambridge, Mass.: Riverside Press, 1912), 18–19.

61. Laura Towne Testimony, AFIC file 3, RG 94 M619, reel 200, frame 253, NARA.

62. Franklin Sanborn, "Harriet Tubman," *Commonwealth,* July 10, 1863, in Lois E. Horton, ed., *Harriet Tubman and the Fight for Freedom: A Brief History with Documents* (Boston: Bedford/St. Martin's, 2013), 132–33; Manuscript history concerning the Pension claim of Harriet Tubman, written by Charles Wood, Record Group 233, NARA. See also Larson, *Bound for the Promised Land,* chap. 10.

63. Moore, *In Christ's Stead,* 1–2 and 45–75; see esp. "Negro Problem from a Missionary's Standpoint," 252–56.

64. Yearly numbers for 1865 to 1870 compiled from data in *American Missionary, Freedmen's Record,* and *American Freedman* and arranged in app. E of Jones, *Soldiers of Light and Love,* 224. For Northern/Southern comparisons, see Ronald Butchart, *Schooling the Freedpeople: Teaching, Learning, and the Struggle for Black Freedom 1861–1876* (Chapel Hill: Univ. of North Carolina Press, 2010), esp. app. A, 179–80 (tables 2-A and 3-A).

65. See Willie Lee Rose, *Rehearsal for Reconstruction: The Port Royal Experiment* (Athens: Univ. of Georgia Press, 1998).

66. List of Local Affiliates of the Pennsylvania State Equal Rights League, 1865; Business Committee Report, Aug. 9, 1865, Proceedings of the Annual Meeting of the Pennsylvania State Equal Rights League, Held in Harrisburg, Aug. 9 and 10, 1865, Papers and Proceedings of the Pennsylvania State Equal Rights League, Leon Gardiner Collection of American Negro Historical Society Records, reel 1, Historical Society of Pennsylvania, Philadelphia; Pennsylvania State Equal Rights League Memorial to Congress, Feb. 20, 1866, ibid.; Proceedings of the Annual Meeting of the Pennsylvania State Equal Rights League 1866 (and all successive

years), ibid.; William Nesbit and Jacob C. White correspondence (about the Fourteenth Amendment) in 1868, ibid. The emphasis on black men's military service and voting also grows stronger and more exclusive in the proceedings of 1866 and later, in Philip S. Foner and George E. Walker, eds. *Proceedings of the Black National and State Conventions, 1865–1900* (Philadelphia: Temple Univ. Press, 1986). Much of the secondary literature on black citizenship and suffrage in Reconstruction reflects this emphasis on former soldiers and voting rights. See, e.g., Mary Frances Berry, *Military Necessity and Civil Rights Policy: Black Citizenship and the Constitution, 1861–1868* (Port Washington, N.Y.: Kennikat Press, 1977); Christian Samito, *Becoming American Under Fire: Irish Americans, African Americans, and the Politics of Citizenship During the Civil War Era* (Ithaca, N.Y.: Cornell Univ. Press, 2011); and Brian Taylor, "'To Make the Union What It Ought to Be': African Americans, Military Service, and the Drive to Make Black Civil War Service Count" (Ph.D. diss., Georgetown Univ., 2015).

67. See Lori D. Ginzberg, *Elizabeth Cady Stanton: An American Life* (New York: Hill & Wang, 2011).

68. Angelina Grimké, May 14, 1863, quoted in Lerner, *Grimké Sisters from South Carolina*, 263.

Wartime Relief

Needles as Weapons

Southern Women and Civil War Relief

LIBRA HILDE

As sectional tensions erupted in armed conflict, Union and Confederate women translated avid political interest in the war into concrete labor to aid their respective causes. In the South, as Confederate leaders invoked defense of women and female sacrifice to mobilize the population, women capitalized on this symbolic role to shape their practical involvement.[1] Using the language of sacrifice enabled women to move into public discourse and activity. Confederate women organized local soldiers' aid and relief societies and defense societies, and as the casualties mounted, they established hospitals and hospital kitchens, cared for the sick and wounded, and provided emergency relief. Through relief efforts that saved lives and bolstered morale, women became increasingly political, organized, and willing to move beyond the confines of traditionally accepted female behavior. Women's wartime activities paved the way for an increasing engagement in clubs and voluntary associations in the decades after the Civil War.[2] White women appropriated the language of patriotic and dutiful service, framing their labors as an extension of their domestic responsibilities, whereas African American women went to work on behalf of the Union or resisted the Confederacy and did not feel the same need to publicly justify themselves. The war and wartime relief work politicized both groups of Southern women. They labored for opposing causes and emerged from the war with different political goals, and yet their wartime work and experiences led to a new sense of women's capabilities, citizenship, and importance in national life.

The Confederacy never developed an umbrella aid organization along the lines of the United States Sanitary Commission, but because the South lagged behind the Union in industrial capacity, and the fledgling government always struggled to organize effective relief, women's associations were critical to maintaining the war effort. Women's voluntary labor kept troops and hospitals supplied and provided medical care and emergency relief when states and the central government failed to do so in a timely manner. The Confederacy established a comprehensive medical and hospital system later than the Union, and this gap in care created an opening for enterprising civilian women, who established and ran a number of early hospitals. When the government assumed control of private medical institutions at the end of 1862, many women stayed on as hospital matrons, continuing their nursing work in an official capacity. While women on both sides initially engaged in similar relief work, as the war escalated Southern civilian women had greater access to hospitals and to volunteer and casual hospital labor because of their proximity to the fighting.[3]

In 1861 the outbreak of fighting brought white women together in a whirlwind of activity to equip their departing soldiers, supply hospitals, and care for the sick and wounded. The prewar South was more agricultural than the North, limiting the formation of women's associations, but those living in towns and urban areas had considerable experience with antebellum benevolent reform and charity.[4] The war spurred a more overt and independent community organization, as women established Ladies' Aid Societies across the South.[5] Such groups attempted to appeal to a broad cross-section of white society, but middle- to upper-class women were most likely to become involved in wartime relief, serve as officers, and sustain a high level of commitment. These women more often had leisure time due to the presence of domestic slaves in their households, and they benefited from and took credit for the slave labor that augmented their relief efforts.[6] The excitement surrounding mobilization and the trend toward urbanization caused by the war facilitated women's relief work. As the war continued longer than expected, however, the South's dire material and food shortages and waning morale complicated relief efforts. Southern relief efforts declined, though never completely collapsed, for a number of reasons. It was impossible to continue the initial fervor indefinitely, and women simply could not sustain the same level of material production due to a lack of supplies, even when their ideological commitment remained steadfast.

The Confederacy also fractured internally along class lines, with a similar development among the female population. While many elite women, particularly dedicated nurses and hospital matrons, maintained their labors and devotion to the cause, women of all class backgrounds increasingly turned their relief efforts inward. As the war lengthened, poor and yeoman women engaged in political activity designed to alleviate the intense hardships they faced. While not traditional "relief," these women became willing to engage in political behavior meant to achieve a measure of relief for themselves and their own families, including petitioning local and state governments for public assistance and engaging in armed bread riots. Although intimately tied to maternal and domestic concerns and based on their dependent status and sacrifice as "soldiers' wives," poor women's behavior was highly organized and assertive. According to Stephanie McCurry, poor and yeoman women's "mass politics" led to "a complete rewriting of Confederate welfare policy."[7] These women assumed responsibility for protecting their own families, a typically masculine role. In this volume, Jeanie Attie similarly explores how donations declined as Union women, particularly of the working class, became suspicious of state policy and corruption in supply lines.

In addition, from the outset of the war, Southern women displayed an overriding concern with the defense of their homes, their liberty, their soldiers, and themselves.

This is not surprising, given the geography of a war fought mainly on Southern soil, but it also reflected the siege mentality and inherent violence of a slave society. Patriarchal, proslavery ideology stressed women's dependence on white male authority and the need to protect female purity from black men, and secessionists fanned these fears of rape in the drive toward disunion.[8] Southern white women had been raised in a culture of paranoia, and faced with an imminent threat to their homes and institutions and a perceived threat to their very bodies, they reacted in ways that pushed the boundaries of the female sphere into masculine affairs. As a result, Southern white women's wartime efforts usually focused on relief and defense rather than reform or change. Elite women had conservative and preservationist political goals that aligned with those of planter men. However, war has a tendency to lead to unexpected outcomes, and planter and poor women engaged in relief efforts and political behavior that challenged traditional Southern gender roles, even as their reasons for doing so and their goals increasingly diverged.[9] In their focus on maintaining the status quo, Southerners unwittingly hastened the demise of the Old South.

The gravity of war gave women a sense of ownership over their soldiers, their homes, and matters related to the cause that affected their lives and the lives of their loved ones. When facing issues of life and death, Southern women seemed unwilling to place their trust entirely in men and male institutions, and thus the war ushered in a more aggressive and public form of patriotic domesticity under the guise of feminine sacrifice. Early in the war, Susan Smith, determined to contribute to the cause, started nursing as a volunteer at the female-run Southern Mothers' Hospital, in Memphis, Tennessee. She learned to handle "scenes of distress" without "flinching," aid the physicians during amputations, and comfort the dying, the special province of women. "I would become so fatigued that I could scarcely walk; yet duty urged me forward, and kept me moving," she recalled. "Sleep was almost a stranger to me for weeks at a time." After the Battle of Shiloh in April of 1862, armed with her volunteer training and worried about her Confederate soldier son, Smith hurried to the makeshift hospitals around Corinth, Mississippi. She found him wounded, hungry, and prepared to die. "Many were in a like condition, and doubtless perished upon that spot," she wrote. "This . . . would have been my son's case, if I had not come to his relief." According to Smith, men who received personal attention during the evacuation of the wounded had a higher chance of survival, and she took credit for saving her son's life.[10] In the antebellum South, men had protected weak and defenseless women. During the war, in aid and defense societies and in hospital work, women actively protected themselves, their homes, and their suffering men.[11] This subtle shift in gender behavior, though couched in traditional terms as an extension of women's domestic talents, carried over into the postwar period.

For the most part, love of country shielded women from criticism as they became increasingly public participants in the unfolding wartime drama.[12] When men framed the revolution as being driven by and about defending women, they provided women with a convenient platform from which to expand their political involvement. South Carolinian George Anderson Mercer believed the work and support of women motivated men to fight: "They make the soldier's uniform and accouterments, they inspire him with courage and chivalry, they give him the flag he would rather die than disgrace, they pray for him in the field, shelter and nurse him when sick, surround him with comforts and kindness when he lies wounded and dying." Mercer credited women with inciting the struggle, stating, "Our dear, noble ladies who pioneered this revolution are bravely supporting it."[13] Texas governor Francis Lubbock agreed. "The noble women, too, of our country are ever in advance of the men. They are imbued with the conviction that submission would leave them the slaves of most miserable and cowardly taskmasters," he declared. "Hence they are prepared to make every sacrifice on the altar of freedom." Women manufactured supplies, nursed the sick and wounded, and offered up "their fathers, husbands, brothers, sons, and lovers, preferring to be orphaned, widowed, and brotherless to seeing their country overrun and reduced by a people as demoralized, infidel, and barbarous as our Northern foes." By defining the enemy as irreligious and morally depraved, Southerners elevated the significance of women, who had long been associated with religious piety.[14]

Even the most basic supply activity, such as knitting socks for soldiers, had political implications and meaning for women. "Our needles are now our weapons," proclaimed Lucy Wood of Charlottesville, Virginia.[15] Diaries, letters, and memoirs attest to the ubiquity of women's aid work, particularly sewing and knitting, as relief associations proliferated across the Confederacy in the early days of the war. "I do not know when I have seen a woman without knitting in her hand," Mary Boykin Chesnut observed, and another added, "Even at evening parties the knitting needle was a regular attendant."[16] Early in the war, those living on plantations channeled slave labor into relief efforts. Susan Eppes noted that her mother had sent all of their linen sheets to Richmond's Reid Hospital and slave women were carding wool for replacements. Her father taught another slave to make salve for wounded soldiers, which they shipped weekly.[17]

Ladies' Aid Societies raised funds through direct appeals for donations, dues, and raffles and by organizing fairs and bazaars and staging entertainments. Women used newspapers and personal correspondence to stimulate group efforts and disseminate information.[18] Southerners recognized the material and psychological importance of women's labors. "Our Southern women are doing everything: their 'Soldiers Aid Societies' are hardly less important than our armies," George Mercer noted. "I read the address of one of these Societies in the Charleston Courier, and tears came to my eyes: how noble and holy its sentiments: who would not fight bravely to defend the honor and happiness of such women!"[19] Women not only inspired men's martial spirit, they made up for the deficiencies of the young state. Emma Holmes highlighted the appeal Rev. R. W. Barnwell made to the women of Charleston to engage in hospital work. "WITHOUT YOU, THIS WAR COULD NOT HAVE BEEN CARRIED ON, FOR THE GOVERNMENT WAS NOT PREPARED TO MEET ALL THAT WAS THROWN UPON IT," he insisted.[20] A newspaper editor in South Carolina, commenting on the work of the ladies' gunboat society, wrote, "This spirited action of our women has roused the Governments, State and Confederate, from their torpor, to the construction of these two noble iron-clad steamers."[21]

Libra Hilde

The elite women of the community typically served as officers of relief and defense societies, but any woman could join, and in some cases those unable to afford a monetary contribution provided labor in lieu of dues.[22] In addition, some aid societies provided a form of local welfare. According to Kate Cumming, the ladies of Mobile, Alabama, "formed themselves into a body, called the 'Military Aid Society,' for the benefit, not only of the soldiers but their families. They have clothes made for the soldiers, and their families, who need employment, make them. In that way the war has not been felt as much by them as it would otherwise have been."[23]

Aid and hospital societies functioned with remarkable similarity across the South. As soon as the war began, women gathered to form a society, electing officers and often adopting a constitution. In some cases, they formed more than one society, with different functions and overlapping membership.[24] They met regularly, monthly or even weekly, and they often shifted their focus as the war continued, responding to changing conditions. The homes of the most active officers and members became focal points of activity. One daughter recalled that "my mother was the Treasurer and Secretary of our Aid Society; therefore, our home was the depot for the supplies sent through that channel."[25] Early in the war, before shortages plagued the South, aid societies purchased large quantities of cloth that managers distributed to members to sew into garments and bedding for soldiers in camp and hospital. One young woman claimed her society "made as many as one thousand pieces in three weeks."[26] While there was no national organization coordinating aid, women did cooperate on a local level. Aid groups in smaller South Carolina towns, for instance, sent their boxes of supplies to aid societies in Charleston or Columbia, which then forwarded them to the front as needed or directed.[27]

Ladies' gunboat societies started in coastal areas vulnerable to Union naval attack and spread inland, as women in New Orleans, Richmond, Charleston, and Mobile inspired those in landlocked areas to raise money for building ironclad gunboats in the defense of Confederate waters. Like relief efforts aimed at equipping the troops or supplying hospitals, women displayed an ability to organize their communities and extend those appeals outward to rural social networks. Gunboat and defense societies collected significant sums of money from men and women by reminding their compatriots of the need for patriotic sacrifice, in this case, in the name of self-preservation. Gunboat societies invoked domesticity in the call to defend home and hearth, but they also pushed women's involvement into military matters typically the exclusive arena of men.[28] Ladies' aid, hospital, and defense efforts often overlapped. For example, Maria Clopton established a private hospital in Richmond and later served as a head matron at Winder Hospital as well as acting as president of the Ladies' Defense Association of Richmond.[29]

Officers used newspapers to advertise for donations and labor and attract new members by exerting a form of nationalistic peer pressure. The "patriotic ladies of Georgia" spread word of their defense fund with the help of the *Daily Columbus Enquirer*. The women "proposed to name the Gunboat 'Bartow'—a name synonymous with chivalry and daring. Should it be her fortune to 'illustrate Georgia' as gloriously upon the water as her gallant prototype did upon land, what Lady will not rejoice that she 'took stock' in the enterprise."[30] Just as men did not want to incur the shame of shirking duty or miss the adventure of military service, the editor made a romantic and class-based appeal to women to invest in their own protection for fear of being excluded from communal glory. Women responded to such published appeals and added their own. "Having observed a few days since in the *Courier* that the ladies of New Orleans had given an order for a gunboat, and also the idea suggested to the ladies of Charleston to emulate their example, I immediately concluded to send you my mite to assist in the good cause," Sue B. Geyber of South Carolina wrote. She contributed a small sum and suggested that "if every true woman in our beloved State" did the same, "we would soon be enabled to give an order for more than one gunboat."[31] Mary Chesnut believed the exigencies of war had altered women's priorities. She donated "a string of pearls to be raffled for at the Gunboat Fair. Mary Witherspoon has sent a silver tea-pot. We do not spare our precious things now. Our silver and gold, what are they?—when we give up to war our beloved."[32]

Women justified this militant endeavor by framing it as defensive and invoking the political language of slavery and potential violation that framed the Confederate experiment. For women long steeped in fears of slave revolt and the need to uphold the social and racial hierarchy and now faced with the supposed threat of rape, extreme times demanded extreme measures. The Ladies' Defense Association of Richmond called upon women to donate their valuable decorative objects to raise money to build an ironclad. "That the work and contributions may be more peculiarly ours as women, we will give such ornaments of gold, and articles of silver, as are our personal property," the society declared in its minutes. "For should it be our sad fate to become slaves, ornaments would ill become our state of bondage; while if God in his infinite mercy shall crown our efforts with success, we will be content to wear the laurel leaves of victory."[33] When discussing the Union foe, these elite women adopted the same political references to slavery employed by Southern men. They also declared their intention to relinquish their markers of gender and class to ensure their own defense and the preservation of their society, and they fully expected to share the rewards of any future victory. Ladies' gunboat societies are thus an excellent example of how the Confederate political experiment had unintended consequences, as women became increasingly assertive, political actors with shifting expectations of their future place in the nation. As men praised women's endeavors, they contributed to these shifting expectations. Newspaper editors lauded donations and endorsed the tangible results of women's organizing and labor as essential to national security. "To your patriotic and noble efforts, Ladies of Georgia, is the port of the city of Savannah indebted for this powerful engine for its defence [sic] against the hateful foes," the *Yorkville Enquirer* declared. "Could it have been completed before the capture of Port Pulaski, the loss of that fortress would not have occurred."[34]

In addition to raising funds to build an ironclad, the ladies of Georgia hoped to collect the materials to manufacture a cannon. "The ladies of this City and vicinity propose, with your aid, to have one or more small brass cannon cast, for the defence [sic]—if

Libra Hilde

needed—of our homes. . . . We ask you to send in, for this purpose, all the articles of brass and copper which you can spare, to help to make a sufficient amount."[35] Women manufactured needed goods such as bandages for hospitals, but they also made items intended for military use, including "cartridge bags & sand bags for batteries."[36] In a culture that associated women with religious piety and had long used Biblical scripture to bolster white authority and justify the physical punishment of slaves, the blending of feminine and martial elements did not seem incongruous. George Mercer defined the war as a "contest between faith and infidelity. . . ." He saw nothing untoward about women handling the instruments of death. In his mind, female patriotic zeal made the Confederacy morally and militarily stronger. "Only this morning I was in our drill room assisting a number of ladies to make cartridges: among them were my sweetheart, my sister and six cousins," he recorded in his diary. "There they were patiently cleaning the greased balls, filling the paper caps with powder and tieing up the missiles of death. While such a spirit animates our women can the northern mobocrats subdue us?[37] As Jeanie Attie notes in this volume, Northerners stressed women's "disinterestedness" and apolitical voluntarism, whereas Southerners considered women's partisan wartime engagement a source of national strength.

Because white Southerners hoped the new nation would embody their vision of the founding ideals, including religious faith, women's piety imbued them with symbolic power in the political enterprise of independence. According to visiting Englishman William Russell Howard, "all the ladies in Mobile belong to the 'Yankee Emancipation Society.' They spend their days sewing cartridges, carding lint, preparing bandages, and I'm not quite sure they don't fill shells and fuses as well. Their zeal and energy will go far to sustain the South in the forthcoming struggle, and nowhere is the influence of women greater than in America." Surely the "ladies of Mobile" were being ironic with the title of their society—or Howard was.[38]

In response to secession and war, women engaged in a range of nation-building activities, including sewing flags, writing poetry and songs, and equipping departing troops, forms of symbolic and ancillary support. Once the troops left, women continued to collect donations and manufacture supplies, shipping boxes to camps and hospitals. Feeding and caring for the sick and wounded, however, required a heightened level of community organization and direct contact with the repercussions of war. When sick and wounded men passed through towns and villages on their way to and from the front, many aid societies became hospital associations, establishing wayside hospitals to accommodate traveling soldiers or kitchens to feed the sick and wounded in local institutions.[39] In these endeavors, women distributed tasks and shared the labor, with rotating daily or weekly committees appointed to pack and send boxes, visit local hospitals, staff the kitchen or wayside hospital, or provide meals from home kitchens. Women spearheaded local hospital organization and served as the administrative force, with men following their lead. In the summer of 1861, the Ladies' Aid Society of Montgomery, Alabama, until then a sewing society, decided to establish a hospital, calling on local physicians to provide medical expertise. The physicians then met, created a corollary society, resolved to appoint a weekly visiting committee, and formed another committee to "confer" with the women "in regard to such other arrangements as they may propose." The Confederate government frequently assumed partial control of community and wayside hospitals established in high traffic areas, with local women continuing to provide extra nursing care and food. Other wayside hospitals remained private institutions throughout the entirety of the war.[40]

Southern women also provided emergency relief when the government struggled to respond effectively to medical crises. After the Battle of Chickamauga in September of 1863, for instance, women in Georgia mobilized to aid the wounded amid disorder and shortages. Samuel Stout, the medical director for the Army of Tennessee, believed that such relief groups prevented many men from dying of hunger following the battle. On another occasion, when an army hospital burned down, civilians "came in from miles in the country, and took the patients to their houses."[41] Throughout the war, thousands of civilian women visited train depots and hospitals individually, rather than as members of hospital associations, and nursed sick and wounded men in private homes. Civilian women provided significant resources and labor to the Confederate medical system as they extended their domestic skills beyond the realm of the household and in support of the nation. They understood and took pride in the vital contribution they made. The women of Greenville, South Carolina, referred to their wayside hospital as a "necessity."[42]

In September 1862, nearly a year and a half after the conflict began, the Confederate government established a comprehensive medical system. In the interim, state governments and citizens responded to the ongoing medical crisis of camp and campaign, establishing state-sponsored and private hospitals. This lag in centralized oversight created an opportunity for charismatic women to establish positions of authority and deploy their formidable administrative skills. Juliet Opie Hopkins traveled from her home in Mobile, Alabama, to Virginia in June of 1861 to offer aid to Alabama soldiers. The governor of Alabama, responding to citizens who urged state action on behalf of the sick and wounded, appointed her husband, Judge Arthur Hopkins, as the state agent in charge of hospital funds. Judge Hopkins turned the money over to his wife, who founded the Alabama Hospitals in Richmond, set up several field hospitals in Virginia towns, and coordinated the distribution of donations from Alabama to the various hospitals housing Alabama men. Juliet Hopkins used a combination of personal funds, state appropriations, and charitable donations to run the Alabama hospitals in Richmond until the fall of 1863.[43] She also became a visible symbol of relief work and a target of requests from surgeons in the field and women on the home front. After reading of Hopkins's efforts on behalf of the sick and wounded in the papers, Sally B. Manning wrote to ask for directions as to what was most needed and how it should be prepared. "It would be giving me so much pleasure to be able to work in this way for our soldiers, where I cannot give them assistance personally," she noted. Surgeon C. J. Clark of the 10th Alabama thanked Hopkins for supplies she forwarded to his field hospital. Knowing that she drew on a reservoir of donations sent by individuals and aid societies, he referred to Hopkins as the "representative of a noble set of women," praised the "importance of the actions of our heroic and devoted countrywomen," and insisted her intervention would "lessen the mortality among our troops." Several Alabama surgeons, unable to procure needed supplies through military channels, relied on Juliet Hopkins as they endeavored to care for their troops.[44]

As the wounded poured into Richmond in 1861 and the government struggled to organize an effective response, women in Richmond stepped in to address the medical crisis. Sally Tompkins, Lucy Webb, Caroline Mayo, and Maria Clopton all established private hospitals. Because civilian women felt more comfortable visiting such hospitals and bringing delicacies, female-run institutions had higher numbers of caregivers and better food. Many women who later served as matrons, such as Fannie Beers, started nursing as volunteers in such hospitals.[45] When the government assumed control of the hospital system, closing smaller institutions and taking over state hospitals, legislators took note of the low mortality rates at several Richmond hospitals founded and run by women. The report of a committee investigating medical care claimed women made better nurses than men and "when men have charge, the mortality averages ten percent; where females manage, it is only five percent." An act passed on September 27, 1862, "to better provide for the sick and wounded of the Army in hospitals," called for the hiring of matrons to supervise kitchens and linen departments. Matrons' official duties stressed supervision and management of departments that corresponded to typically domestic concerns. Their unofficial duties encompassed direct patient care.[46]

While nursing was part of women's antebellum domestic responsibility to kin and neighbors, caring for strange men in hospitals challenged notions of female respectability. Concerns over propriety limited the number of elite white women willing to engage in official hospital labor, yet many women also felt pressure to contribute meaningfully to the cause. The war generated tangible and distressing medical needs that compelled many women to act. They also firmly believed that women's pious, compassionate natures made them inherently more capable than men of soothing pain and distress. "In the sick room was the place where the ladies were most needed," matron Susan Smith declared, "and where they could accomplish the most good."[47] Women who nursed unofficially, or took positions as matrons, justified their work as a patriotic calling for which they were specially suited, as well as a form of reciprocity. Soldiers fought to defend women, home, and country, and women had a duty to mend and thus protect sick and wounded men. Alabaman Kate Cumming, who started nursing as a part of a volunteer effort in Corinth, Mississippi, following the Battle of Shiloh, and then sought and obtained an official position as a matron in one of the mobile hospitals established by Samuel Stout, medical director for the Army of Tennessee, defined nursing as women's particular duty to the cause. "I can not see what else we can do," she noted, "as the war is certainly ours as well as that of the men. We can not fight, so we must take care of those who do." In addition, women hoped that if their own male relatives fell ill or wounded far from home, they would receive tender care from another woman. The thousands of women who nursed Southern soldiers applied a maternal role to a novel setting and in defense of their political goals.[48] Southerners increasingly perceived nurses as the female equivalent of soldiers. "I had nothing to do but stand with those to whom I had pledged my fidelity," Susan Smith noted, "so long as they offered up their lives upon the altar of their country, and I contemplated myself, or my position, as being one of them, and subject to whatever suffering or hardship that they were."[49]

Regardless of the comparisons to women's traditional duties, hospital nursing presented novel challenges, exposing women to graphic sights and sounds, suffering, and constant death. They improved hospital care by overseeing kitchens and often personally preparing food sick and wounded men could actually eat and soliciting donations from aid groups at home and surrounding communities to better supply their patients. They provided individualized care, sitting by men's bedsides and alleviating their sense of loneliness and fear. Nurses wrote letters for patients unable to do so and thereby served as a vital link between front and home front. Matrons and nurses considered attending to dying patients one of their most important duties, as they endeavored to uphold nineteenth-century standards and rituals of a good Christian death, guiding men to a satisfactory relationship with God and counseling families at home in their death notices. Amidst the physical and emotional stress of their work, women derived satisfaction from the gratitude of their patients and felt that they made a significant contribution to the cause. The positive reactions of her patients at the hospital started and run by the South Carolina Hospital Aid Association in Charlottesville, Virginia, made ward nurse Ada Bacot feel that she was "of some use to my country." "No happiness which any thing earthly could give could compare with the pleasure I have experienced in receiving the blessings of the suffering and dying," Kate Cumming declared. After briefly visiting her wounded son, Susan Smith returned to Tunnel Hill, Georgia, because she felt it was "my duty to return to my post, for well did I know that I was needed."[50]

The Southern press reinforced a vision of nurses as "ministering angels," publishing laudatory articles about women's contributions to the cause.[51] Commanders offered public testimonials to women's supply and nursing efforts through letters to the editor.[52] Such public gratitude for women's work raising supplies and caring for the sick and wounded helped to legitimize hospital labor. Generic articles praised group efforts, but editors and correspondents also singled out particularly dedicated nurses by name. One editor praised the "self-sacrificing" efforts of Hattie Foster of Florence, Alabama, who for several months tended to the wounded from Shiloh in Corinth, Mississippi. "Let the land re echo with the praises of this noble pattern of Southern woman," the author stated.[53] While such paeans emphasized traditional feminine qualities, they also equated male and female patriotism. An article about the nursing work of Felicia Grundy Porter in the hospitals of Knoxville and Nashville, Tennessee, in 1861 declared: "The war in which we are now engaged has done more than to develop the gallantry and self-sacrificing patriotism of the sons of the South. It has illustrated to an eminent degree, the noble qualities, and the generous devotion of the daughters of our sunny clime, to the cause of our common country."[54] An article detailing the labors of Mrs. Elizabeth Norris emphasized her "heroism and devotion," combining typically masculine and feminine qualities.

Norris, the author claimed, left her Stewart County, Tennessee, home to nurse sick men of the 14th Tennessee Regiment camped in West Virginia. "She made her way there, unattended by anyone, walking every foot of the seventy-five miles of hilly and mountainous land-travel. . . . All honor to her name!" The author celebrated her fortitude and never chastised her for traveling without a chaperone.[55]

Whereas elite white women's relief work earned high praise, the press ignored the slave labor in these women's households that made this voluntary work possible. Even as enslaved women refused to work for their mistresses and ran away, something explored by Rebecca Capobianco in this volume, unfree labor continued to undergird relief efforts. Slaves ran households and prepared the material goods and delicacies their mistresses donated to camps and hospitals. Former slave Nellie Hill blamed her mother's wartime death on the additional burdens created by the mistresses' wartime relief efforts on behalf of soldiers stationed nearby. "Mis Betsy she always sendin' stuff to de camp, an' mamma work so hard cookin' up stuff, it kill her," Hill recalled.[56]

Confederate military hospitals became battlegrounds over enslaved women's labor. Hospitals generally used convalescent soldiers as labor, but white manpower shortages in the Confederacy meant that slave labor necessarily powered Confederate hospitals.[57] Head surgeons employed male and female slaves as laundresses, cooks, nurses, and attendants; and many surgeons and matrons brought their own slaves with them into hospitals as personal attendants and aides. When Ada Bacot traveled from South Carolina to Charlottesville, Virginia, to work as a volunteer ward nurse, she took with her a female slave, Savary. Savary found herself in the middle of a struggle between Bacot and another enslaved woman employed at the boarding house where the white volunteers lived, a cook called "Old Willie." Bacot, acting more like a mistress than a nurse, slapped Willie's son, William, for failing to clear the dinner table and being "impertinent." William reported the incident to his mother, whom, Bacot recalled, reacted "like a lioness," insisting that "no one should tutch either her or William." The doctors whipped William and then Old Willie because she tried to protect her son. When Old Willie fought back, the doctors had her taken to jail to await the arrival of her owner. Old Willie's resistance illustrates Capobianco's argument about how, during the war, enslaved women attempted to negotiate the terms of their servitude. Bacot saw it another way, regretting the need to sacrifice Savary's presence in the hospital to serve in Willie's place. "It will inconvenience me very much," she noted, "but I feel in some way bound to do what I can to lessen the expence [sic] of getting another cook."[58] Bacot did not think to record Savary's thoughts about the doctors' and nurses' treatment of Old Willie.

In any case, Savary soon made her own sentiments clear. According to Bacot, Savary began "giving me trouble," and she worried she would have to sell her.[59] Like Old Willie, Savary may have resented her treatment at the hands of white doctors and nurses or she may have simply wanted to return to her family, from whom she had been separated by Bacot's decision to volunteer as a nurse. Alternately, Savary may also have seen the move to Virginia as an opportunity to exert agency and redefine her working conditions and relationship with her mistress. Few former slaves commented on hospital labor itself. Ella Belle Ramsey was an exception. Ramsey disliked accompanying her mistress to a soldier's hospital in Atlanta. "I always hate to go dere. . . . de men was always screaming an' groaning an' . . . it stuck in my ears," Ramsey remembered. "I could hear 'em all night when I wen' dere in de day time." Many white women felt ashamed when they discovered in themselves a similar aversion to hospitals. Some quit and some, motivated by a sense of duty and desire to contribute to the cause, persevered. Ella Ramsey had little choice in the matter.[60]

Matrons found it frustrating to train convalescent soldiers as cooks, nurses, and attendants only to lose them to field duty, yet they still preferred white labor, claiming soldiers required less oversight. When the cooks at Newsom Hospital were "all negroes" rather than detailed soldiers, Kate Cumming's workload increased because "they have to be told the same thing every day, and watched to see if they do it then."[61] Cumming expressed attitudes typical of Southern white women, assuming the incompetence of slaves unless properly supervised and complaining, in their memoirs, about the extra effort involved in such oversight—even as they depended on their labor. Worried that their owners would remove the slaves working at Richmond's Chimborazo Hospital to the interior, in 1862 head surgeon James B. McCaw asked the Surgeon General to use impressment to militarily commandeer his laborers, "as it will be utterly impossible to continue the Hospitals without them."[62] The authorities also employed threats to compel labor from the free black population. In May of 1862 the Richmond Whig called for a hundred free black men to apply as nurses at Winder Hospital. "If the parties go willingly, good wages will be paid and kind treatment afforded them," the paper announced. "If they do not volunteer they will be impressed, and run the risk of receiving such treatment and pay as is generally awarded under such circumstances."[63] Confederate hospital administrators had to rely on laborers whom they never trusted yet on whom they were nonetheless dependent.[64]

Free and unfree black hospital workers resisted authority, abandoned their posts when the opportunity arose, and showed little allegiance to the Confederacy. Kate Cumming grumbled that hired free blacks "give no little trouble." When Richmond fell to the Union, Chimborazo Hospital matron Phoebe Pember lost her soldier nurses to Robert E. Lee's retreating army and lamented that the black cooks "deserted me."[65] As slaves fled bondage and coerced wartime employment, hospital matrons, like slaveholders throughout the South, felt betrayed by slaves whom they believed were "loyal." Despite the reliance on slaves and free blacks to keep hospitals running, racial prejudice prevented white Southerners from fully utilizing black labor in positions of authority or skill. Administrators relegated black women to menial tasks, especially sewing and laundry, despite their extensive prewar experience with nursing.[66] Susan Smith and Phoebe Pember noted that male slaves, even when referred to as nurses, mainly performed heavy hospital labor, including cleaning the wards and hauling fuel and water, whereas soldiers and white nurses were involved in patient care.[67]

Union hospitals and ambulance trains located in occupied areas also exploited black labor, as Northern authorities commandeered Confederate property. "Tonight a hospital was made of an old secesh house & a darky . . . was used to get supper for the poor fellows in the ambulances," Union nurse Samuel C. Hunt, of the 45th Massachusetts Infantry wrote. On another night in the field he brandished a gun and set the slaves to "killing poultry" to feed the wounded men who would arrive behind him. "We have a couple of darkies who make a deal of sport," he told his father when settled and serving as a ward master in a hospital in New Berne, North Carolina, "beside doing the dirty work in the morning before I get up Major builds a big fire, & Warren blacks my boots." Though they clearly lightened his workload and provided critical medical support, Hunt treated these men with contempt.[68] As in the South, Northern white racism limited the use of and potential productivity of African Americans as nurses, and condescending white attitudes limited recognition of the substantial aid they provided in hospitals. Southern black women sometimes earned praise, however, as personal nurses. Maj. Oscar Jackson, 63rd Ohio, attributed his recovery from a wound at the Battle of Shiloh to the assiduous attention and cooking of "my colored woman, Jane," who nursed him "with as much care as if I had been a brother." "Determined she should have a good home for her kindness," Jackson brought Jane north when he was able to travel. Jane was likely bound for the household of the 63rd's Col. John W. Sprague, where Jackson said he left the woman. The grateful veteran did not record whether, when she arrived in Ohio, Jane was alone or accompanied by family members or whether the nurse had consented to the move. Gen. Philip Sheridan lent his cook, a "faithful old colored woman" and "expert nurse" to a member of his staff sick with yellow fever during the Shenandoah Valley campaign in the fall of 1864. In response, Capt. Lemuel Abbot, of the 10th Vermont, declared that Sheridan had been "instrumental in saving his life," indirectly honoring the care of Sheridan's black servant.[69] In all of these examples, Union soldiers acknowledged the critical nursing work of black women even as they employed the same paternalistic and possessive language used by slaveholders.

Many Southern slaves who escaped to Union lines worked in Union hospitals, motivated by the desire to provide for themselves and their families, support the Union war effort, and destroy the institution of slavery.[70] Generally relegated to menial positions, African American cooks and laundresses received low pay if compensated at all; more often black hospital workers received rations only. Despite their precarious position, black men and women embraced and furthered the Union cause as their own. Escaped slave Lydia Penny made her way into Union lines near Memphis, Tennessee, met and married a black soldier from Pennsylvania, Thomas Penny, and volunteered as a regimental nurse when he reenlisted in the 5th U.S. Colored Troops in Ohio. According to a letter from another black soldier, QM Sgt. James H. Payne, of the 27th U.S. Colored Troops, Penny "said that she felt it to be her duty to go along with her husband, not merely on account of the love she had for him, but also the love which she had for her country—that the cause which nerved the soldiers to pour out their life-blood was her cause, and that of her race." Nursing enabled Penny to aid the Union and the cause of emancipation, and she told Payne that she would "not think of leaving the field until the last gun is fired and peace is declared, and every slave is freed from captivity."[71] Shortly after the fall of Fort Pulaski in April 1862, teenager Susie King Taylor escaped from Savannah, Georgia, with her uncle and his family. Taylor, who had been clandestinely educated as a child, taught in a school for freed people on St. Simon's Island until August, when her new husband, Edward King, also a literate former slave, joined the Union army.[72] The commander of the 1st South Carolina Volunteers, or 33rd U.S. Colored Troops, Col. Thomas Wentworth Higginson, enlisted Taylor as a company laundress. "I gave my services willingly for four years and three months without receiving a dollar," she recalled. "I was glad, however, to be allowed to go with the regiment to care for the sick and afflicted." When the men of other companies asked her why she treated them so well, she answered: "You are all doing the same duty, and I will do just the same for you."[73] Though officially a laundress, Taylor's varied duties mirrored those of white regimental nurses. Early on she offered reading and writing lessons to off-duty soldiers and nursed the sick in camp, and later she accompanied the men on expeditions; cleaned, tested, and loaded weapons; helped the soldiers pack and prepare for battle; and cared for the wounded.[74] At the end of her memoir, Taylor praised the unsung efforts of "hundreds" of Southern black women who aided the Union cause, taking significant risks to help hide and aid in the escape of Union soldiers and feeding prisoners.[75]

Like Penny and Taylor, some Southern white women aided the Union cause through hospital labor. Fannie Oslin Jackson was drawn into nursing in 1864 when Union officials seized her home near Resaca, Georgia, as a field hospital. "I had always liked nursing the sick but this was a new experience," wrote Jackson, who offered her assistance. "I found plenty to do to keep mind and hands employed." Surprised by her help, three grateful Union surgeons of the 12th Illinois gave her letters commending her abilities as a nurse. The Union troops, part of Sherman's Atlanta campaign, soon withdrew, leaving her crops destroyed and taking with them the army provisions that Jackson had been using to feed her three children. Faced with mounting concerns over survival, Jackson admitted, "If it were not for my children I would rather die."[76] Unable to rely on her husband, a Confederate soldier whom she feared dead, Jackson made a pragmatic and independent decision. She left her son with a neighbor, journeyed to a nearby Union hospital, applied for, and received a nursing position with the help of her recommendation letters. Her two daughters joined her at the hospital. As a young wife with a young family, Jackson had "vowed to God many times that if we could all be spared as a family and reunited, I would never murmur."[77]

In late September of 1864 Jackson located her husband, a prisoner in Atlanta, and Union surgeons and post officers secured his release from the Confederate army, arranged for him to come through the lines and take the oath of allegiance, and found him government work making coffins. Husband and wife boarded at the hospital, and her income helped support the family through the war. After the conflict ended, Jackson and her husband reunited with their son, decided living in the war-torn South would be "unpleasant," and moved to the North. Their home had been destroyed, and as Jackson stated, "We do not feel as if we have the courage to begin life there again and then our children so much need to be in school." During the war, Unionists often faced violence from their neighbors, and Jackson's family may well have understood that their switched allegiance could lead to postwar social ostracism, or worse.[78]

As the war imposed hardship on poor and yeoman women, they prioritized the survival of their families over loyalty to the Confederacy. Relocating within Union lines offered food and stability. While Jackson's late and perhaps practical Unionism differed in some critical ways from the approach of poor and yeoman women who petitioned state officials for aid based on their loyalty to the Confederate cause, her actions paralleled those of women who encouraged their men to desert. Jackson assumed control of her family's destiny, and she did so by making a decision that was at once highly political and yet based on domestic concerns.

The deteriorating material situation in the South during the war caused many white women "to look after the welfare of home matters," and civilian relief efforts suffered. "This little hospital was kept up until poverty closed its door, for we had not so much as a pot of cowpeas to send down," one such woman noted.[79] Yet even amid failing fortunes, white women retained the community organizing skills and confidence they developed in the course of their wartime relief. When Confederate forces evacuated Charleston on February 18, 1865, they deliberately set fire to the CSS *Palmetto State,* the ironclad warship financed by the ladies of South Carolina in order to prevent its capture by advancing and occupying Union forces. Women's double sense of loss at that moment highlighted their shifting definition of female citizenship. "Women who had worked and striven and contributed to its building stood at their windows and viewed the flames from the burning boat color the sky, and lo! as the last detonation sounded, the smoke arose and, upon the red glare of the heavens, formed a palmetto tree, perfect and fair, that stood out against the sky, then wavered and broke apart as we watched it through our tears, then crumbled into wreck and ruin and was lost in the darkness and gloom!"[80] The explosion figuratively represented the condition of the state of South Carolina. The struggle, and the loss, belonged to women as much as it did to men.

In the postwar period, middle- and upper-class white women redirected their efforts into memorial work. When the war ended, aid societies that had become hospital societies transferred their work yet again. Many did not disband, becoming ladies' memorial associations, and members turned their energy to marking graves, erecting monuments, and promulgating and protecting a distinctly Southern white memory of the war. As Caroline Janney has argued, under the cloak of mourning white women engaged in highly political work, playing a significant role in redeeming Southern politics and reconstructing the racial hierarchy.[81] White women, and particularly former aid and hospital workers, were critical agents in the postwar creation and dissemination of Lost Cause memory and thus the maintenance of white supremacy.[82] Hospital matrons, many of whom remained at their posts until the bitter end, were particularly active agents in the preservation of Confederate identity and honor. They were accustomed to dealing with vulnerable men, and the humiliation of military defeat left men in need of continued attention. Matron Kate Cumming called on women to aid in rebuilding the South and to take up the "important work" and "sacred duty" of veterans' care, helping "thousands of men almost as helpless as they were in infancy." According to Fannie Beers, former matron of Buckner Hospital, women emerged from the war stronger, emotionally steeled, and ready to lift their defeated men up "from the apathy of despair."[83] During the war, matrons and nurses had cared for sick and wounded soldiers, and they intended to continue to care for their suffering, defunct nation. Former matrons used their published memoirs to vindicate the Confederacy. "We will never cease to worship, next to Divinity, the banner of the Confederate States," matron Susan Smith proclaimed, as she counseled Southerners to renew their religious faith and await God's "retribution."[84] Despite the omnipresent pain and death they had witnessed, dedicated hospital workers remained staunch Confederates, emboldened by their own pivotal wartime contributions and a communal bond with their patients.

Middle- and upper-class women active in wartime relief developed a new sense of women's capabilities and influence. In their eyes, women were no longer weak and completely dependent but were instead central to fomenting and maintaining the war effort and safeguarding the Confederate legacy. "Not once did they spare themselves, or complain, or evince weakness, or give way to despair," Sara Pryor said of Richmond's female volunteers. Fannie Beers defined women as "the power behind the throne," and according to Phoebe Pember, Southern women "incited the men to struggle in support of their views and . . . sustained them nobly to the end. They were the first to rebel—the last to succumb."[85]

Due to elite white women's postwar conservatism, several historians have stressed continuity in gender conventions. Drew Faust argues that women's ambivalence about the changes wrought by the war led to a retreat into familiar gender roles. Faust discusses the "prerogatives of race . . . weakening and retarding the development of southern feminism, and subordinating its agenda to the seemingly more pressing concerns of reestablishing class and racial privilege."[86] Elite women certainly did focus on restoring the class and racial hierarchy, but if the standard of change is feminism, we miss the substantive shifts in white women's self-perception and the ways in which they used their status as "ladies" and female mourning as powerful political tools. In her work on Virginia ladies' memorial associations, Caroline Janney has documented the expansion of elite women's postwar political activity as well as how women used their "class status as a political shield." The war "politicized" white women and led them to "redefine the very nature of southern femininity," even as their politics remained preservationist. According to Janney, women of the memorial associations not only honored Confederate men and memory but also worked toward "securing their own legacy as devoted citizens and participants in the cause" and "pushed the boundaries of the domestic sphere outward to fill the space left vacant by the Confederate government."[87] Through relief and memorial work, Southern white women developed a new sense of female citizenship based on equal sacrifice. "Many of us are veterans," Lizzie Pollard declared in 1900 when discussing the members of ladies' aid and memorial associations, "veterans as much as the gray, battle-scarred old soldiers, tho' we bided at home."[88]

White women of the South felt that their relief work gave them a sense of shared ownership over the cause and the right to speak publicly in its defense. Southern black women who labored for the Union developed a similar sense of importance, even as African Americans were excluded from the commemoration of the war.[89] After the war, Susie King Taylor returned to Savannah, Georgia, to teach freed people. Unable to survive financially, she eventually worked as a domestic and moved to the North. Taylor was a founding member, in Boston, of an African American branch of the Women's Relief Corps, an auxiliary to the Grand Army of the Republic—a veterans' group that admitted black members. Taylor served as guard, secretary, and treasurer, and in 1893 she became president. She believed that women's wartime work "should be kept in the history before the people."[90] If Taylor is at all representative of the hundreds of Southern black women who worked in the field and in Union hospitals, it can be said that these women took pride in their contributions to the cause and used their work as a springboard to postwar activism in their neighborhoods and communities. Taylor wrote and published her memoir to demonstrate "what sacrifices we can make for our liberty and rights, and that there were 'loyal women,' as well as men, in those days, who did not fear shell or shot, who cared for the sick and dying; women who camped and fared as the boys did, and who are still caring for the comrades in their declining years."[91]

The war politicized a diverse array of Southern women. When in June of 1865 Richmond's African American residents protested abuses against their community to President Andrew Johnson, they emphasized that black men and women had actively supported Union troops. "We have given aid and comfort to the soldiers of Freedom," they told Johnson.[92] African Americans had supported the Union war effort and felt invested in the war's outcome. Elsa Barkley Brown has examined black women's postwar political engagement, including their active participation in Republican and constitutional conventions. Although denied the franchise, African American women established political societies and expressed their politics in a variety of ways.[93] At a political gathering during Reconstruction, African American women in South Carolina "had an especially important—and dangerous—role. While the men participated in the meeting, the women guarded the guns—thus serving as the protectors of the meeting." White and black women assumed the role of protecting their families, communities, and men, though they did so with opposite goals. African American women across the South accompanied men to the polls, participated in mob actions, expressed their political preferences, and ostracized those who voted for Democrats. Brown writes that African American women "understood the vote as a collective . . . possession and . . . unable to cast a separate vote, viewed African American men's vote as equally theirs."[94]

Pro-Confederate white women and pro-Union black women who engaged in wartime relief saw themselves as veterans of the war, and both groups used that service to publicly assert their political beliefs. For Susie King Taylor, that meant an appeal for racial justice in the post-Reconstruction era: "Justice we ask,—to be citizens of these United States, where so many of our people have shed their blood with their white comrades, that the stars and stripes should never be polluted."[95] Rose Russell, a slave living in Vicksburg, Mississippi, volunteered and served as a Union army nurse. When interviewed later in life, she proudly displayed her "badges of honor," from Grand Army of the Republic conventions, and declared herself "loyal to the flag" and "A Veteran of Wars."[96] Confederate relief workers wanted historical justice for the white South. Former nurse Kate Mason Rowland declared that the South had been right and the North wrong and denounced the "iniquitous amendments forced on the South, which remain there as a blot upon the Constitution, an ever-threatening menace of negro equality."[97] Relief work on behalf of the Union and Confederate causes expanded Southern women's political engagement and sense of citizenship. Women who had devoted themselves to relief work felt strongly invested in the meaning of the war. In the postwar period, Southern white and black women used their political voice to fight the continuing war over memory—a memory with vastly different implications for the people and the pasts it represented and protected.

NOTES

1. Drew Gilpin Faust and Stephanie McCurry discuss the rhetoric of womanhood used to mobilize for war. Drew Gilpin Faust, "Altars of Sacrifice: Confederate Women and the Narratives of War," in Catherine Clinton and Nina Silber, eds., *Divided Houses: Gender and the Civil War* (New York: Oxford Univ. Press, 1992), 171–77; Stephanie McCurry, *Confederate Reckoning: Power and Politics in the Civil War South* (Cambridge, Mass.: Harvard Univ. Press, 2010), 24–30, 94.

2. Ann Firor Scott, *Natural Allies: Women's Associations in American History* (Urbana: Univ. of Illinois Press, 1991); Caroline E. Janney, *Burying the Dead but Not the Past: Ladies' Memorial Associations and the Lost Cause* (Chapel Hill: Univ. of North Carolina Press, 2008); Anastasia Sims, *The Power of Femininity in the New South: Women's Organizations and Politics in North Carolina, 1880–1930* (Columbia: Univ. of South Carolina Press, 1997); Marjorie Spruill Wheeler, *New Women of the New South: The Leaders of the Woman Suffrage Movement in the Southern States* (New York: Oxford Univ. Press, 1993).

3. Libra Hilde, *Worth a Dozen Men: Women and Nursing in the Civil War South* (Charlottesville: Univ. of Virginia Press, 2012).

4. Several scholars argue that the doctrine of separate spheres had limited influence in the South and as a result women's benevolent reform lagged behind and was less autonomous and more paternalistic than women's benevolence in the North. This group includes Elizabeth Fox-Genovese, *Within the Plantation Household: Black and White Women of the Old South* (Chapel Hill: Univ. of North Carolina Press, 1988), 61–66, 232–35; Jean E. Friedman, *The Enclosed Garden: Women and Community in the Evangelical South, 1830–1900* (Chapel Hill: Univ. of North Carolina Press, 1985), 6, 19–20; Barbara L. Bellows, *Benevolence Among Slaveholders: Assisting the Poor in Charleston, 1670–1860* (Baton Rouge: Louisiana State Univ. Press, 1993); Stephanie McCurry, *Masters of Small Worlds: Yeoman Households, Gender Relations, and the Political Culture of the Antebellum South Carolina Low Country* (New York: Oxford Univ. Press, 1995), 188–90; and Gail S. Murray, "Charity Within the Bounds of Race and Class: Female Benevolence in the Old South," *South Carolina Historical Magazine* 96 (Jan. 1995): 54–70. Another group of scholars argue that Southern women successfully used the ideology of domesticity to form an array of antebellum voluntary associations that enabled them to exert their moral authority and engage in public activity. See Suzanne Lebsock, *The Free Women*

of Petersburg: Status and Culture in a Southern Town, 1784–1860 (New York: W. W. Norton, 1984), 195–236; Scott, *Natural Allies*, 19–20, 195; John W. Quist, "Slaveholding Operatives of the Benevolent Empire: Bible, Tract, and Sunday School Societies in Antebellum Tuscaloosa County, Alabama," *Journal of Southern History* 57 (Aug. 1996): 481–526; Elizabeth Varon, *We Mean to Be Counted: White Women and Politics in Antebellum Virginia* (Chapel Hill: Univ. of North Carolina Press, 1998), 10–70; Timothy Lockley, *Welfare and Charity in the Antebellum South* (Gainesville: Univ. Press of Florida, 2007). Cynthia Kierner mediates between the two groups, arguing that Northerners and Southerners shared the ideology of domesticity, but after 1830 that language "increasingly coexisted with a more explicitly patriarchal rhetoric that signaled the emergence of an avowedly proslavery ideology," in response to abolitionism. However, "the increasing prevalence of paternalistic and even patriarchal ideals did not extinguish women's public activities," and some groups "continued to form their own relatively autonomous benevolent associations." She does note that the "marginal place of women in the early southern temperance movement suggests that females attained access to the public sphere only to the extent that their activities were consistent with white male dominance." Cynthia A. Kierner, *Beyond the Household: Women's Place in the Early South, 1700–1835* (Ithaca, N.Y.: Cornell Univ. Press, 1998), 216, 202, 215, 6, 180–81, 189–93, 202–3.

5. In her study of Augusta, Georgia, LeeAnn Whites notes links between prewar women's charity and church organizations and wartime organizing. She argues that the antebellum activities enabled planter women to "develop as self-conscious political agents—a development that would remain largely invisible until the traumas of wartime breached the walls of the male-headed household structure. So while the initial meeting of the Ladies' Volunteer Association took an obligatory bow in the direction of patriarchal authority when the minister opened their meeting, this was the beginning and end of male oversight." LeeAnn Whites, *The Civil War as a Crisis in Gender: Augusta, Georgia, 1860–1890* (Athens: Univ. of Georgia Press, 1995), 52.

6. Walter Johnson, *Soul by Soul: Life Inside the Antebellum Slave Market.* (Cambridge, Mass.: Harvard University Press, 1999), 102.

7. McCurry, *Confederate Reckoning*, 192, 180, 133–217; Faust, "Altars of Sacrifice," 193–97; Whites, *Civil War as a Crisis in Gender*, 64–95; Victoria E. Bynum, *Unruly Women: The Politics of Social and Sexual Control in the Old South* (Chapel Hill: Univ. of North Carolina Press, 1992).

8. For a discussion of proslavery ideology and female weakness and vulnerability, see Fox-Genovese, *Within the Plantation Household*, 29–45, 232–35; Catherine Clinton, *The Plantation Mistress: Woman's World in the Old South* (New York: Pantheon, 1983), 87–89, 204–10. In the drive to achieve disunion, "the specter of rape loomed larger in appeals to the people as secessionists became more desperate," McCurry notes. "Vague insinuations about pollution and dishonor had long been a part of the political discourse. The idea that so-called Black Republicans would rape the South itself was sometimes ventured." Fire-eaters also used visions of rape to appeal to the nonslaveholding majority. McCurry, *Confederate Reckoning*, 27, 45–46.

9. McCurry writes that Confederate leaders "provoked precisely the transformation of their own political culture they had hoped to avoid by secession, bringing into the making of history those people—the South's massive unfranchised population of white women and slaves—whose political dispossession they intended to render permanent." According to McCurry, "it was yeoman and poor white women who moved decisively into the practice of politics in the Civil War South reshaping labor and welfare policy in their own image." McCurry, *Confederate Reckoning*, 1, 7. While yeoman women's political activity undermined the state, many planter women worked in support of the state, and in doing so both groups altered the gender expectations and roles upon which the Confederacy had been founded.

10. The Southern Mothers' Hospital, founded and run by the Southern Mothers' Society, disbanded when Union forces occupied Memphis, and Smith went on to serve as a matron in

the mobile hospitals of the Army of Tennessee. Susan E. D. Smith, *The Soldier's Friend: Being a Thrilling Narrative of Grandma Smith's Four Years' Experience and Observations, as Matron, in the Hospitals of the South, during the Late Disastrous Conflict in America* (Memphis,: Bulletin, 1867), 47, 48, 54, 58–59.

11. According to Whites, the war "empowered the domestic labor of Confederate women" and altered the normal hierarchy of protection and dependence. Whites, *Civil War as a Crisis in Gender,* 12, 47, 41–63.

12. Whites includes an interesting example of a man reacting negatively to women's expanded and public wartime activities. "Gray Beard" wrote to the local newspaper in response to women's efforts to raise money to build a gunboat, claiming that such masculine pursuits violated appropriate female concerns. Defining reliance on women for defense as "shameful" to men, his appeal targeted men, hoping to rouse their patriotism to assume control of the project. As Whites notes, in the realm of patriotism the editor backed the women, and despite this complaint, "men seemed to have been content to allow the women to run the show." Whites, *Civil War as a Crisis in Gender,* 59–60.

13. George Anderson Mercer Diary, 00503, Aug. 17, 1861, Southern Historical Collection, Wilson Library, Univ. of North Carolina, Chapel Hill, 2:107–8; ibid., Sept. 8, 1861, 118.

14. Francis Richard Lubbock, *Six Decades in Texas: or Memoirs of Francis Richard Lubbock, Governor of Texas in War Time, 1861–1863,* ed. C. W. Raines (Austin: B. C. Jones, 1900), 522–23.

15. For a Union example, the famous abolitionist Lydia Maria Child informed John Greenleaf Whittier that "this winter I have for the first time been knitting for the army; but I do it only for Kansas troops. I can trust them, for they have vowed a vow unto the Lord that no fugitive shall ever be surrendered in their camps." Lydia Maria Francis Child to John Greenleaf Whittier, Jan. 21, 1862, in *Letters of Lydia Marie Child with a Biographical Introduction by John G. Whittier and Appendix by Wendell Phillips* (Boston: Houghton, Mifflin, 1883), 161; Lucy Wood to Waddy Butler, May 2, 1861, Lucy Wood Butler Papers, Univ. of Virginia Library, Charlottesville.

16. Mary Boykin Chesnut, *A Diary from Dixie,* ed. Isabella D. Martin and Myrta L. Avary (New York: D. Appleton, 1905), Aug., 1861, 113; Memoir of Miss S. C. Waring, in Mrs. Thomas Taylor and Sallie Enders Conner, eds., *South Carolina Women in the Confederacy,* (Columbia, S.C.: State Company, 1903), 1:57.

17. Diary of Susan Bradford Eppes, June 1861, Jan. 1863, in Susan Bradford Eppes, *Through Some Eventful Years* (Macon, Ga.: J. W. Burke, 1926), 155, 192.

18. *Daily Columbus* (Ga.) *Enquirer,* Mar. 15, 1862; *Macon Daily Telegraph,* Apr. 3, 1862; George Anderson Mercer Diary, May 24, 1861, 90; ibid., Sept. 18, 1861, 127.

19. George Anderson Mercer Diary, Aug. 17, 1861, 108.

20. Emma Holmes, *The Diary of Miss Emma Holmes, 1861–1866,* ed. John F. Marszalek (Baton Rouge: Louisiana State Univ. Press, 1994), Dec. 3, 1861, 102.

21. *Edgefield* (S.C.) *Advertiser,* Oct. 22, 1862.

22. Minutes of the Proceedings of the Greenville Ladies' Association in Aid of the Volunteers of the Confederate Army, Aug. 20, 1861, Greenville Ladies' Association, Greenville, S.C., 1:112–14, Duke Univ., Durham, N.C.; "The Ladies' Relief Association of Charleston," Snowden Collection, South Caroliniana Library, Univ. of South Carolina, Columbia.

23. Kate Cumming, *Kate: The Journal of a Confederate Nurse,* ed. Richard Barksdale Harwell (Baton Rouge: Louisiana State Univ. Press, 1998), 55 (July 1862); Memoir of Mrs. J. P. Adams, in Taylor and Conner, eds., *South Carolina Women in the Confederacy,* 81.

24. "I was president of our clothing society, and vice-president of our hospital committee," one woman recalled, noting that she visited the hospital daily. Memoir of Miss S. S. Seabrook, in Taylor and Conner, eds., *South Carolina Women in the Confederacy,* 63.

25. Memoir of A. S. Arnold, in ibid., 180.

26. Memoir of Miss S. C. Waring, in ibid., 57.

27. Memoir of Mary Simpson Williams, in ibid., 31; Hilde, *Worth a Dozen Men,* 106–33.

28. In her master's thesis on ladies' gunboat societies, Cara Vandergriff argues, "Confederate women's remarkable expansion into this most masculine province of military and public policy foreshadows the many forays into forbidden rhetorical territory that would later be attempted by the women of the postbellum South." According to Vandergriff, women raised all or part of the funds for six of the twenty-two ironclad ships commissioned by the Confederacy during the war, and they also played a role in selecting the officers who would command the ships they built. John M. Coski argues that the Ladies' Defense Association of Richmond built the C.S.S. *Virginia II* rather than the *Fredericksburg,* as has been previously claimed. Cara Vandergriff, "'Petticoat Gunboats': The Wartime Expansion of Confederate Women's Discursive Opportunities Through Ladies' Gunboat Societies" (master's thesis, Univ. of Tennessee, 2013), 72, 1–2, 32, http://trace.tennessee.edu/utk_gradthes/1691; John M. Coski, *Capital Navy: The Men, Ships and Operations of the James River Squadron* (Campbell, Calif: Savas Woodbury, 1996).

29. Ellen Elmore noted that her society gave its first concert to "help the hospital service" and later put on a "splendid Gunboat Fair." Memoir of Ellen S. Elmore, in Taylor and Conner, eds., *South Carolina Women in the Confederacy,* 200.

30. The paper referred to Francis S. Bartow, a Confederate politician who died at the First Battle of Manassas, the first brigade commander of the Confederacy to fall in combat. Cass County, Georgia, was renamed Bartow County in his honor. *Daily Columbus* (Ga.) *Enquirer,* Mar. 15, 1862; see also *Macon Daily Telegraph,* Mar. 15, 1862, Mar. 24, 1862; *Daily Dispatch* (Richmond), Apr. 19, 1862. For long lists of contributors and the women who collected the funds, see *Macon Daily Telegraph,* Mar. 27, 1862, Apr. 2, 1862. The society managed to collect over $2,500 in several weeks. The ironclad they built was ultimately named the *C.S.S. Georgia.* Martha Calhoun Burn informed the *Courier* editor that "the ladies of Abbeville and the vicinity have placed in my hands the sum of $437, for the building of a gunboat." Letter from Martha Calhoun Burn, Apr. 2, 1862, in Taylor and Conner, eds., *South Carolina Women in the Confederacy,* 132.

31. Letter from Sue B. Gebyer, Mar. 3, 1862, in Taylor and Conner, eds., *South Carolina Women in the Confederacy,* 127–28.

32. However, when later faced with the needs of suffering soldiers, she declared, "Oh, that we had given our thousand dollars to the hospital and not to the gunboat!" Mary Boykin Chesnut, Mar., 1862, *A Diary from Dixie,* 155, 172.

33. Minutes of the Ladies' Defense Association, Eleanor S. Brockenbrough Library, Museum of the Confederacy, Richmond, ca. 1862–1863.

34. The article continued, "We believe if the enemy should now attempt an attack by water, they will meet with such a reception from the powerful guns of 'The Georgia Ladies' Iron Clad Battery' as will convince them that a country where the women are so decidedly intent upon resistance, cannot be conquered." *Yorkville* (S.C.) *Enquirer,* July 17, 1862. Whites argues that the reality of war led to men's dawning realization of their dependence on women's "love and labor in ways that had hitherto been obscured by the latter's subordination within the household." As women's labor became public, they "seized this opportunity to lay claim to a more *reciprocal* basis for gender relations." Whites, *Civil War as a Crisis in Gender,* 54.

35. "Every family has some article of brass and copper ware which can be spared, such as Andirons, Knobs, Candlesticks, Weights, Mortars and Bells," the appeal continued. *Daily Columbus* (Ga.) *Enquirer,* Mar. 21, 1862.

36. George Anderson Mercer Diary, Apr. 20, 1861, 70–71.

37. Ibid., 70; ibid., Apr. 23, 1861, 73; ibid., May 30, 1861, 95–96.

38. William Howard Russell, *My Diary North and South* (Boston: T.O.H.P. Burnham, 1863), May 1861, 226.

39. *Macon Daily Telegraph,* July 15, 1862. In areas of the Carolinas, the need for hospitals arose only late in the war. Women started wayside or regular hospitals when they began to

experience an influx of sick and wounded men. Virginia Tarrh stated, "At first we had no need of a hospital, so a committee of two ladies was appointed to go each week to the hospital in Florence. . . . Towards the end, however, when many sick and wounded were at our doors, we converted our Town Hall into a hospital. . . ." Memoir of Virginia C. Tarrh, in Taylor and Conner, eds., *South Carolina Women in the Confederacy*, 29.

40. "Physicians Meeting," *Daily Post* (Montgomery, Ala.), June 18, 1861, Civil War and Reconstruction, Confederate Hospitals, folder 3, Alabama Department of Archives and History, Montgomery; Minutes of the Proceedings of the Greenville Ladies' Association in Aid of the Volunteers of the Confederate Army, Greenville Ladies' Association, Greenville, S.C., vol. 1, Duke Univ., Durham, N.C.; Memoir of Jane Carson Brunson, in Taylor and Conner, eds., *South Carolina Women in the Confederacy*, 28; Memoir of Mrs. Campbell Bryce, in ibid., 82. For examples of locally run institutions, see Union Point, Georgia, and Greenville, South Carolina.

41. Cumming, *Kate*, 148, 231, 150, 154, 156.

42. Minutes of the Proceedings of the Greenville Ladies' Association, 2:163. For a detailed discussion of civilian women and medical care in the South, as individuals and groups, see Hilde, *Worth a Dozen Men*, 106–33.

43. The First Alabama Hospital was not in operation for long, so Hopkins's work focused on the Second and Third Alabama Hospitals and on supplying physicians in the field. The hospitals were disbanded and the couple left Richmond after the Confederate government consolidated control of hospitals and the Surgeon General refused to transfer Alabama soldiers from general hospitals to state-run institutions. Hilde, *Worth a Dozen Men*, 19–22.

44. Sally B. Manning to Juliet Opie Hopkins, July 8, 1861, Alabama Hospitals in Richmond, Va., Administrative Files, Correspondence, folder 1, 1861, Alabama Department of Archives and History, Montgomery; C. J. Clark, Surgeon, 10th Alabama Regiment, Virginia, to Juliet Opie Hopkins, Sept. 9, 1861, in ibid.; L. H. Anderson, Surgeon, 9th Alabama Regiment, to Juliet Opie Hopkins, Sept. 1, 1861, in ibid.

45. Beers was a regular visitor at the Soldier's Home Hospital, run by group of women. Fannie A. Beers, *Memories: A Record of Personal Experience and Adventure During Four Years of War* (Philadelphia: J. B. Lippincott, 1889), 38–42; "Ladies' Hospital in Richmond for the Sick Soldiers," *Daily Dispatch*, Oct. 2, 1861.

46. "Journal of the Confederate Congress, First Congress, Second Session," in *Southern Historical Society Papers* 46:237, Senate, Sept. 25, 1862; "An act to better provide for the sick and wounded of the army in hospitals, Sept. 27, 1862, in John Sheldon Moody et al., eds., *The War of the Rebellion: A Compilation of the Official Records of the Union and Confederate Armies* (Washington, D.C.: Government Printing Office, 1900), ser. 4, vol. 2, 199–200; Hilde, *Worth a Dozen Men*, 17–34.

47. Smith served as a matron in several different mobile hospitals associated with the Army of Tennessee, all of which moved periodically throughout the war. Smith was originally from Memphis and was posted mainly in Tennessee and Georgia. Smith, *Soldier's Friend*, 45.

48. Based on Medical Department appropriations for pay, I have estimated that approximately twelve hundred to seventeen hundred women served as official Confederate hospital matrons in 1863 and 1864. But this is an extremely low number that does not take into account the women who nursed prior to 1863 and those matrons who worked without pay. More important, it does not account for the significantly higher numbers of unofficial nurses and hospital visitors, including those who worked at wayside hospitals. Thousands of women volunteered informally, as individuals or as members of hospital associations. Many nursed unofficially throughout the war, while others nursed briefly or sporadically in reaction to a medical crisis or battle, and numerous women took sick and wounded men into their own homes. Hilde, *Worth a Dozen Men*, 3.

49. Cumming, *Kate*, 38–39; Smith, *Soldier's Friend*, 120.

50. Cumming, *Kate,* 178–79; Ada Bacot, *A Confederate Nurse: The Diary of Ada W. Bacot, 1860–1863,* ed. Jean V. Berlin (Columbia: Univ. of South Carolina Press, 1994), 82; Smith, *Soldier's Friend,* 73; Hilde, *Worth a Dozen Men,* 35–56, 74–105.

51. The sobriquet "ministering angel" invariably came up, linking nursing to women's piety and compassion. *Daily Dispatch,* Oct. 26, 1861; *Memphis Daily Appeal,* Aug. 9, 1862; *Weekly Standard* (Raleigh), Aug. 27, 1862; *Athens* (Tenn.) *Post,* Sept. 26, 1862. The one example I have seen of the term being applied to a man was in an obituary for a man training for the ministry. *Semi-Weekly Standard* (Raleigh), Jan. 2, 1863.

52. *Wilmington* (N.C.) *Journal,* Dec. 25, 1861. Men also used the papers to appeal to ladies' aid societies for needed items. *Daily Dispatch,* Dec. 25, 1861.

53. *Chattanooga Daily Rebel,* Mar. 19, 1863.

54. *Nashville Daily Patriot,* Dec. 27, 1861.

55. *Clarksville* (Tenn.) *Chronicle,* Oct. 11, 1861.

56. Hill grew up in Texas and until her mother's death lived with her parents and siblings. While she never mentioned wartime escape attempts, the fact that her parents had nine young children would have complicated any such potential plan. Nellie Hill, in George P. Rawick, ed., *The American Slave: A Composite Autobiography,* suppl., ser. 2, vol. 5, *Texas Narratives,* pt. 4 (Westport, Conn.: Greenwood Press, 1979), 1728.

57. In his book on Georgia slaves during the war, Clarence Mohr estimates that approximately five hundred slaves worked in twenty-nine Georgia hospitals in 1863. His figure does not include wayside hospitals, and he argues that that number may have doubled by the end of the war. An inspection report for fourteen Alabama hospitals in Mobile and Montgomery from the end of 1864 underscores the dependence on black labor, with a 1 to 4 ratio of detailed soldiers to black attendants. Clarence Mohr, *On the Threshold of Freedom: Masters and Slaves in Civil War Georgia* (Athens: Univ. of Georgia Press, 1986), 128–35; R. L. Brodie, Medical Director, Division of the West, Report of Inspection of the Hospitals situated in Montgomery and Mobile, Montgomery, Alabama, Dec. 26, 1864, Civil War and Reconstruction, Confederate Hospitals, folder 3, Alabama Department of Archives and History, Montgomery.

58. Bacot, *Confederate Nurse,* Sept. 8–9, 1862, 144–145, 65n; ibid., Sept. 13, 1862, 147.

59. Bacot provided no background information about Savary. Bacot, *Confederate Nurse,* Oct. 31, 1862, 158.

60. For a discussion of women's guilt over their distaste for hospitals, see Hilde, *Worth A Dozen Men,* 72–73. In their WPA slave narratives, Allen Price related his father's memories of serving with his master in the Civil War, including some time helping in a hospital, but he never commented on how his father felt about the work. Fannie Minter noted that she "served four years in the Confederate army as a nurse," ending the war working in a hospital in Atlanta, but said nothing more. Ella Belle Ramsey, in Rawick, ed. *American Slave,* suppl., ser. 2, vol. 8, *Texas Narratives,* pt. 7, 3231; Allen Price, in ibid., 3159; Fannie Minter, in ibid., ser. 1, vol. 9, *Mississippi Narratives,* pt. 4, 1510.

61. Cumming, *Kate,* 121.

62. Surgeon James B. McCaw, Chimborazo Hospitals, Richmond, to Surgeon General S. P. Moore, May 17, 1862, Letters Received and Sent, Chimborazo Hospital, 1861–1864, RG 109, ch. 6, vol. 707, National Archives and Records Administration, 101.

63. *Richmond Whig,* May 10, 1862.

64. For a discussion of slave impressment and how the failed policy revealed the weaknesses of a slave regime at war and how slavery emerged as a military liability rather than strength, see McCurry, *Confederate Reckoning,* 263–88.

65. Cumming, *Kate,* 70; Phoebe Yates Pember, *A Southern Woman's Story: Life in Confederate Richmond* (New York: G. W. Carleton, 1879), 98. For more examples, see Hilde, *Worth a Dozen Men,* 146–49.

66. For a discussion of black labor in Confederate hospitals, see Hilde, *Worth a Dozen Men*, 138–49. See Jane Schultz, *Women at the Front: Hospital Workers in Civil War America* (Chapel Hill: Univ. of North Carolina Press, 2004), for a discussion of black labor in Union hospitals. Schultz has analyzed the Carded Service Records of Union hospital attendants and found that black women comprised approximately 10 percent of Union female hospital labor. They were usually designated laundresses and cooks, whereas white women were more likely to be given the "higher prestige jobs." Schultz, *Women at the Front*, 22, 19–33.

67. Smith, *Soldier's Friend*, 182; Pember, *A Southern Woman's Story*, 22.

68. Southern blacks also provided another category of demeaning labor in hospitals in the form of comic entertainment. "There was a delightful black boy scuffling on a spring-board," Union nurse Jane Woolsey recalled. "The wards were continually sending up to borrow him, and offering to 'whistle all day' for him to dance." Samuel C. Hunt, New Berne, N.C., to Dearest, Dec. 23, 1862, Samuel C. Hunt Letters, Hay Manuscripts, John Hay Library, Brown Univ., Providence; Samuel C. Hunt to My Dear Father, Feb. 3, 1863, in ibid., ; Jane Stuart Woolsey, *Hospital Days: Reminiscence of a Civil War Nurse* (1868; repr., Roseville, Minn.: Edinborough Press, 2001), 50.

69. Oscar Lawrence Jackson, *The Colonel's Diary: Journals Kept Before and During the Civil War by the Late Colonel Oscar B. Jackson . . . Sometime Commander of the 63rd Regiment O. V. I,.* ed. Dr. David P. Jackson (N.p.: Privately printed, 1922), 88; Lemuel Abijah Abbott, *Personal Recollections and Civil War Diary, 1864* (Burlington, Vt.: Free Press, 1908), Sept. 19, 1864, 152.

70. McCurry refers to the war as a "massive slave rebellion" and discusses the "central role slave women played in the destruction of slavery on Confederate plantations during the Civil War." McCurry, *Confederate Reckoning*, 259, 246, 218–62. For a discussion of black women in Union hospitals, see Jane Schultz, "Seldom Thanked, Never Praised, and Scarcely Recognized: Gender and Racism in Civil War Hospitals," *Civil War History*, 48 (Sept. 2002): 220–25; and Jane Schultz, "Race, Gender, and Bureaucracy: Civil War Army Nurses and the Pension Bureau," *Journal of Women's History* 6 (Summer 1994): 45–69.

71. Edwin S. Redkey, ed., *A Grand Army of Black Men: Letters from African-American Soldiers in the Union Army, 1861–1865* (New York: Cambridge Univ. Press, 1992), 124. A white Union female transport nurse reported that nine black women doing hospital washing "'wish on their souls and bodies' that the Rebels could be 'put in a house together and burned up.'" Frederick Law Olmsted, *Hospital Transports: A Memoir of the Embarkation of the Sick and Wounded from the Peninsula of Virginia in the Summer of 1862* (Boston: Ticknor & Fields, 1863), 124.

72. Suzie King Taylor, *Reminiscences of My Life in Camp: With the 33rd United States Colored Troops Late 1st S. C. Volunteers* (1902; repr., New York: Arno Press, 1968), 5–6, 10, 15. For other examples of women who served black regiments, see Ella Forbes, *African-American Women During the Civil War* (New York: Garland, 1998), chap. 4; and Joseph Glatthaar, *Forged in Battle: The Civil War Alliance of Black Soldiers and White Officers* (New York: Free Press, 1991), chap. 5.

73. Taylor, *Reminiscences of My Life in Camp*, 17, 21, 29–30. Thomas Wentworth Higginson discussed another escaped slave woman he hired as a laundress, Fanny Wright. "Fanny was a modest little mulatto woman, a soldier's wife, and a company laundress. She had escaped from the main-land in a boat, with that child and another. Her baby was shot dead in her arms, and she reached our lines with one child safe on earth and the other in heaven. I never found it needful to give any elemental instructions in courage to Fanny's husband, you may be sure." Thomas Wentworth Higginson, *Army Life in a Black Regiment* (Boston: Fields, Osgood, 1870), 247.

74. Taylor, *Reminiscences of My Life in Camp*, 24, 26, 32, 37–39.

75. According to Taylor, black women in Savannah aided Union men in the local stockade, where they were kept "worse than pigs, without any shelter from sun or storm, and the colored women would take food there at night and pass it to them, through the holes in the fence. The soldiers were starving, and these women did all they could towards relieving those men,

although they knew the penalty, should they be caught giving them aid." Taylor, *Reminiscences of My Life in Camp*, 67–68.

76. Fannie Oslin Jackson, *On Both Sides of the Line*, ed. Joan F. Curran and Rudena K. Mallory (Baltimore: Gateway Press, 1989), 60, 55–56.

77. Jackson sought and obtained a job in Resaca with the Union Department of the Cumberland. Jackson, *On Both Sides of the Line*, 98, 41, 92, 93, 107, 109, 116, 126.

78. Ibid., 103, 96–101.

79. Memoir of Miss S. C. Waring, in Taylor and Conner, eds., *South Carolina Women in the Confederacy*, 58; Memoir of Mary Simpson Williams, in ibid., 31.

80. Memoir of Lee C. Harby, in ibid., 165.

81. Janney, *Burying the Dead*.

82. Hilde, *Worth a Dozen Men*, 204–21.

83. Cumming, *Kate*, 5; Beers, *Memories*, 197.

84. Smith, *Soldier's Friend*, 175.

85. Pryor was herself a volunteer hospital visitor but never an official matron. She referred to the general relief work of civilian women. Mrs. Roger A. Pryor, *My Day: Reminiscences of a Long Life* (New York: Macmillan, 1909), 169; Beers, *Memories*, 199; Pember, *A Southern Woman's Story*, 16.

86. Faust does note women's growing lack of trust in men and increasing assertiveness, yet she prioritizes what was retained rather than what changed. "Doubting the competence of their men and recognizing the necessity of defending their own interests, women were at the same time reluctant, especially in the face of postwar racial upheaval, to abandon the possibility of white male power and protection entirely and forever," she writes. Faust, *Mothers of Invention*, 253, 254; George C. Rable, *Civil Wars: Women and the Crisis of Southern Nationalism* (Urbana: Univ. of Illinois Press, 1991), 240–64; Whites, *Civil War as a Crisis in Gender*, 132–98.

87. Janney, *Burying the Dead*, 55, 57, 87, 92; Hilde, *Worth a Dozen Men*, 10–15, 181–221.

88. Mrs. William J. Behan et al., *History of the Confederate Memorial Associations of the South* (New Orleans: Graham Press, 1904), 34.

89. Jane Schultz notes that wartime division of labor, with black women often relegated to jobs as cooks and laundresses, later put them at a severe disadvantage when seeking pensions. In addition, the postwar commemoration of Northern women's wartime work elevated white women and left black women "to fend for themselves." Schultz, *Women at the Front*, 215, 200–9.

90. Taylor, *Reminiscences of My Life in Camp*, 68, 75–76.

91. Ibid., vi.

92. *New York Tribune*, June 17, 1865; Elsa Barkely Brown, "Negotiating and Transforming the Public Sphere: African American Political Life in the Transition from Slavery to Freedom," in Charles M. Payne and Adam Green, eds., *Time Longer than Rope: A Century of African American Activism, 1850–1950* (New York: New York Univ. Press, 2003), 68–110, 72–73.

93. Janney makes a similar argument, though she also points out that during Reconstruction Southerners deliberately masked white women's political activity so as to avoid the charge of treason. Janney, *Burying the Dead*, 6–7.

94. Like white women, these African American women did not intend to entirely upend gender roles, but they did intend to exercise their voice and vision of freedom and democracy. "Clearly for them the question was not an abstract notion of gender equality but rather one of community," Brown concludes. Elsa Barkely Brown, "To Catch the Vision of Freedom: Reconstructing Southern Black Women's Political History, 1865–1880" in Ann Gordon, Bettye Collier-Thomas, John H. Bracey, Arlene Avakian, and Joyce Berkman, eds., *African American Women and the Vote, 1837–1960* (Amherst: Univ. of Massachusetts Press, 1997), 66–99, 81, 82, 85.

95. Taylor, *Reminiscences of My Life in Camp,* vi.

96. Russell received a pension. Rose Russell, in Rawick, ed. *American Slave,* suppl. ser. 1, vol. 9, *Mississippi Narratives,* pt. 4, 1902–1906.

97. Taylor, *Reminiscences of My Life in Camp,* 75–76; Kate Mason Rowland, "Comments on Objectionable Sentences in the Essay Awarded the Prize in Columbia University, New York, by the U.D.C. of that City," *Richmond Times-Dispatch,* Jan. 31, 1909, folder 31, box 2, Rowland Collection, Museum of the Confederacy, Richmond.

Real Women and Mythical Womanhood

War Relief at the Northern Home Front

JEANIE ATTIE

The American Civil War was a military event that depended on the mass mobilization of home fronts. For the Union that meant the formation and maintenance of an army of unprecedented size reliant on financial support from private sources of wealth and the voluntarism of millions of men and women. When war broke out, the federal government had only a minimal military apparatus, and the formation of a military force far larger than any the United States had before required a citizenry willing to offer resources, labor, and even their bodies to put down the Southern rebellion. Voluntarism was more than a necessity, however; it formed an indispensable component of Americans' relationship to the state and was at the core of their understanding of nationalism.[1]

With Lincoln's first call for troops in April of 1861, the voluntarism of Northern white men acquired an obvious public identity. That of women, however, required a more elaborate definition. While visual and literary imagery positioned women at the center of the domestic worlds that Union soldiers sought to defend, real women wrestled to make apparent the reasoned nature of their politics and the sacrifices they made for the war effort. A narrative that formed early in the war and appeared in numerous postwar tributes was that of massive support flowing from Northern households to the military. The ideal female patriot was a white woman moved by a gendered form of nationalism to extend her charitable instincts and to transform surpluses of time and energy into needed supplies. Though she did not enjoy the full benefits of citizenship, the mythical woman patriot formed a personal identification with the Union cause and appreciated her efforts as a civic duty. Images of industry emanating from private homes by women who had no relation to partisan politics or to the market played into a wartime discourse about the disinterestedness of Northern female patriotism. Indeed, Frances Clarke argues that Northern benevolence itself became a justification for the Union cause, a measure of political righteousness.[2]

Many women made evident throughout the war years that they were prepared to perform their citizenship in public ways and welcomed opportunities to act on their political values. Though, as Stacey Robertson describes in her essay in this volume, countless Northern women were vocal and active participants in national politics throughout the antebellum era, the outbreak of war jolted others into becoming politically proficient. Some admitted surprise at their sudden interest in national politics. "We read newspapers and discuss the war from morning till night," wrote a young Martha Keyes of Massachusetts a few weeks after Fort Sumter. The *Mayflower,* a midwestern feminist newspaper, summarized correspondence from its readership, observing that "nearly every letter we receive breathes a spirit of deep feeling upon the war question. Mothers, wives and daughters are no less interested than their sons, fathers and husbands. There seems to be little disposition to think, speak, read or write of anything else."[3] Throughout the war women paid close attention to federal war policies and the fate of Union forces, with an eye to assessing their own fortunes as well as to enacting their politics. For abolitionist women, a war about the future of slavery made their emancipationist commitments evident. As Chandra Manning recounts in her essay in this volume, once emancipation became the war's end, abolitionist women moved quickly to provide relief to contraband slaves and freed people.

The conflicts that emerged over women's patriotic labors were less about the duties of women and the needs of the army than about the distance between the realities of women's lives and the expectations formed by idealized notions of womanhood. Narratives about home front women depicted selfless wives and sisters compelled by nature and devoid of partisan rancor to offer steady support of the military. Such characterizations not only served the construction of Northern nationalism, they also reinscribed the antebellum ideology of domesticity that attributed women's household labors and charitable acts to their biological natures. As one women's publication argued, "Heroisms of the home" were "natural . . . nothing more than . . . spontaneous impulses." Southern women too, as Libra Hilde details in her essay in this volume, worked under essentialized notions of female nature. Arguably, both Southern and Northern women who redirected their domestic skills to advance nationalist purposes accomplished the perfect symbiosis of public and private arenas of production, the fulfillment of the ideal gender division of labor.[4]

Although postwar tributes cast Northern women's voluntarism as one of unflagging dedication and unremitting work, such accounts obscured a chronology to relief efforts that saw political commitments and household capacities rise and fall over the course of the war. They also masked wartime commentaries that alternately claimed women were doing too much, that their undisciplined efforts resulted in more harm than good, or when concerns about military setbacks worried political and social leaders that donations were insufficient, that women lacked the requisite patriotic ardor or might even be actively undermining the Union cause. The reality was that doing relief work was contingent upon women's assessments of the legitimacy of the claims made upon them as well as their abilities to offer assistance. An appreciation of what they accomplished has to take into account the constraints under which they worked, how they measured their own efforts, and how their work was valued by others. Women labored under a narrative about female patriotism that often ran counter to their own understandings of their politics and their obligations. The distance between those realities meant that the shifting nature and level of women's support left them vulnerable to either public rebukes or a devaluation of what they contributed to the war effort.[5]

Compounding the personal difficulties and political discontent that punctuated home front support was the fact that the military struggle was a distant, largely unseen event. While Union military strategy eventually targeted the entire South—civilians, infrastructure, and the agricultural landscape—it had a far different impact on those in the North who were distant from marching armies, encampments, and battlefields. For a sizable minority of Northerners, most obviously soldiers but also hospital workers and women who traveled to the war front to tend to enlisted men, the brutality of the war became all too real. For most, however, warfare was experienced through press accounts and artists' renderings of battles and campaigns, organizational reports, lectures, sermons, and stories from returning soldiers.

Not that Northerners did not crave a closer affective connection with the war. Many women remarked upon their eagerness for the latest military news and first-hand accounts from the front. Joshua Brown has analyzed the significance that the illustrated press played in bringing the war home, a fact that led newspaper editors, anxious to bolster the value of their publications, to go to great lengths to assert the accuracy and truthfulness of their papers' renderings. The popularity of Matthew Brady's photographs of battlefield dead, on view for some metropolitan audiences by 1863, lay in their ability to provide visceral experiences of death. The challenge both for those producing as well as consuming such images was making the war a "reality."[6]

If the actual war felt remote, few remained impervious to its impact. Whether by an economy that produced increased levels of insecurity and hardship, the political repercussions of conscription, or the absence of a family member, Northerners found their lives shaped and reshaped by the conflict. The wartime economy increased production and lifted the country out of the financial doldrums left by the 1857 panic. But it was not until 1863 that economic expansion began to show tangible gains. Those effects, however, were uneven, generating unprecedented inequalities of wealth and rates of inflation that all but wiped away wage increases. For those women who already existed on the margins of the economy, their plights most closely approximated those in the Confederacy, where the war made lives desperate. Hilde's essay in this volume describes how Southern women from all social classes were not only compelled to turn relief "inwards" but also took up political agitation to address the war-induced hardships they faced. Judith Giesberg likewise has provided powerful accounts of Northern rural and working-class women forced to make excruciating calculations in order to maintain farms and families. Women dependent upon and frequently denied support by local relief boards articulated understandings of an implicit contract they had with government, one that equated relief owed to them with the husbands they had relinquished to the military.[7]

Most in the North experienced the wartime economy as one that made their liveli-hoods more precarious, and the consequences for relief work were significant. House-hold donations that began to fall in 1862 likely never regained their early abundance, and local aid societies as well as national relief organizations turned to cash donations to buy the goods that women could no longer produce at home. In the last years of the war, those monetary contributions increasingly relied on wealthier sectors of society.

By 1862, when home front donations began to decrease, Northern women became targets for those ready to blame military setbacks on waning public support. With the Union army's initial strategy of capturing Virginia proving catastrophic and with little progress in the West, the female public was often admonished for what was portrayed as a collective failure of heart. Lincoln went so far as to characterize Northern disaf-fection as "the fire in the rear," implying that the home front, not the army, might become responsible for Union defeat. If his charge of disloyalty was directed at the antiwar "Copperhead" faction within the Democratic Party, it was significant that women were often accused by contemporaries as being at the forefront of the Copper-head movement. Even women active in relief work took to maligning uncooperative neighbors as disloyal or politically defiant. "Our own immediate vicinity is very much tinctured with Copperheadism," explained one woman about the ungenerous peers in her town. Yet such charges did not capture some of the personal reasons women had for refusing to support the war effort. Nina Silber argues that opposing the war was one of the few levers women had to protest war policies or shield menfolk from battle. For the preservation of their own households, some became inured to patriotic appeals, and in individual acts of resistance, urged husbands to abandon the fight and return home.[8]

Public criticisms of women took a more pointed turn by 1863, when the Northern press and even some female writers cautioned Northern middle-class women to take up the task of supporting the army and combating disloyal elements in their com-munities while steering clear of the shrill politics attributed to Confederate "secesh" women. The pseudonymous Gail Hamilton published an admonition to Northern women about their responsibility for raising the army's morale. If Union forces were to win, women had to mask their economic anxieties in letters to soldiers. "Make a mock of your discomforts," she wrote, warning women that if they filled letters with "tears and sighs . . . loneliness and fears," the South would never be conquered. The popular press singled out wealthy women for their extravagances, judging their consumption habits as unpatriotic acts. It was striking that critiques of the newly rich in the "age of shoddy" often fell on women and their expensive apparel, suggesting that they might be the agents of increasing inequality or war profiteering. But the wealthy were not the only women who came in for public censure. During the 1863 New York Draft Riots, the Northern press gave outsize focus to the violent acts of working-class women who protested conscription and the prospect of racial equality.[9]

Jeanie Attie

Women's mobilization and relief work covered a broad spectrum of labor: organizing soldiers' aid societies; directing national charitable organizations; becoming nurses, laundresses, and cooks in military and contraband hospitals; working on hospital transports; providing aid to refugeed former slaves; and caring for impoverished families in their own localities. Just as in the Confederate states, where Libra Hilde in her essay cites the self-mobilization of Southern women to create aid societies in order to assist a nascent state apparatus, Northern women also accustomed to voluntarism and localism took matters into their own hands. The difference, of course, lay in the language of defense and self-preservation that marked Southern entreaties to provide relief. Many of the Northern mobilization initiatives undertaken during the first weeks of the war drew upon the social networks and organizational know-how that white and black middle-class women had developed in antebellum sewing groups, church associations, and reform movements. In the decades before the war, thousands of women across the North had committed themselves to benevolence and reform societies in the causes of temperance, pacifism, women's rights, and the abolition of slavery. But the war soon eclipsed other causes; even feminists—notably Elizabeth Cady Stanton—decided to suspend the quest for expanded citizenship to focus on the national struggle. The suddenness of war and expectations of a brief struggle drove women to embrace the Union cause as their primary obligation. Even when motivated by anxieties about male kin and neighbors recently become soldiers, few couched their loyalties in personal terms. Rather they made public a reasoned loyalty to the federal government, defense of the Constitution, and opposition to the Southern threat.[10]

While women initiated their own forms of mobilization, they were also on the receiving end of an onslaught of injunctions about how to assist, what sorts of relief they should provide, and the appropriate ways to enact their patriotism. Entreaties emanated from magazines, broadsides, editorials, sermons, and speeches for organizing, producing, and donating to sustain the citizen army. Editors of popular women's magazines such as the *Sibyl, Godey's Lady's Book,* and the *Ladies' Repository,* as well as national papers such as *Leslie's Monthly,* exhorted middle-class white women to transform their households into centers of production. Local newspapers took the message to their readers, as when the *Poughkeepsie Daily Eagle* insisted that women "go to work *immediately,*" to produce two hundred shirts, noting "you can do a great work, and *now is the time.*" Playing to local pride and notions of women's parochialism, some publications goaded women into outdoing their neighbors, as when one local newspaper offered news of a woman from a "country town" who reputedly knitted one hundred pairs of mittens for the soldiers: "Can any young lady show a more patriotic record than this!" the paper queried.[11]

Invariably these appeals were expressed in the language of domesticity, the ideology that had emerged in the prior half century that defined women's household and charitable labors as extensions of their "nature." The antebellum gender ideology mystified the economic value of housework and shaped a wartime narrative that cast female patriotism and labor in service to the Union as acts of love and not work, as sacrifices driven by biology rather than politics or calculation. For work that was rarely translated into economic value, household labor was not labor at all. As the demands for women's products persisted, however, war relief work opened up the intellectual cracks of what had been an unstable set of ideas and presented possibilities for weakening the ideological fictions about gender. In home front organizing, some women saw a chance to shape new civic identities that might take seriously their political commitments as well as the evident economic value of their unpaid labor.[12]

Though it was easy to modify the object of a local sewing group to serve mobilization needs, the war prompted many to create organizations specifically for the war effort or to rename existing groups to mark such benevolence with political intent. The first dedicated soldiers' aid society was constituted on April 15, 1861, in Bridgeport, Connecticut. Others quickly followed suit. The "leading" ladies in Peekskill, New York, arranged to receive contributions and prepare supplies before the first volunteers departed from town. The women of Rockdale, Pennsylvania, began war relief within days of the South's insurrection and extended their labors to the military hospital in nearby Philadelphia. Women not only sewed hospital garments, prepared bandages, and canned food, they also employed strategies for raising money, through the staging of local fairs, bazaars, and themed festivals. The women in Melrose, Wisconsin, were particularly resourceful, garnering donations of wheat from regional farmers that they sent "eighteen miles to market, sold it, and bought materials."[13]

African American women also drew on a long history of charitable and reform work to mobilize support for the Union. From early in the nineteenth century, African Americans had created what historian Craig Wilder characterized as a "web of associations" that provided social services in black communities while also forming connections to the abolitionist movement.[14] When the war erupted, black women, largely excluded from white women's social worlds, created their own relief societies focused on aiding former slaves, and once black men were recruited as soldiers, to giving them support. A number of prominent African American women took charge of groups committed to relieving wartime distress of the black poor. Abolitionist and teacher Sarah Mapps Douglass became vice chair of the women's Pennsylvania branch of the American Freedmen's Aid Commission. Former slave and activist (and dressmaker to Mary Todd Lincoln) Elizabeth Keckley founded a branch Contraband Relief Association in 1862 that later changed its name to the Ladies' Freedmen and Soldier's Relief Association to reflect its expanded mission of aiding black soldiers. She also joined the National Association for the Relief of Destitute Colored Women and Children in Washington, D.C. Other formerly enslaved women, including Harriet Jacobs and Sojourner Truth, worked with Southern refugees and escaped slaves.[15]

Working-class women also participated as members of local aid societies or as paid laborers to produce garments from materials purchased by wealthier neighbors. Mary Marsh reported that at Henry Ward Beecher's Brooklyn church "a dozen sewing machines [were] hard at work ever since Sumter," allowing the wealthier women to boast that they had accomplished "heaps of work." Some were called upon by middle-class women to take advantage of state subsidies—such as the 25 cents that Pennsylvania offered for every pair of knitted socks—to both knit and donate their money so aid societies could buy more supplies. Far more women were employed by the army in munitions plants, which, as Judith Giesberg points out, blurred the line between women's work and war making. Even new avenues of employment did not relieve the plight of poorer women who appealed to local governments, relief agencies, and their richer counterparts for their own relief.[16]

Barely a few months into the conflict, however, women at the Northern home front learned that the organizational skills they had accrued before the war apparently were ill suited to a national crisis. No sooner had they outfitted troops and shipped handmade garments and foodstuffs than stories began to surface that their efforts were proving counterproductive. By the end of the summer of 1861 reports about useless clothing, ill-fitting uniforms, spoiled food, and overstocked hospital supplies flowed from military camps and hospitals back to the home front. Abolitionist and reformer Mary Livermore claimed in her postwar memoir that "baggage cars were soon flooded with fermenting sweetmeats, and broken pots of jelly. . . . Decaying fruit and vegetables, pastry and cake in a demoralized condition, badly canned meats and soups . . . were necessarily thrown away *en route*."[17]

For a number of professional and upper-class women in New York City, such accounts threatened to erase the impact of women's efforts, not to mention the viability of the army. More than anyone else, Dr. Elizabeth Blackwell—the first woman to receive a medical degree in the country—saw an opportunity for supervising a major female intervention in the war, and together with other women from New York's elite families, formed the Women's Central Relief Association (WCRA), whose goal was to systematize female war work by acting as a depot for home front donations, a clearinghouse for reliable information on army needs, and an agency for the recruitment of nurses.[18] These female leaders both employed and ignored cultural fictions about essentialized womanhood, resorting to gendered language in mobilization pitches but recognizing the reality of women's lives when confronted with female resistance to relief work.

The association was barely in operation, however, when Henry Whitney Bellows, minister of the prestigious First Unitarian Church in New York City, took actions to supplant it with an organization that would coordinate donations throughout the North and provide expertise to the management of military hospitals. With the support of a group of physicians and prominent New Yorkers, Bellows launched a plan for mobilizing the female home front into a disciplined entity, and the United States Sanitary Commission (USSC) was born. The men who headed the commission had more ambitious goals than merely making home front relief more efficacious; behind their actions lay a belief that promoting a national organization would loosen people from their narrow, communal ties and demonstrate the value of an activist state guided by disinterested elites. With a vehicle like the Sanitary Commission, they envisioned a unique opportunity to present themselves as organic leaders for a nation in crisis.[19]

After seven months in operation the WCRA was subsumed by the national group and made into a branch of the Sanitary Commission. Losing their autonomous identity, the women leaders rushed to publicize an account of their accomplishments, enumerating the 30,000 hospital garments, 15,000 gifts of bedding, and over 2,000 packages of jelly they had collected and sent to the warfront. Though other regional branches also led by upper-class women soon emerged, it was telling that the professional woman who created the idea of a national clearinghouse for wartime benevolence, and who hoped to elevate the standards of medical care and the training of nurses, was soon shunted to the margins of the organization. Elizabeth Blackwell, together with her physician sister, Emily Blackwell, was prevented by male doctors from any participation in the medical care of soldiers and by their male Sanitary Commission colleagues from a position in the new organization. Their names disappeared from all published USSC records.[20]

Determined to exercise a masculine discipline over female charity, the USSC reiterated stories that the women's "impulses" were creating "immense mischief" by inundating the army with "a flood of public bounty, wasting itself where it was not wanted." With the public's anxieties about the Union war effort heightened by early military defeats, the commission's offer to systematize war relief work struck a responsive chord. "Responding at once . . . the ladies . . . met and organized themselves. . . . Scarcely any opposition was manifested," reported Mrs. Ira Abell of Antwerp, New York. The president of the Ashville, New York, Soldiers' Aid Society recalled that about ten women met for their first meeting in October of 1861: "Our village having but few inhabitants the prospects were rather dark but we resolved to do all we could." The women in Adams, New York, boasted that "about seventy became members of the society," eventually recruiting eighty women from a town of fifteen hundred inhabitants.[21]

Because most soldiers' aid societies were formed by white Protestant women, when African American, Jewish, and Catholic women formed their own organizations, they chose names that proclaimed their identities and difference. The Hebrew Women's Aid Society of Philadelphia reported that it corresponded with thirteen other Jewish groups in Pennsylvania. Philadelphia was also home to the Colored Women's Sanitary Commission and the Ladies Sanitary Association, composed of elite black churchwomen. In cities both large and small, black women organized care at the warfront and home front. In St. Louis, though white women had attempted to create a society for black women within their own organization, the city's middle-class black women insisted on a group of their own; the Union Society gained access to Benton Barracks Hospital in the city, to visit black soldiers, as well as the "privilege" of riding on public streetcars on Saturdays.[22]

Regardless of the forms they assumed, soldiers' aid societies were fragile entities sustained with considerable difficulty. The process of organizing neighbors, canvassing for money, buying raw materials, sewing clothing, canning food, packing boxes, and shipping them to assigned depots required sustained time and energy. "I must say," wrote one woman, "that when the call for lint and bandages was made I

Jeanie Attie

invited the ladies to meet at our house." Yet after successfully collecting three boxes of donations, her attempts to form a permanent society failed; "the interest died out with those articles." Mrs. Waters reported that the women of her Willink, New York, society determined soon after "the interest first evinced began to wane," that "*one half day* every week was more time than they could give." "Our obstacles were many and almost insurmountable," reported Mrs. M. H. France of the Eddy Aid Society of Pennsylvania, noting, "Our place of meeting was very far from many of the member's homes." Even a home front husband felt compelled to write to the WCRA to convey the onerous nature of relief work, explaining in 1864 that his wife and other women of Vernon, New Jersey, no longer sent contributions because "you have no idea what hard work those ladies found it."[23]

Beyond the personal difficulties women encountered in sustaining relief work lay deeper issues about the propriety of exploiting household economic resources in light of the other ways in which the war was impinging on family livelihoods. A crisis erupted when, in 1862, Congress imposed taxes that targeted lower incomes than those imposed in the first year of the war. Together with the flood of paper money, known as greenbacks, that fueled speculative activities, the new taxes also created inflationary pressures. Peter Parish calculates that by July 1863, with "coal prices . . . up by a third, wood by a fifth, clothing by a similar amount," the income tax "profoundly affected" citizens' relationship to the government. For some on the home front, demands for household surpluses were viewed as an additional, perhaps illegitimate, form of taxation. Citing the feeling that the wives of "hard toiling farmers & mechanics, feel that their husbands are to be heavily taxed for the support of the Government," a woman from Oneida, New York, stated: "We need to be convinced that ours is not government work." A resident from Pawlet, Vermont, captured the new concerns: "The farmers say it takes all they can make to pay their taxes and the wives feel as poor as the husbands."[24]

The pressures of the wartime economy together with growing evidence of corruption among war contractors led many to question the legitimacy of demands for homemade donations. Not long after it began operations, the Sanitary Commission faced an onslaught of accusations that it was another site for war-induced fraud. By late 1862 USSC officers were on the receiving end of stories that the organization was a ruse perpetrated by scheming men bent on selling women's homemade gifts for profit. Throughout the North, women claimed to have heard accounts of soldiers being forced to pay for donated supplies and of USSC agents lining their own pockets with the value of voluntary labor. One woman summarized what she heard: "The general practice of all the officers of the Commission 'defrauding the people and appropriating the result thereof to themselves,'" while another reported that "the common people have the impression that every thing is converted into money, *even the lint and bandages are sold for paper rags.*" "A returned soldier says that *every thing* is *sold* by the Commission to the patients," and as a result, the people in her town "positively *refuse* to contribute the least delicacy." "Some think the Commission a speculation," reported Mrs. Dales of Bloomville, New York, while Lydia Batty told of her neighbors in Easton who "talk of it being a lucrative business," and those in Churchville labeled it "a swindling concern."[25] Popular apprehensions that the USSC was a money-making scheme were embedded in larger fears about the ways in which the war was upending so many lives, bringing death and misery to some and great riches to a few. As one female correspondent explained the widespread belief that donated goods were being sold, "Nor need you wonder at this lack of trust. For no time in the world's history was there ever more treachery than at the present."[26]

By 1863, with donations in apparent decline and home front women in defiance, the Sanitary Commission developed new strategies to sustain operations. It sent lecturers to meet with local organizers and rebut rumors, distributed publications to highlight its accomplishments, and called upon branch leaders to provide an accounting of failures. It also found itself relying on cash contributions to purchase supplies. Branch officers reached out to wealthy women in their own social circles, while male Sanitary leaders called upon business leaders to donate significant sums to keep the operation afloat. To many home front women, this turn was just. Nina Silber observed that a number of female writers began to argue that war relief work should properly fall upon those who had prospered in the wartime economy.[27] But even the privileged recalculated the destinations for their charity, dividing their contributions among private and state and local agencies and hoping such strategies would serve as a hedge against fraud.[28]

Hospital Workers

A similar chronology of early zeal followed by institutional struggle marked the story of the thousands of women who became hospital workers. Many of these women had not waited for any War Department directives but transformed themselves into nurses as soon as the war began, descending upon the military to offer their services with regiments, in general and field hospitals, and on army transports. Professional women took the lead in attempting to systematize the efforts of female nurses. After a career in reform work and prisons, Dorothea Dix volunteered her services to Secretary of War Simon Cameron, proposing to set up a nursing corps—the Office of Army Nurses—in exchange for authority over the hiring and direction of nurses.[29] But Dix's authority was compromised from the outset. Not only did her plan run headlong into those of the Blackwell sisters, who had put in place their own recruitment system, but in late 1863 it was opposed by Surgeon General William Hammond, who gave U.S. surgeons the authority to appoint female workers. While both Dix and the WCRA continued to recruit and transport nurses to the front, neither exercised much authority over hospital staff. As superintendent, Dix appointed over three thousand nurses according to her guidelines that permitted only older white, "matronly" women to work in hospitals. In the end she hired only 6 percent of the over six thousand nurses who worked in Union hospitals, less than 2 percent of the over ten thousand matrons and a much smaller percentages of the cooks and laundresses.[30]

Jeanie Attie

Thousands of Northern women—middle class and working class, urban and rural, free blacks and contraband—labored in military hospitals, on transport ships, and with regiments. While the government later recognized that 21,208 women were employed as Union hospital attendants (and thus provided with pensions), hundreds more remain invisible in the historical record. With little nursing training in existence, any woman employed as a laundress, cook, or "nurse" in a hospital setting could be called upon to do nursing. Whether ministering to injured and dying men or the less visible but more extensive menial labor needed in all medical settings, these women encountered horrors they could rarely imagine before the war. Their work was made more onerous by the resistance they encountered from medical supervisors, as well as by the class and racial conflicts that erupted. The obstinacy of medical staffs, bureaucratic mazes, and the grueling nature of nursing resulted in high turnover rates and a decline in volunteers after the first year of the war.[31]

African American women faced the most resistance to being admitted as hospital workers, and the majority had to accept work as cooks and laundresses. Not until January 1864 did the War Department rule that general hospitals could hire African American women as cooks or nurses. Many were former slaves who had offered themselves as contraband to gain protection and freedom within Union lines. As hospital workers, they received government contracts that promised $10 a month. But, mirroring the inequities faced by black soldiers, their wages proved hard to collect and were often stolen, leaving them to subsist on small army rations. African American soldiers routinely endured months before they were paid, making the food and cooking services offered by black cooks critical to their survival. In fact, as Ella Forbes uncovered, enterprising African American women used their considerable cooking skills to sell to white soldiers the decent fare they craved while in hospital or in camp. Even former slave and Underground Railroad operative Harriet Tubman attended wounded troops and cooked for the Union army on the South Carolina Sea Islands. While she used her post to also act as a spy, she taught freedwomen how to launder for Union soldiers and spent her own money to build a washhouse for them.[32]

Going It Alone

Just as with women who invented themselves as nurses and insisted upon their places at the warfront, there were others who acted on their own and traveled to encampments to offer aid or a semblance of domestic comforts to husbands, sons, and neighbors. Wives of enlisted men and officers as well as women from village aid societies journeyed to military camps to bring supplies directly to men in arms or to offer their company. In 1863 British journalist George Augustus Sala reported that "at least fifty fair dames and damsels" were with the Army of the Potomac, some wives of soldiers and military officers there on request of their husbands, others who came without invitation. Some women appeared at military hospitals after battles to search for their men. Others, unable to survive at home without male breadwinners, also traveled to camps, often with children in tow, to survive on what the military could offer.[33]

The realities at military encampments, however, proved far different than some had imagined. Women struggled in militarized settings that prevented them from cooking for their husbands or from caring for children in safety. Jane Schultz uncovered the particular burdens that family members posed for nurses and hospital staff that included pregnant women giving birth in military wards and grieving wives so distraught that they also demanded nursing care. Meanwhile, husbands worried and were sometimes embarrassed by the presence of female kin in rough military settings, some expressing fears of being emasculated in front of their comrades.[34]

RELIEF FOR THE HOME FRONT

Relief went in two directions during the Civil War, from households and localities to sustain the war effort and from welfare organizations and local governments to assist families in need. From the earliest days of the war, women's aid societies appropriated some monies to provide for the families of soldiers. But the local, small-scale nature of such efforts proved inadequate to meet growing levels of distress. As middle-class women sustained home fronts with work and sacrifices, others appealed to local governments, relief agencies, and their richer counterparts for their own relief.

State governments, such as that of Massachusetts, established methods for soldiers to direct some or all of their monthly pay to their dependents. Yet when black men were finally recruited in the 54th Massachusetts Regiment, the Commonwealth excluded their families from state aid. The result was catastrophic for some black families, who were compelled to bind out their children, and for soldiers who deserted and returned home to support their households.[35]

While mid-century women were routinely portrayed as the "natural" providers of charity, they were often in need of charity themselves. Even as middle-class women made explicit that their household labors represented real work and produced measurable economic value, it was still the case that war work depended upon having some means and the time to accomplish it. For elite women who ran Sanitary Commission branches and hosted extravagant benevolent fairs, their relative leisure afforded them the chance to assume full-time, sometimes exhausting work. For poor women the war was less a space for personal agency and political expression than an event that befell their lives.

Those women, whether in agricultural areas or urban centers, who faced severe economic deprivations had to develop a range of strategies to sustain their households, including tending gardens, selling produce, taking in boarders, putting children to work, working on others' farms, or taking paid factory work. But each avenue for subsistence had its limits. Though more than 100,000 factory, sewing, and arsenal jobs mushroomed to meet the military's requirements, most were poorly paid and beholden to the exploitative system of subcontracting. Seamstresses in New York City

Jeanie Attie

saw a decrease in their wages from 17.5 cents per shirt in 1861 to 8 cents per shirt in 1864. Cincinnati women complained that while contractors took in $1.75 per dozen gray woolen shirts, they paid their stitchers only $1 per dozen. Hundreds of thousands of Northern women experienced the war years as ones of poverty and insecurity.[36]

Women in agricultural areas faced particular hardships, with modest local aid societies unable to offer them much assistance and having fewer opportunities for employment outside the home. Numerous rural wives and mothers with male kin in the army relied on monthly allotments from enlisted men to keep their families afloat. In recounting stories of poorer rural women who struggled to maintain farm production and their families, Judith Giesberg argues that for farm women the war provoked ongoing family crises. Given that one-half of all Civil War soldiers were farmers and one-third were married, the removal of men from the household economy required thousands of women to take on field work, sustain agricultural production, fight for husbands' wages, and agonize over the payment of taxes. Some made personal appeals to state governors for aid, providing intimate accounts of their privations and concerns about male kin in the military.[37]

As economic distress deepened, some desperate women became refugees from the home front as they moved to live with their husbands' regiments. More common among those facing severe deprivation was relocating to find shelter and aid. Some moved near friends who could help; others sought outdoor relief, while still others presented themselves at hospitals, asylums, jails, and almshouses. Though embarrassed by having to apply to agencies associated with poor relief, women in economic despair calculated that such relief was a just entitlement during wartime. Yet, while many white women found relief, Northern African American women were usually barred from such support.[38]

Over the course of the war women across the North accomplished impressive feats of organization and production, volunteered for dangerous work in hospitals, and assumed the task of assisting the poor at home and the freed people in the South. They proved adept at working within complex organizations, confronting government bureaucracies, and sidestepping such entities when they impeded charitable aims. They also endured the everyday practical struggles of maintaining family economies under severe strain.

Through all these means, women raised their political visibility and found ways to enact their politics. Whether they found any permanent increase in their political status is questionable. Praise for women's wartime work abounded in the years afterward in volumes that offered narratives of unstinting voluntarism and unqualified devotion but in which real women's experiences more often than not disappeared. The genre of the postwar tribute provided readers with depictions of heroic, though modest, women who relieved suffering and asked for nothing in return. Erased were the moments when women were alternately praised, criticized, or scolded. What also disappeared was an accounting of the actual sacrifices relief work demanded and the economic value that women created. Whether making clothing or food, raising money, working in hospitals, or supporting home front families, the worth of women's labors was effaced by a rhetoric that characterized their efforts as instinctual. Such depictions not only expunged those who experienced deprivation and fear, they were also racialized, leaving black women to seek their own means of self-representation. Even the professional women who put so much of relief work in place and who faced special forms of resistance by male colleagues were rarely acknowledged.[39]

The postwar memorialization of women performed a particular kind of reactionary intervention. Images of brave wives, tender mothers, devoted nurses, and selfless charity workers offered psychic assurance that all was not lost of the prewar world. For a conflict that became a revolution—ending chattel slavery and auguring new powers of the federal government—serving up formulaic representations of noble women may have provided a means for assuaging those who feared more social upheaval. Invoking the antebellum domesticity ideology may have acted as a curative—a way for those who had seen the horrors of war, who had experienced violence and loss, to feel the imaginary soothing hand of the mythical woman. Perhaps, contemplating the self-sacrificing middle-class woman—not the scrappy nurse, the black female entrepreneur, rioting women, or combative home front volunteers—invoked not just the sentimental but needed sentiments.

Perhaps because at the outset of the conflict society had elevated the mythic "female" as the embodiment of a cause, the source of all that was worth defending, the demands made by real women often went unheeded. Indeed, the recording and memorializing of women's wartime labors became another site of contest between those who wanted to celebrate a few individuals and others who wanted to see an emphasis on the efficient, collective nature of their work. Though misty-eyed tributes to female valor, kindness, and generosity abounded in print, in images, and from pulpits and podiums, such portrayals invoked the formulaic contours of the essentialist ideology about gender difference.[40]

But it is also true that something ruptured during the war, and the gendered crises that the war provoked reverberated in the postwar decades. Women's collective efforts to sustain the army and the Union fractured in ways that were not immediately evident in the claims that the prewar gender ideology promised. In the postwar years, the careers of women who gained skills in wartime shaped a new definition of female citizenship. Countless women altered estimations of their abilities as well as their rights to claim greater political clout. The American Civil War disrupted the idealized male and female citizens. Whereas legitimate political power had been located in a masculinized, racialized body before the war, the need for black men's military service and women's labor to win that war held the possibility of rupturing notions of the body politic. Though essentialist ideas about women's capacities endured, what shattered may have been the distance between idealized notions of womanhood and the real women of the Civil War era.

1. Edward K. Spann, *Gotham at War: New York City, 1860–1865* (Wilmington, Del.: Scholarly Resource Books, 2002), 24–25. Spann notes that by early 1862 bankers, investors, and private groups had loaned the federal government $260 million.

2. See Nina Silber, *Gender and the Sectional Conflict* (Chapel Hill: Univ. of North Carolina Press, 2008), 1–13; Jeanie Attie, *Patriotic Toil: Northern Women and the American Civil War* (Ithaca, N.Y.: Cornell Univ. Press, 1998), 19–33; Frances Clarke, "'Let All Nations See': Civil War Nationalism and Memorialization of Wartime Voluntarism," *Civil War History* 52 (Mar. 2006): 76–78; Jane E. Schultz, *Women at the Front: Hospital Workers in Civil War America* (Chapel Hill: Univ. of North Carolina Press, 2004), chap. 7.

3. "Martha" to Captain Prescott, May 9, 1861, Mrs. Prescott Keyes, "Soldiers Aid Society 1861–1865, Concord Massachusetts," Alice Reynolds Keyes Papers, Schlesinger Library, Radcliffe College, Boston; *Mayflower*, May 15, 1861. The semimonthly paper was edited by Miss Lizzie Bunnell and Mary F. Thomas, MD, and published in Peru, Indiana.

4. "Heroism of Home," *Arthur's Home Magazine*, June 1862, 357.

5. Lyde Cullen Sizer, *The Political Work of Northern Women Writers and the Civil War, 1850–1872* (Chapel Hill: Univ. of North Carolina Press, 2000), 114–33; Attie, *Patriotic Toil*, chap. 4.

6. Joshua Brown, *Beyond the Lines: Pictorial Reporting, Everyday Life, and the Crisis of Gilded Age America* (Berkeley: Univ. of California Press, 2002), 33, 52–57.

7. When the wartime economy heated up, high prices and inflation meant that wages did not keep pace. Despite a rise in wages in 1864 and 1865, real earnings declined between 16 and 20 percent. Women had more access to industrial jobs but also extremely low wages. See Peter Parish, *The American Civil War* (New York: Holmes & Meier), 339–44; 362–65; Judith Giesberg, *Army at Home: Women and the Civil War on the Northern Home Front* (Chapel Hill: Univ. of North Carolina Press, 2009),

8. Mary L. Barstow to Louisa Lee Schuyler, Jan. 29, 1863, box 669, United States Sanitary Commission Papers, New York Public Library, New York (hereafter cited as USSC Papers); Silber, *Gender and the Sectional Conflict*, 50–52; Giesberg, *Army at Home*, 30–34.

9. Gail Hamilton, "A Call to My Country-Women, *Atlantic Monthly*, Mar. 1863, 347; Nina Silber, *Daughters of the Union: Northern Women Fight the Civil War* (Cambridge, Mass.: Harvard Univ. Press, 2005), 2–6, chap. 4; Giesberg, *Army at Home*, 124–27.

10. Lori Ginzberg, *Women and the Work of Benevolence: Morality, Politics, and Class in the 19th-Century United States* (New Haven, Conn.: Yale Univ. Press, 1990), chap. 2.

11. For a discussion of the popular entreaties that shaped wartime propaganda about sacrifice and duty, see J. Matthew Gallman, *Defining Duty in the Civil War: Personal Choice, Popular Culture, and the Union Home Front* (Chapel Hill: Univ. of North Carolina Press, 2015), chap. 4; *Poughkeepsie* (N.Y.) *Daily Eagle*, Apr. 24, 1861; Feb. 18, Sept. 11, 1862; Attie, *Patriotic Toil*, chap. 1.

12. See Jeanne Boydston, *Housework, Wages, and the Ideology of Labor in the Early Republic* (New York: Oxford Univ. Press, 1990), chaps. 6, 7, on the ideological shift that accompanied early industrialization and produced the idea that women's household labors produced no economic value, that they were a form of leisure that flowed forth from their natures. Attie, *Patriotic Toil*, 30–33.

13. Attie, *Patriotic Toil*, chap. 3; Silber, *Daughters of the Union*, 171; Judith Ann Giesberg, *Civil War Sisterhood: The U.S. Sanitary Commission and Women's Politics in Transition* (Boston: Northeastern Univ. Press, 2000), 70–71; Colin T. Naylor Jr., *Civil War Days in a Country Village* (Peekskill, N.Y.: Highland Press, 1961), 60; Anthony F. C. Wallace, *Rockdale: The Growth of an American Village in the Early Industrial Revolution* (New York: Alfred A. Knopf, 1978), 460–64.

See also Mrs. Prescott Keyes, "Soldiers Aid Society 1861–1865, Concord Massachusetts," Alice Reynolds Keyes Papers, Schlesinger Library, Radcliffe College, Cambridge, Mass.

14. Craig Steven Wilder, *In the Company of Black Men: The African Influence on African American Culture in New York City* (New York: New York Univ. Press, 2001), 103–19, 127–29; Ella Forbes, *African American Women during the Civil War* (New York: Garland, 1998), 4–5.

15. Silber, *Daughters of the Union,* 166–67; 232; Forbes, *African American Women,* 20–21, 31–33, 66–67, 73–84.

16. Attie, *Patriotic Toil,* chap. 1; Silber, *Daughters of the Union,* 171; Giesberg, *Army at Home,* chap. 3.

17. Mary Livermore, *My Story of the War: A Woman's Narrative of Four Years Personal Experience* . . . (Hartford: A. D. Worthington, 1896), 122.

18. Blackwell hoped that under her training a corps of female nurses would be sent to military hospitals and through their work demonstrate the professionalism that women could bring to the practice of medicine. Attie, *Patriotic Toil,* 38–42.

19. Ibid., 52–57.

20. Ibid., 82–86; Giesberg, *Civil War Sisterhood,* 22–24.

21. Mrs. Ira P. Abell to Blatchford, Apr. 17, 1866; Mrs. R. Roselle Ticknor to Mr. Blatchford, Apr. 16, 1866; Carrie Z. Webb to J. Blatchford, Apr. 5, 1866; Mrs. Henry Rue to USSC, Nov. 20, 1866, box 981, USSC Papers.

22. Rebecca Moss to Jno. S. Blatchford, Mar. 29, 1866, box 980, USSC Papers; Silber, *Daughters of the Union,* 167; Attie, *Patriotic Toil,* chap. 3.

23. H. L. Boyer [to Louisa Lee Schuyler (LLS)], Mar. 29, 1866, Miss Clara C. Reed to J. S. Blatchford, Mar. 29, 1866, Mrs. C. Waters [to LLS], 1866, Mrs. M. H. France to Jn. Blatchford, Jan. 2, 1867, box 980, USSC Papers; C. Allen, MD, to Miss Marshall, Jan. 25, 1864, WCRA, box 671, USSC Papers.

24. In 1862 the federal government passed legislation to tax incomes over $600 (though the taxes were not due until June of the following year); see Parish, *American Civil War,* 356–59, 363; Mrs. S. L. Beardsley to L. Schuyler, June 23, 1863, box 669, USSC Papers; Miss L. B. Fitch to L. Schuyler, May 18, 1863, USSC Papers.

25. Mrs. Proudfit [to LLS], Feb. 26, 1863, Caroline Sherman to L. Schuyler, Jan. 24, 1863, Ophelia Wait to L. Schuyler, Jan. 30,1863, Mrs. C. Dales [to LLS], Feb. 3, 1863, Mrs. Lydia Batty to Louisa Lee Schuyler, Jan. 29, 1863, Mrs. Alanson Tuttle [to LLS], Jan. 29, 1863, Mrs. Folney [to LLS], 1863, box 669, USSC Papers.

26. Mrs. H. P. Green to L. Schuyler, Jan. 26, 1863, box 669, USSC Papers; Attie, *Patriotic Toil,* 166–69.

27. Giesberg, *Civil War Sisterhood,* 78–79; Silber, *Daughters of the Union,* 37–38.

28. Aid societies diverted their donations to the rival United States Christian Commission, which exploited its religious identity to offer an alternative to the United States Sanitary Commission, as well as to an array of local and state relief agencies. Attie, *Patriotic Toil,* chap. 5.

29. Thomas J. Brown, *Dorothea Dix: New England Reformer* (Cambridge, Mass.: Harvard Univ. Press, 1998), 273–79.

30. Schultz, *Women at the Front,* 15, 21. Schultz makes the case that because laundresses, cooks, and other women in military hospitals also carried out nursing tasks, all such workers should be identified as "hospital workers," 4–5, 15; for recruitment of nurses by state governments and women who, defying Dix's orders, invented themselves as nurses, see Peggy Brase Seigel, "She Went to War: Indiana Women Nurses in the Civil War," *Indiana Magazine of History* 86 (Mar. 1990): 1–97.

31. Schultz, *Women at the Front,* 4–5, 16–17, 20, 44.

Jeanie Attie

32. Schultz, *Women at the Front,* 16–17. The contracts the government made with freed-women, to pay them $10 a month, were often broken. Black women had to file formal applications for wages owed and were frequently defrauded of their pay. See Forbes, *African American Women during the Civil War,* 51–55; Eric Foner, *Gateway to Freedom: The Hidden History of the Underground Railroad* (New York: W. W. Norton, 2015), 227.

33. George Augustus Sala, *My Diary in America in the Midst of the War* (London: Tinsley, 1865), 1:294–95; Silber, *Daughters of the Union,* 92–96.

34. Schultz, *Women at the Front,* 88–90; Silber, *Daughters of the Union,* 93–99.

35. Richard F. Miller, "For His Wife, His Widow, and His Orphan: Massachusetts and Family Aid During the Civil War," *Massachusetts Historical Review* 6 (2004): 71, 79–80, 101.

36. Silber, *Daughters of the Union,* 60–63.

37. Ginette Aley, "Inescapable Realities: Rural Midwestern Women and Families During the Civil War," in Ginette Aley and Joseph L. Anderson, eds. *Union Heartland: The Midwestern Home Front during the Civil War* (Carbondale: Southern Illinois Univ. Press, 2013), 131–32; see letters from Isabella A. Ruoff to Massachusetts governor John A. Andrew asking him to explain why she had not heard from her husband and pleading for help with her sick children. Miller, "For His Wife," 71; Giesberg, *War at Home,* 17–34.

38. Silber, *Daughters of the Union,* 51–52; Giesberg, *Army at Home,* chap. 1.

39. See, e.g., Frank Moore, *Women of the War: Their Heroism and Self-Sacrifice* (Hartford, Conn.: S. S. Scranton, 1866); and L. P. Brockett and Mary C. Vaughan, *Woman's Work in the Civil War: A Record of Heroism, Patriotism, and Patience* (Philadelphia: Zeigler, McCurdy, 1867); Clarke, "Let All Nations See," 76–80.

40. Frances Clarke, "Forgetting the Women: Debates over Female Patriotism in the Aftermath of America's Civil War," *Journal of Women's History* 23 (Summer 2011): 64–86.

Women and Families

Women and Families on the Southern Home Front

JACQUELINE GLASS CAMPBELL

With three out of four eligible men away from home fighting, the Southern home front quickly became a world of women who were challenged in ways that far exceeded and in critical ways differed from the experiences of their Northern counterparts. The enemy was on their doorstep, sometimes even within their very homes, and they faced rampant inflation, food shortages, and the breakdown of slavery. Women's varied and diverse responses to the South's ordeal by fire were shaped by a host of variables, including race, class, gender, geography, proximity to the enemy, and even age. Their personal dramas became central to the national drama of creating a Confederate state and sustaining slavery.[1]

For white Southern women, regardless of their social standing, family held a central place, not only in their immediate and extended kin networks but also in defining the very structure of the Old South itself. Family was a great deal more than a biological connection; it was also a social, economic, and political structure. As such it was both the matrix and the nexus of identity for white Southern women. It also provided the model on which white Southerners built the idea of a new nation, thus projecting family interests into the heart of politics and making family a vital arbiter in defining the expectations of behavior in the service of both community and nation.[2]

Familial and gendered language permeated the public discourse in the Civil War era. The nation was a house divided, the war was fratricidal, and the Southern states were the erring sisters. In the spring of 1861, as the country stood on the brink of war, South Carolina diarist Mary Boykin Chesnut, for one, discussed secession and war using a marriage metaphor. Chesnut wrote that North and South were now "divorced" because of incompatibility of temper and, she added sarcastically, the North was only willing to risk war to keep the Southern states because "they love us so." But, she continued, "we are an unwilling bride." Domestic imagery and familial language remained recurrent themes throughout a struggle that many believed was about the meaning of home.[3]

But home, and family, had different meanings to Northerners and Southerners. The industrializing and urbanizing areas of the North encouraged the development of a separate sphere ideology where the home was a private world under the moral guardianship of women. The political focus consequently shifted from personal influence to public institutions highlighting the exclusion of women, though Northern women extended the home into the public square by claiming interests in education, social reforms, and moral crusades. Not so in the South, where the political significance of the Southern household endured as the center of both production and reproduction and race was the primary determinant of social and political power. Both areas of the country placed great importance on women's outward display of submission to male authority. In the South, however, this was not based on a belief that women were inherently delicate creatures but that they chose to restrain their inner strength for the benefit of social harmony and family honor. During the war, when white women of the South were alone on farms and plantations, they saw themselves as responsible for the material and cultural survival of the family, which meant assuming new roles, at least for a time. And, as was frequently the case, when threatened by an invading army, they might respond with a passion worthy of both mothers and warriors.[4]

There had been much discussion in the 1850s about perceived dangers to the family unit, which had come to represent the cornerstone of society and of the Union. Americans viewed the family as the microcosm of the nation, and without sound families the country could not produce virtuous citizens. And then in 1852 a powerful critique of Southern society entered private homes as Northern families eagerly read *Uncle Tom's Cabin*. Harriet Beecher Stowe, a mother of seven, aimed hard blows at slavery's destructive influence on the family. Her novel made "real" the longtime abolitionist charge that a master might break apart a slave family on a whim and sexually abuse his female slaves. Stowe asked readers to consider how such men could be good husbands and fathers. And in such corrupt surroundings, she added, how could white women raise good republican citizens? Slavery had for some time been a political and territorial problem; Stowe now cast it as a domestic problem also.[5]

At the same time Southerners were embracing their paternalistic notion of families "black and white." This term was used across the South and was more than mere defensive propaganda. Slavery was a fundamental part of the Southern household, and the Southern household was a reflection of the political structure of the South. In the agricultural South family meant household, and the household often included slaves. As such, the destruction of slavery threatened not only the nation but also the family. The Southern slave household rested on the assumption that everyone knew and accepted their place, whereby slaves supposedly accepted the unspoken reciprocal agreement that promised their loyalty in exchange for the protection and nurture of their white masters.

Plantation mistresses were also bound by a code of reciprocity to and with their fathers and husbands. Their acceptance of a subordinate role, however, came with expectations that their men would be men—honorable, strong, and brave. To cite one example, on the eve of the Civil War a South Carolina planter's wife wrote that there was nothing a woman dreaded more than to lose respect for her husband. "We are willing to be second" she wrote, "but second only to the first." How, she wondered would men and women be able to face each other if "the men failed or compromised." Southern white women's willingness to accept their subordinate position placed a great burden on their menfolk, who were about to be called upon to display their manliness in defense of their newly created nation and family—indeed their very way of life.[6]

In the course of the war new necessities challenged old assumptions. The material world changed much faster than the deeply internalized Southern worldviews. Even as women of the planter class actively encouraged their men to display their courage and manhood, they also found themselves deprived of the protection and privilege that had been part of that reciprocal bargain. Still, Confederate women clung to their old identities for as long as they could. A young planter woman in North Carolina, for example, spoke for many of her class when she quickly found herself overwhelmed by the burdens of running a plantation alone. While she complained about the difficulties she encountered in having to "lug about the ladder upon which man plants his foot and ascends," she sought to reassure herself of the legitimacy of prevailing ideology. "Rightly managed, prayerfully taken," she continued, "women also may ascend using each of their petty cares as an advance toward that heaven which is governed by self-conquest, self-abnegation."[7]

Women encouraged their men to fight—to defend their way of life and the integrity of the Southern family. Rich or poor, it was a man's duty to protect his home and family, but now many men had to carry out that duty from a distance, which left women vulnerable to a host of dangers and a lack of steady support. But while soldiers hardened to military life and the immediate goals of killing the enemy and surviving the battle, women at home were having to adapt to changing conditions. Wives, sisters, and daughters had to take on increased physical and emotional responsibilities. Some rose to the challenge, especially in the early days when they received regular advice from their husbands. But the irregularity of correspondence and the inconsistency of the mail service forced them to learn on their own. Some struggled to survive while maintaining their loyalty to the Confederacy. Others became desperate and disillusioned and begged their men to return home.[8]

The stability and control of the antebellum years was challenged by trauma and dislocation that impacted all Southern families. For some white women, the burden of sacrifice proved too great. Some became increasingly disillusioned and disaffected from all things military. But frequently those who had firsthand experience facing the enemy rededicated themselves to the Confederate cause. Union soldiers were frequently surprised by the level of defiance displayed by many white women of the South—a defiance that seemed to them to cross the boundaries of acceptable feminine behavior.[9]

Two seeming contradictory commentaries on Southern women's behavior highlight the different understanding North and South of what constituted appropriate female behavior. Early in 1862 Union general Thomas Williams was astounded by the fierce secession sentiment displayed by Confederate women in Louisiana. "Such venom . . . such unsexing," seemed to him unprecedented. "I look at them," wrote

Williams, "and think of fallen angels." On the other side of the lines Confederate soldiers advised their female kin that boldness was the key to weathering the storm. If any Yankee "scoundrel" should attempt to enter their South Carolina home, wrote one soldier to his mother, "don't hesitate to shoot." The explanation for these conflicting views rests in the different ways Yankees and Confederates interpreted woman's nature. The emerging Northern urban, middle-class ethos cast women as inherently physically and intellectually delicate while also emphasizing their moral strength. The South acknowledged that women, at least white women of means, chose to restrain an inner strength for the benefit of social harmony and family honor. Consequently, it was permissible for a Southern white woman.to display passion and proficiency when faced with the imminent dangers of war.[10]

Southern white women displayed a variety of reactions to Union soldiers, ranging from curiosity to apathy and even outright hostility. They could freeze Yankees with a look or ignore them with an aura of disdain. As noted above, Union soldiers were frequently perplexed at the defiant behavior of Southern women, who were quick to show their contempt for them. Such behavior earned these women the nickname "she-devils." A British journalist wrote how astonishing it was when "ladies throw aside all scruples" how they could "baffle and perplex the most resolute men.[11]

In the spring of 1862, when the city of St. Augustine, Florida, fell to the Union navy, the commanding officer noted in his report "much violent and pestilent feeling among the women . . . [who] seem to mistake treason for courage, and have a theatrical desire to figure as heroines," thus disgracing their family name. Two months later a group of girls gathered around the remnants of the flagpole and began kissing it in front of Union soldiers, who burned the stump in frustration. The girls promptly gathered the remains as mementos. Although the troops were amused at these female antics, their commander was not. He ordered that in the future any woman deemed guilty of an "offensive exhibition of disloyalty" would be arrested, having "forfeited immunity from punishment by reason of her sex."[12]

It was relatively easy for Union soldiers to define Southern white women who eschewed the role of passive victim as aberrant. On one particular occasion the North had officially equated Southern women's patriotism with prostitution. Exasperated by Southern women who took every opportunity to insult or humiliate Union soldiers, Gen. Benjamin Butler, Union commander of occupied New Orleans, issued an order that called for any woman displaying such behavior to be "regarded and held liable to be treated as a woman of the town plying her avocation." The widespread expression of Confederate outrage at this order suggests that, in Southern minds, the behavior of these women fell within the limits of gentility—one could be rude and insulting to an enemy and still be a lady.[13]

No one expressed this sentiment in clearer fashion than Confederate captain John Bratton, who encouraged his wife to defend the family honor in very specific terms. He advised her to be cautious, but he continued, "There must be no cringing, no timidity." She should not allow herself to be "irritated" but to keep control of her emotions and display polite behavior. Although she should refrain from expressing her sentiment if possible, "if it should be necessary," he urged her, "speak the truth and the whole truth [even] if you die for it."[14]

Many Union soldiers were deeply perturbed by those Southern white women who refused to be cowed and humiliated but rather lashed out with vitriolic tongues. One Union officer expressed sympathy for those women who sat "with grief depicted on their countenances, or the tears rolling down their cheeks," but those Southern women who "vent[ed] their feelings in curses and rude epithets" made it difficult for him to overlook "what the women of the South have done to keep up this war."[15] Not only had Confederate women stepped beyond the pale of appropriate female behavior, they had also failed in their duties as republican mothers. This role that channeled women's moral superiority into the production of patriotic citizens had clearly gone awry in the South.[16] Union major Henry Hitchcock rationalized the situation to his wife. "Even in the case of women," he wrote, "what they received was but a just retribution for the large share they personally had in bringing on and keeping up this war."[17]

Some white women struggled with what constituted appropriate responses to the invading Yankees. Often they expressed an inner struggle to balance freedom and female subordination and wondered how far they could step out of the confines of the antebellum limitations and still maintain their family honor and the integrity of their sex. While Confederate women certainly did not embrace the role of passive victims, they found it difficult to transcend the hierarchical system in which they had been raised.

Sarah Morgan of Baton Rouge, Louisiana, provides a fine example of a young woman who struggled with the balance between freedom and subordination. Like other young women of her race and class, Morgan had been taught to play a subordinate role to male authority and to acquire the skills to be a good wife and mother. Early in the war Morgan used her diary to work through some of her feelings on men and marriage. She knew that any possible suitor would have to be her intellectual equal, as she could never respect a "fool." Moreover, she insisted he must be "brave to madness," for if he was a coward she would hold him in "unspeakable contempt." Above all he had to be successful, for "woe be to me," she wrote, "if I could feel superior to him for an instant." Sarah was young, spirited, and highly intelligent and yet deeply enmeshed in the cultural conventions that constrained Southern womanhood. She had on one occasion walked outside sporting a Confederate flag, but when federal soldiers watched her pass, she felt ashamed of unnecessarily attracting attention by an unladylike display of defiance. How dreadful was this war that had "brought out wicked, malignant feelings" that did not belong in women's hearts, she lamented.[18]

Nevertheless, the widely publicized behavior of these Southern "she adders," as they were sometimes called, politicized Confederate womanhood and provided grist for wartime propaganda. Many in the North actually blamed defiant and vituperative Confederate women for keeping up the war by displaying a vindictiveness and zeal for blood that crossed the boundaries of acceptable feminine behavior. Rumors even circulated that Southern women collected Yankee skulls and bone fragments to mount on pieces of jewelry. Yet at the same time these examples were used to criticize the level of commitment shown by Northern women, who allegedly lacked sufficient ardor and patriotism, thus cheating the Union cause and their menfolk of vital moral support.[19]

In response to the accusation that Northern women showed less fervor than their Southern counterparts, the Northern Women's Loyal National League took pains to point out the difference between women of the two regions. While they admitted that it might be natural to assume that those who were more "demonstrative" might have a deeper commitment to their cause, this was not the case. On the contrary, they explained, "the feelings of Northern women are rather deep than violent; their sense of duty is a quiet constant rather than a headlong or impetuous impulse."[20]

In many areas of the Confederacy, women were faced with difficult choices. The most pressing problems were financial, but opportunities for women to earn money were limited. Poor women struggled, the majority on farms but others as seamstresses, clerks, and factory workers. Like Northern women, they suffered from low wages and dangerous working conditions. Sewing was poorly paid and undependable work, and as the South had few factories, most sewing was done in private homes as piece-work. There were a few factories that employed women, but several did not survive invasion, fire, or other disruptions. Two felt the hard hand of William T. Sherman's invading army. Twenty miles north of Atlanta Sherman's men destroyed Roswell Mill and forcibly evacuated its extensive female workforce. And again outside Columbia, South Carolina, Sherman's force burned down another mill, in Saluda, and left four hundred unemployed women weeping over their lost income.[21]

Some elite women initially volunteered as nurses, and by 1862 the Confederacy authorized the hiring of women as hospital staff. One exceptional woman, Phoebe Pember, the daughter of a wealthy planter, successfully ran Chimborazo Hospital in Richmond that cared for more than 76,000 Confederate soldiers. Many other women, however, found the horrors of hospital work too much to bear.[22]

For the most part, however, Confederate women did not welcome taking on paid employment, viewing it as humiliating to their station. Cornelia McDonald, for example, came from a slaveholding family, but by 1864 she was a war widow, in dire financial straits, with seven young children to care for. Although McDonald was reluctant to engage in paid work, seeing it as a public declaration of poverty, her circumstances forced her to swallow elite pride. Because her privileged background had not equipped her to run a kitchen, she desperately needed money to hire a cook, and so McDonald became a teacher. Teaching was one of the few occupations open to educated women in the South, but it was not necessarily a welcome career. One Confederate mother declared she would rather suffer than have her daughter on the "treadmill life of a teacher." Another young woman declared that although she "would rather die than be dependent," she would "rather die than teach." "My soul revolts from the drudgery," she added.[23]

The largest employer of elite women was in fact the Confederate government, which employed them as note signers for the Treasury Department and in other office work. As references were required for all government jobs, many women from prominent families used their personal connections to gain these choice positions, and the government was inundated with applications. Circumstances dictated such appeals. Judith McGuire resented having to take a mathematical test before being offered a position, and after she got the job she wrote that no lady "would ever bind herself to keep accounts for six hours a day without dire necessity." To make enough money amid rampant inflation, she took a second night job, making soap at home that she sold to a Richmond merchant. Young Malvina Gist was more enthusiastic about her work in the Treasury Department in Columbia. Until February 1865, the heart of South Carolina had seen little evidence of war, and Gist enjoyed spending her money for vocal lessons and even made a $200 payment on account for her new bonnet. When news came that Sherman's army was a threat to the city and the Treasury Girls were ordered to evacuate, Gist wished she could have stayed. She longed for some excitement and a story "worth relating to her grandchildren." But her youthful enthusiasm for war was born of both privilege and innocence. She left with six gold watches sewn into her clothes and one of her two large trunks packed with "more miscellaneous articles of jewelry than would fill a small jewelry shop." The other trunk held provisions that her father insisted she take. On arriving at Richmond, Gist realized how wise his advice had been. "I wish I had been taught to cook instead of how to play the piano," she wrote. "I adore music, but I can't live without eating—and I'm hungry."[24]

Much unpaid work could not be avoided. Yeoman farm families and poor whites were likely more capable than more affluent and privileged women at performing tasks required to keep the family going. But plantation mistresses frequently lacked the many practical skills required for day-to-day survival.[25] Parthenia Hauge of Alabama, for example, recalled having to pick up the slack on the plantation with field work and learning how to make clothes and shoes. She wrote extensively about trying to find a substitute for coffee that had risen from thirty, to sixty, and then to seventy dollars a pound and even then was in short supply. She also wrote of using cotton-seed oil and ground peas mixed with lard as fuel for lights. Although in the early days ladies celebrated taking on supportive tasks such as sewing uniforms, they soon found it much more challenging when the soles of their shoes wore out. As there was no leather available, some women knit slipper-like footwear, while others used lint, old felt hats, or pieces of carpet. Judith McGuire used an old canvas sail, while Susan Bradford turned to her cousin, who showed her how to tan squirrel skins. Sarah Morgan searched the town of Baton Rouge in vain for about a week until she eventually found a pair of boots that had been made for a slave. Although the footwear fell far short of the quality or style to which she was accustomed, she nevertheless was relieved, as she "had such a terror of anyone seeing my naked foot."[26]

Of all the plantation demands, slave management most tested planter women. The war's unsettling effects on slavery both challenged the South's paternalistic ethos and eroded the foundation of its wealth. Mistresses did not command the same authority as masters, and slaves knew it. Slaves disappeared, left work undone, ignored orders, and drove their mistresses to distraction. Planter women found these changes difficult to grasp. Many could not, or would not, accept that slavery was crumbling.

They clung desperately to the belief that slavery was really in the best interests of all Southerners, black and white, and that slaves were truly the passive, faithful, helpless people planters imagined them to be. Occasionally there was a flash of insight that slaves might desire freedom, or that they were rejecting their owners' authority, but Confederate women could only push these thoughts so far. The conclusions were too disturbing—denial was easier. That denial, combined with years of seeing slaves as extensions of themselves, left slaveholding women unprepared to deal with African Americans outside the institution of slavery. African Americans became the enemy, sometimes even more menacing than the Yankees. Fear and frustration led some planter women to conclude that slavery was more trouble than it was worth. This, however, was an extreme expression of disillusionment, not that they entertained the possibility that slavery was morally wrong. Ironically, as the institution broke down, those once affluent women were simultaneously becoming more and more dependent on their slaves. A young planter woman noted the irony of the situation, commenting that "those whom we have so long fed and cared for now help us." Others, like Grace Elmore of Columbia, South Carolina, clung to her sense of racial superiority. Elmore expressed gratitude to the slaves who refused to let her into the downstairs billiard room until they had wiped the coarse messages some of Sherman's soldiers had written on the walls. Still she insisted that her slaves must remember "they belong to me now as ever." A Union soldier commented with derision that regardless of the privations rich white South Carolinians would suffer in the wake of Sherman's forces, "there is one thing they invariably do, no matter how great the cost; they cling to the *niggers* as the visible proof of their respectability and chivalry."[27]

When African Americans saw their owners suffering the same types of personal tragedies that they had inflicted on others, slaves' reactions spanned a spectrum from delight to ambivalence, and sometimes compassion. For the most part, however, they kept their feelings hidden. Mary Chesnut was aware that her slaves must be contemplating freedom, yet outwardly they remained "more obedient and more considerate than ever," giving no inclination that they "knew freedom was at hand."[28] But one thing was surely clear: slave owners were losing power and becoming vulnerable. Privation, separation from beloved family members, and fear of the future may have been new experiences for elite whites, but they were all too common in slaves' daily lives.

Slaves felt the disruption of war almost immediately, as planters might move them out of the path of Union soldiers. Slave men, too, were taken by the Confederate government to dig trenches, build forts, haul goods, and do all manner of menial work, and many slaves, predominantly men, fled to Union camps. But the disappearance of black men did not have the same impact on female slaves as it did on white women. Slave marriages were not recognized under law, there was little or no property to lose, and slave women had never been able to depend on the constant presence and support of their husbands and fathers. Slave women lived in a matrifocal world where the mother-child relationship was central. And because slave families were so vulnerable to the whim and demands of the master who could break them up at a moment's notice, they had to be flexible and to depend on extended kin networks to sustain family coherence and continuity.[29] Such survival strategies may have even been an advantage during the upheaval of war. Nevertheless, slave women frequently suffered during the war years, not just at the hands of their owners but also by cruel treatment from Northerners. Black women who fled to Union camps to be with their menfolk or to claim their own freedom seldom found the welcome they anticipated from Union officials and soldiers, and those who chose to remain with their owners and wait for liberation often suffered the hard hand of war exercised by Union armies.[30]

When the Union occupied the Sea Islands off the coast of South Carolina early in 1862, planters fled, leaving behind thousands of slaves. The area soon became the site of the first experiment for overseeing the transition from slavery to freedom—a "rehearsal for Reconstruction." The Union saw the need for missionaries to help in this process, and large numbers of women from New England and Pennsylvania eagerly sought the opportunity, not only to educate freed people, but also to establish the integrity of the black family. These Northern women were especially alarmed at the seizure of black men to serve in the military, leaving behind overburdened black women who were also vulnerable to sexual assault by Union soldiers. The Union authorities acknowledged the problem but shifted the blame onto black women, whom they saw as "jezebels" displaying a rampant sexuality. Some white soldiers viewed black women as the "legitimate prey of lust." Union general Rufus Saxton went so far as to assert publicly that colored women were "proud to have illicit intercourse with white men."[31]

A Northern missionary based in South Carolina reported that "no colored woman or girl was safe from the brutal lusts of the [white] soldiers—and by soldiers I mean both officers and men"; she further complained that offenders were seldom punished. One historian has found sufficient evidence of sexual victimization to argue that "the abuse of black women by Union soldiers at Beaufort [S.C.] was endemic."[32] However, when Northern missionaries tried to protect black women from these assaults, they displayed sympathy but also retained deep-seated racial and class prejudices.

In their attempt to support the integrity of the black family, Northern women judged black women's housekeeping according to white middle-class domestic standards. Simultaneously, they insisted that black women work outside the home and contribute financially to the upkeep of the family. Black women were in a no-win situation—if they failed to live up to these standards, they could never be considered true women; if they failed to be self-supporting, they were deemed lazy.[33]

As Union armies advanced through the Confederacy, slaves recognized their opportunity to escape a life of bondage. With federal camps close by, Union soldiers sometimes marched by enslaved people's homes, and slaves followed them. Initially it was mostly single black men who escaped toward Union lines, but later more women and children also became fugitives. Some were forced to leave their plantation homes when their masters saw them as burdens; others fled cruel treatment. A slave woman wrote to her soldier husband that she had nothing but trouble since he left. "They abuse me because you went and . . . will not take care of our children . . . and beat me scandalously." Patsey Leach from Kentucky ran off to a nearby contraband camp because her master had vented his pent-up wrath on her back with a cowhide. After he eventually threatened to kill her, Patsy, fearing for her life, fled, taking her baby but leaving four more children behind. Other women sought to join male kin who were being processed as soldiers in Union camps or desired to claim their own freedom.[34]

When black women ran away, they were taking an active role in claiming their own freedom. They also hurt their owners both materially by withdrawing their labor and psychologically by challenging the misguided belief in slave loyalty. Frequently, however, they became victims. Camp Nelson, Kentucky, a "contraband camp" where large numbers of black soldiers were processed, serves as a good example. Although black women who came to join their menfolk cooked and did laundry at the camps, they were often viewed as burdens by white officers who also believed they were dangerous and immoral women who might pose a sexual danger to the white soldiers. The commanding officer at Camp Nelson repeatedly expelled women from the camp, threatening them with a lashing should they return. The worst atrocity occurred in November 1864, when 400 women and children were expelled, many without shoes or adequate clothing. Of these, 150 perished in the freezing temperatures, and half of those who returned subsequently died. Joseph Miller, who had enlisted as a soldier in October of that year, recounted the fate of his wife and child in an official inquiry. At the time of Miller's enlistment, his master refused to keep his wife and four children and threatened to abuse them, whereupon, with the permission of his lieutenant, they had joined him in camp. A few weeks later he received notice that his family had to leave the following day. Miller appealed, but his wife and four children, one of whom had been sick for some time, were forced out on a freezing November morning. Miller tried to follow and eventually found them taking shelter in an old meetinghouse about six miles from camp. "I found my wife and children shivering with cold and famished with hunger . . . my boy was dead," stated Miller's affidavit. Miller returned to camp and then the next day walked back and buried his child alone.[35]

The Union army was allegedly the vanguard of freedom, but anticipation among the enslaved that their bondage would soon be over was frequently replaced with a sense of betrayal, complicating their decision of whether to flee with or from Union troops. Many African Americans became angry and perplexed when Northern troops destroyed their property, stole their goods, and assaulted black women. Despite repeated orders to attempt to curb the indiscriminate pillaging of black homes, these infamous practices continued. One slave remembered the coming of the Yankees as "scandalous days." Heddie Davis thought Yankees "was de worst people dere ever was." "Every Yankee I see had de stamp of poor white trash on them," recalled another. The ingenuity of one slave simultaneously saved his own possessions and protected the female house servants. When he saw Yankees carrying off his blankets along with those from the main house, this slave begged the soldiers in a terrified tone "not to mix them [the blankets] with his as all the house girls had some catching disease."[36]

At the start of William T. Sherman's Carolina campaign, Maj. Gen. O. O. Howard expressed concern over the mistreatment of blacks and the "many depredations . . . that would disgrace us even in the enemy's country, e.g. the robbing of some negroes and abusing their women."[37] An ex-slave from Winnsboro, South Carolina, echoed these sentiments many years later, when she remembered the Yankees as "a bad lot dat disgrace Mr. Lincoln dat sent them here. They insult women both white and black."[38]

The majority of firsthand evidence from African Americans comes from reminiscences collected during the 1930s. Most of the witnesses who contributed to these narratives were children during the war and so offered their own unique perspective. Unlike their parents, who may have suffered the worst of atrocities under slavery, many black children had valid reasons to distrust a band of ferocious white soldiers. Slave owners frequently terrified these children with stories of Yankee atrocities. Sometimes these fears were allayed. Capt. David Conyngham heard one black child say, "Mamma, the Yanks have good feet; not like de debbil as massa says." Another was so frightened that she hid in a tree until a Union soldier coaxed her down with the offer of money. Others found their suspicions validated. Nancy Washington recalled seeing "uh big blue cloud comin' down dat road en we chillun was scared uv em . . . in some uv de places dey jes ruint eve't'ing." One child saw the Yankees take her mother's moss mattress that had been a gift from her mistress, rip it open, empty out the moss and fill it with meat. Another soldier took her mother's "red stripe shawl" and put it on his horse as a saddle cloth. After choking this child's mother to find out where the whites' valuables were, the Yankees took her mother away, although she subsequently escaped and returned to her daughter.[39]

White families also faced the decision of whether or not to flee from invading armies. At least a quarter of a million Southerners left their homes during the war, and "to refugee" became a verb. Women most often headed refugee families and had to make the initial decision about whether or not to leave. The crisis began almost immediately after the war began, when many Virginia women left their homes. By 1862 the early trickle had swelled to a flood across the Confederacy. Women often packed up and fled two or even three times. Mrs. Emily Goodlett fled from Midway, South Carolina, and arrived in Columbia only two weeks before Sherman threatened that city. The Hamilton family acted as a "sort of avant courier" of the Yankee army. "By incessant hurrying [and] scurrying from pillar to post" over a five-week period, they ran from Columbia, South Carolina, as far as Fayetteville, North Carolina, unable to escape the imminent arrival of Sherman's men.[40]

These refugees came from all walks of life, although each wave contained a large number of wealthy. To "refugee" began as a choice—one that only the wealthy could make as poorer women could not easily afford to abandon their homes. Most refugees fled to cities; Richmond, Raleigh, Columbia, and Atlanta became overcrowded with refugees, who suffered from insufficient housing, food, or public services to accommodate such a rapidly increasing population. Refugees were extremely vulnerable, not only to enemy soldiers but also to deprivation and disease. When these families did return to their homes, they frequently found them destroyed or ransacked. They also found rotting carcasses of dead animals that soldiers had been unable to take with them and left unburied. These depredations only increased Southerners' hatred of the Yankee foe.[41]

Some of these women became disaffected from the Southern cause. Over time there seemed to be a growing contradiction between supporting the principles of the Confederacy and maintaining enthusiasm for an ongoing effort on the one hand and sustaining families on the other. By November 1864 Emily Harris, struggling alone with eight children on her farm in Spartanburg, South Carolina, had lost faith in the Confederacy. "I almost hate the word," she wrote. Another woman told her son that she could see nothing but sacrifice, victims, ruin, and misery. Others urged their husbands to come home.[42]

Some white women looked to the authorities for the support they needed to maintain their loyalty. A poor widow with two sons in the army complained of the "number-less frauds practiced upon civilians by Government officials." Still, she did not object to her sons' military service. "Had I more," she wrote," they should all go." A woman who signed herself "Nina" told Gov. Zebulon Vance, of North Carolina, that she had lost her oldest son and had three others in service. She expressed her frustration at the injustices of the system, but she declared, "My sons are for you no matter what you ever offer—for I have six."[43] Many women sent similar letters and petitions in which they expressed their discontent with the conduct of the war yet simultaneously stressed their loyalty. When they asked for a discharge or a furlough for a male family member, women remained convinced that this would be beneficial to the greater cause. One such woman stressed the need of her entire community for her father's mechanical skills. She had often heard it said that her father "would do more good to be at home an' work for the people than 20 good soldiers would do in the field."[44]

Some white women became increasingly disillusioned and disaffected from all things military, though disillusionment did not necessarily translate into disloyalty. Civilians had their own link to cause and comrades and were subject to the same fluctuations in morale that affected soldiers. And nowhere was this clearer than in war-torn parts of the country where women came into direct contact with the enemy. Enduring and surviving the depredations of an army of invasion might actually stimulate commit-ment to the cause.[45] Instead of calling their men home, many of these women urged their menfolk to exact vengeance on the enemy. "Let me entreat you not to seek a place here, with a view to give us security," wrote one such woman to her husband, ending her letter with the words "Don't Come!" Susan Cheves similarly assured her husband that there was no reason for him to be "uneasy" about her well-being. Emma Holmes called for all Southern soldiers to "die in defense of their country [rather] than live under Yankee rule." Lilly Logan encouraged her soldier brother to keep up his spirits and "whip" the Yankees. She assured him of her own enduring confidence in an early victory, claiming that they should all be "ready to bear even more for our glorious cause." Such tactics obviously had the desired effect on one Confederate soldier, who thanked God for such a "brave mother and sisters." "With such a spirit emanating from you how could we do else but perform our duty nobly and manfully," he wrote.[46]

In areas where the Southern home front was spared the ravages of invasion, isolated women and families suffering from wartime deprivations may have increasingly seen personal survival and Southern nationalism at cross purposes. But William T. Sherman's strategy of targeting the Confederate home front rendered the civilians in those areas as political actors in their own right. The women in Sherman's path who put up a valiant defense identified the family as nation writ small, eschewed their perceived roles of passive victims, and demanded protection as their right rather than resort to prayers and tears, which could only have added humiliation to their condition. In this context, moral outrage, material suffering, and strongly internalized cultural values encouraged many women to resist with whatever power they could muster.

Sherman's men frequently complained that Southern whites refused to recognize either the cultural or military superiority of the North and expressed astonishment at the intensity with which Confederate women fought to maintain both their dignity and their property. A New Jersey lieutenant remarked on how "determined" and "resolute" he found the white women of the Palmetto State. One of his comrades commented that this so-called tender sex was the match of the "roughest and most brutal" soldier when it came to the use of "obscene words."[47]

Confederate women, for their part, were also able to discriminate between the legitimate duty of a soldier and the reprehensible conduct of Yankee invaders who entered private homes and put their "vile touch" on cherished personal possessions. They described Yankees scattering and trampling upon "pictures, old letters, locks of hair, pressed flowers and other hallowed mementos of the dead." A Georgian woman wrote of how wretched she felt when Yankees pried into "sacred" items, "even into father's papers and relics of the dead." "If I live a thousand years I shall never forget the enemies of our country," she continued.[48]

A devastated home front was Sherman's most immediate goal. He trusted that his invasion would leave in its wake a population focused on the need for food and shelter, rather than on supporting further political and military conflict. Many civilians were both materially and spiritually exhausted and concerned over shortages of food but frequently moved beyond this initial feeling of despondency into a new resolve: although defeated, they would never be subjugated. Women who had encountered and survived the enemy now filled their correspondence with vows to continue the struggle. While in other places women's commitment to the cause waned in the final months of the war, as their many sacrifices seemed increasingly useless, women who confronted Sherman's men and other invaders felt that they had shared in an active defense of the Confederacy. They now called upon Southern soldiers to remain at their posts and exact vengeance on the enemy. Of course it was too late for such remonstrance, but even the news of Robert E. Lee's defeat and surrender did not entirely quash their hopes. Many remained convinced that, while the South might be overpowered, it would never be conquered and that the next generation would see an independent Confederacy. In fact, they believed it was their duty to become guardians of the war's memory and teach their children to hate the Yankees.[49]

Once negotiations for peace were underway, a growing disparity of reactions along gender lines emerged. A seeming camaraderie sprang up among war-weary veterans as they waited to hear the peace terms confirmed. Soldiers noted how remarkable it was that men who had been prepared to kill each other just hours before were now acting like brothers—at least for a time. Yet it was clear that women were not as eager to extend a hand of friendship. "I have seen ladies who would treat you to two moral hours' bitter invective against the Yanks," commented one Union officer.[50]

As Confederate women struggled to come to terms with Lee's surrender and military defeat, their grief turned to anger. They expressed hatred of the name "Yankee" and prayed for divine retribution—that the North be rendered "one vast scene of ruin and desolation." In Georgia, Eliza Andrews pronounced herself "more of a rebel today" than she had ever been. One Union soldier encountered a particularly bitter North Carolina woman who declared that she would not give a cup of water to a Yankee, even if he was dying. After some conversation with the soldier in question, she relented. "I would give you a cup of water to soothe your dying agonies," she told him, adding "and, as you are a Yankee I wish I had the opportunity to do so."[51]

In North Carolina Elizabeth Collier shuddered at the thought of "reconstruction." Had it not been a mortal sin she would "pray God to die—anything rather than live to endure the disgrace and degradation in store for us." Another young woman could find no words to express the "bitterness" and "hatred" she felt toward the "despicable conquerors." In South Carolina Eliza Fludd vented her wrath in a letter that took ten days to compose and was so fat that she had to mail it in two separate envelopes. She trusted that once Southerners had written their history of the war, the North would "blush with shame."[52]

Women's determination to win the peace was born of a unique blend of hatred and nostalgia, and nowhere was this more apparent than in Columbia, South Carolina, a city that now stood in ruins. When Mary Chesnut returned to South Carolina from her North Carolina refuge, she could not help weeping "incessantly" at the blackened track left behind by Sherman and his men. Closing her eyes, she vowed that even if they were "a crushed people" she would never be "a whimpering, pining slave." In similar vein, Emma Holmes exclaimed, "our Southern blood rose in stronger rebellion than ever, and we all determined that, if obliged to submit, never could they *subdue* us." Grace Elmore wondered whether they were to "give up war, yet have no peace?"[53]

The only question now, it seemed to Emma LeConte, was "not 'what hope?' but 'what new bitterness?'" For two weeks following this entry, LeConte felt such anger that she feared to express her sentiments in words. Finally she steeled herself to walk among the ruins of her once grand city of Columbia, South Carolina. It was a moonlit night, and her mind waxed poetic: "As far as the eye could reach only specter-like chimneys and the shutter walls, all flooded over by the rich moonlight which gave them a mysterious but mellow softness and quite took from them the ghastly air which they wear in the sunlight. They only lacked moss and lichens and tangled vines to make us believe we stood in some ruined city of antiquity."[54] In these romantic images lay the seeds of the Lost Cause ideology that was to flourish in the ensuing years.

In the postwar world Southerners struggled to recreate family life. Recent scholarship suggests that young white women's fear that they would be unable to find husbands proved unfounded and that over 90 percent who reached eligible age for marriage during the war years did indeed eventually marry. Black families also

Jacqueline Glass Campbell

sought to establish a domestic order that had been refused them before the war. But while African Americans sought a new familial model free of white intrusion, white women struggled to reestablish their antebellum world.[55]

When defeated Southern soldiers returned to their families, they looked to their female kin to reassure them of their manhood. But women would not go gently into their roles as rehabilitators of Southern men and guardians of Southern memory.[56] Mary Chesnut believed that women were forced to be realistic when it came to material losses, for men had the option to "die like a patriot." Another tried to explain the gendered nature of the healing process. All women, in her opinion, preferred "death" or "annihilation" over reunion, and she suspected most men felt the same way. It was, however, impracticable for Southern men to express such opinions, and they therefore associated with Yankees for purely pragmatic reasons. If women were to criticize their menfolk for such actions, it would only "increase their pain." Women's duty then, was to "keep pure the fire of patriotism" on behalf of a "conquered people."[57]

No one encapsulated this suppressed bitterness more accurately than Elizabeth Meriwether, who observed that, while Southern men were occupied with rebuilding their fortunes, "women had more time to brood over the wrongs that had been done them." She could not bring herself to forgive the Yankees, but her husband ,who had fought against them, seemed to have let go feelings of bitterness. Writing some fifty years after Lee's surrender, she noted that, were he still living "he would probably be as kindly and as just in his estimate of a Northern, as of a Southern solder." She could not feel that way.[58]

In the postwar period, soldiers could identify with comrades, even across enemy lines, by mutual recognition of duty fulfilled; women were denied a similar sense of closure. Husbands and sons, who once urged their wives and mothers to meet the Yankee invader with defiance and even with firearms, now exhorted them to honor the dead and place flowers on their graves. No longer vital players in their own right, Southern women had become the appendages of heroes who had glorified themselves on the battlefield. This image of a dedicated and loyal white Southern womanhood fed into a Lost Cause rhetoric. Ironically, and tragically, it was a rhetoric that the North would eventually come to embrace.

Notes

1. A wealth of evidence exists that helps us piece together the mosaic of Southern women's lives. But like all historical portraits, there are missing fragments. Most of the sources come from women of the propertied classes, although poorer women also left voluminous correspondence, not least in their communications with military and political authorities. Neither have the enslaved been silent, and historians have found creative approaches to ensuring that their voices have also been heard. Nevertheless, poorer white women who were illiterate and free black women have been, and will remain, the most neglected subjects of historical investigation, often only making their mark in the historical records as "unruly" women who defied the authority of the Confederacy.

2. The historiography of Southern women in the Civil War era is vast. Important works include George C. Rable, *Civil Wars: Women and the Crisis of Southern Nationalism* (Urbana: Univ. of Illinois Press, 1989); Victoria Bynum, *Unruly Women: The Politics of Social and Sexual Control in the Old South* (Chapel Hill: Univ. of North Carolina Press, 1992); Drew Gilpin Faust, *Mothers of Invention: Women of the Slaveholding South in the American Civil War* (Chapel Hill: Univ. of North Carolina Press, 1996); Leslie A. Schwalm, *A Hard Fight for We: Women's Transition from Slavery to Freedom in South Carolina* (Urbana: Univ. of Illinois Press, 1997); Catherine Clinton, ed., *Southern Families at War* (New York: Oxford Univ. Press, 2000); Jacqueline Glass Campbell, *When Sherman Marched North from the Sea* (Chapel Hill: Univ. of North Carolina Press, 2003); LeeAnn Whites and Alecia P. Long, eds., *Occupied Women: Gender, Military Occupation, and the American Civil War* (Baton Rouge: Louisiana State Univ. Press, 2009).

3. Isabella D. Martin and Myrta Lockett Avery, eds., *Mary Boykin Chesnut, A Diary From Dixie* (New York: D. Appleton, 1905), 20, 72. For an overview of the gendered language of secession, see Nina Silber, *Gender and the Sectional Conflict* (Chapel Hill: Univ. of North Carolina Press, 2009).

4. On the political nature of the Southern household, see Elizabeth Fox-Genevose, *Within the Plantation Household: Black and White Women of the Old South* (Chapel Hill: Univ. of North Carolina Press, 1988), 38–39. On honor, see Bertram Wyatt-Brown, *Southern Honor: Ethics and Behavior in the Old South* (New York: Oxford Univ. Press, 1982), 227.

5. Reid Mitchell, *The Vacant Chair: The Northern Soldier Leaves Home* (New York: Oxford Univ. Press, 1993); Harriet Beecher Stowe, *Uncle Tom's Cabin; Or Life among the Lowly* (Boston: John P. Jewitt, 1852).

6. Eugene Genovese, "Our Family White and Black": Family and Household in the Southern Slaveholders' World View," in Carol Bleser, ed., *In Joy and in Sorrow: Women, Family, and Marriage in the Victorian South* (New York: Oxford Univ. Press, 1991), 69–87. Martha de Saussure letter written on the eve of secession, n.d., qtd. in Rosser H. Taylor, *Antebellum South Carolina: A Social and Cultural History* (Chapel Hill: Univ. of North Carolina Press, 1942), 70.

7. Catherine Edmondston Diary, qtd. in Faust, *Mothers of Invention*, 138.

8. Stephanie McCurry, *Confederate Reckoning: Power and Politics in the Civil War South* (Cambridge, Mass.: Harvard Univ. Press, 2010).

9. The strongest argument for Confederate women's disaffection is Faust, *Mothers of Invention;* see also Rable, *Civil Wars*, which finds Confederate women's relationship to Southern nationalism equally fragile. For arguments that common suffering could lead to greater resolve on the home front as well as the battlefront, see Gary W. Gallagher, *The Confederate War* (Cambridge, Mass.: Harvard Univ. Press, 1997); and William Blair, *Virginia's Private War: Feeding Body and Soul in the Confederacy, 1861–1865* (New York: Oxford Univ. Press, 1998). For specific studies of gendered responses, see Campbell, *When Sherman Marched North;* and Lisa Tendrich Frank, *The Civilian War: Confederate Women and Union Soldiers during Sherman's March* (Baton Rouge: Louisiana State Univ. Press, 2015).

10. "Letters of General Thomas Williams, 1862,"*American Historical Review* 14 (Jan. 1909), 320; Captain Elliot Stephen Welch to "My Dear Mother," Feb. 14 and 24, 1865, Elliot Stephen Welch Papers, Perkins Library, Duke Univ., Durham, N.C. (hereafter cited as DUL). On the inner strength of Southern women, see Wyatt-Brown, *Southern Honor*, 227.

11. George Augustus Sala, *My Diary in America in the Midst of the War* (London: Tinsley Brothers, 1865), 2:351–54.

12. *The War of the Rebellion: A Compilation of the Official Records of the Union and Confederate Navies* (Washington, D.C.: Government Printing Office, 1880), ser. 1, vol. 12:596 (hereafter cited as *ORN*]; Tracy J. Revels, *Grander in Her Daughter: Florida's Women During the Civil War* (Columbia: Univ. of South Carolina Press, 2004), 116. Stephen Ash argues that

Jacqueline Glass Campbell

three images recurred in Southerners' descriptions of occupying soldiers, namely "violation, pollution, and degradation" and that women were particularly virulent in articulating these themes. See Stephen V. Ash, *When the Yankees Came: Conflict and Chaos in the Occupied South, 1861–1865* (Chapel Hill: Univ. of North Carolina Press, 1995), 41–43.

13. *The War of the Rebellion: A Compilation of the Official Records of the Union and Confederate Armies* (Washington, D.C.: Government Printing Office, 1900), ser. I, vol. 15:426. (hereafter cited as *O.R.*); Jacqueline G. Campbell, "'The Unmeaning Twaddle about Order 28': Benjamin F. Butler and Confederate Women in Occupied New Orleans, 1862," *Journal of the Civil War Era* 2 (Mar. 2012): 11–30; see also Faust, *Mothers of Invention*, 207–12.

14. Captain John Bratton to his wife, Feb. 17, 1865, John S. Bratton Papers, Southern Historical Collection, Univ. of North Carolina, Chapel Hill (hereafter cited as SHC).

15. Edward W. Benham to "Dear Jennie," Feb. 19, 1865, Edward W. Benham Papers, DUL.

16. Reid Mitchell, "'Not the General But the Soldier': The Study of Civil War Soldiers," in James McPherson and William J. Cooper Jr., eds., *Writing the Civil War: The Quest to Understand* (Columbia: Univ. of South Carolina Press, 1998), 91–92.

17. Henry Hitchcock, *Marching with Sherman,* ed. M. A. DeWolfe Howe (Lincoln: Univ. of Nebraska Press, 1995), 224.

18. Sarah Morgan, *The Civil War Diary of a Southern Woman,* ed. Charles East (New York: Touchstone Press, 1992), 60–62, 68–69, 122.

19. Mitchell, *Vacant Chair,* esp. 89–113.

20. *A Few Words in Behalf of the Loyal Women of the United States by One of Themselves,* Pamphlet 33, Loyal Publication Society No. 10. (New York: Wm. Bryant, May 1863); see also Silber, *Gender and the Sectional Conflict.*

21. Sala, *My Diary in America,* 2:365; Hartwell T. Bynum, "Sherman's Expulsion of the Roswell Women in 1864," *Georgia Historical Quarterly* 54 (Summer 1970): 169–82; Charles Royster, *The Destructive War: William Tecumseh Sherman, Stonewall Jackson, and the Americans* (New York: Knopf, 1991), 13–14; Marion Brunson Lucas, *Sherman and the Burning of Columbia* (Columbia: Univ. of South Carolina Press, 2000), 83–85; Mary Elizabeth Massey, *Women in the Civil War* (Lincoln: Univ. of Nebraska Press, 1994), 149.

22. Katherine M. Jones, ed., *Heroines of Dixie* (New York: Bobbs-Merrill, 1955), 317–25.

23. Massey, *Women in the Civil War,* 113, 109; Morgan, *Civil War Diary,* 152–53.

24. Massey, *Women in the Civil War,* 139, 213; Jones, *Heroines of Dixie,* 359–60.

25. See Faust, *Mothers of Invention;* and Elizabeth Fox-Genovese, *Within the Plantation Household.*

26. Jones, *Heroines of Dixie,* 133, 259, 261–64, 277.

27. Earl Schenck Miers, ed., *When the World Ended: The Diary of Emma LeConte* (New York: Oxford Univ. Press, 1957), 41; Grace Elmore Diary, Feb. 19, and Mar. 6, 1865, Special Collections, Univ. of South Carolina, Columbia (hereafter cited as USC); Captain David P. Conyngham, *Sherman's March Through the South* (New York: Sheldon, 1865), 346.

28. C. Vann Woodward, ed., *Mary Chesnut's Civil War* (New Haven, Conn.: Yale Univ. Press, 1981), 699.

29. See Deborah Gray White, *"Ar'n't I a Woman?": Female Slaves in the Plantation South* (New York: W. W. Norton, 1985).

30. See Jim Downs, *Sick From Freedom: African-American Illness and Suffering during the Reconstruction Era* (New York: Oxford Univ. Press, 2015); Chandra Manning, *Troubled Refuge: Struggling for Freedom in the Civil War* (New York: Random House, 2016).

31. Willie Lee Rose, *Rehearsal for Reconstruction: The Port Royal Experiment* (New York: Oxford Univ. Press, 1964); Saxton, qtd. in Schwalm, *A Hard Fight for We,* 102–3.

32. Schwalm, *A Hard Fight for We,* 141.

33. Nina Silber, "A Compound of Wonderful Potency: Women Teachers of the North in the Civil War South," in Joan Cashin, ed., *The War Was You and Me: Civilians in the American Civil War* (Princeton, N.J.: Princeton Univ. Press, 2002), 35–59.

34. Ira Berlin and Leslie S. Rowland, eds., *Families and Freedom: A Documentary History of African-American Kinship in the Civil War Era* (New York: New Press, 1997), 97, 102–3.

35. Ibid., 199–201; M. B. Lucas, "Camp Nelson Kentucky during the Civil War: Cradle of Liberty or Refugee Death Camp?" *Filson Club Historical Quarterly* 63, no. 4 (1989): 439–52; Amy Murrell Taylor, "How a Cold Snap in Kentucky led to Freedom for Thousands: An Environmental Story of Emancipation," in Stephen Berry, ed., *Weirding the War: Stories from the Civil War's Ragged Edges* (Athens: Univ. of Georgia Press, 2011), 191–214.

36. George P. Rawick, ed., *The American Slave: A Composite Autobiography* (Westport, Conn.: Greenwood, 1972), vol. 2., pt. 1:235, 259, 77; John F. Marszalek, ed., *Diary of Miss Emma Holmes* (Baton Rouge: Louisiana State Univ. Press, 1979), 403.

37. Maj. Gen. O. O. Howard to Maj. Gen. F. P. Blair Jr., Beaufort, S.C., Jan. 10, 1865, *O.R.*, ser. 1, vol. 47, pt. 2:33.

38. Rawick, ed., *American Slave*, vol. 2, pt. 2:256.

39. Peter Bardaglio, "The Children of Jubilee: African American Childhood in Wartime," in Catherine Clinton and Nina Silber, eds., *Divided Houses: Gender and the Civil War* (New York: Oxford Univ. Press, 1992), 213–29; Rawick, ed., *American Slave*, vol. 3, pt. 4:186–206; Campbell, *When Sherman Marched North*, 48–49.

40. Emily Geiger Goodlett, "The Burning of Columbia by Sherman, February 17, 1865," n.d., Emily Geiger Goodlett Papers, USC; Woodward, ed., *Mary Chesnut's Civil War*, 767. See also Yal Sternhell, *Routes of War: The World of Movement in the Confederate* South (Cambridge, Mass.: Harvard Univ. Press, 2012).

41. William Gilmore Simms, *Sack and Destruction of the City of Columbia, South Carolina*, ed. Alexander Samuel Salley (1865; repr., Atlanta: Oglethorpe Univ. Press, 1937), 53–54, 82; Katherine M. Jones, *When Sherman Came: Southern Women and the "Great March"* (Indianapolis: Bobbs-Merrill, 1964), 284, 362–63; Rawick, ed., *America Slave*, vol. 2, pt. 1:432; ibid., vol. 15, pt. 2:190; Testimony of Violet Guntharpe in Belinda Hurmence, ed., *Before Freedom* (New York: Penguin, 1990), 96; excerpt from Winnsboro (S.C.) *Courier*, n.d., typed manuscript in Mordecai Family Papers, SHC; see also Emily Geiger Goodlett Papers and Grace Elmost Diary, Mar. 6, 1865, both USC; Elizabeth to My Darling Child, Mar. 23, 1865, Hinsdale Family Papers, DUL.

42. Emily Harris Diary, qtd. in Faust, *Mothers of Invention*, 238; A. Grima to Alfred Grima, Nov. 27, 1863, Grima Family Papers, Historic New Orleans Collections, New Orleans.

43. A Southern Woman to Governor Z. B. Vance, Dec. 12, 1864; Nina to Gov. Vance, Dec. 30, 1864; H. Nutt to Gov. Vance, Dec. 12, 1864, all in Governor Zebulon Vance Papers, North Carolina Division of Archives and History, Raleigh (hereafter cited as NCDAH).

44. Sue O. Conly to Governor Z. B. Vance, Jan. 5, 1865; Harriet S. Briley to Governor Z. B. Vance, Dec. 30, 1865; see also Mrs. Richard Drake to Governor Z. B. Vance, Dec. 27, 1864; M. L. Wiggins to Governor Z. B. Vance, Jan. 1, 1865; Mary Newton to Governor Z. B. Vance, Jan. 10, 1865, all in Governor Zebulon B. Vance Papers, NCDAH.

45. Blair, *Virginia's Private War*, 79; Gallagher, *Confederate War*, 56, 78; Campbell, *When Sherman Marched North*; Frank, *Civilian War*.

46. Unsigned to My Dear Willie, Mar. 31, 1865, Henry William DeSaussure Papers, DUL; R.S.C. to Husband, Feb. 27, 1865, Rachel Susan Cheves Papers, DUL; *Diary of Miss Emma Holmes*, 407; Miers, ed., *When the World Ended*, 90–91; Harriott Middleton to Susan, Mar. 2, 1865, in Isabella Leland, ed., "Middleton Correspondence 1861–1865," *South Carolina Historical Magazine*, April 1964, 104; Lily Logan to My Precious Brother, Mar. 2, 1865, in Jones, *When Sherman Came*, 194; Elliot Welch to Mother, Feb. 24, 1865, Elliot Stephen Welch Papers, DUL.

47. Garret S. Byrne Diary, Feb., 1865, qtd. in Joseph T. Glatthaar, *The March to the Sea and Beyond: Sherman's Troops in the Savannah and Carolinas Campaigns* (Baton Rouge: Louisiana State Univ. Press, 1985), 72; William Grunert, *History of the One Hundred and Twenty Ninth Regiment Illinois Volunteer Infantry* (Winchester, Ill.: R. B. Dedman, 1866), 181–82.

48. Mrs. J. J. B., in Jones, *When Sherman Came,* 143; Loula to Poss, May 22, 1865, qtd. in Ash, *When the Yankees Came,* 40. These actions may have been intended to destroy Southern cultural identity, but in fact they often served to actively form a renewed Confederate identity, especially in the postwar world. See Campbell, *When Sherman Marched North,* 105–10. See also Anne Sarah Rubin, *Through the Heart of Dixie: Sherman's March and American Memory* (Chapel Hill: Univ. of North Carolina Press, 2014).

49. See, for example, Miers, ed., *When the World Ended,* 95–96; Woodward, ed., *Mary Chesnut's Civil War,* 800; Marszalek, ed., *Diary of Miss Emma Holmes,* 436–37.

50. Oscar Lawrence Jackson, ed., *The Colonel's Diary: Journals Kept Before and During the Civil War* (Sharon, Conn.: Privately published, 1922), 209; Captain George W. Pepper, *Personal Recollections* (Zanesville, Ohio: Hugh Dunne, 1866), 403; Conyngham, *Sherman's March Through the South,* 384.

51. Nellie Worth to My Dear Cousin, Mar. 21, 1865, in Jones, *When Sherman Came,* 261; Eliza Andrews, *Wartime Journal of a Georgia Girl* (Macon: Ardivan Press, 1960), 172; OTC to Father, April 21, 1865, qtd. in Glatthaar, *March to the Sea and Beyond,* 72.

52. Elizabeth Collier Diary, April 25, May 9, 1865, SHC; Ellen Mordecai to Emma Mordecai, 1865, Mordecai Family Papers, SHC; Eliza Fludd to her sister, Dec. 11, 1865, Eliza Burden Fludd Papers, DUL.

53. Woodward, ed., *Mary Chesnut's Civil War,* 800; Marszalek, ed., *Diary of Miss Emma Holmes,* 436–37; Grace Elmore Diary, May 2, 1865, USC.

54. Miers, ed., *When the World Ended,* 97, 99.

55. J. David Hacker, Libra Hilde, and James Holland Jones, "The Effect of the Civil War on Southern Marriage Patterns," *Journal of Southern History* 86 (Feb. 2010), 39–70; Giselle Roberts, *The Confederate Belle* (Columbia: Univ. of Missouri Press, 2003); Jane Turner Censer, *The Reconstruction of White Southern Womanhood, 1865–1895* (Baton Rouge: Louisiana State Univ. Press, 2003); Nancy Bercaw, *Gendered Freedoms: Race, Rights, and the Politics of Household in the Delta, 1861–1875* (Gainesville: Univ. Press of Florida, 2003).

56. LeeAnn Whites, *The Civil War as a Crisis in Gender: Augusta, Georgia, 1860–1890* (Athens: Univ. of Georgia Press, 1995).

57. Woodward, ed., *Mary Chesnut's Civil War,* 716; Marli F. Weiner, ed., *A Heritage of Woe: The Civil War Diary of Grace Brown Elmore, 1861–1868* (Athens: Univ. of Georgia Press, 1997), 176.

58. Elizabeth Avery Meriwether, Recollections, SHC.

Women and the Family
at Home in the North

NICOLE ETCHESON

During the Civil War, Mary Livermore and Jane Hoge hired a builder to do construction for the United States Sanitary Commission fair they were planning in Chicago. The builder, however, told them their signatures on the contract were worthless. Under Illinois law, he needed their husbands' signatures as well. In her memoirs, Livermore wrote of her outrage: they were legal adults, efficient administrators who had raised the necessary funds. But, as Livermore recalled, "Our earnings were not ours, but belonged to our husbands." Needing the construction done, Livermore and Hoge sent for their husbands and procured the necessary signatures. Livermore's biographer, Wendy Hamand Venet, argues the legal subordination of women to their husbands was probably not the revelation that Livermore claimed, although Livermore recalled in her memoirs that this incident caused her to vow that after the war ended she "would take up a new work—the work of making law and justice synonymous for women." According to Venet, Livermore had "led a reasonably conventional life" before the war, "one that was defined by her husband's professional duties and by her commitment to their daughters," the expected domestic role of child-rearing. Incidents such as the building contract helped make her into an advocate for women's rights as well as for the more conventional woman's reform of temperance. For Venet, Livermore is a "prime example" of the "many women who had led traditional lives before 1861 [but] were transformed by their experiences in the Civil War."[1]

African American women could not live out nineteenth-century gender ideals as easily as white women. The black middle class might aspire to the ideals of domesticity, but the reality was more difficult to fulfill. Black families' survival often required women to work outside the home, and Northern white supremacy denied even free blacks equality. Since black women often worked in other people's homes, they were subject to sexual advances that called their virtue into question. Like working-class whites, black families might not be able to achieve the middle-class ideal of the nuclear family. They might also need to rely on relatives or friends to raise children while they worked. Higher rates of poverty, illness, and death rendered the black family less stable than the white.[2]

Generations of historians have emphasized how the Civil War altered women's role by opening up new professions to them in nursing and clerical work, thereby challenging assumptions of both men and women's innate characteristics and stimulating the movement toward women's rights. But the literature on Civil War women has not explored how women's life stages determined their war experience. Mary Livermore, for example, was a middle-aged matron with a supportive spouse and children old enough not to require constant care. The Civil War transformed her understanding of women's roles, but she experienced the Civil War as she did because of her age. Study of the "life course" acknowledges that one's roles change many times in a lifetime. The expectations of those roles differ not just with age but with the cultural norms of the historical period in which one experiences childhood, young womanhood, marriage, and motherhood.[3]

The Civil War challenged the gender order by taking men out of the home. Ginette Aley writes that "nineteenth-century gender norms defined a woman's life almost entirely by her relationships and in terms of her family."[4] However, the experience of individual women depended greatly on their life stage. The experience of a sweetheart was different from that of a wife, the experience of a sister different than that of a daughter. Peter S. Carmichael calls his study of young Virginia men a collective portrait of a generation. He seeks to use age "as a category of analysis" akin to the perennial standbys of race, class, and gender. Rather than following a generation through the war, as Carmichael does, I seek to represent women at different points in life during the same event, the national Civil War. Historians of women are familiar with the concept of separate spheres, with woman's sphere being the home. But Steven Mintz and Susan Kellogg argue that the idea of spheres applied not just to gender but to age. Girls had different roles than did young women or matrons. By capturing the experience of women at many different stages of life, one can get an idea of the impact of the Civil War on Northern women. The majority of my case studies come from rural and middle-class women. Even though the United States was fast urbanizing in the first half of the nineteenth century, 80 percent of the population still lived in the countryside or in towns with under 2,500 people.[5]

Mary Livermore chose to begin her account of the Civil War years with her experience as a daughter. Before the firing on Fort Sumter, she had gone to Boston to care for her elderly father. But Livermore was a grown woman with a husband and children of her own, and she lived in a country where children were one-third of the population. Since the median age of Civil War soldiers was twenty-three to twenty-four, those who were fathers were likely to have young children. As Catherine A. Jones points out, historians have preferred to study cultural constructions of childhood that are more fully documented than the actual experience of being a child. The younger the girl, the less likely she was to leave a record of her Civil War experience, although comments in parents' letters help fill the gap. Nonetheless, children experienced the war differently than adults did. Anne Scott McLeod argues that nineteenth-century girlhood was remarkably free from constraints. Little girls ran and played, fished, and climbed trees, as did boys. According to McLeod, the anguish that Jo March, Louisa May Alcott's alter ego in *Little Women,* experiences arises from the knowledge that adulthood costs "the freedom to behave according to her nature than to a prescribed code for her sex."[6]

Nevertheless, childhood was the period when girls learned womanhood's "prescribed code." As James Marten has written, Civil War fathers still tried to be "fathers in function as well as in name" despite their absence, substituting advice on child rearing for their presence at home.[7] Alcott dramatized the importance of a father's letters in the opening chapter of *Little Women.* Writing from the front, the Reverend March advises the girls to be "loving children" to their mother, "do their duty faithfully, fight their bosom enemies bravely, and conquer themselves so beautifully that when I come back to them I may be fonder and prouder than ever of my little women."[8] Col. Aden Cavins, an Indiana lawyer before the war, certainly advised his children to form their character and their sentiments as well as intellects. But these admonitions had more effect on his four sons—aged twelve to five—than they would have had on his daughter, who was only a toddler. Marten notes that fathers had less advice for daughters than for sons, feeling that they did not know the appropriate advice to give a daughter. Aden Cavins could only commiserate with his boys that their infant sister must indeed be a "secesh" if she pulled their hair: "I suppose she conquers, and wins every battle."[9] Tillman Valentine, a black sergeant in the 3rd U.S. Colored Troops, expressed his desire to see his wife and children, writing, "Kiss little girl," meaning his daughter Ida. He urged his wife, Annie, to "teach the children good maners" and "to reade and wright." He wanted a "likeness," or photograph, of the children.[10]

Mintz and Kellogg argue that the nineteenth-century family viewed children as "distinct individuals with unique needs." Cavins tailored his advice to the particular personalities of his children. His "earnest wish" for his daughter, Jodie, was "that war may never cloud her happiness and that life may be to her as mild as her infant slumber and as beautiful as the radiant sparkle of the dew drop hanging up flowers fresh and full-bloom in May." Her infancy precluded specific advice, but he enjoyed receiving news of Jodie's development.[11] Similarly, John Peirce, a Massachusetts artilleryman, whose daughter Clara had just started to talk, was "glad she is well and fat."[12] Fathers asked that daughters write them, although children's letters rarely survived. John Applegate, an Indiana cavalryman, instructed his daughter, Allie, "I want you to wright as often as you can if it is only one line it will pleas me."[13]

Nine-year-old Allie Applegate, whose father had been away at the war for three years, evidently missed him deeply. At the end of the war, her mother wrote, "Allie is nearly crazy to hear from you she said this morning if you was only home to go to sunday school with her she would be so glad she promises herself nice times when you come home." Allie's longing to see her father was a theme her mother repeated in letters throughout the war.[14] Iowa soldier John Larimer's daughter Clara promised that when her father was home, "I will sleep with him & hug him & kiss him ever so mutch."[15] Both of Larimer's children, Clara and Eddie, frequently expressed their wish for him to come home. Historians of the family who have emphasized a father's authority obscure the genuine affection fathers and daughters felt for each other.[16]

Children left orphaned by the war numbered in the thousands. Many Northern states opened orphans' homes. But more fatherless children probably continued to live with their mother or other family members. Aden Cavins returned safely from the war when Jodie was three years old. John Applegate came home, but he had been so severely weakened by imprisonment at Andersonville that he died two years later. Elizabeth Applegate, in order to support herself and her daughter, secured a widow's pension and a dependent child's pension, took in boarders, and did sewing. Allie attended school, including the woman's college at Indiana Asbury, and eventually married a minister. She left no record of the impact of losing her father as a child, but in her papers was a newspaper clipping from 1863, "A Soldier's Letter to his Children," in which the absent father longs for his family and finds renewed strength in the letters from home. Perhaps the clipping's presence among later papers, dating from the 1880s and afterwards, indicates Allie's continued sense of the loss both she and her father had suffered in their separation.[17]

The emotional closeness of the nineteenth-century American family appeared not just in the relationships between parents and children but also in those of sisters and brothers. By embodying loyalty and selflessness, sibling relationships took on emotional importance in an increasingly individualistic society. Although sibling rivalry existed, historians emphasize the "mutual succor" siblings provided each other. Sibling relationships were relatively egalitarian, but older sisters in particular might function as "deputy mothers" to younger siblings. Sending a brother to war, and having him die, increased a sister's tendency to idealize what was already a close relationship.[18] Iowa soldier Ortus C. Shelton valued letters and visits from his sisters, Mary and Amanda. He noted in his diary when he received letters, the length of time between letters, and how the letters made him feel. A June 1864 letter from Mary "was of great interest to me. Some things giving me pleasure and others subject for thought." At the end of August, the "most important event today was the receipt of three letters," including one from Mary. Mary made note of Ortus's enlistment and departure for the front: "Sad! Sad! Now I can weep with those that weep. My noble brother gone into the Army. God save and keep him!" She found it "lonely without Brother."[19] Sallie Stafford in Ohio understood the sentiment: "It is hard to part with brothers to go to the army I went with Brother Sam when he went to Camp and I never will forget the looks of him and my feelings when I bid him Good by."[20]

In September 1864 Ortus Shelton became ill while still in camp in Iowa. Amanda sent Mary a letter telling her "of the serious illness of our darling Brother" and cried "to God in his behalf." A week later, a telegram came "that Bro is dangerous." Mary, working as a nurse in Tennessee, rode through the night, her "heart almost bursting with anxiety," desperate that "God will only spare him till I can see him once more." Four days later, "Thank God! Reached home in time to see him die. . . . God help us in our great sorrow!" Amanda wrote a great deal about her hospital work during the war, but at its close she paused to reflect on her "terrible anxiety" at two times during the war: when Mary was in Union lines threatened by Confederate cavalry and "my Brothers sickness and death."[21]

Ella Hawn in Ohio also mourned for "those Dear Brothers of mine." Her brother John was in the army, "exposed to all the hardships that a Soldier must endure." The family worried that his failure to write indicated that he was sick. Another brother, Marion, "sleeps in death beneath a Southern Soil." The family had made repeated and unsuccessful efforts to get his remains returned. "We sometimes fear we will never get him & . . . this was his last request & we should & will use every effort to get him & this is all we can do."[22] Adelia Shroyer bemoaned the death of her brother Newton: "O what a horrible sight [to] look upon and to think that was all that was left of the once merry-hearted bright eyed Boy, my Dear Brother, it is dreadful to contemplate, but alas how frail is life."[23] Fannie Meredith also lost her brother, John, who accidently shot himself in the head while on guard duty. Fannie took comfort that letters from the captain and others "said he was much loved by all his comrades and the officers." The letters gave a complete account of the burial, including "what pieces the Band played." She regretted that the family had not been able to bring the body home and reflected, with conventional religious sentiment, on the fragility of life: "Oh! Death is there no power to stay thy relentless hand and snatch the gay, the beautiful, from thy embrace."[24]

Although Meredith's religious sentiments appear to be conventional pieties rather than deeply felt, the Shelton sisters seem to have possessed a profound religiosity. Sean A. Scott and George C. Rable have shown how Americans viewed the war as providential, as the working out of a divine plan only dimly understood by mankind. Religion provided consolation. Scott, in particular, argues that historians have slighted how "devout" Northern women "emphasized the value of prayer, the importance of spiritual growth, and the necessity of relying completely on God when suffering through trials."[25]

As they feared for absent brothers or mourned their deaths, sisters also lived their own lives. Both Shelton sisters were active in nursing during the war, having been recruited by Annie Wittenmyer, head of the Iowa State Sanitary Commission. Amanda even seemed to lament the end of the war for forcing her to leave the hospital in Washington, D.C., "in which I have spent some of the happiest as well as some of the most sad hours of my life." Both sisters pondered the state of their immortal souls in their diaries. Their concern for their brother appeared in their wartime diaries along with religious musings and accounts of hospital work. Both young women had romances, although Amanda's may have contributed to those "sad hours," for she resisted the advances of "a finished flirt." As wrenching as Ortus's death had been, the war was Amanda's coming of age: "In the last year I have lived more myself and seen more of life than in all the former years."[26]

Unlike the Shelton sisters, Lydia and Aramenta Rader spent the war at home on the family's Henry County, Indiana, farm. They kept their brother, George, a soldier in the 84th Indiana, informed of affairs at home: the corn harvest, threshing, the hogs, the family's health, elections, and Sunday preaching. They relayed admonitions for him to write his father and send a miniature to their mother. Lydia sent him a box of "victuals." Both sisters wanted to see him—Lydia, more than anything in the world. Aramenta wrote she had trouble enjoying herself with George gone. She "hope[d] that the time will soon come when you will be set free from the duties of the country and then you can join the little family circle once more." Both worried about him. Lydia feared he might have to stand picket in the rain after having contracted the measles. Some of her fears were carelessly expressed: that he might never come home to go to Sunday services with her, or that the only furlough he would be able to get would be "in the shape of a coffin." Aramenta was more tactful, but even she had "almost given up all hope of ever seeing you anymore" and was concerned that the South would kill every prisoner taken after the Emancipation Proclamation.[27]

George's absence caused an increased workload, but not for his sisters.[28] There was sufficient male labor in the family that Lydia and Aramenta were not called upon to fill their brother's place. A New York farm wife noted that she and her daughters had to help her husband in the fields after all their sons enlisted, not because the family lacked money to hire farm help but because there were no men to hire.[29] In Fort Wayne, Indiana, Mary Hamilton found herself threshing wheat while her younger sister drove the horses, and her oldest sister pitched the sheaves up to Mary. Their brother raked the straw from the machine their father had built to save labor and Mary unbound the sheaves. "I do not know what he would do if it was not for his girls," Mary said.[30] Farm machinery helped fill the labor gap. Advertisements showed young women operating the machines with captions such as "My brother has gone to the war."[31] The Rader and Shelton sisters, however, did not see an alteration in the work expected from them because of their brother's absence. Their work as sisters was largely emotional: missing him, worrying about him, and perhaps grieving for him.

Sisters cared about brothers, but not in the same way that sweethearts cared for absent lovers. Nineteenth-century Americans valued romantic love as the moment when one revealed the true self to one's beloved. Courtship had long been conducted through correspondence, so the Civil War did not provide an innovation in that regard. In their letters, men and women showed their most intimate thoughts and feelings as they sought to discern the suitability of a prospective marriage partner.[32] During the Civil War, however, courtship became politicized, as one's choice of a suitor was accompanied with professions of support for the war.

A burgeoning romance played out in the letters between Hattie F. Kemper and her "Dear Friend" and distant cousin, G. W. H. ("Tip") Kemper, an assistant surgeon in the 17th Indiana. Hattie offered to send news and learned Civil War songs to play when he returned to visit. She called him a friend and teasingly offered to find a suitable wife for him among her acquaintances. He granted her the "privilege" of calling him "brother." When she didn't hear from him, she "almost concluded some rebel had captivated you, or, some of those beautiful ladies down in Dixie, had stricken your heart." On another occasion, she "came to the conclusion you had fallen with the noble slain." But in each case letters came, renewing their relationship. By the end of 1864, after over a year of correspondence, Hattie was writing of "*love*." Now she teased him about the "*kiss*" he had enclosed in his letter: "Some one else must have taken it, or you forgot to put it in." Hattie had almost decided that they should cease corresponding because the relationship seemed to have stalled, when Tip surprised her by proposing. During their following engagement, she felt uncomfortable going out in company while he was away. The two then granted each other the privilege to socialize even though separated. In January 1865 Hattie was planning their wedding and worrying about her future as a doctor's wife.[33]

If Hattie occasionally expressed concern that Tip would be lured away by a Southern belle, Tip evidently fretted about the "old bachelors." Hattie reassured him that she would prefer spinsterhood to such "stay-at-home rangers."[34] As Hattie's contempt for "stay-at-home rangers" indicated, granting romantic favors became a politically charged act for women in the Civil War. Ohioan Emma A. Moody wrote she would never marry either "An Abolition or a home coward," as she "dispise[d] . . . these two classes of men."[35] When Tip's service expired, he evidently felt unsure whether the patriotic Hattie would support his decision to leave the army and return to medical school. But Hattie insisted, "I think the same as you do, I think you have stood by the flag of our country nobly and protected as a good Union soldier should. Now let some of those *Stay-at-home rangers* go and do something."[36]

Whatever misgivings Hattie harbored during their courtship, Tip Kemper was not playing the field. Ohioan Edwin Lewis Lybarger, however, not only corresponded with a number of female friends and relatives during the war, including his future wife, but placed an advertisement soliciting female correspondents. The girl he eventually chose, Sophronia Rogers, was painfully aware of his correspondence with another young woman, Ella Hawn, who taunted Phrone about Ed's letters. Lybarger eventually broke off the relationship with Ella, writing her to end their correspondence and signing himself as her "friend" but "no longer . . . Lover." Meanwhile, Phrone was dallying with Dawson Critchfield, whom she pointedly called "*My* Critchfield" in letters to Ed. Echoing the language of Ella's letter, perhaps to let Ed know she was aware of it, she closed, "I remain as ever your friend but no longer a lover." In later letters, she daringly assured Ed that she "had quite as much experience" in flirting as he did, and she made him aware that she knew of his letters to yet another young woman. Ed replied with a long, and apparently, soothing letter. Sophronia did not want to end their correspondence. When a visiting friend said to send Ed her love, Sophronia protested, "I do not allow any one save myself to love you." She vowed that if she ever became angry with him again, "I will hug you to death—so that I will not be punished for crime." But Sophronia soon found it necessary to require Ed to end his correspondence with Lizzie Baker, who was claiming that she, and not Phrone, was Ed's sweetheart. Ed did, however, continue writing to two other young ladies at the same time that he accused Sophronia of flirting with other local swain, and in fact Ed did not break off his correspondence with one young woman until he married Sophronia in January 1867.[37] Martha Tomhave Blauvelt has documented the traps young women faced in discerning whether a suitor's blandishments and importuning for physical intimacy were sincere or would fatally injure one's reputa-

Nicole Etcheson

tion.[38] Enforced separation reduced the risk of seduction, but Lybarger was still able to trifle with the affections of several young women at once.

A single woman at least had choices, but a wife had to accept the decisions her husband made. Marriages might be companionate, but husbands possessed ultimate authority. A proper wife resigned herself and submitted to her husband's will. One officer forbade his wife from becoming a nurse, even though she too wished to serve her country in some capacity. Mary Livermore noted that there were women who followed their husbands into the army. One woman who had disguised herself as a man was discovered and removed from the company, but she escaped and, Livermore suspected, managed to rejoin her husband.[39]

Talk of a draft motivated Samuel Cormany to join the 16th Pennsylvania Cavalry. He wanted to enlist as a volunteer, not wait to be drafted. His wife, Rachel, after much prayer, "agreed that as a loyal, patriotic Man I should Enlist." But he enlisted first and then told Rachel. Samuel wrote that Rachel "calmly consents," but Rachel's word was "resigned." The initial "indescribable heaviness of heart" gave way, although she still occasionally succumbed to bouts of "weeping freely." Even the patriotic song "Soldier's Wife," although it asserted that the "Country has / For him a great claim," greater than "wife and children," depicted the wife as less than reconciled, for when "honor calls—why should I weep, / Tho' I am left behind?"[40] Elise Isely, a Swiss immigrant, wept after her husband, Christian, joined the 2nd Kansas Cavalry. As Christian Isely contemplated whether to enlist, Elise prayed "Daily to our Father in heaven" for guidance. She did not give "vent to her feelings" until after Christian's departure. Although the Iselys were both immigrants, Linda Schelbitzki Pickle argues that Elise was very Americanized. Although she made cheese in the Swiss manner, marked her butter rolls with a mold sent by Swiss relatives, and was multilingual, she had joined the Congregational church and the Isely children married native-born Americans.[41]

Good wives deferred to their husband's judgment. Clara Vinson Weaver clearly wanted her husband, Iowa major James B. Weaver, to return home. But she demurred, writing, "But not for one moment would I dissuade you from doing your duty. I dare not counsel you in any way for I do not know. . . . My feelings say come & so does my judgment as far as I am capable of judging, but you know best, & what is honorable & becoming a Christian."[42] Mary S. Logan viewed her marriage as close to the companionate ideal: "Our marriage was a real partnership for thirty-one happy years." She shared her husband's "thoughts and plan," and they worked "in the harmony of a common purpose." She had, however, a good idea of how gender roles affected women, referring, perhaps mockingly, to women's admiration of militia drill by "their lords and masters." Because she had helped her father when he held public office, she was able to aid her husband in his legal career. When war broke out, John Logan was a congressman from southern Illinois. He returned to Washington, leaving her behind to keep his constituents "as nearly as I could in the channel in which Mr. Logan had adroitly drawn them"—that is, in support of the Union. He returned to do recruiting, and he trusted only her as courier for his dispatches. "He had resolved to enter the army . . . with no alternative but to leave me to do the best I could."[43]

Rachel Cormany, with their baby daughter, stayed initially with Samuel's mother and stepfather, but she did not like Samuel's stepfather. She boarded then with the Ploughs, but found John Plough overbearing. Her letters to Samuel were "so blue" they made Samuel weep. Plough was not doing promised chores for Rachel, causing Samuel to have a long talk with him while home on furlough. Although Samuel felt "quite certain maters will now and hereafter be more satisfactory," Rachel still lamented having been left with strangers, being unable to go out much because of the baby, and living as "a hermit in a large town."[44] In Elise Isely's case, she lived with a school friend of her husband's and his wife in Leavenworth. She got along well with the family, and it was there that she gave birth to her first child in June 1862.[45]

A husband's absence also meant the lack of a breadwinner. Even so, Ann Larimer competently ran her Iowa household and cared for the children while her husband, John, was away at war. Although she asked his opinion about selling cattle and other business matters, she clearly made her own decisions. John advised selling, but Ann wrote, "If I have a chance to sell them for a good price, I will do so, & if not, why, I will keep the[m] until fall & see if you are not home to attend to them." Ann also borrowed money, and knowing that other wives were getting relief funds from the county, speculated that "if Unckle Sam or one of unckle sam's boyes did not forke over pretty soon I would have to apply to the county."[46] But in some cases, women could not make a livelihood without their husbands. As R. Douglas Hurt points out, farm women often had enough work raising young children and carrying out their share of the farm's tasks such as raising poultry, canning food, and gardening. Although one Iowa farm wife and her children managed to rake and bind twenty acres of wheat in hundred-degree temperatures, another woman might find that ordinary chores rendered such an extra task impossible.[47]

As Mary Livermore noted, well-to-do women might experience "hours of dreadful suspense" worrying about their husbands, but poorer women suffered real destitution. One woman found the promises of better-off men for support while her husband fought to be unreliable. She narrowly avoided the poorhouse when her husband sent his back pay. Money from soldier husbands might be "irregular and small remittances." Women tried to provide for their children by sewing, but often found they could not earn enough to pay the rent and feed their children. As Judith Giesberg has documented, the war brought poverty to many women.[48]

Black women suffered not just the effects of worry about their menfolk and loss of the breadwinner but also the financial hardship that occurred when black soldiers took a principled stand about unequal pay. Soldiers of the 54th Massachusetts Infantry refused their pay until they were compensated at the same rate as white soldiers. Although admirable, this stance often imposed great suffering on their families, despite the efforts of Massachusetts governor John A. Andrew to provide relief. One former slave was turned out by her landlady and lost her child. Another had four children to support. The pay boycott lasted over a year, until Congress provided equal pay for black soldiers. Governor Andrew complained to President Lincoln that the families of black soldiers had been "driven to beggary and the almshouse."

Nonetheless, historian Ella Forbes argues that black women supported black men's war effort, viewing the sacrifice as necessary for the advancement of their race.[49] Cpl. Henry Harmon of the 3rd U.S. Colored Troops told readers of the *Christian Recorder*, "When you hear of a white family that has lost father, husband, or brother, you can say of the colored man, we too have borne our share of the burden."[50] Harmon voiced an ideal of sacrifice. Annie Valentine, however, was apparently less patient with her husband's absences. While promising to send her money, Tillman scolded, "Dear wife you aske a very hearde [hard] thing when you aske for us to come home on forlow [furlough] for we can not come it is in posable [impossible]."[51]

Mary Logan "made the best" of her husband's military service by helping with the war effort. She raised supplies for Logan's troops, and for as much of the war as possible, she lived in an army camp with her husband. In camp she nursed at the hospital, cared for her husband during an illness, "acted as amanuensis and messenger for him," worked with war refugees, and even buried the dead. But although the Logans were evidently comfortably situated, she hired a black war refugee, Albert, to do the man's work about the house. Albert took care of the livestock and the garden. She taught him to read and write, and she successfully defended him from local Copperheads, who resented the residence of a "nigger" in their neighborhood.[52]

Some wives obviously missed the physical intimacies of marriage. Clara Weaver instructed her husband in a letter, "O Weaver hug me up closely to you & let me kiss you a thousand times ten thousand." Only two days later, she was writing, "I love you so good this morning, Sit down here by me & lay your head in my lap & let me kiss you & so fondly & smoothe your hair back, & look straight into your eyes & then just smother you with kisses."[53] When John Larimer sent his family a photograph, Ann liked the look of his eyes and mouth: "I certainly think you must have been thinking of what those lips would receive when I got the picture."[54]

In addition to the economic and emotional deprivation wives endured during the war, there was the added fear for their husbands. In May 1863, once "the fighting had commenced in earnest," Rachel Cormany felt "uneasy about [Samuel] all the time." Another worried wife walked miles, carrying her baby, to see if Rachel had news from the battlefield about their husbands. "What will woman not do or endure for the man she loves," Rachel commented. Perhaps comforted by her religious faith, Rachel became resigned to Samuel's danger; her fears "diminished" and she became "confident that he will return."[55] Martha Blauvelt argues that religion helped women achieve an attitude of "resigned gratitude": submission to life's hardships, including the death of children, and gratitude for the blessings they enjoyed. But when a rumor circulated that communication between home front and army was to be stopped, Rachel fell into a profound depression, confessing herself "tired of living," until news came that the rumor was false.[56]

Clara Weaver tried to reassure her husband that she was not excessively worried. Not wishing to "borrow trouble," she remained "cheerful" but insisted that "it would be unnatural were I not troubled about you."[57] The song "Soldier's Wife" asked listeners to "Think of the agonizing fear, / The deep suspense of mind—" felt by the wife,

"For, he may fall—Then I must weep / for I am left behind!"[58] After the death of her infant son, Elise Isely also wrote poetry: "One friend is left most dear of all / It is my husband far away / What Oh! If he yet too should fall / O God have pitty when I pray, hear me pray."[59] Anxiety was a common word in Mary Logan's memoirs: "unspeakable anxiety" during the Vicksburg campaign, "midnight hours of sleepless anxiety" during the Atlanta campaign, and "a long and anxious winter" of 1864–1865.[60] One Maine wife signed her letter, "So good night from your anxious wife anxious for your safe arrival home."[61]

As Rachel Cormany's depression revealed, failure to receive letters caused wives enormous emotional distress. Ann Larimer, not having received a recent letter, told her husband, "I should like to know where you are & how you are." By early April, Ann had not gotten a letter in nine weeks. When one arrived, it relieved her fear that he was dead.[62] However, wives read the newspapers and therefore understood which military engagements involved their husbands. Clara Weaver knew her husband was in the Battle of Corinth even as she wrote.[63] And when her husband's tardy missive arrived, Ann Larimer knew that Richmond had fallen and the Union armies were in pursuit of Robert E. Lee's army: "What a bloody battle will be fought & how many brave men will fall, will it be possible for you to get through safe? I cannot think so but there will be some come out safe & perhaps you may be one of the numbers."[64]

Rachel Cormany's initial joy at Samuel's safe return from the war turned to sadness when Samuel confessed "a few lapses" during his military service. These involved drinking and perhaps some dalliances with Southern women. "Almost heartbroken over his missteps," Samuel "vowed" to Rachel "that henceforth no such misteps shall befall him." Rachel "prayed God for grace to overcome," to hide "the anguish of my heart," and "save him from despair." A few days earlier, Rachel had been rejoicing at Samuel's safe return and the end to the loneliness she had borne for three years. She still hoped for them to have their "own home" for their family.[65] On the other hand, Elise and Christian Isely's reunion in the fall of 1864 seems to have been unmarred. Although Elise professed to "love our cause dearly," she was gratified when Christian did not reenlist because "it would almost have broken my heart to think that I should wait so long again before seeing you."[66]

Like wives, mothers could influence but not control male family members. Mothers who themselves could not vote or hold office were expected to inculcate the virtues necessary to republican self-government in sons who would exercise political power. Mothers might lament their sons' departure for war but were expected to take pride in their willingness to fight for their country.[67] When Mary Livermore took her father to see the 6th Massachusetts Infantry depart after Fort Sumter, she saw a woman who had fainted. A bystander explained that the woman had just learned of her son's enlistment that morning. Livermore tried to comfort the woman but found that "the pallid middle-aged mother was weak in body only." "If the country needs my boy . . . I am not the woman to hinder him," the mother said. Her other son having drowned, she said, "He's all I've got . . . but when he told me he'd enlisted, I gave him my blessing, and told him to go—for if we lose our country what

Nicole Etcheson

is there to live for?"[68] A New York farm woman sent three sons to the war and lost the youngest: "It came very hard on us to let the boys go, but we felt we'd no right to hinder 'em. The country needed 'em more'n we."[69] A Lynn, Massachusetts, mother was more nuanced in her willingness for her son to go to war. She thought it strange that he could "love military life so dearly and still stranger that now [he] wish[ed] to be in battle I hope the Lord may prevent it is my Daily Prayer." Shuddering at the "inhuman Butchery" of Fredericksburg and Vicksburg, she admonished him, "only if you are called to go do your duty my Darling son."[70]

Alice Fahs has written that "Civil War America was in fact a deeply maternalist culture." Popular songs, such as "Just Before the Battle, Mother," emphasized the soldier's maternal tie. As women moved into nursing, they justified this new role as one previously carried out by women in the home. One of the most famous Union nurses was "Mother" Ann Bickerdyke.[71] Louisa May Alcott said she felt "a motherly affection" for her patients, and even her "manliest" patient answered her, "'Yes, ma'am,' like a little boy."[72]

As the number of children declined in the middle-class family, child-rearing and socialization were left increasingly to the mother, whose duty it was to build the "character" of her children while the husband was largely absent earning the family's living. As Mary P. Ryan has documented, women cared for the physical well-being of their children and strove to inculcate the virtues for a moral and successful life, such as the prudence and sobriety valued by an emerging middle class.[73] When war came, women were still concerned with physical and moral well-being. While at camp in Indianapolis, William H. Anderson observed female visitors teaching the new soldiers how to cook and do dishes: "I have often saw the mother in camp wat[c]hing her sone, and [rest] of the boys cooking; and looking at them with a longing look, as if she thought that I never raised you to be a cook."[74] George Rader's mother tried to provide for his comfort and maintain contact. She made socks for him—his father made his boots since the army's were too small—and also sent yarn and a darning needle, so he could mend them himself, as well as stamps and advice on avoiding illness.[75]

By young manhood, however, a soldier might be less attached to his mother. Edwin Lybarger saved the letters from his numerous female correspondents but not those from his mother, nor was he as conscientious in writing to his mother as he did to his young female pen pals. Sophronia Rogers repeatedly reminded Ed of his failure to write and his mother's anxiety. "It almost killed your mother when she heard you were wounded," Sophronia wrote in November 1862. A month later, Sophronia continued, "Your Mother talks of you all the time & very often cries about you. She is very uneasy about you." Amelia Lybarger's lamentations seem to have been extreme; she failed to resign herself as a proper mother should. Sophronia noted that she could not enjoy their visits "on account of her grief." Ed apparently complained that he had received only one letter from his mother, but Sophronia insisted his mother had written more. "You have a dear kind mother who cares for you. . . . Think not that your mother had not written to you because you received but one letter from home. I hardly ever go down but what your mother is writing to you." Amelia Lybarger eventually recovered her composure. "Your mother is looking quite well," Sophronia reported, "& I think all that prevents her from being perfectly happy is your absence from her."[76]

Samuel Cormany "had a long talk with Mother seeking to get her reconciled to my going into the Army." Samuel had to convince his mother, a member of the United Brethren, that fighting would not endanger his immortal soul if he was "defending my Mother and Home and Country."[77] But like wives, mothers often realized they had little control over grown sons. A Vermont woman admonished her son that he didn't need the enlistment bounty to make a living: she and his father "would rather that you would not [reenlist] for i cannot think of you going back there again, but i suppose you wil make up your mind to do none or the other before this reaches you."[78] Heinrich Bruns had to slip away quietly and join the Union army to avoid attracting the attention of Jefferson City, Missouri, secessionists. He left his father an envelope containing a lock of his hair, saying, "Give this to Mother."[79]

Sick or dying soldiers, however, often longed for their mothers. One such soldier, feverish, "fancied himself at home with his mother" and called to her for water. Mary Livermore noted that in the hospital men would claim to have the best of mothers, who would come if they knew their son was sick, but they often refused to contact them for fear of causing worry. One mother did not recognize her son, who looked far older than twenty-two, until the hospitalized man exclaimed, "I *am* your boy! Don't you know your Willie?"[80] Louisa May Alcott took a less sentimental view of mothers than did Livermore. One was "an acid, frost-bitten female," whose "anxious fussiness" did her son more harm than good. Nonetheless, Alcott admired her endurance—"she slept on the floor, without uttering a complaint"—and showed "never-failing patience" with her "petulant" son.[81] Jette Geisberg Bruns nursed her nephew Caspar after he lost his arm at Fort Donelson. Her husband brought Caspar back to Jefferson City, Missouri, where "the Turners," members of the German American social and political club, transported Caspar to the Bruns's house. Jette tended him and reassured the dying youth, "Caspar, in Heaven it will be better." Although historian Linda Schelbitzki Pickle believes Jette Bruns never assimilated to the United States—she failed to learn English well and continued to long for family and life in Germany—her experience as the maternal figure for Civil War soldiers matched that of many native-born American women.[82]

Mothers as well as wives might face hardship from the war. Nancy Needham in Delaware County, Indiana, sought money from the county board of commissioners to support her family. One son had been killed in the war and another was in the army, leaving her with four children to support: "She says she is in very needy circumstances."[83] Lydia Bixby, a working-class Irish widow, needed more than an eloquent condolence letter. When her sons died, she needed money to support her younger children.[84] Leading men in Greencastle, Indiana, tried to persuade Gov. Oliver P. Morton to have Lucius Chapin stationed closer to home because he was the "only reliable support" of his widowed mother, Sarah, two other of her sons having died in the war.[85] After her husband's death, Jette Bruns hoped to receive a pension

Nicole Etcheson

for both Dr. Bruns, who had been a medical officer in the Union army, and their fallen son Heinrich, but the sums were insufficient to pay her husband's debts.[86]

Mary Livermore described the white-faced mother who came every day seeking news of her son, who had been wounded at Gettysburg. When the papers reported his death, U.S. Sanitary Commission officials helped secure a free railroad pass for her journey to recover the body. "There are no tears, no words of grief," Livermore claimed, "only a still agony, a repressed anguish, which it is painful to witness." Another mother greeted the news that her son was dead with relief that "he will never have to suffer as his father and I are suffering now."[87] Amelia A. Lewis attempted suicide and was committed to the insane asylum. The cause was listed as "her son being in the Army . . . supposed him dead."[88] Jette Bruns was "frightened . . . tremendously" by the sight of her son Heinrich's corpse after he was killed at the Battle of Iuka in Mississippi. Time and summer heat had rendered the body almost unrecognizable. She prayed for strength "to suffer the first pain calmly," eventually becoming "resigned" and grateful that his body had been returned home.[89]

Charity Townsend left no diaries or other written records of her thoughts. As a girl she had been a slave in Kentucky, but was freed while traveling through Indiana, en route to be sold in Missouri. She married another former slave, Luke Townsend, and they had eleven children. Luke was a strong man who hired out himself and their oldest son, Robert, as farm laborers. The Townsends also owned a small property of two to three acres and belonged to the local church, along with whites. The census listed their children as attending school.[90] Despite the prevalent racism of the society in which they lived, the Townsends were generally respected as hard-working and Christian people.

In 1864, when Indiana finally created a black regiment, Robert Townsend enlisted. He never saw combat but fell ill in camp and returned home, where he died in May 1865. Charity's sorrow went unrecorded, but the family's financial difficulties were documented because of Robert's Civil War service. Luke suffered from rheumatism, and his inability to work was the source of their declining fortunes. But once Luke died, Charity was able to apply for a mother's pension based on Robert's service. The application initially failed, but in 1887 Charity received a back payment of $1,900 as well as a regular monthly income. The newspaper called her "one of the most worthy colored ladies of our city." Charity had been supporting herself and the younger children as a laundress, a back-breaking occupation for an aging woman.[91]

The pension system codified Charity Townsend's experience of the war. Little of Charity's personhood survives except for the record of her piety. The affidavits in the pension file speak mostly about Luke and Robert's labors to support the family. And the pension file even strips away Charity Townsend's identity as a black woman who must have followed the war's impact on African Americans. Charity's own race consciousness is evident in that she and Luke, when Greencastle's black population grew in the 1870s, helped found a local black church, abandoning the white-dominated church in which they had long worshipped.[92] For the purposes of the pension system, Charity Townsend was a mother. Of her eleven children, the only one that the government seemingly took notice of was the son who served, however briefly, in the Civil War army. African American women experienced the war through their race as well as their gender and life stage.

Northern women were expected to demonstrate their patriotism not just through acceptance of their menfolk's decision to go to war but through working for the war themselves. Mary Livermore was both a wife and a mother, yet she was able to devote herself to the U.S. Sanitary Commission, eventually becoming a paid agent. Many wives and mothers, however, lacked the time—especially if they cared for young children while supporting their family in their husband's absence. Livermore's salary was controversial because critics argued that "true" women volunteered their services. Jeanie Attie notes that women were expected to contribute to war work as an extension of their household duties, which were often too pressing to allow time for aiding the war effort.[93] Single women may have been better able to contribute to the war effort than women with families, even if members of those families were in the army.

When the war broke out, Caroline Cowles Richards was nineteen years old and living in Canandaigua, New York, with her grandparents and younger sister. As much as any young man, she was caught up in the *rage militaire* after the firing on Fort Sumter. As the men left to join the army, it seemed to Caroline "very patriotic and grand when they are singing, 'It is sweet, Oh, 'tis sweet, for one's country to die,' and we hear the martial music and see the flags flying and see the recruiting tents on the square and meet men in uniform at every turn and see train loads of the boys in blue going to the front, but it will not seem so grand if we hear they are dead on the battlefield, far from home." She went with other girls "down to the train and took flowers to the soldiers as they were passing through and they cut buttons from their coats and gave to us as souvenirs. We have flags on our paper and envelopes, and have all our stationery bordered with red, white and blue. We wear little flag pins for badges and tie our hair with red, white and blue ribbon and have pins and earrings made of the buttons the soldiers gave us." Both young women and matrons would sew for the soldiers. After the "older ladies' society" cut out the cloth, Caroline and other members of the Young Ladies' Aid Society sewed the garments. Members of the society explained their work: "We are an association whose object it is to aid, in the only way in which woman, alas! can aid our brothers in the field. Our sympathies are with them in the cause for which they have periled all." "We are going to write notes and enclose them in the garments to cheer up the soldier boys." Like many on the home front, Caroline rejoiced at news of Union victories, attended patriotic services, and admired the young men who "offer themselves upon the altar of their country." She read the Emancipation Proclamation to her grandfather. And she mourned the young men who perished. The service for Charlie Wheeler, killed at Gettysburg, was "the saddest funeral and the only one of a soldier that I ever attended," she wrote, although she knew many local men who died. "This cruel war is terrible and precious lives are being sacrificed and hearts broken every day," Caroline reflected in December 1863. "What is to be the result? We can only trust and wait." Although Caroline never articulated the purpose of the war—beyond "The right and the North will surely triumph!"—she took her flag and bell to "make

Nicole Etcheson

all the noise I can" in the celebrations at the war's end. Bells and gongs supplied the noise for the celebration; red, white, and blue bunting, the scenery. Days later, the bells tolled again, this time for Lincoln's death. The flags flew at half-staff, and Caroline felt sick at the news of the assassination.[94]

Emilie Davis was a young black woman living in Philadelphia during the Civil War. She worked as a domestic and dressmaker. Her diary recorded the social and church life of the black community, along with her reaction to seminal events such as Lincoln's issuing the Emancipation Proclamation on January 1, 1863: "*a memorable day*" that she thanked God she had been "sperd to see." She frequently heard Frederick Douglass lecture, and she admired the "colred recruits they looked quite war like," although within weeks black troops were no longer a novelty. Her anxiety, however, was for her father, who visited her in Philadelphia at the outset of the Gettysburg campaign. As refugees poured into the city from the countryside, she worried that he would not make it safely home, although she did not explicitly mention the Confederate army's seizure of Pennsylvania blacks. She found the political campaign of 1864 interesting but stayed away from meeting on election day "for fear something might happen."[95]

Like Caroline Cowles Richards, Emilie Davis rejoiced "over the *good newes* Richmond had fallen." She attended a parade of the 24th U.S. Colored Troops and felt the "excitement" and "holidy" spirit. A week and a half later, she waited four and a half hours to see Lincoln's body when it went through Philadelphia. She thought "the coffin and hearse was beutiful" and the funeral "the gravest . . . i ever saw." But she also memorialized moments in the war that whites did not. In the aftermath of the New York City draft riots, Emilie Davis recorded that "the Colored People suffrd most from the mob." She saw a parade of black troops on November 1, 1864, because "6000 slaves have bine Declard free in the State of Maryaland." This, too, was a significant "holliaday." She belonged to the Ladies Union Association, which collected clothes for the freedmen, went to lectures about them, and—long after white women might have considered the war over—participated in "a Donation Party for the freed" in December 1865.[96]

The war changed Emilie Davis and Charity Townsend's status in ways it did not alter that of white women. Already free, Davis and Townsend nonetheless gained citizenship and civil rights with the Reconstruction laws and amendments. But like white women, they were still subordinated politically to men. Frederick Douglass, in fact, justified denying women the vote by arguing that black men would represent their families as white men did.[97] In Canandaigua the Young Ladies' Association had determined that every girl who sent a soldier to war would receive a flag bed quilt. Caroline had a "soldier . . . down in Virginia," and at war's end she received the quilt, with the words "Three rousing cheers for the Union." A year after the war, she married her soldier and embarked on a life of domesticity.[98] The Civil War had shaped her life, but the contours it took on remained those of woman's sphere: marriage and motherhood.

Our understanding of the Civil War's impact on Northern families, including women, is incomplete. James Marten has examined the impact of the war on children, and Nancy F. Cott has explained how secession further delegitimized free love, divorce, or extramarital relations. But sociologist Glen H. Elder Jr. noted that while scholars have charted the impact of processes such as urbanization and industrialization on the family, "little is said about the impact of such major historical locations as depressions, wars, mass migration, and commercial intrusions." While family historians have looked at the nature of the family before and after the Civil War, they have not fully examined the impact of the Civil War as a factor in changing the Northern family.[99]

Nonetheless, it is clear that women's experience of the war was frequently determined by their life stage and relationship to men in the service. Mary Livermore recalled a note included in a package from a local aid society. The note told the soldier recipient, "You are not *my* husband nor son; but you are the husband or son of some woman who undoubtedly loves you as I love mine. I have made these garments for you with a heart that aches for your sufferings, and with a longing to come to you to assist in taking care of you."[100] Studying the U.S. Sanitary Commission, Judith Ann Giesberg argues that male leaders sought to channel what they saw as a natural "motherly love" into necessary war work.[101] Both women aid workers and their male counterparts understood that women's relation to soldiers was mediated not only by gender but also by age. They might be mothers, wives, daughters, sisters, or sweethearts. The war's impact on them depended in part on whether they lost a father's protection, a brother's companionship, a husband's income, or a son's love and support. It brought varying degrees of hardship and anxiety, depending on whether they and their menfolk survived the war and on the work they undertook either inside or outside the home. The roles expected from women influenced their wartime experiences, but so did their life stage, because nineteenth-century society dictated different roles for women at different points in their lives.

NOTES

1. Wendy Hamand Venet, *A Strong-Minded Woman: The Life of Mary Livermore* (Amherst: Univ. of Massachusetts Press, 2005), ix, 5–6, 105–6.

2. Leslie M. Harris, *In the Shadow of Slavery: African Americans in New York City, 1626–1863* (Chicago: Univ. of Chicago Press, 2003), 98–99, 181; Steven Mintz and Susan Kellogg, *Domestic Revolutions: A Social History of American Family Life* (New York: Free Press, 1988), 77–78.

3. Jane E. Schultz, *Women at the Front: Hospital Workers in Civil War America* (Chapel Hill: Univ. of North Carolina Press, 2004); Catherine Clinton and Nina Silber, eds., *Divided Houses: Gender and the Civil War* (New York: Oxford Univ. Press, 1992); Nina Silber, *Daughters of the Union: Northern Women Fight the Civil War* (Cambridge, Mass.: Harvard Univ. Press, 2005), 10; Venet, *A Strong-Minded Woman*, 87; Tamara K. Hareven, "Introduction: The Historical Study of the Life Course," in Tamara K. Hareven, ed., *Transitions: The Family and the Life Course in Historical Perspective* (New York: Academic Press, 1978), 1–16.

4. Ginette Aley, "Inescapable Realities: Rural Midwestern Women and Families during the Civil War," in Ginette Aley and J. L. Anderson, eds., *Union Heartland: The Midwestern Home Front during the Civil War* (Carbondale: Southern Illinois Univ. Press, 2013), 125–47.

5. Peter S. Carmichael, *The Last Generation: Young Virginians in Peace, War, and Reunion*

(Chapel Hill: Univ. of North Carolina Press, 2005), 7–8; Mintz and Kellogg, *Domestic Revolutions,* xv–xvi; James M. McPherson, *Battle Cry of Freedom: The Civil War Era* (New York: Ballantine, 1988), 9.

6. Mary A. Livermore, *My Story of the War* (1889; repr., New York: Arno Press, 1972), 85–87, 90; James Marten, *The Children's Civil War* (Chapel Hill: Univ. of North Carolina Press, 1998), 10; Louisa May Alcott, *Hospital Sketches,* ed. Alice Fahs (Boston: Bedford/St. Martin's, 2004), 37; Catherine A. Jones, *Intimate Reconstructions: Children in Postemancipation Virginia* (Charlottesville: Univ. of Virginia Press, 2015), 7, 10; Anne Scott McLeod, "The *Caddie Woodlawn* Syndrome: American Girlhood in the Nineteenth Century," in Miriam Forman-Brunell and Leslie Paris, eds., *The Girls' History and Culture Reader: The Nineteenth Century* (Urbana: Univ. of Illinois Press, 2011), 199–221.

7. Marten, *Children's Civil War,* 70, 89.

8. Louisa May Alcott, *Little Women* (1869), http://www.literatureproject.com/little-women/little-women_1.htm.

9. Feb. 8, 1863, Dec. 26, 1864, in Aden G. Cavins, *War Letters of Aden G. Cavins, Written to his Wife Matilda Livingston Cavins* (Evansville, Ind.: Rosenthal-Kuebler, n.d.), 37–38, 100–101; Marten, *Children's Civil War,* 70, 89.

10. Tillman Valentine to My Dear Wife, Dec. 26, 1863, in Jonathan W. White, Katie Fisher, and Elizabeth Wall, eds., "The Civil War Letters of Tillman Valentine, Third US Colored Troops," *Pennsylvania Magazine of History and Biography* 139 (Apr. 2015): 171–88, esp. 181; Tillman Valentine to Ever-Dear Wife, Apr. 25, 1864, in ibid., 184–85; Tillman Valentine to Wife, June 14, 1864, in ibid., 188.

11. Mintz and Kellogg, *Domestic Revolutions,* 43, 48–49; Dec. 2, 1862, Jan. 14, 1864, in Cavins, *War Letters of Aden G. Cavins,* 27, 76–77.

12. John Peirce to My Dear Wife, June 23, 1864, in Nina Silber and Mary Beth Sievens, eds., *Yankee Correspondence: Civil War Letters between New England Soldiers and the Home Front* (Charlottesville: Univ. Press of Virginia, 1996), 149–50.

13. Pa [J. S.] Applegate to Daughter, Mar. 1, 1864, Applegate Manuscripts, Lilly Library, Indiana Univ., Bloomington; Mar. 31, 1865, in Cavins, *War Letters of Aden G. Cavins,* 109.

14. E. S. Applegate to Husband, May 28, 1865, Applegate Manuscripts; E. S. Applegate to Dear Husband, May 8, 1863, Applegate Manuscripts; E. S Applegate to Husband, July 26, 1864, Applegate Manuscripts.

15. Ann Larimer to Husband [John W.], Feb. 17, 1865, Civil War Diaries and Letters, Univ. of Iowa Libraries, Univ. of Iowa, Iowa City, http://digital.lib.uiowa.edu/cdm/compoundobject/collection/cwd/id/20001/rec/5.].

16. On the patriarchal father, see Bernard Wishy, *The Child and the Republic: The Dawn of Modern American Child Nurture* (Philadelphia: Univ. of Pennsylvania Press, 1968), 25.

17. Marten, *Children's Civil War,* 211–12; *Putnam Republican Banner* (Greencastle, Ind.), Dec. 4, 1867; John Applegate Pension File Folder, n.d., Applegate Manuscripts, National Archives, Washington, D.C.

18. Carl N. Degler, *At Odds: Women and the Family in America from the Revolution to the Present* (New York: Oxford Univ. Press, 1980), 107, 158; Leonore Davidoff, *Thicker Than Water: Siblings and Their Relations, 1780–1920* (New York: Oxford Univ. Press, 2012), 31–38, 329–31; C. Dallett Hemphill, *Siblings: Brothers and Sisters in American History* (New York: Oxford Univ. Press, 2011), 6–8; Steven Mintz, *A Prison of Expectations: The Family in Victorian Culture* (New York: New York Univ. Press, 1983), 146–50.

19. May 31, June 13, June 17, Aug. 26, Aug. 27, 1864, Diary of O. C. Shelton, Shelton Family Papers, Univ. of Iowa, Iowa City, http://digital.lib.uiowa.edu/cdm/compoundobject/collection/cwd/id/4275/rec/168; Apr. 29, May 18, May 20, 1864, Mary Shelton Diary, ibid.

20. Sallie A. Stafford to Mattie V. Thomas, Mar. 22, 1863, Prairie Settlement: Nebraska Photographs and Family Letters, 1862–1912, http://memory.loc.gov/cgi-bin/query/r?ammem/ps:@field(DOCID+l004).

21. Sept. 24, Sept. 30, Oct. 1, Oct.4, 1864, Mary Shelton Diary; Feb. 11, 1865, Amanda Shelton Diary, Shelton Family Papers.

22. Ell Hawn to Friend, Dec. 8, 1862, in Nancy L. Rhoades and Lucy E. Bailey, eds., *Wanted—Correspondence: Women's Letters to a Union Soldier* (Athens: Ohio Univ. Press, 2009), 126–27.

23. Adelia [Shroyer] to Ed, Dec. 14, 1862, in ibid., 129–30.

24. Frank Mared [pseudonym for Fannie Meredith] to Ed, Sept. 30, 1864, in ibid., 279–80.

25. Sean A. Scott, *A Visitation of God: Northern Civilians Interpret the Civil War* (New York: Oxford Univ. Press, 2011), 4, 72; George C. Rable, *God's Almost Chosen Peoples: A Religious History of the American Civil War* (Chapel Hill: Univ. of North Carolina Press, 2010), 1, 4, 5.

26. May 2, 1864, Mary Shelton Diary; Feb. 11, 1865, Amanda Shelton Diary.

27. Lydia Rader to Brother [George Washington Rader], Sept. 20, 1862, U.S. Civil War Resources for East Central Indiana, Ball State Univ. Library, Ball State Univ., Muncie, Ind., http://libx.bsu.edu/cdm/compoundobject/collection/LSTACivWar/id/2447/rec/1463 (hereafter cited as CWR); Lydia Rader to Brother, Nov. 19, 1862, ibid.; Lydia Rader to Brother, Dec. 7, 1862, ibid.; Aramenta Rader to George Washington Rader, Oct. 19, 1862, ibid.; Aramenta Rader to George Washington Rader, Nov. 29, 1862, ibid.; Lydia Rader to Brother [George Washington Rader], Sept. 20, 1862, ibid.; Aramenta Rader to George Washington Rader, n.d. [1861 or 1862], ibid.

28. Aramenta Rader to George Washington Rader, n.d. [1861 or 1862], ibid.

29. Livermore, *My Story of the War,* 147.

30. Mary Hamilton to Cousin Adelia, Mar. 20, 1863, in Richard F. Nation and Stephen E. Towne, eds., *Indiana's War: The Civil War in Documents* (Athens: Ohio Univ. Press, 2009), 94–95.

31. J. L. Anderson, "The Vacant Chair on the Farm: Soldier Husbands, Farm Wives, and the Iowa Home Front, 1861–65," in Aley and Anderson, eds., *Union Heartland,* 148–68. For women's work on Civil War farms, see also R. Douglas Hurt, "The Agricultural Power of the Midwest during the Civil War," in ibid., 68–96.

32. Karen Lystra, *Searching the Heart: Women, Men, and Romantic Love in Nineteenth-Century America* (New York: Oxford Univ. Press, 1989), 3–11; Ellen K. Rothman, *Hands and Hearts: A History of Courtship in America* (New York: Basic Books, 1984).

33. Hattie to Cousin, Nov. 29, 1861, CWR; Hattie F. Kemper to Dear Friend, Nov. 26, 1863, CWR; Hattie to *My* Remembered Friend, June 19, 1863, CWR; Hattie F. K. to Brother Tip, Mar. 20, 1863, CWR; Hattie to *My* Remembered Friend, Aug. 15, 1864, CWR. See also Hattie F. Kemper to G. W. H. Kemper, May 8, 1864, CWR; Hattie F. Kemper to Tip, January 31, 1864, CWR; Hattie to Dearest Friend Tip, Dec. 11, 1864, CWR; Hattie F. Kemper to General William Harrison Kemper, Oct. 30, 1864, CWR; Hattie to Dearest Friend Tip, Dec. 23, 1864, CWR; Hattie to Dearest Friend Tip, Nov. 29, 1864, CWR; Hattie to Dearest Friend, Jan. 15, 1865, CWR.

34. Hattie to Friend, May 8, 1863, CWR.

35. Emma A. Moody to Friend E., Oct. 12, 1862, in Rhoades and Bailey, eds., *Wanted—Correspondence,* 119–20.

36. Hattie to Dear Friend, Apr. 14, 1864, CWR.

37. Rhoades and Bailey, eds., *Wanted—Correspondence,* 5–8; Phrone, Oct. 27, 1863 [1862], in ibid., 121–22; [Sophronia Rogers] to Edwin, Dec. 8, 1862, in ibid., 128–29; Ell H. [Ella Hawn] to Ed, Aug. 13, 1863, in ibid., 165–67; Phrone to Dear Friend Ed, Dec. 23, 1863, in ibid., 204–6; Phrone to Dear Friend, Mar. 9, 1864, in ibid., 219–20; Phrone to Ed, Mar. 12, 1864, in ibid., 225–27; Phrone, May 13, 1864, in ibid., 241–42; Phrone to Ed, June 10, 1864, in ibid., 244–45; Phrone to Dearest Friend Ed, June 20, 1864, in ibid., 251–53; Phrone to Friend Ed, July 31, 1864,

in ibid., 262–63; Lou P. Riggen to Lieut. E. L. Lybarger, Aug. 28, 1864, in ibid., 271–72; Frank Mared [pseudonym for Fannie Meredith] to Ed, Sept. 30, 1864, in ibid., 279–80; Phrone to Ed, Mount Vernon, Ohio, Sept. 19 [1865], in ibid., 324–25, 352–53, 357.

38. Martha Tomhave Blauvelt, *The Work of the Heart: Young Women and Emotion, 1780–1830* (Charlottesville: Univ. of Virginia Press, 2007), 94–97.

39. For marriage, see Degler, *At Odds,* 8–9; Blauvelt, *Work of the Heart,* 147; Livermore, *My Story of the War,* 113–14, 116, 119, 287.

40. James C. Mohr and Richard E. Winslow, eds., *The Cormany Diaries: A Northern Family in the Civil War* (Pittsburgh: Univ. of Pittsburgh Press, 1982), ix, 229, 253; "Soldier's Wife," *America Singing: Nineteenth-Century Song Sheets,* https://www.loc.gov/item/amss.hc00024a.

41. Ken Spurgeon, *A Kansas Soldier at War: The Civil War Letters of Christian & Elise Dubach Isely* (Charleston, S.C.: History Press, 2013), 45, 47; Linda Schelbitzki Pickle, *Contented among Strangers: Rural German-Speaking Women and their Families in the Nineteenth-Century Midwest* (Urbana: Univ. of Illinois Press, 1996), 94–95.

42. Clara V. Weaver to My Own Dear Husband, May 16, 1862, Clara Vinson Weaver Letters, http://digital.lib.uiowa.edu/cdm/compoundobject/collection/cwd/id/5130/rec/115.

43. Mrs. John A. [Mary S.] Logan, *Reminiscences of a Soldier's Wife: An Autobiography* (New York: Scribner's, 1913), vii, 6, 12, 50–51, 53, 91, 96–98, 100, http://babel.hathitrust.org/cgi/pt?id=uc2.ark:/13960/fk03x83m72;view=1up;seq=21.

44. Mohr and Winslow, eds., *Cormany Diaries,* 253, 258, 270, 282, 287.

45. Spurgeon, *A Kansas Soldier at War,* 52–53, 57–58.

46. Ann Larimer to Husband [John W.], Feb. 17, 1865, Civil War Diaries and Letters; Ann Larimer to Husband, July 13 [1865], ibid.; Ann Larimer to Husband [John W.], Apr. 2, 1865, ibid.

47. Hurt, "Agricultural Power of the Midwest," 68–96.

48. Livermore, *My Story of the War,* 586–98; Judith Giesberg, *Army at Home: Women and the Civil War on the Northern Home Front* (Chapel Hill: Univ. of North Carolina Press, 2009).

49. Livermore, *My Story of the War,* 599–600; Earl F. Mulderink III, *New Bedford's Civil War* (New York: Fordham Univ. Press, 2012); Ella Forbes, *African American Women during the Civil War* (New York: Garland, 1998), vii–viii.

50. White, Fisher, and Wall, eds., "Civil War Letters of Tillman Valentine," 174.

51. Tillman Valentine to Ever-Dear Wife, Apr. 25, 1864, in ibid., 184.

52. Logan, *Reminiscences of a Soldier's Wife,* 112, 118, 130, 132–34, 146–53.

53. [Clara V. Weaver] to My Own Dear Husband, May 18, 1862, Clara Vinson Weaver Letters.

54. Ann Larimer to Husband, July 13, 1865, Civil War Diaries and Letters.

55. Mohr and Winslow, eds., *Cormany Diaries,* 290, 378, 407.

56. Blauvelt, *Work of the Heart,* 181; Mohr and Winslow, eds., *Cormany Diaries,* 442.

57. [Clara V. Weaver] to My Own Dear Husband, May 18, 1862, Clara Vinson Weaver Letters.

58. "Soldier's Wife."

59. Spurgeon, *A Kansas Soldier at War,* 67.

60. Logan, *Reminiscences of a Soldier's Wife,* 136, 154, 181.

61. Diana Phillips to Dear Husband, June 10, 1862, in Silber and Sievens, eds., *Yankee Correspondence,* 136–37.

62. Ann Larimer to Husband [John W.], Feb. 17, 1865, Civil War Diaries and Letters, Univ. of Iowa Libraries ; Ann Larimer to Husband [John W.], Apr. 2, 1865, ibid.

63. Clara V. Weaver to My Own Dear Husband, May 16, 1862, Clara Vinson Weaver Letters.

64. Ann Larimer to Husband [John W.], Apr. 2, 1865, Civil War Diaries and Letters.

65. Mohr and Winslow, eds., *Cormany Diaries,* 580, 582.

66. Spurgeon, *A Kansas Soldier at War,* 127.

67. Linda K. Kerber, *Women of the Republic: Intellect and Ideology in Revolutionary America* (New York: W. W. Norton, 1980), 200; Nancy F. Cott, *The Bonds of Womanhood: 'Woman's Sphere' in New England, 1780–1835* (New Haven, Conn.: Yale Univ. Press, 1977), 85.

68. Livermore, *My Story of the War,* 96–97.

69. Ibid., 147.

70. Maria H. Berry to My Dear Son Hun, Jan. 12, 1862, in Silber and Sievens, eds., *Yankee Correspondence,* 132–33.

71. Alcott, *Hospital Sketches,* ix, 27–28, 36–37.

72. Ibid., 80, 89.

73. Mary P. Ryan, *Cradle of the Middle Class: The Family in Oneida County, New York, 1790–1865* (Cambridge: Cambridge Univ. Press, 1981), 157–76.

74. Aug. 20, 1862, William H. Anderson Diary, folder 4, Eleanore A. Cammack Papers, DePauw Univ., Greencastle, Ind.

75. Aramenta Rader to George Washington Rader, Nov. 29, 1862, CWR.

76. Rhoades and Bailey, eds., *Wanted—Correspondence,* 30; Phrone [Sophronia Rogers] to Ed, Nov. . 5, 1862, in ibid., 122–23; [Sophronia Rogers] to Edwin, Dec. 8, 1862, in ibid., 128–29; Phrone [Rogers] to Dear Friend, Feb. 22, 1863, in ibid., 135–38; Phrone to Ed, Millwood, Aug. 21, 1864, in ibid., 269–70.

77. Mohr and Winslow, eds., *Cormany Diaries,* 230.

78. Mother to Frank, Mar. 2, 1864, in Silber and Sievens, eds., *Yankee Correspondence,* 165.

79. Adolf E. Schroeder and Carla Schultz-Geisberg, eds., *Hold Dear, As Always: Jette, A German Immigrant Life in Letters,* trans. Adolf E. Shroeder (Columbia: Univ. of Missouri Press, 1988), 186.

80. Livermore, *My Story of the War,* 204–5, 288–89.

81. Alcott, *Hospital Sketches,* 110–11.

82. Jette to Heinrich, Apr. 3, 1862, in Shroeder and Schultz-Geisberg, eds., *Hold Dear, As Always,* 186–87; Pickle, *Contented among Strangers,* 112–13.

83. Nancy Needham to Delaware County [Indiana] Board of Commissioners, n.d. [1860s], CWR.

84. Giesberg, *Army at Home,* 5.

85. John S. Jennings, J. A. Matson, D. C. Donnohue to O. P. Morton, Dec. 26, 1864, Correspondence of the 77th Indiana Volunteer Regiment, Indiana State Archives, Commission on Public Records, Indianapolis; H. S. Cowgill to Gov. Morton, Dec. 26, 1864, ibid.

86. Shroeder and Schultz-Geisberg, eds., *Hold Dear, As Always,* 14–15; Jette to Heinrich, Jan. 4, 1865, ibid., 199; Jette to Heinrich, May 28, 1866, ibid., 208–11.

87. Livermore, *My Story of the War,* 168–69, 402.

88. Nation and Towne, eds., *Indiana's War,* 97–98.

89. Shroeder and Schultz-Geisberg, eds., *Hold Dear, As Always,* 188–89.

90. Murray L. Townsend Jr., *Townsend-Pittman Family Reunion* (n.p.: Murray L. Townsend Jr., 2005), 23; U.S. Census Office, *Population Schedules of the Eighth Census of the United States, 1860* (Washington, D.C.: National Archives, 1967); Affidavit of John R. Miller, Oct. 8, 1884, Robert Townsend Pension File, Pension Files, National Archives, Washington, D.C.; Mar. 2, 1871 indenture, ibid.; Clifton Phillips, ed., *From Frontier Circuit to Urban Church: A History of Greencastle Methodism* (Greencastle, Ind.: Gobin Memorial United Methodist Church, 1989), 17–21; U.S. Census Office, *Population Schedules of the Seventh Census of the United States, 1850* (Washington, D.C.: National Archives, 1963).

91. Affidavit of D.W. Layman, July 24, 1884, Robert Townsend Pension File; Townsend, *Townsend-Pittman Family Reunion,* 24; Affidavit of Charity Townsend, Oct. [n.d.] 1884, Robert Townsend Pension File.

92. Phillips, *From Frontier Circuit to Urban Church*, 61–62.

93. Venet, *A Strong-Minded Woman*, 112; Jeanie Attie, "Warwork and the Crisis of Domesticity in the North," in Clinton and Silber, eds., *Divided Houses*, 247–59; Silber, *Daughters of the Union*, 1–13.

94. For the *rage militaire*, see James M. McPherson, *For Cause and Comrades: Why Men Fought in the Civil War* (New York: Oxford Univ. Press, 1997), 16–17; for Richards, see Caroline Cowles Richards, *Village Life in America, 1852–1872: Including the Period of the American Civil War as Told in the Diary of a School-Girl* (New York: Henry Holt, 1913), 131, 138–39, 145–53, 160–61, 172, 180, 182.

95. Karsonya Wise Whitehead, *Notes from a Colored Girl: The Civil War Pocket Diaries of Emilie Frances Davis* (Columbia: Univ. of South Carolina Press, 2014), 10; Jan. 1, May 17, June 15, June 29, July 4, 1863, Oct. 14, Nov. 8, 1864, Emilie Davis Diary, Historical Society of Pennsylvania, Philadelphia, http://davisdiaries.villanova.edu/january_1–3_1863. See Margaret S. Creighton, *The Colors of Courage: Gettysburg's Forgotten History* (New York: Basic Books, 2005), on the kidnapping of free blacks during the Gettysburg campaign.

96. Memoranda 3, 1863, Nov. 1, Memoranda 4, 1864, Apr. 3–4, 14, 15–16, 20, 21, 22, 23, 24, Oct. 29, Dec. 14, 1865, Emilie Davis Diary.

97. A. Kristen Foster, "'We Are Men!': Frederick Douglass and the Fault Lines of Gendered Citizenship," *Journal of the Civil War Era* 1 (June 2011): 143–75, esp. 165.

98. Richards, *Village Life in America*, 131, 162, 205, 206.

99. Marten, *Children's Civil War;* Nancy F. Cott, *Public Vows: A History of Marriage and the Nation* (Cambridge, Mass.: Harvard Univ. Press, 2000), 77–84. Cott also notes that the Civil War changed spousal relations for slaves by enabling them to legally marry, a right Northern free blacks already possessed. See also Glen H. Elder Jr., "Approaches to Social Change and the Family," in John Demos and Sarane Spence Boocock, eds., *Turning Points: Historical and Sociological Essays on the Family* (Chicago: Univ. of Chicago Press, 1978), S1–S38, especially S8–S9; Mintz and Kellogg, *Domestic Revolutions;* and John Demos, *Past, Present, and Personal: The Family and the Life Course in American History* (New York: Oxford Univ. Press, 1986).

100. Livermore, *My Story of the War*, 137.

101. Judith Ann Giesberg, *Civil War Sisterhood: The U.S. Sanitary Commission and Women's Politics in Transition* (Boston: Northeastern Univ. Press, 2000), x–xi, 6.

PART

6

Religion

"Hasten the Day"

Slavery's Apocalypse among Enslaved Women and Planter Women in the Civil War South

W. SCOTT POOLE

On July 30, 1864, Mary Maxcy Leverett wrote to her son Milton in the Confederate army a letter containing sadness and hope, coupled with rather strongly worded pleading, that she might "see [him] come up the path to the house" so that they could together mourn the passing of Fredric Leverett, who had recently died in Confederate service in Virginia. In this letter, she made all the necessary linguistic oblations expected of the wife of a respected low-country South Carolina Episcopal clergyman. Using slightly altered language from the New Testament, she mourned for her dead son, "in the full expectation of seeing him again . . . I sorrow not therefore as those without hope."[1]

But another, perhaps discordant, note appears in the same letter. Leverett unleashes emotions that do not touch on the promise of the afterlife or the nearness of God, at least not as a source of comfort. "The Almighty," Leverett asserts, "will surely send some awful judgment on this execrable Yankee nation for their unjust, brutal cruel conduct during the war." Mary Leverett proceeds to excoriate "their women" who are "cold, hard, unfeeling." She clearly had been praying for something more than comfort and the safe return of her living son. She wanted the vengeance of God poured out. A number of her other letters return to this theme and use a language as apocalyptic as anything found in the Book of Revelation.[2]

A vast gulf of enslavement, dehumanization, and violence existed between Mary Maxcy Leverett and a woman known to us simply as Aggy, a house servant on a Virginia plantation forced to watch her daughter sadistically beaten by her master. Aggy shocked Mary Livermore, a native New Englander who later became an abolitionist and women's suffrage activist, when she related the scene to her. Livermore always viewed Aggy as a quiet woman, but the brutal assault on the enslaved woman's daughter brought to the surface a steely assurance that God would pour out his wrath in full on the Southern ruling class; "That day a-coming! There's a day a-coming . . . I hear the rumbling of the chariots . . . white folks blood is a running on the ground like a river . . . Oh Lord, hasten the day!" Aggy concluded her cries by praying that

God allow her to live to see the day when "I shall see white folks" die like wolves shot "when they come hungry out the woods."[3]

Historians have long concluded that the Civil War created a religious crisis, without always explaining what exactly constituted the crisis, or indeed crises. Looking more closely at lived religion among black and white Southern women provides a window into how they read the theological, and spiritual, meaning of the war. A vast literature exists that takes into account race and class in the study of the lives of Civil War women in the South, but the same cannot be said concerning what religion meant to them and how it changed for them under the trials and travails of the era.[4]

The war and its aftermath required a new understanding of biblical apocalypse. Timothy Wesley writes in this volume that Northern women viewed both the war and emancipation "in an eschatological fashion." The same is true for white women and enslaved African American women in the South: the Civil War and the violence of Reconstruction reshaped their theology of the apocalypse, indeed their lived experience of the apocalypse. The conception of themselves as either victimized, or liberated, from powerful, satanic forces initiated a dizzying shift in their world views. Racial and class identity, rather than simply religious belief, profoundly affected how Southern women understood the implications of God's judgment entering history.

This study focuses on the experience of slaveholding women and the enslaved. The essay does not explore sources for nonslaveholding women in part because it seeks to show that the end of slavery, as much as the loss of a war, fomented religious doubt that pushed white Southerners into a very different theological world than the one inhabited in the antebellum era. However, what's elucidated fully in the writings of slaveholding women no doubt resonated with white Southern women generally, most of whom had varying degrees of investment in the slave system.[5]

The ideology of white supremacy papered over the language of class hierarchy for many Southerners, white and black. By the beginning of the twentieth century, the evangelical white "town lady" married to the New South banker or insurance agent had much more in common with the tenant farmer's wife or the female textile worker in their belief in God's coming judgment than either had with the freedwoman who also understood God as both Judge and Deliverer.[6]

Looking at women's experience of apocalyptic thought offers a way to understand the rich and variegated role of religion in their lives. It moves beyond the current historiography that, in the case of white women, often assumes that they exhibited a fairly straightforward devotion to the emerging evangelical consensus that urged them to take a leading role in sustaining Confederate nationalism. In general, they are portrayed as finding in religious faith a significant degree of comfort as they waited by their firesides for news of battles and lists of the killed, wounded, and missing. Doubt raised by the war's outcome troubled them, but they allegedly found renewed faith in the increased scope of their religious activities after the war.

However, just as Timothy Wesley argues in this volume that Northern women became inspired to speak and write and agitate based on a "providentialist emancipationist" vision, Southern women black and white found religion igniting their words and actions. Examining the nature of actual women's religious experience confronts us with a variety of expressions of faith. Although much of the historiography on white and black women takes for granted the comforting nature of religious faith, we must not allow the conventional languages of piety to mislead us, even when women themselves made use of it.

The orthodoxies of institutional religion create a controlled discourse in any culture or subculture, an expectation that particular ideas and phrases appear at certain moments in the narrative of the self in relation to God and God's earthly representatives. Religion probably did comfort enslaved women in their oppression, and it probably did provide solace to white women of all classes during the distress of the war. It is important to keep in mind, however, that religion's orthodoxies told them they should find their faith comforting, that not being consoled by their religion constituted a failing on their part, perhaps even a sinful act. These strictures and warnings pushed white Southern women to create narratives of faith triumphant over doubt when writing to their husbands and children in the Confederate army, or for black Southern women, long after the conflict, responding to questions of a white interviewer from the Works Progress Administration.

Religion creates profound anxiety along with symbolisms in which adherents can unleash their rage and despair at least as often as it provides solace. Apocalyptic religious conceptions that women put forward, and then sometimes tried to soften with more conventional language, offer significant insight into the theological problems that women wrestled with during the Civil War era. What of those moments when women spoke and acted out apocalyptic scenarios and imagined the horrors they experienced as either a prelude to God's judgment or God's deliverance or indeed both? What happens to faith when God's judgments are not manifested in history and the promises are left unfulfilled? Worse, what happens when the final judgment apparently has arrived and then history resumes its normal course of oppression and brutality?

Apocalyptic ideas played a significant, indeed central, role in American religious life in the Civil War era. In nineteenth-century America, however, most white churchgoers, North and South, subscribed to a "millennialist" interpretation of the apocalypse—that is, the notion that the church slowly builds the Kingdom of God on Earth in anticipation of a sublime ahistorical moment in which Christ establishes his reign. The details of what exactly this coming millennium looked like remained a mystery of faith.[7]

This rather optimistic version of millennial belief seems like a lost world today, and as Timothy Wesley points out, it is too often read by current scholars as "purely . . . symbolic" rather than as a thoroughgoing theological vision. Perhaps making matters more complex for contemporary readers, the idea of a different kind of apocalypse has a powerful resonance within American popular culture and has since at least the early 1970s. Readers today have experienced five decades of what's known as premillennialist apocalyptic preaching, writing, and, indeed, filmmaking. Premillennialist belief among many evangelical Protestants asserts an elaborate template for the end of the world that includes "the coming of Christ in the air" to rapture true believers, a period of Tribulation and the reign of antichrist and finally a second (or third?) coming of Christ followed by the creation of his thousand-year reign. A popularized version of this rather well-organized apocalypse seeped into the culture beginning in the 1960s and became especially well-known with Hal Lindsey's best-selling *The Late Great Planet Earth* (1970). The *Sturm und Drang* of the *Left Behind* novels and films in the 1990s made "premillennialism" a staple of evangelical religious thought and mass entertainment.

Churchwomen, white and black, would not have recognized such ideas through most of the nineteenth century. Indeed, the multiplicity of reform movements assumed a gradual, progressive elimination of evil. In North and South, women swelled the ranks of the temperance movement. White abolitionist women in the North, or fleeing from the South like the Quakers Sarah and Angelina Grimké, believed that their work coincided with the advance of God's kingdom on Earth through the elimination of a sinful institution.[8]

Slaveholding women saw in the "plantation mission movement" a similar impulse toward establishing a millennium, a desiderata in which discipline and hierarchy played a central role. They would have shared the views of an 1834 series entitled "Biographies of Servants mentioned in Scripture" that ran in the *Charleston Observer*, a Presbyterian paper. The articles assumed that slavery had a place in God's economy of history—indeed, that enslavement advanced the spread of true Christian civilization.[9]

Millennialism took a decidedly different form in the slave quarters. As the research of numerous scholars and the hints and declarations in postwar slave narratives suggest, enslaved women held to the belief that apocalypse meant liberation. Indeed, God's future embraced the past, and the story of the Exodus conjoined with contemporary visions, prophecies, and images of deliverance.

Enslaved women's theology of apocalypse emerged out of their African roots and assumed different notions about time and history than did Western Christianity. They understood Christianity as both a potentially liberating but also an oppressive force. Out of this array of religious experiences, biblical images, and historical experience they crafted a genuinely new and bracing notion of an apocalypse within history in which God's promised future exploded into the present, not as an "end of time" but as deliverance for them and the destruction of the master class.[10]

The apocalyptic religious imagination, though it may appear as a variety of escapism, actually undermines the idea that women only responded to religious teaching with passivity. Thinking of women turning to religion for either the comforts of heaven or Providence leaves them in the grip of the Victorian America's notions about female passivity and, indeed, replicates those images in the historiography. We must instead see them as grappling with theological questions as they tried to understand and make use of ideas that did not fit their experience of the world, reshaping and reforming those ideas as they faced changing historical circumstances created by revolutionary social forces.

W. Scott Poole

African American women—enslaved, brutalized, and seeking a reckoning—had to create their religious imagination out of a tradition that frequently worked against their interests, both in relation to the master class and even within the slave community. Apocalyptic ideas proved especially fruitful. As Kathryn Gin Lum has pointed out, slave narratives reveal an "ironic reversal" in the use of the language of judgment and retribution. Slaves heard of a hell from which the alleged civilizing and Christianizing mission of slavery saved them. However, numerous slave narratives from men and women make clear that, long after emancipation, they found slavery itself a hellish state and assumed that it was they who would enjoy a future deliverance, without the presence of their masters.[11]

Freedwomen asserted this idea not simply as some kind of spiteful, and understandable, desire for vengeance but rather as central to their theological understanding. "This is one reason I believe in hell," recalled a formerly enslaved woman. "I don't believe a just God is going to take on such a man as that [her master] into his Kingdom." Expressing it in these terms expresses a whole cosmology, a conception of the universe underpinned by a just God who would not only deliver the slave but would, as in the tale of the Exodus, punish the master class.[12]

Maria Stewart, the first African American woman in America to speak to so-called "promiscuous assemblies" (gatherings of both men and women), voiced this belief in the doom of the masters. "Oh America, America," she exclaimed in the tradition of the jeremiad, "foul and indelible is your stain!" Stewart became famous, or perhaps infamous, for her condemning of all of white America, not only the South, and its institutions for what she called "the cruel wrongs and injuries to the fallen sons of Africa." Stewart, though herself the product of free parents in the North, became a trumpet to the nation of ideas that percolated on the Southern plantation, where the master class had damnation waiting in their future, as surely as the slaves had deliverance waiting in theirs.

The Book of Revelation, the template for all Christian apocalyptic, most often provided Stewart with her text and, powerfully, with her imagery. "Ye rich and powerful ones," she proclaimed, "many of you will call for the rocks and mountains to fall upon you and to hide you from the wrath of the Lamb and from Him that sitteth upon the throne." This image, borrowed directly from Revelation 6:16, also included a vision of eschatological hope. "Many of the sable-skinned Africans you now despise, will shine in the Kingdom of Heaven as the stars forever and ever."[13]

The centrality of a theology of apocalypse emerged out of women's own appropriation of Christianity and the exigencies of the slave system. Enslaved African American women found in their religious lives a complex set of expectations and demands that mirrored the essential contradictions of slavery. The institution, after all, assumed certain human behaviors, indeed virtues, from people who from the standpoint of the Southern legal system had all the agency of a bale of cotton or barrel of rice. White Southerners expected honesty, humility, an ethic of work, and, above all, submissive obedience from enslaved African Americans. Meanwhile, the nature of the slave system undermined any concept of personhood and dignity that might serve as the underpinnings for ethical prescription. Religious instruction represented an effort to deal with the implacable ironies of slavery, ironies that the white ruling class arguably sought to navigate by creating a vision of Christianity thoroughly grounded in slavery.

Although they recognized the enslaved as souls in need of conversion and catechism, white Southern ministers attempted to preclude any hint that conversion, baptism, or reception of any religious ritual opened the door to legal, as opposed to an amorphous spiritual, liberation. Many, though not all, planters accepted the admonitions of their churches and clergy that slaves receive instruction in the Gospel. In some parts of the South, a religious tradition going back to the early eighteenth century existed in slave communities. A small number of independent black congregations existed in the urban South, though they faced constant harassment, legal restrictions, and the threat of closure.

Enslaved women attempted to carve out a space for themselves in Southern religious experience amid what Evelyn Brooks-Higginbotham calls "a multiple consciousness" of enslavement and gender proscription, efforts to proscribe their experience both within and without the slave community. Often forced to worship in the segregated galleries of white churches or to listen to white preachers extol the biblical nature of the slave system, enslaved women also found religion acting as a spur for the men they worked with, slept with, and prayed with inside the slave community to assert a limited pose of masculinity in their own search for dignity.[14]

The coming Kingdom that black women in the South prayed for focused on the end of slavery. But there are hints that this religious vision included gender equality and that it informed how enslaved women dealt with the men in their community who assumed religious authority over them. The evidence often appears in subtext. Leslie A. Schwalm argues that freedwomen likely made the considered choice not to "air their grievances" about slave men before white interviewers but suggests the likelihood that they did so within the community itself.[15]

Occasionally, some resistance to the limited authority religion granted a few slave men peeks through in the subtext. Amanda McCray, an enslaved woman on a Florida plantation, remembered a local slave preacher with some appreciation both for how he brought news of the coming of the Civil War and whispered prayers that God would destroy the Confederacy. She also described how he went "all dressed up" in "store bought shoes" and how masters allowed him to move freely from plantation to plantation when preaching. It's difficult to discern whether her reference to his clothing exhibited pride in a community leader, resentment for his privileges, or a bit of both.[16]

Women also became the primary conduits of the folktale within the slave community, and later among freed people, allowing them latitude to mock the preacher's masculine privileges. The trope of the "rascal jackleg preacher" offered women one way to undercut the enormous authority the male preacher assumed both before and after the Civil War (and indeed well into the twentieth century). In many of these humorous tales, preachers are bound to a variety of bad habits, mostly related

W. Scott Poole

to lust, gluttony, and greed. A few such tales focused on hypocrisy and the lack of true faith, completely undermining the preachers as spiritual guides.[17]

Enslaved women also had to deal with the ministry, and the supervision, of the white churches. Masters frequently required their slaves to attend Sunday services in white churches. This demand offered a way to further extend control and supervision of the enslaved through the church. Annie Young Henson, a former house slave from a large plantation in Northumberland County, Virginia, complained that the segregated gallery was frequently "overcrowded with ours and slaves from other plantations." She also recalled that an elderly slave who occasionally shouted "Amen!" had been told by white church leaders to stop "hollering" or he would not be allowed to come to the church. Henson recalled that "he got so full of the holy spirit" that he shouted anyway, and white members became "so tickled with him and his antics" that they told him he could come anytime he wished. A figure of fun, he appears in this account as a symbol of both white paternalism and derision.[18]

Black women also found in their encounter with white Christianity an even more direct version of white discipline. Records from some up-country South Carolina churches show that slaves could find themselves in a double bind, punished for behavior considered at once both sinful and at variance with their place in Southern society. In the ironically named Union, South Carolina, women who took part in a "cake walk" on the plantation of "Sister Cornelia Ray" faced the discipline of Padgett's Creek Baptist Church's congregation in 1864. The "cake walk" had originated in the 1850s and became a stylized form of African American dance often understood as a mockery of the plantation "promenade."[19]

Resistance to such efforts to control their religious and personal lives emerged out of a theology of prophecy and deliverance, and the unraveling of plantation authority during the war provided openings for more assertive, and even public, expressions of such belief. Women assumed religious authority for themselves, although many slave communities only granted such roles to women considered elders. The role of "the spiritual mother" on the isolated rice plantations of the Georgia and South Carolina sea islands, for example, occupied a central place in communal life. They had charge of the spiritual initiation of the young and also interpreted the meaning of dreams and visions.[20]

Spiritual mothers, to a degree not fully recognized, represented an expression of apocalyptic religious resistance. They constituted a vision of religious leadership completely outside the control of white clergy and their churches. Moreover, black women who assumed this role became the medium of divine judgment and deliverance in a way that even the black male preacher did not. The preacher could proclaim the standard gospel message with dynamic and poetic force, but the spiritual mother had divine insight embodied in her ability to both interpret dreams and to declare prophecy. Prophecy embodied a variety of religious proclamations that went beyond the Spirit-inspired oratory of the sermon and assumed a complete immersion in the world beyond, a summoning of transcendence into human experience.[21]

White attempts to define the role of the spiritual mother foundered, their uncertainty perhaps underscoring both the significance and multiple roles played by such women in their communities. Laura Towne, a Northern missionary who came to the South Carolina sea islands after their occupation by Union forces, seemed befuddled by her efforts to explain "Maum Katie," a spiritual elder born in Africa and alleged to have been more than a hundred years old. Towne calls her "'spiritual mother,' a fortune-teller or, rather, a prophetess and a woman of tremendous influence over her spiritual children."[22]

What appeared to Towne as "fortune-telling," when combined with the title of "prophetess," suggests that Maum Katie summoned the forces of a promised future, an important role during the period of emancipation in which some of the enslaved believed that all prophecies of deliverance were coming true. Earlier spiritual mothers sometimes predicted apocalyptic deliverance. Frances Kemble, for one, in her almost certainly incomplete narrative of an elderly spiritual mother named Sinda in the 1830s, observed how Sinda predicted a date for the end of the world and lost significant respect among her fellow slaves when deliverance failed to arrive as announced.[23]

For many slave women, the certainty that God would deliver them from their masters became axiomatic, though frequently, unlike Mother Sinda, they refused to place a date on this apocalyptic event growing within history. One freedwoman known simply to them as "Aunt Ellen" told some Northern missionaries in North Carolina after the war that "when we used to think about it, it appeared like the judgment sure to come, but a powerful step off." This sense of God taking his own sweet time even appears in African American women's celebration of their freedom. A Northern journalist traveling in the South told of an unnamed elderly women who, upon hearing that the new South Carolina state constitution of 1865 grudgingly allowed for emancipation, commented that she "had done prayed for that forty years; but appears he [God] idled by the way."[24]

Their actual experience of deliverance aside, freedwomen also became the subject of various symbolic religious projects of whites, North and South, following the war. Propagandists of Southern white supremacy, many of them connected to the United Daughters of the Confederacy, attempted to transform black female domestics into the image of the "Mammy," a religious icon that served in part to reassure the white South of "the good old time faithful negro," a phrase that frequently crops up in language complaining about the allegedly new generation that had helped shape the politics of Reconstruction. Such imagery literally domesticated the revolutionary promise of African American women's apocalyptic visions.[25]

Meanwhile, well-meaning white abolitionists ignored black women's theology of apocalyptic liberation. They created an image of the long-suffering enslaved woman, one that comported with their tendency to see themselves as saviors of victims rather than common comrades in a struggle. The diaries and journals of Northern teachers and missionaries (many of them prepared for wide circulation by their authors) are filled with accounts wondering at the spirituality of the African American women. These accounts often include condescending contempt for black people's allegedly

W. Scott Poole

simple religious ideas and presented, almost in the tradition of the minstrel show, the dialect of the freed people as both humorous and exotic. It's difficult not to see these sympathetic, if ultimately racist, descriptions as the origin of what filmmaker Spike Lee, and a number of scholars, have termed the trope of the "Magical Negro."[26]

White supremacy shaped white Southern women's theology of apocalypse. Many of them began the war with the near assurance that God would deliver them from the Yankees and preserve their world of social relations grounded in slavery. While punishing the Yankee hordes, they trusted in God to protect their loved ones in the army. Mary Leverett provides one example. Although frequently certain that Confederate commanders had no idea how to properly conduct a war, she told her son Milton that "God will shield [your] head in the day of battle!"[27]

Leverett had reason to doubt God's providence and eventually raised questions about which side He might judge. After the death of one son, she urged the other to resign his commission. However, the idea of faithful womanhood, praying and waiting beside the domestic hearth, had been carefully crafted, both by white women themselves and by the men who needed them to serve as a symbol of the social order they defended. The Civil War produced a massive set of symbolisms about women, especially, but not only, concerned with white women. These symbols in one sense tell us little about the actual experience of faith but, in another sense, tell us a great deal about the expectations that Southern society had for how women should express that faith.

By 1863 tens of thousands of copies of "A Mother's Parting Words to Her Soldier Boy" circulated within the Southern armies. The tract presented itself as the words of a woman of faith who chose to give her son "words of instruction, warning and encouragement" rather than "mingled emotions of love, grief and anxiety" that would have become "only tears." This steely determination to urge faith and responsibility leads the author to write that she "gave up her son without reluctance, indeed I may say with joy, to enter the army of his country." The tract blends a political disquisition on the rights of the Confederate States to govern themselves with motherly encouragement that her son "enlist under the banner of the cross." In fact, she assures him he will not be "a worse soldier for being a good Christian," but that faith, both in God and the justice of the cause, will prepare him "to fill an honored grave" if he does not make it home.[28]

Home waited for the Christian Confederate, both in the form of a pious mother who prayed for his "return in triumph" to "the domestic circle," and according to a coda that appeared with "A Mother's Parting Words," servants who remained loyal and, indeed, prayerful, on behalf of Confederate victory. Written by an Alabama Baptist minister who "preached to the colored people" on Sunday afternoons, the short piece "The Servant's Pray for You" more or less reiterates the message of its title. It includes an early construction of the notion of the "Black Mammy" in its description of an unnamed "old woman," a slave who allegedly contributed fifty cents toward the Confederate cause while "talking much about her master and how she prayed that he might be brought back safe."[29]

As historical forces refused to yield to the power of faith and defeat became imminent, white women's religious imagination sometimes faltered. As Sherman's troops stormed the symbolic Confederate stronghold of Columbia, South Carolina, in November 1864, Elizabeth Logan cried in the arms of Anne DeSaussure, "Oh Mrs. DeSaussure," she exclaimed, "is there a God in heaven?"[30]

When not expressing a desperate sense of doubt about whether or not such a thing as providence even existed, members of the white ruling class became markedly uncertain about where God might decide to pour out his apocalyptic wrath. Mary Leverett, who a few months before had written her son serving the Confederacy at Fort Sumter an assurance that God would destroy "yankeedom," became convinced that the Confederacy had earned this same God's wrath.

On November 8, 1863, Leverett wrote to her son with disappointment that he had not complied with the family's efforts to get him promoted out of Fort Sumter with a political sinecure. Although clearly concerned that young Milton served at a particular point of contest in a besieged city under constant naval bombardment, she spared her greatest anxiety for her son's stories of heavy drinking among the men and officers. "It is no honour to be in Sumter now," she insisted, "and I'm afraid some judgment from the Almighty on a place where so much wickedness is prevailing." While seemingly absurd that Leverett became anxious over the understandable heavy drinking by men under constant bombardment, the nineteenth-century temperance movement had proved amazingly successful in both North and South by the time of the Civil War. Temperance advocates saw the abuse of alcohol as a moral issue rather than a social problem; indeed, alcohol had for many gained a literally diabolical reputation. "Flee from Sodom like Lot," she counseled her son, and suggested that he leave the army and seek a political appointment.[31]

Leverett's uncertainty about the direction in which God's judgment might strike, and her insistence that her son get himself out of the army, marks the beginning of a full-blown crisis of faith. The religious doubts of slaveholding women, underpinned by a new uncertainty about their personal fortunes, often emerged in some startling and deeply revealing admissions. They do not seem to have found in the war a wider scope of independence but rather a pervasive sense of religious dread that arguably played a role in the South's rather decisive turn to "Bible Belt" fundamentalism in the decades following Lee's surrender.

Writing, notably in her journals rather than in the more public arena of correspondence, Ella Gertrude Clanton Thomas told of a dark night of the slaveholder's soul in which she came to doubt the Bible itself, a nightmarish notion for devout Protestant women in the era. Thomas, a prominent Methodist in Augusta, Georgia, belonged to the planter elite; she and her husband owned ninety slaves in 1861. By emancipation she was lamenting that she had been "reduced to comparative poverty."[32]

Thomas's journal explained that before the war her Christian faith had been "intimately" interwoven with her belief "in the institution of slavery . . . if the Bible was right then slavery *must* be (emphasis in original)." This represents one of the clearest statements by a layperson about their faith in a religion of slavery, slavery imagined as essential to God's promises and purposes. Thomas wrote that during her period of doubt at the end of the war, "when I opened the Bible, the numerous allusions to slavery mocked me." Another Georgia woman, Elizabeth Kilcrease, quoted one of her friends as putting the matter more simply: "I have lost my religion since the yankees set my negroes free."[33]

Elizabeth Fox-Genovese once argued that these seemingly straightforward statements of doubt do not suggest a widespread loss of faith. "The Protestant tradition in which they had been reared," in Fox-Genovese's words, taught such women "that faith could never be taken for granted—that it always had to be struggled for." But how exactly did they reclaim that faith? Fox-Genovese believed that the growth of organizations such as the Woman's Christian Temperance Union in the South (which Thomas joined after the war) provided white women with "new opportunities" always pursued "under the mantle of religion." But did women's clubs, new positions teaching in Sunday Schools, and joining national organizations of moral concern really settle an existential struggle for faith?[34]

Doubtless many white Southern women did throw themselves into church work of various kinds in the late nineteenth century. However, such efforts would have given women who took religion seriously only a temporary relief from the questions raised by Confederate defeat. Two changes, one historical and one theological, gave them hope. In both cases, this renewed sense of the divine purpose grew from an embittered reaction against the new social and cultural forces of modernity.

The failure of Reconstruction offered many white Southern women a renewed faith. It was not by accident that white Southerners referred to the overthrow of Reconstruction governments as "redemption." White women believed God had intervened on their behalf during Reconstruction, and as during the war, they became religious symbols themselves. During Wade Hampton's 1876 gubernatorial campaign that effectively ended Reconstruction in South Carolina, young women across the state created elaborate pageants in which they dressed as "Liberty," "Justice," and even a distressed "South Carolina." These elaborate tableaus took place amid the singing of hymns and the prayers by clergy, a defiant assertion of the Lost Cause and a belief in God's intervention on their behalf.[35]

When not appearing as symbols of the Lost Cause, women taught their children hatred and suspicion of "Yankee ways." Sidney Andrews, a correspondent for Boston's *Daily Advertiser* following the war, informed readers that "mothers yet teach their children to hate the north." He asked a six-year-old Charleston girl he saw wandering an alley "whose girl she was" and got the response that she was "a Rebel mother's girl" before the young child disappeared. Although Andrews assured his readers that "spite will bite itself to death in time," he did not take into account that spite could also take on new and terrifying shapes in the postwar era.[36]

Jim Crow segregation and the restriction of African American men's access to the ballot did not completely solve the riddles of faith's promises unfulfilled. The turn in the South toward the brutal clarity and stark claims of premillennialism represents the terror of faith unable to bear the vagaries of history. As early as the

1870s, the "premillennial dispensationalist" interpretation of scripture of the Irish evangelist John Nelson Darby began to circulate among ministers and laypeople in the South. A fascination with the signs of the end of time began to focus around the discovery of "Antichrist," and to feed suspicions about the course of modernity in white Southern religious experience.

Cyrus Ingerson Scofield, a Confederate veteran, completed the Scofield Reference Bible in 1909 and advanced much of the white South's acceptance of millennialist dogma. Scofield blurred the discussion between the biblical text and his copious and lengthy footnotes and creatively shaped even the most obscure biblical passages into the premillennial system. Some Southern Baptist leaders, such as Lewis Sperry Chafer, who became the first president of the enormously influential Dallas Theological Seminary, came close to seeing the Scofield notes as inspired by the Holy Spirit. Chafer called the work "God's gift to the Church in the last days."[37]

Looking at how women in the South perceived their own experience of history points us away from the simplistic assertions that religion offered women on both sides of the color line some variety of simple solace. Future work on the topic must also practice exceeding care in its use of primary sources, and any new efforts to examine the religious experiences of Southern women, black and white, must avoid assuming that reigning theologies or material found in sermons delineates what religious experience meant, how women practiced it, or the fervor with which women even believed it.

Historians should engage in a more thorough examination of black women's theology and how it changed after God's deliverance came in 1865 and then seemingly disappeared with the end of Reconstruction and the coming of Jim Crow. "Pharaoh's Army got drowned" but then reemerged from watery graves as Red Shirts, Rifle Clubs, and the Ku Klux Klan. Black women, and men, watched the prophecies fulfilled and the day of deliverance arriving and then quickly found themselves brutalized and legally segregated by the oppressive system that took the place of slavery. This essay can only offer hints at how they adjusted their religious vision and also wonder aloud whether the concept of African American women and the rejection of Christianity and its "long time coming" promises has been avoided in part because it does not comport with white racial stereotypes of black female religiousness.

The rage of white women directed against the Yankee invaders sought an outlet in the years after the war. They continued to rant against the North in their comments about Reconstruction, and some viewed "redemption" as a literal intervention by God on their behalf.

But they also directed their apocalyptic yearnings in more global directions. Evangelical white Protestants, both men and women, invested themselves heavily in the emergence of premillennial views of the end of the age. Such views held sway within fundamentalism throughout the country, but it arguably found its greatest adherents among the sons and daughters of the defeated. By the twentieth century, premillennial notions had made deep inroads, especially among laypeople and an often poorly educated ministry, within the Southern Baptist Convention, the flagship denomination of particularistic Southern identity in the twentieth century.

African American women had more reason to feel anger as the nineteenth century drew to a close. But apocalyptic stirrings for many of them flowed more in the direction of political action with theological import, a millennialism fueled by belief in their own work of uplift, than in new biblical conceptions of a global apocalypse.

Indeed, African American Christians remained understandably suspicious of premillennialist claims. White fundamentalist leaders' tendency to use their conceptions of an inerrant, unchanging scripture to justify the maintenance of the color line are of a piece with the appropriation of scripture by proslavery forces before the war. The *National Baptist Union Review,* a black Baptist publication, understood this and urged its readers to "beware the dealer in biblical prophecies." African American churchwomen put their energies into social justice and the concept of racial uplift, though the idea of God as deliverer and judge of the wicked remained a part of this theological world view.[38]

The work of the Women's Convention of the National Baptist Convention exemplified this notion with its calls for political work combined with a very this-worldly concern that freedmen and women avoid jazz clubs, the wearing of "gaudy colors," and "boisterous" behavior in the streets. Evelyn Brooks-Higginbotham called this discourse "the politics of respectability."[39]

Brooks-Higginbotham viewed this "politics of respectability" as a counterweapon against the horrific stereotypes of black women in white popular and academic culture. She also notes the class dimension of such notions, since representatives from the tiny African American middle class constituted the leadership of the more than a million strong Women's Convention. These middle-class leaders failed to fully escape "their enormous concern for white perception of black behavior."[40]

However, a millennialist vision remained part of the struggle for uplift, suggesting at least one way that African American Christians reframed their hopes for deliverance. Black Baptist reformer Nannie Burroughs closed, at least rhetorically, class division within the Baptist Women's Convention by suggesting that "any army" made up of "the common people whom God has made more than any other kind are shouting the tidings of salvation . . . and Satan's strongholds shall tumble." She believed the work of racial uplift and the reform of American society represented preparation for the Kingdom of God, a rhetoric of evangelical progress much in line with white millennialist reform and the growth in mainstream Northern white Protestantism of the "social gospel."[41]

Women like Nannie Burroughs further showed that, even as black denominations increasingly emphasized male authority, women could assert themselves using older traditions of the "spiritual mother," women as conduits of the power of prophecy. Following the war, at least one black male Baptist described "gospel mothers" and "Church mothers" who "claim to be under the special influence of the spirit and exercise an authority, greater in many cases than that of the minsters." He grumpily described this phenomenon as "quite outside the New Testament arrangement." Clearly the power of prophecy in the Spirit endured and gave women in the black churches, despite many restrictions, authority to work for the coming Kingdom.[42]

Apocalyptic religious aspiration in the Western world has, since the first century of the Common Era, always faced the challenge of history's refusal to end. White Southern women did not see the Yankee destroyed, and many of them sang a bitter psalm of defeat that found expression in the Lost Cause movement and, for many of their children and grandchildren, in fundamentalist conceptions of God's impending destruction of modernity.

African American women sang different songs in 1865, songs of deliverance and the promises of God, often taught to them by their spiritual mothers, now fulfilled. In a little over a decade, the end of Reconstruction and the beginnings of segregation, lynching, and utter economic disempowerment must have called the fulfillment of prophecy into question. The women of the National Baptist Convention, the African Methodist Episcopal Church, and many other smaller denominations sought to improve the world based on promises that seemed far way. They passed that obligation on to later generations. In the Freedom Struggle of the 1960s, churchwomen like Fannie Lou Hamer and Septima Clarke used a language of deliverance to inspire direct political action.

Women's experience in the South of the Civil War era reminds us that religion refuses consistent analysis, calling forth oppression, liberation, doubt, certainty, and frustration. It's the hammer that built the master's house but also the match that sets it on fire. And, unfortunately, it's also the hammer that rebuilds the master's house with more durable materials.

"We shall overcome," it must be recalled, has apocalyptic portent. But also, like all apocalyptic religion, it places hope in "some day."

NOTES

1. Frances Wallace Taylor, Catherine Taylor Matthews, and J. Tracy Power, eds., *The Leverett Letters: Correspondence of a South Carolina Family, 1851–1868* (Columbia: Univ. of South Carolina Press, 2000), 354.

2. Ibid., 355.

3. Mary A. Livermore, *My Story of the War: A Woman's Narrative of Four Years Personal Experience* (Hartford, Conn.: A. D. Worthington,1889), 260–61. Livermore wrote in dialect, a practice that white interviewers followed in the Works Progress Administration narratives. In this essay I have spelled words accurately that white interpreters intentionally misspelled. I have not corrected grammar or changed word usage.

4. Found throughout the literature on postwar Southern religiousness, Thomas L. Connelly and Barbara Bellows made the most straightforward pronouncement on the question in *God and General Longstreet: The Lost Cause and the Southern Mind* (Baton Rouge: Louisiana State Univ. Press, 1982), describing the South as "spiritually unprepared for Appomattox" (14).

5. This idea, of course, draws on the idea that the logic of slavery held sway even among many nonslaveholders and that its end, the end of a social system rather than the end of

simply a labor system, turned the world of Southern whites upside down. Here I'm really following Elizabeth Fox-Genovese's idea of how the class structure of Southern white society helped to inculcate a widespread slaveholding ethos, often closely related to religious belief and instruction. See Elizabeth Fox-Genovese, *Within the Plantation Household: Black and White Women in the Old South* (Chapel Hill: Univ. of North Carolina Press, 1988), 42–48.

6. Although often very theoretically sophisticated, historians of the American South often write as if they assume race as an inviolable category, rather than an ideology that masks more complex social arrangements.

7. There are, of course, very famous alternative movements, such as the Millerites of the 1840s. The Mormon movement also held a much more complex theology of the end times related to Joseph Smith's early reflection on the role of native peoples in eschatology and "the founding of a new nation." See Jared Farmer's *On Zion's Mount: Mormons, Indians and the American Landscape* (Cambridge, Mass.: Harvard Univ. Press, 2008). Catholicism held an essentially millennialist conception as well, though biblical interpretation since the fourth century viewed the Church itself as the "thousand year reign of Christ" (interpreting "a thousand years" as an idiom for an unknown quantity of time), with the Second Coming of Christ a promise to be fulfilled in an unknown, and occluded, future. Joachim of Fiore, around the year 1000, initiated one of history's few "Catholic apocalyptic" movements.

8. Ronald G. Walters, *American Reformers: 1815–1860* (New York: Hill & Wang, 1989), 21–26; see also examples excerpted by Joshua D. Rothman from Catherine Beecher and Charles G. Finney in *Reforming America, 1815–1860* (New York: W. W. Norton, 2010), 5–8.

9. Albert J. Raboteau, *Slave Religion: The Invisible Institution in the Antebellum South* (New York: Oxford University Press, 1980), 154.

10. Readers aware of twentieth-century theology will note an interesting congruence of these ideas and the post–World War II German theologian Jürgen Moltmann. Moltmann suggested that concepts of eschatology had to be pondered in the light of the victims of history. See esp. Moltmann's *Theology of Hope* (New York: Harper & Row, 1967), 266–70, and his *The Crucified God* (New York: HarperCollins, 1991), 162–76.

11. Kathryn Gin Lum, *Damned Nation: Hell in America from the Revolution to Reconstruction* (New York: Oxford Univ. Press, 2014), 181.

12. "Slavery Was Hell without Fires" in George Rawick, ed., *God Struck Me Dead: Religion Conversion Experiences and Autobiographies of Negro Ex-Slaves* (1945; repr., Westport, Conn.: Greenwood, 1972), 215.

13. Maria Stewart, *Productions of Mrs. Maria W. Stewart, Presented to the First African Baptist Church & Society, of the City of Boston* (Boston: Published by Friends of Freedom and Virtue, 1835), 49.

14. Evelyn Brooks-Higginbotham, *Righteous Discontent: The Women's Movement in the Black Baptist Church, 1880–1920* (Cambridge, Mass.: Harvard Univ. Press, 1993), 13–18. Brooks-Higginbotham describes "the multiple consciousness and multiple positionings" in relation to social power in the postbellum era. However, enslaved women arguably faced as many, if not more, complex arrangements of hierarchy, patriarchy, and attempts to create patriarchy during the history of slavery.

15. Leslie A. Schwalm, *A Hard Fight for We: Women's Transition from Slavery to Freedom* (Champaign: Univ. of Illinois Press, 1997), 68.

16. Amanda Cray interview, *Born in Slavery: Slave Narratives from the Federal Writers' Project, 1936–1938*, vol. 3, *Florida Narratives,* Library of Congress American Memory Project, http://memory.loc.gov/ammem/snhtml/snhome.html.

17. See Lawrence W. Levine, *Black Culture and Black Consciousness: Afro-American Folk Thought from Slavery to Freedom* (New York: Oxford Univ. Press, 1978), 324–27.

18. Annie Henson interview, *Born in Slavery,* vol. 8, *Maryland,* http://memory.loc.gov/ammem/snhtml/snhome.html.

19. "Padgett Creek Baptist Church Records, Union District, SC," microfilm, South Caroliniana Library, Univ. of South Carolina, Columbia. The "cake walk dance" or "the chalk line" originated on Florida plantations. The 1864 incident shows that it came to South Carolina very early. Its heyday is often described as being after 1890.

20. Schwalm, *A Hard Fight for We,* 69.

21. The "Conjure woman" in plantation life and, in New Orleans and southern Louisiana, the role of the Vodou or Vodun priestesses such as Sanite Dede and the famous "Marie Laveau" (mother and daughter) go beyond the space of this essay but raise questions for further research about how African American hopes for deliverance blended with, or became muddled in, these religious systems. See Raboteau, *Slave Religion,* 75–78. See also Yolanda Pierce's enthralling discussion of the lay preacher Zilpha Elaw in *Hell without Fires: Slavery, Christianity and the Antebellum Spiritual Narrative* (Gainesville: Univ. Press of Florida, 2005), 87–110. Elaw was a free black woman in Pennsylvania and took her commission to preach during an apocalyptic vision. Pierce does not focus on her millenarian teachings, however.

22. Rupert Sargent Holland, ed., *Letters and Diary of Laura M. Towne* (Cambridge, Mass.; Harvard Univ. Press, 1912), 176–77.

23. Incident regarding Mother Sinda described in Raboteau, *Slave Religion,* 238.

24. Quoted in Raboteau, *Slave Religion,* 312; Sidney Andrews, *The South Since the War* (Boston: Houghton Mifflin Company, 1971), 68.

25. A good brief discussion appears in Karen L. Cox, *Dreaming of Dixie: How the South Was Created in American Popular Culture* (Chapel Hill; Univ. of North Carolina Press, 2011), 7, 33, 65.

26. See Matthew Hughey, "Cinethetic Racism: White Redemption and Black Stereotypes in 'Magical Negro' Films," *Social Problems* 25 (Aug. 2009): 543–77.

27. Taylor, Matthews, and Power, eds., *Leverett Letters,* 98.

28. [Mrs. Frances Blake Brockenbrough], *A Mother's Parting Words to her Soldier Boy* (Petersburg, Va.: n.p., 186–). Repr.; no. 18 (author's collection).

29. Ibid., 6–7.

30. Taylor, Matthews, and Power, eds., *Leverett Letters,* 386.

31. Ibid., 370.

32. Virginia Ingraham Burr, ed., *The Secret Eye: The Journal of Ella Gertrude Clanton Thomas, 1845–1889* (Chapel Hill: Univ. of North Carolina Press, 1990), 276–77.

33. Quoted in Fox-Genovese, "Days of Judgment, Days of Wrath: The Civil War and the Imagination of Women Writers," in Randall Miller, Harry S. Stout, and Charles Reagan Wilson, eds., *Religion in the American Civil War* (New York: Oxford University Press, 1998), 240.

34. Ibid.

35. Alfred Brockenbrough Williams, "Scrapbook," South Caroliniana Library, Univ. of South Carolina, Columbia,; see esp. "Hampton Campaign Opens in Anderson" and "Hampton Receives Ovation in Yorkville."

36. Andrews, *South since the War,* 10.

37. Matthew Avery Sutton's *American Apocalypse: A History of Modern Evangelicalism* (Cambridge, Mass.; Belknap Press of Harvard Univ. Press, 2014) brilliantly interprets the emergence of premillennialism as intertwined with the rise of evangelicalism. He convincingly pushes back the timeline of the birth of Fundamentalism from the 1920s. However, he puts a great deal of emphasis on premillennialism as a national movement, much more than I would. Fundamentalism in the North and Midwest struggled with modernism and became a somewhat marginalized movement in much of those regions, due in part to continued loyalty to mainline denominations

W. Scott Poole

and the influx of immigrants who retained their traditional religious ties. Meanwhile, a kind of folk fundamentalism in the Southern Baptist Convention, soon to become America's largest Protestant religious body, found ready and widespread acceptance. Dallas, Texas, a center of premillennial thought, also became one of the meccas of Southern Baptist life. Somewhat oddly, Sutton gives almost no attention to the Southern Baptist Convention even in discussions of the influence of Dallas Theological Seminary (where Hal Lindsey studied before beginning his successful writing career). See 27, 28, 33, 44, and 345.

38. Quoted in ibid., 65; Sutton has a series of important discussions of race and fundamentalism, as well as the role of prophecy in African American church life. In reference to the ideas expounded in this essay: see esp. 109–12.

39. Brooks-Higginbotham, *Righteous Discontent,* 186–96, 204–5.

40. Ibid., 194.

41. *National Baptist Convention, Journal of the Eighth Annual Assembly of the Woman's Convention held in the First Baptist Church of Lexington Kentucky, September 16–21, 1908* (Nashville: National Baptist Publishing Board, 1909), 240–44.

42. Quoted in Steven Hahn, A *Nation Under Our Feet: Black Political Struggles in the Rural South from Slavery to the Great Migration* (Cambridge, Mass.; Harvard Univ. Press, 2003), 233. A detailed discussion of gender dynamics and the black church also appears in Bettye Collier-Thomas, *Jesus, Jobs and Justice: African American Women and Religion* (New York: Alfred A. Knopf, 2010), 124–38.

"I Can Read His Righteous Sentence"

Female Christian Abolitionists and the Millennium

TIMOTHY WESLEY

I have seen Him in the watch-fires of a hundred circling camps,
They have builded Him an altar in the evening dews and damps;
I can read His righteous sentence by the dim and flaring lamps:
His day is marching on.
    —"The Battle Hymn of the Republic"
    Julia Ward Howe, 1862

The most anticipated consequence of the Civil War was the emancipation of over four million African Americans held in bondage throughout fifteen American states. And at least outside of the anti-reformist South, the dominant impulse in antebellum Christianity was postmillennialism, the belief that mankind could hasten Christ's return and the establishment of his earthly reign by perfecting humanity. As an essayist in the *American Theological Review* observed in 1859, postmillennialism was by then the "commonly received doctrine" among American Protestants.[1] Given the shared importance of emancipation and millennialism during the Civil War era, it was all but inevitable that many Christians framed the end of American slavery in millennialist terms.[2] Appropriately therefore, historians have of late considered several providentialist interpretations of slavery's demise.[3] But even though the majority of church people during the period were female, examinations of the eschatological fashion in which scores of abolitionist women on the Union home front understood emancipation are largely missing from the scholarly literature on religion during the Civil War.[4] Such efforts are long overdue. In their animating trust that God was an intervening yet entreatable agent in their lives and in the life (or, alas, death) of the nation, the female activists who warned of a world ablaze were identical to the wives and mothers who kept the home fires burning and to the benevolent fairgoers, nurses, and other relief-minded women whose patriotic hearts burned for the soldier and his cause. The story of female and millennialist Christian abolitionists, therefore, is a quintessential story of Northern women and religion during the Civil War. By placing these reformist women of faith squarely within the chaotic public marketplace of religious ideas that was mid-nineteenth-century America, it will be possible to reveal much about their formative impact upon the sacralized politics of the Civil War era.[5]

In religiously pluralistic and comparably reform-tolerant northern environs since before the American Revolution, women commonly grounded their activism in some version of progressive millenarian thought.[6] Female Christian activists in America were typically affiliated with evangelical traditions that endorsed providentialism as dogma, but they nevertheless identified with a female-empowering strain of postmillennialism that had been handed down to them from English reformers of an earlier age. The predecessors of religiously inspired women abolitionists in America, chiefly Quakers and Baptists of the seventeenth and early eighteenth centuries, had believed in the egalitarianism of creation. That belief shaped their prominent roles in their respective traditions, their confidence that the awaited utopian society would realize important equalitarian objectives including the political and ministerial parity of the sexes, and their selfless intercession on behalf of the lowliest of the low within English society.[7] In that tradition and throughout the century before the Civil War, female emancipationists awaited the end of slavery in America as part of an assumed preordained progression toward the perfection of mankind and the millennial kingdom.[8]

Scripture-spouting "Comeouter" Maria Weston Chapman was, for example, convinced of emancipation's providential significance.[9] Encouraging recently "converted" antislavery radicals in 1855, Chapman remembered that when she joined the "grandest undertaking of any age, this effort to elevate a whole people in the scale of moral being" in the early 1830s, she had "longed for this coming of millennial glory" and, in organized abolitionism, "found the road on which to go forth to meet it."[10] With a self-described "head full of plans" and "heart of devotedness," the young Chapman was confident that emancipation and then the millennium were imminent, and in that certainty she was not alone.[11] The editors of the Methodist monthly the *Ladies Repository* representatively prophesied in 1850 that in short order "wrong and injustice" would be "forever banished. Every yoke shall be broken, and the oppressed go free . . . then shall come to pass the millennium."[12] Importantly, while Maria Weston Chapman and other providentialist women were more egalitarian than their male abolitionist counterparts as a group, they were far from being anomalies. Had postmillennialist female reformers been genuine spiritual outliers and supposed heretics, their ultimate impact upon wartime popular opinion would have been negligible. As it was, female antislavery crusaders effectually pushed the boundaries of an existing eschatological framework already familiar to evangelical Protestants on the home front.

A palpable degree of abolitionism was apparent in American branches of almost every Protestant denomination including Northern Methodists, Baptists, and Presbyterians. Arguably, however, the Quakers, Congregationalists, and Christian Universalists were most associated with the Christian antislavery movement by the middle of the nineteenth century.[13] And adherents within each of these traditions invested in the ideas of postmillennialism and the perfectibility of humanity.[14] Congregationalists were markedly postmillennialist in part because of their identification with the civil millennialism of the eighteenth century. They embraced the practicability of Christian labors to bring the millennial kingdom into being on Earth and were convinced that the United States was preordained to be the feature player in God's endtime plans.[15]

So too was the Civil War era millennialism of Universalists (and Unitarians) linked to Revolutionary-era America. According to historian David Robinson, American millennialists anticipated an earthly Kingdom of God fashioned by the Almighty working "through the power of a new democratic citizen in a new world. Even though this expectation was attuned to the here and now (or the here and soon to be), and was political in its orientation, it shared the essentially optimistic faith of the Universalists, who were sure of God's ultimate power and will to save."[16] The inherent "earthly" optimism of postmillennialism, in essence, jibed well with what Robinson has labeled the Universalists' "other-worldly optimism."[17] And reformist participants in the Quaker "evangelical renewal" of the nineteenth century "adopted the millennialist teachings of the wider Protestant scene," historian Douglas Gwyn posits, and "at least in some ways, harkened back to the eschatology of early leader George Fox."[18] Admittedly, plenty of Quakers were premillennialists who believed the world would grow worse and worse until Christ returned. That said, reformist Society of Friends members—the variety of Quakers who founded several utopian communities and launched (as with American abolitionism) an impressive number of reform movements—understood the progression of history in much more hopeful terms and endorsed the postmillennialist idea that God was even then at work evolving his divine government on earth.[19]

No matter their denominational affiliation, and like their male colleagues, the majority of female abolitionists always doubted that the millennial process would unfold peacefully.[20] Formerly enslaved Christian poet Phyllis Wheatley, for example, prophesied in 1774 that decades of military subjugation would be visited upon independence-seeking American colonists, who would never witness what one historian has called the "paradisiacal transformation" into enlightened harmony and peace until they ended slavery.[21] Antislavery providentialists like Wheatley routinely infused their rhetoric with forewarnings of Christ's vengeance against the wickedness of slavery and the slaveholding South, seemingly all but conflating post- and premillennialist tenets in the process.[22] Too much should not be made of this, however, for postmillennialists before and during the Civil War era developed a more expansive theology than is routinely recognized by lay commentators and church scholars today. As historian James Moorhead has rightly observed, "much of the cultural power of postmillennialism came from its evocation of cataclysmic images of the End whose energy was then harnessed in service to the incremental construction of an evangelical empire."[23]

More than a half-century after Phyllis Wheatley's predictions, African American evangelist and abolitionist Maria Stewart expected that slavery would soon bring God's fiery judgment upon America, followed by catharsis and the millennial kingdom. "O, ye great and mighty men of America, ye rich and powerful ones," she wrote in 1835, "many of you will call for the rocks and mountains to fall upon you, and to

Timothy Wesley

hide from the wrath of the Lamb . . . whilst many of the sable-skinned Africans you now despise, will shine in the kingdom of heaven as stars forever and ever."[24] The first song in Maria Weston Chapman's *Songs of the Free and Hymns of Christian Freedom,* published in 1836, was titled "The Advent of Christ," and it revealingly envisaged that "The Lord will come! A dreadful form, / With wreath of flame and robe of storm: / Master and slave alike shall find / An equal judge of human kind."[25] And anticipating the Almighty's blistering retribution upon the United States, Harriet Beecher Stowe in *Uncle Tom's Cabin* (1852) likewise blamed America's most egregious national sin for the coming apocalypse as foretold in the Book of Revelation.[26]

Stowe's powerful scriptural allusions and references throughout her classic abolitionist novel reveal the degree to which her social consciousness was informed by a belief in prophetic Christianity, a characteristic she shared with other radical women of the day.[27] "It is time to prepare to die," Stowe wrote in 1842, "the lamp has not long to burn—the hour is flying—all things are sliding away and eternity is coming."[28] Stowe's postmillennialism was initially rooted in the belief that individuals must strive toward perfection as part of the ultimate sanctification of mankind.[29] In the 1840s, however, she disavowed the doctrine of individual perfectibility and instead embraced her own helplessness and imperfectability.[30] She now believed that the "perfect" Kingdom of God would be brought about not by vain attempts at personal purity but by the Christlike sacrifices *of and for* the poorest and most oppressed among men. Thus the shared destiny of mankind was not mutual flawlessness but universal Christian humility and meekness, and courage and resolve in faith of God's saving grace, as exemplified for instance in the titular character of her most famous literary offering. Such an "apostolic experience," she wrote in 1853, must "become the common experience of all Christians, before Christ can subdue the world."[31] The individual could not hope to obtain faultlessness, but through mankind's collective and earnest piety, submission to God's will, and "constant sympathy and communion" with the Savior, the world would yet be transformed.[32]

Because Harriet Beecher Stowe infused all of her writings of the late 1840s and 1850s with this millennialist prescription and wrote so prolifically, she informed the efforts of late-antebellum female reformers as much or more than anyone else. Truly, it is all but impossible to imagine how Stowe could have set a more viscerally effective example for emancipationists who were both Christians and women.[33] All of Stowe's perfectionist endeavors were now redirected away from herself and outward onto the world in a way that simultaneously vilified slavery and lionized the enslaved. "By identifying herself with the Man of Sorrows," scholar Joan Hedrick offers, "Stowe turned her human weakness into a source of divine strength and fixed on a historical and religious reality that linked her experience as a woman with that of a slave."[34] And because all things were thought possible in God, the prerequisite perfection of mankind and the resultant millennial age remained equally viable goals. What man could not achieve, God could, and as Stowe and other abolitionist women agreed, the most essential millennium-facilitating achievement that the Almighty would soon sanction was the eradication of slavery.

By the end of the antebellum era moreover, Stowe and other laborers in the field of Christian abolitionism (including some within pacifistic traditions) believed not only that the redemption of humanity hinged upon the downfall of the South's infernal institution but also that God would use the traditionally slavery-enabling federal government in bringing about such redemption as well.[35] Christian abolitionist, teacher, and poet Lucy Larcom, for instance, observed in late 1860 that "freedom takes long strides in these better days." Liberty's projected ascendency was not random, however, for Larcom was certain that God had at last "turned the heads of our democratic people" to bring about the election of a Republican president in the person of Abraham Lincoln. "That is glorious!" Larcom proclaimed, convinced that Lincoln's victory foreshadowed a governmental offensive against slavery and thus that "the millennium is not so far off as we feared."[36] Moral suasionist Maria Weston Chapman spurned organized religion and the federal government and instead looked to the largely female American Anti-Slavery Society, in her judgment "the only American institution founded on the Christian and republican idea of the equal brotherhood of man." As the war began in earnest, however, even Chapman took satisfaction in knowing that she and the other members of her organization had played an important role in obliging the American state to serve as freedom's champion. Asserting that the American Anti-Slavery Society had at long last "done its work. It had borne the Lord into Jerusalem," Chapman apocalyptically rejoiced over "the signs of the times" and their millennial implications.[37]

More than a few antislavery women were surprised by the sentiments that the government's newly righteous role stirred in them. Lillie Chace, raised by her Quaker mother and father to be both an "obedient" member of the Society of Friends committed to the "tenets of her birthright religion" *and* a devotee of William Lloyd Garrison, was customarily no cheerleader for the American state.[38] Upon finding herself staunchly supporting "the stars and stripes" in June 1861, she therefore confessed, "One year ago, I could not have been made to believe that I should do even that, or in the slightest degree render aid to our government, but—times have changed."[39] Christian Universalist Mary Livermore expressed a similar degree of astonishment at her 1861 conversion to patriotism. "Never before had the national flag signified anything to me," she recalled in her 1887 memoirs, but that was before the American government assumed the role of protagonist in a war against slavery, to her mind mankind's vilest sin and the chief impediment to humanity's redemption. "As I saw it now, kissing the skies," Livermore remembered, "all that it symbolized as representative of government . . . became clear to my mental vision." Most important, Livermore believed the flag and the government it represented "signified an advance in human government, for it had been adopted by millions of men, who stepped out before the on-looking world, and wrote out a declaration of human rights as the basis of national life."[40]

Female emancipationist critics of the federal power like Chace and Livermore for the most part joined their spiritual sisters in welcoming the war as the state's providential opportunity to end slavery. Other Americans who awaited the government's facilitation of the millennium were less persuaded that slavery was the most important issue at hand. A substantial number of evangelicals began the war confident that the preservation of the Union itself was millennialism's sine quo non, the essential and indispensable element of the Almighty's eschatological designs. As a religious essayist from Delaware observed in late 1861, "If we understand the prophetic destiny of America she will come forth like a polished gem from the fiery ordeal, fledged with victory and radiant with glory. Then will the millennium star dawn upon the world and the word of God be unbound."[41] But as prospects for a quick restoration of the Union became evermore bleak, moderate Northerners of every faith tradition increasingly adopted the opinion of their antislavery countrywomen, abandoning their expectations to reestablish the prewar nation "as it was" and accepting the premise that a more righteous providential plan was unfolding.

Numerous devout women on the Union home front acted out of compassion for the victims of slavery without referencing eschatological concerns. As historian Judith Giesberg has noted, the war saw a broader "coming of age of emancipationists sentiment" that made African Americans "the beneficiaries of the white middle class's sympathetic imagination."[42] Rather than hoping to hurry the millennium with their altruism, female workers in such organizations as the United States Sanitary Commission and the United States Christian Commission often took up the cause of the enslaved because abolitionists had, as author Beth Salerno notes, "finally succeeded in portraying assistance to African Americans as being part of women's moral responsibilities."[43]

Other religious women served their country through efforts that they imagined were independent of the slavery question altogether. Hundreds of Northern Catholic women won distinction as nurses during the war, as was true of sisters from at least twelve separate orders of nuns. A lesser but still noteworthy number of Catholic women became important home front benefactors of the soldiers. Laywoman Mary Brady founded Philadelphia's Soldier's Aid Society, for example, while Ellen Ewing Sherman, William Tecumseh Sherman's wife, developed a nationwide reputation for fundraising in support of the troops.[44] And just as the seven thousand Jewish men who served in the Union Army were more than their limited presence in the population demanded, so too did Jewish women offer succor to the Union in measure far greater than their numbers required. The women of Congregation Mikveh Israel in New York turned their synagogue into a hospital for wounded soldiers, for instance, while several Jewish female benevolent societies sponsored sewing circles and other philanthropic efforts.[45] Importantly, scores of "conventional" Protestant women within conservative traditions (such as Episcopalianism and Methodism) hoped simply to convince their countrymen that the Almighty was on their side but that they must all act in ways sure to keep him there.[46] As scholar Scott Cole insists, their moralistic nationalism eventually permeated established venues of female service, displacing "discussions of slavery and states' rights as central themes of the war effort" at sanitary fairs throughout the North.[47]

And finally, many women within those same conservative faith camps (especially in politically contentious states like Indiana and Ohio) belonged to Democratic families who disparaged the war effort from the start as an unwarranted, unnatural, and unholy emancipationist campaign.[48] Plagued by the same sense of religious dread that beset their proslavery counterparts in the South, as profiled by W. Scott Poole in this volume's counterpositional essay on Southern women and apocalyptic thought, Northern Democratic churchwomen were sometimes disloyal. But like most of their neighbors, many more Democratic churchwomen remained true to the Union, even while dismissing the hopeful postmillennialism of Christian abolitionism as so much claptrap. Counterintuitively perhaps, the voices of these chattel-championing but otherwise loyal churchwomen were heard now more than ever before, certainly more than they had ever sounded within the walls of their own conservative churches or paternalistic homes. Because Republicans throughout the North increasingly painted all Democrats with the same broad brush of Copperheadism, in regions "where support for antiwar Democrats was high," Nina Silber writes, there likely developed "a tendency for women to assume a greater burden in articulating the Democratic position because men feared being targeted as traitors or draft resisters."[49] Be they disloyal churchwomen who opposed the war because of its perceived antislavery objective or loyal (if partisan) congregants who supported the war in spite of their aversion to emancipation, such women serve as unmistakable reminders that the reach and transformative influence of abolitionist millennialism had its limits.

All that said, thousands and thousands of women *and* men unquestionably saw the Almighty's millennial handiwork in everything that was transpiring, including the changes then underway in the hearts and minds of white Northerners. As posited by the eloquent Sarah Grimké in 1863, "The eyes of the nation are being anointed with the eye-salve of the King of Heaven."[50] Given the sacralized mood of the home front, this pervasive understanding of abolition's oracular value was essential in producing the level of public support for emancipation that ultimately afforded President Lincoln the latitude to move directly against slavery.[51] It was a conviction developed first and foremost within the ranks of progressive churchmen and women and disseminated largely through agitation. Just as assuredly then, Christian abolitionist women played a leading role in its development and expansion.

Throughout the war's first year and a half, exasperated female activists rebuked the Lincoln administration by linking their prognostications of a dreadful judgment by fire with the federal power's hesitation to make emancipation the primary war aim of the Union.[52] "This country will have to pass through shameful stages of degerance [sic]," Unitarian Lydia Maria Child wrote in 1861, "if we blindly and recklessly throw away the glorious opportunity for atonement which the Divine Ruler has placed within our reach."[53] Radical Quaker abolitionist Amy Post of Rochester, New York, echoed such fears. Observing that the nation "must suffer for all these multiplied wrongs for how long or how severely is not seen as yet" and that the war was in God's hands, she nevertheless noted that military defeat after military defeat had followed Lincoln's revocation of Gen. David Hunter's emancipation of enslaved men and women in several Southern states. Post ventured therefore that perhaps "defeat is the means to bring the nation to its senses."[54] Burgeoning abolitionist Lizzie Little was convinced that nothing could be "nobler than purchasing Freedom for all mankind." In that certainty, she likewise worried that Lincoln's hesitancy to act against slavery was thus rendering the Union's chances for victory "uncertain" at best. "If our Administration does not declare the slaves emancipated ere four weeks pass by," she wrote in early 1862, "I fear we are lost."[55]

Religiously fervent abolitionist Maria Patec held similar views. Welcoming God's final judgment on the evils of slavery even if it necessitated catastrophic death and destruction, Patec wrote in 1861 that "the time has come . . . when the battle of Armageddon is to be fought, the day of preparation is at hand, the irrepressible conflict has begun as in the days of the Israelites in Egypt."[56] Rhoda Southworth, divining that Lincoln courted calamity in his failure to "embrace the great principle[s] of humanity and liberty," believed the president was like the wicked fool in Psalms 52:7, a man who "made not God his trust." Unless and until the nation and its leader stopped "clinging to the great sin which has brought upon the nation His righteous judgments," Southworth dolefully observed, such wickedness "makes Him our enemy."[57] These and similar expressions of dissatisfaction by Christian antislavery women in the war's early stages sowed seeds of doubt about the war's progress in the minds of many on the home front. Abraham Lincoln was keenly aware of such abolitionist criticisms. As numerous biographers have demonstrated and in the words of author David Von Drehle, "Not a day passed in the first nine months of 1862 without Lincoln hearing from these passionate, idealistic men and women . . . and they were fed up with the president's cautious approach to the matter of emancipation."[58]

President Lincoln knew well the sentiments then circulating within abolitionist circles.[59] Nevertheless, several abolitionist women warned the president directly about providential will and the growing discontent of the people. Harriet Tubman stated plainly in a letter to the president that "God won't let Master Lincoln beat the South until he does the right thing." With perhaps too much deference, Tubman added that while "Master Lincoln, he's a great man, and I'm a poor Negro," nevertheless on the matter of emancipation "this Negro can tell Master Lincoln" much that he needed to know.[60] In another highly publicized missive in August 1862, Lydia Maria Child alerted the president that "Everywhere I hear men saying: 'Our President is an honest, able man, but he appears to have no firmness of purpose. He is letting the country drift to ruin for want of earnest action and a consistent policy.'" Adopting a bellicosity that likely stunned the president, Child asked, "What fatal spell is cast over your honest mind, that you hesitate so long to give such orders? Be not deceived; God is not mocked." Still, hope remained. Because the Almighty had placed him in his current position, Child reminded the president, victory would follow when and if Lincoln embraced providential will. "Lay out [your] right arm on the buckler of the Almighty," Child urged, "and march fearlessly forward to universal freedom in the name of the Lord!"[61] A collection of female Christian abolitionists from the Old Northwest likewise observed (in a petition that originally circulated in the *Northwestern Christian Advocate*) that

President Lincoln seemed "to hesitate as though waiting for an expression of the sentiments of the country." Noting that soldiers in the ranks were proscribed and could not speak freely, these "wives, daughters, and mothers" of Wisconsin thus felt compelled to offer such an assessment. "The other sex," their petition read, "in civil life has various modes of expressing views which are fast becoming unanimous in loyal portions of the country." Linking the fate of the nation with the ultimate fate of all mankind, they asked, "Is it not our duty . . . to speak out unitedly and unmistakably in behalf of our army, our country, and humanity?"[62]

And as thousands of Christian women joined the chorus of providentialist emancipationists during the war's first half, Julia Ward Howe provided them the sheet music. Just as Harriet Beecher Stowe's prose helped infuse antebellum abolitionism with the zeal and immediacy of millennialism, Howe's lyrics helped drive wartime public opinion toward a millennialist understanding of emancipation.[63] Certainly nothing more expressly joined together the Book of Revelation's foretold judgment at the end of time, the death of slavery, and the terrible war in which the Union was then engaged than did her transformative anthem "The Battle Hymn of the Republic." Howe's providentialist Christianity was a conglomeration of numerous religious ideas and antecedents, as was true of many abolitionists of the day. Not coincidentally, then, in one lyrical offering and with equal force, she combined the sacrificial Christ of love and charity who was born in the beauty of the lilies and who died for all mankind *and* the apocalyptic Christ of vengeance and retribution who crushes the serpent with his heel, writes his fiery gospel in burnished rows of steel, and is soon to make the world his footstool and the soul of wrong his slave.[64]

In this fashion Howe deftly played upon the various spiritually inspired enthusiasms of a religious people in the midst of their greatest existential crisis while leaving the particular details of application open to denominations, local churches, and even individuals. Her essential message was that Godly intervention in the affairs of men, by and through the American government and toward a millennial end, was at work. Everything else, from the order of millennial events to the literalness of Christ's Second Coming or whatever the case may have been, was open to interpretation but was by no means prohibitive in its vagueness. "The Battle Hymn of the Republic" was consequently malleable to the variables of the war and to the doctrinal peculiarities and unconventionalities of each group of believers in the Union.[65] When initially published in the *Atlantic Monthly* in February 1862, it resonated with a diverse but discouraged public steeped in apocalyptical postmillennialism and increasingly convinced that a nobler purpose for the war must soon be embraced lest the blessings of the Almighty fall disproportionately upon their Southern foes.[66] As scholar Ernest Lee Tuveson has noted, the millennialism of the prewar decades had included an expectation of a future war to fulfill prophecy and complete society's perfection. After Fort Sumter, then, a "new rationale of national mission" was fashioned, derived from millennialist interpretations of scripture and "epitomized for all time" in Howe's verses, a rationale that rendered the war against slavery and its secessionist champions not just understandable but unequivocally

Timothy Wesley

necessary.[67] If the claim made by scholar Mary Jo Miles that "Howe gave the Union the emotional boost it needed to legitimize and continue the war by proclaiming it a crusade to end slavery" is an exaggeration, it is surely not so by much.[68]

Finally, the "Battle Hymn of the Republic" provided desperate Americans a framework in which to resolve the emerging but paramount internal paradox of the war while avoiding, for the most part, societal fragmentation or outright rupture. Because many started the conflict convinced of the eschatological primacy of the Union, it was essential that the "emancipationist turn," in reality a necessary change in the central meaning of the war, somehow not diminish or call into question the importance of Unionism. Thus, that the collective agent of providential realization in Howe's ballad is the nation—as embodied by the soldiers in the circling camps, the "holy" soldiers who build their altars in the evening dews and damps, indeed, the soldiers who are marching on—struck a chord with patriotic Northerners. And because the effort in which they toiled, the cause to which the federal power would soon be formally committed, was to "make men free," Union and emancipation became part and parcel of the same postmillennialist blueprint. "The Battle Hymn of the Republic" in effect predicted and articulated Abraham Lincoln's conviction during the war's latter stages that any struggle to end American slavery and any struggle to preserve the American nation was, by definition, the same struggle, one and inseparable.[69] Sung to the tune of an existing abolitionist marching song about John Brown and his martyred body, Howe's stanzas expressed in verse what Lincoln's Emancipation Proclamation would soon offer in promise. "Mine eyes have seen the glory of the coming of the Lord, / He is trampling out the vintage where the grapes of wrath are stored," Howe offered in her first verse, and continued, "He hath loosed the fateful lightning of his terrible swift sword, / His truth is marching on." Facilitated by the American state, it was to be a future of both transcendent beauty and absolute righteousness. Indeed, it was to be the millennium.

Thanks in large part to the public prayers, petitions, musings, poems, and songs of female abolitionists like Howe, Stowe, Mary Livermore, and others, Northerners by the score were convinced by the summer of 1862 that the setbacks and embarrassments routinely visited upon their nation were more than random. Reconsidering the meaning of the war and why their military efforts consistently yielded bitter fruit, many concluded at last that God would not sanctify any effort that failed to target slavery in earnest.[70] Importantly, this new accord could be found in every quarter of the Union home front. Loyal Democrat Robert Dale Owen of Indiana, for instance, granted in early August 1862 that "the people are ready" and "are today prepared for emancipation." In the end, an attack on slavery was a providential likelihood demanding Northern compliance. "Let us do what we can," Owen wrote, "and leave to God the issue." Recognizing the plan of the Almighty in emancipation, Owen observed, "I see no other road out of the darkness."[71] By roughly the beginning of September 1862, a full-fledged "Emancipation Movement" had all but taken over the public's imagination and was the subject of much analysis in the home front press.[72] And, of course, many now supposed that the antislavery trend was providential. "Our emancipation scheme was planned by God who is leading us to it," a columnist in the *New York Tribune* offered in mid-August, "by a path that we knew not . . . when we entered it; and it is baptized, and to be baptized, in rivers of blood."[73]

Abraham Lincoln's understanding of the influence that female emancipationists had on such home front belief by the end of 1862 is suggested by both his appreciation of Harriet Beecher Stowe's role in the divisive politics of the age and his reckoning of the popular impact of Julia Ward Howe's divinatory ballad.[74] And while Lincoln had always been suspicious of the threat to constitutionalism that radical abolitionism presented, he had similarly always acknowledged the importance of religious sentiment and the church in shaping popular opinion.[75] Moreover, the president was by that time drawing heavy fire from immediatists like Wendell Phillips, who offered as late as a month and a half before the preliminary Emancipation Proclamation that Lincoln was "conducting the war, at present, with the purpose of saving slavery," and thus "if he had been a traitor, he could not have worked better to strengthen one side, and hazard the success of the other."[76] In essence, just as the position proffered by Christian abolitionists became evermore agreeable to wartime Northerners, the president came under scathing levels of very public abolitionist scrutiny. Who can doubt therefore that such trends played a role in presidential deliberations and executive policy? Some in fact suspected then and since that President Lincoln endorsed emancipation in late 1862 *entirely* for political expediency after having experienced little if any personal or political evolution on the subject. In that attitude, Sarah Hildreth Butler wrote to her by then ardently abolitionist husband Gen. Benjamin Butler on September 28, 1862, that "the President's Proclamation of Emancipation was made directly on the heels of this [Antietam] as a concession to the Abolitionists."[77]

But such an attitude is unduly cynical, and the historical Lincoln (circa 1863) deserves more generosity. Two truths suggest this point. First, the formerly religiously skeptical president's understanding of the war and his role in it grew more spiritual with each passing day of the conflict. Speaking to cabinet members five days after the federal victory at Antietam, for example, he described his decision to issue the Emancipation Proclamation as the fulfillment of a solemn promise he had made to God if the Almighty would drive rebel forces from Maryland.[78] The trend did not abate. By the end of the war and as exemplified in his masterful Second Inaugural Address, Lincoln centralized God's will and referenced his righteousness as an explanatory element in most of his public orations. Lincoln the master politician was too astute not to anticipate how such providential language would resonate with Americans of the war era, to be certain, but he was also too principled to lean upon such constructions for political convenience alone.

And second, Abraham Lincoln was after all a Republican dedicated to stopping slavery's expansion and convinced of its depravity. If radical abolitionists found him disappointingly hesitant in attacking slavery from the war's outset, it was because of his understanding of border state politics and not because of his insensitivity to the enslaved. Lincoln told Illinois politician Wait Talcott in 1860 that "I know you Talcotts are all strong abolitionists, and while I had to be very careful in what I have said, I want you to understand that your opinions and wishes have produced a much stronger impression on my mind than you may think." And a longtime friend of Lincoln's, Springfield builder John Roll, told of hearing Lincoln respond to a question about whether or not he was an abolitionist by saying, "I am mighty near one."[79] Certainly by the close of the contest's second year, Abraham Lincoln understood the Civil War as a purification by fire from which a new nation, purged of its original sin, might emerge, and he hoped soon to exercise his executive authority toward that end.[80]

For most of his political career, Abraham Lincoln had been a pragmatist certain of the damnable yet undeniable constitutionality of slavery where it existed and thus convinced that the troublesome institution was best confronted through reserved measures, including compensated emancipation and colonization.[81] President Lincoln's ultimate conceptualization of freedom as both a moral imperative and a prerequisite for providential success—that emancipation was what the nation owed a beset humanity and a just yet demanding God—was absorbed in large part from abolitionists, including many female and millennialistic adversaries of bondage.[82] By the late summer of 1862, an attitude once associated with radical antislavery "pariahs" prevailed throughout the Union, and Abraham Lincoln was but one of millions who saw God's hand in emancipation. According to an essayist in the *Liberator*, "many, including Mr. Lincoln" seemingly thought that by achieving the removal of slavery, "we should enter an American millennium of peace and union."[83] Thus, when it finally arrived (or was at least implied) in the form of the preliminary Emancipation Proclamation, the federal power's pledge to end American slavery was hailed by Christians in the Union as a means to affect what most by now believed would be the central millennialist accomplishment of the Civil War.

Accordingly, scores of women abolitionists celebrated the proclamation as something akin to scripture. Mary Livermore and Jane Hoge, organizers of a great sanitary fair in Chicago in 1863, certainly believed that the Emancipation Proclamation was a holy writ. After they asked Owen Lovejoy to intercede for them in procuring a copy from President Lincoln, Lovejoy relayed their sentiments to the president by avowing that "if you do not deposit in the Archives of the Nation, it seems to me that Illinois would be a very suitable resting place for a document that ought to be laid away in some holy place like the ancient Jewish symbols."[84] Antislavery Unitarian Serena Wright believed the document was transcendent and crowed that England or France now dared not come to the sinful South's aid. "Abraham Lincoln with God on his side," she proclaimed, "is mightier than the[m] all."[85] Although she was always "willing to make sacrifices for our beloved country," the preliminary Emancipation Proclamation stirred Christian Rhoda Southworth to even greater heights of devotion. One week after the president's initial pronouncement in September 1862, Southworth explained to her soldier son that because the country was finally "taking steps in the right direction," now more than ever she was "anxious to do what I can to advance the cause of freedom."[86] Upon the proclamation's announcement in September 1862, antislavery Quaker Anne Ferris immediately resounded its providentialist implications in observing, "Today appears the President's Proclamation of Emancipation," and while "its effects no one can perhaps foresee," nevertheless "our party hails it as the dawn of the millennium." "It is surely a measure of justice and right," she continued, "and I cannot but rejoice that we have, as Gasparin says, 'put ourselves right with God.'"[87]

In the months that followed its preliminary issuance, Ferris further came to believe that the Emancipation Proclamation had a liberating effect on whites as well as blacks. After attending a celebratory and multidenominational abolitionist meeting, she pronounced, "Nothing makes me realize more fully the great revolution through which we are living than to attend one of these meetings and listen to the utterances of the clergy on the subject of slavery. A few years ago it would have been martyrdom for anyone of them to have breathed such sentiments, and now they can scarcely go far enough to meet the popular wishes." Remarking on both their long and "criminal silence" on the slavery issue and their newfound boldness and eloquence in denouncing "the great wrong," Ferris suggested that Union clergymen were now "doubtless thankful for their own emancipation as well as the freedom of the slave."[88]

Finally, and arguably even more so than white women abolitionists, African American female antislavery crusaders praised the Emancipation Proclamation and were convinced of its millennialist value. Onetime Underground Railroad conductor, vociferous political activist, and poet Frances Harper, for instance, reminded an assembled crowd in Ohio that via the Emancipation Proclamation President Lincoln had, "in the hour when the nation's life was convulsed," heroically "reached out his hand through the darkness to break the chains on which the rust of centuries had gathered."[89] In her later 1863 poem "The Contraband's Answer," Harper both anticipated the new and glorious day of freedom that the proclamation presaged and glimpsed the related "lovely" kingdom so eagerly awaited by millennialists. "Oh! Never did the world appear / So lovely to mine eye and ear!" she penned in 1863. "Till freedom came with joy and peace, / And bade my hateful bondage cease."[90]

Not all religiously associated female reformers were as optimistic, and some thought the Emancipation Proclamation too limited in its scope. Amy Post, for instance, opined that the decree was "more than I feared but much less than I hoped."[91] Lydia Maria Child was likewise only mildly encouraged, admitting, "I was thankful for it, but it excited no enthusiasm in my mind," and concluding that "the ugly fact cannot be concealed from history that it was done reluctantly and stintedly" by President Lincoln. The president's hand had been forced "by our own perils and necessities," Child stressed, but "no recognition of principles of justice or humanity surrounded the politic act with a halo of moral glory."[92] Lukewarm responses of this sort to the Emancipation Proclamation were apparently far from anomalous. Sanitary Commission organizer Louisa Lee Schuyler, for example, noted such mixed reactions in commending a colleague's more suitable celebration of the measure. "I hear your house was illuminated in honor of the President's Proclamation," she wrote in the days before the proclamation's January 1, 1863, inauguration. "It is delightful to find some public expression of sympathy with what should have been hailed as the new birth of liberty in our land."[93] In both her desire to "refer to the Emancipation Proclamation as a reality and a substance" and her fear that its critics might cause the initiative to "fizzle out at the little end of the horn," Harriet Beecher Stowe made a trip to Washington to "see the heads of departments" and "have a talk with 'Father Abraham' himself." Voicing the concerns of many and identifying the sense of commonality that American female abolitionists shared with their joint heirs in England, Stowe reckoned that "I should be sorry to call the attention of my sisters in Europe to any such impotent conclusion."[94]

Several Christian abolitionist women appreciated the Emancipation Proclamation for its effectual reconception of the war but nevertheless recognized that their work was far from complete. Ardent New England Unitarian Ella Lowell Lyman voiced a commonly heard pragmatism just days after the Proclamation's commencement. Noting that the "New Year opened with the President's Emancipation Proclamation" and that it was received as "a cause of real rejoicing to many," she nevertheless cautiously observed in early January 1863 that "to me, it seems far wiser to wait until something is accomplished before rejoicing."[95] Universalist Unitarian Frances Gage dedicated herself to "inspiring confidence in the Emancipation Proclamation" as dictated by her belief in an all-encompassing and feministic providentialism that anticipated the millennial kingdom's rapidly approaching dawn. "Temperance, Freedom, Justice to the negro, Justice to woman," she avowed, were "but parts of one great whole, one mighty temple whose maker and builder is God."[96] Prophetic language and providential responsibility infused the encouragements of Congregationalist antislavery activist Mary Abigail Dodge. Writing a few weeks after the Emancipation Proclamation's commencement in a piece that would appear in print that spring, Dodge (under the pseudonym Gail Hamilton) reminded her readers that the war was of monumental importance. "It is the question of the world that we have been set to answer," Dodge offered, and in this "great conflict of ages" and "through the Providence of God we are placed in the van-guard."[97]

As encouraging as the Emancipation Proclamation was for female Christian abolitionists then, few if any of them assumed it was the fulfillment of their largely providentialist objectives. Thus the emancipationist women who founded the Women's Loyal National League in May 1863 used millennialist rhetoric at every turn.[98] The organization, established and directed by Susan B. Anthony and Elizabeth Cady Stanton, conducted the largest petition effort the nation had witnessed to that time, ultimately delivering some 400,000 signatures on entreaties to Congress in support of the enactment of a constitutional amendment to end slavery outright.[99] Tellingly, the effective and passionately written missives offered to members of the League for circulation commonly featured providentialist language and played upon the ubiquity of postmillennialist sentiment on the home front. A petition penned by Elizabeth Cady Stanton in January 1864, for instance, predicted that with the eradication of American slavery in its entirety, "our country, free from the one blot that has always marred its fair escutcheon, will be an example to all the world that 'righteousness exalteth a nation.' The God of Justice is with us, and our word, our work—our prayer for freedom—will not, can not be in vain."[100]

As was true of many abolitionists, Stanton often espoused providentialist viewpoints that were manifestly egalitarian in their conceptualization. She anticipated the new utopian age to come as an "amphiarchate" in which men and women of every race would rule together as equals, and as leader of the League she routinely drafted resolutions linking antislavery and gender equity.[101] Nevertheless, Stanton was vehemently critical of Lincoln's seemingly cautious approach to emancipation, was distrustful of established churches and denominations for most of her adult life, and was never particularly religious in a traditional sense. That she, Susan B. Anthony, and others within the Women's Loyal National League peppered their appeals to the American public with postmillennialistic references and providentialist language therefore suggests much about the resonance and grip of such sentiment in the North by 1864. Moreover, that 40,000 of the signatures came from states of the Old Northwest suggests that millennialistic female abolitionism was much more than an eastern singularity but instead was significant throughout the Union.[102]

The presidential election of 1864 forced female emancipationists to take stock in both their providentialist convictions and their support of Abraham Lincoln. Susan B. Anthony, for example, believed Lincoln had proved an unwilling and faltering friend of the enslaved and thus supported John C. Frémont's potential candidacy.[103] Other antislavery women, dissatisfied with the war's progress for much of the first half of 1864 and disappointed with the pace of emancipation in areas of the nation not affected by the Emancipation Proclamation, endorsed Lincoln's candidacy with notable tentativeness. Lillie Chace dedicated herself to focusing on the war's higher moral purpose, and was sure moreover that even if Democrat George McClellan won in November, God's will would still triumph. She was, however, less enthusiastic than she had once been, and she confessed that "it is hard now to tell what is right."[104] Others joined Chace in wondering if their long-held emancipationist vision of the millennium's advancement remained viable, but they trusted nevertheless that divine retribution would still rule the day. "It is my humble opinion," Catherine Peirce wrote in the spring of 1864, "that [God] formed this earth for the good and brave and if this war do[es] not exterminate all cowards and cop[perheads] that he will send another flood or something else in its place."[105]

But most female abolitionists, with Harriet Beecher Stowe chief among them, continued to support the president and remained convinced of both Lincoln's and the war's providential importance. The Civil War was no "mere local convulsion," Stowe posited, for the fate of mankind hung in the balance. Abraham Lincoln, in Stowe's enthusiastic reckoning, was a servant of God whose "clearness of vision" would soon lead the world into the "promised land of freedom which is to be the patrimony of all men, black and white."[106] Taken altogether, the record suggests that Lincoln remained a worthy figure in the opinion of female emancipationists, even though by the fall of 1864 more than a few were disappointed that his Emancipation Proclamation had not been followed by greater progress toward the total eradication of slavery everywhere in the country.[107] Equally evident is that postmillennialist female abolitionists continued to view the developments of their world through the same providentialist lens, if for many their vision of the approaching millennial kingdom was less clear than it had once been.

Critics of Abraham Lincoln in 1864 were correct in one respect. His reckoning of emancipation as the holy writ of a sovereign God had indeed changed since the issuance of the Emancipation Proclamation. It had not wavered, however, but had grown evermore tangible and determinative. For example, Lincoln's prewar political oratory emphasized contingency, and he frequently spoke of the American state as a "trial" or "experiment" that could still fall short.[108] Such rhetorical insecurity about the government's future was admittedly the custom of the day, but in Lincoln's case it was sincere and occasionally delineated, as in his "House Divided" speech to Illinois Republicans in 1858. Yet in his latter days the president spoke with assurance of the conflict and the fruits it promised to bear—a "new birth of freedom," for example, and a "more perfect Union"—as heaven-sent and unimpeachable instruments of human advancement. He therefore continued to work for the rest of the war (truly, for the rest of his life) to marshal support for such measures as the Thirteenth Amendment, sacred efforts in his estimation that championed liberty and pledged the nation to the protection of freedmen and women. By the time of his assassination, Lincoln was convinced that any abandonment of emancipation on his part would both "ruin the Union" and damn him "through time and eternity."[109]

The president's expressed ideas about the nature of divine will underwent a similar progression. Lincoln memorably believed that the desires of God, while unfaltering, were also all but unknowable. He said in 1862 that "the will of God prevails. In great contests each party claims to act in accordance with the will of God. Both may be, and one must be wrong. God cannot be for, and against the same thing at the same time. In the present civil war it is quite possible that God's purpose is somewhat different from the purpose of either party."[110] Nevertheless, by war's end Lincoln espoused the opinion long held by evangelical reformers throughout the Union that to fail *in the attempt to know* and then consent to God's will, to fail to act "with firmness in the right as God gives us to see the right," would devastate the nation.[111] Abolitionist Methodist bishop Gilbert Haven representatively offered in late 1863, God was "pushing us forward to His, not our, millennium." Lincoln may or may not have embraced every aspect of Haven's eschatological point of view, but he certainly agreed with the bishop that while the Almighty "is using and blessing us if we choose to work with him," the nation will be "broken in pieces" should such submission cease.[112] Abraham Lincoln ultimately claimed "not to have controlled events, but confess plainly that events have controlled me." Noting that the successes and failures of the war to date were for "God alone" to own, the president proclaimed in the middle of 1864 that "If God now wills the removal of a great wrong, and wills also that we of the North as well as you of the South, shall pay fairly for our complicity in that wrong, impartial history will find therein new cause to attest and revere the justice and goodness of God."[113] To realize emancipation, the greatest accomplishment in the history of American classical liberalism—a tradition that stressed individual human agency and autonomy—the onetime religious skeptic in the end surrendered himself to the

direction of an overruling and irresistible divine will.[114] Female Christian abolitionists were certainly not the sole agents of this change within the heart of America's
sixteenth president. But, just as assuredly, they were important and (at least to date)
underappreciated contributors to the apparent wartime evolution of what can rightly
be called the providentialism of Abraham Lincoln.

We take these women at their word and thus avoid the presentist temptation to
view their postmillennialist rhetoric as purely representative or symbolic and thus
less than earnest.[115] Female Christian abolitionists varied in how literally they applied
their particular millennialist beliefs in interpreting the events of the age, but in that
variance they were no different than believers of every ilk. Nor were postmillennialist
abolitionists myopic spiritual elitists interested in African American freedom *only*
because they understood slavery's eradication as a component of the Almighty's
providential plan. While they did imagine that slavery's ruination would facilitate a
millennialist future, most were equally motivated by what emancipation would mean
for the nation in the present. Both female activism and providentialist Christianity
were multivariate and comprised of several constituent strains of thought, resulting
in numerous directives and responsibilities for their respective adherents. Thus the
"admission" of sorts that female Christian abolitionists were at least in part seeking
a greater eschatological end does not negate the animating impact of other tenets
of their activist Christianity, such as caring for the well-being of the oppressed and
doing unto others as they would have done unto themselves. Importantly, other
Christian perfectionists loathed slavery as well, but not enough to actively take up
the cause of abolitionism or vociferously champion the emancipationist Union war
effort.[116] And even if advocates of absolute social and political equality were perhaps
rare among (white) providentialist abolitionists, such is not enough to question their
earnest burden for the enslaved.[117]

Finally, because the political impact of abolitionist women can be difficult to discern in the historical record, it is easy to assume that the only "movers and shakers"
within the Christian emancipationist camp were the affiliated politicians and national
church leaders who most resemble influential conservative religious and political
figures today. To the contrary, Bible-privileging and religiously motivated everyday
emancipationists of both sexes deserve further study because they exercised real
and important agency in home front politics and, by extension, federal policy, but
they did so in ways that have largely escaped historians and bear little resemblance
to the highly organized and oppositional politicking of modern-day fundamentalist
evangelical activists.[118] Certainly the elusory yet real historical influence of female
Christian abolitionists upon Abraham Lincoln and American emancipation, an
impact motivated by a dual and equally sincere desire to affect freedom for millions of enslaved Americans and direct the nation down a providential path that
they believed would end in the dawning of the millennial age, merits such ongoing
historiographical attention.

1. "History of Opinions Respecting the Millennium," *American Theological Review* 1 (Nov. 1859): 644–55. For more on postmillennialism as the central theme of antebellum Protestantism, see Ben Wright and Zachary W. Dresser, "Introduction," in Ben Wright and Zachary W. Dresser, eds., *Apocalypse and the Millennium in the American Civil War Era* (Baton Rouge: Louisiana State Univ. Press, 2013), 1–12; Stanley J. Grenz, *The Millennial Maze: Sorting Out Evangelical Options* (Downers Grove, Ill.: InterVarsity Press, 1999), esp. 65–90; see also James H. Moorhead, "The Erosion of Postmillennialism in American Religious Thought, 1865–1925," *Church History* 53 (Mar. 1984): 61–77. As W. Scott Poole chronicles in his chapter in this volume, while millennialist thought was much more limited in its prewar influence upon Southerners, it was present, a precursor of white Southern women's postwar interest in apocalyptic premillennialism. See also Walter Conser, *Southern Crossroads: Perspective on Religion and Culture* (Lexington: Univ. Press of Kentucky, 2008), 221. Dominant antebellum Christian millennial perspectives can essentially be divided into three categories based upon their anticipated order of events. Posttribulational premillennialism = (1) Tribulations, (2) Second Coming of Christ, (3) Millennium, (4) Last Judgment; Postmillennialism = (1) Millennium, (2) Second Coming/Last Judgment; Amillinnealism = (1) Symbolic Millennium, (2) Second Coming/Last Judgment. Note: Although first enunciated in the late 1830s by Plymouth Brethren Reverend John Nelson Darby, pretribulational (or "dispensational") premillennialism did not become popular among Southern Christian theorists until late in the nineteenth century. It was/is sequenced: (1) Second Coming of Christ *for* Church or "Rapture," (2) Tribulations, (3) Return of Christ *with* Church, (4) Millennium, (5) Last Judgment. See Amy Johnson Frykholm, *Rapture Culture: Left Behind in Evangelical America* (New York: Oxford Univ. Press, 2004), 15–16.

2. See Victor B. Howard, *Religion and the Radical Republican Movement, 1860–1870* (Lexington: Univ. Press of Kentucky, 1990), esp. 7–10; James Brewer Stewart, "Reconsidering the Abolitionists in an Age of Fundamentalist Politics," *Journal of the Early Republic* 26 (Spring 2006): 1–23, 5–6.

3. Slavery and freedom for instance feature prominently in Terrie Dopp Aarnodt, *Righteous Armies, Holy Cause: Apocalyptic Imagery and the Civil War* (Macon, Ga.: Mercer Univ. Press, 2001). For a consideration of African American interpretations of abolition, see Matthew Harper, "Emancipation and African American Millennialism," in Wright and Dresser, eds., *Apocalypse and the Millennium,* 154–74; Beth Barton Schweiger, *The Gospel Working Up: Progress and the Pulpit in Nineteenth-Century Virginia* (New York: Oxford Univ. Press, 2000), 87. That Christian abolitionists linked emancipation and the ultimate return of Christ together is further suggested by the masthead of William Lloyd Garrison's paper the *Liberator,* which associated the end of American slavery with the gathering together of all believers at the Christian end of time. See also Janet Gray, *Race and Time: American Women's Poetics from Antislavery to Racial Modernity* (Iowa City: Univ. of Iowa Press, 2004), 77. Providentialism is the belief that God's will is and has always been at work in every event, and that no occurrence is or has ever been independent of divine foresight.

4. Catherine Clinton, *The Other Civil War: American Women in the Nineteenth Century* (New York: Hill & Wang, 1984), 43–44. Eschatology is that part of theology that focuses upon the death, judgment, and final destiny of mankind.

5. Millennialist thought shaped female reform efforts on other fronts as well. For millennialism's role in female temperance efforts, see Patricia Dockman Anderson, "'By Legal or Moral Suasion Let Us Put It Away': Temperance in Baltimore, 1829–1870" (PhD diss., Univ. of Delaware, 2008), 11, 16, 31. For female millennialism and its manifestations in anti-Catholic

literature (including in the novels of Harriet Beecher Stowe), see Claudia Stokes, *The Altar at Home: Sentimental Literature and Nineteenth-Century American Religion* (Philadelphia: Univ. of Pennsylvania Press, 2014), 103–42. Millennialism was also present in campaigns to censor illicit sex and prostitution. See Barbara Meil Hobson, *Uneasy Virtue: The Politics of Prostitution and the American Reform Tradition* (1987; repr., Chicago: Univ. of Chicago Press, 1990), 40–41.

6. Rosemary Radford Ruether, "Eschatology in Christian Feminist Theologies," in Jerry L. Walls, ed., *The Oxford Handbook of Eschatology* (New York: Oxford Univ. Press, 2008), 328–42. See also Rosemary Reuther, *Women and Redemption: A Theological History* (Minneapolis: Fortress Publishing, 1998), 136–44. The terms "millenarian" and "millennialistic" refer to belief in the Christian doctrine of the millennium.

7. The link between millennialistic abolitionism and feminism in America was always strong as well. Sojourner Truth, for example, believed that millennialism, abolitionism, and women's rights were in fact one issue, intertwined and inseparable. See Jeffrey C. Stewart, "Introduction," in Olive Gilbert, *The Narrative of Sojourner Truth: A Bondswoman of Olden Time, with a History of Her Labors and Correspondence Drawn from Her "Book of Life"* (New York: Oxford Univ. Press, 1991), xxiii–xlvii. For more on the feminist and often providential abolitionism of average women, see Julie Roy Jeffrey, *The Great Silent Army of Abolitionism: Ordinary Women in the Abolition Movement* (Chapel Hill: Univ. of North Carolina Press, 1998), 37–52. Among the most forceful statements of the connection between abolitionism (of every ilk) and feminism is Keith E. Melder, *Beginnings of Sisterhood: The American Women's Rights Movement, 1800–1850* (New York: Schocken Books, 1977), 77–159.

8. The broader Civil War itself was viewed by the leaders of Northern evangelicalism as a millennial step. See Howard, *Religion and the Radical Republican Movement,* 37.

9. Comeouters were antebellum Christian activists who dissented from church orthodoxy and thus withdrew from their respective memberships. The term is based on the admonition in II Corinthians 6:17, "Wherefore come out from among them, and be ye separate, saith the Lord, and touch not the unclean thing, and I will receive you." For more on the Comeouters, see John R. McKivigan, "The Antislavery 'Comeouter' Sects: A Neglected Dimension of the Abolitionist Movement," *Civil War History* 26 (June 1980): 142–50.

10. Maria Weston Chapman, "Anti-Slavery Tracts No. 14, How Can I Help to Abolish Slavery? or, Counsels to the Newly Converted" (Office of the American Anti-Slavery Society, No. 138 Nassau Street, New York, N.Y., 1855), 1. Chapman in time grew disenchanted with churches because they had, as she stated in the 1830s, "lost sight of what they were formed for." Nevertheless, she remained an ardent Christian Unitarian in belief. "Maria Weston Chapman," in Mark C. Bodanza, *Resolve and Rescue: The True Story of Frances Drake and the Antislavery Movement* (Bloomington, Ind.: iUniverse LLC, 2014), 40.

11. Chapman, "Anti-Slavery Tracts No. 14," 1.

12. Steven Mintz, *Moralists and Modernizers: America's Pre-Civil War Reformers* (Baltimore: Johns Hopkins Univ. Press, 1995) 36; Robert R. Mathisen, *Critical Issues in American Religious History: A Reader* (Waco, Tex.: Baylor Univ. Press, 2001), 204.

13. See John R. McKivigan, *The War Against Proslavery Religion: Abolitionism and the Northern Churches, 1830–1865* (Ithaca, N.Y.: Cornell Univ. Press, 1984), 161–82.

14. For more on the extent to which each of the traditions most commonly associated with Christian abolitionism invested in the ideas of postmillennialism and the perfectibility of humanity, see, e.g., Randall Balmer, "Casting Aside the Ballast of History and Tradition: White Protestants and the Bible in the Antebellum Period," in Vincent L. Wimbush, ed., *African Americans and the Bible: Sacred Texts and Social Structures* (New York: Continuum International Publishing, 2003), 193–200.

15. W. Michael Ashcraft, "Progressive Millennialism," in Catherine Wessinger, ed., *The Oxford Handbook of Millennialism* (New York: Oxford Univ. Press, 2011), 44–65.

Timothy Wesley

16. David Robinson, *The Unitarians and Universalists* (Westport, Conn.: Greenwood Press, 1985), 54.

17. Ibid.

18. Douglas Gwyn, "Eschatology," in Margery Post Abbott, Mary Ellen Chijioke, Pink Dandelion, and John William Oliver Jr., eds., *The A to Z of the Friends (Quakers)* (Lanham, Md.: Scarecrow Press, 2003), 92–93.

19. Ibid.

20. John Saillant, "Millennialism and Abolitionism," in Peter P. Hinks and John R. McKivigan, eds., *Encyclopedia of Antislavery and Abolition* (Westport, Conn.: Greenwood Press, 2007), 2:473–75. They were not premillennialists, however, essentially in that they did not believe such tribulations would be preceded by Christ's return to Earth.

21. Zachary McLeod Hutchins, *Inventing Eden: Primitivism, Millennialism, and the Making of New England* (New York: Oxford Univ. Press, 2014), 226.

22. George McKenna, *The Puritan Origins of American Patriotism* (New Haven, Conn.: Yale Univ. Press, 2007), 143.

23. James Moorhead, "Apocalypticism in Mainstream Protestantism, 1800 to the Present," in John Joseph Collins, Bernard McGinn, and Stephen J. Stein, eds., *The Enclopedia of Apocalypticism* (New York: Continuum, 1998), 3:83.

24. Eric J. Sundquist, *Empire and Slavery in American Literature, 1820–1865* (1995; repr., Oxford, Miss.: Univ. Press of Mississippi, 2006), 178.

25. Reginald Heber, "The Advent of Christ," in Maria Weston Chapman, *Songs of the Free, and Hymns of Christian Freedom* (Boston: Isaac Knapp, Washington Street, 1836), 10.

26. For instance, when an enslaved man is sold away from his family and to his ultimate death, the white master repeats the phrase "It's done." Stowe thus references the scriptural prediction of the violent judgment of God in Revelation 16:17–19, "And the seventh angel poured out his vial into the air; and there came a great voice out of the temple of heaven, from the throne, saying, It is done." Saillant, "Millennialism and Abolitionism," 474. Stowe infused the book with numerous such scriptural references, and in her closing chapter called upon readers to "read the signs of the times!" Harriet Beecher Stowe, *Uncle Tom's Cabin; or, Life Among the Lowly* (1852; repr., New York: Dover Thrift Editions, 2005), 378.

27. For more, see Nancy Koester, *Harriet Beecher Stowe: A Spiritual Life* (Grand Rapids,: Wm. B. Eerdmans, 2014); and George M. Fredrickson, "The Coming of the Lord: The Northern Protestant Clergy and the Civil War Crisis," in Randall M. Miller, Harry S. Stout, and Charles Reagan Wilson, eds., *Religion and the American Civil War* (New York: Oxford Univ. Press, 1998), 110–30. Fredrickson writes that those who "believed the millennium was so close at hand that Christians should act as if it had already arrived were spurred to radical abolitionism" (115).

28. Harriet Beecher Stowe to Charles Edward Stowe, Sept. 4, 1842, folder 67, Beecher-Stowe Collection, Schlesinger Library, Harvard Univ., Cambridge, Mass., repr. in Joan D. Hedrick, *Harriet Beecher Stowe: A Life* (New York: Oxford Univ. Press, 1994), 149.

29. Stowe's father Lyman Beecher was one of the forces behind the American Female Moral Reform Society movement, which encouraged the formation of women's groups to help eliminate the besetting sins of American society in the campaign to bring about God's Kingdom in America. Steven K. Green, *Inventing a Christian America: The Myth of the Religious Founding* (New York: Oxford Univ. Press, 2015), 213–15.

30. Numerous iterations of Christian Perfectionism were in play in early to mid-nineteenth century American religious life. Douglas Strong has observed that very popular among evangelicals and reformers was the notion of entire sanctification via the "second blessing"—that Christians could move beyond the initial step of "new birth" toward exaltedness via an additional convictional step, and that via the "experiential spirituality and volitional commitment" that the second step facilitated, it then became possible "for each believer—and, by extrapolation, all of

society—to obey the moral law of God completely." Douglas M. Strong, *Perfectionist Politics: Abolitionism and the Religious Tensions of American Democracy* (Syracuse, N.Y.: Syracuse Univ. Press, 1999), 4.

31. Harriet Beecher Stowe, "The Interior Life: Or Primitive Christian Experience," *General Baptist Repository and Missionary Observer*, n.s., 14 (1853): 77.

32. Harriet Beecher Stowe, "Harriet Beecher Stowe," *New York Evangelist*, Sept. 11, 1845, repr. in Hedrick, *Harriet Beecher Stowe*, 157.

33. The impact that Stowe had upon her community of activists cannot be overstated. Stowe, of course, was not the only practitioner of this doctrine that so inspired reformers to help *improve* the world rather than *perfect* the self, but she was among the most influential. "Out of the contradiction between expectation and human reality grew up a radical brand of Christianity that had transformative implications for American culture," Joan Hedrick writes, as "Stowe replaced perfectionists strivings with the imitation of Christ." Hedrick, *Harriet Beecher Stowe*, 156.

34. Ibid., 157.

35. Elizabeth D. Young, "The Role of Religion in the American Civil War" (MA thesis, American Public Univ. System, Charles Town, W. Va., 2008), 20. The belief that the American government would play an indispensable role in the millennial plans of God was so widespread among religious abolitionists that the founders of the Christian antislavery Liberty Party declared that a "democratically reorganized" American government would prove itself the "visible government of God," a precursor of the millennial age "embodied in human forms." Strong, *Perfectionist Politics*, 80; see also McKenna, *Puritan Origins of American Patriotism*, 142–43.

36. Diary of Lucy Larcom, Nov. 1860, in Daniel Dulaney Anderson, *Lucy Larcom: Life, Letters, and Diary* (Boston: Houghton, Mifflin, 1894), 295.

37. Chapman, "Anti-Slavery Tracts No. 14," 5; Maria Weston Chapman to Anne Greene Chapman, June 21, 1862. Weston Family Papers, Boston Public Library. For more on how and why Chapman (who was dedicated to the idea of nonresistance and against war in principle) ultimately embraced the war as a providential necessity, see Catherine Clinton, "Maria Weston Chapman," in G. J. Barker Bernfield and Catherine Clinton, eds., *Portraits of American Women: From Settlement to the Present* (New York: Oxford Univ. Press, 1998), 147–67. See also Susan Anthony to Elizabeth Cady Stanton, Jan. 15, 1861, Stanton Collection, Library of Congress, Washington, D.C., repr. in Wendy Hamand Venet, *Neither Ballots Nor Bullets: Women Abolitionists and the Civil War* (Charlottesville: Univ. Press of Virginia, 1991), 29.

38. Mothering Diary, Chace Family Papers, repr. in Elizabeth C. Stevens, "Elizabeth Buffum Chace and Lillie Chace Wyman: Motherhood as a Subversive Activity in Nineteenth Century Rhode Island," *Quaker History* 84 (Spring 1995): 38.

39. Letter of Lillie Chace, June 17, 1861, Papers of Anna Dickinson, Harvard Univ. Libraries, Harvard Univ., Cambridge, Mass., microfilm, repr. in Nina Silber, *Daughters of the Union: Northern Women Fight the Civil War* (Cambridge: Harvard Univ. Press, 2005), 226.

40. Mary A. Livermore, *My Story of the War: A Woman's Narrative of Four Years Personal Experience* (1888; repr., New York: DaCapo Press, 1985), 91–92.

41. "God's Rule in America a Subject of Thanksgiving," *Peninsular News and Advertiser* (Milford, Del.), Dec. 6, 1861, 1.

42. Judith Giesberg, *An Army at Home: Women and the Civil War on the Northern Home Front* (Chapel Hill: Univ. of North Carolina Press, 2009), 122.

43. Beth A. Salerno, *Sister Societies: Women's Antislavery Organizations in Antebellum America* (DeKalb: Northern Illinois Univ. Press, 2005), 152.

44. Holly Folk, "American Catholic Women, 1820–1900: From the Jacksonian Period to the Progressive Era," in Rosemary Skinner Kelly and Rosemary Radford Ruether, eds., *Encyclopedia of Women and Religion in North America* (Bloomington: Indiana Univ. Press, 2006), 152–53. Nev-

ertheless, and as Folk argues, Catholic women were largely absent from the abolition movement owing to "longstanding tenets within Catholic theology regarding the naturalness of servitude, sharp social differentiation, and the separation of earthly and temporal powers" (152).

45. Hasia R Diner, "Civil War in the United States," in *Jewish Women: A Comprehensive Historical Encyclopedia* (Mar. 1, 2009), Jewish Women's Archive, jwa.org/encyclopedia/article/civil-war-in-united-states. Although numerous Jewish men (particularly politicized rabbis) were abolitionists, Jewish women played essentially no role in organized abolitionism, with the notable exception of outspoken activist and atheist Ernestine L. Rose, the only known female Jewish abolitionist. Jayme A. Sokolow, "Revolution and Reform: The Antebellum Jewish Abolitionists," in Jonathan D. Sarna and Adam Mendelsohn, eds., *Jews and the Civil War* (New York: New York Univ. Press, 2010), 125–44.

46. For more, see Lorien Foote, *The Gentlemen and the Roughs: Violence, Honor, and Manhood in the Union Army* (New York: New York Univ. Press, 2010), esp. 17–40.

47. Scott N. Cole, "Nationalism, United States," in Lisa Tendrich Frank, ed., *Women in the American Civil War* (Santa Barbara: ABC-CLIO, 2008), 1:419.

48. Silber, *Daughters of the Union,* 128–29.

49. Nina Silber, "The Problem of Women's Patriotism," in Michael Perman and Amy Murrell Taylor, eds., *Major Problems in the Civil War and Reconstruction: Documents and Essays,* 3rd ed. (Boston: Wadsworth, 2011), 225.

50. Sarah M. Grimké to William Lloyd Garrison, Nov. 30, 1863, in Henry M. Parkhurst, *Proceedings of the American Anti-Slavery Society at its Third Decade* (New York: American Anti-Slavery Society, 1864), 145.

51. Beth Salerno explains this female abolitionist impact on society, for instance, by positing that by the time of the Civil War many activist women had carried the message of their antislavery societies into other areas of their lives and thus "'abolitionized' their churches and local benevolent organizations, or that their efforts to portray antislavery as a benevolent cause had finally succeeded." Salerno, *Sister Societies,* 149.

52. For a useful overview of the ways in which evangelical ministers in the Union similarly linked slavery and setbacks in the field, see Andrew R. Murphy, *Prodigal Nation: Moral Decline and Divine Punishment from New England to 9/11* (New York: Oxford Univ. Press, 2009), esp. 44–76.

53. Lydia Maria Child to Jessie Fremont, *Liberator,* Oct. 11, 1861.

54. Amy Post to Isaac Post, 16 Aug. 1862, Post Family Papers, Univ. of Rochester Libraries, Univ. of Rochester, Rochester, N.Y., repr. in Venet, *Neither Ballots Nor Bullets,* 36.

55. Lizzie Little to George Avery, Jan. 12, Jan. 16, Feb. 24, 1862, George Smith Avery Papers, Chicago Historical Society, all qtd. in Sean A. Scott, *A Visitation of God: Northern Civilians Interpret the Civil War* (New York: Oxford Univ. Press, 2011), 52, 53.

56. Letter of Maria Patec, Jan. 1, 1861, American Antiquarian Society, Worcester, Mass., repr. in Nina Silber, *Daughters of the Union,* 225.

57. Rhoda Southworth to Eli Southworth, Sept. 9, Sept. 16, 1862, Newton Southworth and Family Papers, Minnesota Historical Society, St. Paul, qtd. in Scott, *A Visitation of God,* 69.

58. David Von Drehle, *Rise to Greatness: Abraham Lincoln and America's Most Perilous Year* (New York: Henry Holt, 2012), 64, 65. For further insight into Lincoln's consciousness of abolitionist criticism, see Eric Foner, *The Fiery Trial: Abraham Lincoln and American Slavery* (New York: W. W. Norton, 2010), esp. 84–91; Jean Baker, "By No Means Excluding Women: Abraham Lincoln and Women's Suffrage," in Karl Weber, ed., *Lincoln: A President for the Ages: Essays from Leading Writers and Scholars That Offer Fresh Insights Into the Complex Legacy of America's Most Fascinating Icon* (New York: Participant Media, 2012), 65–79, 73–76.

59. See, e.g., Barbara A. White, *Visits With Lincoln: Abolitionists Meet the President at the White House* (Plymouth, UK: Lexington Books, 2011).

60. Harriet Tubman to President Abraham Lincoln, Letter, 1862, qtd. in Letter from Lydia Maria Child to John Greenleaf Whittier, Jan. 21, 1862, in Lydia Maria Child, *Letters of Lydia Maria Child with a Biographical Introduction by John G. Whittier and Appendix by Wendell Phillips* (Boston: Houghton Mifflin, 1883), 159–62.

61. Lydia Maria Child, "Letter to the President of the United States," *National Anti-Slavery Standard* (New York), Sept. 6, 1862. In reference to the letter's public notoriety, see, e.g., "General News Summary," *Springfield* (Mass.) *Weekly Republican,* Aug. 30, 1862, 8; "Various Items," *Lowell* (Mass.) *Daily Citizen and News,* Aug. 27, 1862, 2.

62. "Let the Women of the Nation Speak" (Petition to the President of the United States), *Wisconsin Chief* (Milwaukee), Sept. 3, 1862, 3. Millennialism, abolitionism, and women's rights were intertwined in the states of the Old Northwest from relatively early in the antebellum period. See Stacey M. Robertson, *Hearts Beating for Liberty: Women Abolitionists in the Old Northwest* (Chapel Hill: Univ. of North Carolina Press, 2010), 33, 53–54; Stephanie Elise Booth, *Buckeye Women: The History of Ohio's Daughters* (Athens: Ohio Univ. Press, 2001), 103; Sandra L. Myres, *Westering Women and the Frontier Experience, 1800–1915* (Albuquerque: Univ. of New Mexico Press, 1982), 206; Daniel S. Wright links the exaggerated correlation between Female Moral Reform Societies and abolitionism in the western states (particularly in Ohio, and as compared to New England) with the nature and composition of support for the Liberty Party in the region. David S. Wright, *"The First of Causes to Our Sex": The Female Moral Reform Movement in the Antebellum Northeast, 1834–1848* (New York: Routledge, 2006), 89–92, 102; See also Vernon L. Volpe, *Forlorn Hope of Freedom: The Liberty Party in the Old Northwest, 1838–1848* (Kent, Ohio: Kent State Univ. Press, 1990); and Strong, *Perfectionist Politics,* 84. Christian women in the western states were likely to be abolitionist or not based on their family's point of origin. Ronald W. Lackmann, *Women of the Western Frontier in Fact, Fiction, and Film* (Jefferson, N.C.: McFarland, 1997), 122.

63. Paul Boyer, *When Time Shall Be No More: Prophecy Belief in Modern American Culture* (Cambridge, Mass.: Harvard Univ. Press, 2009), 229. Boyer references Stowe's *Uncle Tom's Cabin,* Howe's "Battle Hymn of the Republic," and Lincoln's Second Inaugural Address as a rhetorical triumvirate that, over time, "distilled the conviction that the nation's history had a sacred meaning transcending the mundane world of political maneuvering and battlefield encounters," (229). The link between abolition and the millennium had been made in several popular songs before the Civil War, but Howe's effort introduced the United States and its military might as the agent of providence. The most widely known musical precursor of the "Battle Hymn of the Republic" was a song performed by the abolitionist Hutchinson Family Singers. Titled "The Millennium" and penned by Calem and Joshua Hutchinson in 1847, it asked, "What do I See! Look, behold! / The Glorious day by Prophets told, / Has dawn'd and now is near, / Me-thinks I hear from yonder plan, / With shouts of gladness loud proclaim, / The Millennium is here! / See freedom's star that shines so bright, / It sheds its ray of truth and light, / O'er mountain, rock, and sea, / And like the mighty march of mind, / Had sought and bless'd all human kind, / And set the bondman free." Scott Gac, *Singing for Freedom: The Hutchinson Family Singers and the Nineteenth-Century Culture of Reform* (New York: Oxford Univ. Press, 2017), 251–52.

64. See McKenna, *The Puritan Origins of American Patriotism,* 142.

65. John Stauffer and Benjamin Soskis, *The Battle Hymn of the Republic: A Biography of the Song That Marches On* (New York: Oxford Univ. Press, 2013), 10.

66. Julia Ward Howe, "Battle Hymn of the Republic," *Atlantic Monthly* 9 (Feb. 1852): 10.

67. Ibid., 191.

68. Mary Jo Miles, "Julia Ward Howe (1819–1910)," in Junius P. Rodriguez, ed., *Slavery in the United States: A Social, Political, and Historical Encyclopedia* (Santa Barbara: ABC-CLIO, 2007), 1:341–42.

Timothy Wesley

69. Stauffer and Soskis, *Battle Hymn of the Republic,* 104–5; Ernest Lee Tuveson, *Redeemer Nation: The Idea of America's Millennial Role,* 2 vols., (Chicago: Univ. of Chicago Press, 1968), 2:191, 197–99. See also Christine McWhirter, *Battle Hymns: The Power and Popularity of Music in the Civil War* (Chapel Hill: Univ. of North Carolina Press, 2012), who holds that the ballad did not become truly popular until the last months of the war. However, more representative within the literature is the assertion that the ballad's impact, shortly after its initial publication, was transformative. For one such interpretation, see Randal W. Allred, "'The Battle Hymn of the Republic' (Song)," in M. Paul Holsinger, ed., *War and American Popular Culture: A Historical Encyclopedia* (Westport, Conn.: Greenwood Press, 1999), 83–84.

70. According to historian Elizabeth Young, by late August 1862 a majority of home front Christians had concluded that "God was punishing his people for their sin. Searching their lives for an evil that would so anger the Almighty, one sin stood above the rest: slavery. The North had only two choices. They could repent and destroy Southern slavery, or they could continue to suffer God's wrath." Elizabeth Young, in "Role of Religion in the American Civil War," 20.

71. "An Old Democrat Speaks," *Lowell Daily Citizen and News,* Aug. 12, 1862, 2.

72. "The Abolition of Slavery," *Barre* (Mass.) *Gazette,* Aug. 29, 1862, 2.

73. "Our Great Natural Ally," *New York Daily Tribune,* Aug. 7, 1862, p. 4.

74. Although Abraham Lincoln's appreciation of Harriet Beecher Stowe's national importance is unquestionable, he likely never offered Stowe the oft-repeated greeting about being the "little lady who started the big war." See Daniel R. Vollaro, "Lincoln, Stowe, and the 'Little Woman/Great War' Story: The Making, and Breaking, of a Great American Anecdote, *Journal of the Abraham Lincoln Association* 30 (Winter 2009): 18–34; For Lincoln's appreciation of Howe, see V. Neil Wyrick, *The Spiritual Abraham Lincoln: New Insights Into America's Favorite President* (Carlsbad, Calif.: Magnus Press, 2004), 72. See also Joe Wheeler, *Abraham Lincoln, a Man of Faith and Courage: Stories of Our Most Admired President* (New York: Simon & Schuster, 2008), 204; and Ace Collins, *Stories Behind the Hymns That Inspire America: Songs That Unite Our Nation* (Grand Rapids: Zondervan, 2003), 42.

75. See Lucas E. Morel, *Lincoln's Sacred Effort: Defining Religion's Role in American Self-Government* (Lanham, Md.: Lexington Books, 2000), 10, 103; See also Foner, *Fiery Trial,* 85.

76. Wendell Phillips, "The Cabinet: Speech at Abington, in the Grove, Aug. 1, 1862," in Wendell Phillips, *Speeches, Lectures, and Letters* (Boston: James Redpath, 1863), 450, and qtd. in Allen C. Guelzo, *Abraham Lincoln as a Man of Ideas* (Carbondale: Southern Illinois Univ. Press, 2009), 91.

77. Letter from Sarah Hildreth Butler to Benjamin Franklin Butler, Sept. 29, 1862, in Benjamin Franklin Butler with Jessie Ames Marshall, *Private and Official Correspondence of Gen. Benjamin F. Butler During the Period of the Civil War* (Springfield, Mass.: Plimpton Press, 1917), 2:629.

78. Thomas G. Mitchell, *Antislavery Politics in Antebellum and Civil War America* (Westport, Conn.: Praeger, 2007), 205.

79. Don Fehrenbacher and Virginia Fehrenbacher, eds., *Recollected Words of Abraham Lincoln* (Stanford, Calif.: Stanford Univ. Press, 1996), 442, 383.

80. William C. Kashatus, *Abraham Lincoln, the Quakers, and the Civil War: A Trial of Principle and Faith* (Santa Barbara: ABC-CLIO, 2014), 74; Philip Lamy, *Millennium Rage: Survivalists, White Supremacists, and the Doomsday Prophecy* (Berlin, Germany: Springer Press, 1996), 59.

81. Kenneth J. Winkle, *Lincoln's Citadel: The Civil War in Washington, D.C.* (New York: W. W. Norton, 2014), 250. See also Abraham Lincoln, "Lincoln-Douglas Debate at Galesburg" (Oct. 7, 1858), in Roy P. Basler, ed., *The Collected Works of Abraham Lincoln* (New Brunswick, N.J.: Rutgers Univ. Press, 1953), 3:208–43; and Darryl Pinckney, "The Invisibility of Black

Abolitionists," in Andrew Delbanco, ed., *The Abolitionist Imagination* (Cambridge, Mass.: Harvard Univ. Press, 2012), 109–34.

82. Philip Lamy, *Millennium Rage,* 58–66. Lamy posits that the "millennial myth" took on "secular elements in adaptation to the [then] current age" and thus became a significant component of the civil religion of the war era. He further motes Lincoln's increasingly prevalent usage of apocalyptic and end-time language (as in the Second Inaugural Address) "just as the evangelical abolitionists did." (59)

83. "Abolitionism," *Liberator,* Jan. 2, 1863, 1.

84. Owen Lovejoy to Abraham Lincoln, Oct. 21, 1863, qtd. in Jane Ann Moore and William F. Moore, *Collaborators for Emancipation: Abraham Lincoln and Owen Lovejoy* (Urbana: Univ. of Illinois Press, 2014), 150; see also Harold Holzer, *Emancipating Lincoln: The Proclamation in Text, Context, and Memory* (Cambridge, Mass.: Harvard Univ. Press, 2012), 107–8.

85. Serena Wright to George Wright, Jan. 4, 1863, George Burdick Wright and Family Papers, Minnesota Historical Society, St. Paul, qtd. in Scott, *A Visitation of God,* 108.

86. Letter of Rhoda Southworth, Sept. 28, 1862, Newton Southworth and Family Papers, Minnesota Historical Society, St. Paul, qtd. in Silber, *Daughters of the Union,* 228.

87. Diary of Ann M. Ferris, Sept. 23, 1862, in Harold B. Hancock, ed., *The Civil War Diaries of Anne M. Ferris* (Wilmington: Historical Society of Delaware, 1961), 44. Gasparin was a French statesman, author, ardent Protestant, and abolitionist. Living in Geneva from 1848 until his death in 1871, he was widely published in the United States and elsewhere.

88. Diary of Ann M. Ferris, Dec. 30, 1862, in ibid., 247.

89. Letter of Frances Ellen Watkins Harper, qtd. in William Still, *From the Underground Rail Road: A Record of Facts, Authentic Narratives, Letters, & c: Narrating the Hardships, Hairbreadth Escapes and Death Struggles of the Slaves in their Efforts for Freedom* (Philadelphia: Porter and Coates, 1872), 766.

90. Frances Harper, "The Contraband's Answer," *Anglo-African* (New York), Dec. 19, 1863, 1.

91. Amy Post to Isaac Post, Jan. 13, 1863, Post Family Papers, Rochester Univ. of Rochester Libraries, Univ. of Rochester, Rochester N.Y., repr. in Venet, *Neither Ballots Nor Bullets,* 184.

92. Lydia Maria Child to Sarah Blake Sturgis Shaw, Oct. 30, 1862, in Lydia Maria Francis Child, *Lydia Maria Child: Selected Letters, 1817–1880* (Amherst: Univ. of Massachusetts Press, 1983), 419.

93. Louisa Lee Schuyler to Various Correspondents, Schuyler Letter Copy Book, Dec. 1862, United States Sanitary Commission Papers, New York Public Library, New York, repr. in Judith Ann Giesberg, *Civil War Sisterhood: The U.S. Sanitary Commission and Women's Politics in Transition* (Boston: Northeastern Univ. Press, 2000), 66.

94. Letter from Harriet Beecher Stowe to Annie Adams Fields, Nov. 1862, in Annie Fields, ed., *Life and Letters of Harriet Beecher Stowe* (Boston: Houghton, Mifflin, 1897), 406.

95. Ella Lyman to Elizabeth R. Lowell, Jan. 5, 1863, in Ella Lyman Cabot, ed., *Arthur Theodore Lyman and Ella Lyman: Letters and Journals* (Menasha, Wis.: George Banta, 1932), 2:148–49.

96. Frances D. Gage, qtd. in L. P. Brockett and Mary C. Vaughn, *Woman's Work in the Civil War: A Record of Heroism, Patriotism and Patience* (Philadelphia: Zeigler, McCurdy, 1867), 689, 690.

97. Ibid., 348–49.

98. See Venet, *Neither Ballots Nor Bullets,* 102–8.

99. Sue Davis, *The Political Thought of Elizabeth Cady Stanton: Women's Rights and the American Political Traditions* (New York: New York Univ. Press, 2008), 122.

100. Elizabeth Cady Stanton, "The Women's Loyal National League, to the Women of the Republic," in Elizabeth Cady Stanton, Susan Brownell Anthony, Matilda Joslyn Gage, and Ida Husted Harper, eds., *History of Woman Suffrage,* vol. 2, *1861–1876* (Rochester, N.Y.: Susan B. Anthony, 1881), 895–96.

101. Elizabeth Cady Stanton, *The Women's Bible* (, 1895; repr., New York: Arno Press, 1974), 25; Robert J. Dinkin, *Before Equal Suffrage: Women in Partisan Politics from Colonial Times to 1920* (Westport, Conn.: Greenwood Press, 1995), 56–57.

102. Venet, *Neither Ballots Nor Bullets,* 122.

103. Frederick J. Blue, *No Taint of Compromise: Crusaders in Antislavery Politics* (Baton Rouge: Louisiana State Univ. Press, 2005), 261–63.

104. Letter of Lillie Chace, Aug. 21, 1864, reel 8, Anna E. Dickinson Papers, Library of Congress, Washington, D.C., qtd. in Silber, *Daughters of the Union,* 149.

105. Letter of Catherine Pierce, in Richard L. Kiper, ed., *Dear Catharine, Dear Taylor: The Civil War Letters of a Union Soldier and His Wife* (Lawrence: Univ. Press of Kansas, 2002), 285–86; Silber, *Daughters of the Union,* 149.

106. Harriet Beecher Stowe, "Abraham Lincoln: From the *Watchman and Reflector,*" *Littell's Living Age,* Feb. 6, 1864, in Venet, *Neither Ballots Nor Bullets,* 139.

107. Venet, after chronicling the various dissenting positions staked out by Anna Dickinson, Elizabeth Cady Stanton, and others, concludes that most female abolitionists ended up supporting President Lincoln's reelection campaign in 1864, in large part because his platform called for a constitutional amendment to end slavery. Venet, *Neither Ballots Nor Bullets,* 123–50.

108. Peter J. Parish, *The North and the Nation in the Era of the Civil War* (New York: Fordham Univ. Press, 2003), 13–14.

109. From the draft of a letter to a Wisconsin War Democrat penned in August 1864 and repr. in part in the *New York Tribune,* Sept. 10, 1864, and qtd. in James M. McPherson, *The Battle Cry of Freedom: The Civil War Era* (New York: Oxford Univ. Press, 1988), 769.

110. Abraham Lincoln, "Meditation on the Divine Will, September 30, 1862," qtd. in Joshua Wolf Shenk, *Lincoln's Melancholy* (New York: Houghton Mifflin, 2005), 198.

111. Abraham Lincoln, "Second Inaugural Address, Saturday, March 4, 1865," in John Grafton and James Daley, eds., *28 Great Inaugural Addresses: From Washington to Reagan* (Mineola, N.Y.: Dover, 2006), 53–54.

112. Gilbert Haven, "The War and the Millennium," *National Sermons* (Boston: Lee & Shepard, 1869), 384.

113. Abraham Lincoln, "To Albert G. Hodges," in Basler, ed., *Collected Works of Abraham Lincoln,* 7:281–82.

114. Allen C. Guelzo, *Abraham Lincoln: Redeemer President* (Grand Rapids, Mich.: Wm. B. Eerdmans Publishing Co., 1999), 447. On Lincoln's early skepticism, see Ferenc Morton Szasz and Margaret Connell Szasz, *Lincoln and Religion* (Carbondale: Southern Illinois Univ. Press, 2014), especially 66–72. Historian Paul Harvey has pointed out that Frederick Douglass "drew (as did most antislavery activists) from the classical liberal tradition, and the contribution of classical liberalism to the antislavery movement stands as its proudest moment." Paul Harvey, "Inventing a Tradition: Race, Liberty, and Classical Liberalism," in *Christianity Today,* Nov. 2009, "Books and Culture: A Christian Review" section., http://www.booksandculture.com/articles/webexclusives/2009/November/inventingatradition.html.

115. For more, see Mark David Hall, "Beyond Self-Interest: The Political Theory and Practice of Evangelical Women in Antebellum America," *Journal of Church and State* 44 (Summer 2002): 477–99.

116. Thomas F. Curran, "Pacifists, Peace Democrats, and the Politics of Perfection in the Civil War Era," *Journal of Church and State* 38 (Summer 1996): 487–505.

117. See Saillant, "Millennialism and Abolitionism," 475.

118. See Stewart, "Reconsidering the Abolitionists," 5.

PART

7

Reconstruction

"In Times of Change and Trouble Like These"

Commonalities among Southern Women during Reconstruction

Elizabeth Parish Smith

A missing breast pin and a ladies' railroad car begin to tell the complex and contentious story of Southern women's experiences of Reconstruction. A black woman named Caroline Johnson stood accused of stealing the pin from her employer, a white woman who had hired her as a nurse, and faced up to two years' imprisonment at Louisiana's state penitentiary if convicted. But justice in this New Orleans courtroom in 1870 looked different from justice in either earlier or later eras of Southern history. As in other courtrooms across the South, black and white men sat side by side among the jury, and black witnesses could testify in Johnson's defense, as her friend Mary Burke did. Burke had a job sweeping railroad cars, a relatively better position than Johnson's in a private home, so she was glad to lend an ear—and a broom—when Johnson came to the railroad and told her friend that she had "left her place." As they swept the cars together, Johnson suddenly exclaimed, according to Burke, "Mary! look what I found, then she showed me a Breast Pin . . . [and] told me that she found it in the Ladies Car." Johnson then apparently handed the pin to her friend. Whatever its provenance, the pin, Burke claimed, had since gone missing after she "droped it in the Gutter and could not find it." Lacking evidence, the court dismissed the charge against Johnson within a month.[1] However unique this case was in its particular circumstances, the friendship between Caroline Johnson and Mary Burke, their shared work and sympathies and their treatment by the law, and the frustrations of Johnson's white female employer—all reveal important dimensions of women's experiences of Reconstruction in the postwar South.

In 1935 W. E. B. Du Bois identified Reconstruction as "the greatest critical period of American history," a fulcrum on which hinged understandings of American citizenship, law, and labor that reverberate through the present day.[2] As with other aspects of the Civil War era, historians long neglected the experiences of women and the role of gender in their examinations of Reconstruction, omissions that recent generations of scholars have made remarkable efforts to correct. Their fields of vision are as vast and varied as the women of the postwar South: planter-class women recalibrating their households and social status without the brace of slavery, freed-women claiming a womanhood attendant to their own needs and aspirations, and poor and middling white women navigating the transition to a New South economy. Historians have also examined black and white women's contributions to their churches as well as their political activism alongside men in community mobilizations and in separate, sometimes auxiliary, organizations. These stories and more begin to explore how women experienced Reconstruction, how gender shaped Reconstruction in turn, and how "critical" or transformative the period ultimately proved to be.[3]

The judge before whom Johnson and Burke appeared had spoken three years earlier of living "in times of change and trouble like these," and indeed Southerners across the racial spectrum shared that characterization during Reconstruction, albeit with vastly different meanings.[4] Reconstruction was fundamentally the effort to "reconstruct" Southern society after the Civil War and emancipation, but just what form the South should take was fiercely debated by politicians and often violently contested by ordinary Southerners in their homes, neighborhoods, churches, fields, and polling places. Reconstruction had to address many pressing questions at once: What would be the status of former Confederate states in the Union, and what over-sight could the federal government now claim over them? How would the law regard former Confederates and, perhaps more tellingly, the four million formerly enslaved people who secured freedom with Union victory and the Thirteenth Amendment? What social, economic, political, and legal systems would replace slavery? So complex were these questions and the various answers that emerged to them that historians struggle even to assign definitive dates to the Reconstruction period. Many begin it during the war itself rather than after Appomattox in April 1865, and some continue it past the standing down of the last federal troops in the South in April 1877 and through the slow, painful construction of a Jim Crow South in the 1880s and 1890s.[5]

Whatever its bookends, the major legal milestones of Reconstruction attest to its peak in the late 1860s and early 1870s. Many white Southerners wished the postwar South to resemble the antebellum South as closely as emancipation would allow, and as a result the oppressive Black Codes enacted by Southern states in 1865 and 1866 significantly replicated earlier slave codes. In these years President Andrew Johnson, who assumed the helm of Reconstruction following Lincoln's assassination, steered a surprisingly lenient course that allowed former Confederates to return to power across the South and bring with them laws and practices meant to protect whites' economic and political supremacy. Such open disregard for African Americans' most basic rights—and the overt violence whites employed to ensure their oppression—provoked a sweeping shift away from this so-called Presidential Reconstruction policy. By 1866 a Republican-run Congress had wrested control of policymaking away from Johnson and embarked on a more comprehensive Reconstruction program that was brought to fruition by the work of black Southerners and their white Republican allies on the ground in the South. Under this so-called Radical (or Congressional) Reconstruction, the Civil Rights Act of 1866 and the

Reconstruction Acts of 1867 and 1868 affirmed the citizenship and civil rights of African Americans and forced Southern state governments to do likewise, while the Fourteenth and Fifteenth Amendments in 1868 and 1870 established and protected basic civil and political rights across race, including black male suffrage, at the highest level of American law. These accomplishments, all revolutions in American law, remain among the great legacies of the Reconstruction period.[6]

These laws or other Republican initiatives did not stifle Southern white opposition to blacks' economic aspirations, civil rights, and political participation. Indeed, Southern whites used any means possible, even violence and murder, to reassert white rule over black lives and to gain control over local and state governments. To cite one example, among many, of whites' practices: a foreign observer, sympathetic to the freed people, described postwar New Orleans in a manner familiar across the South. "Terror continued to weigh on the city," he wrote. "Isolated killings or at least attempted killings, in lonely streets, were reported every day. It was clear that the weak Federal garrison could not withstand a concerted attack by the Confederate elements. . . . At this time in Louisiana, the conqueror was at the mercy of the conquered."[7] Through the 1860s and 1870s planters aimed to secure cheap, compliant labor however they could, and Democrats rallied around the banner of white racial unity, trying to fracture Southern Republican coalitions and suppress black voting. With few formal protections at their disposal, freed people and their allies endured campaigns of violence and terror intended to disrupt their efforts "to build new lives on the ground of freedom," in historian Thavolia Glymph's powerful phrase.[8]

Amid such consequential and deadly events, the missing breast pin and ladies' railroad car can be overlooked as objects that precipitated a few days' drama in the lives of three New Orleans women. Like the pin, the case itself dropped away, simply dismissed by the court without either an acquittal or a conviction. The network it reveals, though, among these three women—a white housewife and employer and two black friends and workers—speaks to the many overlaps and contradictions in the ways women in the South experienced the Reconstruction period.

First, there was simply an intimacy among women that a wider historical lens cannot easily detect. They moved into each others' spaces with some degree of familiarity, if not necessarily ease: Caroline Johnson into her employer's home and then into Mary Burke's place of work, and the employer first to Johnson's house and then Burke's residence after she believed her pin stolen. Lines of private and public blurred in the women's everyday lives and movements. Bringing their disputes and alliances into the very public space of the courtroom arguably dissolved these distinctions entirely.[9]

Second, the lack of a conviction exemplifies the far reach of Reconstruction's legal transformations into people's daily lives. All the women called upon the law to act in ways much expanded from its antebellum functions, albeit for conflicting ends. The employer looked to the law as an ally—or at least a last resort—in regulating free labor in her household, while Johnson and Burke demanded the right to speak against a white woman's accusations. Just as the different stories of the pin's disappearance could not be reconciled, neither could these two claims to justice. While many white employers did get satisfaction in Reconstruction-era criminal courts, Johnson and other women of color also found the South's legal system more responsive to them than at any other point in the nineteenth century (and for much of the twentieth century, too). Mary Burke, testifying in her friend's defense, was likely the difference between the two outcomes in this case.

At the heart of studies of Reconstruction is the question of how radical the period ultimately was—how much it diverged from previous practices in American life and law and how much it transformed these practices in the years to follow. Placing women at the center of our analysis helps us to address this crucial question. For all the continuities across the nineteenth century and into the twentieth, Reconstruction brought a substantial transformation in Southerners' lives. Commonalities in women's lives stretched across racial lines as the region underwent economic devastation and legal revolution in the years following the Confederacy's defeat. This essay will focus on three important themes in Southern women's lives during Reconstruction—labor, law, and violence—that highlight the many experiences women shared in common across lines of race, an extraordinary testament to just how radical Reconstruction was in many respects. At the same time, ever-present intimidation and violence showed how race continued to differentiate the experiences of black and white women in the South, especially as Reconstruction faltered in the 1870s. In the end, the "times of change and trouble like these" only extended so far, to some Southern women's relief and to others' sorrow.

Women labored in a myriad of ways in the antebellum South as determined by their race and social position, but the forms, frequency, and political importance of their work all expanded during the postwar period. Most often, simple economic necessity caused these changes for women across the social spectrum. Poverty gripped the region after the war, and survival itself was sometimes at stake for women.

In cities crowded with refugees and desperate people looking for work, conditions were especially trying. Memphis, Tennessee, was a case in point. In November 1865, a Memphis newspaper marked the death of an unknown black woman who had been living on the street. "Before death the woman had crawled from her blankets," the paper surmised, "and she was found naked and dead."[10] Days later it tried to alert city authorities to a white woman in similar danger: "that poor demented woman, in her dejected, ragged, and almost naked state, wander[ed] about the principal streets of the city."[11] Not all women were in such desperate straits, but the collapse of the Southern economy forced all but the most fortunate of women to consider their financial, if not physical, survival.

The first task after the war for many families, black or white, was reuniting their households—a difficult, sometimes futile effort after losses and disruptions in war and decades of separation under slavery. Nevertheless, the household remained critical to Southerners, not just for its emotional bonds but as a social and economic unit in which men's and women's work, while often differentiated, were both essential. According to the Southern ethos, family ties and pooled resources would protect

Elizabeth Parish Smith

against such tragic fates as befell the two women in Memphis, described above, while also allowing men and women to claim political and social rights and duties premised on the independence of their individual household units. Households thus functioned, in LeeAnn Whites's words, as "the core organizational structure of race, gender, and class relations" in the nineteenth-century South and, if anything, became even more economically and socially important during and because of war, emancipation, and Reconstruction.[12]

For black families, to construct a household was to claim the companionship, self-sufficiency, and privacy that had been impossible under slavery; it was, in short, to affirm dignity as a family and as a race. The absence of such a unit was damning. As one South Carolina woman recalled of life after emancipation, "De birds had nests in de air, de foxes had hoes in de ground, and de fishes had beds under de great falls, but us colored folks was left without any place to lay our heads."[13] Whether taking possession of former slave cabins or migrating to Southern cities or other sites of community, freed people built their families and homes with creativity, daring, and determination. For men, their ability to claim positions as independent heads of household confirmed their manhood and, they argued, the political and voting rights such positions traditionally conferred. At times, as Faye Dudden observes, the primacy this gave men in their individual households rankled their wives and partners as well as women's rights activists in the North.[14] Nevertheless, household formation was an intentionally political act for freedmen and their families.

Despite limitations, women played central roles in this struggle as they reallocated as much of their labor as possible to sustain themselves and their families. Susan O'Donovan samples some of the work black women performed for their households, allowing us to glimpse how necessary—and exhaustive—their responsibilities were. Women busied themselves "milking cows, churning butter, tending chickens, hauling firewood to feed kitchen stoves, and then stirring the pot that simmered on top. They bent their backs over washtubs, burned their fingers on hot irons, carded wool, spun thread, wove fabric, and sewed."[15] Whether paid or unpaid, such labors helped to sustain black households amid economic hard times that lingered through the 1870s. In all this, black families sought to minimize women and children doing field work for white employers whenever possible by contracting as whole household units rather than as individual laborers. If they had to find work in the fields, blacks protected their family's unity and social ordering, even women's bodies, by attempting to limit white men's direct control over them. Doing so was a demonstration of their claim to rights and respect, however much refused by angry whites wanting to command every aspect of blacks' lives.

Blacks' commitment to create and control their own households deprived white households and farms of black women's labor, and getting black families back to the fields was a near-obsession for whites in the South throughout the Reconstruction era. Rather than recognizing the material and reproductive needs shared by all families, whites instead bemoaned black women's insolence. One Georgia planter complained to local federal officials in 1866 that few married freedwomen, especially those with children, were signing labor contracts. "Their husbands are at work," he wrote, "while they are nearly idle as it is possible for them to be, pretending to spin—knit or something that really amounts to nothing." Consequently, the husbands, he continued, could not support their families by themselves "without stealing," thus simultaneously refuting black men's abilities to be independent breadwinners and women's to be family caretakers. The planter then added, "Besides [women's] labor is a very important percent of the entire labor of the South."[16] At stake in black women's attempts to minimize field work were thus their constructions of womanhood, their husbands' claims to manhood and its attendant political rights, and much of the production of Southern agriculture.

Whatever idleness whites feared, most black households could not afford a complete withdrawal of women from the paid workforce, and single women or female heads of household certainly depended on earning a wage. When possible, women preferred work that could be combined with familial responsibilities. Washing is perhaps the best example; though their work was grueling and poorly paid, washerwomen could pick up the clothes and linens from customers and wash, dry, and iron them in their own homes and yards. Taking work as a seamstress or cook or for a business rather than a white family (as did Mary Burke at the railroad) also might provide relatively better pay or more independence from constant white supervision.[17]

Like Caroline Johnson, many black women had little choice but to enter domestic service in white households. An 1866 newspaper advertisement suggests the dilemma many women faced. It read, "Wanted—A situation by a woman having a baby 7 months old, as washer and ironer, in a family, or to do general house work in a small family, is willing to go for small wages." The next year, a similar ad read, "Wanted—By a respectable widow woman, a situation as a Cook or Washer and Ironer, also for her daughter a situation as Nurse in the same house." In 1875 an ad was taken by "a respectable girl want[ing] a situation, in a good family, as child's nurse, or is willing to do chamber work and sewing. Not so much wages as a good home."[18] All three advertisements suggest situations in which black women needed to find work, stated certain preferences, and yet knew they might have to make sacrifices to survive.

Freedwomen tried to negotiate better wages, hours, and working conditions from their employers, who were themselves as dependent on this domestic labor as their employees were on its scant compensation. Many of the cases of alleged thefts by servants such as that against Johnson may have involved these taut negotiations gone awry or otherwise (willfully) misinterpreted by employers. In 1868, for example, a Louisiana employer accused Adeline Johnson of stealing ninety dollars' worth of her dresses, a very valuable collection. The employer testified that the dresses disappeared when Johnson "came to [my] house on that day to get a Certificate of Good conduct" and depart the position. Court records did not include Johnson's version of the interaction.[19] Yet just as this employer could charge her former servant, black women, now able to testify against whites, occasionally brought suit against employers for various wrongs. In 1866, in the same New Orleans court, a woman named Elizabeth Conrad charged her white female employer with assault. As Conrad testified, "The accused called witness [Conrad] into her room to bring brandy for her. Witness refused saying that accused had [too] much Brandy. Accused threw a tumbler into witness . . . and struck witness on the forehead. Witness Bled freely."[20]

Elizabeth Conrad succeeded in her case, likely aided by a white witness's corroboration, but her employer's sentencing is instructive. Conrad's employer received a fine of only one dollar, a small penalty from the court. Adeline Johnson, by contrast, received a sentence of two years at the State Penitentiary for her theft of the dresses. The defendants' race and social position clearly distinguished the two cases.[21] White employers still held the clear upper hand, even as black women had more opportunities and resources than under slavery. Historians grapple with both sides of black women's experience of paid labor in the postwar period. On one hand, their options for employment remained sorely limited, and they were vulnerable to many kinds of abuse and exploitation. On the other hand, by negotiating with employers, leaving bad positions, and even calling upon legal protections, black women exercised rights unthinkable before Reconstruction and fought to secure and expand these rights in the future. As Thavolia Glymph notes about changes in domestic service during Reconstruction, "The costumes and the sets may have been old, but the dialogue and the actions were new."[22]

White women also struggled to adapt to changes in work and workers in their postwar households. During and after the Civil War, one immediate lesson for white women, especially those of the planter class, was their hatred for housework. For former plantation mistresses especially, the drudgery of housework was new and disparagingly associated with black women. These changes did not wait for national policy but began as soon as black women left white households during wartime emancipation. An Arkansas girl named Mary Adelia Byers quickly found that "housework is my abomination" after her family's slaves, a couple named Leanna and Purnell, departed in 1864. Tellingly, Byers commented on Leanna's absence much more frequently in her diary than Purnell's. It was the loss of Leanna's domestic work—cooking, cleaning, washing, and ironing—that most affected the teenage girl and her mother and sisters. "I hate washing worse than anything else," she complained, and she was not alone among white women of all ages.[23] Even when white women were able to hire workers back into their households, they viewed the labor as uneven and undependable and so still carried an enlarged share of housework, even if largely in supervision of others' work.[24]

Women clearly understood this expanded domestic work as tied to larger political forces in the Reconstruction-era South. An unnamed white woman wrote a letter in late 1865, reprinted in a Tennessee paper, about "the poverty of the people of South Carolina." "When I know that the most refined and intelligent women in the State, deserted by their deluded servants, are doing all sorts of housework—sweeping, dusting, making beds, and even in some cases, cooking and washing—it is much easier for me to iron the towels my little son has washed," the woman wrote. While she joked that "we make merry over it, compare notes with our friends and boast of our success in these untried fields," she closed her letter on a bleaker note, observing that "so wide spread is the ruin that even if the new system works well, it will take at least half a century to put us where we were."[25]

The closing of the South Carolina woman's letter suggests just how much white women knew the postwar South had changed, not just in their individual households but as a total society. The same letter remarked that "Innumerable widows, orphans and single women . . . are seeking employment of some kind for bread," and this paid employment for white women, along with increased domestic work, confirmed a new economic and social reality for women in the South, especially for those without the resources men were expected to provide their families.[26] It was not that white women had not engaged in waged work in the antebellum South; it was that paid employment now extended beyond women of the poor and middling classes and to the planter elites for the first time.

White women found employment in a wider range of jobs than did women of color, including clerical positions and jobs in burgeoning Southern industries. The most important field for white women was education. The postwar period represented their first entry into teaching in large numbers, at least in Southern schools. Anya Jabour observes that young women in particular looked to education "as the key to financial independence."[27] This was Arkansan Mary Byers's experience. At the same time that she began housework, she faced another challenge when "Tomorrow I commence school teaching. I do not expect to like it very much, yet I need money badly."[28] With more or less enthusiasm, many other white women took teaching positions across the South. Importantly, such employment received widespread social sanction, not as a postwar aberration but as a new, beneficial option for women. One newspaperman even paid them his highest compliment in observing one teacher "whose fair face and golden hair fascinated us this morning. . . . It is no wonder," he decided, "that the little public school children love their teachers so devotedly."[29]

On the surface, this discussion of women's labor in the postwar South tells a story of difference. White women regularly mistreated and exploited the women of color they hired to work in their homes, and discrimination closed many other types of jobs to black women. Certainly freedwomen found white women to be no more understanding or sympathetic to them given their shared gender. Nevertheless, women's labor within individual households became more politically important during the period, as men and women had to sort out new roles and responsibilities in partnership, strife, and absence.[30] At the same time, more women entered the paid workforce in the Reconstruction-era South either by working outside their families or finally receiving some compensation for doing so. Women's work became enfolded in the politics of the period as freedwomen connected their fight for dignity as workers with their race's struggle for rights, and white women adjusted, however fitfully, to the new Southern social and economic order. These were certainly not the same politics, but they confirmed women's engagement in larger political matters.

If experiences of work forged some commonalities among women, Reconstruction-era reforms in Southern law created even greater leveling. In fact, at the formal level of the law distinctions among women fell away entirely at the peak of Radical

Reconstruction. Changes began during the war and its initial aftermath as freed people gained confidence in the transformative power of the law through emancipation, legalized marriage, and the freedmen's courts that operated across the region by the Bureau of Refugees, Freedmen, and Abandoned Lands (or, more simply, the Freedmen's Bureau). Against widespread white opposition to such an "iniquitous measure," Congress passed its first Civil Rights Act in 1866, granting "that all persons born in the United States and not subject to any foreign power, excluding Indians not taxed, are hereby declared to be citizens of the United States" and were entitled "to full and equal benefit of all laws and proceedings for the security of person and property, as is enjoyed by white citizens."[31] So began a legal revolution in the postwar South that affected women of all races. As Laura Edwards describes the period, "Reconstruction fundamentally altered the dynamics of law and governance in ways that transformed the lives of all Americans."[32]

These transformations rewrote the scripts of Southern lives, opening up new possibilities for many women. In 1867, for example, two young white women from rural Louisiana, nineteen-year-old Martha Long and eighteen-year-old Mary Glover, disguised themselves as boys and ran away to New Orleans with "their black paramours . . . for the purpose of marrying in this city," as a local conservative paper recounted. The foursome was arrested upon arriving in the city, and their stories tumbled out under police examination. Martha Long recounted that her lover "was hired at her father's [farm] as a laborer [and] she had been familiar with him for two years." Her father had discovered the relationship a year before when Long gave birth and "her father made Ben leave and take the child away." Nevertheless, Long "had always intended to marry Ben when opportunity afforded." Her friend Mary Glover had similarly had a two-year-long relationship with a black man who worked in her father's house and told police that "the elopement had been agreed on some time ago."[33]

Although the paper declared the incident "extremely repugnant to the community," there was little that could be done legally against the two couples. Police discharged the men two days after their arrest, and the court assigned a fine of ten dollars each to Long and Glover "for donning breeches in contravention of law" and sent them back home in "striped red calico dresses . . . [and] blue sunbonnets" provided by the police. A case "naturally calculated to shock the morals of the Southern community" thus ended rather tamely. It was a scandal for "young ladies of very respectable standing and good family," but the only line they had crossed according to the law was in their masculine dress, not in sex across the color line. The men had violated no laws at all.[34]

Such colorblind outcomes continued to be resisted by many Southern whites, including judges, police, and legislators, which explains why black Southerners and national Republican politicians alike pushed for further legal protections. These efforts culminated in the so-called Reconstruction Amendments (or Freedom Amendments) and the Reconstructions Acts. Joining the Thirteenth Amendment abolishing slavery in 1865, the Fourteenth Amendment confirmed the citizenship granted across race in the Civil Rights Act of 1866 and guaranteed "due process of law."[35] The same year of its ratification, 1868, Congress completed the four measures collectively called the Reconstruction Acts. In effect, the acts provided a blueprint for former Confederate states to be "reconstructed" and reenter the Union. Central to this process was the rewriting of Southern state constitutions to include civil rights for freed people and suffrage for black men, a process completed across the South by 1870. Finally the Fifteenth Amendment, ratified in 1870, famously declared that "The right of citizens of the United States to vote shall not be denied or abridged . . . on account of race, color, or previous condition of servitude."[36]

Political and legal historians have long studied these developments as the principal events of Reconstruction, as have many historians of women and gender. Outside the South, the Fourteenth and Fifteenth Amendments led to lasting divisions within the women's rights movement as the political interests of white women and men of color were seemingly placed at odds.[37] Perhaps even more particularly in the South, though, this legal revolution exposed what Mary Farmer-Kaiser labels "the interconnectedness of public policy and private lives."[38] Whether it was young Mary Glover hoping to run away with her black lover—and, as she told police, to "cast [her lot] with those of her paramour's own class"—or Elizabeth Conrad suing her white employer for assault, legal reforms reshaped the possibilities of Southern women's lives in often unprecedented ways.[39] Even the vote, designated for "male inhabitants" in the Fourteenth Amendment and not extended by sex as it was for "race, color, or previous condition of servitude" by the Fifteenth Amendment, was widely celebrated by freed people across gender as a political tool for the entire community, not just individual men.[40]

On the everyday level of local law, women of all races crisscrossed courts as claimants, defendants, and witnesses. Moreover, they sometimes received remarkably colorblind verdicts. Michael A. Ross, for example, examines a fascinating case in which two women of color were acquitted in the kidnapping of a white toddler in New Orleans. As he notes of their sensationalized 1871 trial, "It would be almost a hundred years before black defendants in the South would be guaranteed the same due process."[41] Nor were such outcomes restricted to Deep South or urban courtrooms. In her study of Granville County, a tobacco-producing area of North Carolina, Laura Edwards finds that black women as well as common white women used local courts widely, and frequently with success. In prosecuting allegations of sexual assault, for instance, black and white women alike were often able to secure convictions. As Edwards observes, "Each victory delivered a blow to the racial and class hierarchies that had kept these women outside the legal status of womanhood for so long."[42]

Women across the region used the courts to chastise meddlesome neighbors, discipline employees (or employers as the case may be), shame derelict husbands, break from abusive marriages, or protect children seized into apprenticeships. These legal options may have been especially important to women outside elite circles who had fewer social resources to resolve or escape conflicts. Some conservatives might complain of their local courts that "Hundreds of negroes come daily to have some real or fancied wrongs redressed," as did a Tennessee reporter of early freedmen's courts, but in such grumblings we can also read the faith ordinary Southerners had in postwar law to address the realities of their lives and, hopefully, provide them some measure of justice.[43]

Elizabeth Parish Smith

Legal reforms, especially the revised state constitutions of the late 1860s, created extraordinary—and sometimes long-lived—ties among women across race. Louisiana's Reconstruction-era constitution, for example, prohibited racial discrimination in "all places of business, or of public resort."[44] One outcome of this statute was the erasure of legal distinctions among women by race in New Orleans's large and infamous regulated sex trade. Earlier city ordinances had required some degree of segregation among brothels and their residents, but now women (and customers) of all races lived and worked together openly.[45] As a newspaper said of one fight involving these "frail women," "There were black women and white men, white women and mulattoes, rolling, tumbling, screaming and biting, while others stood by enjoying the scandalous encounter."[46] This lack of racial distinctions, moreover, endured unaltered until 1917, when the city's demimonde was closed down. In this half-century of regulation, racial segregation was never reimplemented. New Orleans's integrated demimonde represented a rather extreme example of what the city's paper called "the common status of the white and black population" under Reconstruction-era laws, but it was one way shared bonds among women endured for decades after Reconstruction.[47]

The shortcomings of these legal reforms are also of great interest to historians. In criminal courts women of color were still more likely to face conviction than white women and, as we have seen, had a harder time securing convictions for offenses against them, especially if the accused were white. The inherent limitations of Reconstruction's focus on civil rights also became apparent. Despite people's optimism, there was only so much law itself could accomplish. Laura Edwards explains that in Reconstruction freed people "became legal individuals with the same civil and political rights as all other legal individuals, as if they had never been anything else."[48] Lingering structural inequalities, especially by race, class, and gender, remained largely untouched by legal reforms, which bypassed issues of economic justice or women's rights.[49] Failure to address these fundamental inequities in society automatically truncated the social effects of these otherwise profound legal transformations.

The limits of Reconstruction are most clearly revealed by another, more tragic shared experience in Southern women's lives: violence. Violence tore through postwar Southern society in a variety of forms, from drunken street brawls such as that described above among New Orleans prostitutes to abuses within families—husbands to wives, mothers to children, and more. Coercion and punitive discipline had undergirded the institution of slavery and remained a part of labor relations after emancipation. Women, especially those who were black, poor, or otherwise vulnerable, endured rape and sexual violence and, moreover, often faced blame for somehow inviting or deserving these attacks. Finally, political violence by the Ku Klux Klan and other vigilante groups consumed the region in deadly incidents large and small as part of what Catherine Clinton labels "this exceptionally savage era of racial realignment."[50]

Women faced violence in all its many forms, and experiences of violence were widely shared by women across the South. Importantly, women also acted as perpetrators of violence in ways that historians have sometimes underestimated. Women, especially among the poor and working classes, clashed with neighbors over causes such as an unreturned washtub, the sale of a sick turkey, or uncollected "dog dirt" in a shared yard.[51] The confrontations were sometimes vicious and even escalated to murder, especially in incidents involving sexual jealousies or property disputes. Women struck, slapped, punched, ripped, pulled, kicked, and bit at each other and at men and sometimes children too. They were less likely to have guns than men, but they used all kinds of blades from kitchen knives to hatchets as well as brickbats, brass knuckles, and everyday objects readily at hand, such as pokers, broomsticks, and cotton hooks. A newspaper might remind readers of "the injunction that little 'female hands were never made to tear a body's eyes out,'" but many women across the races brazenly ignored such advice.[52]

Women as perpetrators of violence, however, were not treated alike. Under slavery white women, like men, used violence to discipline African Americans and assert their racial dominance. In the Reconstruction-era South black women could press charges against such violent white women, as did a Louisianan named Amelia Place, who alleged in 1866 that she was "unprovokedly Assaulted and struck on the hand with a tumbler by one Lizzie Harris who also threw a brick Bat and Smoothing Iron at [her]." Place's charge carried great political significance as resistance to white violence, but it may not have provided much personal satisfaction, as the court dismissed the case against Harris.[53] Many women of color found themselves in similar situations during Reconstruction: they used the Southern legal system in unprecedented ways but were too often unable to check the behavior of abusive whites.

The relative difficulty of convicting white women or the unequal sentences received when they were convicted helped to feed associations of aggression and criminality with blackness, a perception of violence in the postwar South that obscured its complicated everyday realities and its political dimensions. Newspaper coverage routinely highlighted violence among black women, racializing behaviors that were perfectly common, but less commonly broadcast, among other women. An 1876 headline, for example, trumpeted, "A Bloody Affair: A Rencontre Between Two Colored Women, in Which One is Cut Fourteen Times."[54] One hardly needed to read the rest of the article to form an opinion of the women involved and their savagery. Newspapers' practice of rarely identifying whiteness only reinforced the link between violence and blackness as white women's race seemed to disappear in discussions of their crimes and transgressions.

Denying that white and black women shared experiences as victims and especially as perpetrators of violence thus became a way of denying them equal womanhood and ultimately equal rights. It became a way to beleaguer the entire Reconstruction enterprise. When a newspaper reported on a black woman poisoning her lover's wife so that he could marry her instead, it impugned all black marriages and households. When it recounted "Harriet, a colored servant" threatening her employer with an ax when asked "to set the dinner table," it negated black employees' real labor complaints and instead cast domestic workers as uncooperative, irrational, and dangerous. Finally, when a paper complained of "the evidently greater proneness to crime manifested by the colored race," as did a Memphis newspaper in April 1866, it helped to ignite large-

Elizabeth Parish Smith

scale racial violence such as the Memphis Massacre in May 1866, which resulted in the deaths of forty-six African Americans, several rapes, and the physical destruction of much of the city's black community.[55]

By so identifying criminality and danger with freed people, Southern whites in effect conflated African Americans' equality under the law with total *lawlessness*.[56] One Georgian, for example, protested in 1872 that "the truth is, for three years our people have not had confidence in the execution of the laws of the State in such a manner as to protect person and property."[57] Southern law, as they saw it, had been so perverted by Reconstruction that law itself was practically absent, and any means were justified to restore the region to Democratic "home rule." White political rhetoric in the 1860s and 1870s overflowed with racial paranoia and calls to violent counterrevolution. A conservative editorial against Louisiana's Reconstruction-era state constitution, for example, proclaimed that it "introduced an oppressive desire to crush out the old white population, and to place them socially and politically at the mercy of blacks." Racial equality remained too difficult to comprehend, much less to accomplish; the outcome must be only total domination by one or the other. The editorial made clear both the menace white Southerners faced and the means necessary to address it. "The white man," it concluded, "cannot long be induced to keep hands off the wolf which invades his sheepfold and would carry away his lambs."[58]

As historians have explored in many rich, complex ways, this political rhetoric depended on gender but in ways that carved all but insurmountable divides among the diverse women of the South. Not only were white women as perpetrators of violence largely ignored, but so were black women as victims of violence. The testimonies of women of color to rape and sexual violence, especially by white men, were among the most powerful political acts of the period. Women testified to such violence in front of local courts, Freedmen's Bureau officials, and congressional committees, and their courage at times created real change for all freed people. This was demonstrated by the five women who testified about their rapes amid the Memphis Massacre. In doing so they helped secure greater congressional protections for Reconstruction in its early years. Hannah Rosen emphasizes how both historically unprecedented and politically important these actions were, observing that "their testimony reveals how new rights to refuse the demands of white men for sex, and thus to control their bodies and sexual relationships, were for African American women a central part of the meaning of freedom."[59]

Such actions, however, were too often obscured by the slow, toxic construction of the so-called rape myth that convulsed the South by the final decades of the nineteenth century. Increasingly only white women could be victims of rape and then overwhelmingly at the hands of black men. No longer could the two young white runaways dream of a life with their black lovers (not to mention their children together) as had seemed possible in 1867. Penalties for all parties, especially the men, would far exceed a fine for cross-dressing by the 1880s and 1890s. As these new scripts on Southern women and violence began to take hold during Reconstruction, many whites echoed the fears of a Georgia woman in 1871: "One hears so many dreadful things of them now, that I would sooner meet a lion in a lonely place, than a 'nigger fellow.'"[60] As Faye Dudden notes of the Reconstruction-era North in her essay in this volume, "The trope of the black rapist," widely publicized in newspapers across the country, crippled support for Reconstruction even among its earlier supporters. It also fractured relations among Southern women. In this racialized construction of sexual violence and its victims, the bond of shared experiences among women that had seemed possible, if difficult, during Reconstruction shattered against the persistent barriers of racism, fear, and separate womanhoods.

Viewing Reconstruction from the distance of a century and a half, it is easy to see its pitfalls and inherent flaws. They are well worth noting. The redistribution of land and various other efforts to modernize the Southern economy swiftly collapsed, national political will in favor of rebuilding the region buckled by the 1870s, and the resolute opposition of many Southern whites—and their flagrant use of violence and terror—overpowered weak federal authorities and the laws they ultimately could not enforce. Reconstruction persisted for varying lengths of time in different pockets of the South. Susan O'Donovan notes of rural southwestern Georgia that the radical potential of Reconstruction foundered "before the third year of freedom was out." By contrast, Laura Edwards observes aspects of Reconstruction persisting in central North Carolina through the late 1880s.[61] However you define Reconstruction's remainders and legacies, historians agree that the peak of Reconstruction was relatively short-lived and was cast into deep shadows by the Jim Crow period to follow. Such limitations pared down the transformative potential of the postwar period for women across the races and across the country.

All that said, it is worth refocusing the spotlight on the Reconstruction era so we do not lose the remarkable achievements of the period, including those by women, and the striking historical records women like Caroline Johnson left behind. The lives, labors, and rights of American women may not have been permanently transformed by Reconstruction, but the diverse women of the South drove Reconstruction and resistance to it in complex, even contradictory, ways that historians should continue to scrutinize. As we have seen, Southern women experienced "times of change and trouble like these" in various ways. The many overlaps in their experiences, though, are as significant as the differences among them. Women shared the importance of households and the value (and difficulties) of their labor in and out of their homes, and they used a legal system that crafted unprecedented formal equalities among them. Violence marred many of their everyday lives as both victims and perpetrators, even as it simultaneously drew stark distinctions among them. Yet even as we see Jim Crow overtake Reconstruction in the late nineteenth century, the commonalities that were possible for women across race during this period help us to recognize the radical potential that existed, if too briefly and too precariously, to reconstruct a very different South.

Elizabeth Parish Smith

1. *State of Louisiana v. Caroline Johnson,* case no. 1774, Jan. 21, 1870, First District Court, Louisiana Division, City Archives and Special Collections, New Orleans Public Library (hereafter Louisiana Division).

2. W. E. B. Du Bois, *Black Reconstruction in America: 1860–1880* (1935; repr., New York: Free Press, 1992), 725.

3. A selection of the many works to add women and gender to the study of Reconstruction in the South includes Jane Turner Censer, *The Reconstruction of White Southern Womanhood, 1865–1895* (Baton Rouge: Louisiana State Univ. Press, 2003); Catherine Clinton and Nina Silber, eds., *Battle Scars: Gender and Sexuality in the American Civil War* (New York: Oxford Univ. Press, 2006); Laura F. Edwards, *Gendered Strife and Confusion: The Political Culture of Reconstruction* (Urbana: Univ. of Illinois Press, 1997); Laura F. Edwards, *Scarlett Doesn't Live Here Anymore: Southern Women in the Civil War Era* (Urbana: Univ. of Illinois Press, 2000); Carol Faulkner, *Women's Radical Reconstruction: The Freedmen's Aid Movement* (Philadelphia: Univ. of Pennsylvania Press, 2004); Noralee Frankel, *Freedom's Women: Black Women and Families in Civil War Era Mississippi* (Bloomington: Indiana Univ. Press, 1999); Thavolia Glymph, *Out of the House of Bondage: The Transformation of the Plantation Household* (New York: Cambridge Univ. Press, 2008); Caroline E. Janney, *Burying the Dead but Not the Past: Ladies' Memorial Associations and the Lost Cause* (Chapel Hill: Univ. of North Carolina Press, 2008); Hannah Rosen, *Terror in the Heart of Freedom: Citizenship, Sexual Violence, and the Meaning of Race in the Postemancipation South* (Chapel Hill: Univ. of North Carolina Press, 2009); Leslie A. Schwalm, *A Hard Fight for We: Women's Transition from Slavery to Freedom in South Carolina* (Urbana: Univ. of Illinois Press, 1997); Amy Dru Stanley, *From Bondage to Contract: Wage Labor, Marriage, and the Market in the Age of Slave Emancipation* (Cambridge: Cambridge Univ. Press, 1998); and LeeAnn Whites, *The Civil War as a Crisis in Gender: Augusta, Georgia, 1860–1890* (Athens: Univ. of Georgia Press, 1995).

For more specifically on women and postwar Southern churches, see Edward J. Blum and W. Scott Poole, eds., *Vale of Tears: New Essays on Religion and Reconstruction* (Macon: Mercer Univ. Press, 2005); Paul Harvey, *Redeeming the South: Religious Cultures and Racial Identities among Southern Baptists, 1865–1925* (Chapel Hill: Univ. of North Carolina Press, 1997); and David W. Stowell, *Rebuilding Zion: The Religious Reconstruction of the South, 1863–1877* (Oxford: Oxford Univ. Press, 1998).

4. "Charge to the Grand Jury," *Daily Picayune* (New Orleans), Apr. 2, 1867, 8.

5. Among the works to address the pressing questions of Reconstruction and its contested chronology are Bruce E. Baker and Brian Kelly, eds., *After Slavery: Race, Labor, and Citizenship in the Reconstruction South* (Gainesville: Univ. Press of Florida, 2013); Ira Berlin, Barbara J. Fields, Steven F. Miller, Joseph P. Reidy, and Leslie S. Rowland, *Slaves No More: Three Essays on Emancipation and the Civil War* (New York: Cambridge Univ. Press, 1992); Paul A. Cimbala and Randall M. Miller, eds., *The Great Task Remaining Before Us: Reconstruction as America's Continuing Civil War* (New York: Fordham Univ. Press, 2010); Gregory P. Downs, *Declarations of Dependence: The Long Reconstruction of Popular Politics in the South, 1861–1908* (Chapel Hill: Univ. of North Carolina Press, 2011); Gregory P. Downs, *After Appomattox: Military Occupation and the Ends of War* (Cambridge, Mass.: Harvard Univ. Press, 2015); Du Bois, *Black Reconstruction in America;* Eric Foner, *Reconstruction: America's Unfinished Revolution, 1863–1877* (New York: Perennial Classics, 2002); Douglas R. Egerton, *The Wars of Reconstruction: The Brief, Violent History of America's Most Progressive Era* (New York: Bloomsbury Press, 2015); Steven Hahn, *A Nation under Our Feet: Black Political Struggles in the Rural South from Slavery to the Great Migration* (Cambridge, Mass.: Belknap Press of Harvard Univ. Press,

2003); Thomas Holt, *Black Over White: Negro Political Leadership in South Carolina During Reconstruction* (Urbana: Univ. of Illinois Press, 1977); Leon F. Litwack, *Been in the Storm So Long: The Aftermath of Slavery* (New York: Vintage Books, 1979); Kate Masur, *An Example for All the Land: Emancipation and the Struggle over Equality in Washington, D.C.* (Chapel Hill: Univ. of North Carolina Press, 2010); Susan Eva O'Donovan, *Becoming Free in the Cotton South* (Cambridge, Mass.: Harvard Univ. Press, 2007); Michael Perman, *Road to Redemption: Southern Politics, 1868–1879* (Chapel Hill: Univ. of North Carolina Press, 1984); and Elliott West, "Reconstructing Race," *Western Historical Quarterly* 34 (Spring 2003): 6–26.

6. For more on the legal revolution of the Reconstruction period, see Peter W. Bardaglio, *Reconstructing the Household: Families, Sex, and the Law in the Nineteenth-Century South* (Chapel Hill: Univ. of North Carolina Press, 1995); Laura F. Edwards, *A Legal History of the Civil War and Reconstruction: A Nation of Rights* (New York: Cambridge Univ. Press, 2015); Sally E. Hadden and Patricia Hagler Minter, eds., *Signposts: New Directions in Southern Legal History* (Athens: Univ. of Georgia Press, 2013); Joseph A. Ranney, *In the Wake of Slavery: Civil War, Civil Rights, and the Reconstruction of Southern Law* (Westport, Conn.: Praeger, 2006); Michael A. Ross, *The Great New Orleans Kidnapping Case: Race, Law, and Justice in the Reconstruction Era* (New York: Oxford Univ. Press, 2015); Stanley, *From Bondage to Contract;* and Robert J. Steinfeld, *Coercion, Contract, and Free Labor in the Nineteenth Century* (New York: Cambridge Univ. Press, 2001).

7. Jean-Charles Houzeau, *My Passage at the New Orleans Tribune: A Memoir of the Civil War Era,* ed. David C. Rankin (Baton Rouge: Louisiana State Univ. Press, 1984), 133.

8. Glymph, *Out of the House of Bondage,* 1.

9. Women's and gender historians of Reconstruction strongly emphasize how little the dichotomy of private and public was realized in women's lives, especially among African American and poor white women. For this scholarship, see Edwards, *Gendered Strife and Confusion;* Mary Farmer-Kaiser, *Freedwomen and the Freedmen's Bureau: Race, Gender, and Public Policy in the Age of Emancipation* (New York: Fordham Univ. Press, 2010), 37; and Glymph, *Out of the House of Bondage.*

10. "Incredible," *Daily Appeal* (Memphis), Nov. 17, 1865, 3.

11. "Query," *Daily Appeal,* Nov. 28, 1865, 3.

12. LeeAnn Whites, *Gender Matters: Civil War, Reconstruction, and the Making of the New South* (New York: Palgrave MacMillan, 2005), 6. For more work on the importance of the household in the postwar South, including its political importance, the divisions of labor within households, and violence within families, see Bardaglio, *Reconstructing the Household;* Nancy Bercaw, *Gendered Freedoms: Race, Rights, and the Politics of the Household in the Delta, 1861–1875* (Gainesville: Univ. Press of Florida, 2003); Catherine A. Jones, *Intimate Reconstructions: Children in Postemancipation Virginia* (Charlottesville: Univ. of Virginia Press, 2015); Jacqueline Jones, *Labor of Love, Labor of Sorrow: Black Women, Work, and the Family, and Slavery to the Present* (New York: Basic Books, 1985); Amy Feely Morsman, *The Big House after Slavery: Virginia Plantation Families and Their Postbellum Domestic Experiment* (Charlottesville: Univ. of Virginia Press, 2010); O'Donovan, *Becoming Free in the Cotton South;* Schwalm, *A Hard Fight for We;* and Whites, *The Civil War as a Crisis in Gender.*

13. Qtd. in Farmer-Kaiser, *Freedwomen and the Freedmen's Bureau,* 37.

14. See Faye Dudden, "Women and Reconstruction in the North," in this volume.

15. O'Donovan, *Becoming Free in the Cotton South,* 174.

16. Qtd. in Ira Berlin and Leslie S. Rowland, eds., *Families and Freedom: A Documentary History of African-American Kinship in the Civil War Era* (New York: Free Press, 1997), 185.

17. For more on black women and work, see Tera W. Hunter, *To 'Joy My Freedom: Southern Women's Lives and Labors after the Civil War* (Cambridge, Mass.: Harvard Univ. Press, 2003).

18. "WANTED," *Daily Picayune,* Oct. 28, 1866, 5; ibid., Jan. 13, 1867, 5; ibid., Dec. 26, 1875, 7. We can presume that women of color took out these advertisements, since these were generally the types of positions open to them. Advertisements by or desiring white or European women typically stated such.

19. *State of Louisiana v. Adeline Johnson,* case no. 445, Oct. 18, 1868, First District Court, Louisiana Division. For discussions of domestic workers and alleged larcenies, see Edwards, *Gendered Strife and Confusion;* Glymph, *Out of the House of Bondage;* and Hunter, *To 'Joy My Freedom.* For an exploration of similar issues outside the South, see Kali N. Gross, *Colored Amazons: Crime, Violence, and Black Women in the City of Brotherly Love, 1880–1910* (Durham: Duke Univ. Press, 2006).

20. *State of Louisiana v. Mrs. E. Tooms,* case no. 1727, Apr. 2, 1866, First District Court, Louisiana Division.

21. It is difficult to explain sentencing in individual criminal court cases. Tooms's trial took place in 1866; perhaps her sentencing would have been harsher after reforms to Louisiana's justice system following the state's required revision of its constitution in 1868. Assault, the charge against Tooms, was also much less severely punished by nineteenth-century courts than larceny, the charge made against Adeline Johnson. Nevertheless, the defendants' race and social status likely affected the disparate sentences they received.

22. Glymph, *Out of the House of Bondage,* 9. Also see Hunter, *To 'Joy My Freedom.*

23. Samuel R. Phillips, ed., *Torn by War: The Civil War Journal of Mary Adelia Byers* (Norman: Univ. of Oklahoma Press, 2013), 99 and 140.

24. See Censer, *Reconstruction of White Southern Womanhood;* Edwards, *Scarlett Doesn't Live Here Anymore;* and Anya Jabour, *Scarlett's Sisters: Young Women in the Old South* (Chapel Hill: Univ. of North Carolina Press, 2007).

25. "The Women of South Carolina and Their Poverty," *Daily Appeal,* Jan. 14, 1866, 1.

26. Ibid.

27. Jabour, *Scarlett's Sisters,* 279.

28. Phillips, ed., *Torn by War,* 102.

29. "Pay Day for the Ladies," *Daily Picayune,* June 3, 1866, 10. For more on white women and work in the postwar South, see Censer, *Reconstruction of White Southern Womanhood.*

30. The incidents of domestic violence in this period tragically reveal the degree to which both black and white families struggled to adapt to the postbellum South. See Edwards, *Gendered Strife and Confusion;* Frankel, *Freedom's Women;* and Schwalm, *A Hard Fight for We.*

31. "President Johnson's Veto," *Daily Appeal,* Mar. 30, 1866, 2; and "The Civil Rights Act of 1866," in *A Just and Lasting Peace: A Documentary History of Reconstruction,* ed. John David Smith (New York: Signet Classics, 2013), 186.

32. Edwards, *A Legal History of the Civil War and Reconstruction: A Nation of Rights* (New York: Cambridge Univ. Press, 2015), 10.

33. "Elopement: Two Young Ladies and Two Negroes," *Daily Picayune,* Mar. 12, 1867, 9; and "The Elopement Case: Human Nature—The Effects of War," *Daily Picayune,* Mar. 12, 1867, 8. According to Alecia Long, Louisiana law did not permit interracial marriage until 1870. It may be that the two couples wished to marry or elope either without official legal sanction or by the women passing as black or the men as white. See Alecia P. Long, *The Great Southern Babylon: Sex, Race, and Respectability in New Orleans, 1865–1920* (Baton Rouge: Louisiana State Univ. Press, 2004).

34. The Elopement Case," *Daily Picayune,* Mar. 12, 1867, 8; "The Four Runaways," *Daily Picayune,* Mar. 14, 1867, 9; "The Two Runaways," *Daily Picayune,* Mar. 20, 1867, 10; and "Elopement," *Daily Picayune,* Mar. 12, 1867. In her study of interracial sex in the nineteenth-century South, Martha Hodes emphasizes that there was often considerable toleration of relationships

between white women and black men before emancipation. In this way, these two relationships may illustrate some degree of continuity with the antebellum South. Martha Hodes, *White Women, Black Men: Illicit Sex in the Nineteenth-Century South* (New Haven, Conn.: Yale Univ. Press, 1999).

35. "Amendment 14," in *A Just and Lasting Peace*, 348.

36. "Amendment 15," in ibid., 372.

37. See Ellen Carol DuBois, *Feminism and Suffrage: The Emergence of an Independent Women's Movement in America, 1848–1869* (Ithaca, N.Y.: Cornell Univ. Press, 1978); Faye E. Dudden, *Fighting Chance: The Struggle over Woman Suffrage and Black Suffrage in Reconstruction America* (New York: Oxford Univ. Press, 2011); Sally McMillen, *Seneca Falls and the Origins of the Women's Rights Movement* (New York: Oxford Univ. Press, 2009); and Lisa Tetrault, *The Myth of Seneca Falls: Memory and the Women's Suffrage Movement, 1848–1898* (Chapel Hill: Univ. of North Carolina Press, 2014).

38. Farmer-Kaiser, *Freedwomen and the Freedmen's Bureau*, 9.

39. "The Elopement Case," *Daily Picayune*, Mar. 12, 1867, 8.

40. "Amendment 14," in *A Just and Lasting Peace*, 349; "Amendment 15," in ibid., 372. For discussions of male suffrage and the black community, see Edwards, *Scarlett Doesn't Live Here Anymore*; and Rosen, *Terror in the Heart of Freedom*.

41. Ross, *Great New Orleans Kidnapping Case*, 207.

42. Edwards, *Gendered Strife and Confusion*, 206–7.

43. "Freedmen's Court," *Daily Appeal*, Nov. 15, 1865, 3. For more on common people's use of local law in the nineteenth-century South, see Laura F. Edwards, *The People and Their Peace: Legal Culture and the Transformation of Inequality in the Post-Revolutionary South* (Chapel Hill: Univ. of North Carolina Press, 2009).

44. *Constitution Adopted by the State Constitutional Convention of the State of Louisiana, March 7, 1868* (New Orleans: Republican Office, 1868), 4.

45. Henry J. Leovy and C. H. Luzenberg, *The Laws and General Ordinances of the City of New Orleans, Together with the Acts of the Legislature, Decisions of the Supreme Court and Constitutional Provisions Relating to the City Government* (New Orleans: Simmons, 1870), 201–6.

46. "A Scuffle on Dryades Street," *Daily Picayune*, Oct. 4, 1870, 2.

47. "Becoming Serious," *Daily Picayune*, May 7, 1867, 8. For more on prostitution in nineteenth-century New Orleans, including its regulation, see Emily Epstein Landau, *Spectacular Wickedness: Sex, Race, and Memory in Storyville, New Orleans* (Baton Rouge: Louisiana State Univ. Press, 2013); Long, *Great Southern Babylon;* and Judith Kelleher Schafer, *Brothels, Depravity, and Abandoned Women: Illegal Sex in Antebellum New Orleans* (Baton Rouge: Louisiana State Univ. Press, 2009).

48. Edwards, *Legal History*, 124 (emphasis mine).

49. Historians who have explored married women's property rights, for instance, find that, though such reforms were often implemented in the South during Reconstruction, legislators' motivations were less to extend rights to women than to provide economic protections for men. As Suzanne Lebsock explains, "Married-women's property reforms stood a chance for the same reasons that woman suffrage did not—there was something in them for men, and they had nothing to do with feminism." Suzanne D. Lebsock, "Radical Reconstruction and the Property Rights of Southern Women," in *Half Sisters of History: Southern Women and the American Past*, ed. Catherine Clinton (Durham, N.C.: Duke Univ. Press, 1994), 112. See also Bardaglio, *Reconstructing the Household*.

50. Catherine Clinton, "Bloody Terrain: Freedwomen, Sexuality, and Violence during Reconstruction," in Clinton, ed., *Half Sisters of History*, 137.

51. *State of Louisiana v. Lizzie Scott,* case no. 934, Mar. 13, 1869, First District Court, Louisiana Division; "Serious Charge," *Daily Picayune,* Dec. 30, 1866, 11; and *State of Louisiana v. Octavia Edwards,* case no. 10373, 15 Mar. 1878, First District Court, Louisiana Division.

52. "Females on the Muscle," *Daily Picayune,* July 4, 1868, 2.

53. *State of Louisiana v. Lizzie Harris,* case no. 17323, Aug. 3, 1866, First District Court, Louisiana Division. We do not know the relationship between the women in this case. For more on white women's use of violence against black women as their household workers, see Glymph, *Out of the House of Bondage.*

54. "A Bloody Affair: A Rencontre Between Two Colored Women, in Which One Is Cut Fourteen Times," *Daily Picayune,* Mar. 31, 1876, 1. For more on the popular depictions of women and violence in the South, see Clinton, "Bloody Terrain."

55. "The Alleged Poisoning Case," *Daily Picayune,* Apr. 19, 1867, 8; "First District Court," ibid., Dec. 5, 1866, 8; and "Colored Criminals," *Daily Appeal,* Apr. 11, 1866, 4. For more on women and the Memphis Massacre, see Rosen, *Terror in the Heart of Freedom.*

56. Hannah Rosen notes that white newspapers presented "freedom as a license for lawlessness." Rosen, *Terror in the Heart of Freedom,* 47. See also Edwards, *Legal History.*

57. Qtd. in Diane Miller Sommerville, *Rape and Race in the Nineteenth-Century South* (Chapel Hill: Univ. of North Carolina Press, 2004), 162.

58. "White and Black Radicalism," *Daily Picayune,* July 15, 1868, 1.

59. Rosen, *Terror in the Heart of Freedom,* 9. Martha Hodes identifies such rhetoric as part of "the broader sexualization of politics in the Reconstruction South." Hodes, *White Women, Black Men,* 171. For more on rape as a tool of racialized terror during Reconstruction, also see Farmer-Kaiser, *Freedwomen and the Freedmen's Bureau;* Elain Frantz Parsons, *Ku-Klux: The Birth of the Klan during Reconstruction* (Chapel Hill: Univ. of North Carolina Press, 2016); and Sommerville, *Rape and Race in the Nineteenth-Century South.*

60. Qtd. in Censer, *Reconstruction of White Southern Womanhood,* 146. For more on women and the "rape myth" in the Jim-Crow South, see Crystal N. Feimster, *Southern Horrors: Women and the Politics of Rape and Lynching* (Cambridge, Mass.: Harvard Univ. Press, 2009); Jacquelyn Dowd Hall, *Revolt Against Chivalry: Jessie Daniel Ames and the Women's Campaign Against Lynching* (New York: Columbia Univ. Press, 1993); Hodes, *White Women, Black Men;* and Sommerville, *Rape and Race in the Nineteenth-Century South.*

61. O'Donovan, *Becoming Free in the Cotton South,* 268; and Edwards, *Gendered Strife and Confusion.*

Women and Reconstruction in the North

FAYE DUDDEN

In the North, Reconstruction (1865–1877) was a pivotal interval in the history of the women's rights movement because after the Civil War destroyed slavery, Reconstruction-era politicians were obliged to define the rights of free people. A window of opportunity opened for political outsiders, especially on questions of the franchise, and women's rights activists, whose antebellum movement had been confined entirely to the North, plunged into a complicated political landscape to fight for the vote. Their women's *rights* movement became a women's *suffrage* movement, and women actually did gain the right to vote in two western territories, Wyoming in 1869 and Utah in 1870. But on the suffrage question they also faced exhausting and futile state referenda, pushback from an increasingly organized opposition, and roadblocks erected by a conservative Supreme Court. The Reconstruction years in the North saw important trends in women's history unrelated to the South, including increased activism among working women, new opportunities to pursue higher education, the women's club movement, and a women's "crusade" against alcohol that led to the formation of the Woman's Christian Temperance Union.[1] Yet those years are mostly remembered for the way Northern woman suffrage activists quarreled bitterly amongst themselves.

As they tried to capitalize on the opportunities of Reconstruction, Elizabeth Cady Stanton and Susan B. Anthony parted company with long-time abolitionist allies and fell into disputes marked by strong personal antagonism and appalling racist rhetoric. They disagreed over whether to cede priority to black men's rights, and the suffrage movement itself split into two rival organizations; Stanton and Anthony's National Woman Suffrage Association rejected the Fifteenth Amendment, which expressly prohibited governments from denying a citizen the right to vote on the basis of "race, color, or previous condition of servitude" but implicitly confined that protection to males, while Lucy Stone and Henry Blackwell's American Woman Suffrage Association supported it. These feminists came to rhetorical blows over Southern Reconstruction policy, debating what freedmen thought about women's rights, and how black men would act if they were enfranchised before women.[2] But what did

Northern activists really know about the freed people or situation on the ground in the South? The fundamental conflicts that fractured the woman suffrage movement during Reconstruction were largely based on what Northern activists saw—or thought they saw—when they looked south. Black activists probably derived accurate information from sources within the black community, though they lacked the numbers and power to set the direction of human rights activism. But white women's rights activists, like the North in general, never saw the postemancipation South clearly because they looked at it in part through the distorting lens of the mainstream press.

FREEDMEN'S AID

Northern women doing freedmen's aid work, discussed at length by Chandra Manning in this volume, provided direct, unfiltered news about the Southern situation when they wrote home. Thousands of women went south as teachers under the auspices of an array of national religious organizations like the American Missionary Association (AMA), affiliated with the Congregational Church, and its nondenominational rival the American Freedmen's Union Commission (AFUC), as well as local associations and denominational groups that recruited teachers and gathered donations and supplies.[3] Freedmen's aid built on patterns developed during the war in soldiers' aid, when elite white men took charge and pursued an ideological vision while depending largely upon women workers to effect it.[4] Eager to vindicate free labor, these men focused on black men's ability to support their families and optimistically stressed that aid would be temporary.[5] But women who went south could not ignore the orphaned, disabled, and elderly, who had little prospect of self-support. They told of a situation "when one pair of shoes is in the storeroom, and one hundred feet go bare," and while they taught school, they also solicited and distributed badly needed clothing and supplies.[6] In their letters home, which were often published or publicized, freedmen's aid teachers wrote of primitive facilities, spartan living conditions, and white Southerners who ostracized them.[7] They also remarked on eager and apt students, and they tried to show progress to encourage support.[8] Nevertheless, public enthusiasm for freedmen's aid fell off quickly from its peak in 1865 and 1866, as both donations and press coverage diminished.[9] In 1869 the AFUC dissolved outright, and though its denominational competitors lasted longer, the AMA was in trouble too, facing "burdensome debt" as donations in 1869 fell to half those of the previous year.[10]

Even during this brief tenure, the freedmen's aid teachers were not working for organizations devoted to equal rights. Both the AMA and the AFUC aimed to teach the freed people basic skills and habits of order and diligence, while the AMA also stressed Christian redemption and tried to inculcate the piety and propriety of true womanhood among Southern black women.[11] The AFUC's idea was that education would reform race relations and thus the whole of Southern society, because as black people learned hard work and "correct deportment," they would "compel the respect and win the cooperation" of Southern whites.[12] Though the AFUC's head, abolitionist J. Miller McKim, insisted that his program was "not an Eleemosynary movement; not an 'old clo' movement merely to relieve physical want and teach little negroes to read," the AFUC did not promote black civil rights—or women's rights.[13] Lucretia Mott criticized McKim for the way "woman was ignored" in his AFUC and was disgusted when the AFUC, despite its name, provided aid to Southern *whites* on an equal basis with the ex-slaves.[14] Caroline Putnam, a veteran radical abolitionist, refused to work with these freedmen's aid organizations because of their "servile policy that doles out charity and education and religious instruction to the freedman as a dependent, instead of demanding his rights as an equal." Instead she went to Virginia independently to work in freedmen's aid.[15] Thus the channels of North-South communication opened up by white freedmen's aid organizations were limited in both duration and focus.

Free black women from the North participated in integrated freedmen's aid organizations like the AMA, but inspired by a sense of mission to help the freed people, the black community also created its own organizations, such as the Contraband Relief Association. Black women who were qualified as teachers had often been prepared at Oberlin, or the Institute for Colored Youth in Philadelphia, and they tended to share other prewar experience in abolitionist, benevolent, or mutual aid organizations.[16] They found that every institution in the black community of the South, including both schools and churches, had to be built up from scratch. The *Christian Recorder,* the official organ of the AME Church published in Philadelphia, reported extensive efforts to establish and regularize black churches and the black ministry in a context in which no less than four different societies, all calling themselves "Methodists," were competing to enroll the freed people.[17] In the antebellum years, free black women in the North had pressed for the advancement of women and the black community through a range of different organizations, including churches, benevolent and mutual aid groups, and fraternal organizations, as well as political groups devoted to the advancement of black rights. In these endeavors, which provided models for freedmen's aid work, black women's interests tended to coincide with those of black men, and black interests were "all bound up together" as everyone worked to meet urgent needs and move forward on diverse fronts.[18]

Black women who went south found that their aid work extended far beyond education; they became "fund-raisers, construction contractors, bookkeepers, nurses, and recruiters," as well as social workers and community organizers.[19] Sojourner Truth said that many of the freed people in the refugee camps near Washington, D.C., were "entirely ignorant of housekeeping" and wanted to learn "the way we live in the North." Truth felt she was able to "tell the colored people things that they had never heard."[20] Bridging the gap was even harder for a middle-class black woman like Charlotte Forten of Philadelphia, as Chandra Manning explains, and yet Forten and others persisted. Anecdotal evidence suggests that Northern black women who went south in freedmen's aid tended to stay longer than white women, and many who returned to the North later went south again to take up permanent or regular teaching posts.[21] Black women's letters, sometimes reprinted in the black press and in the journals published by the freedmen's aid societies, kept North-South communication lines open longer, and black church and community groups in the North passed along information and sponsored speakers who had come from the South. The most prominent of these was Frances E. W. Harper, who addressed black audiences in both the North and South.[22]

While it lasted, freedmen's aid provided a vantage point from which a few Northern abolitionist-feminists, including Frances Dana Gage, Josephine Griffing, Frances E. W. Harper, and Sojourner Truth, could assess the Southern situation while keeping an eye out for women's rights issues. Frances Dana Gage, for instance, contributed a series of letters to the *National Anti-Slavery Standard*, most of which emphasized the capacity and potential of the freed people. In November 1865, however, Gage reported on a new theme: "The negro men of Paris Island insisted (the smartest and most knowing ones) that the money for the women's labor should be paid over to the husband instead of to the laborer herself. Because, 'you know, missus, de woman she have short sense, and don' know how to spend it.'" These men were, Gage remarked dryly, "very much like white folks you see."[23] A year later, at the November 1866 meeting of the Pennsylvania Anti-Slavery Society, Gage described how freedwomen refused to be married in the church, saying, "When we are married in the church, our husbands treat us just as old massa used to, and whip us if they think we deserve it."[24] Gage's reporting stressed her concerns about freedwomen's status within the family. Susan B. Anthony echoed Gage's concerns, worrying that as husbands the freedmen might become "the greatest tyrants the world has yet seen."[25] As Amy Dru Stanley explains, married freedwomen were just then discovering that they were not entitled to the proceeds of their own labor—such were the contradictions involved in "freedom" for wives who were still subject to their husbands under the legal doctrine of coverture.[26] A few years later Frances Harper would similarly report that in the South she spent "part of my time in lecturing to the men about the treatment of their wives," condemning black men who felt entitled to "whip them or leave them."[27] These observations, though scanty and impressionistic, suggested that as gender relationships were changing among the freed people in the South, black women's interests were not always identical with those of black men. As Elizabeth Smith notes in this volume, Reconstruction-era changes in the status of black labor affected black families, and reports that came through to Northern activists could hardly do justice to a complex picture.

RIGHTS AND PRIORITIES

As the war ended, most former abolitionists, both black and white, believed they should stick together to fight for equal rights, but they disagreed about priorities.[28] Wendell Phillips, the new leader of the American Anti-Slavery Society (AASS), announced, "One question at a time. This hour belongs to the negro," implying that women should fall silent about their own claims to rights lest they spoil black men's chances.[29] But Elizabeth Cady Stanton, Susan B. Anthony, and other suffragists challenged Phillips's strategy; their idea was that agitating for both causes simultaneously would not hurt, and might even help, black men's rights. Naturally, both groups focused on news that came out of the South. In the summer and fall of 1865 the *National Anti-Slavery Standard* reprinted many reports from the mainstream press describing how Southern whites victimized and terrorized the freed people with impunity. As Frances Dana Gage commented, "The most startling articles detailing the wrongs done to the Freedmen are extracts from journals read by the millions."[30] President Andrew Johnson pardoned ex-Confederates and returned them to power, where they imposed Black Codes that denied African Americans basic civil rights and failed to extend the franchise. In response, Wendell Phillips tried to arouse the Northern public with a new speech entitled "The South Victorious."[31] Radical Republicans in Congress were soon sparring with President Johnson over civil rights, and the Northern Republican press made the increasing oppression of the freed people one of the major issues of the 1866 elections.[32]

The immediate problem was to protect blacks' civil rights, yet voting rights were unavoidably on the national agenda because emancipation ended the Constitution's three-fifths clause. By counting the ex-slaves as whole people, the ironic result was to *increase* the representation and the power of Southern whites—the same men who had plunged the nation into civil war and whose loyalties were far from secure.[33] With their national majority at stake, Republicans had to do something, and one obvious solution was to enfranchise black men, thereby creating a new, loyal voting bloc in the South.[34] Anticipating this move, Elizabeth Cady Stanton observed in December 1865 that the black man was "in a political point of view, far above the educated women of the country," and she asked, in words designed to appeal to white racism, if black men were to get the vote, should women "stand aside and see 'Sambo' walk into the kingdom first?"[35] Stanton feared that if the "degraded" and "ignorant" freedman went first, women's cause might be set back: "Are we sure that he, once entrenched in all his inalienable rights, may not be an added power to hold us at bay?"[36]

Thus human rights activists in the North began to disagree about suffrage and whether black men ought to go first to the polls. Activists who agreed with Stanton that voting was the right of all citizens, male or female, black or white, formed a new organization, the American Equal Rights Association in May 1866, with some encouragement from Frederick Douglass.[37] But both groups of former abolitionists—Stanton and Anthony's AERA and Wendell Phillips's AASS—were destined for disappointment by the Fourteenth Amendment that emerged from Congress in June 1866.[38] It defined citizens as "all persons born or naturalized" (thus including women and African Americans) and guaranteed citizens "equal protection of the laws" and "due process," but although twentieth-century jurisprudence would make much of the amendment's "equal protection" clause, these promises did not excite much comment at the time and certainly no great radical enthusiasm.[39] Instead, like most legislators and journalists, human rights activists focused on the section that, instead of granting the franchise to African Americans, imposed a representational penalty for *not* doing so. Because the amendment inserted the word "male" into

Faye Dudden

the Constitution, women's rights advocates were dismayed, and advocates for the rights of black men were equally disgusted to find that black voting rights were left unsecured. Wendell Phillips called it "a fatal and total surrender," and Frederick Douglass blasted the contrast between sections one and two: "To tell me that I am an equal American citizen, and, in the same breath, tell me that my right to vote may be constitutionally taken from me by some other equal citizen or citizens, is to tell me that my citizenship is but an empty name."[40] Thus, until 1866, disagreements among Northern activists about radical priorities remained muted and hypothetical. But when the South remained intransigent and rejected the Fourteenth Amendment, Congress imposed a further set of measures, known as "Radical" Reconstruction, including one that required that black men in the South be granted voting rights. This was the development Stanton had anticipated—Congress had enfranchised black men, if only in the Southern states, before women.

Under Radical Reconstruction, Southern black men began to go to the polls and joined with white "scalawags" and carpetbaggers to form a Southern Republican Party where none had been before, and the news coming out of the South began to change. Republican papers, eager to see signs that their policy was working, described black men voting, acting as delegates in constitutional conventions, being elected to office, and holding Union League meetings.[41] "The Negro in the Enjoyment of His Rights" headlined the *Chicago Tribune*.[42] Even conservative Republican papers portrayed calm and hoped that freedmen could defend themselves when armed with the ballot.[43] Soon the Northern mainstream press shifted focus away from the South to Washington, D.C., and the unprecedented drama of a presidential impeachment. Southern outrages continued, but they were less and less covered.[44] Caroline Putnam eventually complained that even the best of the mainstream Northern press had turned away from Southern realities and compiled "a record of vacillating, time-serving, compromising barter of the negro's rights."[45]

In 1867 Northern activists debated the implications of Reconstruction policy. Wendell Phillips sought to push the Northern Republican Party to take a principled stand in favor of black men's right to vote nationwide, since only Southern black men had been covered by the Reconstruction measures.[46] But AERA activists thought that woman suffrage was the next logical move, as Sojourner Truth argued in the AERA convention: "Now colored men have the right to vote, and what I want is to have colored women have the right to vote."[47] In the same speech, Truth described the vote as a remedy for freedwomen who were victimized by husbands who "go about idle, strutting up and down; and when the women come home, they ask for their money and take it all, and then scold because there is no food." The previous winter, after Gage reported that freedwomen were refusing to be legally married, the *Christian Recorder* indignantly denounced the report as a slander on black women, but Gage repeated the charge and Truth's comments now seemed to confirm the nature of the situation.[48] In response, the veteran African American abolitionist Charles Lenox Remond defended the freedmen and predicted that enfranchised black men would "heartily acquiesce in admitting women also to the right of suffrage," while Lucretia

Mott disagreed, saying "the colored men would naturally throw all their strength upon the side of those opposed to woman's enfranchisement."[49] Elizabeth Cady Stanton commented (about black men), "I would not trust him with all my rights; degraded, oppressed himself, he would be more despotic with the governing power than even our Saxon rulers are."[50] But this debate among activists was theoretical because, as Parker Pillsbury observed, "Government is never going to ask us which should enter into citizenship first, the women or the colored men, or whether we prefer one to the other."[51]

The debate became practical in Kansas, which scheduled referenda in November 1867 on both black and woman suffrage. The situation in Kansas looked promising to AERA radicals because it was a new state with a two-to-one Republican majority, a strong radical tradition, and an electorate small enough to be reached by face-to-face "retail politics." Activists needed to mount a vigorous "Vote Yes" campaign for both measures, and they hoped do so by bringing in a corps of charismatic speakers from back East. But Wendell Phillips used his position as a trustee of a bequest to deny the AERA women funds to which they were clearly entitled by the terms of the will. He would not release funds to campaign for woman suffrage, nor even to campaign for black male suffrage in a situation like Kansas, where it would have to "mix" with woman suffrage. Kansas radical Republicans who favored both measures were left underfunded and understaffed, and then outmaneuvered by their local conservative rivals, who spread false reports that black men condemned woman suffrage and white women condemned black suffrage. The conservative politicians and newspapers both attacked woman suffrage and also failed to mount a positive campaign for black suffrage—a fatal move since, as modern political scientists tell us, referenda need vigorous "Vote Yes" efforts to pass. Both measures went down to defeat, and the conservative white men who took control of the Kansas Republican Party were happy to divvy the spoils of office among themselves, unencumbered by women or black people. The flamboyant racist George Francis Train joined Anthony and Stanton to campaign for woman suffrage in Kansas, but he arrived just two weeks before Election Day, too late to affect the results but just in time to confuse the picture.[52]

Woman suffrage agitation had not ruined black men's chances in Kansas, but the state's largest paper, the *Leavenworth Daily Conservative,* put out the story that black suffrage had been defeated by the "side issue" of woman suffrage, and its interpretation of Kansas events was transmitted back East.[53] Wendell Phillips and other old allies, horrified by Train, concluded that Stanton and Anthony had indeed "killed negro suffrage."[54] Stanton and Anthony tried to explain that a faction of the Republican Party had been treacherous, but they could not dislodge the press narrative that made woman suffrage the enemy of black men's voting rights. Thus as activists began to enter into an increasingly hostile dispute about the "lessons" of the Kansas referenda and what they meant about the relationship between black and woman suffrage, they were working from different accounts of what actually happened.[55]

Partisan reporting on the Kansas suffrage referenda was not an isolated problem. In Kansas that same summer, Ohio senator Ben Wade, perhaps the women's most

Faye Dudden

important political ally, suffered a similar press ambush. Wade had been elected president pro tem of the Senate—a significant seat as talk of impeachment heated up—and he was a strong supporter of votes for both black men and for women.[56] In June 1867 Wade gave an impromptu speech in Lawrence, Kansas, and as reported in the *New York Times*, Wade called for the redistribution of wealth.[57] The *Times*, leading the conservative wing of the Republican Party, sandbagged Wade as a wild-eyed radical, and the Democratic press picked up on the story to illustrate Republican perfidy.[58] Wade denied having said any such thing, and the local journalists who were present at the speech supported Wade's denial, but to no avail.[59] There was no stenographic report of the speech, but after a few weeks of the Democratic and conservative Republican press pounding on the story, Wade's "agrarian" remarks were accepted as fact, and Wade was decisively discredited.[60] Ironically, the one part of his speech that all reporters agreed upon was Wade's warm endorsement of woman suffrage.[61] As activists' theoretical disagreements about priorities finally became practical matters and broke out into open sniping in 1867, the warping lens of the mainstream press deepened and complicated resentments and hostilities.

The Power of the Press

The same newspapers that distorted Kansas events were also reporting on the Reconstruction South, and newspapers of the day had little inclination to objective or balanced reporting. On the contrary, they flourished by "slang-whanging" without regard to the facts.[62] As one contemporary journalist remarked coolly, the power of the press consisted "not in its logic or eloquence, but in its ability to manufacture facts, or to give coloring to facts that have occurred."[63] Major papers consolidated their power in the face of rising costs and increased competition with the help of membership in the Associated Press, with its monopoly of telegraphy and thus news that came from a distance.[64] It was important to have press allies, but at this moment reformers and Radical Republicans had lost their only reliable friend among the major New York dailies. Horace Greeley's *New York Tribune* had won its reputation as the most progressive of the great national papers in antebellum days, but Greeley turned against the women's movement, and under the influence of Greeley's postwar political ambitions, the *Tribune* moved away from radicalism. Caroline Putnam and others who were in the South working for the freed people used the pages of the *National Anti-Slavery Standard* to protest bitterly that the *Tribune* was covering up violence and doing them "infinite harm."[65] More accurate reports came from many small Republican papers that had been started all over the Reconstruction South, but they were starved for subscriptions and advertising while their editors faced grave threats, and most quickly disappeared.[66]

Meanwhile, the radical or alternative press stumbled. After the *Liberator* folded, a major effort to replace it went astray. Although former abolitionists invested their hopes and their financial support in the *Nation*, a new weekly journal launched in

July 1865, the editor, E. L. Godkin, hijacked editorial policy and took a conservative stance toward reform.[67] Other sources of Southern news included the freedmen's aid journals, but they too were hard pressed to continue after 1868 or 1869. The radical abolitionist George Luther Stearns began publishing the *Right Way* in 1865 to support black rights in the South, but it ceased publication in April 1867. The *National Anti-Slavery Standard* did its best to spread the word of Southern "outrages," but it could not afford to send its own reporters, and it found less and less Southern news to reprint from the mainstream press. By 1869 the *Standard* had grown noticeably thinner and more dependent on letters from individuals.

On the other end of the political spectrum, Manton Marble took over the *New York World* and built circulation by making the paper clever, lively, and readable. But Marble was a cunning partisan and a relentless racist, a Democrat who attacked radicalism on all fronts.[68] Following Marble's lead, Northern Democratic papers fabricated a Southern narrative in which "outrages" were all committed by black people. On one particularly busy day, August 7, 1868, a single page of the *World* carried articles with the following headlines: "The Texas Negro Insurrection," "Negro Riot in Mobile—Street Cars Seized by Black Radicals," "Negro Riot in Macon—Murderous Assault on a White Cripple—White Radicals Instigate the Riot," "Tragedy in Mississippi—A Man Shot Down in the midst of his Family—The Assassination Instigated by the Loyal League." The *World*'s racism was particularly egregious, but according to a *National Anti-Slavery Standard* correspondent, "Dozens of Democratic sheets" that followed its leadership "teem with perverted accounts varnishing over the disorders and atrocities constantly occurring."[69]

Woman suffrage activists in the North understood that press coverage was becoming an increasingly severe problem for their own movement. "We have decidedly lost [ground] in connection with the daily press," declared Boston activist Caroline Dall in 1866.[70] Susan B. Anthony confronted a *Tribune* editor when she could not get the paper to run a call for an AERA meeting, telling him, "A good wholesome abuse by acknowledged enemies is a thousand times more desirable than this *chilling letting alone of professed friends.*"[71] Mary Livermore complained that New York papers reported AERA members to have said "what they did not say."[72] Lucretia Mott was distressed by the *Nation*'s "base" and "hateful" comments about the women's movement.[73] These sorts of concerns led Stanton and Anthony to start their own newspaper, the *Revolution,* in 1868, but Stanton and Anthony's *Revolution* provided little corrective information about the situation in the South. Unable to pay reporters to travel south, they mostly printed the letters they received. In the first issue they noted that "black men [are] already at the ballot box, exercising the right of suffrage, in constitutional conventions, framing the fundamental laws of states, in courts of justice, pleading at the bar, and sitting in the jury-box."[74] But they ran no coverage about how these nominal rights were threatened in practice by violence and intimidation. When Edmonia Highgate, an African American teacher from Upstate New York, paid a call at their offices, the *Revolution* reported what she told them about her experience as a teacher in Mississippi: Highgate said the freedmen themselves generally supported woman suffrage; it was their leaders who were opposed.[75] And when Parker Pillsbury traveled south to visit his brother in South Carolina, they carried his letter as well.[76] But this sort of reporting was episodic and fragmentary, and it certainly had little impact on Stanton, who editorialized, "We have no reason to suppose that the black man understands the principles of equity, or will practice the Christian virtues better than his Saxon masters," and concluded that "educated women first, and ignorant men afterwards."[77] Thus Stanton moved away from an embrace of equal rights for all, and saw black men in the South as empowered, not endangered.

African American women, who had less reason to trust the mainstream press, so habitual was its misrepresentation of black women, could benefit from the freedmen's aid pipeline of information longer than whites had done. The black press expanded in this period and gave coverage to Southern events that probably escaped the attention of Northern whites, including black women's political presence.[78] For example, Louisa Rollin spoke in favor of universal suffrage on the floor of the South Carolina House of Representatives.[79] As Elsa Barkley Brown has shown, freedwomen showed extraordinary engagement in the political life of the community of freed people.[80] This suggested to some activists that, if enfranchised, black women would be more apt to go to the polls than white women, and thus woman suffrage could help to secure black power. Therefore it made sense when black activist John Willis Menard argued that "they had but one voice in the South, and that was to know no distinctions of color or sex. Unless they concentrated their power they would never attain to any political power."[81] Of course, other Southern black men chose to eschew woman suffrage and even to interpret voting rights as male privilege.[82] Thus even if Northern black women were better informed about the South, the Southern black community did not speak with one voice, as splits opened along lines of class, color, and pre-emancipation status.[83] And little of this was reflected in the press narratives being developed in the mainstream Northern newspapers that catered to white audiences.

THE MYTH OF THE BLACK RAPIST

1868 was a presidential election year, and news out of the South had powerful implications for national affairs. As the presidential campaign heated up in the late summer of 1868, Manton Marble's *New York World* cooked up an especially pernicious disinformation campaign. He had long reported that a massive wave of "negro outrages" was sweeping the South, purportedly the work of black rioters, thieves, thugs, arsonists, and assassins, but in mid September 1868 a new type of black criminal appeared in the pages of the *New York World*: black rapists suddenly became prominent.[84] Many of the alleged rapes happened in the North, but no matter, editor Marble drew the connection anyway, and warned soberly of a supposed upsurge in these rapes:

> Since this devilish work began of stimulating the southern negroes into envy, hatred, and jealousy of their former masters, negro outrages upon whites at the

North also have been enormously more frequent than of old. This is especially true of the worst form of such outrages. Scarcely a week has passed since the spring began that the public press has not been called upon to chronicle one or more instances of hideous outrage perpetrated upon white women in lonely places by negro scoundrels.[85]

The trope of the black rapist had not been commonly invoked in antebellum times but became prominent after the war and eventually would become white Southerners' key excuse for lynching.[86] Stanton read the *World* regularly, since it was the only major New York daily that gave extensive or favorable coverage to the women's rights movement, and she soon showed she had been influenced by the *World*'s disinformation campaign when she repeated a *New York World* report on a black-on-white rape.[87] And she urged every woman in the country to read Democratic vice-presidential candidate Frank Blair's Indianapolis speech in the *World*, "showing most clearly and conclusively what is to be the fate of American women under the radical policy of manhood suffrage."[88] Blair's speech echoed the *World*'s line, arguing that, with the vote, black men would impose a "despotism of bestial passions." Would not black men who could vote, Blair asked, "use that power to the worst extremity that their passions may suggest toward the softer sex?"[89] Stanton seized upon a passage in Blair's speech where he appeared to endorse woman suffrage, though he did so only by way of scoring points against radicals. Eager to accept the seeming endorsement, she apparently bought in to the accompanying premises about rape. The original AERA idea of simultaneous rights for all was losing out to fears of a mythic black rapist.

The Democratic ticket of Horatio Seymour and Blair lost the 1868 election, but Ulysses S. Grant's margin of victory was so thin that Republicans were prompted to draw up a Fifteenth Amendment. Radical Republicans who had long favored black male suffrage on principle were now joined by party hacks who conceded the necessity of protecting black men's right to vote in the South, and extending their right to vote in the North, where it was still illegal in many states. The Fifteenth Amendment that emerged from Congress in February 1869 forbade states to deny the right to vote on grounds of race. Wendell Phillips praised the amendment as "the grandest and most Christian act ever contemplated or accomplished by any nation" and urged AASS members to mobilize for its ratification.[90] But stung by unfair criticism from former allies and poisoned by false information about the South, Stanton refused. She slammed the "unwashed and unlettered ditch-diggers, bootblacks, hostlers, butchers, and barbers" who would precede women and cried, "Think of Patrick and Sambo and Hans and Yung Tung" making laws for educated, refined women.[91] Stanton proceeded to repeat Blair's argument and make it her own. She claimed that the Republican cry of manhood suffrage created an "antagonism between the negro and the woman" in the South and predicted that the Republican policy of enfranchising black men would "culminate in fearful outrages on womanhood especially in the southern states."[92]

This appalling rhetoric shattered the AERA. At its final, stormy meeting in May 1869, Stanton led off with a lengthy speech that began by deploring the Fifteenth

Amendment and included a nasty crack about the "African" from the Southern plantations "in whose eyes woman is simply the being of man's lust." "Manhood suffrage is national suicide and woman's destruction," she warned.[93] Frederick Douglass disagreed and made Klan violence in the South the fulcrum of his argument. He asked how anyone could claim that woman suffrage had the same urgency as black suffrage. "When women, because they are women, are hunted down . . . when they are dragged from their houses and hung upon lamp posts," only then, Douglass declared, will women "have an urgency to obtain the ballot equal to our own."[94] Even in making this case, Douglass's language testified to the difficulty of seeing the South clearly from a distance, since the image of black people being hung from *lampposts* owed more to the New York City draft riots than to the Reconstruction South.

Efforts were made to discredit the rape charges: black legislators James M. Simms and H. M. Turner made their way from Georgia to New York and wrote public letters to explain that "rape is invariably charged upon every colored man who is shot or hung for his politics . . . these men have all been brutally slaughtered because they dared to be Republicans."[95] But the charge of rape had staying power, at least until Ida B. Wells examined the evidence and demolished the story decades later.[96] As a speaker at the AASS meeting in May 1869 commented, the Radical Republican press was not interested in investigating and only bothered to publish reports of Southern "murders and outrages" on the eve of elections, to "wave the bloody shirt" in order to gain votes.[97] The *National Anti-Slavery Standard* continued to alert its readers to Southern conditions and warned of warped coverage in mainstream sources, as when it headlined, "One of the Worst Enemies the Colored and White Loyalists of the South Have to Contend with is the Associated Press."[98] But the *Standard* itself ceased to publish in early 1870, prompting Caroline Putnam to tell a friend, "I could weep and wail to have the *Standard* stop now!"[99]

As Lori Ginzberg comments, Northerners lost interest in the former slaves "astonishingly soon" after the war.[100] Perhaps their declining interest can in part be explained by the mainstream press's negative coverage of Reconstruction. The major metropolitan papers in the North had less and less sympathy for the freed people after 1867, and Democratic papers traded in disinformation and fabricated tales in which blacks were perpetrators, not victims. As Elizabeth Smith observes, newspaper reporting that associated criminality with blackness was "a way to beleaguer the entire Reconstruction enterprise." Competing narratives about the South created a situation in which, despite massive public testimony documenting Ku Klux Klan violence, Northerners as a whole remained unsure about whether the Klan actually existed.[101] As parts of the South were "redeemed," white supremacists took control of more and more Southern newspapers, which put them in a position to feed biased reports to the nation at large via the AP.[102] Northern Democratic papers could then piously explain, "The established press of the South contradicts these reports [of outrages against negroes] and flames with accounts of gross crimes committed by blacks against whites."[103] Soon the *New York Tribune*—a Republican paper with a supposed sympathy for reform and human rights—would be telling its readers that at the end of the war, freed slaves refused to work and as a result, died of starvation by the thousands; that whites generally were kind to blacks, whereas blacks were "insolent" and "provoking in conduct"; that cotton planting failed to pay simply because blacks stole one-fourth of the crop and every pig or chicken they could lay their hands on; that the Alabama legislature of 1868 was almost entirely composed of "illiterate black or white thieves and murderers", etc.[104]

Meanwhile, the alternative press continued to shrink and stumble. As Stanton and Anthony's *Revolution* failed, Lucy Stone's *Woman's Journal* started from a basis of support for the Fifteenth Amendment, but it also began in January 1870 with an editorial stating that race was an inappropriate topic for discussion in its pages.[105] And while the *Woman's Journal* often printed items from all over the country under the heading "Concerning Women," the South was distinctly underrepresented. One of the few items referencing the South in the *Woman's Journal*'s first year of publication described a New York City organization designed to assist Southern women who came north to be educated or to work.[106]

African American newspapers and speakers who circulated through black church and community groups in the North probably provided the most accurate Southern news, but very few Northern whites were alert or open to these sources.[107] Frances E. W. Harper worked tirelessly to speak across the color line, addressing both black and white audiences. She also used fiction and poetry to dramatize the issues at stake and draw her readers into the realities of the freed people's experiences. In her novel, *Minnie's Sacrifice,* Harper's heroine speaks eloquently about how black women and men both need the vote to defend themselves, and ultimately Minnie is murdered by the Klan. Harper's poem "Appeal to the American People" warned that "the traitor" South was still subtly battling the North by oppressing the freed people: "Asking you to weakly yield / All we won upon the field."[108] In "Aunt Chloe" Harper assumed the voice of a Southern black woman who acted as an enforcer, forbidding men from selling their votes. The ex-Confederates might have prevailed at the polls, Aunt Chloe declares, "Had not we women radicals / Just got right in the way."[109]

During Reconstruction, white woman's suffrage activists in the North had little direct communication with the South, and they bought into disinformation spread by bigoted Northern journalists. Northern black women almost certainly understood the Southern situation better, relying upon sources within the black community, but they were far fewer in number and had a broader agenda—focused not only on the right to vote but also on Southern education, public accommodations, social uplift, and the organization of the black church. Try as they might, and Frances Harper made a determined effort, they could not correct the false narratives that had captured the press and their white peers.

As Mark Wahlgren Summers argues, Northern journalism bears "a heavy responsibility for the [Northern white] loss of faith in the Reconstruction experiment in general and the Negro voter in particular."[110] False reports in the Northern press also inflicted collateral damage among Northern woman suffrage activists, who could not agree on strategy in part because they could not agree on what was happening. The striking fact about Northern white women during Reconstruction—even radical suffrage activists who were presumably interested in the fate of the former slaves—was how little they knew, and how much of what they "knew" was actually false.

NOTES

1. See Carol Turbin, *Working Women of Collar City: Gender, Class and Community in Troy, New York, 1864–86* (Urbana, Ill.: Univ. of Illinois Press, 1992); Karen J. Blair, *The Clubwoman as Feminist: True Womanhood Redefined, 1868–1914* (New York: Holmes & Meier, 1980); Ruth Bordin, *Woman and Temperance: The Quest for Power and Liberty, 1873–1900* (Philadelphia: Temple Univ. Press, 1981); Barbara Miller Solomon, *In the Company of Educated Women: A History of Women and Higher Education in America* (New Haven, Conn.: Yale Univ. Press, 1985). These and other Reconstruction era developments are ably summarized in Mari Jo Buhle, Teresa Murphy, and Jane Gerhard, *Women and the Making of America* (Upper Saddle River, N.J.: Pearson, 2009), chap. 10.

2. Of course the term "feminist" is anachronistic when applied to the nineteenth century, but it is a useful shorthand.

3. The best single source is Carol Faulkner, *Women's Radical Reconstruction: The Freedmen's Aid Movement* (Philadelphia: Univ. of Pennsylvania Press, 2004). See also Ronald E. Butchart, *Northern Schools, Southern Blacks, and Reconstruction: Freedmen's Education, 1862–1875* (Westport, Conn.: Greenwood Press, 1980); Jacqueline Jones, *Soldiers of Light and Love: Northern Teachers and Georgia Blacks, 1865–1873* (Athens: Univ. of Georgia Press, 1980); Robert C. Morris, *Reading, 'Riting and Reconstruction: The Education of Freedmen in the South, 1861–1870* (Chicago: Univ. of Chicago Press, 1981); Clara Merritt DeBoer, *His Truth is Marching On: African Americans Who Taught the Freedmen for the American Missionary Association, 1861–1877* (New York: Garland, 1995).

4. Lori D. Ginzberg, *Women and the Work of Benevolence: Morality, Politics, and Class in the Nineteenth-Century United States* (New Haven, Conn.: Yale Univ. Press, 1990); Judith Ann Giesberg, *Civil War Sisterhood: The U.S. Sanitary Commission and Women's Politics in Transition* (Boston: Northeastern Univ. Press, 2000); Jeanie Attie, *Patriotic Toil: Northern Women and the American Civil War* (Ithaca, N.Y.: Cornell Univ. Press, 1998). Historians disagree about the long-term impact of women's work in soldiers' aid: women apparently achieved some authority in branch work, or in locally based activities, including the Sanitary Fairs.

5. Willie Lee Rose, *Rehearsal for Reconstruction: The Port Royal Experiment* (New York: Oxford Univ. Press, 1964); Faulkner, *Women's Radical Reconstruction.*

6. Lucy Chase to Dear Ones at Home, Apr. 1, 1863, in Henry Lee Swint, ed., *Dear Ones at Home: Letters from the Contraband Camps* (Nashville: Vanderbilt Univ. Press, 1966), 67.

7. James M. McPherson, *The Struggle for Equality* (Princeton, N.J.: Princeton Univ. Press, 1964), chaps. 7 and 17 generally, 394 and 440, on the journals published by the freedmen's aid groups, where letters were often run.

8. McPherson, *Struggle for Equality,* 172–74.

9. The number of hits in a search of the *America's Historical Newspapers* database for the combination of "freedmen" and "teachers" declined from 651 items in 1866 to 155 in 1868, and to 67 in 1871. McPherson, *Struggle for Equality,* 402–4.

10. McPherson, *Struggle for Equality,* chap. 17; "American Missionary Association, Financial Appeal," *Boston Recorder,* Aug. 19, 1869; "American Missionary Association," *Lowell* (Mass.) *Daily Citizen and News,* May 12, 1869, 1.

11. Butchart, *Northern Schools*, 23–24.

12. Ibid., 22.

13. Qtd. in ibid., 31.

14. Lucretia Coffin Mott to Martha C. Wright and Anna Temple Brown, Apr. 10, 1865, and LCM to James Miller McKim, c. Apr. 15, 1866, in Beverly Wilson Palmer, ed., *Selected Letters of Lucretia Coffin Mott* (Urbana: Univ. of Illinois Press, 2002), 357, 370.

15. Caroline F. Putnam, "The National Situation," *National Anti-Slavery Standard*, Jan. 4, 1868 (hereafter cited as *NASS*). On Putnam, see Faulkner, *Women's Radical Reconstruction*, 36–41.

16. Martha S. Jones, *All Bound Up Together: The Woman Question in African American Public Culture, 1830–1900* (Chapel Hill: Univ. of North Carolina Press, 2007), 133–34; Jones, *Soldiers of Light*, app. B, re AMA teachers in one state, Georgia. .

17. "Christian Fellowship and the Duties of the Hour," *Christian Recorder*, July 27, 1867. These were the Methodist Church South, the Methodist Church North, the AME Church, and the Zion Church.

18. Jones, *All Bound Up Together*, chaps. 1–4.

19. Ibid., 121.

20. Truth qtd. in Dorothy Sterling, ed., *We Are Your Sisters: Black Women in the Nineteenth Century* (New York: W. W. Norton, 1984), 253.

21. Jones, *Soldiers of Light*, 65, 70; Ronald E. Butchart, *Schooling the Freedpeople: Teaching, Learning, and the Struggle for Black Freedom, 1861–1876* (Chapel Hill: Univ. of North Carolina Press, 2010), app. A, table 5-A; Sterling, ed., *We Are Your Sisters*, chap. 16.

22. See Frances Smith Foster, ed., *A Brighter Coming Day: A Frances Ellen Watkins Reader* (New York: Feminist Press, 1990); Farah Jasmine Griffin, "Frances Ellen Watkins Harper in the Reconstruction South," *Sage: A Scholarly Journal on Black Women* (Suppl. 1988): 45–47.

23. "Letter from Mrs. Gage," *NASS*, Nov. 25, 1865. In this same letter Gage complained that the "great advocates of human equality," including Phillips and Garrison, had ceased to speak about women's rights: "Who ever hears of sex now from any of these champions of freedom?"

24. "Twenty-Ninth Annual Meeting of the Pennsylvania Anti-Slavery Society," *NASS*, Dec. 8, 1866.

25. "Remarks of Miss Anthony," *NASS*, Dec. 1, 1866.

26. Amy Dru Stanley, *From Bondage to Contract: Wage Labor, Marriage, and the Market in the Age of Slave Emancipation* (Cambridge: Cambridge Univ. Press, 1998), chaps. 1 and 5.

27. "Communications from Our Correspondent. F. E. W. Harper," *Christian Recorder*, Dec. 24, 1870.

28. "Thirty-Second Anniversary of the American Anti-Slavery Society," *NASS*, May 13 and May 20, 1865; McPherson, *Struggle for Equality*, 287–307.

29. "Thirty-Second Anniversary of the American Anti-Slavery Society" *NASS*, May 13, 1865. Ellen Carol DuBois, *Feminism and Suffrage: The Emergence of an Independent Women's Movement in America, 1848–1869* (Ithaca, N.Y.: Cornell Univ. Press, 1978), 60, notes that Phillips's "unprovoked" announcement shows how "obvious and compelling" the connection between black suffrage and woman suffrage seemed.

30. FDG, "Signs of the Times," *NASS*, 19 Aug. 1865. She mentioned "the Tribune, Times, Herald, Cincinnati Commercial and Gazette, St. Louis Democrat, Chicago Tribune and others of this ilk"—i.e., Northern Republican papers.

31. McPherson, *Struggle for Equality*, 332, 335.

32. Ibid., 358.

33. On "slave seats," the operation of this clause, and the implications of its having been voided by the Thirteenth Amendment, see Garrett Epps, *Democracy Reborn: The Fourteenth*

Amendment and the Fight for Civil Rights in Post-Civil War America (New York: Henry Holt, 2006), 56–59.

34. "Letter from Robert Dale Owen. Negro Suffrage and Representative Population," *Liberator,* July 7, 1865; *Nation* 1 (July 6, 1865).

35. ECS, "This Is the Negro's Hour," *NASS,* Dec. 26, 1865, in Ann D. Gordon, ed., *The Selected Papers of Elizabeth Cady Stanton and Susan B. Anthony,* vol 1., *In the School of Anti-Slavery* (New Brunswick, N.J.: Rutgers Univ. Press, 1997), 564–66.

36. ECS, "This Is the Negro's Hour," in Gordon, ed., *Selected Papers,* 1:564–66.

37. According to Stanton, Frederick Douglass agreed that " the time has come to bury the woman and the negro in the citizen." ECS to Wendell Phillips, Feb. 10, [1866], in Patricia D. Holland and Ann D. Gordon, eds., *Papers of Elizabeth Cady Stanton and Susan B. Anthony* (Wilmington Del.: Scholarly Resources, 1991), reel 11, frames 343–44 (hereafter *Papers of ECS and SBA*).

38. See my *Fighting Chance: The Struggle over Woman Suffrage and Black Suffrage in Reconstruction America* (New York: Oxford Univ. Press, 2011), 73–80.

39. Differing accounts, all of which indicate limited debate over section one, are found in Epps, *Democracy Reborn,* 225–39; Eric L. McKitrick, *Andrew Johnson and Reconstruction* (Chicago: Univ. of Chicago Press, 1960), chap. 11; Joseph B. James, *The Framing of the Fourteenth Amendment* (Urbana: Univ. of Illinois Press, 1956) , 124–31, 142–50; Michael Les Benedict, *A Compromise of Principle: Congressional Republicans and Reconstruction, 1863–1869* (New York: W. W. Norton, 1974), 169–86. Section one seemed only to reiterate provisions of the Civil Rights bill that Congress had just passed.

40. Phillips and Douglass, as qtd. in McPherson, *Struggle for Equality,* 354–55.

41. See, e.g., "The Loyal Doings of Reconstructed Rebels. Old Pro-Slavery Prejudices Going Under," *Chicago Tribune,* Apr. 5, 1867; "The Free South," *Chicago Tribune,* Apr. 23, 1867; "Negro Candidates for Congress," *Chicago Tribune,* Sept. 5, 1867.

42. The Free South," *Chicago Tribune,* Apr. 23, 1867.

43. "The Negro and His Prospects," *New York Times,* Apr. 21, 1867; "Conditions of the South," *New York Times,* Aug. 27, 1867.

44. Charles E. Moss, "Virginia Correspondence," *NASS,* Jan. 4, 1868, concludes, "The people of the loyal North do not and cannot truly appreciate the state of affairs existing in the rebellious states the past two or three years." The *NASS* found less to reprint and had increasingly to rely on private correspondence, sometimes withholding the writer's name "for prudential reasons."

45. Caroline F. Putnam, "The National Situation," *NASS,* Jan. 4, 1868.

46. "The President Impeached!" *NASS,* Feb. 29, 1868; "Impeachment," *NASS,* May 16, 1868.

47. "Proceedings of the First Anniversary of the American Equal Rights Association, May 9 and 10, 1867," 20–21, in *Papers of ECS and SBA,* 12:164.

48. "29th Annual Meeting of the Pennsylvania Anti-Slavery Society," *NASS,* Dec. 8, 1866, 1; "Our Boston Correspondent," *NASS,* Feb. 16, 1867; "Proceedings of the First Anniversary of the American Equal Rights Association, held at the Church of the Puritans, New York, May 9 and 10, 1867" (New York, 1867), in *Papers of ECS and SBA,* 12:167.

49. "Proceedings of the First Anniversary of the AERA, 1867," 53, in *Papers of ECS and SBA,* 12:180.

50. Ibid.

51. Ibid., 61, in *Papers of ECS and SBA,* 12:184.

52. Dudden, *Fighting Chance,* chap. 5.

53. "The West," *Leavenworth* (Kansas) *Daily Conservative,* Nov. 9, 1867; "Oh Yes," *Leavenworth Daily Conservative,* Nov. 12, 1867.

54. Elizabeth Cady Stanton, Susan B. Anthony, and Matilda Joslyn Gage, eds., *History of Woman Suffrage* (Rochester, N.Y.: Charles Mann, 1881), 2:265. In January 1868 Anthony reported that Senator Thayer of Nebraska "said we had killed the negro question in Kansas." "Woman Suffrage at Rahway, N.J.," *Revolution* (New York), Jan. 8, 1868, 3. Horace Greeley even extended the blame to Lucy Stone: "I have always felt that Miss Anthony, Lucy Stone and Mrs. Stanton defeated negro suffrage in Kansas." "Horace Greeley," *Revolution*, Sept. 9, 1869, 152–53.

55. Dudden, *Fighting Chance*, 134–38.

56. *American National Biography Online*, sv. Wade, Benjamin, http:/www.anb.org.

57. "The Union Pacific Railroad. The Senatorial Excursion Party—Speech of Senator Wade," *New York Times*, June 11, 1867, 5.

58. Untitled, *Boston Post*, June 13, 1867, 1; "Agrarianism at Last," *Boston Post*, June 19, 1867, 1.

59. "Another Excursion Party. Speech by Hon. B.F. Wade," *Lawrence* (Kans.) *Daily Tribune*, June 11, 1867; "From the Senatorial Excursion," *Leavenworth Daily Conservative*, June 13, 1867; "Ben Wade's Lawrence Speech," ibid., July 3, 1867.

60. Compare "The Radical Tenets," *Boston Post*, June 21, 1867, 1, "It is to be regretted that a stenographic report could not have been made"; and [untitled], *Boston Post*, July 1, 1867, 1:. "Cunning politicians are trying to drag Senator Wade out of his agrarian swamp, and have sent correspondents to him to persuade him that he didn't say what he did. But it is too late for the Senator to deny the sentiments of his heart and utterance . . . so specific are the statements in the report of his speech."

61. Accepting the *Times* version is William Zornow, "'Bluff Ben' Wade in Lawrence, Kansas: The Issue of Class Conflict," *Ohio Historical Quarterly* 66 (Jan. 1956): 44–52. Eric Foner indicates that the *New York Times* "lambasted the Radicals for desiring 'a war on property . . . to succeed the war on Slavery,' and the *Nation* linked Wade's speech with the confiscation issue." See Eric Foner, *Reconstruction: America's Unfinished Revolution, 1863–1877* (New York: Harper & Row, 1988), 309–10.

62. On the power of the press in this period, see Mark Wahlgren Summers, *The Press Gang: Newspapers and Politics, 1865–1878* (Chapel Hill: Univ. of North Carolina Press, 1994); "slang-whanging," in Henry Meyer, *All on Fire: William Lloyd Garrison and the Abolition of Slavery* (New York: St. Martin's Press, 1998), 40.

63. John W. Forney, *Anecdotes of Public Men* (New York: Harper Bros., 1874) 1:383, as cited in William E. Gienapp, "'Politics Seem to Enter into Everything,'" in Stephen E. Maizlish and John J. Kushma, eds., *Essays on American Antebellum Politics, 1840–1860* (College Station: Texas A & M Univ. Press, 1982), 41.

64. James G. Smart, "Information Control, Thought Control: Whitelaw Reid and the Nation's News Services," *Public Historian* 3 (Spring 1981): 23–42; Summers, *Press Gang*, chaps. 12 and 13. Also useful on the press of the period: William E. Huntziker, *The Popular Press, 1833–1865* (Westport, Conn.: Greenwood Press, 1999); and Gerald Baldasty, *The Commercialization of News in the Nineteenth Century* (Madison: Univ. of Wisconsin Press, 1992).

65. Caroline Putnam, "Affairs in Virginia," *NASS*, Aug. 28, 1869; "A Gentleman Not Unknown in the Nation," *NASS*, Sept. 18, 1869; "The South—Tendencies," *NASS*, July 31, 1869; Parker Pillsbury, "Deceitfulness of the Press," *Revolution*, Apr. 9 1868, 211.

66. Richard H. Abbott, "Republican Newspapers and Freedom of the Press in the Reconstruction South, 1865–1877," in David B. Sachsman, S. Kittrell Rushing, and Debra Reddin van Tuyl, eds., *The Civil War and the Press* (New Brunswick, N.J.: Transaction, 2000), 473–84.

67. "Home Notes," *Commonwealth*, May 13, 1865; *NASS*, June 3, 1865; "The Nation," *Commonwealth*, Feb. 17, 1866, 2; McPherson, *Struggle for Equality*, 323–25.

68. George T. McJimsey, *Genteel Partisan: Manton Marble, 1834–1917* (Ames, Iowa: Iowa State Univ. Press, 1971).

69. "Texas," *NASS*, Aug. 14, 1869.

70. Caroline Dall, "Report Made to the Eleventh National Woman's Rights Convention," 65, in *Papers of ECS and SBA*, 11:507.

71. SBA to John Russell Young, Nov. 16, 1866, in *Papers of ECS and SBA*, 11:645–47.

72. "Battling for the Ballot," *New York World*, May 14, 1869, in *Papers of ECS and SBA*, 13:507.

73. Faulkner, *Women's Radical Reconstruction*, 203.

74. "Are We a Slaveholding Nation?" *Revolution*, Jan. 8, 1868, 9.

75. "Edmonia G. Highgate," and "Woman's Suffrage Meeting," *Revolution*, Oct. 7, 1869, 218, 219.

76. Parker Pillsbury, "South Carolina," *Revolution*, Oct. 14, 1869, 225–26; Stacey M. Robertson, *Parker Pillsbury: Radical Abolitionist, Male Feminist* (Ithaca, N.Y.: Cornell Univ. Press, 2000), 148. Pillsbury's letter was misinterpreted by the Democratic press, and most of the Republican papers as well, leading him to protest the misrepresentation. LCM to Martha C. Wright, Apr. 7, 1870, in Palmer, ed., *Selected Letters of Lucretia Coffin Mott*, 439.

77. ECS, "Sharp Points," *Revolution*, Apr. 9 1868, 212.

78. Steven Hahn, *A Nation Under Our Feet: Black Political Struggles in the Rural South from Slavery to the Great Migration* (Cambridge, Mass.: Harvard Univ. Press, 2003), 325–26; Penn I. Garland, *The Afro-American Press and Its Editors* (Springfield, Mass.: Wiley, 1891), 104–15; Armistead S. Pride and Clint C. Wilson II, eds., *A History of the Black Press* (Washington, D.C.: Howard Univ. Press, 1997), chap. 9.

79. Roslyn Terborg-Penn, "Nineteenth Century Black Women and Woman Suffrage," *Potomac Review* 7 (1977): 16. "Personal," *NASS*, July 31, 1869, reports Rollin was appointed chief clerk in the Adjutant General's office; and "Woman's Rights in South Carolina," *Revolution*, Apr. 29, 1869, 268, reported that "a colored woman spoke very ably" before the legislature but did not name her. On the "celebrated Rollin sisters," see Sterling, ed., *We Are Your Sisters*, 365–69; Lerone Bennett, Jr., *Black Power U.S.A.: The Human Side of Reconstruction* (Baltimore: Penguin Books, 1969), 347–53.

80. Elsa Barkley Brown, "Negotiating and Transforming the Public Sphere," *Public Culture* 7 (1994): 107–46. Earlier scholarship also contained scattered mention of the freedwomen's political activism, e.g., Thomas Holt, *Black Over White: Negro Political Leadership in South Carolina During Reconstruction* (Urbana: Univ. of Illinois Press, 1977), 34–35; and Benjamin Quarles, "Frederick Douglass and the Woman's Rights Movement," *Journal of Negro History* 25 (Jan. 1940): 35.

81. See Philip S. Foner and George E. Walker, eds., *Proceedings of the Black State Conventions, 1840–1865* (Philadelphia: Temple Univ. Press, 1979), 367.

82. Hahn, *A Nation Under Our Feet*, 212–14, infers a consensus among black men on woman suffrage from the fact that it was nowhere enacted in the Reconstruction South. But Roslyn Terborg-Penn notes that, although black men were widely described as opposed to woman suffrage, her research did not turn up many of the "anti-woman's rights speeches or newspaper articles black men had been accused of writing." Roslyn Terborg-Penn, "African American Women and the Vote: An Overview," in Ann D. Gordon and Bettye Collier-Thomas, eds., *African American Women and the Vote, 1837–1965* (Amherst: Univ. of Massachusetts Press, 1997), 12.

83. Holt, *Black Over White*, discusses the political results of these divisions among blacks, which were fatal to Republican control despite South Carolina's black majority. Cf. Hahn, *A Nation Under Our Feet*, 261 and passim; Michael W. Fitzgerald, "Reconstruction Politics and the Politics of Reconstruction," in Thomas J. Brown, ed., *Reconstructions: New Perspectives on the Postbellum United States*(New York: Oxford Univ. Press, 2006), 111–14.

84. George C. Rable, *But There Was No Peace: The Role of Violence in the Politics of Reconstruction* (Athens: Univ. of Georgia Press, 1984), 71. *New York World*, Sept. 10, 15, 16, 17, 1868.

85. Untitled editorial, *New York World*, Sept. 25, 1868, 4.

86. Historians agree that the trope of the black rapist became more common after the Civil War, although the attribution of uncontrolled sexuality to black men dates to the eighteenth century at least. Winthrop Jordan, *White Over Black: American Attitudes Toward the Negro, 1550–1812* (Chapel Hill: Univ. of North Carolina Press, 1968), 473; Peter W. Bardaglio, "Rape and the Law in the Old South: 'Calculated to Excite Indignation in Every Heart,'" *Journal of Southern History* 60 (Nov. 1994): 749–72; Martha Hodes, "Wartime Dialogues on Illicit Sex: White Women and Black Men," in Catherine Clinton and Nina Silber, eds., *Divided Houses: Gender and the Civil War* (New York: Oxford Univ. Press, 1992), 240–41; Martha Hodes, "The Sexualization of Reconstruction Politics: White Women and Black Men in the South After the Civil War," *Journal of the History of Sexuality* 3 (Jan. 1993): 402–17; Diane Miller Somerville, "The Rape Myth in the Old South Reconsidered," *Journal of Southern History* 61 (Aug. 1995): 481–518. Frederick Douglass condemned the rape charge as an invention to justify violence against the freed people in "Why Is the Negro Lynched?" (1894), in Philip S. Foner, *The Life and Writings of Frederick Douglass*, vol. 4, *Reconstruction and After* (New York: International Publishers, 1955), 501–2. W. E. B. DuBois and Ida B. Wells both analyzed the cynicism and functionality of the black-on-white rape charge as a means of race control in "The Reason Why the Colored American is Not in the World's Columbian Exposition," in Trudier Harris, ed., *Selected Works of Ida B. Wells-Barnett* (New York: Oxford Univ. Press, 1991), 56, 74.

87. "Outrage by a Negro in Tennessee," *New York World*, Jan. 13, 1869; "Woman's Protectors," *Revolution*, Jan. 21, 1869.

88. ECS, "Frank Blair on Woman's Suffrage," *Revolution*, Oct. 1, 1868, 200. Stanton referred her readers to the *New York World* of Sept. 26, 1868, which carried the speech in full. The *Revolution* again recommended Blair's speech in "Frank Blair on Woman's Suffrage," *Revolution*, Oct. 15, 1868, 235.

89. "The Indiana Canvass," *New York World*, Sept. 26, 1868, 1.

90. "The Constitutional Amendment," *NASS*, Mar. 20, 1869.

91. "Manhood Suffrage," *Revolution*, Dec. 24, 1868, 392–93, in Gordon, ed., *Selected Papers*, 2:194–98.

92. "The Washington Convention," *Revolution*, Jan. 28, 1869, 56–57; *Washington, DC Daily Morning Chronicle*, Jan. 21, 1869, in *Papers of ECS and SBA*, 13:281; ECS, "Women and Black Men," *Revolution*, Feb. 4, 1869, 88.

93. "Anniversary of the American Equal Rights Association. Address of Elizabeth Cady Stanton," *Revolution*, May 13, 1869, 292; "Women of the Period," *New York World*, May 13, 1869, in *Papers of ECS and SBA*, 13:502.

94. "Women of the Period," *New York World*, May 13, 1869, in *Papers of ECS and SBA*, 13:504.

95. "Affairs in Georgia," *NASS*, May 22, 1869, also published in the *New York Tribune*.

96. The best source is Paula J. Giddings, *Ida, A Sword Among Lions: Ida B. Wells and the Campaign Against Lynching* (New York: HarperCollins, 2008).

97. "Thirty Sixth Anniversary of the American Anti Slavery Society," *NASS*, May 29, 1869; "Speech of Aaron M. Powell," *NASS*, June 5, 1869.

98. "One of the Worst Enemies the Colored and White Loyalists of the South Have to Contend with Is the Associated Press," *NASS*, Aug. 21, 1869; "A Virginia Correspondent," *NASS*, Sept. 18, 1869.

99. "Miss Caroline Putnam . . . to Miss Holley," *NASS*, Mar. 12, 1870.

100. Ginzberg, *Women and the Work of Benevolence*, 179.

101. Elaine Frantz Parsons, "Klan Skepticism and Denial in Reconstruction—Era Public Discourse," *Journal of Southern History* 77 (Feb. 2011): 53–90.

Faye Dudden

102. Nicholas Lemann, *Redemption: The Last Battle of the Civil War* (New York: Farrar, Strauss and Giroux, 2006), is especially sensitive to the way that suppressing certain kinds of information and substituting alternate narratives was central to the process of restoring white supremacy in the South.

103. "The Truth About the 'Outrages' by Negroes and Against Negroes," *Albany* (N.Y.) *Daily Argus,* Oct. 10, 1868, 2; Summers, *Press Gang,* 218–19, regarding the composition of the AP in the South.

104. Summers, *Press Gang,* 204.

105. Henry Blackwell, "Political Organization," *Woman's Journal,* Jan. 8, 1870.

106. "Southern Women's Bureau," *Woman's Journal,* Sept. 3, 1870.

107. The *Christian Recorder* provides an accessible window into these community networks.

108. The *Christian Recorder* mentions her speaking schedule frequently, as does the *National Anti-Slavery Standard.* See also Sterling, ed., *We Are Your Sisters,* 403–6; Margaret Hope Bacon, "'One Great Bundle of Humanity': Frances Ellen Watkins Harper," *Pennsylvania Magazine of History and Biography* 113 (Jan. 1989): 21–43; Melba Joyce Boyd, *Discarded Legacy: Politics and Poetics in the Life of Frances E. W. Harper, 1825–1911* (Detroit: Wayne State Univ. Press, 1994).

109. *Minnie's Sacrifice* was serialized in the *Christian Recorder,* Mar.–Sept. 1869. Poems in *A Brighter Coming Day,* 168, 204. On actual "enforcers" see Hahn, *A Nation Under Our Feet,* 227–28.

110. Summers, *Press Gang,* 192.

Civil War Memory

Southern Memories and Reconstructions

The Shifting Grounds and Contested Places of Women's Civil War Memorial Work

MICKI MCELYA

Standing twenty-two feet high, a bronze figurative sculpture dominates the sight-lines of the Contrabands and Freedmen's Cemetery Memorial dedicated in 2014 in Alexandria, Virginia. The work represents the difficult journeys from enslavement to freedom taken by those who emancipated themselves during the Civil War and headed to Washington, D.C., and surrounding communities under Union occupation. The monument's narrative and visual elements thrust upward. Officially called the *Path of Thorns and Roses* by sculptor Mario Chiodo, this rise is reinforced by the sculpture's dominant organic themes, incorporating a trunk and thorny branches growing from the earth. Several human forms, representing Oppression, Struggle, Sacrifice, Loss, Compassion, and Hope, seem twisted up in the plant or carried by it from the base to the top. The lower figures, embodiments of the hunger, exposure, physical toll, and disease that killed many and necessitated the cemetery in 1864, seem broken, warped, and sometimes difficult to distinguish from the trunk. The three highest figures are fully visible and intact, however. They include a crouched woman who holds an infant high in her left hand while reaching down with her right, and an adult male on his toes, calves tensed and finely articulated within the folds of his trousers that seem whipped by wind. This third fully articulated male figure, the highest on the sculpture and the embodiment of Hope, appears as though he might leap from the structure altogether.

While the sculpture is the site's most visible aspect, necessarily shaping the experience of moving through and around it, the memorial is first and foremost a historic cemetery. Dedicated within the contexts of wider Civil War sesquicentennial events on September 6, 2014, the reclamation and re-marking of the African American burial ground began much earlier when work on the I-95 corridor and Woodrow Wilson Bridge provided a space of opportunity for community organizers. The Contrabands and Freedmen's Cemetery Memorial is a significant contribution to the landscape of Civil War commemoration and Southern memory. As a relatively rare public site devoted to African American Civil War history, it is even more unusual

Mario Chiodo, *The Path of Thorns and Roses,* Contrabands and Freedmen's Cemetery Memorial, City of Alexandria, Va., 2014. Courtesy of Chiodo Art Development.

Micki McElya

for its primary focus on nonmilitary actors. Rather than emphasizing the soldier of the United States Colored Troops (USCT) as the central black agent of freedom, the memorial honors in heroic terms the journeys of the vast majority of the formerly enslaved who claimed their freedom on the move during the war or as the lines of battle found them deep within the Confederacy.

As the new memorial does this important work, it also persists in framing black progress and citizenship as essentially masculine and decidedly patriarchal. The dominant sculptural narrative literally embodies hope and future possibility in a black male figure while framing women's histories and contributions as maternal and mourning; they are vessels of past sorrows whose futures lie with their children and their men, rather than themselves. Women's freedom is denoted in the realization of supportive familial roles, domesticity, and protection afforded by the claiming of black "manhood rights," to use the common nineteenth-century terminology.[1] The history of this site and creation of the Contrabands and Freedmen's Cemetery Memorial highlight persistent gendered and racial limitations of Civil War memorial cultures, particularly where the experiences and histories of formerly enslaved women are concerned.[2]

The story of the Contrabands and Freedmen's Cemetery's recovery and rededication in the twenty-first century, and the historical and activist work of black women it entailed, share certain similarities with the Ladies' Memorial Associations and Southern cemetery organizations of the nineteenth century and Southern white women's postwar labors to find, move, reinter, and honor the Confederate dead. Necessitated by the pointed federal neglect of the graves of vanquished traitors, the meanings and outcomes of these aggrieved white Southern women's work exceeded their immediate concerns. As historians Drew Faust and Caroline E. Janney argue, by tending to and memorializing the dead, these women were doing the work of the state, claiming Confederate ground, and maintaining a sense of enduring Confederate nationalism and their own places within it.[3] But these similarities in black and white Southern women's memorial work across time are profoundly limited by that same Confederate nationalism that sought the very erasure of the black freedom struggles represented in the modern neglect and near loss of the Alexandria cemetery.

Taking the fugitive histories of self-emancipating—or "contraband"—women as a point of entry to considerations of Southern war and Reconstruction memory necessitates renewed attention to *place*. In one sense, this refers to the common roles or scripts attributed to various Southern women in dominant narratives of Civil War remembrance and the Lost Cause. It denotes white and black women's locations within the intersecting hierarchies of race and patriarchy and the work of keeping them in their places. Speaking at the cornerstone laying ceremony for the Confederate Memorial in Arlington National Cemetery in 1912, for instance, William Jennings Bryan denoted the power and limits of that place in his praise of the United Daughters of the Confederacy's efforts as monument builders. "Woman," he opined, "last at the cross and first at the sepulcher—holds undisputed sway on occasions like this."[4]

At the same time, *place* designates the physical locations and contested geographies of remembrance, with an emphasis on the cemetery and public monuments. These are not the only sites of white and black women's memorial work after the Civil War, but they hold primacy in the production of popular Southern memory over time, as well as its historiographies.[5] This is due in part to the types of archives generated by women's activities in loose associations or formal organizations, from the logistics and accounting of collecting and reinterring the dead to the design selection, fund raising, and publicity of monument building. It is also an intended outcome of the women's desire to publicly mourn and honor the sacrifices of their fallen and broadcast their particular versions of the past in order to shape the present and future.

Both arenas are about taking ground, seeking permanent visibility, and cementing particular interpretations of the Civil War and its legacies. In many ways, the dead are the foundations of these claims. Robert Pogue Harrison has argued that at its most fundamental level, burying the dead allows the living "to humanize the ground on which they build their worlds and found their histories."[6] The public monuments to the dead built over these graves or located in community centers transform the landscape and proclaim the honor and authority of the living, including the people who built them. To borrow a phrase from architectural historian Catherine Bishir, they are "landmarks of power."[7] Or they are not. Much of this essay is devoted to historical actors, cemeteries, and public works altered, rarely visited, or disappeared. Stories of continued neglect or the memorial work of recovery and historical re-narration highlight the ways in which the drive to lasting interpretive cohesion and monumental impenetrability is always fleeting. As art historian Kirk Savage argues, the ground on which these monuments were built and bodies interred "perpetually shifts as changes in the landscape and the world around it open up new possibilities of engagement."[8] The foundations of memorial work are always unstable, as are the grounds of our historical investigations of their constructions.

This is perhaps most clear when connecting the structural constraints and memorial silences in representing subjects caught between legal categories and distinct social locations to the literal places between North and South, Union and Confederacy, that comprised the Border States. This essay considers together the persistent absence of formerly enslaved women's complex histories in Civil War commemorative cultures and the contested regional identifications and unruly memorial terrains of Kentucky as such a state in order to highlight the generally unstable grounds of Southern Civil War memory.

Finally, taking the histories of "contraband" women as our point of entry to the subject of women, gender, and Southern memory compels us to consider the stories of self-emancipating women as constitutive of Southern remembrance and regional identifications no matter where we find them. This could be in the region's contraband camps, burial grounds, and abandoned plantations, or among those relocated by the military and then Freedmen's Bureau to far-flung places in the Midwest and New England. Recent scholarship on self-directed as well as coerced migrations of the formerly enslaved and the development of a "contraband" diaspora during the war and Reconstruction is critical to these examinations.[9] So are the words of Eudora Welty, that careful analyst of Southern women, history, and remembrance, who reminds us that "the memory is a living thing—it too is in transit."[10]

The term "contraband" emerged early in the war to describe enslaved people who emancipated themselves and ran to Union lines. First employed as an ad hoc designation in the field by Gen. Benjamin F. Butler to justify putting runaways to work for the Union army at Fort Monroe on the Virginia coast in May 1861, the legal claim, which persisted in framing the formerly enslaved as objects and property, was never formalized but enfolded within subsequent policies, including the First Confiscation Act passed a few months later. As historian Kate Masur has argued, the term remained common in popular Northern usage because it helped to soothe concerns about the national inclusion of four million once-enslaved black Southerners, offering a category between slavery and freedom and suggesting a space of and capacity for transition.[11] As a response to the disruptions and strategic mobility of self-emancipation, however, "contraband" simultaneously marked attempts to contain the places of formerly enslaved black Southerners.

The categorization also persisted officially in the war's rapidly proliferating federal bureaucracy, holding on long after the actions of the enslaved, the Emancipation Proclamation, and the start of the Thirteenth Amendment struggle secured the war's aim of liberation. Confronted with ever-increasing numbers of self-emancipated people seeking shelter and work, the War Department designated civilian superintendents of contrabands for various areas. While Frederick Law Olmsted took leave from his work on New York City's Central Park to head the U.S. Sanitary Commission early in the war, his first hope for participation in the Union effort had been as national supervisor of contrabands. Notably, his work transforming public space and urban terrains intersected with his desire to direct the transformation of African American places in the South in freedom.[12] Writing on June 1, 1861, to a friend who was off to Washington to lobby Lincoln, Olmsted explained his interest and qualifications: "I have, I suppose, given more thought to the special question of the management of negroes in a state of limbo between slavery and freedom than anyone else in the country," a claim he based on his earlier work as a correspondent in the South for the *New York Times* and subsequent publication of *A Journey in the Seaboard Slave States; With Remarks on Their Economy* (1856). "I think, in fact," Olmsted continued, "that I should find here my 'mission,' which is really something I am pining to find, in this war."[13] For a time in November 1861, it appeared as if Olmsted might be tasked with managing attempts to turn more than ten thousand new "contrabands" into free laborers on the captured Sea Island plantations of South Carolina's Port Royal Sound, which historian Willie Lee Rose famously termed a "Rehearsal for Reconstruction."[14]

Olmsted was not alone in his hunger to find his own place and mission among the formerly enslaved. In Alexandria, Olmsted's racial and patriotic ambitions were mirrored in an itinerant Baptist minister from Connecticut, Rev. Albert Gladwin. Thousands of newly free men, women, and children moved into or through the city during the war, most in desperate need of food, shelter, and clothing. Designated

Alexandria's superintendent of contrabands in May 1863, Gladwin had already been raising funds and providing relief for refugees in the area for at least a year as an affiliate with the American Baptist Free Mission Society. He often crossed paths with the wide network of churches, organizations, and individuals doing this work in complex relationship to military authority and occupying Union troops on the ground.

Harriet Jacobs, the celebrated runaway, activist, and recent author of *Incidents in the Life of a Slave Girl, Written by Herself* (1861), was, for instance, also in Alexandria doing relief work and advocating on behalf of former slaves. For free black people working among the "contrabands," negotiating one's place—one's self-presentation and self-preservation—in the face of such need and popular racism, was constant and fraught. This was perhaps even more so for self-emancipated women like Jacobs or Elizabeth Keckley and Sojourner Truth who also both did relief work in the area, as Chandra Manning and Faye Dudden so critically explore in their own contributions to this volume. When Jacobs arrived in Alexandria, Julia Wilbur, a white Quaker serving as an agent of the Rochester Ladies' Anti-Slavery Society, had already been at work in the city for a couple of months. Wilbur was suspicious of Jacobs at first, but the two worked together and soon became friends. They shared not only moral and political commitments but also a marked dislike of Gladwin. The women questioned his goals, methods, and harsh treatment of the formerly enslaved. Writing in her diary on November 12, 1862, in the midst of a number of entries about illness, death, and the particular plight of mothers among the "contrabands," Wilbur remarked, "I don't like the way Mr. Gladwin speaks to these people. Don't treat them as if they were women." This was followed by a note that she and Gladwin had arrived at the hospital to find three more children had died, and that Gladwin had "ordered a colored man" to pray over them. "I was too full & came away," she concluded.[15] Wilbur and Jacobs were appalled when Gladwin was appointed superintendent of contrabands for Alexandria, and later they made a formal protest. Around the same time, complaints from physicians treating the ill and concerned about the general condition of those in Gladwin's care prompted a military investigation of his work. He was ultimately exonerated, to Wilbur's and Jacob's horror. They subsequently devoted much of their energies in Alexandria to helping people outside the chain of official contraband relief, a strategy that helped them avoid Gladwin.[16]

In early 1864, on an abandoned Confederate property at the intersection of South Washington and Church streets in what was then the outskirts of the city, the army established a burial ground for free people who died in Alexandria. Gladwin oversaw burials at the site, which resulted in the death and interment records that comprise its central archive today, popularly known as the "Gladwin Record." The cemetery's creation was prompted by mounting numbers of black civilian deaths, mostly people with limited community networks and no personal or family resources to pay for private burials. Writing in her diary on April 12, 1864, Julia Wilbur described going "to the new Contraband burying ground. 65 graves there already. As good a place as they could get."[17] Federal authorities clearly thought of it as a burial ground for all black people who died in the vicinity. In December 1864, U.S. Colored Troops

Micki McElya

convalescing in nearby L'Ouverture Hospital successfully petitioned for the relocation of recently interred USCT remains to the city's Soldier's Cemetery, which was
among the first cemeteries of the new federal system known today as the Alexandria
National Cemetery. Wilbur had witnessed at least one of the burials on May 5, noting
in her diary that she had gone "to the Funeral of a Colored soldier" and that he had
been "buried in the New Freedmen's B. Ground." Gladwin's officiating at the funeral
had done nothing to shake her low estimation of the man. He had not spoken of the
soldier's bravery, nor given any words of encouragement to his living comrades. Gladwin "shows no sympathy for the people," she concluded, "nor for the Country."[18] The
recovering black soldiers were also furious. After expressing their anger to Gladwin
and refusing to serve as escorts for military funerals in the "Contraband burying
ground" in December, they submitted their protest in a letter to the War Department
that argued in part, "We are not contrabands, but soldiers in the U.S. Army."[19] With
support from the white quartermaster officer responsible for the Alexandria Soldier's
Cemetery, their protests were successful and the remains were moved in January
1865. This protest, which would be repeated by others without success at Arlington
National Cemetery after the war, made clear the personal investments and popular
lines drawn between self-possessed free people, now understood largely to be black
soldiers, on the one hand, and dependent contrabands, on the other.[20]

The gendered frames of this dichotomy, between active masculine and martial
independence and feminized dependency, drew on longer constructs that only
solidified the distinction further in official, reform, and popular perceptions. This
occurred despite the prevalence of formerly enslaved women as critical laborers
for the military throughout the war, primarily as cooks, nurses, and launderers,
and the tens of thousands of men who never served as soldiers counted among the
contraband. Of the more than 200,000 black men who served in the Union Army
and Navy, ultimately constituting about 10 percent of federal forces, roughly 150,000
had been enslaved when the war began. But 3.5 million more enslaved men, women,
and children claimed their freedom and fought their own battles in the transition
from slavery. The vast majority did not do so as soldiers, yet it is the Union soldier
who dominates representations of their histories and popular memory.[21] This further
distances black wartime experiences from constructions of Southern memory by
associating them so tightly with Union—and thus Northern—histories.

This minimizing of contraband histories in dominant commemorative cultures of
black Civil War military experience and its gendered implications are both characterized and facilitated by one of the most iconic images of African American soldiering
to emerge from the immediate aftermath of the war. Having spent much of the war
living and working in Louisville, Kentucky, after moving there from Nashville, Tennessee, Thomas Waterman Wood, a Vermonter by birth, produced his 1866 triptych of
paintings depicting the transmogrification of a black man from former slave to Union
soldier and then veteran in the Border State city before moving to New York. There
he exhibited the paintings, entitled *The Contraband, The Recruit,* and *The Veteran,*
to significant acclaim at the National Academy of Design in 1867. That same year,

Harper's Weekly published woodcut engravings of all three, which broadened their audience significantly and stamped the imagery onto the national visual culture of the war. The paper's short accompanying text said the original paintings were drawn from life studies in Tennessee—were documentary—and suggested they needed little description as they "tell their own thrilling story."[22] The first painting's identification of *the* (rather than *a*) contraband as a male soldier-in-waiting reinforced the exclusion of formerly enslaved black women as agents of their own liberation or as worthy subjects of citizenship earned through service and sacrifice by dropping them from the story altogether. This act mirrored the diverse "contraband" histories of the region in which Wood conceptualized and painted his visual narrative.

While the paintings were completed in Louisville, the assertion or presumption that they depicted a black soldier from Tennessee denoted the complex relationship of Kentucky to the Union, Confederacy, slavery, and black military service. One of the largest cities along the Ohio River that forms the northern and western border of the state, Louisville, largely a Union stronghold during the war, was perched at the edge of the Blue Grass, where most of the state's enslaved people and slave owners were located. Excluded from the provisions of the Emancipation Proclamation as a state that had not seceded, slavery remained legal in Kentucky until the passage of the Thirteenth Amendment in 1865, which the Commonwealth did not ratify. As an occupied state, Tennessee was also outside the purview of Lincoln's proclamation; military governor and candidate for vice president Andrew Johnson freed all those still enslaved there in October 1864. Yet from the start of the war, the region was full of self-emancipated people on the move, and by the end it had produced several units of USCT comprised of thousands of black men.

The Union army sought to manage this movement in part through a large contraband camp at Cairo, Illinois, also the location of Ulysses S. Grant's early command headquarters on the southernmost point of the state, nestled between Missouri and Kentucky where the Ohio and Mississippi Rivers meet. With significant numbers of able-bodied black men put to work as laborers for the army, by the fall of 1862 the camp at Cairo was primarily inhabited by women, children, and the old, many from Tennessee and points deeper south as well as the Border States. In September, it became a central point of departure for relocating "contrabands" further north as laborers. As historian Leslie Schwalm argues, this was a gendered policy aimed at removing women and children considered by the army to be drains on resources, rather than valuable laborers, or later valuable soldiers, like the men.[23] The policy was broadly unpopular in the states receiving migrants and decried as the federal government's importation of needful and dependent black people into Northern communities. It commonly represented demographic shifts in terms of both race and regional identifications and cultures.

The war's dominant geographic binary equating section with Union or Confederate sympathies was perhaps most obviously unsettled in Kentucky. The memorial work that followed in the Commonwealth was a contest to establish clear identifications and secure Kentucky's Civil War legacies. It was a contest, historian Anne

Micki McElya

E. Marshall argues in her account of "creating a Confederate Kentucky," in which glorifying the Lost Cause and the politics of white supremacy seemed to prevail.[24] Furthermore, it was a contest *among* Southerners, black and white, women and men, Union and Confederate.

In Virginia, the Alexandria Contrabands and Freedmen's Cemetery was federally managed until 1869, when it received its last official remains. Based on Albert Gladwin's records, at least eighteen hundred people were buried there in the five years of its federal operation, after which the land reverted to its previous Confederate owner and was increasingly encroached upon by brickyards and railroad tracks. The original wooden headboards, which deteriorated and disappeared over time, were mostly never replaced. While city records continued to show a historic cemetery at the site until the mid-twentieth century, local knowledge of the land's former use and remaining graves similarly dissipated. In 1917 it was transferred to the Catholic Diocese of Alexandria, which sold the "unused" property after it was zoned for commercial use in 1946. By this time the George Washington Parkway cut through the area, part of the growing network of heavily trafficked roadways around Washington, D.C. Ten years later the Old Town Mobil gas station and an office building stood on the property, leaving no sign of the graves beneath them.[25]

The long history of disinterest, neglect, and outright disturbance of these graves and the black lives and wartime struggles they denoted was clearly defined as desecration in the campaign to re-mark and memorialize them. The fate of this federal cemetery was much different from those in the national cemetery system, like the one in Alexandria, which still stand as an enduring legacy of federal authority and obligation emerging from the incredible death toll of the war.[26] The USCT remains that were moved from the ground at South Washington and Church streets during the war to a racially segregated section of the national cemetery were not lost beneath a gas station. Nor for that matter were the area's Confederate dead, which were later collected and reinterred in a new Confederate section of Arlington National Cemetery when the federal government assumed responsibility for the graves of all Civil War military dead at the turn of the last century.[27]

While the army turned fields of battle into federal military cemeteries and scoured farmland and roadsides for isolated Union bodies in order to protect them from desecration and return them to loved ones or inter them together in national cemeteries from 1865 to 1869, white women across the South mourned, despised the presence of federal reburial corps, often comprised of USCT, and feared for their own scattered and hastily marked dead. In the absence of comparable Confederate government or military authority, they organized to collect, rebury, and honor them.[28]

The glorification of the gendered and racialized domestic work of tending to the dead, including the celebration of Southern white women's adaptability and resolve and the faithfulness of the enslaved, began before the demise of Confederate public institutions. This is most notable in William D. Washington's historical painting *The Burial of Latané* (1864) depicting a funeral performed by grieving white women and girl children and enslaved adults. The only living male figure in the painting is an enslaved man resting against his shovel having dug the grave and soon to bury the draped coffin atop which rests Latané's sword, the emblem of his service and chivalry. This image would become even more popular among white Southerners after the war as a mournful celebration of the Lost Cause, women's memorial work, and the fantasy of faithful slavery; the latter aspect itself a part of the intersectional conditions of popular Southern Civil War memory that limit public representations of black women. White Southern women were simultaneously motivated in their early memorial work by revulsion at black Southerners' emancipation celebrations and parades, which were pronounced public rejections of faithful servitude and white paternalism and commonly included uniformed African American men.[29]

As the work of burying the Union war dead was turned into an enduring federal commitment to increasing numbers of veterans and their dependents over time, similar to the expansion of pension benefits in the nineteenth century, organized white Southern women continued their memorial labors, sometimes in concert with the United Confederate Veterans. This constellation of local and regional Confederate organizations would be joined in 1894 by the United Daughters of the Confederacy (UDC), whose swift growth and particular dedication to monument building and "righting" the "wrongs of history," as historian general Mildred Lewis Rutherford later put it, had a profound impact on dominant constructions of Civil War memory within and beyond the South.[30] These groups would also soon be joined by the federal government and War Department when President William McKinley's 1898 promise to share in the care of Confederate graves led to passage of the Foraker Bill in 1906, named for its sponsoring Republican senator from Ohio, Joseph B. Foraker, who, like McKinley, was a Union veteran.[31] White Southern insistence of the dishonor represented in the disproportionate care of Union and Confederate graves prompted McKinley's recourse to the issue while seeking the support of Southern Democrats in the work of overseas empire after the Spanish-American War.

So pervasive was the sentiment, it had become a key facet of the Lost Cause and postwar Confederate identifications. In 1887 a group of white women in Louisville used the occasion of Decoration Day to honor the Confederate dead in the city's Cave Hill Cemetery and announce the creation of the Confederate Monument Association for "the erection of a monument in this city in memory of all the Confederate dead in Kentucky."[32] Building on a legacy of white women's Confederate memorial work in the state reaching back at least to 1869 and the Lexington Ladies' Memorial and Monument Association, the Louisville women were likely also inspired by the dedication just one week earlier of a monument to the unknown Confederate dead in Hopkinsville, Kentucky, a small community to the south and west of the city. More than twenty thousand people were reported to have witnessed the unveiling of the monument in a town of not many more than five thousand residents. Standing thirty-seven feet high and topped by a pyramid of cannonballs, it had been arranged and paid for by local son and Confederate veteran John C. Latham Jr., by then a prominent tobacco broker, investment banker, and long-time resident of New York

City. Claiming no sectional intent on the part of Latham, the *New York Times* noted his original plan for a monument to all unknown Civil War dead in Hopkinsville who, in Latham's words, shared a death "of hardship, heroism, and valor costing the precious lives of true-hearted Americans." But, he continued, since the government had removed the Union dead to the national cemetery at Fort Donelson just over the border in Tennessee, "there were only left my comrades, the Confederate dead, and to their hallowed memory I dedicate this shaft."[33] Given the fact this had been done two decades earlier during the army's initial reburial mission in 1866, Latham's statement seemed mostly aimed at spotlighting the difference in care. The ceremony and subsequent reports depicted the monument as a scene of sectional reconciliation and the shared valor of all white men spun through a narrative of mutual investment, commerce, and the exclusion of African Americans.[34]

While possibly inspired by Latham's monument and its publicity, the Kentucky Women's Confederate Monument Association had different plans for their grand memorial to the Confederate dead of the Commonwealth. In November 1893, the *Confederate Veteran* reported that Louisville sculptor Enid Yandell, daughter of a Confederate veteran and recently celebrated for her bronze sculpture of Daniel Boone commissioned for the entrance to the Kentucky Building at the World's Columbian Exposition in Chicago, was in the early stages of work on a "magnificent Confederate monument, to be erected in one of our Southern States."[35] Her success in winning the Kentucky Confederate Monument design competition from among twenty submissions was announced the following year, as was the monument's planned location in the center of Louisville's Third Street traffic circle. In late September a Nashville paper described the design as "very chaste and original and quite out of the ordinary."[36] It was comprised of a bronze female figure of "Fame" or "Victory" holding a laurel wreath in one hand and Confederate flag in the other, standing atop a column of red granite, with inscriptions at the base. The finished monument was to be seventy-five feet tall. Given that its basic design of a single column topped by a figural sculpture was similar to other Confederate (and Union) monuments, it appears that the choice of a female allegorical figure rather than a soldier or war matériel to represent the Confederacy marked its originality for the Tennessee paper. This became a source of controversy when local Confederate veterans protested the design, arguing that a soldier sculpture should top the monument. Added to this were charges that Yandell's friends in the association had orchestrated her selection. Prompted by these controversies, the women took another vote in October 1894; this time the commission was won by a man from a local monument company who submitted a design including a central pillar holding a mass-produced Confederate soldier bronze.[37]

Created in struggle over appropriate martial and gendered representations of the Confederacy and over who among contemporary Kentuckians was to be honored in building memorials to the war dead, the newly designed monument sparked further controversy the following year. This time the monument's organizers asserted themselves overtly into contests over the state's Civil War identifications and the place of public commemorations of Union military histories. With the national encampment of the Grand Army of the Republic set for Louisville in September 1895, making it the most southern location for the organization's annual meeting yet, the Confederate Monument Association announced plans to schedule the unveiling of its memorial to coincide with the GAR event. In the face of broad protests, local and national, however, the association retreated from its plan. The cornerstone was ultimately laid on May 25, 1895, with an expected completion in thirty days, meaning the monument would be unveiled before the GAR meeting—a fact reported on the front page of the *New York Times*.[38]

The Confederate Monument controversy amplified concerns among African American members of the GAR and its women's auxiliary, the Woman's Relief Corps (WRC), along with many of their white comrades, about the conditions and treatment they would confront while attending the encampment in a segregated Southern city. As Wendy Hamand Venet details in her essay for this volume, the 1890s saw many attempts by white members to segregate WRC events and formally divide the corps of Kentucky and Maryland. They were successful in 1900, but struggles over the meaning of Louisville's Civil War histories continued—and do to this day.

The ground has shifted beneath the city's Confederate Monument in recent years. In the 1940s it was moved from its original location in order to address traffic concerns and make way for roadwork. This move and campus expansion put the city-owned monument within the grounds of the University of Louisville, where it stood when the university was desegregated in the early 1950s. Since that time, it has been the subject both of campus protest and celebration and the scene of several civil rights actions. In 2002 the university's Board of Trustees approved the new Freedom Park at the monument site to detail the long history of the city's African American communities, with an emphasis on twentieth-century civil rights activism.

The late J. Blain Hudson, professor of history and Pan African studies and dean of the College of Arts and Sciences at the University of Louisville, was a leading figure in the success of the Freedom Park initiative. A Louisville native and university alumnus, he had been a student activist with the Black Student Union in the late 1960s and was arrested while occupying an administration building with other students demanding the creation of a black studies program—the genesis of the program he would go on to chair as a professor many years later. It was in this capacity that he addressed the trustees and explained the need for monumental additions and historical corrections at the Confederate Memorial. Describing Louisville's Union military past, he noted, "They were not here as an Army of occupation. They were Union soldiers in a Union City, in a Union state." He added that the Confederate Monument was not without historical basis or meaning but that its representation was incomplete. The memorial context of Freedom Park was needed, he argued, to "put all the historical information on the table and develop an interpretation that reflects as accurately as possible the totality of the Civil War and the late Antebellum experience of this area."[39] Freedom Park was dedicated in 2012 and a memorial panel in Dr. Hudson's honor added after his death in 2013.[40]

Micki McElya

A month after Louisville hosted the GAR encampment in 1895, white women in Lexington, Kentucky, formed the Commonwealth's first chapter of the United Daughters of the Confederacy. It was only the twelfth charter of the new organization.[41] The organization grew rapidly, proliferating across urban areas and smaller rural communities and including many chapters along the Ohio River and in the western part of the state abutting Illinois and Missouri. Between 1900 and 1920 the UDC was responsible for at least twelve new monuments to the Lost Cause and Confederate dead in Kentucky.[42] They were also critical fundraisers for other campaigns, including the enormous Jefferson Davis Memorial at his birthplace in Fairview, Kentucky, near Hopkinsville. Organized by the Kentucky Confederate veterans of the Orphan Brigade Association and modeled after the Washington Monument, the Davis Memorial obelisk stands at just over 350 feet high. With ever-rising costs that rivaled its size, the monument was funded through several organizations, the UDC and women of the Confederated Southern Memorial Associations chief among them. Bringing together Ladies' Memorial Associations from across the South, the CSMA had been founded in 1900, largely in response to the rapid growth and power of the UDC. The women chose Louisville, Kentucky, for their founding meeting to coincide with the United Confederate Veterans annual reunion held there that year. In the end, the Kentucky legislature appropriated $15,000 of state funds to complete the project and became the official custodian of the site. Dedicated on June 7, 1924, the Jefferson Davis Memorial was celebrated in the *Confederate Veteran* as a worthy honor to the first and only president of the Confederate States of America and a meaningful new destination "for visitors from every country—and a shrine for Southern hearts!"[43]

But some of Kentucky's "Southern hearts" sought other shrines. The following month, on the Fourth of July, an African American chapter of the Woman's Relief Corps from the state's capital, Frankfort, dedicated a monument in "Memory of the Colored Soldiers, Franklin Co. Ky. Who Fought in the Civil War, 1861–1865." Located in Greenhill Cemetery, one of the city's African American burial grounds dating to the Civil War era, the flat-topped pillar stands about ten feet high and carries on three sides the names of 142 individual black soldiers of the USCT.[44] Clearly inspired by the memorial listing of names and public accounting for the individual soldier dead after World War I, the remaining side of the squared pillar identifies the monument builders themselves. Above the dedication, and filling the entire surface in large print, the inscription surrounding a bas-relief of crossed rifles and an American flag reads, "Erected by Woman's Relief Corps No 8 GAR July 1924." Below is a list of nine names, identified as the women of the Monument Committee.[45] In this, and similar to Confederate monuments identifying the UDC, the memorial becomes not only an honor to black military service and a claim for Kentucky's Union Civil War memory but a public marker to the local black women of the WRC and their place as the keepers and producers of this memory. It is a monument to their efforts and the WRC and GAR generally. Notably, while the monument makes the women's place in constructing black Civil War memory visible, it does so through decidedly military associations in its broad aims as well as specific details. The listing of committeewomen's names mirrors that of the soldiers. And while the location of the martial bas-relief may signal the designer's desire not to crowd or shrink the soldiers' names on the other sides, it similarly likens the WRC women's work to military service.

Today the Frankfort USCT monument, now called the Kentucky African American Civil War Memorial, serves as the only official state commemoration of the Civil War military service of nearly 25,000 black men from Kentucky.[46] On Memorial Day 1992, members of the Kentucky State University community, a land-grant HBCU (Historically Black Colleges and Universities) also located in Frankfort, honored the USCT soldiers buried in Greenhill Cemetery. They dedicated their own memorial marker beside the 1924 monument that links the Civil War memorial to the university and includes in its inscription the name of its then president, Dr. Mary L. Smith, who was the first woman to hold the position. This coincided with the beginning of efforts in Alexandria, Virginia, to preserve the Contrabands and Freedmen's Cemetery.

Since the late 1980s, when a historian working for the city came across a nineteenth-century reference to the cemetery, various members of the community had been working to publicize the site's African American history and ongoing desecrations. This was catalyzed by plans to reconstruct the Woodrow Wilson Bridge, which would further impact the site, and resulted in a series of community meetings held from 1992 to 1996. In 1997 Alexandria residents and activists founded the Friends of Freedmen's Cemetery to mobilize efforts for research and preservation of the site as a vital part of the city's history.

Both places represent the persistent power of Civil War sites within contemporary racial and gendered struggles for cultural and political representation. They are also emblematic of the continued primacy of the black soldier in African American Civil War commemorations. The Contrabands and Freedmen's Cemetery Memorial that was dedicated in 2014 is quite different from the original design, which had included a central, figurative monument of four uniformed black soldiers, "holding up, in honor, a representative casket" that would carry panels depicting "the trials and tribulations of the people who struggled to reach Alexandria fleeing slavery, and those who fought willingly in the Civil War." While the possible content of the bas-relief panels was not included in the proposal, the overwhelming focus of the commemorative grouping on the black men who served in the military is clear. It was to be joined by another sculpture of a "solemn, singular USCT soldier," at the outside corner of the site, facing the sidewalk.[47] Subsequent steering committee recommendations addressed the disproportionate martial focus of the winning design, calling for a sculptural element that "personifies the freed men, women, and children buried in the cemetery."[48] This was the genesis of a new competition, including community voting, for the sculpture that resulted in the selection of Chiodo's *Path of Thorns and Roses*.

The final memorial is a large commemorative terrain of many parts. It includes a decorative gate; markers for every identifiable grave that are flush to the ground; a walled structure carrying two bas-relief sculptures, interpretive and inspirational text, and a series of bronze panels listing all of the names of individuals once interred at the site; and the large central sculpture.[49] The historical text and wall of names were also mandates from the steering committee after the design competition. This aspect of the memorial is in some ways its most traditionally martial, locating it—like the WRC's 1924 monument in Greenhill Cemetery—within the rich iconographic history of modern nation-states memorializing average soldiers and their individual deaths through public inscriptions of names.[50] More recently, this is clearly shaped by the power and popularity of Maya Lin's Vietnam Veterans Memorial, dedicated in 1982, which has had enormous influence on all subsequent public memorials, including those to nonmilitary dead. The panels of the Contrabands and Freedmen's Cemetery Memorial are made to look like the pages of "Gladwin's Record." This is a compelling aesthetic decision that unsettles the martial connotations and necessarily marks—and makes monumental—the current centrality of genealogy to African American personal and collective memories and the reconstructions of slave pasts, including family histories.

Amidst it all stands Chiodo's sculpture, the tallest and most obvious feature of the memorial and to which the eye is immediately drawn. While nothing in the monument's iconography is specific to the cemetery's history or Alexandria and the memorial site itself contains a number of elements, it is the primary visual marker of the entire memorial park. As one approaches the site to enter, the sculpture is centrally framed by the main gate. The arch of the gate's sign, "Freedmen's Cemetery," mirrors the arc of the monument's ring of thorns. A commemorative souvenir ornament depicts the sculpture framed by the gate, reinforcing its function as the iconic representation of the cemetery.

The top male figure is framed by a large ring of thorny branches and looks down toward his outstretched hands, turned upward to reveal a rose that is not yet open. The artist's corporate webpage describes the figure as Hope, "holding the unbloomed 'rose of freedom' as he stands on his tiptoes to avoid the thorns of oppression beneath him." Noting that more than 40 percent of the known 1,800 graves of the cemetery were for children, the page identifies the female figure as "Compassion" offering a "flower of hope" to another female figure below her, "Sacrifice," who is collapsed across an adolescent child she mourns.[51] Both female figures are definitively marked as mothers, as "Compassion" holds aloft a small infant. There is no iconographic space for an adult, nonelderly woman who is not maternal. Moreover, the lifted infant creates a kind of family group at the top of the memorial, celebrating the patriarchal family as progress. Here and elsewhere, the celebration of heroic black masculinity in the figure of the soldier and/or patriarch is as much a response to popular denigrations of the black family dating to the political culture and social movements of 1960s as it is about popular memories of the 1860s.[52]

On the day of the dedication, the monument was wrapped in a garland of red roses, which made a stark contrast to the dark bronze. This was reminiscent in some ways of nineteenth-century Decoration Days, strewing the graves of the dead with flowers. The holiday itself captures many of the problems of Southern memory and the preservation of Civil War pasts. It originated as a celebration of emancipation organized by formerly enslaved men, women, and children and their white allies in

Charleston, South Carolina, in 1866. By 1868 the Grand Army of the Republic had repurposed the event into a national holiday for honoring the Union dead, which would include black Union veterans in more and less ways over time, but narrowed the holiday into a celebration of martial, and thus men's, histories. The Alexandria memorial is an important addition to public commemoration of diverse Civil War pasts, but it is also an opportunity missed. This is particularly true in its flattened public histories of women like Harriet Jacobs and Julia Wilbur, who left extensive archives and narrow depictions of the thousands of formerly enslaved people who moved through or found their last rest there. It is testament to the complexities of Southern identities and geographies and the ongoing problems of the place of black women in constructions of popular Southern memory and commemorations of the Civil War and Reconstruction. It remains troubled ground.

NOTES

1. Stephanie McCurry examines this patriarchal narrative of emancipation and gendered paths to citizenship in her "War, Gender, and Emancipation in the Civil War South," in William A. Blair and Karen Fisher, eds., *Lincoln's Proclamation: Emancipation Reconsidered* (Chapel Hill: Univ. of North Carolina Press, 2009), 120–50. On nineteenth-century black "manhood rights," see James Oliver Horton, "Defending the Manhood of the Race: The Crisis of Citizenship in Black Boston at Midcentury," in Martin H. Blatt, Thomas J. Brown, and Donald Yavacone, eds., *Hope and Glory: Essays on the Legacy of the 54th Massachusetts Regiment* (Amherst: Univ. of Massachusetts Press, 2001), 7–20.

2. I explore this problem in relation to other public memorials and the film *Lincoln* (Steven Spielberg, dir., 2012) in Micki McElya, "Unknowns: Commemorating Black Women's Civil War Heroism," in Kirk Savage, ed., *The Civil War in Art and Memory,* Studies in the History of Art series (Washington, D.C.: Center for Advanced Study in the Visual Arts, National Gallery of Art, distributed by Yale Univ. Press, 2016), 213–26. On black women's particular histories as "contrabands," see Thavolia Glymph, "'This Species of Property': Female Slave Contrabands in the Civil War," in Edward D. C. Campbell Jr. and Kim S. Rice, *A Woman's War: Southern Women, Civil War, and the Confederate Legacy* (Charlottesville: Univ. Press of Virginia, 1997), 55–70; and Leslie Schwalm, "Between Slavery and Freedom: African American Women and the Occupation of the Slave South," in LeeAnn Whites and Alecia P. Long, eds., *Occupied Women: Gender, Military Occupation, and the American Civil War* (Baton Rouge: Louisiana State Univ. Press, 2009), 137–54.

3. Drew Gilpin Faust, *This Republic of Suffering: Death and the American Civil War* (New York: Knopf, 2008), 82–85; Caroline E. Janney, *Burying the Dead but Not the Past: Ladies' Memorial Associations and the Lost Cause* (Chapel Hill: Univ. of North Carolina Press, 2008). It is important to note that during the war, when the role the federal government and military would assume in identifying, transporting, and caring for the dead remained unclear, Northern women similarly found, moved, and buried their loved ones, often at great risk. See Judith Giesberg, *Army at Home: Women and the Civil War on the Northern Home Front* (Chapel Hill: Univ. of North Carolina Press, 2009), chap. 6.

4. Hilary A. Herbert, *History of the Arlington Confederate Monument* (N.p.: United Daughters of the Confederacy, 1914), 36.

Micki McElya

5. For a discussion of the centrality of *place* and alternative geographies in recent historiographies of women, gender, slavery, and the Civil War, see Lyde Cullen Sizer, "Mapping the Spaces of Women's Civil War History," *Journal of the Civil War Era* 1 (Dec. 2011): 536–48. For a general discussion of place, geography, and Southern memory, see Stuart McConnell, "Epilogue: The Geography of Memory," in Alice Fahs and Joan Waugh, eds., *The Memory of the Civil War in American Culture* (Chapel Hill: Univ. of North Carolina Press, 2004), 258–66. The scholarship on Southern memory, women, public monuments, and cemeteries includes William Allen Blair, *Cities of the Dead: Contesting the Memory of the Civil War in the South, 1865–1914* (Chapel Hill: Univ. of North Carolina Press, 2004); W. Fitzhugh Brundage, *The Southern Past: A Clash of Race and Memory* (Cambridge, Mass.: Belknap Press of Harvard Univ. Press, 2005); Karen L. Cox, *Dixie's Daughters: The United Daughters of the Confederacy and the Preservation of Confederate Culture* (Gainesville: Univ. Press of Florida, 2003); Janney, *Burying the Dead but Not the Past;* Caroline E. Janney, *Remembering the Civil War: Reunion and the Limits to Reconciliation* (Chapel Hill: Univ. of North Carolina Press, 2013); Michelle A. Krowl, "'In the Spirit of Fraternity': The United States Government and the Burial of Confederate Dead at Arlington National Cemetery, 1864–1914," *Virginia Magazine of History and Biography* 111 (2003): 151–86; Micki McElya, *Clinging to Mammy: The Faithful Slave in Twentieth-Century America* (Cambridge, Mass.: Harvard Univ. Press, 2007); Micki McElya, *The Politics of Mourning: Death and Honor in Arlington National Cemetery* (Cambridge, Mass.: Harvard Univ. Press, 2016); Cynthia Mills and Pamela H. Simpson, eds., *Monuments to the Lost Cause: Women, Art, and the Landscapes of Southern Memory* (Knoxville: Univ. of Tennessee Press, 2003); and John R. Neff, *Honoring the Civil War Dead: Commemoration and the Problem of Reconciliation* (Lawrence: Univ. Press of Kansas, 2005).

6. Robert Pogue Harrison, *The Dominion of the Dead* (Chicago: Univ. of Chicago Press, 2003), xi.

7. Catherine W. Bishir, "Landmarks of Power: Building a Southern Past in Raleigh and Wilmington, North Carolina, 1885–1915," in W. Fitzhugh Brundage, ed., *Where These Memories Grow: History, Memory, and Southern Identity* (Chapel Hill: Univ. of North Carolina Press, 2000), 139–68.

8. Kirk Savage, *Monument Wars: Washington, D.C., the National Mall, and the Transformation of the Memorial Landscape* (Berkeley: Univ. of California Press, 2009), 11.

9. Carol Faulkner, "'A New Field of Labor': Anti-Slavery Women, Freedmen's Aid, and Political Power," in Paul A. Cimbala and Randall M. Miller, eds., *The Great Task Remaining Before Us: Reconstruction as America's Continuing Civil War* (New York: Fordham Univ. Press, 2010), 94–97; Janette Thomas Greenwood, *First Fruits of Freedom: The Migration of Former Slaves and their Search for Equality in Worcester, Massachusetts, 1862–1900* (Chapel Hill: Univ. of North Carolina Press, 2010); and Leslie A. Schwalm, *Emancipation's Diaspora: Race and Reconstruction in the Upper Midwest* (Chapel Hill: Univ. of North Carolina Press, 2009).

10. Eudora Welty, *One Writer's Beginnings* (1983; repr., Cambridge, Mass.: Harvard Univ. Press, 1995), 104.

11. Kate Masur, "'A Rare Phenomenon of Philological Vegetation': The Word 'Contraband' and the Meanings of Emancipation in the United States," *Journal of American History* 93 (Mar. 2007): 1050–84.

12. It bears noting that in 1857 Seneca Village, a predominantly black community that represented the largest collection of black land owners in New York City located between 81st and 89th Streets was seized via eminent domain and razed for the creation of Central Park. Diana diZerega Wall, Nan A. Rothschild, and Cynthia Copeland, "Seneca Village and Little Africa: Two African American Communities in Antebellum New York City," *Historical Archaeology* 42, no. 1 (2008): 97–107; *The Seneca Village Project,* http://www.mcah.columbia.edu/seneca_village/index.html.

13. Frederick Law Olmsted to Henry Whitney Bellows, June 1, 1861, qtd. in Witold Ryb-czynski, *A Clearing in the Distance: Frederick Law Olmsted and America in the Nineteenth Century* (New York: Scribner's, 2003), 197.

14. Willie Lee Rose, *Rehearsal for Reconstruction: The Port Royal Experiment* (New York: Oxford Univ. Press, 1964). On Olmsted's involvement, see "Our Port Royal Correspondence," *New York Times*, Nov. 20, 1861, 1; "From Port Royal," *Chicago Tribune*, Dec. 4, 1861, 3; and Laura Wood Roper, "Frederick Law Olmsted and the Port Royal Experiment," *Journal of Southern History* 31 (Aug. 1965): 272–84.

15. Julia Wilbur Diary, Nov. 12, 1862, transcr. by Paula T. Whitacre for the Alexandria Ar-chaeology Museum, original in Special Collections, Haverford College Library, Haverford, Pa. See also Carol Faulkner, *Women's Radical Reconstruction: The Freedmen's Aid Movement* (Philadelphia: Univ. of Pennsylvania Press, 2007); and Jean Fagan Yellin, *Harriet Jacobs: A Life* (New York: Basic Civitas Books, 1995), 165. There is a surprising dearth of scholarship or biographical work on Albert Gladwin.

16. Yellin, *Harriet Jacobs*, 169–74; Ira Berlin, Steven F. Miller, Joseph P. Reidy, Leslie S. Rowland, eds., *Freedom: A Documentary History of Emancipation, 1861–1865*, ser. 1, vol. 2, *The Wartime Genesis of Free Labor: The Upper South*, (New York: Cambridge Univ. Press, 1993), 298–303.

17. Julia Wilbur Diary, Apr. 12, 1864.

18. Ibid., May 5, 1864.

19. City of Alexandria, Va., *Contrabands and Freedmen's Cemetery Memorial 2008 Design Competition Guidelines*, 2.4–2.5. See also Julia Wilbur Diary, Dec. 26 and 27, 1864.

20. McElya, *Politics of Mourning*, 126–28.

21. McCurry, "War, Gender, and Emancipation in the Civil War South," 124. On the gendered parameters of dependency in U.S. history generally, see Nancy Fraser and Linda Gordon, "A Genealogy of Dependency: Tracing a Keyword of the U.S. Welfare State," *Signs* 18 (Winter 1994): 309–36; and Linda Kerber, *No Constitutional Right to Be Ladies: Women and the Obligations of Citizenship* (New York: Hill & Wang, 1999), chap. 2.

22. "The Contraband, Recruit, and Veteran," *Harper's Weekly* (May 4, 1867): 284. On the paintings and their circulation generally, see Masur, "'A Rare Phenomenon of Philological Vegetation,'" 1077–78; and Deborah C. Pollack, *Visual Art and the Urban Evolution of the New South* (Columbia: Univ. of South Carolina Press, 2015), 165–66.

23. Schwalm, "Between Slavery and Freedom," 146–49.

24. Anne E. Marshall, *Creating a Confederate Kentucky: The Lost Cause and Civil War Memory in a Border State* (Chapel Hill: Univ. of North Carolina Press, 2010). See also Aaron Astor, *Rebels on the Border: Civil War, Emancipation, and Reconstruction in Kentucky and Missouri* (Baton Rouge: Louisiana State Univ. Press, 2012).

25. http://alexandriava.gov/FreedmenMemorial#rededication. Later archaeology revealed the remains of stone markers that had been placed by family or friends at some point.

26. Faust, *This Republic of Suffering*; McElya, *Politics of Mourning*.

27. On the continued cost of this policy to the federal government, see Steven I. Weiss, "You Won't Believe What the Government Spends on Confederate Graves," *Atlantic* (July 19, 2013), http://www.theatlantic.com/politics/archive/2013/07/government-spending-confederate-graves/277931.

28. Drew Gilpin Faust, "Battle over the Bodies: Burying and Reburying the Civil War Dead, 1865–1871," in Gary W. Gallagher and Joan Waugh, eds., *War within a War: Controversy and Conflict Over the American Civil War* (Chapel Hill: Univ. of North Carolina Press, 2009), 184–201.

29. Faust, *This Republic of Suffering*, 83–85; Janney, *Burying the Dead but Not the Past*, 34–35; Neff, *Honoring the Civil War Dead*, 150–52.

Micki McElya

30. Mildred Lewis Rutherford, "Wrongs of History Righted," Address of the Historian General to the Annual Convention of the United Daughters of the Confederacy, Savannah, 1914.

31. Gaines M. Foster, *Ghosts of the Confederacy: Defeat, the Lost Cause, and the Emergence of the New South 1865 to 1913* (New York: Oxford Univ. Press, 1987), 153–54.

32. "Confederate Dead Remembered," *New York Times,* May 29, 1887, 2.

33. "Dead Comrades Honored," *New York Times,* May 20, 1887, 3.

34. On the "Latham Monument" and dedication, generally, see "To the Confederate Dead," *Chicago Tribune,* May 20, 1887, 2; and Jack Glazier, *Been Coming Through Some Hard Times: Race, History, and Memory in Western Kentucky* (Knoxville: Univ. of Tennessee Press, 2013), 159–63. On the federal reburial mission in the Ohio River Valley, see Faust, "Battle over the Bodies," 193. On the longer history of Ladies' Memorial Associations in Kentucky, see Marshall, *Creating a Confederate Kentucky,* 84–85.

35. "A Southern Girl at the World's Fair," *Confederate Veteran* 1 (Nov. 1893): 323.

36. Clipping from unidentified newspaper, Nashville, Tenn., Sept. 29, 1894, Enid Yandell Papers, 1878–1982, Confederate Monument Scrapbook, Archives of American Art, Smithsonian Institution, Washington, D.C.

37. Pollack, *Visual Art and the Urban Evolution,* 187–88. It is possible that Yandell's sculpture was incorporated into the United Daughters of the Confederacy's Shiloh Battlefield Confederate Monument (1917). Chicago sculptor Frederick C. Hibbard won the commission with his model for *Victory Defeated by Death.* The large work includes a central grouping of three female allegorical figures in bronze, flanked at each end with a pair of bronze military figures representing each branch of the Confederate service. The UDC's official institutional history, first published in 1938, includes the following note in its detail of the monument and campaign, "'Victory' of the monument, the figure of a woman, modeled by a beautiful Kentucky girl, stands in the center of this group . . ." *The History of the United Daughters of the Confederacy, Centennial Edition* (1938; repr., Richmond: United Daughters of the Confederacy, 1994), 54.

38. "Louisville's Confederate Monument," *New York Times,* May 26, 1895, 1. See also Barbara A. Gannon, *The Won Cause: Black and White Comradeship in the Grand Army of the Republic* (Chapel Hill: Univ. of North Carolina Press, 2011), 76; Marshall, *Creating a Confederate Kentucky,* 104; and Pollack, *Urban Art and the Visual Revolution,* 187.

39. Bruce Schreiner, "Confederate Statue Might Get Company," *Cincinnati Enquirer,* Nov. 27, 2002, http://www.enquirer.com/editions/2002/11/27/loc_kyconfederate27.html.

40. "Charles H. Parrish, Jr. Freedom Park," Univ. of Louisville, https://louisville.edu/freedompark.

41. *History of the United Daughters of the Confederacy,* 23.

42. Marshall, *Creating a Confederate Kentucky,* 160–61.

43. "The Jefferson Davis Memorial," *Confederate Veteran* 32 (July 1924): 253–54. While this article only mentioned the United Daughters of the Confederacy in its reference to women's fundraising, the Confederated Southern Memorial Association had published a detailed accounting of its collections for 1922 and 1923 just two months prior. "Jefferson Davis Memorial Fund," *Confederate Veteran* 32 (Apr. 1924): 154–55. On the CSMA generally, see Janney, *Burying the Dead but Not the Past,* 178–83.

44. Marshall, *Creating a Confederate Kentucky,* 182. On earlier campaigns to represent black men's Civil War military service monumentally, see Kirk Savage, *Standing Soldiers, Kneeling Slaves: Race, War, and Monument in Nineteenth-Century America* (Princeton, N.J.: Princeton Univ. Press, 1997), 180–208.

45. Images and history available at: http://explorekyhistory.ky.gov/items/show/191.

46. Ibid.

47. C. J. Howard, Alexandria, Va., Entry #0161, Contrabands and Freedmen's Cemetery Memorial (winner). http://www3.alexandriava.gov/freedmens/winners.php.

48. "Freedmen's Cemetery Memorial, Project Status," n.d.

49. The Alexandria Contrabands and Freedmen's Cemetery Memorial joins two other historic sites for the history of "contrabands," both of which are additions to extant National Park Service Civil War sites in response to NPS work in the 1990s to incorporate the histories of slavery and diverse people and interpretations and battlefield parks. They are the "First Light of Freedom" (2001) monument commemorating the Roanoke Island Freedmen's Colony at the Fort Raleigh National Historic Site and the Corinth Contraband Camp (2004), including several bronze figures located throughout the site, connected to the Shiloh National Military Park. "First Light of Freedom, Fort Raleigh National Historical Site," *Commemorative Landscapes of North Carolina* (http://docsouth.unc.edu/commland/monument/378/); National Park Service, *Fort Raleigh National Historic Site Long-Range Interpretive Plan* (Manteo, N.C.: National Park Service, U.S. Department of the Interior, May 2010), 47; and National Park Service, Shiloh National Military Park, Tenn., MS, http://www.nps.gov/shil/index.htm. On the Roanoke Island Freedmen's Colony, see Patricia C. Click, *Time Full of Trial: The Roanoke Island Freedmen's Colony, 1862–1867* (Chapel Hill: Univ. of North Carolina Press, 2001).

50. Thomas W. Laqueur, "Names, Bodies, and the Anxiety of Erasure," in Theodore R. Schatzke and Wolfgang Natter, eds. *The Social and Political Body* (New York: Guilford Press, 1996), 123–41.

51. Path of Thorns and Roses: Completed and Installed, http://freedommarchofart.com/thepathofthornsandroses.html. The sculpture was dedicated with the entire memorial park on Sept. 6, 2014, in Alexandria, Virginia. It had been installed the year before in violation of a city limit on public art to fifteen feet. Derrick Perkins, "City Council Resolves Sculpture's Permitting Problems," *Alexandria Times,* Sept. 23, 2013, http://alextimes.com/2013/09/city-council-resolves-sculptures-permitting-problem.

52. Daniel Patrick Moynihan, *The Negro Family: The Case for National Action* (Washington, D.C.: United States Department of Labor, 1965). For critical responses, see Angela Davis, "Reflections on the Black Woman's Role in the Community of Slaves," *Black Scholar* 13 (1971): 2–15; Ruth Feldstein, *Motherhood in Black and White: Race and Sex in American Liberalism, 1930–1965* (Ithaca, N.Y.: Cornell Univ. Press, 2000); Melissa V. Harris-Perry, *Sister Citizen: Shame, Stereotypes, and Black Women in America* (2011; repr., New Haven, Conn.: Yale Univ. Press, 2013); K. Sue Jewell, *From Mammy to Miss America: Cultural Images and the Shaping of U.S. Social Policy* (New York: Routledge, 1993); and Michelle Wallace, *Black Macho and the Myth of the Superwoman* (1978; repr., New York: Verso, 1999).

Micki McElya

Faithful Helpmates and Fervent Activists
Northern Women and Civil War Memory

WENDY HAMAND VENET

In the decades following the Civil War, Northern women played an important role in commemorating the national tragedy. As members of the Woman's Relief Corps, they decorated soldiers' graves, supported male veterans, and lobbied for pension benefits for all who served, including women. Army veterans supported their efforts, praising these women as "faithful helpmates."[1] But women also found ways to commemorate the war independent of men. They published memoirs that recounted both the valor of soldiers and the valor of nurses and benevolent volunteers. They erected public statues to honor women's role in the war. As advocates in the emerging suffrage movement, a small but growing number of activist women used female wartime achievements as the basis to argue for political rights in the postwar period. These fervent activists carried the banner of woman suffrage from the postwar period straight into the twentieth century.

Professional and amateur writers produced some of the first works commemorating the Civil War. Understanding that Northern and Southern partisans would attempt to interpret the history of the recent "rebellion" and anxious to interpret the war in such a way as to reveal the superiority of the Union cause, Northern writers jumped into the fray. As the historian Caroline Janney has noted, "Memory is not a passive act."[2]

Male writers published the first narratives that focused on the Northern war effort. Frank Moore, author of patriotic tomes about the American Revolution, began publishing books about Northern heroism and Southern perfidy in 1862, including *Heroes and Martyrs* and the *Rebellion Record*. In 1866 Moore wrote *Women of the War: Their Heroism and Self-Sacrifice*. In the war's immediate aftermath, Moore solicited stories from women nurses about their experiences. Ignored by several of the most renowned caregivers, including Clara Barton and Mary Ann Bickerdyke, and faced with others who expressed their reluctance to receive public attention for their contributions, Moore nonetheless heard from more than one hundred individuals, including women themselves and soldiers who recalled their efforts. *Women of the War* combined individual narratives with running commentary about women's sacrifice and heroism. Anxious to portray wartime efforts as a temporary departure from women's domestic sphere, Moore emphasized women's "extreme reluctance" to seek publicity for their efforts. One prepublication announcement of the book praised Moore for the "loving task" of assembling the narrative and concluded that the volume "deserves a place in every loyal household in the country."[3]

Moore had a competitor in postwar publishing about women. In 1863 Linus P. Brockett began collecting stories about women nurses. In an effort to complete the work in a timely fashion, he decided to coauthor the volume with Mary C. Vaughan, a writer who aspired to publish her own book. Brockett and Vaughan dedicated *Woman's Work in the War: A Record of Heroism, Patriotism and Patience* (1867) to the "Loyal Women of America." The book consists of chapters dedicated to individual women, including Clara Barton, whose image appears on the inside cover, and also includes chapters devoted to women's collective relief efforts. Although the authors included stories of five hundred women, they excluded African American women altogether.[4]

Women of the War and *Woman's Work in the War* sold well—Moore published five editions in five years—but these books did not bring profits to the hospital workers who provided so much of the material for the books. Indeed, some women who worked with these authors asked them for pay and did not receive it.[5] Desiring to tell their own stories, recognizing that profits could be significant, and also motivated by financial need, women benevolent workers began publishing their own interpretations of the war.

They had to tread carefully. "Moore's war workers were voiceless objects of admiration who had helped their country in its hour of need and then left the stage of history," the historian Jane Schultz wrote. With the public ready to buy books about women's wartime participation but expecting women to appear modest and to mask their financial incentives for writing, authors adopted the stance that they published reluctantly and only at the behest of friends and even the soldiers they had once nursed. Jane Blakie Hoge provides a good example. Hoge joined the U.S. Sanitary Commission (USSC), a quasi-governmental agency that provided nursing and nutritional assistance to enlisted soldiers in the Union army. As associate manager of the Northwestern (Chicago) Branch of the USSC, Hoge spent three years nursing soldiers, organizing civilian volunteers, and raising money through two successful fundraising fairs. Aware that Brockett and Vaughan were collecting stories of women and anxious, no doubt, for both personal recognition and financial gain by publishing a book, Hoge produced a volume in 1867 called *The Boys in Blue* that she dedicated to "the returned, triumphant soldiers" of the Union army. She also wanted to preserve a record of the efforts made by women. Her book recounted many instances of women's commitment, labor, and patriotism in support of the Union war effort. Unconcerned about furthering the cause of sectional reconciliation, Hoge believed that Southern rebels should be "severely condemned, no matter how mistaken, prejudiced or sincere in their course." She also wanted her book to serve as a "warning to future generations" about the threat posed by secessionism.[6]

Nurses in the eastern theater of the war also wrote books, including Sophronia Bucklin, who published *In Hospital and Camp: Woman's Record of Thrilling Incidents among the Wounded in the Late War.* As a nurse whose appointment won the approval of the exacting superintendent of army nurses, Dorothea Dix, Bucklin spent the war years tending to Union soldiers in a variety of hospitals. Like Hoge, she offered praise for the heroism of Union soldiers, while also emphasizing the sense of duty and commitment that propelled nurses such as herself into government service. "I thought it was my duty to go," she wrote. "Home, with its joys and peaceful pleasures, was well-nigh forgotten." Bucklin did not mention that, as a single woman, she needed to earn money after the war. Bucklin conveyed a sense of confidence about her nursing contributions and even demonstrated a willingness to criticize physicians, notably those she observed to be drunk or those who challenged nurses' right to serve in hospitals.[7]

Over time, two organizations took leadership roles in the work of commemoration in the North: the Grand Army of the Republic (GAR) and its female auxiliary, the Woman's Relief Corps (WRC). These organizations honored fallen soldiers, raised funds to support surviving veterans, and promoted patriotism in the postwar period. The Woman's Relief Corps also drew public attention to women's wartime roles.

Founded in 1866 as an organization of Union veterans, the GAR was intended as a fraternal and charitable organization, but one that also provided a platform for former Union general John A. Logan and other soldiers who sought high office on the Republican ticket. In the following years, the GAR's membership grew to the point that major cities throughout the North boasted GAR posts, as did smaller towns. The GAR increased its membership in part because of its policy of inclusiveness. Rejecting the type of grade system that characterized the Masonic order, the GAR welcomed all who served as veterans in the Union Army, men of every military rank, including African Americans. Over time, GAR membership rose to more than 400,000. It advocated pensions for veterans, and its members campaigned for Republican candidates in national elections, including Logan, an Illinois congressman, later senator, and unsuccessful vice presidential candidate who served for several years as commander in chief of the GAR.[8]

The GAR's policy of inclusiveness did not extend to women. Although a significant number of women supported their activities from the 1860s onward and the GAR welcomed their attendance at events it sponsored, it did not admit them to formal membership, arguing that the shared experience of military life defined its mission. In response, women formed their own auxiliary, called the Woman's Relief Corps, as the separate but sanctioned auxiliary to the GAR.[9]

Almost immediately the new organization faced a potentially explosive issue: what constituted a "loyal woman"? In keeping with its status as appendage to the GAR, some WRC women wanted membership to be confined to women with male relatives who served in uniform. Other members of the WRC argued that such restrictions would prevent nurses and aid workers from taking their rightful place in the organization. In the end, the group followed the recommendation of President Florence Barker to admit all women who had not aided the Union's enemies. To do otherwise would be "a stain on our organization should we vote to disbar loyal ladies from our Order."[10]

The WRC's founding in 1883 corresponded with a rapid expansion of interest in women's social and philanthropic clubs throughout the nation, and President Barker bragged that "the growth of our Order during the year has been almost unprecedented." By 1887 the WRC had close to 50,000 members. Populous states in the Midwest and East led with a thousand or more members, but western states also recruited women, including Colorado, Dakota, Oregon, New Mexico, and Washington Territory. Among western states, California boasted the largest membership, with 2,400 women. By 1900 the WRC had attracted 118,000 members nationwide. While other women's groups competed for members, including the Ladies of the Grand Army of the Republic, the Ladies' Aid Society, and the Daughters of the Union, the WRC was the largest women's association dedicated to its mission.[11]

Like the GAR, the WRC was a multiracial organization, one that included African American and a small number of Native American women. However, in the 1890s white members in the Southern states made an effort to detach local black affiliates, known as "corps" by the WRC, from the state organizations. Delegates to the 1897 national convention debated the issue. Following a motion from white women in Kentucky to detach sixteen corps for blacks, a Maryland delegate suggested a similar arrangement for that state. Hiding their true intentions behind arguments involving alleged bookkeeping deficiencies, the segregationists made their case before the assembled delegates. Julia Layton, born in slavery and married to a navy veteran, rebutted them. She gave a powerful speech to the convention.

> I have come this morning, not as a representative of a despised and ignorant race depicted to you this morning, but I come to you as a member of the Woman's Relief Corps, who joined it with the understanding that it was the one organization on the face of the globe that accorded a woman her right, be she black or white . . . Is the colored Woman's Relief Corps dragging the white women down? No; not by any means. What we want in this organization is union, and until we have union this organization will not progress.[12]

Layton's persuasive rhetoric carried the moment; joined by a biracial coalition of members, she prevented the formal separation of black corps in the South. However, white Southern delegates insisted on dining at separate tables during this and future WRC functions, and in 1900 Southern whites made another effort to segregate the Kentucky and Maryland corps. This time they succeeded, in large part because white delegates feared that otherwise "the future of the white Corps is doomed" in the South. While Northern state branches continued to be integrated, similar controversies erupted in other women's clubs and organizations, including the General Federation of Women's Clubs, where the efforts of an African American club in Massachusetts to affiliate with the General Federation led to several years of debate and ultimately to a compromise in which Southern states were allowed to exclude black affiliate clubs and Northern states were allowed to include them. Efforts to create a truly biracial club women's movement did not succeed within the WRC or other organizations in Gilded Age America.[13]

Although Union and Confederate veterans held military reunions that promoted sectional reconciliation in the late nineteenth century, members of the WRC and their counterparts in the South made little effort to interact. Caroline Janney has argued that veterans' shared experience of soldiering helped them to find common ground with former foes, but women felt no such bonds. It appears that the WRC and its Southern counterparts, the Ladies' Memorial Associations and the United Daughters of the Confederacy, had little communication. Janney further posits that while the WRC had more members than its counterparts across the Mason-Dixon Line, Union women held a less prominent role. She concludes that military defeat in the South "may have been easier to share than victory."[14]

Yet a careful study of their activism reveals that the WRC significantly enhanced women's visibility in commemorations of the war; in at least one famous instance, the WRC went toe to toe with the UDC in contesting a Southern interpretation of the Old South. Prior to its formation, women often attended GAR gatherings called "encampments," but their presence barely registered in printed documents of these events. In 1881, for example, the New York Department of the GAR held an encampment at Seneca Falls, New York. Although few if any veterans realized the significance of this location, Seneca Falls had hosted the historic founding convention of the women's rights movement in 1848. The New York GAR meeting referenced women's attendance, but their participation was limited to the brief recognition bestowed upon Mrs. Minerva Kline and two friends for singing "How Sleep the Brave."[15]

Several years later, with the WRC now a fixture in New York and elsewhere, women's profile had strengthened. When the New York Department met at Binghamton in 1889, the WRC included a poem in the printed *Proceedings* of the Department that begins "Last year, you may remember, we crossed your picket line / And entered in your camp, without pass or countersign." The 1881 *Proceedings* failed to mention any role played by women in decorating soldiers' graves, but the 1889 poem noted: "Last year, at 'Seven Pines,' as was never done before / Flowers were placed on every grave by the Women's Relief Corps." The poem ended with an emphatic statement of women's relevance to postwar commemoration. "We believe that generations hence will bless forevermore / The 'Grand Army of the Republic,' and its 'Women's Relief Corps.'" By 1892 the New York GAR was allowing the WRC to print the proceedings of its annual meeting in tandem with those of the GAR, and in 1894 the GAR passed a resolution acknowledging "that we recognize in the Woman's Relief Corps earnest and faithful helpmates" in the work of caring for veterans.[16]

Across the North, newspapers sent reporters to cover WRC elections, projects, and events to help veterans, giving positive publicity to women's commemorative work and attention to their role in the public sphere. Not surprisingly, the WRC received special accolades when it opened soldiers' homes, often in conjunction with the GAR. For example, the Wisconsin State Veterans' Home at Waupaca opened in

1888 with great fanfare, a joint project of the GAR and WRC. Seven cottages for aging soldiers comprised the complex. Five years later, the Waupaca home had forty cottages, with space for three hundred soldiers and their wives, and the complex boasted a reading room (stocked with books gathered by the local Woman's Christian Temperance Union), two hospitals, steam heat, and electric lights. In addition to the Waupaca home, the *Milwaukee Sentinel* wanted readers to know about WRC-sponsored veterans' homes in California, Colorado, Pennsylvania, New Hampshire "and other Eastern states." The Chicago *Daily Inter Ocean* ran a story about Illinois WRC president Sarah Bradford, including her picture, biographical details, and praise for her work as "the Old Soldier's Friend." The *Inter Ocean* also kept readers up to date on the formation of new corps of the WRC in nearby states. Iowa was expected to have two hundred corps by Christmas 1889.[17]

Newspaper coverage of the WRC also revealed the nontraditional nature of women's activism. The *Bangor Daily Whig and Courier* reported in 1894 that Ella Jordan Mason, Maine's WRC state president, "addressed a large audience in the Unitarian church, Ellsworth" seeking charitable donations in support of the state's aging veterans. Before and during the war, few women spoke to large groups in church or elsewhere. This fact was not lost on the Kansas state president, Julia Chase, when she addressed an audience of men and women at the Southwestern Soldiers' Association annual reunion in Arkansas City, Kansas, October 14, 1891. Although her specific words were not recorded, she praised the valor of men in blue and exclaimed on the positive political and social changes brought by the war. Notably, the newspaper also paraphrased this specific comment made by Chase: "Thirty years ago she could never have dreamed she would ever address a body of veteran soldiers." The historian Nina Silber has warned against interpreting the Civil War era as a time of dramatic change in gender roles, citing the WRC's auxiliary relationship to the GAR as one example of women's continuing subordination in American society. Nevertheless, as Silber acknowledges, the WRC provided a platform through which women exerted leadership, including opportunities for public speaking, once considered well beyond women's appropriate sphere. By the end of the century, some WRC members supported the woman's suffrage movement.[18]

Women's visibility increased on the national level as well. When the GAR held its national encampment in Boston during August 1890, it did so in conjunction with the WRC. The festivities opened with a reception for veterans on a Monday evening and a grand parade the following morning, but on Tuesday members of the WRC joined members of the GAR for a "Grand Reception," and the two groups held simultaneous convention meetings on Wednesday and Thursday, before joining again on Friday and Saturday for a series of harbor excursions and clambakes.[19]

In order to boost its national profile, the WRC actively sought the participation of prominent women. When the GAR met in Washington, D.C., for a national meeting in 1892, the WRC showcased the wartime role of Clara Barton, the nation's most famous Civil War nurse and postwar founder of the American Red Cross. Barton was a subcommittee chair for the WRC and Ladies of the GAR, and she also held the honorary title of chaplain for the meeting. Attendees were encouraged to visit Red Cross headquarters at 17th and F Streets. The wives of prominent politicians lent their names to an advisory committee for the meeting, including Caroline Harrison, wife of President Benjamin Harrison, and Anna Morton, the vice president's wife. Mary Logan, whose husband John played a pivotal role founding and leading the GAR, attended national meetings of the WRC long after her husband's death in 1886. At the 1892 meeting, she shared a letter from the widow of Ulysses S. Grant, reprinted in Northern newspapers, that showed her support for the organization.[20]

On the national, state, and local levels, the WRC engaged in a range of activities to support Union veterans and to promote patriotism. On the local level, WRC corps raised money for distribution to indigent veterans and their families. Among African American corps, these efforts often filled a critical need. Throughout the North, the WRC distributed flags to public school classrooms. One of its highest priorities was to promote annual celebrations of Memorial Day. At their national convention in 1885, delegates emphasized the need for local ceremonies of the holiday to be "solemn and reverent," along with the importance of avoiding "needless expense in display," especially when so many widows and orphans were in need of financial help. The historian Cecelia O'Leary has noted that Memorial Day celebrations were a way to "create a cultural bridge between the nation's past and its future."[21]

Members of the Woman's Relief Corps did not apologize for their lack of battlefield participation in the Civil War. At the national encampments, they celebrated the role they played on the sidelines as benevolent volunteers and as keepers of the domestic sphere while men were away at war. In arguing for their vital role in commemorating the war, they emphasized that their very removal from direct combat made them qualified to commemorate the war in its aftermath. According to the "Official Souvenir" of the 1890 national encampment, "The loyal woman gives from a fresh supply, not depleted by . . . long service at the front, or diminished by the ill-health of the veteran." Women's better health gave them the patriotic vigor needed to participate in commemorative activities as well as caring for the widow and orphan.[22]

In the 1920s, the WRC challenged the UDC when the UDC's Washington, D.C., division sought congressional approval to place a statue of the "faithful colored mammies of the South" near the site of the Lincoln Memorial. The black press led the opposition effort, including the *Washington Tribune,* which also decried the lack of access to public transportation, public schools of high quality, and voting rights to the descendants of mammies. The WRC also weighed in, condemning the "sickly sentimental proposition" and adding that the money appropriated for such a statue would be better spent in improving the lives of slavery's descendants. The statue was not erected.[23]

In addition to its work supporting the GAR and challenging the UDC, the WRC also served an advocacy role when female wartime leaders needed financial help. At its early conventions, the WRC selected the cases of Anna Ella Carroll and Mary Ann Bickerdyke for special attention. Carroll alleged that she had provided the Lincoln administration with valuable military and political advice and she was entitled to be rewarded financially by Congress in recognition of her work. The WRC agreed, but Congress did not. Carroll tried for many years without success to receive a congressional appropriation for her war work. The WRC had more success as an advocate for individual nurses seeking pensions. Bickerdyke, a beloved nurse whose age and status as a widow left her in financially reduced circumstances after the war, deserved a pension, according to the WRC, and in 1886 she finally received one. At $25 per month, it was half the sum that her supporters claimed that she deserved. Annie Wittenmyer, a wartime nurse and a postwar president of the WRC, received a similar pension the following decade. The WRC's Committee on Relief for Army Workers, Widows and Orphans emphasized the urgent need to identify all army nurses and benevolent workers who might be "in want." The committee concluded its 1886 report with "the work has only begun."[24]

In 1892 Congress responded to the lobbying efforts of former nurses and the WRC to pass the Army Nurses Pension Act, legislation that gave monthly stipends of $12 to all nurses who worked six months or more during the Civil War. In earlier wars, women might receive survivor's benefits if their husbands served in uniform during wartime; however, this landmark legislation recognized women's wartime efforts independent of men. The policy had limitations. Some women had trouble establishing their war records because of the scarcity of surviving hospital and payroll records. To rectify this, the Pension Bureau began allowing testimony from coworkers, supervisors, and soldiers to establish a woman's claim. In 1895 cooks and laundresses were made eligible to receive pensions. It is not clear whether many of them made claims.[25]

Well into the twentieth century, the WRC continued its efforts to remember women's wartime role, and on notable occasions it raised money to erect public statues. The construction of monuments to honor war dead occurred under the auspices of many civic and religious groups in the late nineteenth century. One of the earliest monuments dedicated to women honors victims of the Washington Arsenal fire of July 1864. Located in Washington's Congressional Cemetery, the marble monument features a female figure representing grief that stands, eyes closed and hands folded, atop a twenty-foot shaft. Side panels depict the explosion on one side and present the names of twenty-one victims on the others.[26] In contrast to this poignant victims' monument is the heroic statue of Mary Ann Bickerdyke erected by the WRC on the courthouse grounds in her hometown of Galesburg, Illinois in 1906. Sculpted by Theo Alice Ruggles Kitson, the statue depicts a larger-than-life figure of a kneeling Bickerdyke, holding a cup to the mouth of a soldier, whose face and figure are intended as the focal point.[27]

In spite of the artist's intended focus on the soldier, her representation of Bickerdyke is powerful and striking, the antithesis of a representation of women as victims or as passive. Instead, Bickerdyke is presented as a strong, competent, middle-aged woman, her no-nonsense attitude revealed by her large, muscular body, simple hairstyle, plain clothing, and rolled-up shirtsleeves. At the base of the monument, Kitson included the quotation, attributed to William Tecumsah Sherman, "She outranks me," a testament to Bickerdyke's tenacity and willingness to challenge military

Wendy Hamand Venet

authorities in support of wounded soldiers. In this instance, the WRC wanted to remember a woman who out-generaled the general.[28]

The following decade, a Boston-based group of Daughters of Veterans of the Civil War, an affiliate of the GAR's Massachusetts Department, unveiled a statue to honor Civil War nurses in the state. Located in the Massachusetts state senate Staircase Hall and sculpted by Bela Pratt, the work is titled *Angels of Mercy and Life amid Scenes of Conflict and Death*. The artist may have been influenced by Kitson's Bickerdyke, for his sculpture is similar in composition—a woman kneeling behind and ministering to a soldier—but very different in conception. Unlike Kitson's sculpture, Pratt's work focuses on the face and figure of the nurse more than the soldier she nurses and represents her as dainty and idealized. The nurse, beautifully draped in classical dress, harkens to nineteenth-century notions of women as passive and nurturing. Among Northern states, Massachusetts stands out in its efforts to honor Civil War women, and the legislature added additional tributes during the succeeding years. In the 1930s, under auspices of the federal Works Progress Administration, Edward Brodney painted a mural honoring "Mothers of the War." More recently, the state added a plaque dedicated to Massachusetts native Clara Barton, who died in 1912, and in 1984 the Massachusetts legislature renamed Staircase Hall, to become Civil War Nurses Hall.[29]

The Clara Barton sculptural relief in the Massachusetts Civil War Nurses Hall honors her career as "teacher, self-taught nurse, women's rights advocate, founder of the American Red Cross." Although Barton was not a representative Civil War nurse, indeed her extraordinary life places her in an elite pantheon of nineteenth-century woman leaders, her Civil War nursing led her to embrace rights for women in the postwar period, and on this path she was not alone. Other women in the North followed a similar trajectory, often citing their Civil War experiences in public speeches and writing, sometimes invoking their wartime experiences as pivotal to their decision to embrace rights for women.

After the war, supporters of rights for African Americans and rights for women joined to create the American Equal Rights Association. Building on the successful prewar pairing of the abolition and women's rights movements, association members hoped to further rights for both groups in the postwar period, but in 1869 it disbanded, after a fractious meeting in which members could not agree on whether to support an amendment to the U.S. Constitution granting voting rights to black men while excluding women. As Faye Dudden points out in her essay in this volume, white women's rights activists were uninformed about the dire situation for freed people in the South, largely because they read mainstream newspapers and failed to listen to what African American activists, including Frances E. W. Harper, and Sojourner Truth, told them. In the aftermath of the schism, separate and competing women's rights organizations formed: the National Woman Suffrage Association, headquartered in New York and focused on a national amendment to the Constitution enfranchising women, and the American Woman Suffrage Association, headquartered in Boston, focused on enfranchisement for women after voting rights for black men had been achieved. Leaders of both groups used women's Civil War contributions as an argument for her enlarged sphere.[30]

Elizabeth Cady Stanton and Susan B. Anthony led the National Woman Suffrage Association and believed that women's wartime contributions created a new climate of acceptance for women's rights in the postwar period. Stanton and Lucretia Mott organized the first women's rights convention at Seneca Falls in 1848, recruiting Anthony to join the movement a few years later. During the war, Stanton and Anthony suspended annual meetings but found another way to support their cause. In 1863 they organized the Woman's National Loyal League, an organization promoting an end to slavery through constitutional amendment. The league gave women an avenue for political activism and organizing. It focused activities around a petition campaign, one that included signatures of both men and women. In the absence of voting rights, the right to petition was an important political outlet for women. By the time it held its anniversary meeting in May 1864, the Loyal League had recruited 5,000 members from Maine to California, collected 265,314 signatures on antislavery petitions, and launched a new conversation about rights for women in the postwar period. Convention proceedings called for women to be "co-workers [with men] . . . in giving immortal life to the NEW nation." Additionally, Stanton and Anthony passed resolutions calling for female nurses to be paid at the same rate as their male colleagues, and calling for the vote for all citizens who served in the military or paid taxes for their country's support. Since women paid taxes, or at least some did so, they would be enfranchised. Without these measures, a "true republic" could never be achieved.[31]

Elizabeth Cady Stanton believed that the public embraced the activist role of women in the Loyal League, and this support helped to soften the image of women's rights. Before the war, suffragists often met with public ridicule. In her memoir, Stanton recalled that prewar suffragists were "uniformly denounced as 'unwise,' 'imprudent,' 'fanatical,' and 'impracticable.'" However, she wrote that "the leading journals vied with each other in praising the patience and prudence, the executive ability, the loyalty, and the patriotism of the women of the League." Stanton believed that this positive image of activist women had staying power.[32] The Loyal League's national network of petition collectors also formed a reservoir of potential recruits for the postwar suffrage movement.

Leadership of the American Woman Suffrage Association fell to a group of men and women who shared editorial responsibilities for the organization's weekly newspaper *Woman's Journal*. Prewar advocates of women's rights Lucy Stone, her husband Henry Blackwell, and William Lloyd Garrison joined forces with newcomers Julia Ward Howe and Mary Livermore, both of whom became public figures during the war and embraced rights for women in the postwar period.

In their inaugural articles for the *Journal*, Howe and Livermore invoked the Civil War in an effort to associate women's rights with wartime patriotism and motivate women to win the vote as they had helped to win the war. Howe, an author of poetry and fiction and wife to reformer Samuel Gridley Howe, wrote the "Battle Hymn of the Republic" in 1861 and published it on the front cover of *Atlantic Monthly* the following year. Sung to the tune of "John Brown's Body," the anthem's soaring lyrics linking the war and the antislavery cause with biblical language about justice led Battle Hymn to become the most stirring anthem of the war. Howe, already a prominent member of Boston society, now became a national figure. In her article for the *Woman's Journal*, she called for a "Grand Army of the Republic of Women" to join forces in support of female voting rights.[33]

As lead editor of the *Woman's Journal*, Mary Livermore began a thirty-year career as a professional editor, writer, and public speaker in support of the cause of women's rights, and she invoked the war frequently. In her inaugural article, Livermore cited General Ulysses S. Grant, who received a telegram late in the war indicating that if the Northern army might "push things," General Robert E. Lee would surrender his army. Grant replied, "Push things!" Livermore believed that if women's rights advocates followed General Grant's advice, they might achieve voting rights for women in the not-too-distant future. Territorial Wyoming had recently granted women the vote, and conversations were taking place across the country about rights for women and for African Americans.[34]

Livermore's wartime experiences with the U.S. Sanitary Commission convinced her that women must abandon notions about separate spheres in the postwar period. A minister's wife active in church affairs, Livermore advocated antislavery and temperance in the prewar period but did so largely behind the scenes. Her work with the Sanitary Commission changed her worldview. As cochair with Jane Hoge of the Northwestern branch headquartered in Chicago, Livermore recruited and organized volunteers, raised money, and by the end of the war she had begun speaking in public. To an audience in Dubuque, Iowa, in March 1864, Livermore admitted that before the war "nothing would have tempted me" to support women speaking in public. But the national emergency convinced her that women must play a public role.[35] She never looked back.

At state and national suffrage conventions, Livermore often focused on her personal decision to embrace women's rights. "It was not Lucy Stone who converted me to Woman Suffrage," she told one audience in 1870. "It was the war and the strength of character which it developed in our women." She continued:

> I could tell you of women who have died from exposure and suffering in the war, and whose graves can be found at Milliken's Bend and other places throughout the country. Hundreds of the very best women in the Northwest went down voluntarily as nurses, and in other capacities, and assisted suffering and dying men, until they themselves were almost at death's door.

Livermore rebutted those who would suggest that women did not deserve voting rights because they had not served in the military.

> "When women do military duty they shall vote!" We *did* do military duty. [Applause]

We did our full share, and we could have done more had it not been for the prejudice of leading men in the army. We could have made out pay-rolls and commissarial lists as well as men did . . . We rebuked treason everywhere. In the Northwest, the women were so positive in their loyalty, that any woman who talked rebellion, immediately lost caste, no matter how superbly she was dressed or how great her wealth.

Livermore concluded by emphasizing women's constancy, declaring, "Never for an instant did we halt in our devotion to our country, or in our efforts to maintain its unity until Lee surrendered to Grant at Appomattox." For Livermore, women's contributions to the war effort proved their ability to play a role in national life, and their contributions meant that the nation owed them access to an enlarged sphere. "Knowing, then, the qualities of woman and her courage and bravery under trials, I can never cease to demand that she shall have just as large a sphere as man has."[36]

In addition to her suffrage work, Livermore became the most successful female lyceum speaker in the nation, making transcontinental trips twice yearly, and her speeches often invoked the role of women in wartime. In a speech called "Sphere of Influence of Woman," she recalled women's contributions "during our late civil war," and their efforts to "save our *national life!*" Other nurses also gave public lectures, including Clara Barton, who shared Livermore's view that the war was a transformative time for American women. Barton befriended suffrage leaders, read their publications, and supported their efforts when her schedule allowed. Barton gave speeches declaring that women deserved "perfectly equal rights" including the suffrage. In 1888 she told an audience in Boston that American women were "fifty years in advance of the normal position which continued peace and existing conditions would have assigned [them]" if the war had not occurred.[37]

Mary Livermore published two volumes of autobiography in the 1880s and 1890s, another vehicle through which to record her own achievements and those of other women in the war and to promote their public role in the late nineteenth century. The publication of Ulysses S. Grant's highly acclaimed two-volume memoir in 1885–1886 helped to stimulate renewed public interest in the war's leaders. Livermore believed that women should be part of that movement. "There is a great demand today for autobiographies of people who have been helpers of the world," she wrote to Clara Barton. Livermore believed that it was important for nurses and benevolent workers to write their histories "for the benefit of women," and she urged Barton to record her own story. Livermore published *My Story of the War* in 1887 and *The Story of My Life* ten years later. Unlike her close friend Jane Hoge, whose memoir *The Boys in Blue* was published twenty years earlier, Livermore dedicated her book to Union soldiers but made clear through its title that this was *her* story of the war. In her second memoir, Livermore adopted the familiar theme that the war caused her to "become aware that a large portion of the nation's work was badly done, or not done at all, because woman was not recognized as a factor in the political world."[38] Livermore, along with Julia Ward Howe, Elizabeth Cady Stanton, Clara Barton, and others, lived into the early twentieth century, carrying a message linking wartime activism with empowered womanhood into the new millennium.

Although she was not a public speaker, Louisa May Alcott invoked her Civil War nursing experiences in her writing and became a public advocate of votes for women after the war. Today Alcott is best known as the author of the novel *Little Women*, set against a backdrop of the Civil War, but Alcott also served as a nurse and published one of the earliest nursing memoirs of the war. Shortly after her thirtieth birthday, she joined the ranks of paid nurses and was assigned to a hospital in Georgetown outside the nation's capital. Thrown into the maelstrom of wartime nursing in the aftermath of the Battle of Fredericksburg, Alcott bathed, fed, and bandaged the wounded, and she held the hands of dying soldiers. Though her career as nurse was cut short because of a life-threatening illness, she recorded her experiences in an autobiographical volume called *Hospital Sketches,* published in 1863. The book did well and helped to launch her literary career. Writing under the assumed name Tribulation Periwinkle, Alcott presented a truthful account of her nursing but told her story in a lighthearted way to deflect anxiety about the perils of hospital life. Periwinkle alleged that she became a nurse simply for something to do, as Chandra Manning shows in this volume, while Alcott wanted to aid the cause of helping others and helping her country, an act that was in and of itself progressive for a woman. Periwinkle likened her experience to that of a soldier by telling her family, "I've enlisted!"[39]

Like many other nurses, including Mary Livermore, Clara Barton, Jane Hoge, and Mary Ann Bickerdyke, Alcott embraced rights for women in the postwar period. In 1879 tax-paying women in Massachusetts gained limited access to the franchise by being allowed to vote in school committee elections, and in March 1880 twenty women cast ballots for the first time in Concord, Massachusetts, including Alcott. By contrast, the Confederacy's iconic nurses did not publicly endorse votes for women, including Phoebe Pember, chief matron of Richmond's Chimborazo Hospital, and Sally Tompkins, the "Angel of the Confederacy." Wartime diarist Mary Chesnut, a volunteer nurse, tried her hand at writing for publication in order to supplement her family's meager postwar income but did not suggest an enlargement of women's sphere.[40]

Although many of the North's wartime nurses and postwar memorialists engaged in women's rights activism, many others chose public lives that did not include the suffrage movement. After her term as the WRC's first president, Florence Barker focused on civic leadership in her hometown of Malden, Massachusetts, as a trustee of the local hospital and a stalwart of the Woman's Club. Annie Wittenmyer had a higher profile than Barker since she joined the national temperance movement, served as founding president of the WCTU, and later became president of the WRC. Wittenmyer did not favor woman's suffrage, but she did use her Civil War memoir *Under the Guns* (1895) as a political platform, warning Americans about two issues that concerned her: foreign immigration and the "accumulation of great wealth" by a small number of avaricious Americans.[41]

Mary S. Logan provides an example of a woman who navigated the issues of Civil War remembrance and woman's appropriate public role with equal finesse. A resident of Washington, D.C., the widowed Mrs. Logan earned money by editing a domestic periodical called *Home Magazine*. She also contributed to her community by serving on the board of directors of a local hospital. Logan promoted Civil War remembrance through her activism in the WRC and by writing *The Part Taken by Women in American History* (1912). Careful to avoid reopening sectional wounds, she did not discuss the causes of the Civil War or its outcome, but she did include chapters about Northern and Southern women and the postwar roles of the WRC and UDC. Additionally, the volume contains sections devoted to Catholic, Jewish, and Christian Science women, women in the professions, women reformers, and the history of the woman's suffrage movement. Although victory in securing a national suffrage amendment was still eight years away when she published her book, Logan offered praise for suffragists and compared them to female supporters of the American Revolution, in their "heroism, steadfastness of purpose, indefatigable industry, conscientious convictions and determination."[42] Logan understood that the balance between women's public and private roles was a topic that must be handled diplomatically; her solution was to celebrate women for their public roles and to applaud suffragists without directly endorsing their cause. Moreover, by involving the patriots of 1776 she sidestepped America's most divisive war. Logan recognized that Civil War remembrance was both an important endeavor and a tricky subject to navigate. It still is.

NOTES

1. *Proceedings of the Twenty-Eighth Annual Encampment Department of New York G.A.R. Held at Rochester* (Albany: James B. Lyon, 1894), 228.

2. Caroline E. Janney, *Remembering the Civil War: Reunion and the Limits of Reconciliation* (Chapel Hill: Univ. of North Carolina Press, 2013), 4.

3. Frank Moore, *Women of the War. Their Heroism and Self-sacrifice* (Hartford: S. S. Scranton, 1867), 593; *Daily Evening Bulletin* (San Francisco), Nov. 24, 1866; Jane E. Schultz, *Women at the Front: Hospital Workers in Civil War America* (Chapel Hill: Univ. of North Carolina Press, 2004), 224, 232.

4. L. P. Brockett and Mary C. Vaughan, *Woman's Work in the Civil War: A Record of Heroism, Patriotism and Patience* (Philadelphia: Zeigler, McCurdy, 1867), 5–6. An announcement of the book and its pricing appeared in the *Wisconsin State Register*, Mar. 23, 1867. Schultz, *Women at the Front*, 237; Thavolia Glymph, "The Civil War Era," in Nancy A. Hewitt, ed., *A Companion to American Women's History* (Oxford: Blackwell, 2002), 169.

5. Schultz, *Women at the Front*, 231, 236.

6. Jane Hoge, *The Boys in Blue or Heroes of the Rank and File* (New York: E. B. Treat, 1867), 14–15; Frances M. Clarke, *War Stories: Suffering and Sacrifice in the Civil War North* (Chicago: Univ. of Chicago Press, 2011), 62; Schultz, *Women at the Front*, 239.

7. Sophronia E. Bucklin, *In Hospital and Camp: Woman's Record of Thrilling Incidents Among the Wounded in the Late War* (Philadelphia: John E. Potter, 1869), 35, 58; Lyde Cullen Sizer, *The Political Work of Northern Women Writers and the Civil War, 1850–1872* (Chapel Hill: Univ. of North Carolina Press, 2000), 208–9.

8. The GAR tried using a grade system in its early years then abandoned it. Stuart McConnell, *Glorious Contentment: The Grand Army of the Republic, 1865–1900* (Chapel Hill: Univ. of

North Carolina Press, 1992), 24–27, 30–31, 38–40, 53–55, 206; Cecilia Elizabeth O'Leary, *To Die For: The Paradox of American Patriotism* (Princeton, N.J.: Princeton Univ. Press, 1999), 35–47.

9. Francesca Morgan, *Women and Patriotism in Jim Crow America* (Chapel Hill: Univ. of North Carolina Press, 2005), 12–13.

10. *Proceedings of the Second National Convention Woman's Relief Corps 1884* (1884; repr., Boston: Griffith, Stillings, 1903), 44; O'Leary, *To Die For,* 77.

11. *Proceedings of the Second National Convention Woman's Relief Corps 1884,* 55. Chicago's *Daily Inter Ocean,* June 11, 1887 provides state-by-state membership totals. Morgan, *Women and Patriotism,* 12–13; Caroline Janney, "Hell Hath no Fury," *Civil War Monitor* 3 (Fall 2013): 63.

12. Morgan, *Women and Patriotism,* 38–39; O'Leary, *To Die For,* 82–89.

13. *Journal of the Eighteenth National Convention of the Woman's Relief Corps* (Boston: E. B. Stillings, 1900), 51, 58; O'Leary, *To Die For,* 82–89; Karen J. Blair, *The Clubwoman as Feminist: True Womanhood Redefined, 1868–1914* (New York: Holmes & Meier, 1980), 108–10. The GAR also debated the issue of integration. See McConnell, *Glorious Contentment,* 213–14; and Barbara A. Gannon, *The Won Cause: Black and White Comradeship in the Grand Army of the Republic* (Chapel Hill: Univ. of North Carolina Press, 2011), 28–34.

14. Janney, *Remembering the Civil War,* 7, 234–39.

15. *Proceedings of the Semi-Annual and Annual Encampment of the Department of New York G.A.R. Convened at Seneca Falls* (New York: Journal Office, 1882), 16, 26.

16. *Proceedings of the Twenty-Third Annual Encampment Department of New York G.A.R Held at Binghamton* (Albany: Troy Press, 1889), 185–89; *Proceedings of the Twenty-Sixth Annual Encampment, Department of New York G.A.R. Held at Buffalo* (Albany: Troy Press, 1889); The WRC's proceedings comprise 154 pages of this 465-page document. *Proceedings of the Twenty-Eighth Annual Encampment Department of New York G.A.R. Held at Rochester* (Albany: James B. Lyon, 1894), 228.

17. *Milwaukee Sentinel,* Aug. 27, 1889, Nov. 18, 1893; *Daily Inter Ocean* (Chicago), Sept. 8, 1888, Feb. 1, Nov. 30, 1889.

18. *Bangor* (Maine) *Daily Whig & Courier,* Oct. 5, 1894; *Atchison* (Kansas) *Champion,* Oct. 15, 1891; Nina Silber, *Daughters of the Union: Northern Women Fight the Civil War* (Cambridge, Mass.: Harvard Univ. Press, 2005), 11–12, 269–84.

19. *Official Souvenir of the Twenty-Fourth National Encampment, Boston, Mass., Aug. 1890, of the Grand Army of the Republic, also Fourth Convention National Naval Veterans Association and the Eighth Annual Convention Woman's Relief Corps* (Boston: Geo. H. Richards, 1890).

20. *Souvenir Program of the G.A.R. Twenty-Sixth National Encampment September 20, 1892, Washington, D.C.* (Philadelphia: D. F. Rowe, 1892). Caroline Harrison died of tuberculosis in October 1892. On John A. Logan, see McConnell, *Glorious Contentment,* 24–27, 193–200. Julia Grant's letter to Mary Logan was reprinted in the *Milwaukee Journal,* Sept. 17, 1892.

21. *Proceedings of the Third National Convention of the Woman's Relief Corps 1885 86* (1885–1886; repr., Boston: Griffith, Stillings, 1908), 120–21; Gannon, *Won Cause,* 48–50, 76; Morgan, *Women and Patriotism,* 12; O'Leary, *To Die For,* 100.

22. *Official Souvenir of the Twenty-Fourth National Encampment,* 20.

23. Micki McElya, *Clinging to Mammy: The Faithful Slave in Twentieth-Century America* (Cambridge, Mass.: Harvard Univ. Press, 2007), 116–18, 145–46, 151–55.

24. *Proceedings of the Third National Convention,* 130–35; Nina Brown Baker, *Cyclone in Calico: The Story of Mary Ann Bickerdyke* (Boston: Little, Brown, 1952), 243; Janet L. Coryell, *Neither Heroine nor Fool: Anna Ella Carroll of Maryland* (Kent, Ohio: Kent State Univ. Press, 1990), 90–109. For a discussion of Wittenmyer, see Elizabeth D. Leonard, *Yankee Women: Gender Battles in the Civil War* (New York: Norton, 1994), 164.

25. Schultz, *Women at the Front,* 6–7, 184–210. The Nurses Pension Act did not include Confederate nurses.

26. The *New York Times,* June 18, 1864, reported that nineteen of the bodies were "so terribly charred as to be almost beyond identification." The monument was erected in 1865. Judith Giesberg, *Army at Home: Women and the Civil War on the Northern Home Front* (Chapel Hill: Univ. of North Carolina Press, 2009), 89–91. Arsenal explosions and fires killed women in other Northern factories, including Allegheny, Pennsylvania, in 1862. A monument to the memory of seventy-eight victims there was dedicated in 1929. Evidently, it replaced an earlier monument. Ibid., 71. Ernest B. Furgurson, *Freedom Rising: Washington in the Civil War* (New York: Vintage, 2004), 303–5. Another monument in Washington, D.C., honors "Nuns of the Battlefield." Erected in 1924 by the Ladies Auxiliary to the Ancient Order of Hibernians, the bronze bas relief depicts twelve nuns nursing soldiers and is dedicated "To the Memory and in Honor of the Various Orders of Sisters Who Gave Their Service and as Nurses on Battlefields in Hospitals During the War." For a discussion of women religious and Civil War nursing, see Sister Mary Denis Maher, *To Bind Up the Wounds: Catholic Sister Nurses in the U.S. Civil War* (Westport, Conn.: Greenwood Press, 1989).

27. Baker, *Cyclone in Calico,* 253–54.

28. Charlotte Streifer Rubinstein, *American Women Sculptors: A History of Women Working in Three Dimensions* (Boston: G. K. Hall, 1990), 99, 104–5; Baker, *Cyclone in Calico,* 253.

29. Polly Welts Kaufman et al., *Boston's Women's Heritage Trail: Seven Self-guided Walks Through Four Centuries of Boston Women's History,* 3rd ed. (Boston: Boston Educational Development Fund, 2006), 10; Edward Brodney obituary in *New York Times,* Aug. 19, 2002. See also the website for Boston Women's Heritage Trail, bwht.org.

30. Jean V. Matthews, *Women's Struggle for Equality: The First Phase, 1828–1876* (Chicago: Ivan Dee, 1997), 116–47. The African American-led National Equal Rights League, founded 1864, supported voting rights for black men and an end to racial segregation. Although black women and men signed its petitions, none of the petitions included provisions for woman's suffrage. The historian Hugh Davis has concluded that woman's suffrage "was the subject of extensive debate among northern African Americans." See Hugh Davis, *"We Will be Satisfied With Nothing Less": The African American Struggle for Rights in the North during Reconstruction* (Ithaca, N.Y.: Cornell Univ. Press, 2011), 67.

31. For the Woman's National Loyal League proceedings, see Elizabeth Cady Stanton, Susan B. Anthony, and Matilda Joslyn Gage, eds., *History of Woman Suffrage,* 2nd ed. (Rochester, N.Y.: Charles Mann, 1899), 2:85. For the origins, structure, and development of the organization, see Wendy Hamand Venet, *Neither Ballots nor Bullets: Women Abolitionists and the Civil War* (Charlottesville: Univ. Press of Virginia, 1991), 94–148. By the time it disbanded, the WNLL gathered close to 400,000 signatures.

32. Elizabeth Cady Stanton, *Eighty Years and More: Reminiscences of Elizabeth Cady Stanton* (New York: European, 1898), 240.

33. *Woman's Journal,* Jan. 8, 1870; Julia Ward Howe, *Reminiscences 1819–1899* (1899; repr., New York: Negro Universities Press, 1969), 275–80, 373–77; Deborah Pickman Clifford, *Mine Eyes Have Seen the Glory: A Biography of Julia Ward Howe* (Boston: Little, Brown, 1979), 144–47.

34. *Woman's Journal,* Jan. 8, 1870; Judith Ann Giesberg, *Civil War Sisterhood: The U.S. Sanitary Commission and Women's Politics in Transition* (Boston: Northeastern Univ. Press, 2000), 164.

35. *Dubuque* (Iowa) *Times,* Mar. 12, 1864; Wendy Hamand Venet, "The Emergence of a Suffragist: Mary Livermore, Civil War Activism, and the Moral Power of Women," *Civil War History* 48 (June 2002): 143–64.

36. Livermore's speech to the American Woman Suffrage Association convention was reprinted in *Woman's Journal,* May 21, 1870. The area identified by Livermore as the "North-west" is today known as the Midwest. Milliken's Bend served as a hospital and supply center during the Vicksburg campaign.

37. Mary A. Livermore, "Sphere of Influence of Woman," unpubl. speech, Livermore Collection, Princeton Univ., Princeton, N.J. For a discussion of Livermore's public career, see Wendy Hamand Venet, *A Strong-minded Woman: The Life of Mary Livermore* (Amherst: Univ. of Massachusetts Press, 2005). Clara Barton speeches qtd. in Stephen B. Oates, *A Woman of Valor: Clara Barton and the Civil War* (New York: Free Press, 1994), 377–78; Elizabeth Brown Pryor, *Clara Barton: Professional Angel* (Philadelphia: Univ. of Pennsylvania Press, 1987), 150–51, 198.

38. Mary A. Livermore, *My Story of the War: A Woman's Narrative of Four Years Personal Experience* (Hartford, Conn.: A. D. Worthington, 1887); Mary A. Livermore, *The Story of My Life; or The Sunshine and Shadow of Seventy Years* (1897; repr., New York: Arno Press, 1974), 479; Mary Livermore to Clara Barton, Sept. 14, 1897, Barton Collection, Library of Congress; Venet, *A Strong-minded Woman*, 242–47; Clarke, *War Stories*, 185–86. Clara Barton waited until age eighty-six to publish a memoir, one that focused on her childhood and was intended for juvenile readers. See *The Story of My Childhood* (1907; repr, New York: Arno Press, 1980). See also Barbara Cutter, *Domestic Devils, Battlefield Angels: The Radicalism of American Womanhood, 1830–1865* (DeKalb: Northern Illinois Univ. Press, 2003), 178–80.

39. Louisa May Alcott, *Hospital Sketches,* ed. Alice Fahs (New York: Bedford/St. Martin's, 2004); John Matteson, *Eden's Outcasts: The Story of Louisa May Alcott and Her Father* (New York: W. W. Norton, 2007), 270–82; Sizer, *The Political Work of Northern Women Writers,* 96–99; Silber, *Daughters of the Union,* 194.

40. *Woman's Journal,* Apr. 19, 1879; Matteson, *Eden's Outcasts,* 396. In 1879 Phoebe Yates Pember published a brief memoir of her wartime activities. See Phoebe Yates Pember, *A Southern Woman's Story,* ed. George C. Rable (Columbia: Univ. of South Carolina Press, 2002). Little is known about Pember's postwar life. Mary Chesnut sold only one story, "The Arrest of a Spy," earning $10. Elisabeth Muhlenfeld, *Mary Boykin Chesnut: A Biography* (Baton Rouge: Louisiana State Univ. Press, 1981), 207.

41. On Barker, see Sarah E. Fuller, *History of the Department of Massachusetts, Woman's Relief Corps* (Boston: E. B. Stillings, 1895), 291–92. Annie Wittenmyer, *Under the Guns: A Woman's Reminiscences of the Civil War* (Boston: E. B. Stillings, 1895), 201, 212.

42. Mary S. Logan, *The Part Taken by Women in American History* (1912; repr., New York: Arno Press, 1972), 15, 347–49, 548. Logan ended the chapter on suffrage with a quotation from Theodore Roosevelt endorsing female suffrage. As an independent candidate for president in 1912, Roosevelt campaigned on this issue. The cover page of Logan's book contains endorsements by several women, including leaders in the temperance and clubwomen's movements, the DAR, WRC, and UDC, and suffragist Harriet Taylor Upton.

Contributors

EDITORS

JUDITH GIESBERG is professor of history at Villanova University and the editor of the *Journal of the Civil War Era*. She is the author of numerous articles and several books on women, gender, and social history in the Civil War era. Her most recent book is *Sex and the Civil War: Soldiers, Pornography, and the Making of American Morality* (University of North Carolina Press). She currently is leading a project entitled "'Last Seen': Finding Family after Slavery," that digitizes Information Wanted advertisements placed in newspapers by African Americans looking for family members lost in slavery.

RANDALL M. MILLER is the William Dirk Warren '50 Sesquicentennial Chair and professor of history at Saint Joseph's University. He is the author or editor of numerous books on a host of subjects, including the Civil War and Reconstruction, slavery, the American South, religion, and race in America. His most recent book, co-authored with Paul Cimbala, is *The Northern Home Front during the Civil War* (Praeger).

AUTHORS

JEANIE ATTIE is an associate professor of history at Long Island University–Post and the author of *Patriotic Toil: Northern Women and American Civil War* (Cornell University Press). She recently served as historical consultant for an exhibit at the Schomberg Center for Research and Black Culture titled *Black Suburbia* and is presently working on a study of race and geography and the lived experience of hypersegregation in northern suburbs.

JACQUELINE GLASS CAMPBELL received her doctorate from Duke University and is currently associate professor of history at Francis Marion University. She has published *When Sherman Marched North from the Sea: Resistance on the Confederate Home Front* (University of North Carolina Press) and is currently completing a book on Benjamin Butler in New Orleans under contract with the University of North Carolina Press.

REBECCA CAPOBIANCO is a PhD student at the College of William and Mary focusing on identity politics in commemorative spaces after the American Civil War. She has previously written on gender, race, and reform while completing her MA at Villanova University, worked developing educational and interpretive material for Fredericksburg and Spotsylvania National Military Park, and served as a park ranger at additional National Park Service units.

FAYE DUDDEN is the Charles A. Dana Professor of History Emerita at Colgate University. Her most recent book is *Fighting Chance: The Struggle over Woman Suffrage and Black Suffrage in Reconstruction America* (Oxford University Press). She is currently researching the women's rights movement in the 1870s.

NICOLE ETCHESON is the Alexander M. Bracken Professor of History at Ball State University. She is the author of numerous articles on the Civil War and on Midwestern history and three books, including *A Generation at War: The Civil War Era in a Northern Community* (University Press of Kansas), which won the Avery O. Craven Award from the Organization of American Historians and Best Non-fiction Book of Indiana from the Indiana Center for the Book at the Indiana State Library.

LISA TENDRICH FRANK is the author of *The Civilian War: Southern Women and Union Soldiers During Sherman's March* (Louisiana State University Press). Since receiving her PhD from the University of Florida, she has published five other books and several articles on American Civil War, Southern, and women's history. She is currently writing a history of the forced evacuation of Atlanta in 1864.

LIBRA HILDE is an associate professor of history at San Jose State University whose work focuses on gender in the American South. She has written on Confederate nurses in *Worth A Dozen Men: Women and Nursing in the Civil War South* (University of Virginia Press) and is currently completing a book on fatherhood and slavery.

CHANDRA MANNING is professor of history at Georgetown University. She has also taught at Pacific Lutheran University in Tacoma, Washington, and served as special adviser to the dean of the Radcliffe Institute at Harvard University. Her most recent book, *Troubled Refuge: Struggling for Freedom in the Civil War* (Knopf), is about Civil War contraband camps and the lived experience—as well as the legal, military, and political processes—of emancipation.

MICKI MCELYA is director of the Women's, Gender and Sexuality Studies program and associate professor of history at the University of Connecticut. She specializes in the histories of women, gender, and racial formation in the United States from the Civil War to the present, with an emphasis on political culture and memory. She is author of *Clinging to Mammy: The Faithful Slave in Twentieth-Century America* (Harvard University Press) and most recently of the award-winning *The Politics of Mourning: Death and Honor in Arlington National Cemetery* (Harvard University Press), which was also a finalist for the Pulitzer Prize.

W. SCOTT POOLE is professor of history at the College of Charleston. He is the author of the award-winning *Monsters in America: Our Historical Obsession with the Hideous and the Haunting* (Baylor University Press). He most recently examined gender, race, and class in the life of H. P. Lovecraft with *In the Mountains of Madness* (Soft Skull Press) and is currently working on a book about the roots of American and European horror in the First World War.

STACEY M. ROBERTSON is provost and professor of history at the State University of New York Geneseo. She has published extensively on abolitionism and women's history; among her books is *Hearts Beating for Liberty: Women Abolitionists in the Old Northwest* (University of North Carolina Press). She is currently working on a book on women and politics in the 1850s.

ELIZABETH PARISH SMITH received her PhD from the University of North Carolina and currently teaches at the University of Central Missouri in history and women's, gender, and sexuality studies. She is completing a book titled "Southern Sirens: Disorderly Women in Post-Civil War New Orleans." Her research focuses on the intersections of marginalized women and larger political, legal, and intellectual trends in the nineteenth-century South.

ELIZABETH R. VARON is the Langbourne M. Williams Professor of History and associate director of the John L. Nau III Center for Civil War History at the University of Virginia. Her most recent book is *Appomattox: Victory, Defeat, and Freedom at the End of the Civil War* (Oxford University Press), which won the Library of Virginia's Literary Award for Nonfiction in 2014.

WENDY HAMAND VENET is professor of history at Georgia State University in Atlanta. A scholar who specializes in the role of Northern women in the Civil War, she is the author of *Neither Ballots nor Bullets: Women Abolitionists and the Civil War* (University Press of Virginia) and *A Strong-Minded Woman: The Life of Mary Livermore* (University of Massachusetts Press). Her current project focuses on the changing nature of Civil War commemoration in Atlanta since 1865.

TIMOTHY WESLEY is assistant professor of history at Austin Peay State University and the author of *The Politics of Faith During the Civil War* (Louisiana State University Press). His research and writing examines the crosscurrents of religion and politics during the antebellum, Civil War, and Reconstruction eras. He is currently at work on a book examining the religious history of African American separatism in the long nineteenth century, under contract with Fordham University Press.

JESSICA ZIPARO earned her JD from Harvard Law School and her PhD in history from Johns Hopkins University. Her work focuses on gender in nineteenth-century America. She is the author of *This Grand Experiment: When Women Entered the Federal Workforce in Civil War Era Washington, D.C.* (University of North Carolina Press).

Index

Abbot, Lemuel, 137

Abell, (Mrs. Ira), 158

abolitionism: abolitionist third parties, 25–26, 35; antislavery societies as precursor to aid societies, 104–6; and apocalypse, 222–23; Fathers and Rulers petition (1830s), 24; Lincoln's support by abolitionists, 238–43, 257n107; literature of, 103–4; Southern women and politics, 4–6; Women's Loyal National League, 34–35. *See also* politics and Northern women; religion and Northern women

"Advent of Christ, The" (Chapman), 235

African American men (Southern): labor of, during Reconstruction, 281; "manhood rights" of, 305, 318n1; rape myth about, 273–74, 289–93, 298n86; as slaves in Confederate army, 83; and three-fifths clause of Constitution, 284; violence toward wives by, 270–72, 283. *See also* gender issues; memorials and Southern women; slavery; *individual freedmen's aid societies*

African American women (Northern): aid societies of, 156–57, 158–59; compensation for labor of, 161; family responsibilities of, 190–91; as government workers, 68; as laundresses and cooks, 66; mobility of, 51–52; as nurses and hospital workers, 67, 161; partisan activism of, 31–34; religious beliefs of, 234–35, 244; social welfare denied to, 163; soldiers' aid by, 64; and soldiers' pay, 162, 198–99; in South, for Reconstruction-era aid work, 282–83; widows' military pensions for, 72, 203–4

African American women (Southern): freedwomen's accusations by employers, 261–64, 266–67, 272, 274, 277n21; freedwomen's jobs without white supervision, 265–66; memorial to, 315–16 (*see also* memorials and Southern women); postwar political engagement by, 141–42; religion of, 219. *See also* slavery

African Methodist Episcopal (AME) Church, 109, 199, 282

age of women, gender roles and, 191–92

Aggy (enslaved woman), 215–16

agriculture. *See* farming; plantations

Agriculture Department (U.S.), 71

aid societies: freedmen's aid, 281–83; fundraising by Southern women, 128, 132–33, 145n30; gunboat societies of Southern women, 129–31, 144n12, 145n28, 145n34; mobilization by Northern women, 64–65, 155; mobilization by Southern women, 45–46, 52; religion and Northern women, 237–38; Southern organization of, 125; war relief by Northern women, 155–60, 204. *See also* hospitals and medicine

Alabama hospitals (Richmond), 132, 146n43

Alcott, Louisa May, 102–4, 105, 192, 200, 202, 335

Alexandria (Virginia) National Cemetery (Contrabands and Freedmen's Cemetery Memorial): burial controversy, 306–9, 311; *Path of Thorns and Roses* (Chiodo), 303–5, 304, 316–17

Aley, Ginette, 70, 167n37, 191

Allan, Elizabeth Randolph Preston, 9

Alsop, Lizzie, 98n34

American Anti-Slavery Society, 104, 236, 283

American Apocalypse (Sutton), 230–31n37

American Baptist Free Mission Society, 308

American Colonization Society (ACS), 4–5

American Equal Rights Association (AERA), 284–86, 288, 290, 331

American Female Moral Reform Society, 251n28

American Freedmen's Aid Commission (AFUC), 156, 281–82

American Missionary Association (AMA), 281–82

American Red Cross, 328–29, 331

American Slavery As It Is (Weld), 104

American Theological Review, 232

American Woman Suffrage Association, 280, 331–32

Ames, Mary, 109, 113

Anderson, William H., 201

Andrew, John A., 167n37, 198–99

Andrews, Eliza, 184

Andrews, Sidney, 225

Angels of Mercy and Life amid Scenes of Conflict and Death (Pratt), 331

Anthony, Susan B.: on Civil War and effects on women, 63, 73; and National Woman Suffrage Association, 280, 332–33; religious beliefs of, 246–47; Women's Loyal National League, 34–35;

Bishir, Catherine, 306
Bixby, Lydia, 202
Black Codes, 262, 284
Blackford, Mary, 4–5, 9
Black Laws, 32
Blackwell, Elizabeth: and Dorothea Dix, 65–66, 160; and United States Sanitary Commission, 157–58
Blackwell, Emily, 158, 160
Blackwell, Henry, 280
Blair, Frank, 290
Blauvelt, Martha Tomhave, 196–97, 199
"Bloody Affair, A" (newspaper article), 272
Book of Revelation, 219, 235
Botume, Elizabeth, 112–13
Boyce, W. W., 93
Boyd, Belle, 55
Boys in Blue, The (Hoge), 324–25, 334
Bradford, Susan, 177
Bradley, Amy, 67
Brady, Mary, 237
Brady, Matthew, 153
Brasher, Glenn David, 96–97n20, 98n33, 101n102
Brattleboro Democrat, 26–27
Bratton, John, 174–75
bread riots, 10, 53
Brent, Linda (Harriet Jacobs), 5
Brockett, Linus P., 324
Brodney, Edward, 331
Brooks, Preston, 6–7, 28–29
Brooks-Higginbotham, Evelyn, 220, 227
Brown, Elsa Barkley, 141, 289
Brown, F. H., 98n43
Brown, John, 8, 32–34, 241
Brown, Joseph, 43
Brown, Joshua, 153
Bruce, Susan, 76n56
Bruns, Heinrich, 202, 203
Bruns, Jette Geisberg, 202–3
Bryan, William Jennings, 305
Buchanan, James, 22–24, 28–31
Buck, Lucy, 47
Bucklin, Sophronia, 325
Buckner Hospital, 140
Bull Run, First Battle of, 55, 83
bummers, 14
Bunnell, Lizzie, 165n3
Bureau of Pensions (U.S.), 72
Bureau of Refugees, Freedmen, and Abandoned Lands (Freedmen's Bureau), 119n40, 269
Burial of Latané, The (Washington), 311–12
Burke, Mary, 261–63, 266
Burroughs, Nannie, 227
Burton, Annie, 94–95
Butler, Benjamin F., 13, 83, 84, 94, 174, 307
Butler, Sarah Hildreth, 242

Byers, Mary Adelia, 267, 268
Bynum, Jesse A., 6

Cairo (Illinois), contraband camp in, 99n54, 109, 112
cake walk dance, 221
Caldwell, Mary, 94
California: Compromise of 1850, 26; Frémont on antislavery status of, 29
Cameron, Simon, 83, 160
Camp, Stephanie, 6, 86–87
Campbell, C. B., 34
"camp followers," 15, 66
Camp Nelson (Kentucky), as contraband camp, 180
Canada, former slaves' emigration to, 28
Capobianco, Rebecca, 102, 135
Carmichael, Peter S., 191
Carroll, Anna Ella, 329–30
Carter, General Samuel P., 51
Catholics, 158–59
Cave Hill Cemetery, 312
Cavins, Aden, 192, 193
Cavins, Jodie, 192, 193
cemeteries. *See* memorials and Northern women; memorials and Southern women
Censer, Jane Turner, 17
Chace, Lillie, 236, 246
Chafer, Lewis Sperry, 226
Chapin, Lucius, 202
Chapin, Sarah, 202
Chapman, Maria Weston, 233, 235, 236, 250n10
Charleston Observer, 218
Chase, Julia, 328
Chase, Lucy, 105, 110, 112
Chase, Lydia, 105
Chase, Salmon, 69
Chase, Sarah, 105, 110, 112
Chesnut, Mary Boykin, 49, 128, 130, 171, 178, 184
Cheves, Susan, 182
Chicago Tribune, 285
Chickamauga, Battle of, 132
Child, Lydia Maria, 16, 104, 105, 144n15, 238, 239, 244
Chimborazo Military Hospital (Richmond), 12, 48, 136, 176
Chiodo, Mario, 303–5, *304,* 316–17
Christian Perfectionism, 235, 251–52n30, 252n33
Christian Recorder (AME Church), 199, 282
citizenship. *See* Fourteenth Amendment
Civil Rights Act (1866), 262–63, 269
civil rights movement: Civil War-era religion, 228; Jim Crow laws, 225–26
Civil War. *See* emancipation and Northern women; emancipation and Southern women; family and Northern women; family and Southern women; memorials and Northern women; memorials and Southern women;

Fanny (enslaved woman), 86
Farmer-Kaiser, Mary, 119n40, 270
farming: by civilian men during war, 195; Northern women's work in, 70, 163, 167n37, 198
Farnsworth, Charlotte, 119n40
father/daughter relationships, 192–93
Fathers and Rulers petition (1830s), 24
Faust, Drew, 9, 17, 140, 149n86, 305
Federal Writers' Project, 91, 98n43
Ferris, Anne, 243–44
Fifteenth Amendment: and Grant's election, 290–91; passage of, 263; ratification of, 270; women's suffrage movement on, 280–81, 292
5th Regiment U.S. Colored Troops Infantry, 137
54th Regiment Massachusetts Voluntary Infantry, 162, 198
First Confiscation Act (1861), 83, 307
First Unitarian Church (New York City), 157
Fludd, Eliza, 184
Foner, Eric, 83–84
food preparation: and nutrition concept, 108–9; by Southern women's aid societies, 46
Foraker Bill (1906), 312
Forbes, Ella, 161, 199
Fort Donelson, 313
Forten, Charlotte, 107, 113, 282
Fort Monroe, 99n50
45th Regiment Massachusetts Voluntary Infantry, 137
Foster, Hattie, 134
Foster, Kate, 93, 98n35
Fourteenth Amendment: passage of, 115, 263; and women's suffrage movement, 284–85
14th Tennessee Regiment, 135
Fox, George, 234
Fox-Genovese, Elizabeth, 225, 228–29n5
France, (Mrs.), 159
Frank, Lisa Tendrich, 14
Fraser, Nancy, 109–10
Fredericksburg, Battle of, 84, 94, 97n22, 335
Fredericksburg, escaped slaves in, 84, 87
freedmen's aid societies: and employment of freed people, 109–11; and freedwomen's dependency, 119n40; inception of, 106; nutrition efforts by, 108–9; sanitation efforts by, 109; teaching by, 106–7, 110–15
Freedmen's Association of New York, 106
Freedmen's Bureau, 119n40, 269
Freedmen's Intelligence and Employment Agency, 119n42
Freedom Park (Louisville), 314
Freehling, William, 16
Free Soil Party, 26–27, 35
Fremaux, Celine, 97n22
Frémont, Jesse, 7, 22–24, 28–31, 35
Frémont, John C., 22–24, 28–31, 246

Friends of Freedmen's Cemetery (Alexandria, Virginia), 316–17
Fugitive Slave Law (1850), 5, 26–28, 103, 105
Fugitive Slave Law (Ohio), 27
Furgerson, Henrietta, 81, 87

Gage, Frances, 108, 245, 283, 284, 285
Garretson, Elizabeth, 69
Garrison, William Lloyd, 22, 25, 236, 332
gender issues: of African Americans during Reconstruction, 283; Civil War memorials and framing of, 303–9, 304, 311, 316–17 (see also memorials and Northern women; memorials and Southern women); domestic ideology, 126–27, 142–43n4, 155–56, 162–64; of escaped slaves, 86; expectations for Southern men, 172–73; gendered notions and social stigma about work, 66–67, 69, 82; in nursing, 201 (see also nursing profession); over life course, 191–92; separate sphere doctrine, 4, 142n4, 172, 191, 333 (see also domestic ideology); and Southern religious views, 221–22, 227–28; Southern white women's changed roles in absence of men, 86, 88, 92–95; Southern women and politics, 4, 6–7, 10–13; United States Sanitary Commission and male authority, 64, 157; and war relief by Southern women, 126–27, 133–36, 140, 149–50n94, 149n86; and Women's Relief Corps (WRC), 328; women's subordination and women's work, 63–65. See also legal system
General Federation of Women's Clubs, 326–27
General Order No. 11 (Ewing), 14
Georgia Ladies' Iron Clad Battery, 145n34
Gettysburg, Battle of, 56, 203, 204
Geyber, Sue B., 130
Giesberg, Judith: on Northern women's labor, 65, 153, 157, 163; on poverty, 198; on rural Pennsylvania women, 70, 71; on working-class families' income, 77n76
Gilmer Hospital (Chattanooga), 48
Ginzberg, Lori, 291
Gist, Malvina, 177
Gladwin, Albert, 112, 307–9, 311, 317, 320n15
Gladwin Record, 308
Glover, Mary, 269, 270
Glymph, Thavolia, 15, 17, 84, 92, 93, 263, 267
Godey's Lady's Book, 155
Godkin, E. L., 288
Gone with the Wind (film), 3
Gone with the Wind (Mitchell), 4, 10
Goode, John, 18–19
Goodlett, Emily, 181
Goolrick, Fanny Bernard, 85
Gordon, Linda, 109–10
government (Confederate): and Jefferson Davis, 44, 48, 52, 54, 55, 315; women's relationship to,

Methodists, Northern, 233, 247, 282
Miles, Mary Jo, 241
military. *See* aid societies; army (Confederate); army (Union); pensions; women soldiers
Military Aid Society (Mobile, Alabama), 129
millennialism: defined, 250n6; feminism linked to, 250n7; on government's antislavery role, 252n35; Abraham Lincoln on, 256n82; postmillennialist beliefs of Northern women, 232–38, 241, 243, 245–46; premillennialist beliefs of Northern women, 243; premillennialist beliefs of Southern women, 217–19, 230–31n37, 249n1; on slavery, 251n26. *See also* apocalypse
"Millennium, The" (Hutchinson, Hutchinson), 254n63
Miller, Joseph, 180
Milwaukee Sentinel, 328
Minnie's Sacrifice (Harper), 292
Minter, Fannie, 147n60
Mintz, Steven, 191, 192
mobilization by Northern women, 62–78; and aid societies, 64–65, 155; as factory workers, 67–68, 157, 338n26; and farming, 70; gender relations and women's subordination, 63–65; as government workers, 68–70, 76n51–54, 76n56, 77n68; as nurses, 65–67; overview, 62; pay for women's work, 67, 69–70, 75n42, 77n76; property ownership by women, 70–71, 73, 278n49; social stigma of women's work, 66–67, 69; social welfare and pensions for women, 71–72; as soldiers, 11, 72–73, 78n84
mobilization by Southern women, 41–61; and agricultural production, 47; aid societies, 45–46; and enlistment of men, 44–45; espionage, 54–55; and factory jobs, 49–50; and labor of enslaved women, 50; and medical aid, 47–49, 54; migration of Southern families, 50–52; overview, 41–42; and secession, 42–43; for and against slavery, 43; women soldiers, 11, 55–56, 61n86; women's relationship to their government, 52–55
Mohr, Clarence, 147n57
Moltmann, Jürgen, 229n10
Moody, Emma A., 196
Moore, Frank, 323–25
Moore, Joanna, 106–7, 110, 114–15
Moore, Rebecca, 114
Moorhead, James, 234
Mordecai, Emma, 91
Morgan, Sarah, 51, 175, 177
Mormons, 229n7
Morton, Anna, 329
Morton, Oliver P., 202
"Mothers of the War" (Brodney), 331

mother/son relationships, 200–203, 223–24
"Mother's Parting Words to Her Soldier Boy, A," 223
Mott, Lucretia, 34, 73, 104, 282, 285–86, 332
Mount Vernon Ladies Association, 3, 7–8
My Story of the War (Livermore), 334

Nation (abolitionist publication), 287–88
National Academy of Design, 309–10
National Anti-Slavery Standard, 283, 284, 287, 288, 291
National Association for the Relief of Destitute Colored Women and Children, 156
National Baptist Convention, 227
National Baptist Union Review, 227
National Equal Rights League, 115
National Era (Washington, D.C.), 27
National Freedmen's Relief Association, 105
National Park Service, 322n49
National Woman Suffrage Association, 280, 331–32
navy (Union), 174, 309
Needham, Nancy, 202
"Negro in the Enjoyment of His Rights, The" (*Chicago Tribune*), 285
Nesbitt, Scott, 84
New England Freedmen's Aid Commission, 107
New Jersey, suffrage in, 23
New Mexico, Compromise of 1850 and, 26
New Orleans: interracial marriage in, 269, 270, 277–78n34, 277n33; legal system in, 261–64, 266, 269, 274; regulated sex trade in, 271
newspapers: Reconstruction-era influence of, 287–93; reporting accuracy asserted by, 153. *See also individual names of newspapers*
Newton, Isaac, 71
New York Draft Riots (1863), 154
New York Times, 287, 307, 313, 314
New York Tribune, 242, 287
New York World, 288, 289
Nichols, Clarina, 26–27
Nina (Southern white woman), 182
Norris, Elizabeth, 134–35
North Carolina: and emancipation, 93; women's relationship to government in, 53, 54
Northern Women's Loyal National League, 176
Northwestern Christian Advocate, 239–40
Northwest Freedmen's Aid Commission, 106, 109
nursing profession: African American and working-class nurses (Northern), 67, 161; and Elizabeth Blackwell, 65–66, 157–58, 160; and Emily Blackwell, 158, 160; Jefferson Davis on, 50; and Dorothea Dix, 65–66, 160, 166n30, 325; enslaved labor in, 48, 135–38, 147n57; and gender roles, 201; mobilization by Northern

women, 65–67; pensions of nurses, 329–30; statistics of, during Civil War, 146n47; status of nurses, 133–34
nutrition efforts, 108–9

Oberlin College, 282
O'Donovan, Susan, 265, 274
Office of Army Nurses, 160
Ohio Fugitive Slave Law, 27
Old Capitol Prison (Washington, D.C.), 55
O'Leary, Cecelia, 329
Olmsted, Frederick Law, 307
"One of the Worst Enemies the Colored and White Loyalists of the South Have to Contend with is the Associated Press" (*National Anti-Slavery Standard*), 291
Orphan Brigade Association, 315
Orphan's Home (Nashville), 118n35
Osterud, Nancy Grey, 70
Owen, Robert Dale, 241

Padgett's Creek Baptist Church, 221
Palmer, Alice, 92
Palmetto State, CSS, 139
Parish, Peter, 159
Park, Lucinda, 105
Parrott, (Miss), 51
Part Taken by Women in American History, The (Logan), 336
Patec, Maria, 239
Path of Thorns and Roses (Chiodo), 303–5, *304,* 316–17
Payne, James H., 137
Peggy (freedwoman), 113
Peirce, Clara, 192
Peirce, John, 192
Pember, Phoebe Yates, 12, 48, 136, 140, 176, 335
Pennsylvania: Confederate army's seizure of African Americans in, 205; women workers in, 70, 71
Pennsylvania Anti-Slavery Society, 283
Pennsylvania State Equal Rights Association, 115, 120–21n66
Penny, Lydia, 137
Penny, Thomas, 137
pensions: for African American women's jobs, 149n89; widows' military pensions, 71–72, 203–4; of women hospital workers and nurses, 161, 329–30
Peters, Margaret C., 69
Philadelphia, aid societies in, 158
Phillips, Wendell, 22, 283–86, 290, 294n23, 295n37
Pickle, Linda Schelbitzki, 197, 202
Pierson, Michael, 26, 27, 37n24
Pillsbury, Parker, 286, 289

Pineville (South Carolina), uprising in (March 1865), 91–92
place, alternative geographies and, 306, 319n5. *See also* memorials and Southern women
Place, Amelia, 272
plantations: managed by women, 47; plantation mission movement, 218; during Reconstruction, 267
Plough, John, 198
politics. *See* politics and Northern women; politics and Southern women
politics and Northern women, 22–38; and abolitionist third parties, 25–26, 35; African American women's partisan activism, 31–34; and early Republican Party, 22, 28–34; and election of 1856, 22–24, 28–31; and Fugitive Slave Law (1850) reaction, 27–28; and Harpers Ferry raid, 32–34; Higher Law position of, 26–27, 32–33; study of, 35–36; and Whig partisanship, 24–25; and Women's Loyal National League, 34–35
politics and Southern women, 3–21; abolition and resistance to slavery, 4–6; contraband camps and, 15–16 (*see also* contraband camps and history); defining politics of, 18–19; dissent among Southern women, 16–17; and female accountability, 13–15; and freedwomen's resistance, 17–18; gender and divergence of conventions, 4; and gender aspersions, 6–7; and gender role conflict, 10–13; and war relief by Southern women, 127–28, 141–42, 143n9 (*see also* war relief by Southern women); white women on Confederate cause, overview, 3–5; white women's partisanship, 7–10
Pollard, Lizzie, 140
Poole, W. Scott, 238
Porcher, Elizabeth Palmer, 92
Porter, Felicia Grundy, 134
Post, Amy, 238–39, 244
postmillennialism: and Northern women's beliefs, 232–34; and Harriet Beecher Stowe, 235
Poughkeepsie Daily Eagle, on mobilization of Northern women, 155
Pratt, Bela, 331
Preliminary Emancipation Proclamation, 84
press, Reconstruction-era influence of, 287–93
Preston, Margaret Junkin, 11
Price, Allen, 147n60
prisoners of war: Northern soldiers supported by enslaved women, 50; and Southern women as spies, 54–55
privacy issues: of Southern women during Reconstruction, 276n9; and widows' pensions, 71–72
property ownership, by Northern women, 70–71, 73, 278n49

prostitution: and "camp follower" label, 66; defiant Southern women accused of, 174; by escaped slaves, 87; segregation of, 271; soldiers' widows accused of, 72

Pryor, Sara, 140

public speaking, by abolitionists, 104–5

Purnell (enslaved man), 267

Putnam, Caroline, 282, 285, 287

Putnam, Sallie A. (Brock), 8–9

Quakers, 233, 234, 236, 238, 243

Quantrill, William, 14

Rable, George, 17, 194

Rader, Aramenta, 194–95

Rader, George, 194–95, 201

Rader, Lydia, 194–95

Radical Reconstruction, 262–63, 285

Ramsay, George D., 68

Ramsey, Ella Belle, 136

Randall, Alexander, 105

rape myth, 273–74, 289–93, 298n86

"rascal jackleg preacher" image, 220–21

Ray, Cornelia, 221

Rebecca (enslaved woman), 88

Reconstruction Acts (1867, 1868), 263

Reconstruction Amendments, 269. *See also* Fifteenth Amendment; Fourteenth Amendment; Thirteenth Amendment

Reconstruction and Northern women, 280–99; freedmen's aid, 281–83; power of press during, 287–93; rape myth, 289–93, 298n86; women's suffrage movement, 280–81, 283–87

Reconstruction and Southern women, 261–79; African American citizenship and voting rights, 120–21n66; effect on Southern white families, 184; family issues of, 264–65; and interracial marriage, 269, 270, 277–78n34, 277n33; labor issues of whites and African Americans, 261–71, 274; and legal system, 261–64, 266–71, 274; Southern religious views about, 225; Southern women and politics of, 18; and suffrage of African American males, 270; and white supremacy, 268, 271; women as perpetrators of violence, 271–73; women as victims of violence, 273–74; women's poverty, 264

Recruit, The (Wood), 309–10

refugee camps. *See* contraband camps and history

Register of All Officers and Agents, Civil, Military, and Naval, in the Service of the United States, 68, 76n52

relief efforts. *See* war relief by Northern women; war relief by Southern women

religion: Higher Law position, 26–27, 32–33; and Northern family relationships, 194, 199; and Reconstruction, 282; United States Christian Commission, 166n28; and war relief efforts in South, 131. *See also* apocalypse; religion and Northern women; religion and Southern women; *individual names of religious groups*

religion and Northern women, 232–57; abolitionist activism, 238–43, 257n107; aid societies, 237–38; antislavery providentialists, 234–37; Emancipation Proclamation reaction, 243–48; eschatological beliefs, 232–38, 241, 243, 245–46, 247 (*see also* apocalypse); women's religiosity, 232–33

religion and Southern women, 214–31, 215–31; anxiety created by religion, 217; biblical apocalypse (*see* apocalypse); and class issues, 215–16, 228–29n5; overview, 215–16; and slavery, 215–16, 218–20, 224–28

Remond, Charles Lenox, 285

Renfro, Maria, 109

Republican Party: antislavery position of, 103; Kansas Republican Party, 286; and Abraham Lincoln, 34; and mobilization of Southern women, 41–42; Northern women and rise of, 22, 28–34; and Radical Reconstruction, 262–63 (*see also* Reconstruction and Northern women; Reconstruction and Southern women); Radical Republicans, 284, 287; Southern Republican Party, 285; supported by antislavery Northerners, 6

Revolution (Stanton, Anthony), 288, 292

Richards, Caroline Cowles, 204

Richmond Bread Riot (April 1863), 10, 53

Richmond Daily Dispatch, 7, 13

Richmond Enquirer, 6

Richmond Whig, 136

Right Way (Stearns), 288

Roanoke Island (North Carolina), contraband camp of, 111

Robert (enslaved man), 88

Robertson, Stacey, 152

Robinson, David, 234

Rochester Ladies Anti-Slavery Society, 308

Rockford (Illinois) Female Seminary, 106–7

Rogers, Sophronia "Phrone," 196–97, 201–2

Roll, John, 243

Rollin, Louisa, 288

Roman, Celina, 85

romantic relationships, of Union soldiers, 195–97

Roosevelt, Theodore, 339n42

Ropes, Hannah, 66–67

Rose (enslaved woman), 92

Rose, Ernestine L., 253n45

Rose, Willie Lee, 307

Rosen, Hannah, 18, 273

Ross, Michael A., 270

Rowland, Kate Mason, 142

Ruoff, Isabella A., 167n37

Southern Mothers' Hospital (Memphis, Tennessee), 127, 143–44n10
Southern Unionists, 9–10, 138–39
"South Victorious, The" (Phillips), 284
South v. The South, The (Freehling), 16
Southworth, Rhoda, 239
Special Diet Kitchen (SDK), 108–9
Spinner, F. E., 63
"spiritual mothers," 221–22, 227–28
Sprague, John W., 137
Stafford, Sallie, 193
Stafford, Sam, 193
Stanley, Amy Dru, 283
Stanley, Henry Morton, 44
Stanton, Edwin, 70
Stanton, Elizabeth Cady: on Civil War and effects on women, 63; Civil War focus of, 155; effect of Civil War on women's rights movement, 73; National Woman Suffrage Association of, 280, 332–33; religious beliefs of, 245–46; Women's Loyal National League, 34–35; at women's rights movement convention (1863), 115; women's suffrage movement during Reconstruction, 280, 283–86, 288–90, 292, 295n37, 296n54, 298n88
Stearns, George Luther, 288
Stewart, Maria W. Miller, 104, 219, 234–35
Stone, Kate, 85, 86, 90, 91, 92
Stone, Lucy, 280, 292, 332
Stoneman, George, 18
Story of My Life, The (Livermore), 334
Stout, Samuel, 132, 133
Stowe, Harriet Beecher: and Abraham Lincoln, 242, 245, 246, 255n74; religious beliefs of, 235, 252n33; on slavery as domestic problem, 172; Uncle Tom's Cabin, 27, 35, 104, 116n7, 172, 235
Streeter, Holland, 111
Strong, Douglas, 251–52n30
Sturtevant, Amanda, 32–33
suffrage: of African American males, 18, 73, 225–26, 263, 270, 279, 287, 296n54; disagreement between advocates for women and African American males, 284–85, 291, 295n37, 297n82; effect of Civil War on women's rights movement, 73; and Fourteenth Amendment, 115; memorials and Northern women, 331–34; in New Jersey, 23; Southern women's partisanship role prior to, 7–8 (see also politics and Southern women); women's suffrage movement during Reconstruction, 280–81, 283–87. See also Anthony, Susan B.; Douglass, Frederick; Stanton, Elizabeth Cady
Summers, Mark Wahlgren, 292–93
Sumner, Charles, 6–7, 28–29
Sutton, Matthew Avery, 230–31n37
Swisshelm, Jane, 26–27

Talcott, Wait, 242
Tarbell, Ida, 73
Tarrh, Virginia, 145–46n39
Taylor, Susie Baker King, 14–15, 45, 138, 141–42
teaching: by Northern women, 106–7, 110–15; by Northern women, in South, 281–82; by Southern women, 176, 268
temperance: and millennialist thought, 249–50n5; movement in North, 7; and Southern religious views, 218, 224–25; Woman's Christian Temperance Union, 280
10th Regiment Vermont Voluntary Infantry, 137
Theatre Hall (Little Rock), 46
3rd Regiment U.S. Colored Troops Infantry, 192, 199
Thirteenth Amendment: and Kentucky emancipation, 310; Lincoln's support of, 247; and Reconstruction era, 262, 269
33rd U.S. Colored Troops, 138
Thomas, (Mrs. F. M.), 119n40
Thomas, Ella Gertrude Clanton, 93, 224
Thomas, Mary F., 165n3
Thompson, Franklin (Sarah Edmonds), 73
three-fifths clause of Constitution, 284
Tidewater (Virginia), emancipation actions of slaves in, 101n102
Todd, David, 119n40
Todd, John, 119n40
Tompkins, Sally, 12, 48, 133, 335
Tooms, (Mrs. E.), 267, 277n21
Towne, Laura, 113–14, 115, 222
Townsend, Charity, 203–4
Townsend, Luke, 203–4
Townsend, Robert, 203
Train, George Francis, 286
Treasury (U.S.): Spinner's report on women workers, 63; women workers in, 68–69
Treasury (Confederate), women hired by, 49, 176–77
"Tribulation Periwinkle" (Alcott), 335
Truth, Sojourner: influence of, 45, 282, 283; public speaking by, 32; relief work of, 308; religious beliefs of, 250n7; and women's suffrage, 285; work with refugees and escaped slaves, 156
Tubman, Harriet: characteristics of, 114; employment of freedwomen by, 110, 161; influence of, 5; pension claim of, 119n43, 119n45; religious beliefs of, 238; spying by, 55, 161
Turner, H. M., 291
Tuveson, Ernest Lee, 240
12th Regiment Illinois Volunteer Infantry, 138
24th Regiment U.S. Colored Troops Infantry, 204
27th Regiment U.S. Colored Troops Infantry, 137

Uncle Tom's Cabin (Stowe): influence of, 35, 104; sales of, 4, 27, 116n7; on slavery as domestic problem, 172; and Stowe's religious beliefs, 235

Underground Railroad, 5. *See also* Tubman, Harriet

Union Circles, 44

Union Hotel Hospital (Georgetown), 67

Unionists (Southern), 9–10, 138–39

Union Society, 158

Unitarians, 234, 238, 243, 248

United Confederate Veterans, 312

United Daughters of the Confederacy (UDC), 17, 222, 305, 312, 315, 321n43, 327, 329, 330

United States Christian Commission, 64, 166n28, 237

United States Colored Troops (USCT), 93–94. *See also individual regiments*

United States Sanitary Commission: and abolitionism, 237; class issues affecting, 162; and Emancipation Proclamation, 244; formation of, 157–58; fraud accusations against, 159–60; and Jane Hoge, 324–25; male authority of, 64, 157; and Frederick Law Olmsted, 307; Southern aid societies' organization compared to, 125; and United States Christian Commission, 166n28; and women's legal status, 190; work of, 203

Universalists, 233–34, 236, 245

University of Louisville, 314

Utah: Compromise of 1850, 26; women's suffrage in, 280

Valentine, Annie, 192, 199

Valentine, Ida, 192

Valentine, Tillman, 192, 199

Vance, Zebulon, 53, 93, 182

Vandergriff, Cara, 145n28

Van Lew, Elizabeth, 9–10, 18, 55

Vaughan, Mary C., 324–25

Venet, Wendy Hamand, 190

Veteran, The (Wood), 309–10

Victory Defeated by Death (Hibbard), 321n37

violence: fear of, among Southern women, 126–27, 143n8; and Ku Klux Klan, 271, 291; lynching, 290; in marriage, 270–72, 283; Memphis (Tennessee), mob violence (May 1, 1866), 273; military invasion of Southern whites' homes, 182–83, 189n48; "rape myth," 273–74, 298n86; toward escaped slaves, 87–88, 91–92; of Union soldiers toward slave women and their families, 178–81; women as perpetrators of, 271–73

Wade, Ben, 286–87

War Department (Confederate), 49. *See also* army (Confederate)

War Department (U.S.): on farm output during Civil War, 71; women workers in, 68–69, 70. *See also* army (Union)

Ware, Harriet, 113

war relief by Northern women, 151–67; aid societies, 155–60, 204; class issues of, 154; economic issues affecting, 153–56, 159, 162–64; fundraising, 154; hospital workers, 157–58, 160–61; overview, 151–52; postwar legacy of, 152–53, 163–64; Union military strategy and support by women, 153–54; women in Union military camps, 161–62

war relief by Southern women, 125–50; and class divisions, 126, 135; and enslaved labor, 135–38; and fears of violence, 126–27, 143n8; fundraising for, 128, 132–33, 145n30; and gender roles, 126–27, 133–36, 140; and medical aid, 127, 131–39; and memorial and legacy work, 139–42; military aid by gunboat societies, 129–31, 144n12, 145n28, 145n34; overview, 125–26; and political involvement, 127–28, 141–42; and Unionism, 138–39

Washington, George, 7

Washington, Nancy, 181

Washington, William D., 311–12

Washington Arsenal, 68

Washington Tribune, 329

Waters, (Mrs.), 159

Watkins, Frances Ellen, 32, 33. *See also* Harper, Frances

Wayside Hospital (Columbia, South Carolina), 49

Weaver, Clara Vinson, 197, 199–200

Weaver, James B., 197

Weld, Theodore Dwight, 104

Wellford, Beverly, Jr., 8

Wells, Ida B., 291

Welty, Eudora, 307

Wesley, Timothy, 216–17

Western Antislavery Society, 104

Wheatley, Phyllis, 234

Wheeler, Charlie, 204

Whig Party, 24–25

Whites, LeeAnn, 143n5, 144n12, 145n34, 265

white supremacy: and Confederate memorials, 139–40; Douglass on, 291; Ku Klux Klan, 271, 291; Memphis (Tennessee) mob violence (May 1, 1866), 17–18

Whittier, John Greenleaf, 144n15

Wide Awake groups, 34

Wilbur, Julia, 111–12, 308

Wilder, Craig, 156

William (enslaved child), 135

William, John, 86

Williams, Thomas, 173–74

Willie (enslaved man), 135